BOLLINGEN SERIES XCVIII

LOUIS MASSIGNON

The Passion of al-Hallāj

Mystic and Martyr
of Islam

Translated from the French with
a biographical foreword by

HERBERT MASON

VOLUME 2

The Survival of al-Hallāj

BOLLINGEN SERIES XCVIII

PRINCETON UNIVERSITY PRESS

CONTENTS OF VOLUME 2

CONTENTS

LIST OF ILLUSTRATIONS
TO VOLUME 2

THE SURVIVAL OF HALLĀJ

VIII

~~~~~~

MODALITIES OF THE HALLĀJIAN
SURVIVAL

I. GENERAL MODALITIES OF THE SURVIVAL

a. *Transmission of the* Isnāds

The execution on 24 *Qa'da* 309/March 26, 922 in Baghdad had a profound effect on people's consciences. It had taken place before "a crowd,
a countless number" (Zanjī); "there was no one in Baghdad who was not
present at his execution" (A. Y. Qazwīnī); "an ominous day" (Mas'ūdī:
using the Qur'ānic phrase from 83:5: *yawm 'azīm*: which, among the
Nusayrīs, is personified by Salsal); "it was said that there was no one
who witnessed the execution who was not overtaken by calamity
(*usiba*)" (Ibn Fadlallāh 'Umarī).

As the tragic conclusion of a resounding preaching, followed by a long
imprisonment, it immediately gave rise to eschatological forebodings,
directed dreams (*istikārāt*) and apparitions, identifying Hallāj with the
awaited Mahdī, obstinately hoping for an impending temporal triumph
by this executed man. This is the way I believe we must interpret the
threat of a riot referred to by a Sūfī source (*Akhbār*, end of no. 1) after the
first blow from the executioner: "there were rumblings of riot, some of
his disciples set fire (to some shops)." And it was in this way particularly
that the Hallājīya group that rebelled in Talaqan reacted from afar upon
learning of his execution, in which they refused to believe (his head had
to be sent there [to convince them]).

Many spectators connected this execution with the preaching in which
Hallāj had offered himself up to suffer and die, struck down by Muslim
law; among his last acts and last words they sought confirmation and
fulfillment of what he had taught. The words about Constantinople that
Zanjī (an enemy) ironically attributes to him already refer to the Mahdī.
Before his gibbet, Qannād is reminded of a verse in which Hallāj had told
him his vow of attaining at any cost "the highest destiny." A closer
friend, Shiblī, was assumed, before 360, to have shouted at the executed
man the Qur'ānic curse of the people of Sodom against Lot: "have we

not forbidden you to receive any guest?" (i.e., "to succumb to the inspiration which revealed to you the Divine Presence in yourself"); as early as 370, one adds that to Shiblī, who was asking "what therefore is Sūfism?" Hallāj, when dying, was supposed to have replied: "you see its beginning here" (Khargūshī; Ibn Bākūyā).

Much earlier, isolated witnesses had affirmed certain things as fact: his face had not turned pale; his cries "O Only One, Only One"; or even "*hasb al-wājid*," or "*ilahya idhā tatawaddad*"; precise details challenged almost immediately, moreover, by others.

Some Hallājians were immediately crystallized in their certainty: Shākir, who, before getting himself killed (in 311: voluntarily, it seems) for Hallāj, was able to "publish his public discourses" (*akhraja kalāmahu li'l-nās*). He was indeed the Mahdī, the prophesized saint who would return as intercessor, for by his death he accomplished the idea that he had preached of a spiritual mahdism, suffering and victimal, destined to perfect the Islam of Muhammad by a consummation in divine love, by a compassion for the Community forced into martyrdom by obedience to Islamic Law. This is what Fāris was to repeat after Shākir, and this is what emerges from the *Akhbār*, the core of which is very early.

The condemnation and execution of Hallāj were not punishments, but acts of grace and blessing; this is what many people began to think, quietly, until in *Sha'bān* 437/February 1045, 122 years later, on the day of his elevation to the vizirate, a Shāfi'ite canonist, a *shāhid* of the court, Ibn al-Muslima, declared publicly:[1] "this is a blessed site" (*makān mubārak*), stopping to make two short prostrations on the knoll where Hallāj, executed, had been exposed on the gibbet (*maslib*).

Most did not dare say it, let alone write it: for example, Harawī Ansārī noted, "I do not mean that his form of death was a grace" (this would be contradictory), yet venerated him as a saint. What was involved was a secret, the very secret of Sūfism (say the Sālimīya), to be transmitted only to trustworthy friends, *qulūb al-ahrār*; Murta'ish had observed it: through a kind of initiation. As long as the legal condemnation remained unrepealed. Shiblī [transmitted] thus (to Nasrābādhī, afterwards to Husrī, founder of the Zawzanī *ribāt*) in Baghdad, Ibn Khafīf in Shiraz (to the Kāzerūnīya), Ibn al-Haddād (to AB Qaffāl); not without speaking of it previously to certain amīrs, such as AH M-b-Ibrāhīm Sīmjūr (d. 377), the friend of Qaffāl and probably the patron of Fāris in Khurasan and Mawaralnahr, and such as M-b-'Abbās Dhuhlī (d. 378), nobleman of Herat, and patron of Shiblī.

---

[1] Form of honorable amends for the *shuhūd* of 309.

The preachers (*wu''āz*) of the *dhikr* sessions in the Sūfī *ribāts* were immediately able to make use of Hallāj's punishment in these gatherings as something conducive to arousing them to ecstasy; it was a tale that was much more moving than the rosaries of fulgurating sentences by Bistāmī, which were disconnected and static, being peddled by Abū Mūsā Dabīlī. Hence, the connected and dramatic accounts of the martyrdom of Hallāj: the one by Razzāz, adopted and circulated by AB Ibn Shādhān Bajalī, and the one that Ibn Bākūyā (and the *Akhbār*) introduce as being by Shiblī. A kind of literary glory tinges the horrible execution: Ibn Abī'l-Khayr says that the gibbet of Hallāj is reserved for heroes; Baqlī will say: the secret of the (royal) tiara with which the one condemned to death is adorned. Finally, in the initiation rite kept in use by the military order of the Bektāshīs, the cell in which the novice must prostrate himself in offering up his life is called "*dār-e Mansūr*" (= the gibbet of Hallāj).

The slow growth, up to the full flowering, of this collective belief in the sanctity of Hallāj, in the efficacy of his intervention, *hic et nunc*, as a witness (*shāhid*) close to God, on behalf of the Community for which he had died, and one of whose spiritual pillars (*abdāl*, *budalā'*) he had been, is conveyed, in the Sunnite milieu, by *isnāds*, or chains of transmission, giving the names of traditionists who were convinced enough to dare, at the risk of their liberty or their life, to transmit, from responsible *rāwīs*, an account concerning Hallāj. The geographical and chronological propagation of these chains permits us to locate exactly the resonating lines of the Hallājian teaching in the Muslim universe.

1. The Eight Basic Testimonial Chains

The first chain, the one for which the transmitters ran a minimum of risks, was that of the juridical *fatwā* in which Ibn Surayj (d. 306), prior to the trial of 301/913, rendered *tawaqquf*, declared the *shar'ī* court (of the qādī) *incompetent* to judge in matters of Hallājian mysticism, for grace (and sanctity) transcends the Law. This chain coincides with the *isnād*, among Shāfi'ites in Baghdad,[2] in Cairo and in Khurasan,[3] of the special *fatwās* of Ibn Surayj (*mas'ala surayjīya*, etc.) via Ibn al-Haddād (d. 344), AB Qaffāl (d. 365), AT Tabarī (d. around 450), A Ishāq Shīrāzī up to M-b-Mubārak-b-Khall (d. 552). Ghazālī, Damīrī, and Khafājī were in this chain.

The second was that of the *tafsīr* (commentary on the Qur'ān) by Ibn 'Atā' (d. 309) containing Hallājian sentences hidden behind the simple

[2] In the Waqf Da'laj.
[3] In Nishapur, in the Waqf Khaffāfī (as far back as the muftī Thaqafī).

first name "al-Husayn"; transmitted, without too many risks, via An-matī and M-b-Abī Mūsā 'Īsā Hāshimī (d. 351) to Sulamī (d. 412), the *rāwīs* of his *ta'rīkh*: AF 'Ushshārī and Ismā'īl Hīrī (d. 430), and to several Khurasanian *rāwīs* of his *tafsīr*, including AB ibn Abī Khalaf (d. 487), M ibn Abī Nasr Tālaqānī (d. 466),[4] Wajīh Shahhāmī (d. 541) (*M*), Tāhir Maqdisī (d. 576) and Baqlī (d. 606), a Shirazian, 'Uthmān-b-M Shahrazūrī and Abū Nasr ibn al-Shīrāzī.

The third was that of the Sālimīya *mutakallimūn* (scholastics) of Basra, AN Sarrāj (d. 377), Ibn Jahdam (d. 414, Mecca), Ibn Bīshrān (d. 430, Baghdad), who canonized Hallāj by name for dogmatic reasons (*tajallī*), which were branded afterwards as heresy as much from the Ash'arite as from the Hanbalite point of view, which finally broke off this chain. It appears to go back to the founder, Ibn Sālim (d. a nonagenarian in 356), via such sermonizers as AB-b-Shādān Bajalī (d. 376) and Amīr Mansūr Dhuhlī (d. 402), and as 'Umar-b-Rufayl Jarjarā'ī and Ma'rūf Zinjānī. It reached as many via the *Bahja* of Ibn Jahdam as via the *Luma'* of AN Sar-rāj in important Hanbalite circles: the B. Manda of Isfahan, Sa'īd 'Ayyār[5] (d. 457) and A Kūfānī (d. 464), Abū'l-Waqt (d. 554) and Karīma Di-mishqīya (d. 641), *rāwī* of the *Luma'*, Azajī (d. 444), Zawzanī (d. 451) and AJ Sarrāj, *rāwī* of Ibn Jahdam (Azajī transmitted the *Bahja* to M ibn al-Battī [d. 564] via A-b-'AQ-b-Yf).

The fourth chain was that of a growing minority of Ash'arite *mutakal-limūn* who canonized Hallāj after Ibn Khafīf (d. a centenarian in 371 at Shiraz); the *isnad* goes from Ibn Ghālib Daylamī and Ibn Bākūyā (d. 428) to Qushayrī (d. 465) and Fārmadhī (d. 477); master of Ghazālī (d. 505), Salmān Ansārī (d. 512), Diyā' D 'Umar Rāzī and his son, the great Fakhr D. Rāzī (d. 606). Ibn Khafīf is at the beginning of the *isnād* of the *Risāla* of Qushayrī and of the *Ihyā'* of Ghazālī[6] (AB-b-'Arabī Ishbīlī, d. 543).

A fifth, a congregationist, chain also starts with Ibn Khafīf, namely: via Hy Akkar and Ibrāhīm-b-Shahryār, founder of the Kāzerūnīya, and the family of Ibn Sālbih (d. 473), coming from Bayda to Shiraz, it reaches R. Baqlī, the passionate commentator on the Hallājian corpus of work (d. 609), the Baydāwīya and Balyānīya, joins both the *qāri'* Shams Jazarī (d. 833) and Abū'l-Futūh Tāwūsī (d. 871), from whence derive all the congregationist Hallājian affiliations, those of the Hijaz with 'Ujaymī (d. 1113), of Hadramut with the B. 'Aydarūs and Zabīdī, of the Maghrib with 'Ayyāshī (d. 1091), and up to Sanūsī (d. 1274).

---

[4] Who went to teach in Syria.   [5] *Lisān al-mīzān* III, 30.

[6] *Ihyā'* in the West: Ibn Hirzahim, Abu Madyan, Ibn Sīd Bono, Shādhilī; *Risāla* in the East: Ismā'īl Jabartī (d. 806), Ibn al-Jazarī (d. 833), Abū Makhrama (*qasīda*).

From Ibn Bākūyā comes the chain of transmission for the *ijāza* authorizing the dictation of his monograph on Hallāj, the only one accepted beyond question in Sunnite circles: this *isnād*, via Mas'ūd Sijistānī (d. 477), Tuyūrī (d. 500), Ibn Muqarrab Karkhī (d. 563), reaches the Hanbalites of Damascus through 'Umar-b-'Alī-b-Khadir Zubayrī (d. 575) and 'Alī-b-Hy ibn al-Muqayir (d. 643).

Another, more complete, biography of Hallāj, inserted by Khatīb Baghdādī (d. 463) in his huge dictionary of the traditionists of Baghdad, no doubt because of his friendship with the Hallājian vizir, Ibn al-Muslima (d. 450), makes the Surayjian thesis party to the diffusion of this dictionary via 'AR Qazzāz (d. 535), Sam'ānī (d. 562) (cf. Ibn 'Asākir), Zayd Kindī (d. 614), Yf ibn al-Mujāwir (d. 690), and Mizzī (d. 742). The 'Abbāsid Court thus seems to have been favorably disposed to the memory of Hallāj, and the official historian Ibn al-Hamadhānī (d. 521) proves sympathetic.

A sixth initiatory chain, which comes from Ibrāhīm Nasrābādhī (d. 369), disciple and *murīd* of Shiblī, Hallāj's friend, reaches, via Ibn Abī'l-Khayr (d. 440) and Harawī Ansārī (d. 481), Yf Hamadhānī (d. 535), 'Abbāsa Tūsī (d. 594), the great Persian poet Farīd D 'Attār (d. 589), author of a monumental (and triple) Hallājian epic; from 'Attār, via Awhad Kirmānī, his disciples of India and Ghawth Hindī (d. 970), it spread throughout the whole of Indian Islam from Delhi to Bengal and to the Deccan; while from Yf Hamadhānī, via A Yesewī (d. 562), it transmitted its basic theme to Turkish mystical poetry. One can connect with Ibn Abī'l-Khayr the biography of Hallāj by Ibn al-Qassās Sharwānī (d. c. 512), diffused by AT Silafī (d. 576) (*M*) [?] as far as the Maghrib: where a pupil of the Baghdadian Ash'arite Shāfi'ite sermonizer Shaydhalā' (d. 494), Hy ibn Sukkara Saraqustī, who died a qādī of Murcia (in 512), an area of the 'Abbāsid *khutba*, may have been the origin of the veneration given to Hallāj by two famous Murcian mystics, Ibn 'Arabī (d. 632) and Ibn Sab'īn (d. 669).

Finally, a seventh chain, and the most profoundly Hallājian, the most discontinuous, is the *isnād* of transmission of the *Akhbār al-Hallāj*, the work that gives his ecstatic prayers and preaching together with the account of his passion.[7]

This *isnād* brings us into contact with a small circle of extremist Hallājians who wanted to transmit his forbidden works and his outlawed teaching inside Sunnite circles at the risk of their lives. Also, this *isnād*

---

[7] Cf. also those of Tawhīdī, Suhrawardī, Ibn Sab'īn.

was broken off (Shākir) and rejoined by genuine renewals on several occasions. It begins with the collection made by Shākir (d. 311), undoubtedly executed for having dared to publish it; resumes with the accounts by Ibrāhīm-b-Fātik, blacklisted for same; continues with Fāris Dīnawarī, taking refuge in Samarqand (d. c. 345), excommunicated *post mortem* for having republished them, and transmitted to Ab Wajīhī, A Hy Fārisī and AB Kalābādhī (d. 380, author of the *Ta'arruf*);[8] resumes with the *Intisār* (Hallājian apologia). Redacted by the well-known Hanbalite Ibn 'Aqīl (d. 513) in his youth, during the vizirate of Ibn al-Muslima, retracted forcibly in 465, this apologia is transmitted secretly by its author to Ibn Marāhib (d. 583), leads to the blacklisting of Ibn al-Ghazzāl, who had intended to reissue it, but inspires the beautiful apologues of 'AQ Kīlānī (d. 561), founder of the Qādirīya, survives in the Hanbalite circles of Damascus: the Shādhilīya order, Najm Rāzī, Kīshī, Semnānī, and the Shuhūdīya (Sirhindī, Bīdil) (Bayrāmīya, Sārī Tchelebī)—a century later, and appears to be the textual basis for the manuscripts of the fragmentary collection that we have published as *Akhbār al-Hallāj*.

An eighth *isnād*, independent, not attacked, because it is merely anecdotal, derives from Qannād (d. c. 325), and from his "Hallājian accounts," whose literary merit was recognized by several *rāwīs*, such as the Mu'tazilite qādī Jurjānī (d. 366), the *muhaddiths* Urmawī (d. 433) and Ibrāhīm Habbāl (d. 482), but which shows only an external and episodic sympathy towards Hallāj.

The centers of dissemination of these eight *isnāds* were Baghdad (1st, 2nd, 5th *c*, 7th, 8th), Nishapur (5th *b*, 6th), Basra (3rd) and Shiraz (4th, 5th *a*). Wiped out in Basra (in 326), persecuted in Baghdad (especially from 334 to 393), the Hallājians were not only tolerated in Khurasan, but were actually supported in Transoxiana, where they took part in the Muslim apostolate on the Turkish and Indian frontiers. Their center in Shiraz died out in the eleventh century (Hijra) when Shī'ism became the official religion of Persia. There were secondary Hallājian centers in Kurdistan (whence the Hallājism of the Yazīdīs), in the Hijaz (with Ibn Jahdam, Ibn Muqarrab, under Abū Numayy, with Nahrawālī, Shinnāwī and Dajjānī), in Yemen, in Jerusalem and Damascus (Ibn Ghānim Maqdisī, Ibn Tūlūn), in Cairo (Ibn al-Haddād, Shams Ikī, Shams Hanafī, Ghamrī Wāsitī).[9]

---

[8] Retraction by Nasrabadhī; retraction by Ibn 'Aqīl.

[9] The ninth artisan and military chain: *Futuwwa: hadīth al-luqma*; Khalaj after Ibn Kundaj up to Ibn Mahlabān Madhkūr. [The list of *rāwīs* who transmitted this *isnād* is found in Chapter XIV.]

Before and after his death, the example of Hallāj propagated Islam in circles that were becoming converted: officers and soldiers of Christian origin, either Byzantine (Nasr, Janissary), Kurd, or Soghdian; either Christian administrative and commercial scribes (Qunnā'īya Nestorians) or Manichaean (Uyghurs); Iraqī (fityān) and Indian (Bengal) artisans; scribes of Jewish origin (Rashīd al-Dīn).

In areas already Islamized and in the lower classes, the cult of Hallāj continued in Kurdistan[10] (Yazīdīs; a number of pro-Hallājian Sunnites were born in Dinawar and Hamadhan), where the Iranian tongue was spoken; it flowered in Turkish lands, Transoxiana and Anatolia, and spread from India (Chittagong especially) to Malaysia. In Arabic-speaking countries, a slender thread of Hallājian popular devotion exists in Syria (Damascus, Druzes of Chouf), in Iraq (cenotaphs in Baghdad and Mosul); in the Maghrib (and Andalusia), as in black Africa, in Sudanese and Bantu regions, only some congregationist texts, reported by pilgrims from the Hijaz, keep alive, from time to time, the memory of Hallāj, which in Arab countries is an intermittent source in a zone of hostile silence: H Qabalān on Hallāj at Shahim. Cf. the Untel (So and so = Jesus) of Judaism—"The one whom we must not speak about."[11]

2. The Hostile Chains of Transmission

Showing a singular perseverence in hatred, the opponents of Hallāj, not content with having sought and obtained his prosecution as an outlaw and his state execution, made every effort to transmit to others their belief in his Satanic evil-doing and their certainty of his eternal damnation.

His first public accuser, the Zāhirite qādī Ibn Dāwūd, instilled in his disciples a hostility which, carried on from generation to generation, from Ibn al-Mughallis (d. 324) to Grand Qādī Bishr-b-Husayn (Baghdad, 369-372), had pursued Ibn Khafīf in Fars, in the person of AH Khurrazī (d. 391), reappeared, with the particular force of a curse in the work of Ibn Hazm (d. 456), and passed with it from M Humaydī (420, d. 488), from the *muqri'* Shurāyh (*khatīb* of Seville; 451, d. 537) to the grammarian and *muqri'* M ibn Khayr Ishbīlī (d. 575) and to Ibn Madā' (d. 592), burst forth a last time in the work of their *rāwī*, Ibn Dihya (d. 633), the first master of the *Dār al-hadīth Kāmilīya* in Cairo; where it became regularized in a systematic anti-Hallājian teaching by his successors, par-

---

[10] Yf Hamadhānī is from Burnzird; Jibrīl→Kīshī; Jāzir→Baqlī.

[11] To be completed via Shawkānī (d. 1250), *Kitāb ithāf al-akābir bi isnād al-dafātir*, written in 1214 (Hyderabad, 1328) (Kattānī II [?], 410).

ticularly Ibn al-Qastallānī (d. 686): whose theory making Hallāj the first Muslim link in a philosophical conspiracy bent on destroying Islam (cf. Nasīr Tūsī) was taken up again by an extreme Andalusian Zāhirite, Abū Hayyān, and especially by the great Hanbalite polemicist Ibn Taymīya (d. 728), precursor of the present-day Salafīya.

A second chain begins with the head of the *Qurrā'*, the Shāfi'ite Ibn Mujāhid, who was assigned the task of examining the conduct and writings of Hallāj at the trial in 308; his opinion created a split in the Shāfi'ite rite, in which the disciples of Ibn Surayj remained favorably disposed towards Hallāj, but many others became anti-Hallājian (cf. Dhahabī). And Ibn Muhāhid's opinion, particularly, was predominant among Reciters of the Qur'ān (a Sālimīyan minority was favorable) and grammarians (cf. Fasawī, Ibn al-Qārih, Ma'arrī); with a touch of caustic irony, of Mu'tazilite origin (cf. the vehemence of two Mu'tazilites, AH Balkhī and AY Qazwīnī, d. 488).

A third chain took shape among the theologians, from a dogmatic source (therefore Mu'tazilite), and at first theoretical in viewpoint among the opponents of the Hallājian Sūfī Shiblī (Muzayyin, Būshanjī, Ibn Yazdanyār), of the Sālimīya, of Ibn Khafīf (ex.: the Ash'arite Bundār, and Yazūl Qazwīnī), the hostility suddenly took on a violent character of *odium theologicum* in Bāqillānī, a Mālikite whom his master, the Grand Qādī Ibn Umm Shaybān (d. 368), son-in-law of Grand Qādī Abū 'Umar, had taught to hate Hallāj at least as much as this latter judge who had condemned him. From Bāqillānī to Abū Ishāq Isfarā'inī and to Juwaynī, the Ash'arite theologians taught that Hallāj was a possessed man and an antichrist ("Dajjāl"); a theme continued by Sam'anī and various Shāfi'ites (Ibn Khallikān, Dhahabī, Ibn Kathīr).

The Hanbalite rite had from the outset the following cleavage: between *mujassima* (Niftawayh, Farrā') and spiritualists (Ibn Abī Dāwūd; Ibn Bashshār, Barbahārī; Ibn al-Mudhahhab); it had started out defending the memory of Hallāj in Baghdad ('Ushshārī) against the Shī'ites; but, suddenly, at the very moment when certain Shāfi'ites were successful, with Vizir Ibn al-Muslima, in predisposing some Ash'arites towards Hallāj (Qushayrī), out of a kind of conservative hatred, a narrow "Baghdadism" erupting against Khurasan and the Turks, there was a strange outburst of anti-Hallājian rage (the trial of Ibn 'Aqīl, 461-465, run by the Hanbalite *sharīf* AJ ibn Abī Mūsā, d. 470), with which the great Hanbalite *khatīb* Ibn al-Jawzī (d. 597) became seized again a century later: in the face of the determined Hallājism of his opponent 'Abd al-Qādir Kīlānī, a Hanbalite beyond question, whose remains he arranged to have thrown into the river, but who is now the saint of Baghdad. We have seen above that the anti-Hallājism of Ibn Taymīya came from another source.

As for the Shī'ites, their canonists had piously reproduced the curses hurled by their *wakīl* Ibn Rawh Nawbakhtī against Hallāj; with a renewed outbreak of hatred under the Buwayhids; by Mufīd, at a time when the name Hallāj must have been used to rally the 'Ayyārūn insurgents; and especially by AQ Tanūkhī, when the Hallājian vizir, Ibn al-Muslima, his enemy, undertook to free the Caliphate from the Shī'ite hold by summoning the Turks. A veritable chain of inflamed hatred against Hallāj, going back from AQ Tanūkhī (d. 384) via his father Muhassin and his grandfather 'Alī (d. 342) to the historian Sūlī (d. 335), whose executor was 'Alī.

The theory of the identification of Hallāj with one of the *"Dajjālīn kadhdhābīn"* (false prophets) of the end of time:

The hadīth collections of the third century of the Hijra refer to the *Dajjālīn*. For example, in Ibn Hanbal, the hadīth of Hudhayfa: "In my community there will be liars, *Dajjālīn*, twenty-seven in number, including four women; but I am the seal of the Prophets, there will be none after me *(lā Nabīya ba'dī)*."[12]

In the wake of Ibn Dāwūd (cf. his *fatwā*) and of Qādī Abū 'Umar (cf. the Qur'ānic form of punishment inflicted on Hallāj), the Zāhirite and Mālikite rites were inclined to give an antichrist apocalyptic character to the personality of Hallāj. That is quite consciously affirmed in the notice by the Zāhirite Ibn Dihya (d. 633) in his *Nibrās*, written in 613.

Hallāj was executed as a *Dajjāl*, as a deceitful rival of the Prophet, and this is why his body was thrown into the fire, a symbol of Hell, after his intercision and his exposure on the cross.

The list of twenty-seven, according to Ibn Dihya, includes Hallāj:[13] it begins with Musaylima, Sabīgh-b-'Isl [?], 'AA Ibn Saba'. The *salafī* M Siddiq Khān Qannawjī (d. 1307), in his essay on apocalyptic history in Islam *(Idhā'a)*, includes among the twenty-seven the extremist Shī'ites, the Bātinīya and Hulūlīya; he refers by name to Ibn al-Kawwā', Aswad, Musaylima, Tulayha, Sajāh Taghlabīya, Mukhtār, the Qā'id al-Zanj,

---

[12] *Nibrās* [bib. no. 251-a], 104; *Ishā'a* [?], 41-43.
[13] Along with nine macrobite false *muhaddithūn* (Sīlafī's list), Ja'far-b-Nastūr, Ashajj; Tanjī, on whom Nasr Qushūrī, Dānī relied; Khirāsh, Dīnār, Ibrāhīm-b-Hadba, Zayd-b-Tamīm, Bābā Ratan (d. 632, Qūsī and Samnānī relied on them), Rabi', Mārdīnī (*Lisān* II, 131, 395, 408, 447, 502; I, 119; VI, 3-76).

four Qarmathian chiefs, Shalmaghānī and Ibn al-Basrī, the Nehavendi (Muhammad) of the year 499, the Magribian Lā', the sorcerer Ghāzārī, and a Maghribian woman; but does not name Hallāj among them. He likens them to the Mehdevi Jawnpūrī, Sayyid Ahmad Khān, founder of Aligarh, and especially the Avicennian Nasīr Tūsī, cursed by Ibn al-Qayīm; and to the historian Ibn Ishāq, whom Mālik denounced as a *Dajjāl*.

It is certain that already during Hallāj's lifetime, the apocalyptical tendencies of his sermons encouraged this interpretation, which his excommunication and his canonical punishment reinforced.

Running parallel to this anti-Hallājian tradition stemming from Zāhirite and Mālikite jurisconsults, a hostile tradition came into being among Ash'arite theologians, thanks to Bāqillānī, who was a Mālikite in law. Transmitted from Abū Ishāq Isfarā'inī to Juwaynī, it links up via the learned Farāwī[14] family of Nishapur with Ibn Dihya and Ibn Khallikān.[15]

b. Criticism of the Validity of the Condemnation

1. As to Its Form: the *Ijmā'*

Hallāj's sentence of condemnation brought about the ruin of the juridical rite that he had founded; but it did not meet with the unanimous approval of Sunnite Muslim jurisconsults, for we see it attacked over the centuries in bold declarations made by authoritative voices. Before examining these in detail, we must inquire if, in terms of Islamic law, according to Sunnite orthodoxy, Hallāj's condemnation was *legal*, legitimate, and if it rendered his excommunication final. Most of the Mālikite (with 'Iyād), Zāhirite (with Ibn Hazm), and Hanbalite jurisconsults[16] (with the *sharīf* Abū Ja'far in 465/1072 and Ibn Taymīya) answer affirmatively. We must, therefore, look at this in more detail.

It is certain, first of all, that the sentence handed down in 309/922 by Sunnite judges goes back to the theoretical powers of the *ijmā' fuqahā' al-zamān*, a kind of concilary authority, *consensus ecclesiae* of jurisconsults,

---

[14] Farāwī (cf. Sam'ānī) [?].

[15] It was perhaps Shāfi'ite in origin: going back to *muqri'* Ibn Mujāhid through his direct disciples, Ibn Umm Shaybān, Malatī, 'Atūfī. Bāqillānī was the pupil of Ibn Umm Shaybān and of the *mutakallim* A'AA ibn Mujāhid (d. after 370): who had him sent on an embassy by 'Adūd al-Dawla. Ibn Dihya said textually that, in his *Shāmil* (*Nubuwwa* chapter missing in the ms. that has recently been discovered in Cairo), Juwaynī "in order to establish the real existence of the Devil, compares Hallāj to him, what a dreadful companion" (*Nibrās* [bib. no. 419-a], 101).

[16] Shādhilī's statement: "I condemn two characteristic marks of the *fuqahā*': of saying that al-khidr is not alive, and of excommunicating Hallāj."

"the fourth basis" of Sunnism, guardian of dogma, infallible safeguard of traditional interpretation, for this sentence was rendered on a point of canon law, that of pilgrimage.

On the other hand, it is historically established that, though *ijmā'* had not yet been formulated as a theoretical concept in law in this period, it was already used, not only for *qirā'a* and *nahw*,[17] but also for *hadīth*.

It already no longer stood for the simple "agreement," postulated by the Zāhirite school,[18] "among *companions* of the Prophet on the question of traditions";[19] it was tending to become the "present agreement among *contemporary jurisconsults* regarding a particular decision to be made in the name of the Muslim community." A century later, Juwaynī did not question it, and, after having formulated—the first, no doubt, to do so—the complete and classical definition of *ijmā'*, the "agreement which contemporary scholars come to regarding a new fact in a legal matter,"[20] he cites as a strange opinion, current in the century with which we are concerned, that was held by Ibn Jarīr Tabarī (d. 310/923), furthered by the Baghdadian Mu'tazilite Abū al-Husayn al-Khayyāt, and adopted by the Hanafite Abū Bakr Rāzī (d. 370/980),[21] that "the opposition of one or even of two, does not invalidate the judgement of *ijmā'*." On that, Juwaynī observes that Ash'arism, on the contrary, recognizes the *liberum veto*.[22] This is the Sunnite tradition.[23]

Let us assume that *ijmā'* had existed: then, unanimity among the consulted legal scholars was required; or at the very least the absence of any declared opposition (*khilāf*); for abstention (*tawaqquf*) was only a means of becoming excluded from the *auctoritas interpretativa* (*ilā inqirād al-'asr*).

Was there a unanimity among Sunnite scholars for condemning Hallāj? In the first place, we have seen that, as far back as the first consultation of

[17] Cf. this edition, 1, 491 (*qirā'a*) and Ibn Jinnī, *Khasā'is* [bib. no. 2106-a], p. 196: *ijmā' ahl al-'arabīya*.

[18] Cf. *Kitāb al-rahn* by Dāwūd [?], including a hundred questions: that Shāfi'ī settled, in opposition to this *ijmā'* (Nābulūsī, *Radd matīn* [bib. no. 842-d], cf. *'Uqūd al-jumān* [?]).

[19] Cf. the trial of Ibn Hanbal. Cf. the book of Najjār (*Fihrist* I, 179). And the criticism that Nazzām directs at the very principle of *ijmā'*. Dirār (followed by Hafs ibn al-Fard) established the idea that after the Prophet, the only proof, *hujja*, is *ijmā'*; the *Akhbār al-Ahād* are to be rejected (Hazm I, 115). Cf. on *ijmā'* the book of Qādī Baydawī (d. 362/972) (Ghazālī, *Faysal* [bib. no. 280-n], 65); and that of the Zaydite Qāsim (d. 246/860), ap. Strothmann, *Kultus* [bib. no. 2221], p. 17.

[20] *Waraqāt*, ms. P. 1266, f. 132b.   [21] *Fihrist* I, 208.

[22] *Waraqāt*, ms. P. 1266, f. 153b.

[23] Cf. in Cairo, in the fifteenth century, the *liberum veto* of al-Mahallī saving an unfortunate fellow condemned by all of the other *'ulamā'* (Sha'rāwī, *Yawāqīt* [bib. no. 741-g], 272); and at Ahmadabad in Gujarat, a little later, the death sentence *fatwā* against Jawnpūrī, rendered invalid by the opposition of only one.

the qādīs, around 296/908, there were *abstentions*, including one, at least, loud and clear,[24] that of the Shāfi'ite Ibn Surayj, a jurisconsult of Baghdad, who seems to have thwarted the preliminary investigation of the trial until his death (d. 305/917). And perhaps also that of the Mālikite Ibn Sālim (d. 297/909) of Basra; but his Sunnite orthodoxy was later to be held in question.[25]

In the second place, with the abstentions disposed of as invalid, was there at least unanimity, as Ibn Abī Mūsā, Tawfī, and Ibn Taymīya were to maintain, among the responses of the scholars who declared themselves? No. Ibn 'Atā', a recognized scholar of the *madhhab* of the *ahl-al-hadīth* (i.e., Shāfi'ite or Thawrite), a traditionist accepted by everyone,[26] was consulted in 309/922, and refused explicitly to join the others in condemning Hallāj's testament of faith (*'aqīda*). Even more, he testified in writing that he considered it orthodox, and we know that he preferred to die from the punishment that the hatred of the deluded vizir had inflicted on him, than to change his mind. The single objection of this witness, only partially stifled by his death, must be sufficient, according to established practice in Sunnism, to render the *fatwā* of condemnation invalid.

In the third place, we note that this *fatwā*, surprisingly rendered, was done so without previous invitation to repentance (*istitāba* by the accused), a prompt procedure peculiar to the Mālikite rite, and one which the Hanifites do not allow.

2. As to Its Content

a. Among Sunnites. It is known that the sentence was guided by considerations of political expediency. But the alleged motive was not a false pretext. The incriminatory proposal applied to the prescription of the *legal pilgrimage* a mystical rule, the *isqāt al-wasā'it*; it declared the omnipresence of God, to Whom the soul must turn to be absolved, to be above the physical act of symbolic rites performed in Mecca.[27] It did not do away with pilgrimage, but affirmed that tradition authorized one to replace it, anywhere,[28] by equivalent and equally efficacious rituals; *when*

---

[24] Damīrī was to compare it to the opinion of 'Umar II regarding the dissensions among *sahāba*. (Cf. this edition, 1, 369-371.)

[25] By Ibn Khafīf, Hujwīrī, and Kīlānī (*Ghunya* [bib. no. 341-h], I, 83).

[26] Even by the Mālikite 'Iyād (*Shifā'* I, 160) and the Hanbalite Ibn al-Jawzī (*Mawdū'āt* [bib. no. 370-l], s.v. *Marad*).

[27] The Hanafites, on the contrary, put such a high value on the materiality of the visit to Mecca that they recognize pilgrimage *by proxy*, to the benefit of the living and even of the dead (ancestors of a convert), for the absolution of their sins. (Cf. Sha'rāwī, *Mīzān* [bib. no. 741-c] [Perron translation, new ed.], p. 154.) Cf. 'Alī Qāri': *bayān fi'l al-khayr idhā' dakhal Makkah man hajja 'an al-ghayr; al-tawāf ba'd al-hadam* (Cairo ms. VII, 130).

[28] "In his house or in the desert," remarks the Shī'ite Narāqī (*Mushkilāt al-'ulūm* [bib. no.

one was unable to go to Mecca. Given the fact of Hallāj's execution, no one dared anymore to revive this old thesis on the juridical plane.[29]

Only one, a philosopher of exceptional originality, Abū Hayyān Tawhīdī (d. 414/1023), wrote a short treatise, no longer extant, "on the intellectual pilgrimage (*'aqlī*), when the physical means is missing for carrying out the legal pilgrimage." It is not certain that this work dared refer to Hallāj; Khuldī, Tawhīdī's master in Sūfism,[30] was hostile to him; Hallāj avoided the word *'aqlī*.[31]

In fact, Hallāj's thesis tended to deprive Mecca of its primacy, the Ka'ba of its holiness. It tended toward the same objective as the violence carried out against pilgrims by the Qarmathian gangs, who succeeded in pillaging Mecca and in carrying off [the Black Stone of] the Ka'ba, in 8-14 *Dhū'l-Hijja* 317/January 930, eight years after the death of Hallāj.[32]

In strict Sunnism, Hallāj's proposition is an error (*bid'a*), not a heresy (*kufr*), for it touches the *furū'*, not the *usūl*.[33] But its consequences made Hallāj's condemnation inevitable and final.[34] The protests that were raised on his behalf were due to the prestige of his scholastic and mystical theses, and have always been refuted by the jurisconsults (*fuqahā'*) in the name of the *res judicata*. The hajj is the one effective coordinating center capable of giving a liturgical structure to Sunnism.[35]

957-a], 309), who states that this is a change in the very content of the ritual set by the lawgiver, thus a *bid'a*. Cf. the little "*ka'bāt*" made of stones set in a row built in the tomb of Buhlūl Dānā. (Cf. *RHR*, 1908, p. 2.) In Johore, prior to 1902, the sultan had a miniature *ka'ba* built for inducing the Malaysians to go on hajj (as related by General Bailloud). In fact, the people of northern Morocco, on the day of 'Arafāt, go to the tomb of Ibn Mshīsh, which is the *hajj al-maskīn* (Nāsirī, *Istiqsā* [?] VIII). And, in Khurasan, there is the daily ritual of the *'īd al-qurbān* (*Moslem World*, October 1921, p. 389): is this perhaps a holdover from the Hallājian preaching?

[29] Sha'rāwī dares not believe it of him. 'Umarī (Amīn al-) and Sayyid Murtadā pardon him. See Makkī, *Qūt al-qulūb* [bib. no. 145-a] I, 92 (Bishr).

[30] Subkī IV, 2.

[31] Cf. *Tawāsin*, 136, 195; Ibn al-Fārid uses it (*Nazm al-sulūk* [bib. no. 403-a], 358, 450). Compare the Hermetic λογιπὴ Θυσία (*Poimandrès* I, 31; XIII, 18), with *hajj ilā ka'bat al-qurb* of 'Ulwān (d. 1531; *Jawhar mahbūk* [?], 56).

[32] Ka'ba removed from 317 to 339, visions of Ibn al-Raqqī (d. 326) and A'A, *Kātib* in 317 (Qush., 128). —Hā Mīm! (Hamīnī?) executed in 325 Hijra in Cordova for having preached the discontinuance of the hajj, according to Hammer (*LGA* [?], IV, 208; taken from Conde [?], p. 79).

[33] Faith in God, the Prophets and judgment (Ghazālī, *Faysal* [bib. no. 280-n], 57).

[34] To deny the Ka'ba is to attack the Prophet (*ibid.*). Compare this with the privilege of the Temple of Jerusalem, upheld against the Jews of Elephantine. The hajj is *fard* (Muslim, *Sahīh* I, 379, 382), hadith stating: *tārik al-salāt aw al-hajj Kāfir* (Hazm III, 229, 236, 247); but Ibn Rāhūya says: *man radda hadīthan sahīhan ('indahu min al-Nabīy fa qad kafar).*

[35] Acceptable spiritual communion, whenever the sacramental is lacking. Jesus at Jacob's well.

b. Among Shī'ites. The Hallāj case troubled deeply the minds of
Shī'ites. We are not referring in this instance to the opinion held by the
Zaydite Shī'ites, which was the same as that of the Mu'tazila,[36] nor to
that of the Qarmathian sects, whose opinion seems to have been at first
favorable,[37] but solely to that of the Twelve Shī'ites, the *Imāmīya*,
whose hierarchical and dogmatic cohesiveness stands in contrast, from
the fourth/tenth century on, to the inconsistency of the Sunnites.[38]

The sentence pronounced by the Sunnite judges in 309/922, in the eyes
of the Imāmites, amounts merely to a political action, decreed by a
usurper without mandate. The condemnation of a heretic, among the
Imāmīya, is a kind of formal excommunication, served in the name of the
Imām by a *tawqī' al-Nāhīya* brief addressed to the leading members of the
party, enjoining them to cease all relations (*tabarrī 'anhu*) with the said
heretic. This is the way in which a dozen heresiarchs[39] in succession had
been excommunicated by name by the sixth Imām, Ja'far al-Sādiq.

Through his sermons among the Imāmites Hallāj had become regarded as one of their own; and two of their leaders, Abū Sahl Nawbakhtī and Abū Hasan ibn Abī Būya, were quick to declare the danger;[40]
before long, it seems, a brief (*tawqī'*) was handed down in the name of the
(absent) Imām for the purpose of excommunicating Hallāj.[41] The text of
this brief, which should have been signed by the third *wakīl*, Ibn Rawh,
has not been found.[42] But Hallāj must have indeed been explicitly condemned. His theory of sainthood, in effect, undermines the foundation
of Shī'ism, the privilege ('*isma*) of the 'Alid Imāms, and the 'Alid

[36] Typical opinion: Abū Yūsuf al-Qazwīnī; but Qannād and Ibn Abī'l-Hadīd are for.
[37] Cf. this edition, 1, 200-204, 280-283; 2, 18, 72, 73; 3, 193-197. *Druzes*: Shihabī (this edition, 3, 194, n. 81; *hurūfīs*: Fadl Allāh *janidān* XXI (this edition, 2, 271-274, and [bib. no.] 1367-a): *ali ilahis*: verse by Khatā'ī (= Shāh Ismā'īl), ap. Turkish ms., ms. P. 1307, f. 15b.
[38] Reciprocal *takfīr* of the Mu'tazila (*qadar, ta'tīl*), Hanbalites ('*ulūw, hurūf*), and Ash'arites (*irjā', tanzīh, sifāt ma'nawīya*).
[39] List, ap. Friedländer, "Shiites" [bib. no. 1693-a] II, 90, 96; compare, for the complete list of heretics excommunicated by the Imāms, with Khūnsārī [bib. no. 923-a] II, 234, and Ibn al-Dā'ī [bib. no. 1081-a], pp. 419-423.
[40] Cf. this edition, 1, 326. Hallāj's teaching on the imminence of the Judgment is close to the Shī'ite *raj'a*. The Yazīdīs have set aside one of their seven *sanjāq* (Dirr) for him.
[41] Jazā'irī (in Khūnsārī [bib. no. 923-a] II, 234) and Hurr 'Amīlī (*Risāla Ithnā 'asharīya* [bib. no. 825-a], ff. 111-112) affirm it.
[42] Tabarsī does not give the text of it; Mufīd gives it [according to] Bihbidāk (*Khayra kya* [?], 43). In his *Ihtijāj* one finds only a *tawqī'* (244) against the *ghulāt* (claiming that the Imām is acquainted with the next world, that he shares in the divine power, and that he can appear in two places) and a *tawqī'* against Shalmaghānī (245) excommunicating him "with his predecessors and peers Sharī'ī, Namīrī, Hilālī, Bilālī and others." Hallāj is not named in this piece, signed by Ibn Rawh.

politico-theological mahdism.[43] And Henceforward, the *akhbārīyūn* Imāmite theologians, from Ibn Bākūyā to Abū Ja'far Tūsī, rank, according to Mufīd, the Hallājīya "children of Cain" among the Shī'ite heretics, in the *Ghulāt* (fanatics) section.

But in the sixth/thirteenth century, Nasīr al-Dīn Tūsī,[44] although an Imāmite, considered Hallāj a saint;[45] the Hallājian ecstasy confirmed for him his own philosophical doctrine of the identification of pure intellect with God.[46] Such was also the opinion of Sadr al-Dīn Shīrāzī,[47] founder of the modern *usūliyūn* Imāmites; [it is found] moreover in the *turuq* (*kasr al-asnām al-jāhilīya*, excerpt in *Safīnāt al-Bihār*).

A very active cult of the memory of Hallāj revived in this way in Persia among the most fervent *mujtahidūn usūliyūn*, Bahā' 'Amilī,[48] Amīr Dāmād and his pupil Ishkaverī, Muhsin al-Fayd—to the great outrage of the *akhbāriyūn* supporters of *taqlīd*, such as Karakī, Miqdādī,[49] and Hurr 'Amilī.

The case of Nūrallāh Shūshtarī is to be viewed separately: this anti-Sunnite[50] polemicist believed that Hallāj had proclaimed, "filled with joy," the coming return of the twelfth Imām, at Talaqan;[51] and that his only crime was in being too hasty in believing the Hour was imminent. Nūrallāh accepts the miracles of Hallāj, and compares him in terms of his zeal and his tragic destiny to the Imāmite Jābir ibn Yazīd al-Ju'fī.[52]

The *Nusayrī* dissident Shī'ites[53] excommunicated Hallāj: as witness this poem[54] by Shaykh Hasan ibn Ajrūd (d. 836/1432):

---

[43] Cf. this edition, 1, 329, n. 151.

[44] Adviser of Hulagu, spurs him on to capture Baghdad.

[45] His friend Shams al-Dīn Kīshī (d. around A.H. 694) taught in the Nizāmiya; —A.H. 665, wrote a laudatory commentary on Hallāj's *Qasīda Uqtulūnī* (*Hindushah* [?], 200).

[46] *Awsāf al-ashrāf*, [by Fakhr Rāzī].

[47] *Asfār arbā'a* [bib. no. 806-a], f. 26, 390, 454: influenced by Ghazālī and Ibn 'Arabī.

[48] *Kashkūl*, [bib. no. 794-a], p. 90, and *Dīwān* [bib. no. 1177-a].

[49] *Salwat al-Shī'a* [bib. no. 1183-a]; cf. this edition, 3, 293ff.

[50] Author of the *Ihqāq al-Haqq*, a refutation of the Sunnite counter by Ibn Ruzbahān to the Shī'ite apologetics of al-Hilli (London ms., Ar. 7493).

[51] He relied on a text of Birūnī (cf. this edition, 2, 72-73).

[52] Khūnsārī [bib. no. 923-a] II, 227. Born in Kufa, died in 128/745, Jābir was the successor of Mughīra, the founder of the Kufa school of hadīth, the master of Sufyān al-Thawrī and the disciple of al-Shu'bī, two Sunnite traditionists. He taught the doctrine of the *raj'a* or resurrection of certain of the dead, especially 'Alī, whom he venerated, before the Judgment (cf. Sam'ānī, Gibb ed., f. 131b; Friedländer, "Shiites" [bib. no. 1693-a], s.v.).

[53] Tabarānī, *Majmū' al-A'yād* [bib. no. 146-a], (ch. IV, *Ghadīr*), lists the heretics, who, like the fallen angels (changed into frogs, falling on the ground with the rain) denied that the divinity of 'Alī was proclaimed to Ghadir: "*Mithl al-ishāqīya wa'l-shārī'īya wa'l-huskīya wa'l-hallājīya wa mā shākalahum*" (Khasībī's answer to Jillī).

[54] Ms. P. 1450, f. 176a; cf. Huart translation, *JAP* (1879), p. 260.

"Put your trust in Khasībī, [55]

—Who has been celebrated in verses and in poems—But those envious of him have said he has hidden himself from view.

—This is the opinion of Husayn Hallāj, the deceit and guile of this traitor, this damned one!

—He believed that Khasībī had needed to see (in order to be a man inspired)! That wretch, that scoundrel, that cursed fellow, that lunatic!

—Before him, Hajjāj[56] also had proved unfaithful and heretical, corrupted like that youth![57]

—God excluded them from His mystery, and threw them into the fires of Hell![58]

More recently, the Bābīs, and afterwards the Bahais, Bahā' Allāh and Gulpaygānī, have honored the memory of Hallāj as a precursor.

Mansūr-i Hallāj, according to the Yazīdīs.

He is the last divine messenger whom they mention before the Judgment and the end of time.[59] In the list of seven *sanjāq* (bronzes? of Tāwūs, the "Peacock," representing his successive manifestations, Dirr[60] noted that Mansūr-i Hallāj occupies the sixth) (the bronze for his image weighed 308 kg. [sic] and the seventh is not named).[61]

In a tale[62] concerning the end of the world, Mansūr Hallāj appears as the seventh and last divine messenger:[63] "he will purify the world and will level it off completely."

c. The Sainthood (Walāya) of Hallāj: Canonization in Islam

Since the last members of the rite that Hallāj had founded disappeared as far back as the fifth/eleventh century, and since the grounds for his condemnation have become since 309/922 *res judicata*, how does it happen that the "Hallāj case" can still today be posed so sharply[64] to the conscience of Muslims? How is it that, given these circumstances, the matter

[55] Abū 'Abdallāh al-Husayn ibn Hamdān al-Khasībī, Persian, third successor to al-Namīrī as head of the Nusayrīs: plants the sect in Syria.
[56] The Umayyad viceroy, cursed in the third *quddās* (ibid. [?], 44).
[57] A reference to Hallāj's early period.
[58] On Ibn Ajrūd, see *Du'd' al-yamin* (*bākūra*, tr. ap. *JAOS*, 1868, p. 280).
[59] Lescot text [?].
[60] *E. I.*
[61] Tchāl [?].
[62] Kurd, *Afnu*, November 1936 (Lescot) [?].
[63] After Ezi (= Yezid), Osmanjek, Jesus (Sherfiddin, Hajāj, and Majāj).
[64] Cf. the controversy between Madārisī, a Shāfi'ite, and Najdī, a Hanbalite, a few years ago (bib. nos. 975, 976); between Shifshawarānī and 'Alaysh-Siddīq Khān; Nadwī.

was not "buried in oblivion," as in the case of so many other heresiarchs who were either more or less cruelly put to death?[65]

We are in the presence here of a very unexpected historical phenomenon, the stubborn survival in the memory of Muslims of a strong moral personality, disfigured in vain by the coalition of political power and religious leaders, and honored as a source of poetry, as a model of beauty and love, in popular[66] legend and erudite literature.

And in a parallel way, in the most diverse of minds, one comes unexpectedly upon the spontaneous, disinterested appearance of a deep-seated adherence, like a conversion, to this outlaw's cause. One can argue that Ghazālī defended Ḥallāj because he was following in this the Sālimīya scholastics and the mystic Fārmadhī; one can argue that the small flock of Ṣūfīs and mystics wished to vindicate Ḥallāj because their cause had been identified with his. But these explanations are of no value in the case of men like Vizir Ibn al-Muslima and the Ash'arite Ibn Khafīf, like the Hanbalites Ibn 'Aqīl Harawī, 'Abd al-Qādir Kīlānī, and Tawfī, like the philosophers Suhrawardī of Aleppo, Nasīr al-Dīn Tūsī and Sadr al-Dīn Shīrāzī, like the Imāmite Nūrallāh Shūshtarī, and the Hanafite 'Alī al-Qāri'.

No self-interest, personal or collective, won these men over to Ḥallāj; quite the contrary. Rather a sudden sympathy felt for the moving story of his life, an admiration, at first perhaps merely aesthetic, for the great stream of poetry of which he was the source, and afterwards a careful reflection on the very engaging tone of his works, poems, and maxims, led them finally to a certitude: they grasped a profound agreement between the condensed essence of his thought and the best of what their personal theories held true. From Ibn Khafīf: "If he were not a believer in one God, then no one in the world is!" Ibn 'Aqīl confessed in his forced retraction: "I believed that Ḥallāj had been a good Muslim." Such must have been, in this era, the firm belief and devotion of many of the common people of Baghdad with regard to Ḥallāj.

So it was that the question of Ḥallāj arose again, brought up again before the court of *fuqahā'* (jurisconsults); the fact that they had proved once that he had been justly condemned was useless when people came forward and affirmed to them that Ḥallāj was a *saint*.

---

[65] And who are rehabilitated only together (theosophists; S. Reinach).

[66] 'Abd al-Mahdī, a bedouin from Salt, said to me in 1917 in Jerusalem: "it is he who used to say: '*man yujīranī min Allāh?*' who will protect me from God?" Cf. Qur'ān 72:22—"*ughīthūnī min Allāh*" ('Amili, *Kashkūl* [bib. no. 794-a], 96): cf. Angelo de Foligno "*Amor incognitus, quare?*"

All of the cleverly conceived and probable accusations put together against him,[67] and even the grounds for the condemnation, mattered little; popular devotion, supported by the religious experience of disinterested scholars, affirmed that Hallāj was a saint and called upon him as such without waiting for the approval of the jurisconsults.[68]

We touch here on a very interesting point of Sunnite law, the *procedure of canonization*. What is the role of the *ijmā' al-fuqahā'* in this matter? Far from being unanimous in this instance as theory would have it, the opinion of the Sunnite jurisconsults appears to be hopelessly divided, and, indeed, from the previous question: along with prophets *are there saints*, *"awliyā"*; "friends of God," to whom one has recourse before and after their deaths, as intercessors (*shafā'a*) for obtaining divine graces, even miracles? Since the fourth/tenth century, the Karrāmīya Hanbalites, followed by the Ash'arites, answer affirmatively and canonize, in accordance with very old traditions,[69] the ten *ashāb*[70] *mubashshara* of the Prophet, with Uways Qaranī and still others,[71] in opposition to the negative conclusion of the Mu'tazila, who condemn the dissensions of the *sahāba* and reserve miracles for the prophets.

In the eighth/fourteenth and twelfth/eighteenth centuries, the negative view is revived, at least in terms of the second part, by the neo-Hanbalites, Ibn Taymīya and the Wahhābites [respectively], who are followed by the contemporary Muslim modernists; to them the cult of saints is only idolatry. The canonization of Hallāj produces in them the twofold exasperation of seeing popular devotion, in the first place, going astray by canonizing someone and, on top of that, by choosing an excommunicate. Hence, the sharp tone of Ibn Taymīya's *fatwā*, which will be analyzed later.

As for the other *fuqahā'*, those belonging to rites that accepted the theoretical possibility of the existence of *saints* and the legal legitimacy of popular devotion to them, the fact that the question of sainthood remains a subject of disagreement between them and other *fuqahā'*, prevents them from formulating a regular *procedure of canonization*. There is no interest

---

[67] Jubbā'ī, Bāqillānī, Juwaynī (cf. this edition, 1, 546-547).

[68] In Sunnism, it is the muftīs, qādīs, and *shuhūd* who are in authority.

[69] Baghdādī, *Farq* [bib. no. 201-a], 344. Qur'ān 48:18. Certain Hanbalites accept it: some *budalā'* and one *mustakhlif* (*Hilya* X, 305, ap. the biography of Badr-b-Mundhir Mughāzilī; A Barmakī, for AH A-b-M ibn Bashshār, d. 313, whose *shafā'a* he puts above that of Uways, in the *maqām al-nabīyīn* (Farrā', *Tabaq.* [bib. no. 2066-a], s.v.). Ibn Batta forbid speaking of the *walāya*, or *barā'a*, of anyone.

[70] Bakrīya, *Farq* [?], 201: Ibn Hanbal.

[71] The contending forces of Badr, the contending forces of Uhud (except for Quzmān), coswearers of Hudhaybīya.

in inquiring into the virtues of a person (one must not reflect on the sins of the prophets,[72] nor in examining the orthodoxy of his writings and his pronouncements; for the saint is basically a "possessed man of God," considered not accountable for anything he might say or do[73] during ecstasy. The only criterion is: whether or not one surrenders to popular religious experience; that is to say, to the proven efficacy of his intercession on behalf of his devotees,[74] and beyond that to intuitions, dreams, or personal visions.[75]

d. Commemorative Monuments

After the burning of Hallāj's torso, his ashes were thrown into the wind from the top of a minaret (at Bab al-Taq)[76] overlooking the Tigris. It was there, on the banks of the river, that people awaited his resurrection, according to Ma'arrī (two accounts of his appearing). Of his head, hands, and feet, exposed on the wall of New Prison, we know only that the head, removed after a year from the "museum of heads" (Khizāna),[77] was dispatched to Khurasan and carried about from district to district; was it then brought back to Baghdad and put with his other remains, was it then buried? No one knows.[78]

The site of his execution, maslib, was venerated early. In 437/1046, Vizir Ibn al-Muslima, coming to pray there, said "hadhā makān mubārak," according to the historian Hamadhānī, who adds "wakāna bayt 'ibāda qadīma," "this had formerly been a place of prayer";[79] it was a "tell" on the procession route going from the palace (Harīm East bank) to the al-Mansūr mosque, therefore near Bab Khurasan. One can pinpoint this, since it is in the same place where Ibn al-Muslima was executed in 450/1059: near the camp, in the al-Māristān (al-'Adudī) sūq, near Bab Khurasan and the Najmī gardens,[80] "opposite the turba of (Gharīb) al-Khāl,"[81]

---

[72] Fakhr al-Dīn al-Rāzī, Tafsīr Kabīr [bib. no. 385-c] V, 363.

[73] Ibn Hajar and Abū al-Su'ūd are in agreement about canonizing Ibn al-Fārid and Ibn 'Arabī, even though blacklisting all of their works (Alūsī, Jalā, 65).

[74] The Baghdadian proverb on the tomb of Ma'rūf al-Karkhī: "a tried and true theriac" (Qushayrī, Risāla [bib. no. 231-a] I, 81).

[75] Haytamī and Nābulusī accept Hallāj on the authority of Kīlānī; Khafājī does so on the authority of Shādhilī; by taqlīd.

[76] Manārat, absolutely = the one of the Sūq al-Ghazl: this edition, 2, Figure 13.

[77] On this museum "cupboard," cf. Tabarī III, 2213. It burned in 601/1204 (the head of Basāsīrī was in it); Fakhrī, 374 [bib. 501-a] (a hand of Ibn Muqla and the head of Hy-b-'UA-b-Wahb).

[78] Nasr, or the Queen Mother, or Maryam, would have preserved them.

[79] Christian church, or Mazdaean fire altar.

[80] Hamadhānī.

[81] His son Hārūn was buried there in 322 (Sūlī, ms. P. 4836, f. 10a: "near Qasr 'Īsā"; cf. ibid., f. 98: tomb of Hārūn-b-Muqtadir).

the brother of Queen Mother Shaghab. The *rahba* where Hallāj was executed was, as we have seen above, at Bab Khurasan, near the Qarār, the destroyed palace where New Prison was built in that period, "between the bridge and Bab Khurasan," according to Niftawayh.[82]

1. The Present-Day *Qabr al-Hallāj* in Baghdad

It is out of the question to identify this *maslib* with the site where, since the year 581, accounts by travelers attest for us to the erection of a tomb, *qabr al-Hallāj*, which still exists, always in the same place, "near the *mashshad* of Ma'rūf Karkhī," Ibn Tiqtaqā specifies (around 680/1281). This [latter] site is in the southernmost end of Baghdad (right bank), to the south of Karkh (Qantarat al-Shawk; Bab al-Dayr, Tutha, Qatufta), to the east of the group of tombs making up the Qabr Junayd (the old Shuniz Madfan Ma'ruf cemetery, Qabr Zubayda.)[83] This is the *qabr* visited by Ibn Jubayr (*Safar* 581), AH Harawī (around 612),[84] Ahmad Badawī (around 630), Semnānī (687), Mustawfī (before 740), Silahlī Matrāqī (942), Sārī 'Abdallāh (probably 1048),[85] Mustafā Siddīqī (1139); which pilgrims still visit, especially Indians; and which Amīn Rayhānī and Kāzim Dujaylī visited in 1924.[86]

I have visited it several times (1907-1908, 1927, 1930, 1934, 1939);[87] it is a cube-shaped structure, [roughly] 26 feet each side, 11 feet high; consisting of only one room, with a window, and, on the left side, a plaster rectangle forming the grave.[88]

Built between 437 ([probably] after 450) and 581; therefore necessarily with the approval, at least tacit, of the *shaykh al-shuyūkh* of Baghdad; on the initiative of an influential family, almost certainly the B. al-Muslima, in memory of the Hallājian devotion of their founder, on an estate belonging to them (they owned one such property at Qatufta), like their other foundations: turba at Bab Abraz, *Ribāt* Ibn Ra'ys al-Ru'asā' in the palace (east bank), turba in the *Ribāt* Zawzanī (opposite the al-Mansūr

---

[82] Khatīb I, 92, line 20 = Salmon, 120.

[83] This pseudo-tomb of Zubayda is probably the *turba* of Saljūqa Khātūn (d. 584, Zumurrud, Hujra and Benefshah) (M. Jawād; *contra*, 'Azzāwī, *Bayn ihtilālayn* I, 406 [bib. 999-01?]).

[84] Harawī [bib. no. 389-a], ms. P. 5975, f. 68b.

[85] Cf. his *Jawhar al-bidāya* (Tāhir bey I, 100: Hālis Ef. ms. Istanbul); cf. the saying of the spirit of Nazmī Zādeh about the *wali Pembūgh*.

[86] *Recueil*, p. 243.

[87] Visits: 12/20 and 29/1907, 1/26/1908, 3/16/1908, 12/14/1927, 12/19/1927, 6/28/1930, 12/16/1930, 3/3/1934, 4/15/1939, 4/29/1939, 4/20/1945, 4/29/1945, 12/12/1951, 3/21/1952, 3/26/1952.

[88] *Missions* II, 114. [See this edition, 2, Figure 19.]

mosque), *Ribāt* Mubārak. Perhaps as early as 479, at the time of the restoration through the good offices of the *shaykh al-shuyūkh*, Abū Sa'd-b-A-b-M Dūstzād Naysābūrī, of the *Madfan* Ma'rūf, damaged by floods; or even, between 567 and 581, at the same time as the *Ribāt* al-Ikhlātīya of the *Madfan* Ma'rūf, by Queen Mother Zumurrud (d. 598), a Turk and a fervent Hanbalite.[89]

Graffiti on the Qabr al-Hallāj
Noted 3/16/1908

A. One graffito in Turkish:
line 1: . . . God . . . "Anā'l-Haqq" . . .
line 2: . . . by this pious visit . . .

B. One graffito in Persian:
line 1: "O God, author of grace and mercy (*keremgar*),
line 2: Lord of mercy, to whom says 'Amen,' You grant one's share of paradise!"
(Signed): "'AR. Ishāq, Ghulām Muhyī al-Dīn, Ghulām M Nasīb al-Dīn, Ghulām Haydar M Khān, servants of the bolt (of the door) of His Highness (= 'Alī), Mullā 'Alī, 'Arab M; may the intercession of the martyr be kind to them!"
This Shī'ite graffito comes perhaps from extremist Hindus (*buhūras*), Ismā'īlīs, employed by a *waqf* in Najaf or Kufa.

C. One graffito in Arabic:
line 1: the director of the quarantine (against the plague) in Kazimayn,
line 2: M. Husayn Khān, the Indian, 13 *Muharram* 1326.
This is probably an offshoot Sunnite (*mehdevi*) from Ghujrat.

D. One graffito in Arabic:
line 1: I have put in writing in this place
line 2: the testimony that there is no god but God.
This is the customary formula for *ziyāra* (cf. Snouck Hurgronje, *Mekke* (Leiden: E. J. Brill, 1931) II, 28, 1; and the graffiti that I saw in 1927 in Jeble in the tomb of Ibrāhīm Adham).

In 1924, K. Dujaylī stated that someone had hung a poster up with the Hallājian "Nadīmi . . . " quatrain. It was no longer there three years later.

[89] Ibn al-Sā'ī IX, 55, 189 [bib. 463-c]; Athīr [bib. no. 420-a], X, 55; XII, 18. In any case, this *qabr* cannot have been usurped from some unknown Hallāj, such as 'Umar-b-'Uthmān, d. 604 (Mansūr mosque), M-b-Barakat, d. 583 (Bab Harb), Hibattallāh, d. 634.

2. The *Maqām*

No *maqām* has been noted in Khurasan, although there was perhaps a reference to Hallāj (spelled Hajjāj, *sic*) in an epitaph in Tashkent[90] dating from 608/1212.

In Mosul, there are two *maqām* dedicated to Hallāj; one in a small mosque in the Hadīthīya suburb (referring to Hadīthat al-Dijla, a ruined city southeast of Mosul), called attention to at the end of the eighteenth century by Amīn 'Umarī.[91] The other, in the Bab al-Masjid quarter (building no. 18/160), the Mansūr al-Hallāj masjid, with adjoining *madrasa*, rediscovered in 1927, according to Dāwūd Çelebī, by the qādī of Baghdad, 'Uthmān Devejī (not far from the Nabī Dānyāl *madrasa*).[92] In Lalish (Jabal Hakkār, northeast of Mosul), adjoining the tomb of Shaykh Adī, there is a *maqāma Hallāj*, crowned with a cupola.[93]

In the tomb itself, of the seven bronze effigies of the "Peacock" Angel (= Malak Tāwūs), the oldest and the heaviest (308 kg) is called Sanjāq Mansūr Hallāj.[94]

In India, there are figured representations of Hallāj in eastern Bengal (cult of Satya Pīr).[95] There is a *maqām-i Hallāj* in Mahmūd Bandar (Porto-Novo) near Madras.[96]

In Damascus, in the Maydan quarter, a Hallājīya *madrasa* was erected in the Mamlūk period, probably dedicated to Hallāj by Sultan AM Ahmad (= al-Mālik al-Mu'ayyad, 815, d. 824) in 818. The epigraphic text, which we have published,[97] records, in fact, the existence of a director of a *waqf* entitled "*al-mashyakha al-masūna*" of the Sūfī Husayn al-Hallāj. Could this have been a convent for women, the kind of which there were several (Hanbalite) at that time? Pilgrims' graffiti will have to be examined on all of these monuments. I had begun the task for the *qabr al-Hallāj* of Baghdad,[98] of which I published a sixteenth-century miniature by Matrāqī[99] and two photos taken in 1907 and in 1957.[100] This *qabr*

[90] Wiet, *Répertoire recueil épigr.* [bib. no. 2251-b] X, 70-71 (no. 3700).
[91] [Cf. *Passion*, p. 398.]
[92] Dāwūd Çelebī, *Makhtūtāt al-mawsil* [bib. no. 999-04], 190, 204.
[93] With a green or yellow cotton flag (Parry, *Six Months* [bib. no. 1644-a], p. 381).
[94] Menzel, ap. *Enc. Isl.*, s.v. Yazīdī.
[95] Oral testimony of M. Suhravardi (May 1940).
[96] M. Hamīdullāh, ap. *REI* (1938), p. 104.
[97] According to MM. Wiet and de Lorey (*Recueil*, pp. 69-70). But this sultan was hostile to mystics (*mudarris* of the anti-Sūfī Mu'ayyadīya; execution of Nesīmī in 817). See this edition, 2, Figure 28.
[98] *Mission en Mésopotamie* II, 114-116.
[99] Ap. *Dīwān al-Hallāj*, p. 122; cf. *Recueil*, p. 244 n.
[100] Cf. this edition, 2, Figures 17, 18, and 19, and *Dīwān*, p. 122.

was restored around 1922 by Sayyid Rashīd-b-Dāwūd Sa'dī, a leading Baghdadi property owner, whose estates were adjacent to the tomb, which was threatened by plans for enlarging the British railway station (West Baghdad). In the cadastral survey, the *qabr* is shown to occupy the northeast corner of the Ibrāhīm Erzeumlī *mazra'a*.[101] The key to the tomb was found in 1939 in the home of the son of the custodian (*qārim*) appointed in 1905 at the time of the restoration by Kāzim Pasha, Sayyid Ahmad: Umūrti-b-Shaykh Ahmad (April 1945).[102]

3. Hallāj Street in Istanbul (October 1927)

In October 1927, the numbering commission for the municipality of Istanbul was obliged to replace a certain number of obsolete names; thus, in the Shahzade quarter, it gave to the ancient *Tekke* Sūqāghī the name *Hallāc-e Mansūr Sūqāghī*; this little street, running parallel to Veznejiler Street, forms, in the north, a quadrilateral with it and with two side streets, Dayruni Street and the Martyrs du XVI Mars Street. This appellation raised an uproar in the press, which was soon quelled by the commission president, 'Usmān bey Cemāl.[103]

4. The Hallājian Memorial in Cemeteries
(Tombs of Hallājians)

EGYPT

Cairo: in the Qarafatayn Misr: (NE: Muqattam): AH Dīnawarī (d. 331), with 'Abd al-Samad (d. 335) and Bunān (d. 316); (SE: Wafā'īya): Ibn 'Atā' Allāh (d. 709); (right in the SSW): Shihāb Tūsī (d. 596); Fakhr Fārisī (d. 622); (W: Imām Shāfi'ī): jawsaq Madharā'yī; (E: Imām Shāfi'ī): Shattanawfī; Taqī ibn Razīn; (the Qāytabāy gate): zāwiya 'Adawīya; (WNW: Sitta Nafīsa): Ibn Murta'ish (d. 328); Zabīdī

at Bab al-Nasr Misr: (Sūfīya): Ibn Ghānim Maqdisī (d. 678)
at Bab al-Sha'rīya Misr: Jāmi' Ghamrī; Sha'rāwī; Ibn al-Haddād
in Damietta: Shushtarī (d. 668)
in Alexandria: Silafī (d. 576); Mursī

IRAQ

in Baghdad: Hallāj (d. 309); Shiblī (d. 334); Kīlānī [d. 561]

---

[101] Letter from the RP. Anastase-Marie de Saint-Élie, 3/20/1911 (cf. *Recueil*, p. 244). *Mazra'a* bought by M. Tenge (west RR Station).

[102] Hemmed in on three sides by a knoll set with nineteen date-palms (in the northeast), to the west of the Isolation Hospital (Mustashfā'l-'azl). [And also a *maqām* at Galibolu (Turkey): this edition, 2, Figure XXI.]

[103] Cf. *Recueil*, pp. 171-172.

ARABIA
in Mecca: Nasrabadhī [d. 367]

SYRIA
in Aleppo: Suhrawardī; ['Imād] Nesīmī [d. 820][104]

TURKEY
in Istanbul: Sārī 'AA Çelebī [d. 1071]
in Limni Kal'e: Niyazī [Misrī, d. 1105][105]
in Brusa: Ismā'īl Haqqī (d. 1137); Lāmi'ī (Naqqāsh 'Alī mosque) [d. 958]
in Aydin: Muridī [d. around 1004]

IRAN
in Shiraz: (Kabirīya): Ibn Khafīf (d. 371); Tawhīdī (d. 414); Rūzbehān
Baqlī (d. 609);[106] Ibn Bākūyā? (Bābā Kūhī?)
in Nishapur: Ghazālī (Tūs); 'Attār (d. 617)

TURKESTAN
in Bukhara: Fāris [Dīnawārī] (or in Samarqand?) [d. 345];
Kalābādhī[107]
in Marw: Yf. Hamadhānī
in Yasa: [Ahmad] Yesewī [d. 561]
in Tashkent: AB Qaffī

AFGHANISTAN
in Herat: Ansārī [d. 481]; Fakhr Rāzī [d. 606]
in Ghazna: Sanā'ī[108]

PAKISTAN
in Lahore: Hujwayrī; Iqbāl

INDIA
in Delhi: Sērmēd [d. 1071]; Bīdil (d. 1133)

MOROCCO
in Fez: AB-b-'Arabī Mu'afirī; 'AQ Fasī; Ibn 'Abbād Rundī

[104] Cf. the epitaph of Nesīmī, ap. Recueil, p. 151.
[105] Limni Kal'e = Kastro, on the Isle of Lemnos (cf. chap. IX). [See also the epitaph of Niyazī Misrī, ap. Recueil, p. 164.]
[106] Cf. Ivanow, 1928: his tomb is at Mahallat Darbeh Shaykh.
[107] [Cf. Ch. IX.]
[108] [Cf. REI (1941-1946), p. 41, n. 1. L.M. visited the tomb of Sanā'ī in 1945.]

e. The Dhikr *of Hallāj and the Neo-Hallājīya*[109]

1. The *Dhikr* According to Nesīmī

On one final point, various later Muslim mystics declared themselves openly to be disciples of Hallāj; on the formula to be adopted for the *dhikr*, "litany." The Hallājian principle of the *isqāt al-wasā'it*,[110] applied to the formulas of ritual prayer, had led to the proclaiming of the superiority of mental prayer (*fikr, tafakkur*) over vocal litany (*dhikr, tadhakkur*); in contrast to the vogue regarding the *dhikr* in most of the Muslim schools of mysticism. However, in order to keep mental prayer from degenerating into a mere philosophical meditation on some metaphysical themes, an exercise of pure intellect leaving the will unaffected, it was necessary to give a rigid framework to prayer, to introduce at the start some very short expressions, always the same, which served as a springboard and as a *formule excitatrice*. That was a circuitous route, which revived the practice of the *dhikr*, as al-Nasafī observes:[111] "the *Fikrīya* say: meditation is worth more than the [prescribed] worship; they do away with four of the five *farā'id*—the legal prayer, alms, fasting, pilgrimage—and they "*dhikr*" merely the *shadāda*: "*lā ilāha illā-llāh!*" There is no document that enables us to ascertain if Hallāj had taught his disciples a special initiatory *dhikr* formula upon their entry into his order.[112] We have shown elsewhere[113] how much the authentic prayers that they have preserved for us by him were free of any formulism, of any repetition. Now one might object that their *dhikr*, if it were *dhikr*, since it had to remain secret, was not recorded in writing.

---

[109] We have no documents enabling us to connect the executions of the following Sūfis directly with the memory of Hallāj: Abū Bakr Nābulūsī, executed in 363/978 (cf. Qush. IV, 188, 189) in Cairo (Sha'rāwī, *Yawāqīt* [bib. no. 741-g] II, 14); Ibn Barrajān, author of a *tafsīr* and herald of the capture of Jerusalem (Subkī V, 210. Asin, *Abenmasarra* [bib. no. 1725-a], pp. 109-110), executed in 536/1141 in Marrakesh with Khawlī and Ibn Qasyī, author of *Khal' al-Na'layn* (Shahīd 'Alī ms., 1174) Sh. *Tab.* I, 17); Murjānī, executed in Tunis in 669/1270 (Sh. *Tab.* I, 203); Qābid (d. 934/1527) and his disciples in Constantinople (Hammer, III, 69; IV, 236, etc. [bib. no. 1602?]); Murshidī (d. 1304/1886) in Mecca (Le Châtelier, *Confréries* [bib. no. 1634], pp. 97-99).
A dervish from Kuki voluntarily offered himself up for punishment, saying *Anā* "in order to imitate Mansūr" (= Hallāj), in Bijapur (India); he was Mahmūd Bahrī Pīshagī (*'Arūs 'Irfān* [?], written in 1117/1705) (f. 26).
—'Ayn al-Qudāt Hamadhānī.
—Hamid-b-Makkī Itfīhī Qassār, a former Ismā'īlī Shī'ite, who became an Ash'arite and afterwards recognized as a *Hallājian*, was crucified and pierced with arrows (cf. St. Sebastian), in Cairo, in Dhū'l-Hijja 516/1123 (Maqrīzī, *Khitat* [bib. no. 2157A-a], I, 459-460).
[110] Cf. this edition, 3, 245 ff.
[111] *Bayān al-madhāhib* [?]: Jabarīya, 10th sect.
[112] Except perhaps *Tawāsin* XI (*Bustān al-ma'rifa*), §23.   [113] *Quatre Textes*, pp. 24-27.

Some believed that the *dhikr* of the Hallājian order was the famous expression: "*Anā'l-Haqq*! I am the Truth!"[114] And that it was through constant repetition of this expression, regarded as [including] one of the ninety-nine names of God, as the *ism a'zam*, that Hallāj had arrived at permanent divine union.[115] This idea begins to work its way into the legends of his martyrdom, where we see him with his limbs mutilated, his head cut off, his ashes scattered, repeating in a loud voice: "*Anā'l-Haqq.*" This is the central theme of the Hallājian epic in the great philosophical poems of 'Attār. And this is the thesis put forward by the great Turkish poet Nesīmī in his *Dīwān*.[116]

'Imād al-Dīn Nesīmī,[117] at first merely in love with mysticism and an imitator of Shiblī, was introduced to the neo-Qarmathian teaching of the Hurūfīs at the same time as were the leaders of the Bektashīya military order.[118] The admiration that he professed in public both for Fadl Allāh Hurūfī and for Hallāj created riots in Aleppo; he was judged, sentenced, and skinned alive in 820/1417.[119] Nesīmī had disciples in Turkey, among others Rāfi'ī (811), who was the author of *Bashārat Name*.

2. The *Dhikr* According to Sanūsī

Present-day Islam knows another form of *dhikr* which claims to have been the initiatory sign of the order founded by Hallāj, of the *tarīqa hallājīya*, thus resembling in an unexpected way the modern type of Muslim congregations.

Here is what Sanūsī (d. 1276/1859), the famous founder of the martial order of the Sanūsīya (Senusis), has to say about it:[120] "The *tarīqa hal-*

---

[114] Ghazālī, *Fadā'ih* [bib. no. 280-l], 30, line 12. In Baghdad there is variety of pigeon called "*haqqī*" because the cry they make is "Haqq!"

[115] Jāmī's thesis (see Probst-Biraben, in *Tawāsin*, 178, n. 9).

[116] Stamboul ed., 1298, p. 52, etc.: "I repeat '*Anā'l-Haqq*!' continually."

[117] The inscription on his tomb, adjacent to a small cemetery near the Farāfira quarter (in Aleppo); wooden boards set on a wooden gallery to the left of Nesīmī's tomb: copied down on December 29, 1918.

[118] Cf. E. G. Browne, *JRAS* (1898), and following numbers. Cf. this edition, 2, 271-274.

[119] One strange legend, current among the Armenians of Aleppo, depicts Nesīmī as having married a crypto-Christian Armenian woman; converted while seeing her father-in-law celebrating Mass, he declared himself a Christian and was skinned alive (Yusufian, in *Machriq* [September 1920], pp. 706, 59). A stone in the Bab al-Nasr (Aleppo) bears the impression of three of his fingers. Sha'rāwī (d. 973/1565, *Yawāqīt* [bib. no. 741-g], 140) rendered a curious account, legendary also, of his trial and of his happy attitude in the face of death. His execution is depicted in two miniatures (ms. P., Persian Supplement, 1559, f. 167; and ms. P., Persian Supplement, 1150, f. 152). Cf. Gibb, *Hist. Ott. Poetry* [bib. no. 1660-a] I, 344-367.

[120] In the *Jawāhir khamsa* of the Shattarīya (ms. BN 5359).

lājīya is founded on the principle of divine union (*jam' bi-llāh*).[121] It teaches how to arrive at it through recitation of the name of Allāh (*dhikr al-jalāla*) by omitting the initial syllable *al* and by giving the three vowels to the final *h* in succession: the *a* (while bending the head) to the right, the *i* to the left, and the *u* to the heart (thus: *Lāha! lāhi! lāhu!*).[122] This method is effective in many ways, but may be used for the *dhikr* only in solitude (*khalwa*) and by a man warned of what will result from it. This is what many initiates have not taken into account, which has resulted in their saying things in public that must be kept secret,[123] to the point that a heretical sect has grown out of it, may God confound it and protect us from the temptation into which it has fallen!"[124] Sanūsī adds: "My[125] shaykh, al-Shinnāwī,[126] was initiated into this *tarīqa*, clothed for it[127] by the authority of Ibn Abī al-Futūh, who took it from the saint, from the man of God (*Amīn al-milla wa'l-Dīn*) Muhammad ibn Mas'ūd Balyānī,[128] who took it from Shaykh Rukn al-Dīn 'Abdallāh ibn Muhammad Baydāwī,[129] whose lineage goes back directly to Hallāj."

It seems that, in the thirteenth century of our era, in Bayda (Fars), Hallāj's native town, there were actually two brothers who claimed to be his direct descendants of the eighth generation:[130] Rukn al-Dīn 'Abdallāh

---

[121] This text appears, more concisely, in the *Adāb al-dhikr* of an Indian Qādirī, Ja'far M (b.) Abū Sa'īd, written in 1097/1686 (Persian ms., Calcutta, o a 30, f. 37, Ivanow).

[122] "*Lāhu lāhi*" is perhaps a distortion of the end of *Bustān al-ma'rifa* (*Lā huwa wa lā hiya*). Cf. Ibn Sab'īn: *laysa illā Huwa* (*Allāh*) (*dhikr*).

[123] Summary of a text by Simnānī on "*anā'l-Haqq*" (*Ta'wilāt*, [bib. no. 522-a], s. CXII). Simnānī took it perhaps from Balyānī, and Balyānī took it, in fact, from Ibn Sab'īn, for Ibn Taymīya (*Rasā'il kubrā* [bib. no. 512-j] II, 97) said "(it seems that Hallāj was *ittihādī*) and this is why the *khirqa* of Ibn Sab'īn included, among a series of bad masters, Hallāj."

[124] Ap. *Salsabīl mu'īn*.

[125] Text from the seventeenth century (Hasan Ujaymī, d. 1113/1702) in his *risāla*.

[126] Son of the master of Sha'rāwī (*Latā'if* I, 11; *Tab*. II, 133), of the Badawīya order.

[127] Al-Sandyūnī, al-Dulunjāwī, and Sayyid Murtadā appear to have been initiated into this brotherhood. Likewise 'Abdarī, one of whose passages (*Mudkhal* [bib. no. 524-a] I, 17) is similar to the one by Dulunjānwī (cf. this edition, 2, 182; apropos of the Prophet).

[128] Awhad al-Dīn (Abū) 'Abdallāh ibn Imām al-Dīn Mas'ūd Balyānī (d. 686/1287), a seventh-generation descendant of al-Daqqāq, who lived in Shiraz (Jāmī, *Nafahāt*, 295) and spoke of Hallāj (see this edition, 2, 227-228).

[129] One must not identify him with the famous Qur'ān commentator Ibn 'Umar Baydāwī. Sanūsī describes him as "*sāhib al-nūr al-mushriq*," which should remind us of the title of a work of which the great Baydāwī was supposed to have been the author; but this, I believe, is a simple laudatory epithet, an allusion to his eastern (Persian) origin, playing on the word "*mushriq*," "he who rises to illumine" (like the sun in the East). Compare the truncated sentence (in the printed edition of Khūnsārī, *Rawdāt* [bib. no. 923-a] II, 235) of al-Jazā'irī on Diyā' al-Dīn, a descendant of Hallāj.

[130] Common genealogy of their father Muhammad; Ibn Ahmad ibn 'Abd al-Rahīm (ibn Husayn ibn Muhammad), ibn Ahmad, ibn 'Abd al-Samad ibn Abī al-Mughīth (= Hallāj).

and Shihāb al-Dīn Ahmad. The first[131] founded the modern Hallājian order. As for the second, Sayyid Murtadā tells us that he was a pure Arab, speaking Arabic,[132] head of an honored and respected family which still had representatives "down to the present time."[133] This family used to say that Hallāj, its ancestor, had been[134] the direct descendant of the *sahābī* Abū Ayyūb al-Ansārī, the Prophet's standard-bearer, killed (52/672) at the first siege of Constantinople; he is the eponym of the present-day cemetery of Eyüp, at the end of the Golden Horn.[135]

II. HALLĀJ AND SPECIFIC CURRENTS OF THOUGHT IN MUSLIM SOCIETY

In the whole of the Islamic world, apart from the circles in which we have just examined the continuing traces of his survival, Hallāj is no more than a name, barely appreciated, labeled and classified under one or another rubric, in accordance with the Muslim discipline in which one is professionally trained.

a. Urban and Peasant Crafts

In the official tradition of the urban corporations, of the early Ottoman Empire (*gedik*, abolished in 1924), of Iran, and of Moghul India, Hallāj is the patron of carders; thus, both of those who begin the cleaning, either of wool, or especially of cotton, by means of iron combs (cards) or a wheel (*dawlāb*) with two nails, iron (fluted) and wooden, and a piece of warped wood around which the cotton is rolled, thanks to a drum (*daff*, *juljul*) beaten by the right foot,[1] and [the patron] of those who finish it, the *naddāfa*,[2] by means of a bow, *mindaf*, which, beaten by a mallet, makes a piercing sound (tr, tqe; tr, tq; tr, tr, tq, tqe); he is not the patron

---

[131] He was the master of the founder of the Safavids: Rukn al-Dīn Baydāwī.

[132] See this edition, 2, Table IV, pp. 116-117.

[133] Taken from whom? —"*ilā-l'ān*."

[134] Al-Husayn ibn Mansūr, Ibn Abī Bakr, Ibn 'Umar, Ibn 'Abdallāh, Ibn al-Layth, Ibn Abī Bakr, Ibn Abī Sālih al-Shāmī, Ibn 'Abdallāh, Ibn Abī Ayyūb (nine generations for three centuries), Sayyid Murtadā, *Ithāf* [bib. no. 862-a] I, 250; IX, 33.

[135] Identified from a vision of Shaykh ĀQ Shams al-Dīn, who spurred Muhammad II on to storm Constantinople in 858/1453 (Hammer, *Gesch. Osm. Reiches* [bib. no. 1602-b] I, 523-524).

---

[1] A kind of roller: Qāsimī, *Qāmūs, sin. shām.*, [bib. no. 2189-a], 18; Wehbī, *Suwarnāma*, ap. *Mejelle Umūr Belediye* ('Uthmān Nūrī), 1922 (II, 590 [bib. no. 1342A].

[2] Baldensperger, *Palest. Expl. Fund* (1903), p. 41; Evliyā, p. 589 (= Hammer [bib. no. 1602-b] II , 474).

of fullers (combined with carders only in the West),[3] considered an impure corporation in Islam (whereas Seth had been a carder).

In Istanbul, Evliyā specifies, in 1048/1638, that the patron of carders (hallājān), after Seth, was Mansūr Zāhid al-Qattān, the twelfth of the pīr initiated by Salmān,[4] buried in Baghdad; and that on their doors they hung, as emblems made of cotton, clubs, arrows, guns, men with black eyes, lions, tigers,[5] and all kinds of animals; each lion is equipped with a chain also made of cotton; "beware of the cotton lion," said the emblem of a hallāj. It may be that these lions are a token of remembrance of the legendary Hallāj "astride the lions with a whip." The provincial origin of the carders of Istanbul should be studied. Perhaps there were Yazīdī Kurds among them, thus extremist Hallājians. Evliyā notes, in the case of the two garlic (sāremsāqjiyān) and onion (sughānjiyān) market corporations, two plants originating under footsteps (garlic right foot, onion left foot) of Iblīs,[6] some connection with the Yazīdī Kurdish tribes (Khāletī, Çekwānī). From these Kurdish elements in the working classes of Istanbul arise certain disconcerting reminiscences concerning Hallāj,[7] like the word uttered by a Turkish woman, noted in passing in the street in May 1940 by a reporter of Aqsām,[8] a typical Yazīdī word.

Artisan folklore includes satires against the hallāj, who is forced to always stand, while the naddāf is always seated;[9] Usāma[10] and Ābī[11] refer obscurely to these satires without clarifying whether Hallāj himself is alluded to in them. In Arabic from the Algerian south, hallāj stands for bardash;[12] in onirocriticism "hallāj al-qutn" stands for the judge, master of settling matters, the money changer who chooses the good coins, the man who has many wives and children.[13] The mihlāj, the carding apparatus, signifies the fact that truth is distinguished from falsehood; this tool and its drums are personified as two partners, one of which is perfidious and the other cruel.[14]

---

[3] Franklin, Dict. hist. arts métiers [bib. no. 2067-a], 1906, p. 126.

[4] Out of fifty-eight.

[5] In Bengal, Hallāj is depicted seated on a tiger.

[6] Anal. Hammer (Constantinople, 1822) II, 435 [bib. no. 1602-c] (passage omitted ap. Evliyā edition).

[7] See the verse [concerning the] wool: Qur'ān 101:4 ["And the mountains will become as carded wool"].

[8] Valā Nūrettin, ap. Aqsām [?], May 17, 1940.

[9] Ikhwān al-safā' II, 29.   [10] I'tibār, Hitti edition, 124.

[11] Lubāb nathr al-durar, ms. P. 3490, f. 54a.

[12] Beaussier [bib. no. 2030-a], p. 136, col. I; Marçais, Tangiers, [bib. no. 1731-b], p. 423, s.v. Qurshul.

[13] Nābulusī, Ta'tīr [bib. no. 842-e] I, 164.   [14] Ibid. II, 251.

b. Female Occupations

There are some slight Hallājian traces: in Istanbul, some Turkish mothers silence the tears of their children by calling upon *Hallāc-e Mansūr*;[15] Yazīdī women must not use narrow-necked jars, in which the voice of Hallāj could reverberate, and would risk making them pregnant, like his sister.[16]

Exorcists in the time of Būnī attributed one of their methods (that of *Khānqātitīya*) to Hallāj. Likewise the alchemists and physicians.

Flutists of the Mevlevi concerts have a flute, *nei Mansūr* (opp. *neye Shāh*), which bears his name: in Turkey and in Iran.[17]

Tahalluljī of Damascus still chant, during nights of mourning, *zajal* by Shushtarī, and Hallāj's name appears in them.[18]

Fadāwī, tellers of sagas in rhyme, itinerant singers, still sometimes sing the popular *Qissa* of Hallāj in the Druze parts of Lebanon.

The corporations of brigands, *'ayyārīn*, *shattārīn*, have for a long time had certain connections to Hallāj, apologues of AQ Hamadhānī, AQ Kīlānī (*Bahja*, [*Bahjat al-Asrār*; see EI², I, 70 and GAL, I, 560; Suppl. I, 777] 121), "Ibn Khafīf."[19]

c. Intellectual Professions (of the Book): Copyists and Reciters

Subject to police supervision from the *muhtasib*, three professions of the book, copyists, booksellers (*warrāqīn*), and school masters, were obliged, in Baghdad, to deal with an index of forbidden books, including those by and about Hallāj; three centuries after his death, Ibn al-Ghazzāl was threatened for having copied some *riwāya* with *isnād* about Hallāj, in Baghdad.

The *warrāqīn* were the publishers, literally the managers of copy shops, expressly empowered by authors to disseminate their works, of which

---

[15] Testimony of Sabri Essad [to L.M.], Istanbul 2/7/40.

[16] Myriam Harry, *Les Adorateurs de Satan* [bib. no. 1739-b], pp. 80-81, transposed it, making Hallāj John the Baptist and his sister Salome.

[17] Villoteau, *Descr. Egypte XIII*, 442; Raouf Yektā, *Encycl. Mus. Lavignac V*, 3018-3019. A verse by Shams 'Uthmān Uskudārī (Tahir bey II, 271): "the jug of wine goes around with the cup—the intoxication of the mystery bubbles over from heart to heart—the voice of the melody with the Shāh flute, turns toward Mansūr—conversation between adepts is united from heart to heart." Testimony of Pr. Şerefettin, Istanbul 2/14/40. Cf. Burhānī, *Qati'* [?], Turkish translation, s.v. Shāhnay, 514 (Deny).

[18] Qasīmī, *Qāmūs* [bib. no. 2189-a], s.v.; *zajal* M 3, footnote 13 and *zajal* F 95a (v. 2) (G. S. Colin [?]).

[19] Abī, *l.c. supra* [see n. 11]. And *futuwwa* (*Taw.*, 170; 'AQ Hamadhānī; Qūsī: according to Ibn Khafīf).

they retained the *asl* (the original text authenticated by *ijāza* and *samā'*). They were concentrated in the areas of Qasr Waddah (Ibn al-Dāya, *Muk Fāh*, [*Kitāb al-Mukhafā'a*; see GAL, I, 155; Suppl. I, 229; EI2, III, 745-756] 16) and Bab al-Taq (Yāq., *Ud.*, VI, 461).[20] Some of them worked for the Caliph: for Mu'tadid (and Muqtadir?), Dhakwān (Kh. VIII, 397), and the Mālikite M-b-Jahm Marwazī (*Furh.*[?], 243). Khayrān was the one for the grammarians (Yāq., *Ud.*, II, 145); the Abū'l-'Abbās brothers and A Ishāq-b-Ibrāhīm published *qurrā'* (such as Khalaf and Ibn Shannabūdh I. Jaz. I, 34); Hy Samarqandī (d. 282) published Zāhirite law (*Lis. Miz.* [bib. no. 632-b] II, 290); AQ ibn Hubaysh, and afterwards AS 'Umar-b-A Dīnawārī, worked for Tabarī (Yāq., *Ud.*, VI, 450, 453); Ismā'īl-b-A Zajjājī was the *warrāq* of Mubarrad (*Fihr.*, 60). The historian Jahshyārī and Abū'l-Tayīb (*Fihr.*, 165), and the mystic Ibn Abī'l-Dunyā Ahmad-b-M, the master of the *nāqid* Ibn Hubaysh (Kh. IV, 391): he is perhaps the one who published Hallāj.

Ibn Mujāhid had a *warrāq* for the text of the Qur'ān who became famous as head of the *shuhūd* of Baghdad from 338 to 370 at least, Talha-b-M-b-Ja'far (b. 288; d. 376); he was already his pupil in the period and the one who was so strict in upholding the ban on copying and selling Hallājian texts (in 367, in Mecca, when the Hallājian *warrāq* Nasrābādhī died, it was discovered that he had forbidden texts in his possession; in 311, one such was found in a box belonging to the former vizir, Ibn 'Isā; it was due to the effects of non-Baghdadī Sālimīya *muhaddithīn* that a Hallājian text was read, for example, by Mansūr Dhuhlī of Herat).

d. Qur'ānic Sciences (Mufassir)

In general those belonging to this discipline, the readers (*qurrā'*), reciters (knowing the entire Qur'ān by heart = *huffāz*), and commentators (*mufassirūn*), are of one mind in either ignoring or condemning (Abū Hayyān)[21] Hallāj.

Exceptions to this, some *qurrā'*: Ibn Mardhānaqā, Ibn al-Haddād, AT 'Ushshārī, Silafī, 'Atūfī (d. 430), Ibn Muqarrab (d. 563), Nasr Manbijī (d. 719), Ibn al-Jazarīd, Zak Ansārī, Shattanawfī, Suyūtī; some *huffāz* (Harawī, Ibn Surayj, Ibn al-Haddād, Sulamī, Khatīb, Mas'ūd Sijzī, Silafī, Ibn al-Sā'ī, Nūr Tāwusī, have defended him. Hallāj (was) regarded as a *hāfiz* by his generation (*Akhbār*, no. 72).

Some Qur'ānic commentators, in the mystical sense, mention him:

[20] They gave their name to the (*rub'*) Warrāqīn quarter, which had a *sūq* (Yāq., *Ud.*, I, 153).

[21] In *Qur'ān* 5:19.

Ibn ʿAtāʾ, AB Qaffāl, Sulamī in the *haqāʾiq al-tafsīr*, with respect to verse 42:17 and 208 passages;[22] also in the *taʾwīlāt* of Kasirqī and Semnānī, after the *ʿarāʾis* of Fakhr Rāzī and Baqlī; and this is all there is, apart from a reference in Kāshifī and two in Ismāʿīl Haqqī.

e. Traditions and Lives of the Prophet
(Hadīth and Sīra)[23]

Hallāj had not been a *muhaddith* (Dhahabī), and the onomastic and traditionist directories, both those of the Sunnites and of the Shīʿites, mention him only to exclude him.[24]

Among the authors of *sīra*, Burhān Halabī (d. 1044), adapting in his *Insān al-ʿuyūn* the *Subul al-hudā* of Sālihī, studies the Hallāj case with respect to the angel "assuming the form of Dihya."

His condemnation, in the *shifāʾ* of Qādī ʿIyād (d. 544), created a stir, as witness the number of its commentaries.

By a rash waiving of the rule, Hallāj's name (Husayn-b-Mansūr) is included in one of the *isnād* of the *hadīth al-luqma*, in the *Musalsalāt* of Saʿīd D Kāzerūnī.[25]

f. Table of Opinions Held by the Leading Scholars of Islam

Arranged in chronological order in the following tables are the names of the learned scholars of Islam who expressed their opinions about the orthodoxy of Hallāj, under the following three rubrics:

1) *Taraddud* (condemnation), subdivided into *radd* (simple rejection) and *takfīr* (excommunication). The scholars mentioned in this group believed that Hallāj's mystical teaching was heretical and that his "miracles" were either prestidigitations or demoniacal marvels (*sāhir*).

2) *Tarahhum* (canonization), subdivided into *iʿtidhār* (justification with excuses) and *qabūl* (complete and unqualified acceptance).

Ibn Taymīya (ap. *Rasāʾil kubrā* [bib. no. 512-j] II, 97) divided them thus.

---

[22] Published in *Essai*.

[23] In the Dār al-Hadīth Kāmilīya of Cairo: ʿA ʿAjūrī Mundhirī, Qutb Qastallānī *contra*; in the Dār al-Hadīth Ashrafīya of Damascus (Nawawī), Subkī: *pro* (1st Ibn Salāh, d. 643, Abū Shāmī, d. 665), Nawawī, d. 676, Mizzī, d. 742, Subkī, d. 756: ʿAbd al-Qādir, *Tuhfat al-zāʾir* II, 76 [bib. no. 969-b].

[24] The Zawzanī *wuʿāz* . . . Ashʿarites—a little before 465—Maqādisa; *Qissa* (one verse quoted by Ibn Taymīya).

[25] Cairo ms., Majm. 403, f. 14a.

a) *i'tidhār*—for Hallāj being *mustalim*, died *shahīd*; his judges being *mujāhidīn*. This is the opinion held by Kīlānī (cf. Hallāj);

b) *qabūl*: (1) Hallāj being *mustalim*, died *mazlūm*: culpability of the executive authority *(ahl al-shar')*. (2) *Id.*, *id.*: culpability of the *fuqahā'* in their *ijtihād* *('ulamā'*; *sharī'a)*. Cf. Pārsā *(Passion*, 1st ed., p. 427) and Yāfi'ī *(ibid.*, p. 356, n. 1). (3) Hallāj died manifesting God through *hulūl* (a secret not to be revealed): this is the opinion held by Harawī (Semnānī). (4) Hallāj died demonstrating that all is God *(zuhūr kullī)*: the view held by the monists, including Ibn Sab'īn.

The scholars mentioned in this group believed that Hallāj's mystical states were consistent with orthodoxy and that his miracles were genuine. Almost all, in point of fact, thought that the public preaching of esoteric truths had been a scandal rightly punished by death by the law.[26]

As for the theological explanation given by Hallāj of his theory of *'ayn al-jam'*, some find it excessive and incorrect; this explanation is only the hyperbole of a fanatic, for the saint cannot unite with the divine essence, but only with one or another of the names or divine attributes;[27] and they excuse him *(i'tidhār)* because of the influence of ecstasy *(ghalaba)*.

Others accept *(qabūl)* the reality of *'ayn al-jam'*, but separate it from the philosophical premises on which Hallāj based it. They connect it with the monist thought regarding the abstract unity of logical Being; since Ibn 'Arabī especially, they consider it a precursory and incomplete vision, a much too "personalized" confession of the impersonal identity of the All, both creator and creatures.

3) *Tawaqquf* (abstention). The scholars mentioned in this group thought[28] that the Hallāj case was a secret, mysterious, and inexplicable case that it was not their business to judge.

Examples will be given later of the most important opinions. We have arranged them in two tables: the *fuqahā'* and the *mutakallimūn* (and *hukamā'*) with regard to the particular nature of their works and of their proofs. But for the great majority of scholars the matter of the litigation was not the whole of Hallāj's life or teaching, but rather the symbolic sentence which was given him, and which epitomizes him for posterity: "*Anā'l-Haqq*," "I am the Truth," or rather "my 'I' is God!"[29] The *sūfīya*

[26] Some of them even pronounced the *takfīr* against him for having violated the "arcanal discipline" (cf. *Der Islam*, 1912, p. 254). All of them vindicate the judges, except for Amīn al-'Umarī and Sayyid Murtadā, to whom Sha'rāwī wrongly adds Ibn Khallikān.

[27] *Sifatite* theory of Wāsitī, Bistāmī, and Jurjānī analyzed by Ghazālī with odd and deliberate stylistic prudence, ap. *Fadā'ih al-bātinīya* [bib. no. 280-1], 30, line 17, and *Maqsad asnā* [?], 73.

[28] Cf. *Passion*, 1st ed., *fatwā* of al-Urdī, p. 395.

[29] Cf. *Der Islam*, 1912, pp. 255-256.

will be examined separately at the end of this chapter and in the next chapter.

1. By the Jurisconsults, According to Rite

(1) *Zāhirites*. It was the head of this now no longer extant rite, Ibn Dāwūd (297/909), who had delivered the first *fatwā* of excommunication against Hallāj. The Zāhirites in general followed his opinion; as witness Ibn Hazm, Abū Hayyān. Only the Sūfī Ibn 'Arabī, who claimed to be a Zāhirite in law, exonerated him.

(2) *Mālikites*. In accordance with the *fatwā* of 309/922, drafted by the Mālikite Abū 'Umar, the great majority of Mālikite scholars (especially in the Maghrib) excommunicated Hallāj and approved of his execution without prior *istitāba*; for example: Qādī 'Iyād, Qurtubī, Ibn Khaldūn, Ibn Abī Sharīf al-Tilimsānī. However, beginning in the eighth/ fourteenth century, before the development of the philosophical and mystical monism of Ibn 'Arabī and due to the influence of the leading orders, we encounter some lapses: 'Abdarī (d. 737/1336)[30] in his *Mudhkal*, Dulunjāwī in his intense manifestations of devotion to Hallāj on the margin of Khatīb's *Ta'rīkh Baghdad*.[31]

(3) *Hanbalites*. It is not certain that the general tradition of the rite was to accept the legitimacy of Hallāj's condemnation;[32] Husrī (Sūfī) abstained;[33] Ibn 'Aqīl, *defender* of Hallāj's sanctity, was forced to retract. Two great mystics, Harawī and 'Abd al-Qādir Kīlānī, both unquestioned Hanbalites, declared themselves for al-Hallāj. And Mar'ī, the conscientious commentator of Ibn Taymīya, aligned himself with the opinion of Ibn al-Ghazzāl and Tawfī, who declared Hallāj innocent, although Ibn Taymīya was dead set against him.

(4) *Hanafites*. Their qādī, Ibn Buhlūl, had not countersigned Hallāj's condemnation.[34] Most of the Hanafites were hostile to Hallāj in the early

---

[30] He was the pupil of Ibn Abī Jamra (d. 675/1276), who had been confined in his house until his death for having claimed to have had a vision of the Prophet when awake (Sha'rāwī, *Tabaqāt* [bib. no. 741-a], I, 202-203).

[31] *Fatwā* of Ibrāhīm Laqānī (d. 1041) (Sirhindī).

[32] Nasr: for; Muflih: against.

[33] Husrī. Ibn Sam'ūn

```
    Harawī        AH Qazwīnī
       \              |
      Kīlānī       Abū'l Waqt
                      |
                  Ibn al-Ghazzāl
```

[34] Condemnation of the Hallājīya (Abū Shakūr, Jabirī, *Tamhīd*), the Karrāmīya create *waqfs*.

TABLE I
OPINIONS HELD BY THE *Fuqahā'* (JURISCONSULTS)
REGARDING THE ORTHODOXY OF HALLĀJ

4th Century. *RHM*: a) No full acceptance. b) Ibn Surayj (*SF*); Ibn al-Haddād (*SF* Tabarite); Muzanī (*HB*).
RDD: a) Ibn 'Īsā (*HF*); Ibn Buhlūl (*HF*); Junayd (as a Thawrite *SF*), b) Ibn Dāwūd (*ZR*); Ibn Rūh (*IM*); Abū 'Umar (*ML*); Ibn al-Ushnānī (*ZD*); Ibn Bābūya (*IM*).

5th Century. *RHM*: b) Harawī (*HB*).
RDD: a) Khatīb (*SF*). b) Ibn Hazm (*ZR*); Tūsī (*IM*); Abū Ja'far 'Abd al-Khāliq ibn Mūsā (d. 470/1077: *HB*).

6th Century. *RHM*: b) Kīlānī (*HB*).
RDD: a) Ibn al-Jawzī (*HB*). b) 'Iyad, Turtūshī (*ML*).

7th Century. *RHM*: b) Ibn 'Arabī (*ZR*); 'Izz Maqdisī (*SF*); Majd Ibn al-Athīr (*SF*).
RDD: a) Ibn Abī'l-Dam (*SF*); Ibn Khallikān (*SF*). b) Ibn al-Dā'ī (*IM*).

8th Century. *RHM*: b) Subkī (*SF*); Tawfī (*HB*); 'Īsā Ruhāwī (*SF*).
RDD: a) Ibn Khaldūn, Ibrāhīm Shātibī (*ML*). b) Jamāl Hillī (*IM*); Ibn Taymīya, Ibn al-Qayyim (*HB*); Dhahabī, Ibn Kathīr, Bulqinī (*SF*); Mughlatā'ī (*HF*).

9th Century. *RHM*: a) Muhammad Hanafī, Ba'iqarā' (*HF*). b) Ibn Hajar, Suyūtī, Ansārī (*SF*). Bukhārī, Shahzādeh Kurkut (*HF*).
RDD: b) Maqrīzī (*SF*); 'Aynī, Bistāmī (*HF*).

10th Century. *RHM*: a) Sha'rawī (*SF*); Shūstarī (*IM*). b) Haytamī (*SF*); Jannābī.
RDD: a) Tilimsānī (*ML*); Diyārbakrī (*HB*).

11th Century. *RHM*: a) Bahā' 'Amilī, Muhsin Fayd (*IM*); Mar'ī (*HB*). b) Dārā', Kātib Tchelebī (*HF*); 'Urdī (*SF*).
RDD: a) 'Akarī (*HB*). b) Tāhir Qummī, Mu'min Jazā'irī, Hurr 'Amilī (*IM*).

12th Century. *RHM*: a) Ibn 'Aqīla (*SF*). b) Sawaydī, 'Umarī, Zabīdī (*HF*).
RDD: a) Bahrānī (*IM*).

13th Century. *RHM*: a) Wardīghī (*ML*); Nabhānī (*HF*); Madārisī (*SF*).
RDD: a) Khūnsārī (*IM*); Nu'mān Alūsī, Rashīd Ridā' (*HB*).

ABBREVIATIONS: *RHM* = *tarahhum* (canonization: a) *qabūl*, b) *i'tidhār*). *RDD* = *taraddud* (condemnation: a) *radd*, b) *takfīr*). *ML* = Mālikite. *SF* = Shāfi'ite. *HB* = Hanbalite. *HF* = Hanafite. *ZD* = Zaydite. *ZR* = Zāhirite. *IM* = Imāmite.

centuries for reasons of dogmatic theology (*mu'tazila*); and accepting the *res judicata*, they did not involve themselves in the question, though the Shams al-Dīn Hanafī and Sayyid Murtadā wanted to pardon Hallāj.[35]

(5) *Shāfi'ites*. Shāfi'ites, at first favorable, were profoundly divided. The average opinion was guided by the *fatwā* of abstention[36] that Ibn Surayj had signed and that Qushayrī, Ibn Hajar, Suyūtī, and Urdī revived. However, there was a deep division between the party of Ghazālī, 'AQ Hamadhānī, Maqdisī, Sha'rāwī, Haytamī, and Ibn 'Aqīla, which canonized Hallāj, and the later group (influences by Ibn Taymīya) of Dhahabī, Ibn Kathīr, al-Bulqīnī, and Sakhāwī, which excommunicated him.

(6) *Shī'ites*: (1) Zaydites. It being the rule[37] for Zaydites to excommunicate Sūfīs, Hallāj was duly[38] condemned by Abū Yūsuf Qazwīnī, pupil of Ibn Kajj; (2) Imāmites. In accordance with the *tawqī'* delivered against Hallāj, all of the Imāmite scholars without exception excommunicated him, save for the *usūlī* author of *Muhhib al-Qulūb*, the history of the sciences of Qādī Qutb al-Dīn Ishkavarī Lālihī in the third part (cf. *Nafas*[?], 65). We set aside the case of his admirer, Nūrallāh Shūshtārī (who was an Imāmite qādī in India), because he died there executed for heresy.

2. By the Theologians, According to School[39]

Only the table of opinions appears here; analysis of criticisms will be found in Chapter XIII.

Because Hallāj had adopted, as we shall see, the Greek (Aristotelian) philosophical vocabulary, he was excommunicated by the early Scholastics, who were upholders of materialistic atomism ever since the Mu'tazilites; except for Qannād, who was also a historian of mysticism; from Jubbā'ī to Abū Yūsuf al-Qazwīnī, down to the Ash'arites, from Bāqillānī to Juwaynī. Ibn Khafīf is an exception whom we shall examine when we come to him.

---

[35] Abū Nu'aym was silent.

[36] Ahmad Māhir Effendi, a Hanafite, a deputy of Kastamūnī, stated to me in 1912 that there was no *ijmā'* against Hallāj. In 1927, the municipality of Stambul was able to succeed in naming a street after him.

[37] Cf. the *takfīr* of Kīlānī and of Ibn 'Arabī by the Zaydite Imām, Mansūr bi-llāh (d. 1029/1620) in his *Qasīda al-kāmil al-mutadārik* (London ms., Or. 3851, ff. 101b-105a).

[38] Also Ibn al-'Ushnānī.

[39] Notice against Hallāj of AZ Balkhī (and not AQB, whose *maqālāt* are earlier than those of Ash'arī).

The supporters of Greek logic, on the other hand, perhaps from Tawhīdī onward, were favorable to him; likewise the neo-Ash'arites, in the person of Ghazālī and Fakhr al-Dīn Rāzī; the pure *hukāmā'*, in the person of Ibn Tufayl and Nasīr al-Dīn Tūsī; and the *ishrāqīyūn*, in the person of Suhrawardī of Aleppo and Sadr al-Dīn Shīrāzī.

Ibn 'Arabī and the Ittihādīya school (until Nābulusī) even attributed to Hallāj the paternity of their own theological teaching.

From the ninth/fifteenth century onward, most of the *mutakallimūn* are careful to distinguish, with Sayyid Sharīf Jurjānī (d. 816/1413)[40] and Ibn Kamālpāshā, the *ittihādīya* thesis (*wahdat al-wujūd*) from that of the *hulūlīya*, in order to help the latter escape the legal excommunication which hung over the former. And the majority, when they seek to absolve Hallāj, act in that attempt in accordance with the opinion they hold on Ibn 'Arabī, who has become the great subject of debate in mysticism among dogmatic theologians.[41]

One exception must be noted: 'Alī Qārī'; this Hanafite *faqīh*, who opposes Ibn 'Arabī and Dawwānī so violently, tries to justify Hallāj (cf. 'Izz Maqdisī). He approves and upholds, in his *risāla* against Ibn 'Arabī, the antithesis of Kīlānī, between Hallāj "whom the contemplation of God caused to forget the creation of himself" and "Pharaoh, who became absorbed in the contemplation of himself"; "this is why the *'ulamā'* are divided on the subject of Mansūr (= Hallāj) and in agreement in condemning Pharaoh." Qārī' feels, even confusedly, that the abstract and logical monism of Ibn 'Arabī has nothing in common with the doctrine of divine union preached with such rapture by Hallāj.[42]

---

[40] *Sharh 'alā tajrīd al-kalām* (*Hāshīya*, Köpr. ms. 800; *cit.* Khafājī, f. 811a).

[41] In chronological order: Defenders of his *sanctity*: Ibn 'Atā-Allāh, Abū al-Qāsim Baydāwī, Ibn Fadl Allāh Yāfi'ī, Fīrūzabādhī, Jurjānī, 'Alī ibn Maymūn, 'Ajam bint al-Nafīs, Jāmī, Dawwānī, Zakarīyā Ansārī, Ibn Kamālpāshā (Shaykh al-Islām from 932/1525 to 940/1534), Sha'rāwī, Haytamī, Muhsin Fayd, Sadr Shīrāzī, Ibrāhīm Kawrānī, Munāwī, Nābulūsī, Ismā'īl Haqqī, Ibn Bahā' al-Dīn, Ibn al-Qādī, Shirbīnī, Khafājī, Tawfīq Tchārkasī.

Supporters of the *excommunication*: Ibn Taymīya, [Ibn Qayyim] al-Jawzīya, Ibn al-Khayyāt, Taftāzānī, Abū Hayān ibn Daqīq al-'Īd, Ibn al-'Irāqī, Nāshīrī, Dhahabī, 'Asqalānī, Bukhārī, Ibn al-Muqri', Sakhāwī, Bulqīnī, Biqā'ī, Qārī' (cf. the work of Tāhir bey, quoted ap. Bibliography, s.v. Ibn 'Arabī).

Supporters of his *sanctity* who put his works on the *index*: 'Izz al-Dīn Maqdisī, Suyūtī (who condemns his disciple 'Abd al-Karīm Jīlī), Ibn al-'Imād 'Akarī, Abū Su'ūd (Shaykh al-Islām from 952/1545 to 982/1570), Haskafī; Ibn 'Abidīn (according to Alūsī, *Jalā'*, 45).

[42] Early defenders: *muzakkī*: Ibn Shādhān; *shāhid mu'addal*: Ibn al-Muslima; in hadīth: Ibn 'Atā'; in *fiqh*: Ibn 'Aqīl-Hamadhānī; in dogma: Ghazālī; in philosophy: Suhrawardī M[aqtūl].

TABLE II

Opinions Held by the *Mutakallimūn* and the *Hukamā'* (Theologians
and Philosophers) Regarding the Orthodoxy of Hallāj

4th Century. *RHM*: a) No certain acceptance. b) Qannād (*MU'TAZ*); Ibn Khafīf (*ASH*); Makkī (*SAL*); Ibn Mamshādh (*KAR*); Tawhīdī (*HAK*). *RDD*: a) Jubbā'ī, Ibn al-Azraq, Ibn Kajj (*MU'TAZ*). b) Mufīd (*IM AKHB*); Baqillānī (*ASH*).

5th Century. *RHM*: a) Ibn 'Aqīl (*HB* in law). b) Qushayrī, Ghazālī (*ASH*). *RDD*: a) Qazwīnī (*MU'TAZ*); Baghdādī (*ASH*); Tabarānī (*NUS*). b) Juwaynī (*ASH*).

6th Century. *RHM*: a) Ibn Tufayl, Suhrawardī Halabī (*HAK*).

7th Century. *RHM*: b) Fakhr Rāzī (*ASH*); Ibn Abī'l-Hadīd (*MU'TAZ*); Nasīr Tūsī (*IM USŪLĪ*). *RDD*: a) Fihrī (*ASH*).

8th Century. *RHM*: a) Rashīd al-Dīn (*ASH*); Yafi'ī (*ASH*); Jildakī (*HAK*).

9th-10th Centuries. *RHM*: a) Maybudhī (*IM US*); Ishkawarī (*IM AKHB?*); Dawwānī (*HAK*). *RDD*: a) Biqā'ī, Sakhāwī (*ASH*); Ibn Kamāl Pasha (*MAT*); Ajrūd (*NUS*). b) Ardabīlī (*IM AKHB*); 'Alī Karakī, Hasan Karakī (*id.*).

11th Century. *RHM*: a) 'Alī Qāri' (*MAT*). b) Sadr Shīrāzī, Amīr Dāmād (*IM USŪLĪ*). *RDD*: b) Miqdādī, Majlisī (*IM AKHB*).

12th-13th Centuries. *RHM*: a) Nābulusī (*MAT*). b) Hamadhān (*BĀBĪ*); Gulpaygānī (*BAHAI*).

Abbreviations: *RHM* = *tarahhum* (canonization: a) *qabūl*, b) *i'tidhār*). *RDD* = *taraddud* (condemnation: a) *radd*, b) *takfīr*). *ASH* = Ash'arite. *IM* = Imāmite (Akhbārī, Usūlī). *MU'TAZ* = Mu'tazilite. *KAR* = Karrāmī. *SAL* = Sālimī. *HAK* = philosopher. *MAT* = Māturīdite. *NUS* = Nusayrī.

g. *Juridical and Dogmatic Texts: Principal* Fatwās

1. Bāqillānī's Theory (d. 403/1012)

This great Mālikite, the second founder of Ash'arism, studied particularly the case of Hallāj: "he credited him with having claimed the gift of marvels (*hiyal*) and of *makhārīq*, for [the Ash'arites] believe in *qadīr*." Also, in the book in which he demonstrates "the incapacity of the *Mu'tazila* to ascertain the distinctive signs of the prophetic mission when applying their principles," Bāqillānī relates the *makhārīq* of Hallāj and the characteristics of his marvels.[43]

Bāqillānī,[44] probably against Rāzī and the "prestidigitations of prophets," responds as follows to the question: how to prove the veracity of prophets by the miracles that they have performed, since you say that there are prestidigitators and charlatans in the world who accomplish similar wonders by their own hands, thanks to their ordinary skill, like those accomplished by Ibn Hilāl and by Hallāj? How do you distinguish them apart?

We have defined "miracles" performed by prophets as everything that cannot be the product of prestidigitators' skill, as sophisticated as it might be, but that is the deed of the one divine power: such as the resurrection of the dead, the creation of bodies, the creation of hearing and of sight, the cure of those born blind and of lepers, the cyclic phenomena (of the stars). The counterfeits of shifting the coils of snakes by feeding mercury into them, and by the use of strings, and the immobilization of animals by a drug and afterwards their revival by another drug, to make people believe in their resurrection, are tricks that can be exposed (in the second case, by asking the charlatans to bring the bodies of animals back to life which have been pronounced dead). Such were the magical tricks of Fir'awn, of Ibn Hilāl, of Hallāj, of Jannābī (and of) Qarmatī: like producing a living lamb (through a trap door) out of a lighted oven, or a fish (from a basement tank) in a room in one's home; or even to draw from a stream or from a well water scented with rose or musk (with the help of a properly anointed jar) or to make their bodies inflate in a room called "the room of immensity": "about which it was told, Hallāj had in Basra a large room specially fitted with tubing devices in the corners and walls, and, underneath, a basement with vents through which air entered the room; he would sit on a raised chair, dressed in a shirt made of silk or some other light material, which made him appear thin when his visitors entered; on such occasions he would order the tubes to be opened, the air passed through the vents and, little by little, flow into his apparel, and inflate his shirt, until it filled the entire room, as was said, 'with his immensity.' "

This is an application of Bāqillānī's particular theory of miracles.[45] He accepts the reality of miracles performed by the sorcerer (*sāhir*) as much as[46] that of miracles performed by the pious man (*sālih*), even if they change the essences[47] (*qalab al-a'yān*) and transform the natures[48] (*ihālat*

---

[43] Baghdādī, *Farq* [bib. no. 201-a], 247, lines 8-11. The ambiguity (intended by Bāqillānī) of the words *makhārīq* and *hiyal*, taken here in the large sense, had led me at first to write that Bāqillānī had been a supporter of the sanctity of Hallāj (*RHR*, 1908, p. 333).

[44] Tübingen ms., f. 24a (Winkler copy); *Ma* [?] VI, 93 (f. 24b, 30b, 31b). Ibn Khafīf's argument is more profound.

[45] Subkī II, 63.   [46] Cf. Hujwīrī, *Kashf*, pp. 151-152.

[47] CF. this edition, 3, 63ff.

[48] "Nature," that which is potentially in a thing, its essence as the primary cause of its activity. Hazm V, 14. Ex.: wine does not have the property of "intoxicating"; God created

al-tabā'i') of things. Because, for him, created essences are reduced to relations (*nasab*), and the natures of things to customary patterns (*'adāt*). Bāqillānī is an *occasionalist*, which is to say that he does not believe in natural laws, nor in real causality in creatures; all phenomena (*a'rād*) derive from the discretion (*tajwīz*) of God Who makes them burst forth instantaneously and thereby breaks "patterns" without departing in that from natural laws that do not exist. This is why he calls miracles *makhārīq*, the "breaking of the pattern" (*kharq al-'āda*), and not *mu'jizāt*. For, according to his theory of ideas (*ma'ānī*), one must not say that one "*can*" or "*cannot*" perform miracles, since one can only talk about power (*qudra*) where one can talk about powerlessness (*'ajz*), and since all of the acts of creatures, whether miracles or not, are pure acts of God's omnipotence.

God performs miracles as He pleases, through sorcerers as well as through saints. The miracle is a proof of the conformity of the former and the latter to the good or bad role that God makes them play; and God withdraws the gift of it from the sorcerer only if he desires to be taken for something he is not, for the miracle is the sign of the sincerity of his mission (*da'wā sahīha*). It is on that that Bāqillānī constructs his theory of the privilege of *tahaddī*,[49] reserved for Prophets; they alone have the privilege of inviting their contemporaries to try to *compete* with them in public, as Moses did with the Egyptian sorcerers before Pharaoh, while being *assured of triumphing over them*. That is the distinguishing sign of their public mission and the thing which makes their marvels unequalled.

Bāqillānī reproached the *mu'tazila* for not having understood the *tahaddī*; according to them, if all men are creators of their acts, there is nothing that could outwardly distinguish the miracles of prophets from the tricks of charlatans. But, in fact, the marvels of Hallāj were real, regardless of whether he was a sorcerer or a saint; this power was removed from him only when he wanted to be taken for a prophet by assuming a public mission; he did not have the privilege of *tahaddī*:[50] and this is what his *mu'tazila* opponents, Abū 'Alī Jubbā'ī and Abū al-Hāshim Balkhī, did not understand.

---

the "intoxicating" accident immediately before the accident "intoxication"; but their sequence is not a natural law, rather only a customary pattern (a category of the being *hadath*, not *mumtanī*). Ibn Hazm believes that only the miracles of prophets are real; those of sorcerers and saints are only illusions.

[49] *Tahaddī*: a word not included in Yāqūt, *Udabā'* I, 177, line 12. Hazm VI, 11; cf. IV, 225, Jurjānī, *Sharh al-mawāqif* [bib. no. 2130-b], 579. Ibn Khaldūn, tr. Slane I, 193 [bib. no. 1590-b]. Cf. this edition, 3, 17.

[50] It was from that that Ibn Fūrak deduced his distinguishing rule: publicity (*izhār*) of the miracle of the prophet, clandestineness (*sitr*) of the miracle of the saint; who must not even be aware of his sanctity (Qushayrī, 1318 edition, p. 187; Ansārī edition IV, 149).

2. Ibn Abī'l-Khayr

It was Abū Saʿīd ibn Abī'l-Khayr Mahnawī (d. 440/1049) who decided definitively in favor of the supporters of Hallāj among Sūfis.[51]

He said of Hallāj:[52] "this reflector of Spirits (sajanjal al-arwāh), this light upon light (Qur'ān 24:35), Husayn ibn Mansūr! He possessed divine grace to the full; no one, in his time, from the east to the west, possessed its gift like him."

And he was often inspired by him in his quatrains, which are among the most beautiful in the Persian language.[53]

The following, perhaps more recent, quatrain is also attributed to Abū Saʿīd:[54]

> Mansūr Hallāj! this "crocodile of the Ocean,"
> He who from the cotton of his body carded the seed of the Soul
> On the day when he cried out: "I am the Truth" in our [human] language,
> Where therefore was Mansūr? God was God!

In close association with Ibn Abī'l-Khayr, Khuttalī and Jurjānī (d. 469) showed their admiration for Hallāj. And their disciple Hujwīrī, whose mind was one of disordered erudition, left us in his *Kashf al-mahjūb* a notice on Hallāj which shows a ludicrous confusion; he tries to split the personality of Hallāj in two, to attribute to the other the acts of sorcery and the heresies of which he was accused, which is only a tactical expedient;[55] he thereby reduces his hero to a kind of puppet, a harmless eccentric, with discourses unbalanced by ecstasy. There as elsewhere Hujwīrī's way of reasoning shows us he is a studious pupil, wanting to understand what his masters have spoken of, but a frivolous mind, lacking analytical firmness, undecided and inconsistent.

3. ʿIyād al-Sibtī

In Spain, the Mālikite qādī of qādīs, ʿIyād Sibtī (d. 544/1149), who had the civil authorities burn the *Ihyā'* of Ghazālī, inserted in his *Shifā'* the following paragraphs, qism VI-3, fasl 5:

> The consensus (ijmāʿ) of the Mālikite fuqahā' in Baghdad, during the reign of Muqtadir, decided in accordance[56] with his qādī of qādīs, Abū ʿUmar, the Mālik-

---

[51] His pupil: Salmān-b-Nāsir Ansārī, master of Fakhr Rāzī.
[52] Bayqarā', 'Ushshāq [bib. no. 1157-a], s.v., summarized in Jāmī, Nafahāt, 169.
[53] Cf. Ethé edition, nos. 17, 30, 12, 18; Azād edition, Gulshān-i maʿrifat, pp. 5, 7, 154, 191, 192, 341. See commentary, Fātih ms. 5365, no. 2.
[54] Ap. JRASB, 1912, no. 230.
[55] That ʿAttār and Mudarris-Zādeh were to revive.
[56] Cf. this edition, 1, 544-545.

ite, to execute Hallāj and to expose him on the gibbet:[57] (1) for having pretended to divinity (ilāhīya); (2) for having affirmed the doctrine of hulūl (incarnation); (3) for having declared: "I am the Truth," (4) while continuing to carry out the legal observances. (5) And they did not judge it lawful to accept his retraction.

The immense reputation of the Shifā' in Islamic countries gives this text a considerable importance. It must be examined point by point:

(1) This is an excerpt from the early questioning, by Hāmid, at the last trial; (2) is an allusion to the thesis of the Mu'tazilite and Shī'ite mutakallimūn, adopted by the early Ash'arites; (3) is a direct criticism of Ghazālī and of the justifications that he presented of this famous saying, particularly in his Ihyā'. (4) This clause is remarkable; it discards the hypothesis put forward by so many of Hallāj's supporters, that of an amorous rapture which should have rendered him unaccountable in the eyes of the law. And it argues from the standpoint of his fidelity itself in continuing to practice the legal observances, the prayers and fasts, to prove that he was fully accountable. He was the master of his acts, as Ibn Khaldūn was to put it. (5) This is a question of the Mālikite practice of refusing to invite the zindīq to show repentance, and of depriving him of the benefit of istitāba. A little further on, 'Iyād cites a fatwā of Abū Hasan al-Qābisī that allows the istitāba in the case of the drunkard who, as a joke, shouts "I am God!" "But this decision does not apply in the case of 'mystical intoxication,' and is not inconsistent with the aforesaid Mālikite practice, in spite of what was said," notes al-Khafījī.

Most[58] of the commentators of the Shifā' restrict themselves to collecting texts consistent with the argumentation of 'Iyād. Three, Qārī', 'Urdī, and Khafājī, undertook to refute it in detail and to justify Hallāj.[59]

4. Tawfī

Tawfī (d. 716/1316), a paradoxical mind, who tried to reconcile Ash'arism and Zāhirism, and combined the teaching of the strict Hanbal-

---

[57] The theory that Hallāj was put on the cross only after he was decapitated. In order to deny that he had spoken and may have repented (cf. Kīlānī, Passion, 1st ed., p. 388, n. 1).

[58] Sibt ibn al-'Ajamī, Ibn Khalīl, Shumunnī, Ibn Abī Sharīf, Daljī.

[59] In a charge renewed by the historian Ibn Khudhyān al-Farghānī, and which Ibn Khallikān seems to make his own, 'Iyād compared Hallāj's teaching with that of the heresiarch Shalmaghānī, the Imāmite executed in 322/934 in Baghdad; the two teachings have in common only the fact of their having been officially persecuted, one after the other; Shalmaghānī is a pure Imāmite, who seems to have been renounced by his sect for political reasons (cf. this edition, 1, 315-322), and the accusations of his claiming to be God and of his having admitted to immorality come from too suspect a source to be accepted, so long as

ite law with a respect for 'Alids, who regarded him as an Imāmite[60]—
and who criticized the Sunnites' principle of variation, *ikhtilāf*,[61] left the
following *fatwā*:

> I have seen many things attributed to Hallāj in the way of written works,
> maxims and treatises, all of it apocryphal. People have begun to attribute to Hal-
> lāj everything they can find in the way of *shath* (ambiguous expressions) and of
> *tāmāt* (echolalias), for he seems to lend himself to them more than any other.
>
> None of the shaykhs of the mystic way, neither the greatest nor the least, ap-
> proves of *everything* that Hallāj said. On the contrary, the masters agreed to say:
> he has fallen into error, or: he has rebelled, or: he has inured himself to sin, or: he
> is an impious man.
>
> And whoever claims that all of the sayings that have come down to us as being
> by him must be approved, that person is a heretic, to be excommunicated by all
> Muslims.
>
> Hallāj was executed for *zandaqa* on a basis of the *fatwā* of the *'ulamā'* of his time;
> and the best that his defenders could say is what one of them said:[62] "He was
> wrong to use certain expressions; but he was a pious man, guided by a sound
> conscience; however, ecstasy overcame him, and in this state he stumbled, not
> knowing what he was saying; words spoken in intoxication are not taken down
> nor are they reported; the victim is a martyr, and his executioner a fighter of the
> holy war on behalf of God,[63] for he upholds tradition!"
>
> This thesis doesn't contravene excommunication brought against one who
> claims to believe in the outward meaning of these words; they were blurted out
> by Hallāj, either because he was overcome by ecstasy, or because he had fallen
> into error; in both cases he remains pardonable. For if the faithful who uses his
> entire strength to find God falls, God forgives him for his error, though it reveals
> a certain inadequacy (*taqsīr*) on his part; that is not an error that makes an impious
> man out of him.

5. Ibn Taymīya

Ibn Taymīya (d. 728/1328), the penetrating and intolerant opponent of
the monism introduced by Ibn 'Arabī, regarded Hallāj as the forerunner
of this heresy. He therefore persecuted his memory with particular intensity, inflamed perhaps by the persistent devotion that some Hanbalites
still had for this condemned man. His *fatwās* on the matter, moreover,
are a model of clear focus. On this "matter of Hallāj," Ibn Taymīya is the
only jurisconsult who took a coherent and logical position. We shall
analyze only three of his *fatwās*:

---

we lack fragments of his works (cf. *Farq*, 249; Friedländer, "Shiites" [bib. no. 1693-a] II,
s.v.).

[60] Cf. the Hanbalite Sarsarī (d. 656) and his "*al-'adhāb al-wāsib 'alā arwāh al-nawāsib*" (cit.
Alūsī, *Jalā'* [?], pp. 2, 3).

[61] [I.] Goldziher, *Katholische tendenz und Partikularismus in Islam* (Upsala, 1913), p. 136.

[62] Probably Tawfi himself, in accordance with Ghazālī.

[63] Cf. this edition, 1, 288-289; 2, 386.

(1) The answer to two questions concerning Hallāj:[64]

1st question: Is this an honest (*siddīq*) or perfidious (*zindīq*) man? Is this a venerable saint (*walī muttaqī*), the possessor of a divine grace (*ḥāl rahmānī*), or an adept of magic and charlatanism?

2nd question: Was he executed for *zandaqa* in accordance with the opinion of the assembly of *'ulamā'* of Islam? or was he in fact unjustly [executed]?

Answer: Hallāj was justly condemned. And anyone who is not of this opinion is either hypocritical or ignorant; and whoever approves of him must be killed like him.

Ibn Taymīya then goes on to recount his life, his journey to India to learn magic, his satanic utterances, his false miracles, his trial, and his punishment. As regards the way juridically to treat the *zindīq*, some consider it proper to invite him to repent, others do not. In any case, whether one accepts or not, the execution is necessary; it is a fruitful penance for the true repentant, a just punishment for the false penitent.

There were no miracles after his death; what his blood wrote and what caused the flooding of the Tigris are stories made up by those impious people who say that "the law of Muhammad kills the saints."[65]

In fact, Hallāj was a satanic being who displayed a false repentance. Not only did he do conjuring tricks, but he was also served by demons, like other contemporary possessed men whom Ibn Taymīya knew, consulters of idols, visited by satanic apparitions; like the possessed man whom he had executed in 715/1315 and who had had visions of a demon who had told him to be the Prophet.[66] Satan rewards these possessed people with miraculous gifts. They are the antichrists of whom the Prophet spoke, forerunners of the one-eyed antichrist. Hallāj was one of them. What difference does it make that he seemed to repent. He spoke and acted in such a way as to get himself condemned and executed by unanimous consent of the Muslims.

(2) *Fatwā* concerning the sanctity of Hallāj:

The opinion that affirms the sanctity (*walāya*) of Hallāj is blasted by his own principles:

---

[64] Later, in his *Al-Irāda wa'l-amr* (*Rasā'il Kubrā* [bib. no. 512-j] II, 95-100), Ibn Taymīya made a subtler study of Hallāj's case apropos of the famous dialogue between Adam and Moses (on the sin of Adam), cf. this edition, 2, 34-35.

[65] Cf. this edition, 2, 264-265; and Rūmī, *Mathnawī*, based on Qur'ān 3:112.

[66] Not, notes Ibn Taymīya, that he could have assumed his true appearance; for God would not permit it. Cf. this edition, 1, 117 ff.

A. It is *ijmā*[67] that endorsed the formula "it is lawful to shed the blood of Hallāj and those like him."

B. Sanctity involves faith and fear of God to the highest degree, it demands that the saint be protected from heresies like those of *hulūl* and *ittihād*. Whoever, on these two points, approves of Hallāj, shows himself incapable of perceiving true sanctity.

C. Let him, therefore, knowingly embracing the heresy,[68] continue to affirm the sanctity of Hallāj! His testimony is only personal, like that of the Jew, the Christian, and the Rāfidite; like them, he is subject to condemnation by the Qur'ān, by tradition, and by *ijmā'*.

D. To plead on a basis of the repentance that Hallāj may or may not have shown *in extremis*,[69] is to pretend to know what God alone knows.

E. To excuse him on grounds of an ecstatic trance (*istilām*)[70] is to ignore the facts; he wrote and spoke with full presence of mind.

F. Indeed, even if the confusion of ecstasy could be an excuse for his inner conscience, it would not justify his attitude; it would not authorize one to say: "he was executed unjustly, he remained true to his faith," things that are ignored.

G. In fact, the reality was quite different. Given these conditions, what believing Muslim would agree to let Hallāj profit from the excuse of ecstasy?

H. As for the one who approves of Hallāj for the ideas that got him executed, he behaves like an infidel and a heretic.

I. Similarly, the one who does not approve of the execution of those like him, proves himself a rebel against Islamic orthodoxy.

J. As for us (*'ulamā'*), we have the formula of divine unity (*tawhīd*) which has been prescribed for us, the way of God that has been laid down for us, and from both we have learned that "what Hallāj said is only falsehood,"[71] and that those like him deserve death.

K. As for his personal fate, for him, and as for the question of knowing if, in his conscience, he experienced some occurrence of repentance or something else that caused him to be absolved by God, that is God's affair, no one can verify it. And God knows all about it.

---

[67] *Imām* and *fuqahā'*.
[68] An allusion to Ibn 'Arabī.
[69] The thesis of 'Īsā al-Qassār and of Kīlānī (*Kasb al-wājid . . .*), this edition 1, 614-615. Cf. Ibn 'Arabī and al-Shādhilī.
[70] An allusion to A Hamid Ghazālī; cf. this edition, 2, 170.
[71] A text of Ibn Dāwūd; cf. this edition, 2, 345-346.

(3) Though the two preceding *fatwās* are an especially brutal way of posing the previous question, we know that Ibn Taymīya also became interested in certain verses by Hallāj, and here follows a third *fatwā* by him in which he agrees to examine the problem in depth apropos of the divine decree (*irāda*) and precept (*amr*).[72]

Ibn Taymīya, whose moral teaching is very firm on this point, refutes any attempt to pardon transgressions against the Law based on the decree foredooming them, or on a momentary paralysis of reason that renders the sinner unaccountable. The ticklish case of Khadir (Qur'ān 18:64-81) is explained, according to him, by a profounder Law than that known to Moses; and the words condemned in Hallāj could not be pardoned on grounds of their being uttered in ecstasy; they were reasoned.

At this point Ibn Taymīya, who seems to be attacking the school of Shādhilī,[73] lists the different attempts to justify Hallāj:

A. Ecstasy had temporarily cut off his reason (*fanā' al-'aql*), he spoke in amorous delirium. We must look upon him either (a) as pardonable (*ma'dhūr*), and thus his judges rightly condemned him (*ijtihād musīb*), "they being fighters for the faith, he being a martyr";[74] or (b) as wronged (*mazlūm*), and thus his judges erred (*ijtihād mukhtī*),[75] or the Muslim Law itself is unjust in the world, because "it kills the saints."[76]

B. He was lucid and he revealed the mystery, even that of *Tawhīd*, which made his execution necessary (*wājib*), according to some famous verses dealing with the discipline of the arcanum.[77] What is this mystery?

The adepts of *hulūl* think that Hallāj was "possessed of God" Who spoke through his tongue, just as the demon speaks with the tongue of the possessed (*masrū'*):[78] temporarily annulling his personality (*fanā' nāsūtīya*) without ecstasy: God alone can declare through our voice that He is One; which is Harawī's thesis; and this is why Kīlānī contrasts the inspired "I" of Hallāj to the arrogant "I" of Satan.

The adepts of monism (*ittihād mutlaq, wahdat al-wujūd*) think that Hallāj, by speaking in this way, wanted to show that every creature is a form

---

[72] *Majm. rasā'il kubrā* II, 87-100, concerning the hadīth in which Adam proves to Moses that his sin was an act of the divine decree (add. by us).

[73] See Mursī here; and 'Izz Maqdisī, *Sharh al-awliyā'* [bib. no. 441-b]. Ibn 'Abdallāh, Mawā'iz ms. 1299.

[74] Kīlānī ('*Athara* [?]).

[75] Yasawī.

[76] Cf. 'Izz Maqdisī [bib. no. 441-b]: Khadir says to Hallāj on the cross: "Such is the reward of the saints of God."

[77] Of Suhrawardī Halabī, this edition, vol. 2.

[78] Ibn Taymīya, letter to Nasr Manbijī.

of expression of the divine essence.[79] "And this is why in the *isnād* of his *khirqa*, Ibn Sab'īn included, among other impious men, Hallāj." According to them, the "I" of Satan is identical with the "I" of Hallāj.

Ibn Taymīya concluded by affirming his thesis: since Hallāj did not speak in ecstasy, it is not a question here of *Tawhīd al-rubūbīya*; Hallāj, condemned for blasphemy against the Qur'ān and the hajj, by *ittifāq* of the jurisconsults, was only a sorcerer served by demons.

Not only in Persia, but also in Africa, the Ash'arite disciples of Ghazālī brought about a reaction among jurisconsults against his attempts to rehabilitate Hallāj.

In Egypt, where the official state teaching was still that of Ismā'īlī Shī'ism, Shāfi'ite propaganda filtered in, through the collusion of certain officials. The Fātimid state had a missionary college, a central house of learning, for training propagandists in all countries, the *Dār al-'ilm*, inaugurated in 395 by Hākim in Cairo at Bab Tabbanin (= Khoronshif, before the Aqmar mosque): where the grand *dā'ī* Mu'ayyad Shīrāzī was buried.[80] Now, in the time of Vizir Afdal (487-515), we find that a Sunnite nucleus of professors and students, called "al-Badī'īya," had formed within it, which forced the college to close (513). When it reopened in 515, the surviving head of this group, Hamīd-b-Makī Itfīhī, undaunted by the death of his colleague Barakāt and by the executions of five disciples, resurfaced and resumed his position of influence. The grand Fātimid *dā'ī*, Ibn al-Haqīq, denounced him to Vizir Batā'ihī in the following terms: "(Itfīhī) learned a little of Ash'arite dogmatics, after which he forsook Islam to follow the way of Hallāj and to deceive the credulous; for Hallāj, in the beginning, called himself a *dā'ī* of the Mahdī, and afterwards the Mahdī himself; after that he laid claim to divinity, saying that the *jinn* were in his service; he also had restored some birds to life"; in much the same way Qassār, a former Shī'ite, lays claim to the *rubūbīya*, obtains food for his disciples in the Jebel, and resuscitates birds after having slit their throats; his disciples are afraid to commit the sin of looking at his face, and do not dare lean against a wall (to rest) in his presence.

Qassār, who was arrested and put in prison (where he pretended to be dead) with his disciples, was nailed with them on the cross where they were finished off with arrows (in *Hijja* 516; in the beginning of 517 it was his disciple Khayyāt's turn).

This hostile account, by the historian Ibn al-Ma'mūn, son of Vizir

---

[79] Ibn 'Arabī's view.
[80] Mu'ayyad Shīrāzī appropriated to himself a poem by Hallāj.

Batā'ihī,[81] does not gratuitously connect the name of Hallāj with the Ash'arite[82] offensive at the very heart of Ismā'īlī Shī'ism.[83]

6. Dhahabī

The great Shāfi'ite historian Dhahabī (d. 748/1348) was the first to try to give a psychological explanation for the behavior of Hallāj. A systematic mind and passionate defender of strict orthodoxy, he applied to his writing of history the principles of critical analysis, assuredly rudimentary and biased, but clearly articulated, that he used in the exegesis of tradition, following Ibn Taymīya.

He summarily dismisses 'Alī-b-Ahmad-b-'Alī al-Wā'iz ibn al-Qassās Shirwānī, the author of *Akhbār al-Hallāj* written around 490/1097 and unknown in any other connection, as a "liar, for most of his *isnād* derive, says Silafī (d. 576/1180), from a book lacking authority."[84]

When he reproduced in his *ta'rīkh* the historic texts of Ibn Bākūyā and others, which he collected on Hallāj, he followed them with his own brief scoffing and cutting remarks: concerning the miracle of the blood,[85] the testimony of Ibn Khafīf,[86] the statement that "the mark of the wise man is being empty (of desire) for this life and the next,"[87] and the testimony of Ghazālī,[88] "who excuses him at the expense of Arabic grammar!"

In *Mīzān al-i'tidāl* and in *Kitāb al-'ibar*, he presents his personal view: Hallāj had started out well; but after brilliant beginnings in asceticism and contemplation, the spirit of pride and ambition took hold of him; he departed for India to learn magic; then, he became possessed by a demon, and seduced many people with that magic that one learns to perform miracles; just as the antichrist will do. "Those who called him a 'magi-

---

[81] He is the one who, according to the Būhuras (Dāwūdīya), was responsible for the drama of 522, in which their mahdī, Tayīb, the legitimate heir of Āmir (they believed in his *ghayba*), disappeared.

[82] Reproduced ap. Maqrīzī *Khitat* [bib. no. 2157A-a] I, 459-460 (noted by G. Wiet). On the *masjid* built in 458 by Vizir Afdal I for Wihāta-b-Sa'd Itfihī, cf. *ibid.*, II, 451.

[83] Which was to triumph with Shihāb Tūsī (this edition, 2, 171); cf. the *Mustazhirī* of Ghazālī, and, from 450 on, the role of Vizir Ibn al-Muslima.

[84] *Mīzān al-i'tidāl* [bib. no. 530-d], no. 1706 (II, 218).

[85] "This is false!" (*Ta'rīkh al-Islām*.)

[86] Translated *supra*, 1, 507-509.

[87] "Filthy language!" (contrary to Qur'ān 17:20; 3:146), from a "vainglorious, boastful, useless man." Note that the statement is by Ibn Adham (Qushayrī III, 214), repeated by Kilānī (*Bahja* [?], 56); was to become a hadīth, according to the *Jadhb* of the pseudo-Suhrawardī (p. 21 [?]). *Gharīb fī'l-dunyā wa'l-ākhira*: revived by Harawī (*Manāzil*), as ap. Ibn al-Qayīr, *Madārij* [?] III, 129.

[88] *Mishkāt al-anwār*.

cian' were right; those who said he was the slave of the *jinn* were close to the truth, for what he did no reasonable man would undertake, since it was bound to get him killed; especially as he was unlike the possessed or the wretched man who gives prophecies about hidden things,[89] without being given ecstasy, revelation or the gift of miracles to help him. Some men, a stupid breed, have said: 'No, he was a wise man, a saint of God; he performed miracles; let him speak as he pleases.' They give thereby a double proof of their ignorance, by declaring: (1) that he was a saint; (2) that a saint can speak as he wishes. No, quite the contrary, for he must speak only the truth! Such a state of mind is a disaster, a deep-seated malady, which defies the cures of physicians; it spreads everywhere and brings fame to anyone who catches it."

7. Shams al-Dīn M-b-H Hanafī

This descendant (d. 847/1443) of Abū Bakr, this restorer of Shādhilism in Egypt, did, according to his son, Abū al-Khayr,[90] express his opinion of Hallāj in the following terms:

We had formed a group which accompanied the master; he had gone on horse-back to the Tāj and the seven Wujūh. Returning the next day to the city [Cairo], I was walking beside the master's stirrup. Next to me was Sīdī Shams al-Dīn M-b-A-b-Mūsā Sakhāwī,[91] surnamed Ibn al-Qasabī,[92] and this was before he was appointed qādī of Medina in 860; and he said to me: "I would like to question my master about Shaykh Husayn al-Hallāj." "Come forward," I told him, "and ask." We were to the right of the master, who was on his mare. Sakhāwī kissed his stirrup, the master turned to him, and [Sakhāwī] said to him: "Master, what is your opinion of Hallāj?" "May God bless him and allow us to benefit from his protection! If he spoke, it was in a state of rapture (*ghalaba*). That is our opinion of him. But others, like Shaykh Sirāj al-Dīn 'Umar-b-R Bulqīnī and others, on the contrary, hold the opposite opinion."[93]

8. Ibn Hajar 'Asqalānī

The following points had been put to him (d. 852/1449):

(1) A man declared that Husayn al-Hallāj is not a saint; (2) a *faqīh* declared that whoever believes in his sanctity is an impious man, (3) adding that 'Umar ibn al-Fārid is not a saint, and that his language is monistic; (4) Yahyā-b-Yūsuf Sar-

[89] The gypsy woman tells fortunes to others, and the poor woman does not know her own (*Prov. fr.* [?], I, 191).
[90] Batanūnī, *Al-Sirr al-safī* [bib. no. 677-a] II, 16, 34; Sha'rāwī II, 99.
[91] Born in 819, died in 895, he arrived in Cairo between 831 and 839 and remained there for more than seven years; Hajj 840 (*Dawī* [?] VII, 110, 111).
[92] See the work by him, Cairo ms. VII, f. 204.
[93] The Commentary of Muhammad Hanafī on the "*al-nās niyām*" hadīth, As'ad ms. 1513.

sarī[94] believed in the absolute eternity of the letters [of the alphabet], which led him to be disowned by certain Sūfīs.

He responded: "(1) What this man reported concerning Hallāj is the opinion of the *'ulamā'* and *fuqahā'*; followed by most of the Sūfī ascetics, just as it appears in the *risāla* of Qushayrī (God's blessing be upon him)." But some of them disagreed with it, especially among those Sūfīs who had mixed philosophy with mysticism, such as Ibn 'Arabī and Ibn al-Fārid;[95] and their language is obviously monistic. . . . (2) As for the aforementioned sentence by the *faqīh*: 'Whoever believes in the sanctity of Hallāj and of Ibn al-Fārid is a blasphemer,' it does not do him honor; for to call a supportable thesis an impiety is a mistake. (3) As for his statement about Sarsarī, it is correct: the verses of this poet prove it: in this he was following the Hanbalite rite, where the opinion is current. (4) As for his denial of the sanctity of Hallāj, it is based on appearances: but God knows consciences the best."[96]

9. Sha'rawī

Sha'rawī (d. 973/1565), a conscientious and honest scholar, but a credulous spirit, did not leave us a systematic presentation of his ideas concerning Hallāj. He included him in his catalogue of the "persecuted saints" of Islam, and adopted the *fatwā* of Ibn 'Arabī on his case as his own. He assembled in his works many testimonies in favor of Hallāj that are valuable from the standpoint of the history of ideas. But the arguments that he adds to them are quite weak: he says, apropos of the proposal that led [Hallāj] to be condemned: "God knows whether it was made by him!" suggesting thereby that it might have been forged; and he canvasses Ibn Khallikān's text to make him say that such a proposal did not deserve the death penalty.[97]

10. Ibn Hajar Haytamī

Haytamī (d. 973/1565), a respected scholar of the Shāfi'ite rite, whose authority in the present day extends to [Saudi] Arabia, Afghanistan, India, and Java, was obliged to look into the Hallāj case.

In a first *fatwā* concerning the meaning to be given to his saying "I am the Truth," he asserts that, when the mystic man is dominated by the signs (*shuhūd*) of the divine presence, he forgets all the rest . . . and that such utterances translate the following line of reasoning:[98] "The signs of

---

[94] This is a tactic on the part of Ibn Hajar: in order to more fully discredit the opinion of the Hanbalite Ibn Taymīya concerning Ibn al-Fārid, he has himself questioned here about another poet, a Hanbalite, quite damaging for this rite.

[95] Ibn al-Fārid discussed *"Anā'l-Haqq"* (*Nazm al-Sulūk*, verses 277-279).

[96] Alūsī, *Jalā'*, 53.

[97] *Tabaqāt kubrā* [bib. no. 741-a], I, 16, 107.

[98] The philosophical theory of ecstasy; cf. A. Hamid Ghazālī in this edition, 2, 171.

the divine presence are so transfigured to me that I believe I am transformed in them"; when he is speaking in this way in a state of recall. But if he were in [a state of] rapture, this utterance would be a *shath*, which there would be no way to analyze, for we only analyze words uttered in a state of "soberness" and free will.

In a second *fatwā*, he agrees with the opinion of al-Suhrawardī of Baghdad, explaining this expression as implying "God says . . . ," and he cautiously restricts its legitimate use to the second instance mentioned in the first *fatwā*: to the instance of rapture that paralyzes the will.

In a special notice in which Haytamī concludes in favor of the sanctity of Hallāj, he mentions the affirmation of Kīlānī: "Such an affirmation coming from such a Pole, and assigning to him such a high rank, is sufficient for the glory of Hallāj!"[99]

11. The *fatwā* of Abū'l-Faraj Nahrawālī

In *Kitāb anīs al-jalīs wa nadīm al-ra'īs*, a compilation designed to give moral edification, recopied in 1015 by a Hanafite jurisconsult affiliated with the Qādirīya order,[100] and the author of which was Abū'l-Faraj Nahrawālī,[101] whom I believe to be identical with Qutb al-Dīn Nahrawālī Ikhwānabādhī, a "Hanafite jurisconsult affiliated with the Qādarīya order," who taught in Mecca in 988,[102] and whom A Khafājī has chronicled as one of his Meccan masters,[103] we are given, in the form of a quasi *fatwā*, the general opinion of Hallāj's execution among the religious élite of Mecca in the seventeenth century of our era:

Question: we know that God "created His servants that they should be sincere and speak the truth. What did His Wisdom mean (*mā'l-hikma fī* . . .) therefore by allowing eighty-four ('*ulamā*')[104] to render a *fatwā* condemning Hallāj to death for having spoken the truth and declared 'I

---

[99] *Fatāwā hadīthīya*, 213-214, 223, 224; excerpts ap. Bītāwarī, *Tuhfat al-ikhwān* [bib. no. 928-a]. Note that Haytamī is hostile to Ibn Taymīya.

[100] Habīb Ghazzī, a Hanafî Qādirī (Berlin ms. 8914-1; cf. ms. 8913-2, ap. *Ahlwardt cat.* VII, 781).

[101] Ms. P. 1317, f. 124a (pointed out by G. Vajda), whose title changed, reads "*Durar wa la'ālī* by A Faraj [and A Ma'ālī = 'AR?]-b-Zakariyā Nahrawālī," and is described rather strangely as a "collection of excerpts from the works of Sakhāwī" (M-b-'AR, d. 902; an enemy of Ibn 'Arabī, and hardly inclined to express himself in this way).

[102] Berlin mss. 175-1 and 7414 (Ahlwardt) = Qutb Nahrawālī, d. 990 (nephew muftī in Mecca).

[103] Berlin ms. 7414, f. 62b. Note that Khafājī was pro-Hallājian, like the very Turkish and Indian-oriented Meccan milieu of the seventeenth century (cf. Shinnāwī, Qushāshī).

[104] Ms. P. 1317: "*anna arba'a nafar min aftū*" (*sic*: for: "*anna arba'a wa thamānīn aftū*"): according to the figure from the legendary *Qissa*.

am the Truth'; they killed, crucified, and burned him, he who was consumed with love ('ishq). What was His Wisdom in doing that?"
Answer:

Know that the threshold of the Lord of Glory and the audience of the King of Kings are not like the thresholds of sultans. As long as one does not gamble one's soul[105] on this threshold, he cannot join the Master; but when one has sacrificed his head,[106] his self, and his soul, one joins Him and sees Him. And so, don't imagine that the one who has been burned for his Master has actually been burned. No, the one who has been burned for Him is ablaze with His light. Don't you see how the vagabonds, when they set out, carry a firebrand; if you ask them: what are you going to do with that firebrand, one will tell you: I carry it with me so that, if I find myself in a dark place, I can use it to light it up. Accordingly, therefore, don't believe that they had burned Hallāj: no, they set him afire like a torchlight, so that on the Day of Judgment he may illumine the Assizes, guiding sinners by his light, for whom he will intercede (*yashfaʿfihim*). But if he who spoke the truth is burned, what will happen, do you think, to the one who uttered falsehood (*bātil*).

Now, know that Mansūr Hallāj, God hold him in His mercy, was in the audience of His glorious majesty like a butterfly before a candle. The moth that sees a candle in the night imagines it to be a shining star; it goes toward it, and rushes into the flame, wanting to taste the full brightness of the candle; but it is immediately set on fire without succeeding in grasping a particle of light, and it falls, burned, before the taper; it realizes its powerlessness then and confesses: "I who had thought I could be something in the presence of the light know now that I am nothing." And as soon as it has recognized its powerlessness, its eyes open and it sees the top of the taper, lopped off and fallen down beside it. That is to say, that from the moment that it realized its lowness and humbled itself, it reached its Goal. Hallāj, in the same way, had imagined he could be something in the audience of the Divinity when he had perceived its light. Once burned, he recognized his lowness, and, in the same way, he reached his Goal.

12. ʿUmar al-ʿUrdī

In the eleventh and last volume of his *Sharh al-Shifāʾ*, completed in 1019/1610, ʿUrdī (d. 1024/1615), after presenting the short passage by ʿIyād dealing with Hallāj, follows it with the long attack directed against Hallāj by Dhahabī in his *ʿIbar*, then undertakes to build his personal thesis of the *sanctity* of Hallāj on a refutation, point by point, of Dhahabī and ʿIyād.

Against the first, he argues: from the masters of Hallāj, who were Sunnites; from Shiblī, who admitted sharing his ideas; from Ibn ʿAtāʾ, Ibn Khafīf, and Nasrābādhī, who defended him; from Kīlānī, who

---

[105] A Turco-Iranian expression (*jānbāz*; Sārī ʿAA: *derbāz*).
[106] This is ʿAttār's idea, traditional in Turkish lands (Yesewī: *bāshenin bīr*).

affirmed that Hallāj was a passionate lover of God, and that desire had made him lose sight of created things (mystical state called *al-jam'*). He concludes that the anecdotes told against Hallāj are the fruit of hatred, and must be rejected along with those of the Nusayrīs against the first three Caliphs,[107] those of the Shī'ites against the first two, and those of the Khārijites against 'Alī. Wasn't Moses himself accused of murder by the Israelites? Hallāj, though less highly placed than Moses, could not escape slander. Besides, Dhahabī died beaten and blinded as punishment for his attacks against the great Sūfīs.

From this first refutation, he deduces a *fatwā* of *tawaqquf*:[108] "As for Hallāj and Dhahabī, and, more generally, for the one who affirms the sanctity of Hallāj and the one who denies it, we have this to say: these Muslim generations of the past have seen the fate of the perishable goods they had acquired; pay attention to your own, and stop asking what these dead men have done."[109]

Turning to the second, he expresses his regret that 'Iyād did not keep quiet: for he was wrong on every point: a) in accusing Hallāj of having proclaimed himself God, nonsense which he could not have said; b) in accusing him of having taught the heresy of *hulūl* (the inclusion of divinity in his humanity); for, in plain logic, in order to justify this inclusion, he had to affirm the existence of his *self*; but, since he denied his *self*, how could he have spoken of an inclusion of the presence of God in pure nothingness? c) Dhahabī's accusing anecdotes are refuted by 'Iyād's own testimony, by the fact "that he continued to practice the legal observances"; d) the only basis [of accusation] which remains is the saying "*Anā'l-Haqq*" (I am the Truth), which can be explained as expressing the mystical state of union (*jam'*);[110] in an explanation related to this, al-Ghazālī saw in it the mystical state of annihilation (*fanā'*).[111]

h. The Role Played by the Karrāmīya Theologians in the Indictment of Hallāj as a Hulūlī[112]

The heresiographical manual, of Ash'arī, the *Maqālāt*, written prior to his conversion, adheres to a Mu'tazilite classification, in which the charge of *hulūl* ("localization" of God in a human being) is referred to only in passing, Mu'tazilism accepting some *sifāt makhlūqa lā fī mahall*; some ex-

---

[107] The curses in the third Nusayrī *quddās* (*Bākūra* [?], 44).
[108] Reproduced by Khafājī.
[109] Qur'ān 2:134, 141: a generalization of personal responsibility.
[110] Here, some verses.   [111] Cf. this edition, 2, 170-171.
[112] 'Alī-b-'Īsā against them (*Lisān* V, 356).

tremist Shī'ites (pp. 14-15) and some ascetics (pp. 13 and 288) were briefly charged with *hulūl* (localization of the Spirit of God). The word originated perhaps with the polemics of Warrāq against the Nestorians; for the heresiographical manual of Khashīsh (d. 253), which is older, prefers to characterize this category of heretics as *rūhānīya*.

The heresiographical manual of Baghdādī, the *Farq*, written around A.H. 410, contains a special rubric for *hulūlī* sects; under which, after the extremist Shī'ites, he inscribes, not without embarassment for him, an Ash'arite Shāfi'ite, two ascetical sects, the Hulmānīya and Hallājīya (p. 241; cf. his *Usūl al-Dīn*, p. 316); about which Hujwīrī speaks again, around A.H. 470, in his *Kashf* (tr., p. 260): in restricting the *takfīr* to the Hallājīya Fārisīya. The *Farq* and the *Kashf* were both written in Khurasan, the region where the Karrāmīya theologians were powerful (primacy in the periods 370-388, 405-413, 421-456). They seem to refer to a kind of official catalogue of heresies established by official *mutakallimīn usūlī* qādīs, thus for the most part Hanafites, who could not have been Mu'tazilites (the Mu'tazilites having been stamped with *takfīr* by the edicts of Qādir [408, 413], carried out by the Ghaznavids), but rather Karrāmīya.

The *Farq* contains a very elaborate theological definition of the Hallājian *hulūl*, which had appeared already in the "geography" of Balkhī-Istakhrī, ninety years earlier, and which Bīrūnī, again in Khurasan, was also to reproduce "*man hadhdhaba. . . .*" I do not believe that it originates with the manual by the Mu'tazilite AS Balkhī (d. 319), and it could not have been made up by the philosopher-geographer AZ Balkhī. Its similarity to two Karramīyan theological attacks against the Hallājian *hulūl*, that of AB-b-Mamshādh Dīnawarī (trial of 308), and that found in the *Maqālāt* of Ibn al-Haysam (written against the Ash'arite Ibn Fūrak, before A.H. 405: cf. Ibn Abī'l-Hadīd [bib. no. 431-a] I, p. 297), leads me to attribute it to a mystic from Armenia (whose capital, Dabil, was Karramīyan), Ibn Yazdānyār, who came to attack Shiblī and other Sūfīs in Baghdad between 315 and 325 (the departure of Murta'ish), and a descendant of whose referred to Ibn Karrām (*Rawda* [?], ms. P. 1369, f. 163b). Qannād, pro-Hallājian, was very severe in his judgment of Ibn Yazdānyār, in some verses in which he naturally did not dare to mention Hallāj, since the latter was a condemned man; after this attack, pro-Hallājian Sālimīya theologians avoided mentioning Hallāj by name when they quoted the "*Anā man ahwā*" piece in which the word *hulūl* appears (*Luma'*, *Ta'arruf*). The Hanbalite manual *Sharh al-Sharī'a* of Ajurrī (d. 360) contains a chapter against the *hulūl* (of the uncreated Spirit, *Rūh qadīma*). Around 365, the young Ash'arite Abū Ishāq Isfarā'inī (340, d. 418), arriving in Nishapur, forced the Hallājian Nasrabadhī to retract the thesis of the *Hulūl al-Rūh al-qadīma* which, moreover, only the Hallājian Fāris Dīnawarī had dared defend. A Shāfi'ite, Maqdisī (surely Nasr M, 415, d. 490, a pupil of Abū Hāmid Isfarā'inī via Salīm Rāzī, d. 447), after reproducing in his *Kitāb*, around 445, the condemnation of the two *hulūlīya* ascetical sects, the Hulmānīya and the Hallājīya, and the head of the Hallājīya of Iraq, Abū Ja'far Saydalānī, published a declaration asserting that this *takfīr* was directed only at Fāris.

Only mystical theologians concerned with asceticism like the Karrāmīya, explaining sanctifying graces, not as actualizations transforming the human subject (Hallājian *ma'rifa*, real, but infixable *"lā tastaqarr fī'l-qalb"* [*Taw. XI*] against the Karramīyan *ma'rifa*, permanent quality), but as innovations in the divine essence (*ihdāth fī'l-dhāt*), considered the possibility of using the weapon of *takfīr bi'l-hulūl* to the utmost to combat, in Khurasan, not only Fāris, but also Ibn Abī'l-Khayr.

i. Hallāj's Consciousness of the Veracity of His Testimony and His Apocalyptic Cry: "Anā'l-Haqq" ("My 'I' is God")

The fulfillment of Abrahamic monotheism in the believer is his worshipping of God alone" (= having shattered all idols) and obeying God at all costs (= loving Him above all else). There can be no doubt that Islam presents this goal to sincere Muslims in an abrupt and threatening manner; and the entire life of Hallāj is bent like a bow toward this target.

Can the problem of the ultimate success of the venture of those who set out to capture sanctity be resolved in such a way as to convince a public that is understandably skeptical, *a priori*, in view of the impudence of this statement?

The maximum sympathy that the historian could show them is to concede that their intellectual plane is unified and that they increasingly "realize" their responsibility for the contradiction[113] that exists between the Commandment of God that they feel in themselves and their present failure to accomplish it, through the increasing devotion that they give to Him. All that would be required for their success to be genuine would be the verification of a real psychic fullness consistent with the outward admission of a lack, of a disappointment.

Hallāj is original among Muslim mystics for not having brushed away

---

[113] A.H.T., *Basā'ir* [Abū Hayyān Tawhīdī].

the difficulty of explaining mystical union by imputing his theopathic utterances to his irresponsible state of intoxication during ecstasy. God, in Himself, is not unconsciousness; His supremely simple Truth expresses itself eternally, and the human language uttered "beyond time" is destined to connect us personally with this Witness of the One, when our soul is unified.

In this regard, Hallāj sketched out a philosophy of language, in Arabic: a philosophy not static and existential, like the monism of Ibn 'Arabī (*wahdat al-wujūd*), but dynamic and testimonial (*wahdat al-shuhūd*). He believed that Arabic, as a Semitic language and as the language of revelation, was predisposed to conceive the mental word in the first person, under the influence of the Spirit: in the recollected state of silence, of fasting, of poverty, and of tears. This idea was disputed by literalistic grammarians, and mused upon by philosophical grammarians.

Experimentally, he practiced "breaking (mental) idols" of worship (destroying the Ka'ba mentally in himself in order to enter the immediate presence of its Founder) and obeying God at all costs, breaking family ties, yearning to die accursed for his Muslim brothers.

The crucial sentence of his experiment, "*Anā'l-Haqq*," "I am the Truth," or "my 'I' is God," is not a metaphysician's monistic formulation; it is an "outcry for justice" (*sayha bi'l-haqq*, Qur'ān 50:41) cried out in full lucidity. Nor is it the magical formulation of the *dhikr* that was popularized by a later Hallājism.

We have discussed the circumstances in which it was uttered; it sums up, in any case, the teaching found in many passages of his works (*Taw.*, 215). More serious is the attack against the real authenticity of this utterance made by those who point out that his vocabulary changed, chronologically and apologetically: his choice between *haqq* and *haqīqa*, *'ishq* and *mahabba*, his meaning of *shāhid*, his meaning of "*ahl*"; he made Shī'ites think that his devotion to the "*Ahl al-bayt*" was a devotion to the physical lineage of the Prophet; when his *nasab* with the Prophet was *siddīqī*,[114] kinship in spirit, *ghurba* solitude, in *al-ghār*, the "cave of the hijra";[115] there was his act of contrition, at the trial, his literalistic "Sunnite" protest while awaiting his sentence, his mental debate, the last night, in prison (*makr*, *haqq*).

But there is no contradiction in this, if, as we believe, his vocation, of which he was increasingly conscious, was to fulfill the Prophet's last prayer at 'Arafat—the *waqfa* of the farewell pilgrimage—by dying for all of his brothers.

[114] Qur'ān 2:146; 33:4.   [115] Qur'ān 9:40.

1. How to Express Theopathic Locution Correctly, According to Ibn 'Arabī

Given his theory of a universe that has emanated from God in a descending hierarchy of five superimposed planes (hadarāt) or "worlds,"[116] men living on earth on the fifth plane can be reached there by the divine word through the fourth plane, that of ideas (mithāl), by means of fahwānīya, which he defines as follows: "direct divine locution expressing itself in the world of ideas."[117] Can it be perceived and expressed as theopathic, does the mystic achieve divine union by it, and can he utter in the first person the "I, it is I" of God? Ibn 'Arabī thinks not, the initial monism of his teaching (wahdat al-wujūd) excludes the possibility, and he attempts to prove that this pseudo problem cannot be formulated, reviewing each of the pronominal words that the Arabic language provides us to personalize the subject speaking the sentence, and testing, both in prose (analyses) and in verse (attempts at invocations) the situations in which our corresponding psychic states place us vis-à-vis God. The words examined are: huwa (he; huwīya, his ipseity), anā (I; anānīya, my ipseity), anta (you), nahnū (we), inn (it is, here is, indeed; innīya, hecceity; the word "ecceity" would be better).

He argues for the exclusive use of the word "huwa, He, Him" in sentences in which the mystic intends to give an account of his personal divine locution. Huwa is the exclusive name of the absolute Essence, the name of the moneity (ahadīya); it is he who flows in all of the physical beings that he supports (thubūt) and gives existence to (wujūd). Huwa has a synonym, the affix-ī (my, mine),[118] which is the fahwānī of the moneity for it alone, whereas huwa is the fahwānī of the Lord in relation to His creatures. The faithful can immerse himself quietly in his invocations to "Him" (huwa), for God answers "the one who is in everything," "god for God, man for man, call for call"; this is the state of 'ayn al-jam'.

The use of the word "anta, You" (syn: laka, to you) has many pitfalls, introduces a thicker veil; it opposes huwa, emphasizing in dialogue the other of two persons without defining which of the two it means. This is why only those who can abstract (tanzīh, out of khayāl, the imaginative) are allowed to use it; it is not for the mujassima, who delight in using it. How, when calling upon God, can we ask Him to say "O you" to us on the same level of reality and not on the simple order of the wad' (situa-

---

[116] Kitāb al-Huwa, Sirr al-Yā', ms. P. 6640 f. 72ff.
[117] Jurjānī [bib. no. 2130-a or b], 176, 197.
[118] -ī: in lī, darabnī, innanī in which the first n = lilwiqāya, the second khafīfa.

tion). Metaphor (*majāz*) is not permitted in *hadra*. To delude oneself with it is to be taken in by one of God's tricks (*makr*).

The word "*nahnū*, we" among pronouns, is only a collective word (*mujmal*), like "Allāh" among external objects.

The word "*anā*, I, me." Here Ibn 'Arabī attacks Bistāmī and Hallāj without naming them:

some people, oblivious to the high position of *huwa* and to the distinction to be made between essence modalized into forms (multiples of existence), between modalization (*tahawwul*) and absolute essence (*mutlaqa*), thought that "I" (*anā*) was the noblest of appropriate symbols (*kināyāt*) for expressing mystical unification (*ittihād*), without discovering that this unification is *a priori* impossible. When you say "I," the idea (*ma'nā*) communicated thus to the One with Whom you wish to be united is "you, who have said 'I' "; it is an expression coming from you, and not you. As regards the idea itself, you have formed it, either with your *anānīya* (the ipseity "mine" of your created form, *sūra*), or with His; which creates a dilemma: either it is you alone, or you no longer exist, and, in both cases, there is no unification. One is not permitted to cry out "*Anā*, I" in *sahw* (= outside of ecstasy); if the mystic ignores *huwa*, he becomes subject to the provisions of the law, and must show repentence.[119]

To speak to "*anā*, I" when invoking Him is folly (*hawas*);[120] to call God "I" when praying to Him draws His response "your status is contradictory; if it is your *anānīya* (the ipseity of your I) that you call upon, then it is up to it to respond to you, through you. — And what if You responded to Yourself through me? — I will never reveal Myself to you through My "I," the exclusive privilege of the moneity" (*ahadīya* = *jam' al-jam'*).

The enunciative particle "*Inn*, it is, here is," (syn: *'iyyā*): this expresses the personal and spontaneous first impulse of the sentence, prelude to the pronoun subject (cf. in Latin: *ecce*). Ibn 'Arabī points out that this word, closer (like *nahnū*) to *huwa*, is weaker (and more discreet) than "*anā*." But to call upon God Himself asking Him to release this "*inn*" in us makes the construction of the prayer very difficult. For example: "O, it is I, I realize myself in you emanating from me without going out of me, when You have come forth emanating from me in this 'it is I' just as Your 'it is you' emanates from You. Look for me emanating from me through 'it is I,' out of fear that through jealousy You may leave me, and that this 'it is I' may leave me. For the only 'it is I' in me emanates from Your 'it is I'; this 'it is I' is one which is not mine, for the 'it is' is Yours and mine insofar as it is in You, not in me." To which God responds: "there is both truth and fallacy in your words: for *inn* (it is) can never stop revealing the two hecceities; if you put yourself in the 'it is You,' I am with you

---

[119] *Hū, hā, hī* = *k* + *n* + their ligature (*kun!*).
[120] *Hawas*: cf. Hallāj, *Akhbār*, nos. 12, 47.

in order to help you; if you put yourself in yourself through a 'it is I' by withholding the 'it is you,' you will appear outwardly to be revealing me, and the observer will imagine that you are the locus in which the appearance (mazhar 'an innaka) of 'it is You' occurs, whereas you remain the locus of 'it is I.' I warned you: if you desire 'it is I,' your hecceity will stop being in you; I cannot coexist with another essence (kiyān)."

In chapter 428 of the Futūhāt (IV, 42-44), which is undoubtedly dealing with the use of "innī" by Hallāj both in the Tawāsīn (I, 14; II, 5-6) and in a famous quatrain,[121] he smoothes down the rough edges of the passage just translated. To ask to be stripped of one's own "innī, it is I" is to fulfill the sacrifice (īthār) and to become the ransom (fidā'); it is no longer the ordinary shuhūd, the annihilation of the statute (fanā' hukm, fanā' na't), without the annihilation of the essence (fanā' 'ayn); it is the highest degree of union (wasla) in which the shuhūd (of the 'abd) joins the wujūd (of God); it is the highest of the maqāmāt: the shuhūd al-'abd keeps him united with other men (as men) at the very moment when it binds him essentially to the divine Existence (rabt al-wujūd bi 'ayn al-shuhūd); and God, out of respect for his sacrifice made for Him, gives him joy (farah).

It should be noted that Ibn 'Arabī is inserting here precisely into his theory of existential monism, as an abnormal case, the very theory of Harawī and Simnānī justifying Hallājian ecstasy in terms of "testimonial monism" (wahdat al-shuhūd).[122]

2. Grammatical Analysis of the Sentence "Anā'l-Haqq"

It was two famous Basrian grammarians, Sirafī (d. 368) and Fārisī (d. 377), both disciples of M-b-'Alī Mabramān, who were the first to publish the sentence in question, according to the interpretation given them by their master Zajjāj; judging it, after careful analysis, to be bordering on blasphemy. Classical grammatical analysis of "Anā'l-haqq" presents us with only three possible interpretations:

a) It is a narrative (ikhbārīya) nominal clause (jumla ismīya), declaring an ideal objective connection between "I" and "God"; this conditional connection does not make the clause "flexible." "My 'I' is God" = I personally imagine God to be the only possible subject of any logical utterance. —The static theory of existential monism (wahdat al-wujūd).

b) It is a declarative (inshā'īya) nominal clause, affirming a subjective connection between "I" and "God"; which does not make the clause any more "flexible." "My 'I' is God" = I imagine God to be speaking my

---

[121] "Fa'rfa' . . . innīyī min al-baynī" (Dīwān, no. 55, p. 90).

[122] Aniyatak hiya huwīyatī (Jīlī I, 48). God is threefold quwwa (I, 8: ahadīya, huwīya, anīya).

sentence in me. By the supposition of the Qur'ān reciter (hikāya; by metonymy, kināya); or by an inner pleasure felt (ishrāb; intussusception); or by an "elucidation" (tajāwuz: a transfiguring metaphor).

c) It is an *active* [French = *effective*] (īqā'īya) verbal clause (fi'līya), validating a canonical connection between "I" and "God" (like "anta hurr" setting one free, and "anti tāliqun," repudiating one): which makes the clause "flexible" (lahā mahall fi'l-i'rāb), for its khabar (inchoative) makes *explicit* its elided (mahdhūf) mubtada' (inchoative), implied (muqaddar) necessarily (li'l-ta'adhdhur): a flexible damīr al-sha'n ("Huwa" = He). "My 'I' is God" = I swear that my "I" has become (anā sirtu) this "He" Who is God. In an outcry for justice announcing the Last Judgment, identifying this present reciter of the shahāda, this present Witness, with the Shāhid al-qidam, the Eternal Witness, the Spirit-Word. "Innanī 'anā' sirtu'lladhī Huwa'l-Haqq." It is clear "Huwa" must be implied and that "this He" is not an ordinary "harf al-fasl" separating "I," "anā," from "God," "al-Haqq," to prevent "al-Haqq" from being made into an attribute (sifa) or appendage (tābi') of "anā," which would be absurd. And to prevent "Huwa" from being made either a "tābi' mu'akkad" or an implied "second declarative."

This grammatical analysis of the incriminatory sentence led to its being made a classical example of the teaching of the "qa'ilūn bi'l-shāhid," professing that God has Present (apotropaic) Witnesses on earth, particularly on the day of 'Arafat (yawm shāhid). In grammatical terminology, a "shāhid" is a particular verse, conclusive in itself, which one uses as a basis for formulating a rule. This was, indeed, the way in which Zajjāj understood "Anā'l-haqq": a usurpation of the supreme power of God. And Tabarī could say with Ibn Surayj, the only canonist who had defended Hallāj's innocence, that his boldness had left room between himself and God only for His Judgment, (daynūna). This is testimonial monism (wahdat al-shuhūd).

j. The Social Centers of the Tradition and Diffusion of Hallājian Thought

1. The Imperial and Princely Courts (and Their Waqfs)

In Baghdad, after the drama of 309, we find the secret preservation of a Hallājian tradition within the Court, despite a hundred years of Shī'ite proscription (334-437): on the part of the hājib Nasr and his son Ahmad; and in the household of the Queen Mother, Shaghab, whose waqfs (where Mutī' and several caliphs among his descendants were buried) seem to have been administered by Shāfi'ite (Surayjian, hence pro-Hallājian) *shuhūd*. This would explain the resurgence of Hallājian devotion under Caliph Qāyim (422-467), who seems, indeed, to have personally venerated Hallāj, since he allowed his confidants to do so (Vizir Ibn al-Muslima, Ibn 'Aqīl, the adopted son of his friend Abū Mansūr, whom he was to defend and lodge for over a period of four years). Likewise Muqtadī (467-487); and his mother Urjuwān and her *waqfs*, where two of his descendants, Muqtafī and Mustadī', were buried (a "tomb of Hallāj" was *waqfed* between 437 and 581—[Harawī]); and Mustazhir (487-512) and his mother Tayf al-Khayāl; and their occupants of the position of *ustādh al-dār*, the B. al-Muslima. After the sack of 656, two 'Abbāsid princesses, Shāhilatī and Rābi'a, married to Mongol viceroys of Baghdad, the Juwaynīs, were surely involved in the Hallājian revival signaled in their court by the works of Kīshī and N Tūsī.

The librarian (*khāzin al-kutub*) of Mustansir (d. 641), Ibn al-Sā'ī (d. 674), wrote some *Akhbār al-Hallāj*; and his successor, the musicologist Safī Urmawī (d. 693) was connected with the Juwaynī viceroys (private tutor). The *muhtasib* of Nāsir, Harawī, refers to the tomb of Hallāj among the *waqfs* of Baghdad (612).

In *Nishapur*, *khatīb* of the mosque.

In *Isfahan*, by tradition Turkish, Saljūq princesses patronized pro-Hallājian preachers like Ahmad Ghazālī (d. 517); as did certain Saljūq vizirs like the Rudhrawarī (patrons of Ibn al-Hamadhānī and of Farīd 'Attār) and Ibn Rajā' (patron of 'AQ Hamadhānī, d. 531). The tradition passed from there to the Saljūqs of Konya, since the Baghdadian *waqf* of their daughter Saljūqa Khātūn (d. 584) became the Tekkē of the Bektāshīs. Revived in Isfahan in the seventeenth century.

In *Bukhara*, the lasting attachments that Hallāj had won for himself in the court of the Sāmānids seem to have been centered around Vizir Bal'amī (308, d. 329), his disciple the muftī Su'lūkī, his descendants, and especially his friends the B. Simjūr, amīrs, of Quhistan, who, for three generations, governed the leading cities and protected Hallājians like Qaffāl in them. Four centuries later, the Timūrids, for example, Abū'l-Ghazī Hy-b-Mansūr Bayqarā, prince of Herat (d. 912), extolled Hallāj in their court (Jāmī, Kārizgāhī). It should be added that, from the years 317-405, Amīrs Dhuhlī and Dabbī of Herat, benefactors of Shiblī, had known of the latter's friendship with Hallāj.

In *Tabriz*, under the pagan Mongol ruler Abaqa (672) and the Juwaynī viceroys, there was a Hallājian revival in the court; indicated, as we have seen, by N Tūsī, inspector general of all of the denominational *waqfs*; indicated even more in the works of the great vizir, Rashīd al-Dīn (698, d. 718), edited by his son, Vizir Ghiyāth al-Dīn (728, d. 738), in which the author speaks to Emperor Ghāzān (694, d. 703), a recent convert, about "Hallāj, Pole of the saints."

In *Cairo* and *Damascus*, in the court of the Kurdish (Ayyubid) and Turcomen and Circassian (Mamlūk) princes, the Hallāj case was often discussed, but as a symbol of opposition; Saladin bestowed favors on two rivals at the same time, the Ash'arite Sh. Tūsī, who was pro-Hallājian, and the Hanbalite Ibn Najīya; Baybars had as his spiritual director Khadir Mihrānī Kurdī (d. 676), a Yazīdī (pro-Hallājian), but he appointed Qutb Qastallānī (662), a bitter foe of Hallāj, professor in the *Dār al-hadīth kāmilīya*. Confronted with Ibn Taymīya's attacks on the Sūfīs, the high officials of Cairo and of Damascus were divided, which proves that there was no decisive state tradition regarding the lawfulness of this Sūfism; the grand qādī of Damascus and Cairo, Jalāl M-b-'AR Qazwīnī (d. 739), wrote a commentary on Ibn al-Fārid.

In *Mecca* and *Medina*, the Shārifian Court occasionally authorized Hallājians to speak in the Haram[123] before the Ka'ba; in 553 one such was the Hanbalite *qāri'* Ibn Muqarrab (under the sharif Qāsim Ibn Fulayta); in 670 or thereabouts, there was the preacher Ibn Ghānim Maqdisī (d. 18 *Shawwāl* 678), who preached before the historian Ah-b-Ibrāhīm Tāj Fazārī (d. 690), the jurisconsults Ibn Ajīl Yamanī and Taqī ibn Daqīq al-'Īd (d. 702): under the sharif Abū Numayy (652, d. 701), who was already the patron of Ibn Sab'īn and of Shams Ikī (cf. also Ibn 'Alawān): thus clearly pro-Hallājian.

In *Spain*: the rallying of Muslim principalities in the southeast (Murcia, Valencia) to the 'Abbāsid *khutba*, and the affiliation of Prince Ibn Hūd (d. in Damascus in 699) with the Sab'īnīya, suggests the possibility of a pro-Hallājian mystical tradition in these small courts (Shūdī, qādī of Seville!).

In *Istanbul*: the extent to which the poetic interest usually given to the subject of the martyr Hallāce Mansūr was seen to revive in the Osmanli court depended on which of the influences fell upon the *Dīwān* (or *Haram*), that of the Bektāshīs from Murat II and Mehmet II; under Bayezid II[124] especially (Balim Sultan) and Selim I; the Mevlevīs under

---

[123] The *shaykh al-haram*: Ibn al-Mundhīr (d. 318), Ibn al-'Arabī (d. 343), Nasawī (d. 396) pro-Hallājian, Ibn Jahdam (d. 414) pro-Hallājian, Abū Dharr Harawī (d. 434), Sa'd Zinjānī (436, d. 476) (despite the Fātimids).

[124] His name might derive not from Bayēzid Bistamī, but from the "messenger" of Bektāsh; whose *turba* he rebuilt.

Majīd (Besme Sultan) (under Sulaymān I, with Sururī [d. 969], private tutor); the Khelwetīs (under Ahmad I); or the Rifā'īya (under Hāmid II). Two grand vizirs, Shehīd 'Alī Pasha (Damad: 1125, d. 1128) and Rāghib Pasha (1170, d. 1176), and a *ra'īs al-kuttāb*, Sārī 'AA Tchelebī (1038-1039)[125] were pro-Hallāj.

In *Shirwan*: the redaction of the *Akhbār al-Hallāj* by Ibn al-Qassās that Silafī came to consult directly in Chemakha around 506, states that the author was a preacher in the court of the last Shaybānid amīr, Feridūn-b-Feribūrz, the son-in-law of the king of Georgia, David II (483, d. 519).

In *Shiraz*: after 140 years of Shī'ite official persecution of the Hallājian Sūfīs under the Buwayhids, and a hundred years of Saljūq truce, the Salgharid state was established and the patronage of the court under Takla-b-Zengī (570, d. 590) enabled R Baqlī to write his Hallājian works; the atabeg AB Qutlugh-b-Sa'd venerated his memory (it was in his reign that the *tarīqa Hallājīya* was founded in Bayda—628, d. 658; and in the reign of Abish Khātūn, d. 686). And as long as the Court of Shiraz remained Sunnite, under the Injūids (703-754) as well as under the Muzaffarids (754-795: Shāh Shiya, patron of AF Tawūsī), Hallāj's memory was revered (Hāfiz).

In *Delhi*: Iltutmish venerated Hāmid Nāzūrī, a Hallājian. The only prince who may have been interested particularly in Hallāj (as a *qādirī*) was the emperor, Dārā Shikūh (1069); the influence of the Chishtīya under Akbār (who, like Aurengzeb, was fond of the works of Sharaf Minyarī from Menair, Behar).[126]

2. Public Institutions of Learning

a. Madrasas

In Baghdad, in the *Nizāmīya*: the *mudarris* AH Ghazālī (484-488) and Ahmad Ghazālī (488-492), as we know, were pro-Hallāj in writing and in teaching. As were Ismā'īl Ru'yānī (d. 502: comm. on Qushayrī's *Risāla*) and Ibrāhīm Nufaylī (d. 529: comm. on Sulamī's *Tafsīr*). Lastly, Shams Kīshī (665-672: *Risāla fī du'ā' al-Hallāj*); in the *Mustansirīya*: 'AR-b-Yf ibn al-Jawzī (d. 656); in the *Tājīya*: Shihāb Tūsī (around 565: *fatwā fīdam al-Hallāj*); in Bab Azaj: Shaydhalā' Jīlī (d. 494: *khutab*) and the *naqīb* of the Hāshimites, Hibatallāh ibn al-Mansūrī (d. around 635: *Qādirī*).

In Cairo, in *al-Azhar*: Itfayhī, Ibn 'Atā'llāh, Laqānī, Bashbīshī; in

---

[125] Cf. Mhd Thurayya, *Sijill 'Uthmānī* [?], 1257, 4 vols.

[126] Princess Zeb al-Nisa' had the *Tafsīr kabīr* [bib. no. 385-c] of F Rāzī (favorable to Hallāj) translated into Persian.

Manāzil al-'Izz: Shihāb Tūsī (with the philosopher Āmidī), and his deputy 'AR-b-M Qurushī (d. 616).

In Qaysārīya, in the first Osmanli *madrasa*: Dāwūd Qaysārī (d. 751; pro-Hallājian).

In Istanbul, in the *madrasa Ayā Sūfīya* (the *wā'iz* 'Abd al-Ahad Nūrī, d. 1061); in *Sahne Themānīya (Fātih)*; Akhawayn (d. 904), Kamālpāshāzāde (d. 940), Jānīzade (d. 954), Abū'l-Su'ūd (d. 982): all hostile to Ibn 'Arabī and to Hallāj; in *Dār al-Mathnawī* (Ismā'īl Anqirawī, d. 1042); in the *madrasa Qalenderkhāne: Mu'ayyadzādd* (f. 888) favorable, for a student of Dawwānī; Tāshköprüzāde (d. 968; hostile, for he was the translator of Ibn Khallikān).

In India, in the *madrasas* of Delhi (Mu'izzīya 620, Nāsirīya 650, Fīrūzīya) the programs of study (in Arabic) at first only touched lightly on the name of Hallāj in the *'Awārif* of Sh. Suhrawardī (and accidentally in the *Fusūs* of Ibn 'Arabī; and (in Persian) in the *Dīwān* of Hāfiz (cf. Dawlutshāh in Persia). After Aurengzeb, the manual of Sadr Shīrāzī (philosopher) became a standard work, and encouraged the study of the works of Suhrawardī Maqtūl (as in Persia) and of Nasīr Tūsī: in which Hallāj was admired by a Sunnite and by a Shī'ite. In the modern universities, the Nizāmīya of Farangi Mahal (Lucknow, f. 1114), Deoband (Dār al-'ulūm), Aligarh (1875), Nadwa of Lucknow (1894), Osmania of Hyderabad (1917), apart from the *Ta'rīkh al-khulafā'* of Suyūtī, one finds hardly any mention of Hallāj in a manual.

b. The Dār al-Hadīth

Designed exclusively for the teaching of the traditional maxims of the Prophet (and of the related sciences, *jarh wa ta'dīl*, etc.) the *Dār al-Hadīth* represented an even stronger reaction of a Sunnism threatened, no longer only by Shī'ism, but now also by the Crusades, and trying to draw the Muslim Community even tighter around its founder. They were official foundations that supported the hadīth studies which private efforts were carrying on in the leading centers (the B. Manda in Isfahan, Khatīb in Baghdad, the Sam'ānī in Marw, Ibn al-Bayyi' in Nishapur, 'Abd al-Ghānī-b-Sa'īd in Cairo). The majority were founded by Kurdish amīrs for the Shāfi'ites.

The first was the Madrasat Ibn Sallār, founded in 546 by this vizir in Alexandria for AT-b-M Silafī (d. 576); he transmitted there on Hallāj the *Hikāyat* of Qannād and the *Akhbār* of Ibn al-Qassās.

The second was the Dār al-Hadīth Nūrīya, founded around 551 by Nūr al-Dīn (d. 569) in Damascus ('Asrūnīya), for the famous *muhaddith* and Ash'arite 'Alī-b-H ibn 'Asākir (d. 571): who pardoned Hallāj (ap. *Ta'rīkh*, biography of Shiblī), following Qushayrī's example, from whom his nephew A-b-Hibatallāh ibn 'Asākir received the *Risāla* of Mu'ayyad Tūsī (d. 617).[127]

The Nūrīya was soon replaced in Damascus by the Dār al-Hadīth Ashrafīya, founded in 696 by Mālik Ashraf (d. 635) for Taqī D ibn al-Salāh Shahrazūrī (d. 643), *rāwī* of the *Risāla* of Qushayrī, whose successors were eminent masters, AK Harustānī (643, d. 662), followed by the historian Abū Shāma 'AR-b-Ismā'īl Dimishqī (d. 665), Yahyā Nawawī[128] (d. 676), Mizzī (d. 742), and Dhahabī (742: not appointed), 'Alī Subkī (742, d. 750), A-b-Ismā'īl-b-Khalīfa (d. 818), and Sharā'ihī (d. 821). Probably Mizzī (*rāwī* of Khatīb), a friend of Birzatī (d. 739), and surely Dhahabī were anti-Hallājian; but Subkī, a pupil of Ibn 'Atā'llāh, was pro-Hallājian; he had to be not only a Shāfi'ite, but also an Ash'arite, to teach there.

The third was Dār al-Hadīth Muhājirīya, founded in Mosul by the very pious amīr Isbil Gökbüri (563, d. 630), the brother-in-law of Saladin (m. Rabī'a, d. Damascus 643), around 580, for some Hanbalites, 'UA-b-A ibn al-Samīn, pupil of Qazzāz, master of Ibn al-Sahīh (d. 588), Ibrāhīm Ibn al-Baranī (d. 622) and Hy-b-'Umar ibn Bāz (d. 622; pupil of Shuhda); Ibn Dihya came there in 604; and the father of Ibn Khallikān taught there around 622; it was also there that Ibn Khallikān became anti-Hallājian.

The fourth, whose influence was considerable in a time when Egypt was saving Islam, crushed between the Mongols and the Crusaders, was the Dār al-Hadīth Kāmilīya, founded in 622 in Cairo by Mālik Kāmil (d. 635): for his former tutor 'Umar-b-H ibn Dihya (d. 633), a Valencian, a Zāhirite (like Ibn Hazm, he accepted unconditionally the hadīth of Muslim which placed the relatives of the Prophet in hell), a mad anti-Hallājian, foe of Fakhr Rāzī, a learned *hāfiz* whose unscrupulous pugnacity (cf. his biography by M-b-Yh 'Utāridī and Tāj Kindī) brought about his dismissal; he was replaced by his brother 'Uthmān ibn Dihya, a grammarian (d. there in 634); followed by A 'Azīm Mundhirī, a former Hanbalite gone over to Ash'arism (634, d. there in 656); who allowed, as Ibn Rāfi attests, Ibrāhīm Taghlabı to comment there on a sentence by Kīlānī pardoning Hallāj; AB-M-b-M-b-Ibrāhīm ibn Surāqa Shātibī (b. 592, d. 662), an Andalusian mystic, a Suhrawardian, whom Shustarī left to

---

[127] Burhānī, *zahra* who delivers a *fatwā* permitting *al-tabarruk*, a suspect use of the *isnād* H[asan] B[asrī]—'Alī.
[128] Anti-Avicennian.

follow Ibn Sab'īn; Rashīd Yh-b-'Alī 'Attār Misrī (660, d. 662), a Mālikite; Tāj 'Alī-b-Ibrāhīm al-Qastallānī, an Andalusian Mālikite (662, d.
there 665; b. 588); M-b-'Umar ibn Dihya (665, d. 667); Qutb A-b-M
Tūzarī ibn al-Qastallānī (667, d. 686; b. 614); M-b-Ibrāhīm ibn Jamā'a
(710-727); the Kāmilīya was put to another purpose in 786, after having
been the center of this anti-Hallājian movement, whose doctrinal influence, through Abū Hayyān (Zāhirite), Dhahabī, and especially Ibn
Taymīya, has continued down to the present-day Salafīya. This movement was based on a formal criticism of the hadīths invoked by Sūfīs: Ibn
Dihya was the first to expose the falseness of the Hasan Basrī-'Alī isnād
for the khirqa (Simt, 103: the Shādhilīya also put = H.B.-'Alī); and, being
Zāhirite, it was anti-Hallājian. Ibn Surāqa, author of the oldest treatise on
the Labs al-kirqa (Katt.[?] I, 337), rejected, as had Suhrawardī, both the
futuwwa of the calendars and philosophical Hellenism; finally Qutb Qastallānī, author of the Irtiqā"'l-rutba fī'l-libās wā'l-suhba on the khirqa ('Iqd,
p. 3), directed his polemics against the philosophical and Hellenizing
mysticism of Ibn Sab'īn on the censure of Hallāj, seen as the founder in
Islam of the monist heresy (cf. Von Kremer), and against the "spiritual"
isnād invented by Ibn Sab'īn in order to link himself to this precursor.
Qutb Qastallānī, both a Mālikite and a Shāfi'ite, was placed by Baybars
at the head of the Kāmilīya after his return from the hajj; he had been
initiated by Nāsir 'AA-b-'AR 'Attār into the Sahramanīya tarīqa ('Iqd, p.
61). Ibn Taymīya was only reiterating the anti-Hallājian thesis of Qutb
Qastallānī.[129]

In Damascus, there was the Dār al-Hadīth Qūsīya (founder: Ism-b-
Hāmid Qūsī, d. 653).

The different dār al-hadīth in Istanbul and Delhi were less important. In
the one in Adrianople, Kamālpāshāzāde took a position against Ibn
'Arabī and Hallāj.

c. Monasteries (Ribātāt, Khānqāhān)

The early ribāts of the Karrāmīya were private; and the first official attempt to create a Sunnite monastery appears in Baghdad with the Ribāt
Zawzānī, founded around 460 opposite the cathedral-mosque of Mansūr
by Husrī (d. 371), a disciple of Shiblī turned Shāfi'ite; this foundation
could not develop (in view of the hostility of the Buwayhid sultanate)
without the continual support of the Caliphal representative, the khatīb of
the cathedral-mosque, AB A-b-M ibn Abī Mūsā 'Īsā Ma'badī (350, d.

---

[129] [We refer again to] Cairo: madrasa Mansūrīya (founded around 680: hadīth): first sharaf
'A Mu'mīn Dimyātī (d. 705), a disciple of Silafī (indirect) and of Ibn Muqayīr.

386): imitating his predecessor, ʿAA-b-M ibn Burya (329, d. 350) in that respect; the latter having supported, despite the Buwayhid police, the hadīth sessions of AB Shāfiʿī after 334. It is an established fact that this *ribāt*, which had direct contacts with the pro-Hallājian Shāfiʿites of the *Waqf Surayjī*, preserved the memory of Hallāj, and that its second founder, ʿAlī Zawzanī (366, d. 451), transmitted verses of Hallāj: A-b-ʿAR Kirmānī (d. 575) may have been the author of the *Hikāyāt Ibn Khafīf*; Sh. Suhrawardī (600-605) was the author of the *ʿAwārif*.

It was Vizir ʿAlī ibn al-Muslima who officially recognized monastic institutions in Baghdad by placing all private monasteries under an inspector general, a *shaykh al-shuyūkh*, residing in the Nahr al-Muʿallā (in a *waqf* established by a friend of the vizir, the *ʿamīd al-ʿIrāq*, Abū Nasr Ahmad ibn ʿAlī); a *waqf* for refugees from Khurasan responsible for providing funds for the first official Ashʿarite *madrasa* (the future Nizāmīya); reviving the idea of Amīr Ibn Sīmjūr, who in Nishapur had combined the *khānqāh* of Būshanjī (d. 348) with the Ashʿarite *madrasa* of Ibn Fūrak (d. 405). The titulars of the office were: Abūʾl-Barakāt Ism-b-A-b-M ibn Dūst Naysābūrī (d. 441), followed by his brother Abū Saʿd (d. 479: who built the Nizāmīya on orders from Nizām al-Mulk), Ism-b-Abī Saʿd (b. 464, d. 541), Sadr ʿAbd al-Rahīm-b-Ismāʿil (from 541 to 580), ʿAbd al-Latīf-b-Ismāʿil (b. 513, d. 596), their nephew Diyāʾ ʿA Wahhāb ibn Sukayna (b. 519, d. 607), ʿA Razzāq-b-ʿA Wahhāb (d. 625), Qutb M-b-ʿA Razzāq (b. 604, d. 644), ʿAlī Nayyār (644, d. 656), Abū Saʾd Mubārak-b-Yh Mukharrimī (d. 664); Nizām D. Mahmūd, who restored Ghāzān in 696 to the Mustansirīya; his son, Mubārak Shāh, had married the granddaughter of Nasīr Tūsī. They were all very high officials, of a rank equal to the grand qādī and the two *naqībs*, entrusted with diplomatic and arbitral matters. They gave permission for a "tomb of Hallāj" to be erected and maintained as a *waqf*; Ibn Sukayna converted to Sūfism the son of the anti-Hallājian preacher Ibn al-Jawzī, whose grandson collected the Hallājian parables of AQ Kīlānī; its Abū Saʿd predecessors had lodged in a *ribāt* the Khurasanian Ashʿarite preachers sent to Baghdad by the Saljūqs: preachers who, according to Ibn al-Jawzī (*Talbīs*, 183), preached generally about the sanctity of Hallāj.

Among the *ribāts* of Baghdad we call attention to the following: the Ibn Mahlabān Ribāt founded by the Kurdish amīr of this name for ʿUmar Bistāmī (d. 493), member of a leading Shāfiʿite family, backward grandson of M-b-Hy Bistāmī, qādī of Nishapur in 388, died in 407, son-in-law of AS Suʿlūkī, the friend of Nasrabadhī; taken over by Tāhir-b-Saʿd-b-Fadl Mayhanī (d. 542), grandson of the great mystic Ibn Abīʾl-Khayr (a

Hallājian), and his descendants: Muhammad (d. 596) and his son 'Abd al-Mun'im (fell out of favor in 613). Next, the Behrūz Ribāt, where Ahmad Ghazālī spoke; the Dār al-Falak convent for women[130] (where Nizām, the "Beatrice" of Ibn 'Arabī, lived; he recited verses of Hallāj to her; and from where 'Ajība Bāqadārīya must have brought to Damascus a [manuscript] of the *Bidāyat al-Hallāj*); the Marzbānīya Ribāt, consigned to Shihāb Suhrawardī (around 610), who had been dismissed in 605 from the Zawzānī Ribāt for misappropriation of funds, and afterwards to Ahwad Kirmānī, an avid disciple of Farīd 'Attār. Two monasteries in Baghdad appear to have carried on the memory of Hallāj: that of the Turbat al-Jihat al-Saljūqīya (= tomb of Saljūqa Khātūn, d. 584, the mother of [Caliph] Nāsir) = *Ribāt Jadīd*; united as a *waqf* with the Urjuwān Ribāt (= Ikhlātīya? near the tomb of Ma'rūf), the burial place of Muqtafī and Mustadī', according to Harawī; for this turba, visited by Ibn al-'Adīm, became the Tekkē Bektāshī (cf. *Mission* II, 50); and the Hallājian fervor of the Bektāshī poets (Nesīmī, Fuzūlī, Rūhī) is well known. And the unidentified monastery which in 762 became the Qalandarkhāne, in 1017 the Tekkē Mevlevī (and in 1235 the Asafīya mosque, under Dāwūdpāshā), since Qalandars and Mevlevīs both extolled Hallāj.

The mother house of the Qādirīya in Baghdad, the Bab Azaj Ribāt, continued to maintain a *madrasa*, that of, Mubārak Mukharrimī (d. 513) (first *mudarris* 'A Wahhāb-b-'AQ Kīlānī, replaced from 588 to 590 by Ibn al-Jawzī, when the tomb of his father was desecrated, dead in 593; followed by 'A Salām-b-'A Wahhāb, 593-603, d. 611, Nasr-b-'A Razzāq Kīlānī, d. 633, M Tawhīdī, d. 656) where Kīlānī's view of Hallāj was transmitted.

IN DAMASCUS AND CAIRO. From before 517. Nūr al-Dīn, copying Baghdad, established a resident *shaykh al-shuyūkh* in the Sumaysatīya Khānqāh (founded around 430 by 'Alī-b-M Sulamī Habash, d. 453; with Ismā'īl ibn Dūst, who departed for Baghdad; in 561, Sa'īd Falakī): who was 'Imād al-D 'Umar b-Hammūya Juwaynī (567, d. 577; son of the last *shaykh al-shuyūkh* of Khurasan) to whom Saladin gave Cairo in 569; followed by his children: Sadr M-b-'Umar (577, d. 617), 'Imād al-D 'Umar-b-M-b-'Umar (d. 581: 617, d. 636), Tāj 'AA-b-'Umar-b-'Alī (d. 642). The B. Hammūya, whose political influence was great, resided in the Sa'īd al-Su'adā' Khānqāh in Cairo. After that, following an interrup-

---

[130] [Cf.] the convents for women in Damascus. In Cairo (Maqrīzī [bib. no. 2157A-a or b] IV, 293): Ribāt al-Baghdādīya in 684. The convent of the 'Adawīya in Cairo: Yf-b-M-b-'Adī-b-Sakhr 'Adawī, d. 697.

tion (H-b-M ibn 'Amrūk Naysabūrī, 642-647),[131] they kept only Damascus (Sharaf AB-b-Tāj-b-Hammūya, d. 678; Fakhr al-D Yf b-AB, d. 701).

In Cairo, after 658, we find Shams M-b-Ibrāhīm Maqdisī (d. 676; Hanbalite and Qādirī; pro-Sūfī) after Tāj A Wahhāb ibn Bint al-A'azz (d. 665; Shāfi'ite; last grand qādī before the quadripartite division); followed by Shams M-b-AB Īkī, a devout mystic, who was dismissed for having dared to have the *Tā'īya* of Ibn al-Fārid taught in the pro-Hallājian commentary of Farghānī; in 686; died, Mezze 697; next, his foe Taqī 'AR-b-Tāj ibn Bint al-A'azz, d. 695; and 'Abd al-Karīm Amulī (dismissed in 708, d. 740), a disciple of the *kubrawī* Sa'd-b-Hammūya replaced briefly by M-b-Ibrāhīm ibn Jamā'a; and then 'Alā' 'Alī-b-Ism Qūnawī, commention a *Khānqāh Hallājīya* (beginning of fifteenth century), the *waqf* of of Īkī, a mystic, and an enemy of Ibn Taymīya. Beginning in 725, the new Siriyāqūs Khānqāh had some *shaykh al-shuyūkhs* who replaced those of the Sa'īd al-Su'adā' Khānqāh: Majd Mūsā Aqsarāyī (d. 744), first in the Muhsinī Khānqāh in Alexandria, and afterwards in the khānqāh of his master, Karīm al-D (Amalī) in Qarafa; Badr al-D (748), Nizām Ishāq Isfahānī (d. 783) for several years. Since the seventeenth century at least the title of *shaykh al-shuyūkh* belonged in Cairo to the family of Shaykh al-Bakrī and the Wafā'īya.

In Damascus, where the two lacunary epigraphical texts appear to mention a *Khānqāh Hallājīya* (beginning of fifteenth century), the *waqf* of the Diyā'īya Hanbalite *madrasa*, founded in Salhīya by Diyā' al-D M-b-A Wāhid Maqdisī (569, d. 643)[132] for hadīth study, contained on the manuscript of the year 553 of Ibn Bākūyā's *Bidāyat al-Hallāj* mention of a copy made in 638 for Vizir Ahmad Baysanī (son of Qādī Fādil; Vizir designate in 615, and a *muhaddith*; d. 643), father of a qādī, d. 657.

IN TURKEY. Apart from Brusa, where the Tekkē Jelwetī, under Shaykh Ismā'īl Haqqī (d. 1137), emphasized the personality of Hallāj, the various *tekkēs* continued to mention it in accordance with the tradition of their respective orders, the Bektāshīs especially, and the Mevlevīs.

IN IRAN. In Nishapur: the *shaykh al-shuyūkhs* resided in Bāgh-al-Bazzāzīn (after Sahlagī, d. 476).

In Shiraz: the 1st *shaykh al-shuyūkh* came from Bayda: Ibn Sālbīh (d. 473); it was in his khānqāh that Baqlī gathered his documentary evidence.

---

[131] From 615 to 624, according to 'Akarī (s.a. 656).   [132] Ms. P. 5912, f. 226b.

k. The Survival of Hallāj in Toponomastics
and Onomastics

In Turkey, J. Deny has noted sixteen villages[133] named "Hallac, Hallacli, Hallacler," particularly in the areas of Kastamūnī and Ankara (*caza* of Hayamana and Kalecik). It is hard to compare them with the standard Arabo-Persian corporate "Hallacān" model (= "the carders"); but their trade eponym would be Hallace Mansūr (cf. Adharbayjan, Georgia, and Turkestan).

In Muslim onomastics, nothing can be proven with regard to devotion to Hallāj on the part of parents naming their children "Husayn," for this name refers by prior right to the grandson of the Prophet, considered a patron saint ("Abū 'Abdallāh Husayn"). No trace, therefore, in Arab countries. But in the Iranian, Turkish, Albanian, Indian, and Malaysian regions, where Hallāj is referred to by the name of his father, "Mansūr," the search for such traces become possible. We must clearly rule out all the examples in which "Mansūr" is equivalent to the Arabic surname "al-Mansūr" (= the victorious), and not go back before our fourteenth century when the names of Sūfī saints, *Uways*, Qaranī, *Bayezid*, Bistāmī, *Junayd*, *Shiblī* appear as names of princes of Turkoman[134] dynasties allied with the Jelā'irida princesses; an era in which some of them, being constant readers of 'Attār's "Memorial of Saints," may also have chosen *Mansūr* Hallāj as patron saint of his son. A case could be made of the latter for the Muzaffarid prince of Isfahan, Shāh Mansūr-b-Muzaffar (789, d. 795),[135] because of his having been born in Shiraz and being the first cousin of Sultān Shiblī, and also for the Tīmūrid prince, Mansūr-b-Bā'iqarā'-b-'Umar Shaykh-b-Tīmūr, who died in 849 and was buried in Gazirgah (near the pro-Hallājian Harawī, d. 481, venerated with his great uncle, Shāh Rūkh); for he had by Fīrūza Begum a son whom he was anxious to call Husayn: the latter was the prince of Herat (d. 912) who

---

[133] Köylerimizin Ādlawī, pub. by the Interior Ministry of Istanbul, 1929: pp. 136, 156, 158, 174, 383, 406, 474, 511, 577, 626, 781, 861, 901, 909, 1037 (*Halac Engesori*, caza of Kamikh, vilayet of Van), 1046. But the toponym Mansūrīye (*ibid.*, p. 811: caza of Khadak, vilayet of Kodalu) does not refer to Hallāj; and the "*Halacor*" of p. 225 (caza of Olti, vilayet of Erzerum) should be corrected to read "*Salaçor*" (Deny). [Among these villages] there are two *Hallāj*, p. 136 (caza of Finike, vilayet of Antaliya), 406 (Bayezid, *ibid.*). Eight *Hallājlī*, p. 156 (Hayamana, Ankara); 511 (Rechadir, Tokat); 626 (Erezli, Zongouldak); 781 (Kastamūnī, *ibid.*); 861 (Marjidiye, Kirchehir); 909 (Tireboli, Kiresun); 1046 (Yazgat, *ibid.*). Five *Hallājlar*, p. 174 (Tchine, Aidin); 383 (Balikessir, *ibid.*); 474 (Gerede, Bolas); 577 (Inankōy, Denizli); 901 (Ushak, Kutahir).

[134] Cf. the Persian catalogues of manuscripts (Ethé, Ivanow) and the manual of Zambaur [bib. no. 2257] (table k).

[135] Nephew of a Bayezid, first cousin of an Uways and a Shiblī; lord of Baghdad in 776.

showed his exceptional devotion to Hallāj by having a painting made of him by the famous Behzad, and in his "Sessions of Lovers." This Tīmūrid Mansūr's *laqab* was "Ghiyāth al-Dīn," which recalls the *kunya* of Hallāj, "Abū'l-Mughīth."

The last of the B. Ramadān amīrs of Adana (Cilicia), Pīr Mansūr (d. 1017), very likely had Hallāj as his patron saint.

In Iranian Sūfī circles, one can connect with Hallāj the first names of Mīr Ghiyāth al-D Mansūr-b-Sadr al-D Shīrāzī (d. 948), of the following century's poets Ghiyāth al-D Mansūr Harandī, and Ghiyāth al-D Mansūr Fikrat; and of Mansūr-b-Budh.[136]

Lastly, the unusual frequency of the first name "Mansūr" found in the genealogy of the B. Shihāb amīrs of Lebanon beginning with the Turkish domination can be traced, perhaps, to the old popular devotion of the Druzes of Shuf to Hallāj (attested to by the Shihāb ms. of the *Qissat al-Hallāj*).

l. Hallājian Trends in Art

The study of onirocriticism gives us an inkling of the materials that the Muslim imagination of the time was choosing in preference to other experimental data of the five senses.

This provides us with a starting point for examining the kinds of artistic achievement found in Hallāj's era and the interpretation of them that he was advocating.

It seems that if smell acts directly upon the imagination (and the memory),[137] preparing the way for the taste (and vital assimilation [of something]), the sense of sight permits rational coordination of entireties (perceived simultaneously), preparing the way for touch (the methodical apprehension of architectonic and geometric forms); as for the sense of hearing, which apprehends uninterruptedly, it is made in such a way as to be able to detect through the intonations of one's speech one's ultimate, spiritual intention.

1. The Arts of Sight and Touch

There are three different trends in art for representing objects from our field of vision.[138] One that projects them either outside us on a surface

---

[136] Ethé [bib. no. 1681-a], p. 654.
[137] The odor of sanctity (cf. *rawā'ih*), the savor of sanctifying grace. Cf. Cardan, Zimmermann, J.-J. Rousseau (*Émile* II, 261; ap. [Hippolyte] Cloquet, *Osphrésiologie* [Paris, 1821], pp. 20, 28).
[138] *Anwār-hilāl-shams, kawākib*.

(of 2 dimensions) or into a space (of 3 dimensions) by means of orthogonal coordinates (mariners' compass dials or rhumb lines), allowing an indefinite extension of the framework (cf. Egypt).

And one that carries us outside ourselves to the very center of the object—for we do not merely want to know it but to understand it—by identifying us with it in its center, where our thought assembles it. According to this approach, the sea is no longer a series of indefinite horizontal lines, but a closed disc of concentric circles, a framework defining it comprehensively (cf. Babylon).

The third trend is that of a decorative and fortuitous juxtaposition of constant clusters (cf. collars, portulans, caricatures; Chinese and Turkish landscape gardens).

The first trend, that of scientific art, is the most recent; the second is the oldest, but every period of religious revival, aiming at mystical involvement, revives it.

In terms of pure lines, architecture, and sculpture of forms, the Muslim trend is well known.[139] We have no Hallājian documents dealing with monuments, but only instructions concerning *cartography* and *calligraphy*.

The geographer Istakhrī, who became interested in Hallāj and who was the first to place him in the setting of his native town, uses the archaic Babylonian-Sāssānid seven *kishwār* method of representation in cartography. The universe appears in plane projection as consisting of seven interconnecting circles of equal radius, one central (*Bābil* = Eranshahr) and six peripheral; due to the pre-eminent position of the number eight in Euclidian space (cf. the hexagonal honeycombs of bees). This method breaks up space into little pieces and distorts the distances of peripheral points; but the scientific method of orthogonal coordinates (Ptolemy-Mercator) also has its distortions; and one can see that the seven *kishwār* method tends to create a structure independently of a system of spatial references by propounding simply one origin (cf. polar coordinates, vectors, tensors). It must be added that Bīrūnī, in good scientific language, rejects this system.[140]

As for calligraphy, the Arabic script at that time followed two different trends. Either it conformed in its stylized[141] techniques to the very basis of its composition, the "open" linear projection of an indefinite succes-

[139] Cf. our *Réalisation artistique* (ap. *Syria* [1921, II, 47-53 and 149-160]).
[140] Cf. Bīrūnī, ap. Yāqūt, *Buldan* I, 27: the seven being *Bābil* (center), *Hind* (southeast), *Hijāz* (southwest), *Misr* (west), *Rūm* (northwest), *Yajūj* (northeast), *Sīn* (east).
[141] The style of Ibn Muqla.

sion of alphabetical characters, a straight line occasionally provided with secondary parallels for certain complementary signs; or it went back to the archaic and synthetic principle of the ideogram, at least for certain words (especially proper names): using the characteristic volutes of each component letter in order to make the calligraphed word into a monogram, an intricate separate unit, an enclosed interlaced design, having a symetrical structure—a group, not a mass. It is precisely this latter archaistic trend which a document captured at the time of the trial in 309/ 922 proves was the one followed by direct disciples of Hallāj. It shows an interlaced design of letters combining two names (identified spiritually with one another), 'Alī and Allāh. This is the calligraphy used by extremist Shī'ites, of which we have examples in Nusayrī manuscripts;[142] the method consists either of simply reduplicating each name in the design or of repeating a given name (e.g., *qahhār 'Alī*) four times by having it turn around its first letter in four successive rotations of 90° in the design. At a later time, the Bektāshīs, whose cult of Hallāj is well known, used two rotations of 180° around an axis in space, which coupled the revered name with its opposite (like a reflection in a mirror). In both cases,[143] the aim is to make the selected name a radiant center of perspective, to which the artist (and the reader) are transported through contemplation, as Hallāj indicated in his apologues of the crescent moon and the burned butterfly.[144]

With regard to *colors*, there were also two opposing trends, the Newtonian and the Goethean;[145] they were viewed either in open, linear, indefinite sequence (a series of crescent-shaped wave lengths from red to violet; which left out white and black, in accordance with astrology, and Aristotle and Newton), or as a closed cycle of complementary qualities occurring side by side, white-black, red-green, yellow-blue, in accordance with the very old procedure in use with regard to dyes, tattoos, coats of arms, standards and cast marks, in accordance with Taoists, Jainists and Buddhists,[146] following Pythagoras, Democritus, Hippoc-

[142] This edition, 1, Figure 10; Nusayrī ms., Paris 1450, f. 65a: "MS." S. Reich ms. "*Shikl 'Ayn 'Alī*"; cf. Ibn Abī Jamra, ms. P. 695, f. 230b; 'Abd al-Bakī, *Melamiler* [?], 180.

[143] Birge [bib. no. 1797a], Plate 15; [Ernst Emil] Herzfeld, [*Archäologische reise im Euphratund Tigris-gebiet* (Berlin, 1911-20)] II, 158; our *Mission* II, 43.

[144] Sulamī, *Tafsīr Qur'ān* 2:109 (= p. 588); *Tawāsīn* [II, no. 2].

[145] Cf. C. Prantl, *Aristoteles über die Farben*, 1849; Goethe, *Farbenlehre*, 1810 (inadequate analysis in Faivre, 1862). Cf. the colors of the four (or five) elements, those of the four cardinal points (in America).

[146] H. Maspero, *Chine antique* [bib. no. 2158-a], p. 165; ap. *JAP* (1937), p. 368; Dumézil, *Jupiter* [bib. no. 2059-a], p. 66; Leumann, ap. Schubring, *Grundrisse* [?], III, 28 (1935); J[agmanderlal] Jaini, *Outlines of Jainism* ([Cambridge], 1918), p. 45; [Paul] Demiéville,

rates (the theory of the humoral origin of the four color pigments), and the alchemists, and according to Goethe. And the latter, being the trend followed by the illuminator-miniaturists, was the one which the disciples of Hallāj had followed during his lifetime in making deluxe copies of his works. We know the list of their complementary colors from such cartographers of the period as Istakhrī.

This was also the trend followed by calligraphers;[147] we know that they were illuminating manuscripts of the Qur'ān at that time, and therefore also the Qur'ānic quotations with which the Hallājian texts were studded, using the following (extremist Shī'ite) symbolism of complementary colors: on *white* paper, *black* for consonants (= the words' material and inanimate body); above which the vocalic signs were written in *red* (= the soul fortuitously given to the words, which alone enables them to be spoken),[148] *yellow* or *green* for aspiration (hamza = enunciatory inspiration), *blue* for the doubling of consonants.

In heraldry, several texts show us that Hallāj preferred the color *black* (or dark blue); this was the 'Abbāsid dynastic color, in contrast to the green of the Fātimids, the white of the Umayyads, and the red of the Qays tribes.[149]

With regard to *touch*, we have only the brief mention, found in some Hallājian texts, of contrasting tactile[150] sensations (cf. Goethe).[151]

2. The Auditory Arts: Music

The musical theories and education of the elite were already very advanced in Baghdad in Hallāj's time, which is why he had to state his opinion about them. We see him selecting a melodic theme in a concert

---

Hōbōgirin [Tokyo, 1929-   ], fasc. III, suppl. p. 111, add. p. 214; cf. Przyluski, ap. *BSOS* (1930).

[147] De Sacy, *Grammaire*, I, 35, 37, 42, 45, 52, 59.

[148] A Druze explanation (De Sacy, *Druzes*, II, 3, 5, 7, and 481).

[149] Y. Artin Pasha, *Blason en Orient* [bib. no. 2020-a]; *AMM* [?], 3rd ed., pp. 180, 446; Brown-Rose, *Dervishes* [bib. no. 2038-a], p. 56; *Me Elle Belediye* [?], Istanbul, 1922; Desmaisons, *Dictionnaire persan* [bib. no. 2056], s.v. heft rang, *Khatteberzakh*; [Louis Alphonse Daniel] Nicolas, [Essai sur le] *Chéïkhisme* [Paris, 1910-14] III, 43; Jābir, ed. Kraus [?], p. 430; *Umm al-kitāb*, tr. by Ivanow, p. 437; *Amratkund*, ed. by Y. Husayn, ap. *JAP*, 19 [28]; Druze *Risāla fī ta'tīl wa tartīb zuhūr al-sayyid* (Chehab ms.); Kattānī, *Tarātīb idārīya* [?]; Ibn 'Arabī, *Tajallīyat* [bib. no. 421-f], ms. P., f. 47a; Jildakī, ms. P. 6683, f. 236; Hallāj did not know the theory of the colors of the soul's coverings (Semnānī, ap. *Recueil*, p. 144; cf. Khalwatīya, according to Sanūsī, *Salsabīl*, 100, tr. ap. Rinn, *Marabouts* [bib. no. 2193-a], p. 300). Concerning Christian liturgical colors, cf. *The Apocalypse* and Spirago [?], p. 456.

[150] *Taw.* II: *lams*, *massawī*.

[151] [Ernest] Faivre, *Œuvres scientifiques de Goethe* [Paris, 1862], p. 160; cf. Democritus, ap. Theophrastus, *Osm* [?].

program (samā'), though we do not know its mode, which would be an important clue to discovering the corresponding emotion that he wished to arouse.[152] However, it is clear that, as a mystic, he must have been a follower of the old trend, supporting the cyclic theory of complementary and contrasting modes (as opposed to the indefinite melodic linear sequences), perhaps also the cyclic theory of complementary rhythmic patterns[153] (dihāt wa tā'āt) which are to modes what black and white drawing is to color painting. That for successive contrast (cf. light colors).

As for simultaneous contrast, of which music was to become fully cognizant only in the Christian mediaeval West (the "plural voice") with the notion of consonant and dissonant chords (harmony), the idea existed already in the bud at that time in the East in the notion of the *timbres* (dependent on the number of harmonics of its emitted note) of instruments, which is the basis of orchestral instrumentation. Islam of that time grasped perfectly (as onirocriticism shows us) the contrasting nuances of instrumental timbres: percussion instruments contrasting with string instruments, like black (and dark tones) with bright white; wind instruments, and human voices corresponding to various color pigments. Instrumental contrasts arise on several occasions in the life and legend of Hallāj: the horn (būq) heard in Nihawand;[154] the trumpet (nafīr)[155] sounded by custom to signal his condemnation (a sign of the hajj in onirocriticism); the flute[156] (cf. the *nei Mansūr* which the Mevlevīs dedicate to him), whose melancholy sound he criticized in Baghdad; the bass drum (tabl) which Harawī compared to his "Anā'l-Haqq"; the voice of the muezzin which he was supposed to have criticized for half-heartedness. And fifty years before Hallāj, Jāhiz assigned a distinct timbre shade to each of the four strings of the lute.[157]

Hearing perceives time. It might be better therefore to put here, rather than under the rubric of seeing,[158] a remark concerning the modes of artistic representation of *historical time* in the era of Hallāj. Reacting against the occasionalistic tendency of the early Muslim theologians, who viewed historical time as only a linear succession of instants independent of each other, the extremist Shī'ites centered historical time around a supreme divine manifestation, encircled by the converging attitudes of its

---

[152] *Akhbār*, no. [39]; a mode intended to "awaken": thus *hijāz* (= 4, 3, 3, 4 + 2, 6, 2 quarter tones).

[153] Cf. *Enc. Isl.*, art. *tik* [?].

[154] *Akhbār*, no. [22]; cf. yellow.

[155] This edition, 1, 557, cf. red.

[156] This edition, 2, 266, cf. blue.

[157] Cf. Ikhwān I, 117; *Tadwīr* [?], 133. L. Hoffman said the human voice was "green" (Goethe).

[158] Kayyāl puts hearing *above* seeing.

contemporaries both good and bad; and recurring in the same way in cycles.[159] This theory becomes in the hands of mystics, including Hallāj, the doctrine of the *abdāl* and of the *quṭb* (or the "pole"), the spiritual center of gravity of souls in each generation; which leads to a mystical geography of the "seven *kishwār*" sort which we discussed above.[160]

3. The Arts of Taste and Smell

Recent works resulting from advances in the field of organic chemistry have enabled us to determine precisely the scales of sensation for taste[161] and smell;[162] that of tastes is comparable to that of sounds (there are agreements), and that of smells to that of colors.

We know that the art of cooking in the Muslim East is based on very crude contrasts between tastes,[163] and without as much connection as is made in China between nutrition and medicine.[164] It will be noted that the assortment of nutriments (and therefore of tastes) preferred by the ascetics of Baghdad, and by Hallāj (endives, cucumbers, sugared meal) is a "hot" and constrictive vegetable assortment (in contrast to the cold and dilating assortment: wheat, beans).

As for nutritious medicine, which we have discussed previously, the phrase *hadma rūhānīya*, "spiritual digestive juice," is a very strange technical expression.

As for perfumes, their importance, both to Arabia from the beginnings of time and to the Prophet Muhammad, is well known. The tribe from which he came originally, the Quraysh, above all specialized in the perfume trade, dealing, not only in native, but also exotic, and especially Indian perfumes, which they brought back across the desert to Mecca

---

[159] Cf. our *Salmān Pāk.*

[160] Cf. the Shī'ite and Ismā'īlī dioceses, the Indian *kwipu.*

[161] Bitter, alkaline, salty, sweet, sour, flat (Charles Henry, ap. *Bull. Inst. Gén. Psychol.*, 1919, pp. 159-166; classification consisting of increasing lengths of waves). Democritus had used the same scale made up of pairs of complementary tastes: sour, alkaline; salty, sweet; bitter, flat. Ch. Henry inverted salty and bitter. Cf. Theophrastus, *De causis plantarum VI,* 2; Solovine, *Démocrite* [bib. no. 2218], p. 23; cf. Maspero, *JAP* (1937), p. 183.

[162] Alliaceous, terebentheneous (= aromatic), musky (= ambrosial), ethereal, benzolated, aromatic, balsamic (= fragrant) (Zwaardemaker's scale, ap. Larguier des Bancels, *Le Goût et l'odorat,* 1912, p. 45; corrected by Ch. Henry, *loc. cit.*; cf. F. Warrain, *L'Oeuvre psychobiophysique de Charles Henry,* 1931, p. 201). This scale derives from Linnaeus. Ex. of smells: terebentheneous (camphor, cinnamon, lavender, rosemary, anise, cedar, laurel, incense); musky (musk, amber, *asperula, holcus*); ethereal (ripened fruit, wine, wax); benzoline (coffee, tar, hellebore, opium); balsamic (aspen, benjamin, orchids, vanilla, tuberose, jasmine, rose, aloes).

[163] Cf. L. Gauthier.

[164] N. Sakurazwa, *Médecine d'Extrême-Orient.*

from the port of Darin (= the present-day 'Uqayr) in Bahrayn;[165] which explains the pre-eminence of an Indian perfume, musk (misk), in early hadīth literature. The Hallājian texts refer in several places to perfumes: to the mixture of musk and amber (= ghālīya), the favorite perfume of the 'Abbāsid court and the one which, in onirocriticism, presages the hajj[166] and symbolizes, for Hallāj, mystical union; and to the aloes ('ud, yanjūj) used to fumigate mosques, which Hallāj, in his final prayer, made the symbol of his bodily resurrection;[167] and which people lay on graves in Egypt (sabbāra).[168]

The Baghdadi poets of the period, particularly Ibn al-Mu'tazz and Ibn al-Rūmī, had emphasized in their verse contrasts between various flowers[169] which must have derived partly from contrasts between their scents; just as contrasts between varieties of trees[170] arise mostly from their yield. We pointed out in another connection the Hallājian theme of the "red rose" (cf. Baqlī and the Turkish poets).

m. Hallājian Trends in Science

Examination of the main "working" utopian conceptions of an ideal Islamic city in the time of Hallāj provides us with the characteristic basic principles of the philosophical thought of his time.

It is permissible to speak of scientific trend and philosophical reflection with respect to Hallāj; his opponents noted in him an experimental method,[171] and some of his treatises present whole systematic and coherent arguments.[172]

Also useful for illustrating [these principles] are two kinds of traditional technical sigils of Hellenistic science, arithmetic symbols and geometric forms: two methods used simultaneously since the Timaeus of Plato.[173]

---

[165] Bīrūnī, Saydala [bib. no. 190-d], pp. 16, 30.

[166] Nabulūsī, Ta'tīr [bib. no. 842-e] II, 314; Hallāj, Dīwān M 41; Laylat al-sab' bukhār (Légey, Folklore marocain [bib. no. 2148-a], p. 17) for seven times salāmun in Qur'ān; Ghawth, Jawāhir in Hughes [?], s.v. Da'wat; Tamgrūtī, Nafḥa miskīya [bib. no. 2227-a], 93. Hallāj: rawā'iḥ (Sul. Tab.) — yanjūj (cf. ghālīya) — shamm (Isfahan; Akhbār no. [2]; Shath, no. [cf. Taw., 201]) — anbar, misk (Dīwān, no. 41). Hallāj: tu'ūm: hādima khamra, ma' (Dīwān, no. 47); opalization — Nusayrīs = muddy color — Goethe.

[167] Akhbār, no. [2].

[168] Galāl, REI.

[169] Cf. the five floral patterns of Persian rugs.

[170] Cf. the five trees of China.

[171] Ibn Bābawayh: kīmīya, tajallī.

[172] Preface of sayhūr; Taw. III, 1; frag. ap. Sulami, Jawāmi', nos. 7 and 8.

[173] Galen's commentary on it translated into Arabic (edition by Kraus in progress).

1. Arithmetic Symbols

There were two opposing trends in arithmetic symbolism: a nominalistic and atomistic trend, expressed by numbers borrowed from India; and a realistic, algorithmic trend, using the letters of the alphabet (each having its own numerical value), namely, that of *jafr*. Hallāj uses numbers only to "number" certain esoteric sentences; which was a "philosophical" method of working, employed instead of the *qummī* cryptographical method used at the time by extremist Shī'ites.[174] He does not stress the material, quantitative value of numbers; though the liturgy of Islamic prayer gives numbers whose basis is as singular as 5 and 17 (= the first two rhythmical numbers, of the form $2^n + 1$ the first; cf. also 51).[175] Unlike the Khurrāmīya (number 5) and the Ismā'īlīya (Kayyāl; numbers 7 and 9),[176] he does not use a standard divisor number (except for 6, ap. Sulamī, *Tafsīr*, concerning Qur'ān 25:2, no. 113) to classify the elements of his universe. On the other hand, Hallāj resorts constantly to *jafr*, whose letters constitute for him, as they do for the gnostic extremist Shī'ites, a collection of ideograms referring to distinct concepts:[177] 'Ayn, Mīm, Sīn, Tā', Yā, Lām-alif. He used it in this way to analyze the name of the Prophet MHMD, and to define his spiritual character.[178] The same method was used for analyzing the initial letters of the Qur'ān and, in a wider sense, the two numbers, 290 and 309,[179] which refer to the Islamic problem of the numbered crowds.[180]

2. Geometric Symbols

Here also there are two trends: a projective and extensive trend, one that led astrologers to construct great systems of spherical references, *zā'irja li-istikhrāj al-haylāj* (as early as Sinjārī, around 360),[181] in order to work out horoscopes; and an involutive and topological trend, aiming at condensing a space with its structure into the center point of a circle. It is this second trend that Hallāj follows in constructing concentric circles of concepts, which are not spaced out like those of the logicians, but are encased some within others in terms of extension, rising from the center to the periphery, and make us enter, through a deepening, from the pe-

---

[174] Qalqashandī, *Subh* IX, 232.
[175] Charles Henry, *Cercle chromatique* ([Paris], 1889), p. 15; Warrain [?], p. 157.
[176] Ikhwān al-safā' I, 108; II, 20; Shahrastanī, [bib. no. 2210-a] II, 17.
[177] *Essai*, pp. 98-101; *Akhbār*, p. 49.
[178] *Taw*. I, 15.
[179] *Akhbār*, [p.] 48.
[180] Ap. *Archeion* (1932), pp. 370-371.
[181] Ms. P. 6686, f. 26b; cf. 'Attār's theory about Hallāj = *haylāj*.

riphery to the center, into the real. The various circular shapes of the *Tawāsīn* are applications of this dynamic idea: to make one proceed from the obvious meaning to the allegorical meaning, then to the moral meaning and, finally, through the anagogical meaning, to the Real Unique (*zāhir, bātin, hadd, muttala'; ism, majāz* [=*ishāra, ma'nā*], *haqīqa; fahm, safā', harām; maf'ūlāt, marsūmāt, ma'lūmāt*; cf. his definitions, "starting from the point," for the straight line, as well as for the *Lāmalif*).[182]

3. Grammatical Symbols

Various references to the precise meaning of certain grammatical terms (*Taw.* IX, 4): for the demonstrative *hā'* and the conditional substantive *man*, give us an idea of the type of grammatical symbolization adopted by Hallāj. He subordinates the literal meaning of a term to its syntactical function, but places the real meaning above, and renounces any verbal magic.

Because Arabic grammar was based on nunnation, and flexional vocalization, Hallāj, in order to prove the validity of nominal propositions (particularly those in which the attribute, the *khabar*, playing the role of resolvent, is introduced by the analogical particle, *ka'annahu*) introduces, for the indefinite noun (*nakira*, whose attribute is *sifa*) and the definite noun (*ma'rifa*, whose attribute is *hāl*), some precise details that interpose the logic of the propositions.

4. Logical Symbols

Hallāj reasons essentially along lines of a search for a way to find our origin in order to go back to the Real, a way whose steps and perils he describes.[183] Like the Aristotelian or Hegelian syllogism, his argument has three parts, major, minor, and conclusion. But since for him it is not a question of formal logic (of more or less conceptual propositions), but of the concrete logic of problems, his reasoning bears a closer resemblance to the diagnostic syllogism of the Stoics and to the juridical induction of the Hanafite *usūlīyūn*. Like theirs, this argument grows out of that temporary logic of problems which, as Kolmogoroff has demonstrated,[184] moves thought briefly into the domain of Brouwer-Heyting's intuitionism. Since his reasoning leads to God, the real infinite, he cannot deduce from the comparison between the major and the minor a solution

---

[182] This edition, 3, 315-316, *Taw.* [V, 1; cf. *Akhbār*, no. 64].

[183] Cf. this edition, 2, 60, n. 120.

[184] *Math. Zeitschrift* (1932), pp. 58-65; cf. Heyting ap. *Erkenntnis* (1931), p. 106; *Pennsylvania Academy Series* (1930) I, 42; II, 57; III, 158.

per absurdum. The evaluation of the datum being unrealizable, the excluded third part does not occur. Hence, those paradoxical, hyper-dialectical arguments found in the final pages of the *Tawāsīn*; they are not the thoughts of a skeptic on the equiprobability of opposites (*takāfu' al-adilla*),[185] nor a mystic's confessions of deception; they represent a care-fully considered use of argument to prove divine transcendence, and to show that one does not depend on reason but on will to be allowed to be united with the Real, which cannot be presented as being included in the considered datum, *hic* and *nunc.*

A long text of the *Aqālīd Malkūtīya* of Abū Ya'qūb Sijzī (d. 331), pre-served for us by Ibn Taymīya,[186] proves decisively that this type of ar-gument, which Hallāj joins the Qarmathian apologists of the period in using, rejects the principle of the excluded third part as it is suitable to the logic of problems.

III. THE TRUE HISTORICAL IMPORTANCE OF THE
HALLĀJIAN REALITY AND THE
STRUCTURE OF THE ETERNAL CITY

*a. The Personal Arc of Hallāj's Destiny and the
Dramatic Situations That It Intersected*

When comparing the personal arcs of individual biographies, one tends to classify them according to distinct types and different sets of adven-tures, peripeteias, crises, and trials. Such is the aim of a particular science, developing since Galton, which combines sociology (even statistics) with the differential psychology of personalities. By this we are given a crucial perspective on the great aesthetic problem of dramatic situations posed by Aristotle and Goethe.[1] And we obtain a method for the investigation of the social reactions to a specific individual destiny as well as forms of memorization suited to perpetuate his memory from generation to gen-eration.

From the outside and to the observer, the noteworthy and critical points in an arc of destiny look like a succession of points of retrogression

[185] Cf. the *Jābiriyan kitāb al-jārūf* (*Fihrist*, 357; Baghdādī, *Usūl* [bib. no. 201-d], 316); cf. Ash'arī.
[186] Ibn Taymīya, *Sharh al-Isfahānīya* [bib. no. 512-1], pp. 70-71, in which God is defined simultaneously by "*lāsifa*" and by "*lā-lāsifa*": which is *exactly* Brouwer's theorem (Vol. 77a, V 7a). Thabit-b-Qurra accepts transfinite numbers (Pines [?], p. 87).

---

[1] Cf. Polti, *Les Trente-six Situations dramatiques* [Paris, 1912]; Poyer's topological, an-thropographical psychology.

or of rectification, of orientation (sometimes even of nodes), correlative to what the subject feels (and expresses) from within as an increasing series of experiences, trials, birthpangs (ōdīnes, in Greek), and graces. These two directly connected sequences, moreover, are not always simultaneous, and Greek poetics regards separately in dramatic action the external peripeteias and the "recognitions" or internal experiences which, when shared in, confirm understanding among friends and bring out catharsis in spectators.

The succession of peripeteias in the life of Hallāj can be divided according to his five journeys from Ahwaz to Baghdad: (1) at a very young age he comes to Basra to don the Sūfī habit and to get married; (2) after his first hajj and his disputes with 'Amr, he returns to Ahwaz; he breaks [with his masters] and undertakes his first long journey; (3) after his second hajj, he leaves Ahwaz to set up residence in Baghdad,[2] from where he leaves again on his second long journey into infidel lands (India and Chinese Turkestan); (4) after his third hajj, he begins his public preaching in Baghdad; at the end, pursued, he takes refuge in Ahwaz; (5) discovered and captured, he is led back to Baghdad for his two trials and his execution.

The sequence of crises in his vocation occurs as follows: (1) at the time of his first return to Ahwaz; (2) when he discloses publicly the mystical state of union, the beginning of charisms (secrets of hearts he has read, food distributed to the people), and the formation of a group of disciples (in Talaqan and in Fars); after he moves to Baghdad (where he is named "al-Mustalim" by a select group of followers), the use of mysticism on behalf of an apostolate in infidel lands; (3) upon his return from his third hajj; (4) during the period of his great ecstatic preaching in Baghdad, where he expresses his desire to die anathematized for Islam; leading finally to his persecution; (5) and, after the long period in prison, during the last night when he accepts his execution.

The sequence of nodes of action is the following: divisions in his family, unfailing loyalty of his wife when his father-in-law undersigns his excommunication and right up to his execution (and the loyalty of his children even after his execution); divisions concerning him within special groups: public administrators and bankers in Ahwaz (the Sunnite B. Makhlad: pro; Shī'ites: contra), theologians in Basra (Sālimīya: pro; Mu'tazilites: contra), jurisconsults in Baghdad (Shāfi'ites: pro; Zāhirites and Mālikites: contra), and political parties in the court.

---

[2] The rash deeds, the retrogressions.

The tragic dénouement comes about through political pressures on the executive. The far-reaching hatred[3] of the 'Aynīya extremist Shī'ites (from Qumm), who were powerful in the finance ministry, fused successively with the following: the future vizir Hāmid, an extortion manipulated by another prevaricator, Vizir Ibn al-Furāt, and goaded on by three self-interested advisers, his son-in-law Ibn Bistām, and the confused fanatic Shalmaghānī, their hatred's spearhead along with Muhassin and AS Nawbakhtī; Qādī Abū 'Umar, ambitious and lofty, obsequious to those in power; and lastly, the sovereign himself, Muqtadir, haunted by legitimist scruples, besieged by two eunuchs, the commander-in-chief, Mu'nis (guided, in terms of internal policy, by a Shī'ite secretary), and the director of the imperial harem, the corrupt Muflih.

All of the opposing efforts by Hallāj's friends are crushed one by one: to safeguard his own position and to save his cousins, the assistant vizir, Ibn 'Isā allows himself to become disinvolved; Mu'nis, exerting pressure on his old companion in arms, disarms the loyal friendship of Grand Chamberlain Nasr; and the sovereign rejects the final plea of the Queen Mother.

Under pressure from hostile (particularly Zāhirite) Sūfīs, members of Hallāj's group of mystical disciples, like Dabbās and Awārijī, betray him; Jurayrī denies him; and Shiblī temporarily fails him through weakness. However, even before Hallāj is killed, Ibn 'Atā', with dangerous heroism, gives himself up to die for him. Just as Shākir, Haykal Haydara and his friends, and Hallāj's second son will do soon after his death.

The motivating passions of the drama are the following: spiritual jealousy on the part of 'Amr Makkī; spiteful envy on the part of AS Nawbakhtī; a false notion of pure love as loving without being loved on the part of Ibn Dāwūd; the hypocritical hatred of an expert in political trickery like Shalmaghānī allying itself with the cynical contempt professed by a tax collector like Hāmid for all moral purity. All that on the part of his enemies, underlying pretexts of doctrinal orthodoxy and loyalty to the government. And in terms of his friends, all shades of devotion and a discounted temporal victory, right up to the idea of uniting one's intention with his voluntary sacrifice as realized by Ibn 'Atā', and understood *post mortem* by Shiblī and afterwards by Ibn Khafīf ("recognitions").

---

[3] The *jealousy* on the part of Sūfīs ('Amr, Awarijī, Jurayrī); *hatred*: Ibn Abī 'Allām → Jubbā'ī → Nawbakhtī → Ibn Abī 'Awn (avenges Ibn al-Furāt against Ibn Thawāba) → Shalmaghānī. [This hatred has] two sources: Mu'tazilite theology (no mystical union), [and] Shī'ite *kuttāb* against Sunnite *kuttāb* (finance administration).

Neither literature nor popular legend preserved all those dramatic elements found in the actual history. In legend three things are dreamed up as playing deciding roles to explain the tragic outcome: the mother's vow, the spiritual director's (Junayd's) control of the destiny of his disciple (Hallāj), and the divine and fatal philter offered by his sister.

The real history brings three dramatic situations, a trilogy, into relief in Hallāj's destiny: (1) his venturesome departure on his first long journey, when, instead of being discouraged by a quarrel with his father-in-law, and by the mounting hatred of the Shī'ites and Mu'tazilites against him, for his having dared speak publicly of mysticism, he leaves everything to go and preach in Khurasan; (2) during the controversy among jurisconsults in Baghdad over the question of essential union with God through love in which Ibn Dāwūd attacks and fulminates, and in which Ibn Surayj refuses to make a judgment, most of the Sūfīs avoid involvement, but Hallāj, retracting nothing, boldly declares to his audience that he accepts and desires the canonical condemnation with which he is threatened, and to die accursed; (3) the offering of his life to the Beloved, achieved at the end of two trials; after the first, by the loving expectation of "nine years added to 300" (Qur'ān 18) spent in prison following his first exposure in the pillory; after the second, by his slow agony on the cross, forsaken, utterly alone, before the decapitation and the cremation: (1) the bold undertaking; (2) sacrificing himself for the Law; (3) the struggle against God.[4]

b. Heroism in Love: the Holy War with God and the Testimony of Blood

In an effort to characterize the soul of Hallāj, Farīd 'Attār describes him as follows: "this combatant killed by God in the holy war . . . , this fearless and sincere warrior."[5] Kīlānī says: "he stood as a brigand, a highwayman on the route of desire, who made away with the pearl of the mystery of love."[6]

This militant impulse, this passionate intensity, seems very definitely the root of the Hallājian character.[7] One contemporary historian, a hos-

---

[4] [Dramatic situations] IX, XX, and XXXI of Polti [see n. 1]. The crystallizations: *ghulat shi'a ghayba* of the Mahdī, interpreted by a *Sīn*, — Mālikism (after Zāhirism) passes on to the Shī'a — Ismā'īlis: → destruction of the Temple — Hallāj → weeps for the blind — the dynasty loses Sunnite support (Ibn 'Īsā), Muqtadir forsakes Shaghab.

Remembrance of this trilogy: Talaqān 'Attār ("cocking his head," to be killed on *jihād*, explosive uproar [*Anā'l-Haqq*], the sign of blood).

[5] *Tadhkira*, the beginning.   [6] Ap. *Bahja*, 121, line 23.

[7] This is what made him leave the community of Junayd: according to the *hadīth zuhūr 'alā'l-Haqq* (*Nihāyat al-sūl* [?], folio 11b; *Tahrīr* [?], 546).

tile one, Ibn Abī Ṭāhir, had underscored this when he said that Hallāj "showed himself to be bold in the presence of sultans . . . pondering the overthrow of states." More profoundly, Ibn Abī'l-Khayr says that Hallāj's death on the gibbet is the privilege of heroes; Nasrabadhī had said: "if there is one love that forbids the shedding of blood, there is another love that demands it, by the swords of love, which is the highest degree." All of which undoubtedly is a reference to what some direct disciples of Hallāj, like 'Abd al-Mālik Iskāf (after Shiblī) were saying privately about his desire for martyrdom. Thus his word to Nihawand: "when will our Naynūz come?—On the day when I shall be tied to the gibbet and drawn nearer (God)." The central theme of the anonymous collection of Akhbār al-Hallāj is a desire to die accursed for the Muslim Community, struck down by its very laws.[8]

We believe we find the beginning of it in the authentic fragments of Hallāj's work that have survived. The transnatural distance that separates the divine essence from humanity can only be bridged by force; in order to draw ourselves nearer Him, God has obliged us to declare war with Him, for He is ruse, makr,[9] and stratagem, ḥīla, and this obvious ambiguity, talbīs, is only the veil of His holiness, taqdīs, which draws us to itself through the sacrifice of our lives.

His sovereign transcendence leads us into a trap by appearing to us to be accessible: "no ruse is more undeniable than God's, when He deludes His servants into believing that some means of access to Him might be available to them, that the contingent could be connected with the absolute."[10] We must excuse ourselves and protest. But God is the Archer (tīrandāz) Who does not miss the target; the hearts of believers are the target for the arrows of His Wisdom.[11] "When God takes hold of a heart, He empties it of everything other than Himself."[12] "Help, save me from God, O Muslims!"[13] "So, kill me . . . and I shall be freed at last."[14]

This "war with God" is described in metaphors drawn from the military tactics and strategy of that time;[15] for example, the ambush laid by scouts,[16] the rigid motionless standing of the archer,[17] the buckler and the sword of the final duel.[18]

---

[8] Istiqtāl, istimāta.
[9] Akhbār, nos. 37, 47, 50, 52-54, 2; Sulamī, Tafsīr, nos. 4, 45; Tawāsīn IV, 2; VI, 32.
[10] Talbīs, p. 355.
[11] 'Attār, Tadhkira [bib. no. 1101-c] II, app. 86, line 8.   [12] Akhbār, no. 36.
[13] Ibid., nos. 10 (adhīthūnī) and 38.   [14] Ibid., no. 50 and Dīwān, p. 33.
[15] Cf. the treatises (adab al-hurūb) translated from Greek and Persian from the time of Ma'mūn on, and the furūsīya dedicated by Ibn Akh Khizām to Mu'tadid.
[16] Sulamī, Tafsīr, no. 61.
[17] Sulamī, Tabaqāt, no. 10; Qushayrī III, 179.   [18] Dīwān, no. 4.

Since God has the initiative with respect to action and maneuvering, in order to fight against Him, the loving soul, "neither robbed of itself, nor returned to itself,"[19] must especially avoid copying His tactics: "to pretend to know Him is ignorance; to persist in serving Him is disrespect; to refrain from fighting Him is madness; to allow oneself to be deceived by His peace is stupidity; to discourse on His attributes is digression; to abstain from affirming Him is foolhardiness; and to consent to being estranged from Him is baseness."[20] "Do not let yourself be deceived by God, nor despair because of Him. Do not seek His love, nor resign yourself to not loving Him. Do not try any longer to affirm Him, nor feel inclined to deny Him. And, especially, beware of proclaiming His unity."[21] One must endure by playing dead.

Such was the offensive ascetical position taken by Hallāj from the beginning, from the Basra period, when he went into mourning for the 'Īd al-Fitr. And it is even more apparent in Mecca, when he "tested his endurance"[22] with God, according to the hostile remark made by Maghribī.

In Mecca during his three prolonged visits, and later on the frontiers of Islam among the Indians and the Turks, Hallāj combined his violent ascetical impulse with the very deeply Muslim symbolism of two of the fundamental precepts of Islam: hajj (pilgrimage to Mecca) and jihād (holy war).

The call of the jihād brings him to the life of the *ribāt* (the frontier garrison outpost for which Ibn Adham had come to die at Jeble, and in which Ibn al-Mubārak was to live at Tarsus, extolling in verse the glory of this fortified camp of volunteers for the faith).[23] We have some meaningful statements by his friend Shiblī and by Abū 'Uthmān Maghribī on the symbolism of jihād: "for penitents, the jihād of the soul is to be killed by the sword of desire, fallen on the threshold of humility; for ascetics, the jihād of the heart is to be killed by the sword of vigilance and regret, fallen on the threshold of reconciliation; for lovers, the jihād of the mind is to be killed by the sword of attraction, fallen on the threshold of coquetry and liberality."[24] It is a certain way of encountering God that Hallāj goes to find on the remote frontier of the apostolate.

Previously, however, his thought had concentrated on the ultimate theme of the violent death of the *mujāhid*, at the time of his three visits to Mecca when taking part in the hajj rites whose climax, on *Dhū'l-Hijja* 9,

---

[19] *Akhbār*, nos. 10 and 38.
[21] *Ibid.*, no. 41.
[23] *Nihāyat . . . fi'l-furūsīya*, ms. BN 2828, f. 10a.

[20] *Ibid.*, no. 14.
[22] *Yatasabbar.*
[24] *Ibid.*, f. 9a.

is solemnized at 'Arafat, in the *mawqif* of the Jabal al-Rahma, in the *Waqfa* of the *'asr* prayer: when the whole multitude of pilgrims stands in meditation to offer the sacrifice of the sheep which are killed the next day with a view to the pardon of everyone, present and absent, in the Muslim Community, prays two *rak'a* only, listens to a *khutba*, and chants the *talbīya*.[25] We have a *talbīya* in verse by Hallāj[26] which, of all the sites where the *ihrām* is required, seems to allude especially to 'Arafat; we also have two fragments of a *khutba*[27] that he was supposed to have been allowed to deliver at 'Arafat (on the hajj of 288). And above all a famous maxim, perhaps authentic, about the two *rak'a* of the *Waqfa*,[28] in which 'Attār, with a true dramatic sense, perceived the ultimate importance of Hallāj's martyrdom: "in love one prayer of two *rak'a* is enough; but the ablution that precedes them is worthy only if made in blood."[29]

The holy memory that all pilgrims retain of it proves that he is referring here to the two *rak'a* of the *Waqfa*. Algerian pilgrims furthermore refer to them as that pair of doves that drink only once and are thirsty all year.[30]

The prayer of two *rak'a* is shortened at dawn, when traveling, and when engaged in war; however, two witnesses depict Hallāj as praying two *rak'a*, either before he was taken from his cell, or before his intercision.[31] 'Attār, on the other hand, puts this prayer much more fittingly after the intercision, and has him commenting on it, as he rubs his face with his bloody stumps, with the sentence *"rak'atānī fī'l-'ishqi . . ."* translated above.[32] It thus takes on the value of an offertory prayer before the sacrifice, like the *Waqfa* at 'Arafat; in this case, before the end of his martyrdom by the sword. This is true also of Hallāj's poem beginning *"Yā lā'imī fī hawāhu"*:[33]

---

[25] Batanūnī, *Rihla* [?], 188; Gaudefroy-Denombynes [bib. no. 1766-a], p. 249.

[26] *Dīwān*, pp. 11-15.

[27] 'Attār II, 139; cf. Baqlī, *Tafsīr* [bib. no. 380-a], no. 17, and Kal., *Ta'ar*, no. 29, and *Akhbār*, ms. BN 5855, f. 87a.

[28] *Prior to the sacrifice that validates them* (cf. the Last Supper).

[29] 'Attār II, 144; calligraphy by Kāmil Akdik, ap. our *Situation de l'Islam* (1939), plate IX.

[30] Giacobetti, *Recueil d'énigmes arabes populaires* (Algiers, 1916), no. 608: *"zūj hamāmat tū'ām—isberbū marra ū ighebbū 'ām."*

[31] *Akhbār*, nos. 1 and 2.

[32] 'Attār used this theme four times: (1) ap. *Tadhkira*, after the image "I rubbed my face with blood so it would be red to your eyes, for rosy red is the color of the blood of the brave"; (2) ap. *Mantiq al-tayr*: the same image; (3) ap. *Waslatnāma*, after the following: "the sweat of the brave is blood"; (4) ap. *Ilahi-nāma*, before the following: "thus the brave, close to the Beloved, know neither tear nor reproach from anyone; (5) no reference in the great epics (*Jawhar* II, ch. 13; *Ushtūr* III, ch. 18; *Haylāj*, ch. 9).

[33] *Dīwān*, p. 85.

If they offer lambs in sacrifice, I shall offer my heart and my blood.

The prayer of his last vigil seems to indicate that Hallāj had indeed given in 309, with the full thrust of his will, the testimony of blood that he claimed to desire fifteen years earlier during his last public sermon in Baghdad. However, his most zealous supporters, like Harawī Ansārī, do not dare go so far as to say that his horrible punishment was a divine grace granting his prayer. Popular legend believes it to be so, as it read the Divine Name (*Allāh*) in the traces that his spilled blood left on the ground, writing his vindication (*tazkiya*) in this way.

We believe that the particular meaning given to Hallāj's death—both that he was killed as a *mujāhid* (= a fighter in the holy war), hence a *shahīd*, and that he was a sacrificial victim united with the propitiatory victims of the hajj (whose celebration he had specifically wanted to universalize by the legalization of the *ta'rīf*)—account for the rapid spread of Hallājian legend among newly converted Turks and Indians. In the case of the Turks, among whom Shamanism impregnated with accounts of Buddhist jatakas had sown the idea of sacrifice, whereas the military temperament aspired to link it to a holy war symbolism. Hence, the use of the "*dāre Mansūr*" (the gibbet of Hallāj) in the initiation into the Bektāshī order, and the veneration of Hallāj on the part of the Janissaries.

In the case of the Indians, who were much less attracted to the jihād than the Turks, but were very familiar with asceticism's *via negativa*, which leads to a sacrifice of self-annihilation, Hallājian legend enabled them to envision a sacrifice that bears witness personally to a real substantial truth. Hence, the cult of Satya Pīr in Bengal and the Shattārī *dhikr*.

c. The True Historical Importance of
the Hallājian Reality

"Killed by God in the holy war," Hallāj, in witnessing the reality of mystical union, voluntarily went to his martyrdom consigning to Baghdad, the capital of the 'Abbāsid Caliphate, a spiritual combat whose temporal, social, and political consequences shook the entire Muslim world.

[He achieved this] by a personal recalling of the whole divine imperative incumbent upon each person whom His Transcendence wishes to penetrate; by the announcing of the *fiat* that must be offered in the loving visitation of His Spirit. Which is the consolation of broken hearts, and the very anticipation of the Hour of the Last Judgment.

By giving a little bread to poor fellahs of Ahwaz, in time of famine, through a frail charism eluding the big monopolists' hold over everyone;

by declaring to beaten Shī'ite rebels the bitter news that the only true *mahdī* is the Holy Spirit, to those imprisoned with him, penance, and to the sovereign and his mother, that it is useless to try to reassure oneself about one's legitimacy by heaping bounteous gifts upon the Temple from the legal sacrifice when one does not offer the hajj from the heart; by proclaiming to all of the literalists that their sacramental worship of tradition, Qur'ān, and the *shahāda* is but impiety so long as they fail to embody it in themselves by adhering to the commandments with their whole heart; by living it, Hallāj was breaking the mold in which Islam had enclosed itself, like an Israel before the Pentecost, by materializing the *qibla*, the Qur'ānic verses, and the hadīth. He was affirming that the true structure of the Community was built differently, with living stones, with hidden intercessory, apotropaic saints who, from generation to generation, drew divine blessing upon the world, by suffering and gaining merit for everyone.

Hallāj, in that, was only uttering aloud what Sūfism, ever since Hasan Basrī, Ma'rūf, and Muhāsibī, was effecting in silence; but he felt compelled to say it, and the time for it to be said had come, because directed now against the faltering 'Abbāsid universal Caliphate was the conspiracy of a freemasonry of all the disinherited, the anti-Caliphate of the Fātimids, which Sūfism eroded from within, while the Christian Crusades took advantage of it from without.

In a more particular way Hallāj, after Ibn Karrām, was the first conscious and avowed missionary of Islam "*in partibus infidelium*." He involved himself very little in the approaches to the true God of his brothers in Abraham, the Christians and Jews (visit to the Holy Sepulcher, turncoats at court; he condemned an insult to a Jew); he preached to a few Mazdaeans (Behram, Tustar), but he concentrated his efforts on the two countries where Islam since that time has achieved the profoundest conversions: India and Turkestan.

Hallāj, perhaps a Persian, in any case born in Persia, but completely Arabicized, was, even more than Salmān, at the source of the Muslim vocation that Iran, more specifically Khurasan, radiated into India and Turkestan through the Persian language, filling the world for the God of Abraham; this for the second time, after Cyrus and the restoration of the Temple. And this Iranian Islamic propaganda carried as far as China and Malaysia the universalistic imprint of the Hallājian mysticism, with the Name of God as "Truth = Haqq."

In India, the personalistic emphasis in Hallājian mystical thought transcendentalized the deep mystical aspiration sown in Indian souls, Dravidian and Aryan, since the Upanishads. And Hallāj still lives in the heart of Indian Islam, keeping it from becoming ossified, as in so many other countries, either by legalism or by monist aestheticism (Sirhindī). There is a supreme cry of love. It was India that had steered Hallāj to Turkish lands, which were so impregnated with Buddhist ideas of sacrifice.

In Turkish areas, Hallāj's influence is even more evident after ten centuries. In the opinion of the Persian 'Attār, Hallāj became in those areas the Saint *par excellence* who, by his martyrdom, leads souls to union. And it was not by accident that the only Hallājian vizir, Ibn al-Muslima, saved the 'Abbāsid Caliph, Qāyim, from the rival Fātimid Caliphate, by opening Baghdad to the Saljūqs, thereby preparing the way for the Turks' entry into Istanbul and for their accession to the Caliphate (the Ottomans).

In Arab countries, this mystic who spoke Arabic remains suspect, like Christ to the Aramaean members of his race, and like Sakyamūnī to the Sanskrit tradition of his homeland. However, his memory is continually revived as a problem still to be solved, a sign of a possible rehabilitation and of a reincorporation underway (a vision), by pilgrims of Mecca and by Arabicized blacks of both Sudans.

His contemporaries readily sensed the largeness of his mission and his witness, calling him an intercessor and deluding themselves into believing that he would have a direct political influence. In contrast to the purely negative, atomistic conception that many Sunnites have of the history of mankind, and the conception of the eternal return, through cyclical recurrences, of an initial encounter between good and evil which the Shī'ites contemplate, we also find in Islam, thanks to such great mystical philosophers as Ibn 'Arabī, Ibn Sab'īn, Jalāl al-Dīn Rūmī, and Jīlī, the hope of an ascension, a growing trust in the latter-day saints' building of a human spiritual unity that is ever higher, more beautiful, and universal—a building in which Hallāj indeed seems, by their very acknowledgment, to have placed the foundation stone by his martyrdom.

Hallāj was the first of the great Sunnite mystics to teach that the goal of human history is not an ordinary planetary cyclism (Shī'ites), nor [a] return to origins (Junayd), [but] a Judgment confirming the Covenant with an exact compensation. God "forges always ahead"; the Account that His continual creative activity gives of Himself is increasingly vast and serenely beautiful. Though avoiding subdividing into *tajaddudāt* (Ibn Karrām, Abū Barakāt), Hallāj recognized the growth of the divine work, the fecundity of graces divinizing persons. In a hyper-Pascalian expression, he said: "O my God, if contemplation of Your pre-eternity dismays me, how greatly the sight of Your Witness of the Last Day (= *Rūh*) consoles me."[34] And, responding to a questioner: "What has a better taste, the Beginning or the End? —They have no common term leading us to prefer one to the other! The End does not stir us by a mere desire to enjoy; it is the advent of fulfillment!"[35]

d. Hallāj's Social Ideal and the Building of the Eternal Community

Whereas Israel, descended from a patriarchal clan, is established by dint of the exodus and the diaspora as a privileged, exclusive, and dissocial nation guided in its way toward God by the fond hope in the leader who is to come to complete the building of Zion, restored at last; and whereas Christianity, founded on the sacrifice and resurrection of a condemned leader, is a spiritual community, living by present charity, generative of a multitude of consecrated families (nations, religious orders), tested briefly in this world by the laws of states; Islam is a state moving toward a final cohesion, expanded from a city of expatriots (having a fraternity of adoption), claiming before God, in the name of its primordial justice, to bear witness to His truth (hijra, hajj).

Very early the most fervent Muslims differentiated the eternal Community they were building from the temporal form of the Caliphate-Imāmate (Shī'ites, Khārijites) with its incumbents and underlings who were so often unworthy. They had a presentiment that in each generation and according to a precise but secret hierarchy there were intercessory saints associated with this ultimate Islamic Community around whom the mass of sincere believers gathered through love (*hadīth al-ghibta*, *shafā'a* of the saints: *abdāl*). This idea, held both by Sunnites and Shī'ites, from Abū'l-Khattāb to the Druzes, to a schematization of the city beyond that was distinct from the diocesan geographical apportionment of the *wakīls* of their Imāms. But this distinction was made much more sharply by the Sunnite *muhaddithīn*, especially among the Hanabalites and the Sālimīya.

Ibn Hanbal, Badr Mughāzilī, Hallāj, Ibn Bashshār[36] Marubī, and Kharīmī (d. 329) were each venerated during their lifetimes, not only as

---

[34] Sh., f. 174-b.

[35] *Ibid.*, f. 177a. Ibn 'Arabī teaches the *taraqqī* of souls, not their spiritual improvement in this world, but in the next, after death (not only the search for faults, but *raf' al-himma*, the rectification of the conscience of the role, the gradual sanctification of will (Ibn 'Atā', ap. *Tajallīyāt*).

[36] Mughāzilī (d. 282) (*Hilya* X, 305) [bib. no. 2066-a], Farrā', 42; Ibn Bashshār (d. 313) (Farrā', 323, his *Shafā'a*).

one of the *abdāl*, but also as the universal Intercessor (*mustakhlif*; syn: *quṭb*, pole; *ghawth*; Samadānī; Khadir), "the angel of the world,"[37] presiding over a hierarchy of hidden saints who pray for the salvation of the Community (*ibtihāl*: "*aslih*").[38] It even appears that the disciples of Hallāj went so far as to specify the numerical importance of various ranks in this invisible hierarchy (*rijāl al-ghayb*); for example, AB Kittānī (d. 322), who taught[39] that beneath the supreme *Ghawth* in Mecca there are four '*umud* (= *awtād*) in the four corners of the earth, seven wandering *akhyār*, forty *abdāl* (= *budalā*') in Syria, seventy *nujabā*' in Egypt, three hundred *nuqabā*' in the Maghrib,[40] thus giving a purely geographical[41] meaning to categories of positions[42] originally separate (cf. still ap. *sīnīya* Shī'ites),[43] such as priests, doctors of the church, martyrs, and virgins in Christianity (cf. the Manichaeans).[44]

We can further specify some characteristics of this eternal city as conceived by the early Hallājians, at the very time when Fārābī and the Ikhwān al-Safā' also were building their "utopias."

A well-ordered range of occupations in the ultimate Community corresponded to their differentiation in the temporal city of this world. Just

---

[37] *Akhbār*, no. 8; cf. *Riwāyāt*, XXVII (and 'Īsā).

[38] Cf. the sanctoral circle and the feast days of the year [among Christians].

[39] According to Ibn Jahdam: Khatīb III, 75-76.

[40] AT Makkī, *Qūt* [bib. no. 145-a] I, eighty-six *abdāl*; II, 78, 121: one *quṭb* = the *sayyid* (= Khalil, Abū Bakr), three *athāfī* (= the other three Rāshidūn), seven *abdāl* (= the rest of the ten Companions); three hundred *muqarrabūn* (three classes: *siddīq*, *shāhid*, *sālih*); a single *sālih* is worth a thousand *mu'min*) = *badrīyūn*.

Himyarite tradition (Sam'ānī, f. 507b: 1, 8, 70).

The rhythm of the liturgical seasons (*Ikhwān al-safā*').

The Hanbalite liturgical symmetry (Kīlānī, *Ghunya* [bib. no. 341-h] I, 166): Quaternary, including one favorite (*ikhtiyar*, *Taw*. I); four angels, four *anbiyā*' (cf. Ibn 'Atā', Baqlī, f. 357a), four *sahāba*, *masājid*, *ayyām* (*fitr*, *adhā*, 'Arafa, 'Āshūrā'), *laylīā* (*barā'a*, *qadr*, *jum'a*, *qurbān*). four *biqā'*, *jibāl* (Ṭūr), *anhār* (Furāt), four *shuhūr*.

[41] Cf. Qūsī, *Wahīd*, [bib. no. 460-a], f. 69a on their distribution in Egypt, Syria, Iraq, and the Maghrib; cf. the twelve Shī'ite dioceses (*jazīra*). Cf. Suyūtī [see bib. no. 690] II, 244. Cf. Tūsī, *Ghayba*, 299; *badrīyūn* pr. Qāyim = *nujabā*', Egypt; *abdāl*, Syria; *akhyār*, Iraq.

[42] "The trade guilds" of the eternal city, for praise (cf. Ja'far Sādiq).

[43] These five "angelic" and demiurgic functions of Salmān, Miqdād, 'Ammār, Abū Dharr, and 'Amr Damri according to Garmī (Astarabadhī [?], 225); cf. Adhām, *Bāk* [?], 30, *Umm al-kitāb*, 447, 474; Abū Hayyān [?] VIII, 133; *Rūh al-Bayān* III, 782; *Sharh al-nahj* IV, 100, 104; *RMM* XLIV, 24; Kharajite '*Aqīda*, 36-37. Cf. the seven planetary influences.

[44] Home in Nazareth, mission in Galilee, cross, cenacle. Cf. in Israel, patriarchs, Moses and the prophets, Machabaeus, and Essenes. Cf. in Islam, *khalwā*, *taqallub* (Seven Sleepers), *balā*' (*mihna*), *abdāl*.

Early hadiths concerning the seven (in all periods, cf. *ahl al-kahf*) (Suyūtī, *Hawī* [bib. no. 690-g] II, 212): the *abdāl* see Khidr (like Kurz Hārithī, ap. *Ghunya* II, 72), who teaches them to pray "*aslih al-Umma*." Abraham was their precursor, as were the Seven Sleepers. Jesus will proclaim at his return the ultimate reign of this hierarchy.

as the composition of spiritual man resembles the various virtues (*maqāmāt, ahwāl*) that he has cultivated through asceticism, so also the arrangement of the assembly of saints, in the highest meetings held, will be based on the hierarchy of intercessions and substitutions to which love will have inspired fervent souls in this life. Here humanity ceases being labeled externally in terms of confessional denominations (fortuitously incurred and in no way chosen) or intermediary observances (*wasā'it*), which the transforming union allows one to dispense with; the remoteness of souls with regard to the central divine manifestation depends on the "theopathic" quality of the praise that they have shown in this world.

Ghazālī, who considers the same question in his *Mishkāt*, also forgoes classification under outward, confessional rubrics, and arranges souls with regard to the divine home in four categories or "veils," positioned from the periphery to the center as follows: total darkness = men enslaved by their vices; light and shade = those captive to their sensory perceptions, anthropomorphic images, abstract concepts; clear light = the seers, who have become synchronous with the rhythm of the demiurgic Spirit Who moves the universe; fire = those who, consumed in the One, are motionless.

This famous classification[45] is more intellectual than mystical, as evidenced by its radical rejection of any possibility of divine visitation in the soul (which is deifiable, however, by an intelligible actuating form), and by its excluding the idea of any internal richness in the transcendent One: two points affirmed by Hallāj and the Sālimīya.[46]

---

[45] Criticized by Ibn Taymīya.

[46] [This text has been completed with the following final annotations]:
—*Hadra, istifā'īya*; the damned judged with the others; *sūq* of Bistamī.
—The two gardens and the four springs.
—The seven *abdāl* of Ja'far Sādiq (*Qut* II, 125), *'ubbād, 'ulamā', tujjār, khalīfa, wazīr, amīr al-jaysh, sāhib al-shurta, qādī, shuhūd.*
—Shihr-b-Hawshab: *anbiyā', shuhadā', hamalat al-Qur'ān* = learned scholars (ap. *Hilya* VI, 61).
—Ibn 'Atā' (*Ta'arruf*, 42): *mursal, nabī, siddīq, shahīd, sālih, mu'min.*
—*Riwāya* XXII gives the following: *awtād* (4?), *budalā'* (40?), *mutawallihīn* (70?), *mutahajjidīn* (300?).
—Hujwīrī, *Kashf*, 214: 355 (days? cf. Dény): 300 *akhyār,* 40 *abdāl,* 7 *abrār,* 4 *awtād,* 3 *nuqabā',* 1 *qutb.*
—The *abdāl* in the corners of the world (hence, the *mawālī* in the *ribāts,* at the frontiers).
—The sixty names of Ramadān.
—The *rutba khadirīya* (*Qūt* II, 121): Hasan, first *qutb* 'Abd al-'Azīz Manūfī Hasanī (*wahīd, Durar* II, 374) presides over *hadra, ighātha midhūb irshād dāll, bast sujūd shaykh, tawlīyat al-Ghawth.* —Criticized by Ibn Taymīya *Futuwwa* (*Majm.* 1340), 174.
—The *ruhānīyat 'isawīya* in the case of Hūd (Ibn Taymīya, *Sab'īnīya*), Ibn Wātil.

e. The Hallājian Survival in the Futuwwa Guilds

We have pointed out the "militant" and almost insurrectional character of the Hallājian mystical apostolate, combining the sacrificial spirit of the Meccan hajj with his desire to carry on on the frontiers the spirit of volunteers for the jihād (holy war).

The style of his maxims is that of a warlike dynamism (ref. *sayhūr*, "*man 'arafa min ayn jā' . . .*").

Twenty-five years after his death, the party of Shī'ite scribes who had caused his death emerged triumphant for a hundred years in Baghdad with the Buwayhid sultanate. Therefore, it is clear that the Sunnite popular opposition had to form its reactions around small groups of resisters known for their anti-'Alidism, and, primarily, around Hallājian supporters of al-Siddīq, that is, of Abū Bakr (like AB Hāshimī Rab'ī; cf. *Taw*, I, 4-5, concerning the *nasab ruhānī*), at the time when 'Āyisha at the Battle of the Camel was commemorated (in 363), afterwards the Feast of Ghār (389-393, 422), and when the *Ghazw* was preached in Baghdad by the Sūfī Madhkūr (in 422), acclaiming "Abū Bakr and 'Umar"; in full agreement with Caliph Qāyim, who, fifteen years later, authorized his vizir, Ibn al-Muslima, to initiate his anti-Shī'ite action by a public walk to the *Maslib al-Hallāj*.

Any concerted political action by Sunnites ran the risk of being broken up by the Buwayhid police, who kept a close surveillance on Hanbalite preachers (AB Shāfi'ī, AHy ibn Sam'ūn) and Sūfīs (two *ribāts* only: Shūnīz and Zawzanī), and almost confiscated the *Waqf Da'laj* (351); therefore, their organization had to be clandestine and had to be camouflaged under the cover of seeming trade guilds, with their daring and venturesome supporters, *fityān*, '*ayyārīn*. As early as 363, a group of Sunnite *futuwwa* appears in Baghdad, the Nubuwwīya, whom we find again two centuries later in Damascus. A Fātimid *futuwwa* is hunted down in Baghdad in 473. A Hallājian *futuwwa* is definitely referred to prior to 523 by 'AQ Hamadhānī: when he introduces the word "*futuwwa*" at the beginning of Hallāj's *Tā' Sīn al-Azal*, in which the inserted verses 6:20-25 extol Hallāj as the head of a Satanic *futuwwa*, and, even before this, when the Kurd Yf Hamadhānī (d. 535), the transmitter to the Turkish Bektāshīs of a chivalric initiation rite based on the gibbet of Hallāj, attempts to separate him from the "satanic" (this is his own term for it) and the dissenting Hallājism of Ahmad Ghazālī. The most interesting note is that Yf Hamadhānī claims also to be Siddīqī and Salmānī by initiation.[47] There can be no doubt, therefore, that the Bektāshī "gibbet of Mansūr (= Hallāj)" ritual is of Salmānīyan artisanal origin, like that of the Nubuwwīya.

I believe that the Hallājian *futuwwa* was organized from the outset in Baghdad in Turkish and Kurdish military circles; and, specifically, in the circle of long-bow archers, the *rumāt* (sing.: *rāmī*). The Janissaries, all of whom were Bektāshīs, were crossbowmen in the beginning, before they became fusiliers; and in the *"zamjīnamā"* of the Moghul fusiliers of Lahore, the beginning of the initiatory questionnaire refers again to the Hallājian *"Anā'l-Haqq"* in 1140/1728 (*REI*, 1927, p. 264).

As for the early center [of the *futuwwa*], it appears to have been in Khurasan, around Talaqan, where Abū Muslim organized both the eruption of the 'Abbāsid conspiracy and the first regular Muslim army (horse archers; no women, notes Jāhiz), whose members had to be sworn in according to certain rituals.[48] Now, it must be remembered that (1) Abū Muslim appears in the *isnād* of the Baghdadian *futuwwa*, which was as much Hanbalite (Khartabirtī, *Tuhfa* [?], 117) as Nāsirite (Mufaddal, *PO* [?], 12, 426), and even in the *zamjīnamā*; (2) the chief disciples of Hallāj were Turkish and Kurdish military leaders, some of whom were certainly among the Hallājian rebels of Talaqan in 309, and among the officers of Subugtagīn[49] in 362. The uniformity of the initiation rite of the crossbowmen extends the range of this observation to include the Ghuzz of Qaraqan (d. Waddan 604) finally quartered in Fez.

f. Prophesies Heralding the Mahdī and Their Influence on Hallāj during His Lifetime

Recent Sunnite exegesis tends to dismiss the *mahdī* as a Shī'ite invention; it claims that there is no trace of the *mahdī* in the Qur'ān. On the other hand, history and heresiography show that since the time of the Companions of the Prophet, century after century, the Sunnite masses have believed in a number of would-be mahdīs who were often supported by ascetics and mystics of renown.

Just as the source of the "kingdom of God" is found in the "Pater Noster," mahdism originates in a verse of the *Fātiha*: *ihdīnā*, "guide us," meaning "give us a Guide on the straight path."

---

[47] (Baton and turban): like both Ja'far Sādiq (→ Mūsā → Junayd → Qādirīya) and Bistāmī (Jurjānī; Kharqānī).
[48] Cf. the attempt by Abū Kālījār (called several times to Baghdad by the army).
[49] Alptagīn guarded the Shāfi'ite vizir (Bal'amī II).

The Hanbalite rite believes that there is a continuous series of guides sent by God to the Community, pious men who have neither political power nor specialized knowledge. This is the very old idea of the *abdāl*, apotropaic saints, which the mystics were to expand by means of hierarchical numbers and a geographical distribution.

The Shāfi'ite rite limits itself to asserting that in the beginning of each century of the Hijra there is a *mujaddid al-'asr*, "a renewer of the age" for canon law: Ibn Surayj, for the years 300; Ghazālī, in his *Munqidh*, confides to us his desire to become the *mujaddid* for the 500s.

However, neither the *badal* nor the *mujaddid* fulfill the notion, implicit in the Qur'ān, of the *mahdī*. The latter is an inspired leader who will prepare the way for the Last Judgment through a consolidation of the Law and by stunning victories, "filling the world finally with justice as it had been previously filled with iniquity." This is the Jewish idea of the final reestablishment of the suffering Just (whence the post-Mazdaean and Manichaean Iranian theme of the Savior), and it is the Christian idea of the Parousia, of the Second Coming of the Savior Jesus as the universal Judge.

The eschatological sense of Qur'ānic verses dealing with Jesus and the divine *fiat* does not exactly equate Jesus with the *mahdī*, but it does closely connect them, as it does with two others, the "two witnesses" (*waliayn*, *ālayn*) joined in one (Nafs Zakīya, Khadir, Mūsā), and sometimes with seven others, the Seven Sleepers of *sūra* 18; and the Betrothed of Jesus (*Rafīqa*); al-Mathal al-A'lā.

Two traditions about the *mahdī* confronted one another early: one identifying him with Jesus ("no *mahdī* but Jesus"), the other making him an 'Alid blood descendant of the Prophet through Fātima, or a Muslim saint and spiritual descendant of the Prophet who received an "unction" from God.

In the time of Hallāj, every region had its collections of prophesies about the *mahdī*. This was especially so in Khurasan, where Hallāj had his most steadfast group of followers; and where the 'Abbāsid dynastic propaganda of the years 100-130 of the Hijra had sown prophesies. Though unfulfilled by the triumph of Saffāh and Mansūr, they were kept alive among dissidents (Khurramīya, Muqannā'īya), whereas Abū 'Isma Nūh's former secretary, Na'īm-b-Hammād Marwazī (d. 218, imprisoned in Samarra for having refused to admit that the Qur'ān was created) recorded them in his *Kitāb al-fitan*.

We read in this that the initial role, without the triumph of the Hāshimite Mahdī, concealed in Khotan (China), reverts to the head of its advanced guard, who was to raise the black flags in Talaqan (Juzjan) very near the place where Abū Muslim's revolt began in 130 and Yahyā-b-Zayd's in 135; it was there that the Zaydite M-b-Qāsim revolted in 219 and the Hallājians (of Shākir) in 309. Because of the hadīth: "There is a treasure for the Āl-Muhammad in Talaqan; God will reveal it when He so desires, and his preaching will be Truth (Haqq); he will rebel with divine permission and he will preach the divine religion." Haqq is a Hallājian word, and in the text of Na'īm we find two place names, Bayda of Istakhr and Talaqan, both of which figured in the life of Hallāj.

g. *The Hallājian Teaching on Jesus, the Mahdī of Islam.*
Its Origins, Convergences, Importance,
and Personal, Historical, and Legendary Realization

To Hallāj, the return of Jesus is a judicial advent and the beginning of a reign: he will promulgate the definitive Law speaking in the Name of God. He regards Jesus therefore as the Qāyim, his return as the *raj'a*; his Law abolishes (*naskh*) all preceding ones: it is spiritual.

Several of his contemporaries were teaching similar doctrines: two Mu'tazilites, A ibn Khābit and Fadl Hadathī regarded Jesus as the Judge and demiurge, the understanding; the Sunnite Hakīm Tirmidhī (d. 285), a Hanafite and mystic, considered Jesus the Seal of the saints, upon his return, as Muhammad was the Seal of the prophets.[50]

These teachings had a traditional source, the famous hadīth of Shāfi'ī,[51] propagated by Yūnus-b-'Abd al-A'lā (d. 264), who traced it back to Hasan Basrī: "the situation will only grow worse and the world only decay and people only become more avaricious; and the Hour will come only for the most perverse generation; and there will be no other mahdī than Jesus son of Mary," the essential Mujaddid. This hadīth, which was evidently used in polemics against Shī'ite propaganda for an 'Alid *mahdī*, was taught in the time of Hallāj by eminent traditionists. After M-b-Māja Qazwīnī (d. 273; ap. *Sunan*), these were as follows: in Nishapur, by M-b-Ish-b-Khuzayma (d. 311) and AB 'AA-b-M-b-Ziyād (d. 324); in Rayy, by 'AR-b-Abī Hātim M-b-Mundhir (d. 327); in Basra, by Zak-b-Yh Sājī (d. 307); in Damascus and Ramlah, by the Shāfi'ite qādī 'AA-b-M Qazwīnī (d. 315); in Cairo, by A-b-M Tahāwī (d. 321),

---

[50] Cf. Ibn 'Arabī. M Saghīr-b-'AR Farsī (d. 1134) and his disciples, the *Ifrānī* historian (d. 1151) and the Nāsirī M Dar'ī Tamgrūtī (d. 1158), admitted to initiation given by Jesus (Kattānī [?] II, 31).

[51] Subkī, s.v.

Yq-b-Ish Isfarā'inī (d. 316), and H-b-Yf Tarā'ifī (the master of Ibn Manda).[52]

It is known that the 'Alid theme of the *mahdī* has no clearly defined Qur'ānic sources; whereas the return of Jesus is indicated in the Qur'ān: Jesus is the Hour; and the verse of the *"fiat"* (*kun*), which appears six times in it, alludes solely, as Muqātil-b-Sulaymān (master of Shāfi'ī) remarked, to Jesus and the Judgment. The Qur'ān calls Jesus the *"Rūh Allāh*," the "Spirit of God." Hallāj was accused of asking him for the divine inspiration that led to mystical union. Others had preceded him in that, Sunnites and even Shī'ites (Mustansīr, Mansūrīya), because of the *Rūh al-Amr* superior to the Angels. Shalmaghānī was to claim to receive the inspiration of the divinized Masīh. Hallāj seems to have indeed designated Jesus as the human being chosen by God to manifest Himself to the rest of creation, both at the primordial Covenant and at the Last Judgment (the *Suthānā* quatrain; the prayer of the last vigil).

In the political sphere, on the day when the first 'Abbāsid caliph,[53] Saffāh, was installed in Kufa, his brother Dāwūd, from high in the pulpit, declared that "this authority will remain in our family until we surrender it to Jesus son of Mary"; and not to the 'Alids, "whom the perverse Sabā'īya declare to be more worthy than we," Saffāh had added.

During the Baghdad riots of 482 between the Sunnites and Shī'ites of Karkh, the Sunnites were shouting "victory to the Messiah" and the Shī'ites "victory to Mustansir (the Fātimid)," raising crosses in mockery (Habīb Zayyāt, *La Croix dans l'Islam*, p. 50).

[The author thought of going on with this study according to the following plan]:

II. Convergences

(Mansūr al-Yaman Nashwān, *Shams*; Hamdānī, *Iklīl* VIII, 71).

Manichaean legati (3rd: Srōsh). Cf. the Mazdaean Sawshī (Jāhiz, *Tarb.*, 98).

Bēma of Jesus the Judge.

The two Jewish Messiahs: M-ben-Joseph (assassinated,[54] revived by); M-ben-David.

III. Scope

This Hallājian teaching was a reaction against the dissimilation of the *Masīh* (= Christ) separated from the *Mahdī* (Qāyim Qahtānī, afterwards

---

[52] Cf. also Abū Mahdī 'Īsā Tha'ālibī (d. 1080; Kittāni II, 191).
[53] (Tab. III, 33) [no reference].
[54] Nafs Zakīya.

Wasī Fātimī) as conceived by the Himyarites (in memory of their Mansūr) and exploited by the Shī'ites with so much success that the majority
of Sunnites, today, accept a pure-bred 'Alid mahdī.

IV. Personal Realization

Historically Hallāj connected[55] the witness of the saint (badal, shāhid)
closely with Jesus: both were united through the shāhid al-qidam, the divine Spirit in Whom they were joined together, becoming one, for Jesus
as Masīh is Rūh.

The miracles performed during his period of preaching in Ahwaz are
'Isāwīyan (Qur'ān 3:49; hidden provisions). His surname "al-Gharīb"
and the hadīth of Ibn Hanbal concerning the ghurabā' who take refuge
with Jesus at the Judgment (Ibn Q al-Jawzīya, Madārīj III, 123).[56]

The circumstances of the last trial, and of the execution in particular,
give him a close resemblance to Jesus: the prayer of his last vigil = the
uniting with Christ; his ashes[57] will assume at the Resurrection the size of
the body of Christ.

The Qur'ānic verse[58] on the crucifixion of Jesus is quoted as uniting
the dying Hallāj with Jesus.[59]

The text "let his blood fall on us" is applied to him: in an original way
(the responsibility assumed by the learned scholars of the Law).[60]

The theme of the reincarnation of his ashes in a virgin-mother
(Yazīdīs, Nesimī, Bengal, Pajajaram) combines the Islamic and Shī'ite
theme of the living Water (min al-mā' kull shay' hayy, Qur'ān 21:30: on
which the ashes, floating like the spirit, inscribe the words "I am the
Truth") with the hydriophoric Annunciation to Mary. The Child (tifl)
who speaks fī'l-mahd (cf. 'Azāz), who gets burned with him ('Attār).

The princess of Pajajaram and the Christians.

The husbān min al-samā' = reduced to miraculous ashes.

The paradisiacal betrothed of Jesus [who] grazes sheep with wolves,
who has neither hands nor feet nor eyes (Hilya VI, 158; IX, 177;
Naysabūrī, 'Uqalā'; Levi della Vida, Shaydhala [?], p. 154).

---

[55] Amā 'Isā al-Zamān (from the Shī'ite Khutbat al-bayān).

[56] The revived parrot = bird of Jesus.

[57] Anā'l-Haqq.

[58] "The 'ārif must die maslūb." Husayn also said this at Karbala, according to Khasibī,
A'yād, f. 91a.

[59] Ibn Khafīf; Ghazālī, Mustaz. [bib. no. 280-g], 30; Harawī, Tab.; 'Ayn al-Qudāt
Hamadhānī, Raf' [?]; F Rāzī.

[60] "Lā shughla ahammu min qatlī" (in [the mosque of] Mansūr, where he had said Anā'l-
Haqq).

IV. HALLĀJ AND SŪFISM

a. *The Period of the Debates*
(309/922 to 460/1067)

1. His Opponents: from Ibn Shaybān to Ibn Bākūyā

Hallāj was viewed by contemporary Sūfīs as an apostate for having de-frocked himself. The public success of his preaching had lured his mas-ters' best students away from them and embittered them against him. His first denouncers, Makkī, Nahrajūrī, Dabbās, Awārijī, were Sūfīs. Were they sincere?[1] Did they hate his teachings, or were they reproach-ing him merely for the sake of exposing publicly[2] some opinions that ran contrary to the laws and theology of the time but which, from their own mystical experience, they could admit privately were at least possible, if not probable?[3] The legend of the esoteric book stolen by Hallāj from Makkī and published hints at the latter.[4] A certain text of Ruwaym[5] shows us a tendency in this author to "ruminate" privately with himself over the public position of Hallāj. Later, of course, they will use his maxims, his verses, and his example, without naming him; a reading of the *tafsīr* of Qushayrī is particularly suggestive of this attitude.[6-7]

This distorted use removed from Hallāj's personality its essential traits and doctrinal unity. His idea of voluntary suffering chosen and agreed to, and his teaching of the separate and definitive personality of the saint, are

---

[1] We have been unable to clarify this point completely; cf. this edition, 1, 292, 295, 476, 486, and *Essai*, pp. 309-315.

[2] The apostrophe by Shiblī (this edition, 1, 607-612); saying of a Majdhūb, ap. *Essai*, p. 17.

[3] This is what the legend of the *fatwā* of Junayd shows (cf. *infra*, p. 353).

[4] Cf. *infra*, p. 344. Ismā'īl Haqqī will repeat, in accordance with the Ta'wīlāt Najaīya: "whereas the novice whom God instructs without shaykhs needs to deliver himself up to Him like the dead into the hands of the washer completely for *three hundred and nine* years (Hallāj, d. 309), the novice whom God instructs with shaykhs will reach maturity through a retreat lasting *forty days* (*Rūh al-bayān*, extr. ap. *Tarā'iq* III, 287).

[5] Cf. This edition, 1, 76-77.

[6] An anti-*hulūlī* polemic: Bundār, Ibn Yazolānyār-b-B-M-b-Hy Ajurrī Baghdādī (Han-balite, d. in Mecca in 360): (Dh. *'Uluw*, p. 289) includes it [no footnote ref.].

[7] The head of the Imāmite Dhahabīya congregation, Mirza Abū'l-Qāsim Bābā al-Qutb Dhahabī, wrote in 1270/1853 that the mystic would not know how to come forth to enter the gate of 'Alid holiness without being drawn to it by divine grace: the grace which in-spired Bistamī, after his *mi'rāj* to become *saqqā* of the sixth Imām, to say "In my *jubba* . . . ," and to Hallāj, who was prostrating himself, with his forehead on the ground of the Qāyim's threshold, to say involuntarily "*Anā'l-Haqq*." He recalls at this point the double miracle of the ashes writing "*Allāh*" on the river and the blood writing "*Anā'l-Haqq*" to justify his having said a blasphemy voluntarily [no footnote ref.].

gone. To Muslim Sūfism he remains a paradoxical and strange case, a captivating and incomprehensible figure.

During the fifty years immediately following Hallāj's death, the leading spokesmen for Sūfism were very open in their approval of his condemnation. We refer to a group of Sūfī writers basing themselves on the most orthodox traditionism: Ibn Shaybān, Ibn Abī Sa'dān, al-Khuldī, and Ibn Abī Zar'a.

Ibrāhīm ibn Shaybān Qirmīsīnī (d. 337/948), the leader of orthodox Sūfism in the area of Isfahan, used the following arguments in his violent polemic against the supporters of Hallāj:[8] Hallāj was punished for the ascetic extremes to which his pride had pushed him, as Maghribī had forewarned:[9] "Whoever wishes," he added, "to discover where these so-called apostolic missions end up has only to think of Hallāj and what happened to him. These preachings and public demonstrations have always brought shame upon their authors, ever since the day when Iblīs said: 'As for me, I am worth more than Adam.' "[10]

Ibn Abī Sa'dān,[11] whose hostile anecdote we quoted earlier, declared the following, as collected by al-Khuldī: "Husayn ibn Mansūr is a charlatan, a performer of tricks!"[12]

Ja'far al-Khuldī[13] inserted various accounts of Hallāj in his *Hikāyāt al-Mashā'ikh*[14] which depicted him as a gyrovague, a proud and unruly spirit, with a fanatical and disordered imagination;[15] including also accounts of his breaks with Junayd,[16] Makkī, Khawwās and 'Alī ibn Sahl:

[8] *Kāna shadīdan 'alā ashāb al-da'āwā*, Sulamī says simply, copied by Sha'rāwī (*Tabaqāt* I, 113), "he fought intensely against the supporters of a public apostolate of mystical union." AQ Baghdādī, the author of the *Farq*, states that, of the thousand shaykhs whom Sulamī speaks of in his *Ta'rīkh*, all are orthodox except three:
—Abū Hulmān (*hulūlī*);
—Hallāj (his case is difficult: Ibn 'Atā', Ibn Khafīf, and Nasrabadhī revered him);
—Qannād (Mu'tazilite) (*Usūl al-dīn*, Istanbul, 1928, 316).
[9] Cf. This edition, 1, 108.
[10] Naqqāsh, *Tabaqāt* [?]: cf. the *Tawāsīn* interpolation, VI, 20-25.
[11] A friend of Ruwaym, whom Ibn Khafīf saw him with in Baghdad (*Tarā'iq* II, 215).
[12] Naqqāsh, *ibid.*; cf. this edition, 1, 112.
[13] Abū Muhammad Ja'far ibn Muhammad ibn Nusayr ibn al-Qāsim al-Khuldī (and not al-Khālidī) was born in 253/867, died in 348/959 (his biography found in al-Khatīb, s.v.). (Cf. P. Loosen, *ZAW* [?], XXVII, 193); a friend, through his master Ruwaym, of Ibn Dāwūd (Sarrāj, *Masāri'* [?], 256).
[14] Edited by Ibn Shādhān (Qushayrī [?], 33).
[15] He admires, however, his couplet "*urīduka . . .*" (cf. this edition, 3, 116). Cf. the accounts by Ibn 'Atā'.
[16] Cf. This edition, 1, 125. Where we failed to indicate the source: Hujwīrī, *Kashf*, ms. P. Persian Suppl. 1214, f. 133b.

breaks punished by the death penalty. They are, in substance, accurate;[17] and we have used their information previously in this work.[18] But their anecdotal approach, with its style of scornful irony, belongs more appropriately to Khuldī himself, who stated with regard to Hallāj: "This man is a blasphemer and an unbeliever."[19]

His students in hadīth, such as Ibn Jundī, Ibn Hayyawayh, and Dāraqutnī, generally shared his hostility to Hallāj.[20]

Ibn Abī Zar'a Tabarī (d. after 353/964)[21] is less dogmatic in his stated opposition to Hallāj. In his notice on him,[22] the first to give the precise day of his death, he says that his orthodoxy is questionable, but refers only to the condemnations of him by Ibn Abī Sa'dān, Makkī, Aqta', Fuwatī, and Khuldī.

The last Sūfī writers who were hostile to Hallāj are the following: Abū Qāsim Ja'far ibn Ahmad Rāzī (d. 378/988), from whom we learn of the position of Ibn Abī Sa'dān and the account by Ibn Mamshādh; Abū Sa'īd Naqqāsh of Isfahan (d. 412/1021), who uses Ibn Abī Zar'a; Abū Nu'aym Isfahānī (d. 430/1038), a Shāfi'ite and disciple of al-Khuldī,[23] who omitted Hallāj from his great hagiographical collection *Hilyat al-Awliyā'*; and Ibn Bākūyā (d. 428/1037),[24] who collected in his *Bidāyat hāl al-Hallāj wa nihāyatuhu* fifteen texts that were hostile out of twenty-one testimonies in all, thus making his tract the arsenal from which Khatīb (d. 463/1071) and Dhahabī (d. 748/1348) were to draw their arguments against Hallāj.

In point of fact, these authors, beginning with Ibn Abī Zar'a, give more the impression of assenting only for the sake of form to the official and governmental condemnation.

---

[17] [But] his "Anecdotes" tell of visits by Ibn Kullāb and Ka'bī to Junayd that were fabricated.

[18] Cf. This edition, 1, 113, 168 (this last attribution is hypothetical).

[19] Naqqāsh, *ibid*.

[20] Cf. This edition, 1, 161-162.

[21] Ahmad ibn Muhammad al-Fadl Tabarī, after many trips and a stay in Damascus, went to Shiraz, where he died; a student in hadīth of Muhāmilī (ms. P. 2012, f. 242) and in Sūfism of Bundar ibn al-Husayn Shīrāzī (Sha'rāwī, *Tabaqāt* I, 280), a student of Yf-b-Hy Rāzī (*Hilya* X, 225), Khuldī (Kh. VII, 247), and Ibn Yazdānyār, the master of Warthānī.

[22] Published ap. Abū Sa'īd al-Naqqāsh, *Tabaqāt al-sūfīya*; hence fragments in Ibn Bākūyā's *Bidāya* and Dhahabī's *Ta'rīkh al-Islām*.

[23] Subkī III, 10.

[24] It is important to note that Ibn Bākūyā, who liked to retire to a cave called *"maghāra Kūhī"* north of Shiraz, where a spring was said to have burst forth in answer to his prayer, is known in Persian under the name of Bābā Kūhī (Ma'sūm 'Alī Shāh, *Tarā'iq* II, 222). Sa'dī refers to him (*Bustān* V).

2. The Abstentionists: Qushayrī

There were others who avoided stating their positions on this difficult and controversial case, and, whenever asked about it, said they abstained; for example, the Hanbalite Husrī (d. 371/982), whom the government persecuted, and whose silence amounted to a tacit approval, since his disciple Khuttalī declared himself for Hallāj.

Following the example of his master Daqqāq (d. 405/1014),[25] Qushayrī (d. 465/1074) abstained [from declaring his position on the difficult case of Hallāj], and gave his reasons in the following terms: "If Hallāj was a master in the knowledge of ideas and of reality, he would not have been forsaken by some people; and if he was forsaken by grace and reproached by God, others would not have accepted him as an authority."[26]

The upshot was that he excluded Hallāj from the list of Sūfī saints accorded biographical notices in Chapter II of his famous *Risālat ilā jamā'at al-sūfīya bi-buldān al-islām* written[27] in 437/1046.[28] On the other hand, he dared to give his name when he, like Kalābādhī (who had not dared name him), put the text of a profession of faith ('aqīda) ascribed to Hallāj at the beginning of his first chapter, which was devoted to establishing on dogmatic grounds the orthodoxy of Sūfism (such questions as *tanzīh* and the *Khalq al-hurūf*). Ibn 'Arabī explained in detail the reason for this attitude expressed by Qushayrī in his *Futūhāt*;[29] he did not want to revive the hatred caused by Hallāj for fear of bringing divine maledictions down upon his detractors.[30] More to the point, Qushayrī was trying to dodge official hostility and the inquisitional threats posed by Turkish Hanafism aimed against Ash'arites who were demonstrating the relationship between this 'aqīda and the *i'tiqād* of Qādir issued against the Mu'tazilites in 432. His tribulations between the years 440/1048 and 455/1063[31] and the trial of Ibn 'Aqīl,[32] which occurred the same year as his death, proved that his fears were justified.

[25] Who uses his verses and his maxims (Kalāb., *Ta'arruf*, after § 32).

[26] Hujwīrī, *Kashf*, Nicholson's tr., p. 150 (corrected according to the Persian text). 'Attār and Ibn Hajar allude to this. Qushayrī's goal in *kalām*: merely to prove that the Sūfī *tanzīh* is Ash'arite (whereas Harawī . . .): cf. Ibn al-Muslima.

[27] Criticized from the Imāmite point of view by Ibn al-Dā'ī [bib. no. 1081-a] (405-409).

[28] A refugee, he settled in Baghdad between 448 and 455.

[29] IV, 214. Cf. Sha'rāwī, *Kibrīt* [bib. no. 741-b], 272.

[30] Ibn 'Arabī says here with some vanity: It is just the same in my case; I do not reveal the name, which I know, of the present *Qutb* (= the saint who is the Pole of the world) "*out of compassion* for the nation of Muhammad" (who could refuse to recognize him as such).

[31] Told in his *Shakāyat Ahl al-Sunna* (Subkī II, 276-288), written in 446/1054; in which he exonerates Ash'arism from the heterodox inferences drawn from its metaphysical principles.

[32] Cf. This edition, 2, 166-167; 472.

Qushayrī personally considered Hallāj an authority in Sūfism, because he used his verses (without naming him) in commenting on certain verses of the Qur'ān and justified his "*Anā'l-Haqq*" in the following terms: "God speaks to the inner soul in three ways: a) through outward expression which the soul recognizes as divine and to which its interior (*sirr*) responds; b) through fear which forces its interior to be silent; c) through language which itself provides both utterance and response with the faithful being unable himself to explain (what is said). It is to him as if he were seeing himself asleep, and as if it were not God (Who spoke through him). It is certain, however, that the word of God is present in him, though the faithful does not know it, and that the difference (between him and God) disappears. This is 'the supreme union' (*jam' al-jam'*), in which the spokesman of mystics said '*Anā'l-Haqq!*'; words uttered by God when the entire human personality was annihilated."[33] Qushayrī thus appears to be a precursor of Ghazālī, being an author of two kinds of works, exoteric and esoteric, reconciling in the first esoteric mysticism with the atomistic metaphysics of the Ash'arites.

3. His Supporters

Many Sūfīs, without adopting Hallāj's dogmatic principles, felt drawn toward his apostolate and were deeply moved by his death. *Shiblī* (d. 334/945), who had condemned his doctrine of the "'*ayn al-jam'*," and who had insulted him on the day of his execution, confessed privately to his favorite disciple Mansūr ibn 'Abdallāh: "Hallāj and I had only one and the same doctrine. But he made it public, whereas I kept it hidden. My madness saved me, whereas his lucidity destroyed him."[34] Which Sūfī tradition was to relate later as follows: "Hallāj and I drank of the same cup; but he became inebriated (*sukr*) and I remained sober."[35] Certain very old[36] parts of the anonymously composed "Visits from Shiblī" (to Hallāj in prison) give the impression of including, within a conventional framework, some maxims and verses collected and transmitted by Shiblī himself, who through his accounts must have given the Baghdadian legend its early form.[37]

---

33 *Tartīb al-sulūk*, extr. ap. Ibn al-'Azm, *Rawd zāhir* [bib. no. 942-a], II, f. 291.
34 *Quatre Textes* II, no. 8; cf. *supra*, pp. 433-434.
35 Ibn 'Arabī, *Futūhāt* II, 13, 607. 'Alī Khawwās, *Jawāhir*.
36 Already ap. Hamadhānī's *Takmila*.
37 [The study of Nasrabādhī which is found in the first edition (of the *Passion*) has been transferred and enlarged in this edition, 2, 205-208.]

TABLE III
OPINIONS OF THE SŪFĪYA CONCERNING
HALLĀJ'S ORTHODOXY

4th Century
RHM: a) Ibn 'Atā', Haykal, Fāris. b) Abū Bakr Wāsitī, Shiblī, Sayyārī, Kalābādhī, Nasrābādhī, Sulamī.
WQF: Husrī, Daqqāq.
RDD: a) Maghribī, Khawwās, 'Alī ibn Sahl. b) 'Amr Makkī, Nahrajūrī, Jurayrī, Khuldī.

5th Century
RHM: a) Ibn Abī'l-Khayr. b) Khuttalī, Saydalānī, Fārmadhī, Hujwīrī.
RDD: Naqqāsh, Ibn Bākūyā.

6th Century
RHM: a) Shirwānī, Yusūf Hamadhānī, 'Adī Umawī, Ahmad Yesewī, 'Abbāsah Tūsī (d. 549/1154), Baqlī.
RDD: a) 'Abd al-Jalīl Saffār, Rifā'ī.

7th Century
RHM: a) Najm Rāzī (KB), Jalāl Rūmī, Balabānī (HALLĀJĪ). b) Najm Kubrā, Majd Baghdādī (KB), Ibn al-Sabbāgh (QD), 'Alī Harīrī (RF), Shādhilī, Afīf Tilimsānī, Shushtarī, Kāsirqī (KB), Mursī (SD).
WQF: 'Umar Suhrawardī, Qūsī.

8th Century
RHM: a) Yunūs Imre (BABAI), Shābishtārī (MW), Farghānī (SW), 'Alī al-A'lā (HR). b) Simnānī (KB), Shattanawfī (QD), Qaysūrī, Wafā' (SD).

9th Century
RHM: a) 'Imād Nesīmī (HR). b) Pārsā (NQ), Jāmī (NQ), Ibn Zaghdūn (SD).
RDD: a) Makhzūmī (RF), Jīlī (QD).

10th Century
RHM: a) Sandiyūnī (KLH), Nūrī Sīwāsī (KHL).
RDD: a) Ibn Jalāl (RF).

11th Century
RHM: b) Sārī 'Abdallāh (MW), Bandanījī (NQ), Niyāzī (KHL), Dulunjāwī.

12th Century
RHM: b) Siddīqī Bakrī (KHL), Ismā'īl Haqqī, Zabīdī (HALLĀJĪ).

13th Century
RHM: Sanūsī (HALLĀJĪ).
RDD: a) Abū'l-Hudā (RF).

ABBREVIATIONS: RHM = tarahhum [canonization: a) qabūl, b) i'tidhār]. RDD = taraddud [condemnation: a) radd, b) takfīr]. WQF = tawaqquf [abstention]; and SD = Shādhilī, KB = Kubrawī, QD = Qādirī, SW = Suhrawardī, MW = Mewlewī, NQ = Naqshbandī, RF = Rifā'ī, KHL = Helwetī, HR = Hurūfī.

b. The Model of Hallāj and the Religious Orders

After the sixth/twelfth century, no Muslim mystic disavowed Hallāj. His poems, arranged according to the outline of his legend, were freely recited during the sessions of *samā'* (spiritual recital) in the different religious orders that appeared and were well organized in this era. Each of them, however, left its imprint on the legend, and it is these variations that we must examine henceforth.

It is probable that the formation of the religious orders derived, like that of the trade guilds, from the Qarmathian propaganda of the Ismā'īlī *dā'ī*. The Sūfī schools listed in the earlier sources of the sixth/twelfth century[38] were ordinary philosophical schools[39] which involved no initiatory bond between their members. It is a known fact that the Sūfī monastic discipline created a bond of obedience between the master (*shaykh*) and disciples (*khuddām*), but this bond appeared, in the beginning, as something merely temporary and personal, and when the shaykh died, he did not designate his successor. Hallāj seems to have been the first to have gathered disciples (*murīdūn*) who subjected themselves to a rule based on a homogeneous doctrine. His was an order and, even more, a *rite*, both in the juridical and dogmatic sense, which persecutions by the authority crushed, as we have seen, rather quickly. Moreover he did not designate a successor and there is no text that speaks of the transmission of his *khirqa* (habit).[40]

In the sixth/twelfth century, on the other hand, Muslim mystics were grouped together in several permanent guilds that bore the names of their founders; their members were bound to them by a double chain (*silsila*), symbol of a continuous spiritual descendance, the *taking of the hand* ('*ahd al-yad wa al-iqtidā*', later *talqīn*) and the *taking of the habit* ('*ahd al-khirqa*), which corresponds exactly to the '*ahd al-yad wa al-ishāra* and to the *shadd al-mihzam* of the trade guilds.[41]

The earliest author to deal with the monastic habit (*khirqa*), Qurashī,[42]

---

[38] The *silsila* are ordinary *isnāds*: e.g., *isnād* of al-Khuldī (d. 348/959) going back through Junayd, Sarī, Mar'ūf, Farqad Sinjī, Hasan Basrī, Anas ibn Mālik to the Tābi'yūn (*Fihrist*, 183). E.g., the Khurasanian Malāmatīya, a school which lasted three centuries and of whose members two, Khargūshī and the Hanbalite Harawī, were interested in Hallāj (Jāmī, *Nafahāt*, 138, 312). Jāmī was to claim later that the *silsilat al-khirqa* of Ibn Abī'l-Khayr linked him through Sulamī and Nasrabādhī to Shiblī (*ibid.*, 352). *Wa'z* and *wasīya* were to evolve in the same way by *rule* (this edition, 2, 186 ff.).

[39] Cf.: Hanbalites, Qurrā'ite.

[40] Legend has it thrown in the water; cf. this edition, 2, 347.

[41] Cf. This edition, 1, 280-281.

[42] Shihāb al-Dīn Ahmad, Ibn al-Qādī Radi al-Dīn Abī Bakr ibn Muhammad al-Raqqād al-Taymī al-Qurashī, ap. *Al-Qawā'id al-wafīya fī asl hukm al-khirqat al-sūfīya* (extr. ap. al-Aydarūs), = A-b-al-Qādī, Laleli ms. 3747 and 1478.

listed five different types: (1) that of 'Abd al-Qādir Kīlānī (d. 561/1166): *Qādirīya* order; (2) that of Ahmad Rifā'ī (d. 570/1175): *Rifā'īya* order; (3) that of Shihāb al-Dīn Suhrawardī of Baghdad (d. 632/1234): *Suhrawardīya* order; (4) that of Abū Madyān Shu'ayb (d. 594/1197) of Tlemcen: *Madanīya* order; and (5) that of Abū Ishāq Kāzarūnī of Shiraz (426/1034): Kāzarūnīya order. A sixth was added to this list in the work by al-'Aydarūs (d. 909/1503):[43] that of 'Alī Shādhilī (d. 654/1256), the founder of the *Shādhilīya* order, which actually grew out of the *Madanīya*. Also to be taken into consideration are the *Kubrawīya*, the *Chīshtīya* of Mawdūd Tshīshtī (d. 527/1132?), the *Ahmadīya* of Badāwī, the *Dasūqīya*, the *Naqishbandīya*, the *Khalwatīya*, and other modern orders.[44]

[43] *Al-Hirq al-latīf fī 'ilm al-tahkīm al-sharīf.*

[44] [This section IV of Chapter VIII includes the beginning of Chapter IX of the 1922 edition with the insertion of handwritten addenda by the author, constituting a text that he planned to recast under the title of *Résurgences dans les turuq*. The rest of the original Chapter IX can be found either in Chapter VIII of the present edition (the study of Ibn Abī'l-Khayr in section II, g 2), or particularly in its Chapter IX, in which the studies of the *opinions particulières des principaux ordres religieux* are very much expanded and scattered throughout the ten sections of this new Chapter IX:

Kāzerūnīya (III b)
Qādirīya (x a, b)
Rifā'īya (II x)
Kubrāwīya (IV k)
Mēwlēwīya, Whirling Dervishes (v b 8)
Shādhilīya (x a 6, b and c)
Suhrawardīya (IV k)
Naqishbandīya (IV l and VI c)
Chīstīya (x a 6)
Ni'matallāhīya (III d)
Khalwatīya (v b 7)
Bektāshīya (v b 4 and c)
Sanūsīya (x g)
etc.
Lastly, the study of the Qādirīya is repeated here in Chapter X, section III b. See also the author's two studies of *tarīqa* and *tasawwuf* in the Encyclopaedia of Islam.

The author's schema also provided for other studies in Chapter VIII of the present edition of the following subjects:
—Mansūr Dhuhlī, the Maqādisa, Zanzarī, the Ash'arites (Chapter VIII, II e);
—the opinions of the Ismā'īlīs, Nusayrīs, and Druzes (Chapter VIII, II f);
—the *fatwās* of Nūr. Halabī, Siddīq Khān, and Rashīd Ridā (Chapter VIII, II g);
—the philosophers and historians (Kutubī, Khwandemir, Istakhrī);
—the grammarians (Fasawī);
—the literary critics (Kinānī);
—the encyclopaedists (Ibn al-Nadīm Bistāmī).]

IX

THE HISTORY OF THE
LOCALIZATIONS OF HALLĀJIAN
TRADITION

I. The Extinction of the Hallājīya in Ahwaz
(Years 312-334)

"On the last Monday of *Dhū'l-Qa'da* 310 (March 17, 923), the head of Hy-b-M Hallāj[1] was taken down from the Dār al-Sultān to be transported to Khurasan."[2]

a. Their Outlawing

The stringent measures enforced by Vizir Hāmid against Hallāj—his execution and the suppression of his works—accomplished their desired aim: the destruction of the combined theological, juridical, and mystical *madhhab* that he had just founded. Not only could manuscripts of his works not be found, at least not in Baghdad,[3] but one risked death in openly declaring oneself a disciple of Hallāj. Hallāj's execution seems, on the other hand, to have been followed immediately by the temporary freeing of disciples arrested during his trial, men such as Qasrī[4] and Hāshimī, whom we shall meet again in Ahwaz. But from 311/924, Shākir Baghdādī,[5] one of Hallāj's principal agents in Khurasan, was brought to Baghdad, where he was beheaded at Bab al-Taq.[6] There also, in 312/924,[7] three persons, Haydara, Sha'rānī,[8] and Ibn Mansūr were de-

---

[1] Although he was executed, [his] remains [were] respected (contrary to the Mālikite and Zaydite accounts).

[2] Ibn al-Jawzī, *Muntazam* [bib. no. 370-a], ms. P. 5909, f. 128b.

[3] Cf. Hujwīrī, *Kashf*, 344; Baqlī, *Shathīyāt*, f. 146.

[4] Cf. This edition, 1, 509-510.

[5] "Alert, fearless like Hallāj: he is the one who transmitted his words to the public (in Khurasan, in Balkh)": Safadī, *Wāfī*, [cf. this edition 2, 119].

[6] Sulamī, *Ta'rīkh al-sūfīya*, extr. ap. Ibn Taghrībirdī, *Nujūm* [bib. no. 660-a], II 218-219 (or Salāmī, here, bib. no. 137).

[7] 23 *Muharram* 312/May 1, 924: Ibn al-Jawzī, *Muntazam*, s.a.; 312 (ms. P. 5909, f. 140a) (following Sujzī, *Jami' shāhī* [?]).

[8] (*Tarā'iq* II, 316) Sha'rānī Istakhrī, a Sūfī friend of Ibn Khafīf or of one of the families of Khurasanian ascetics of this name (Sam'ānī, f. 334b).

nounced as being disciples of Hallāj to the police commissioner Nāzūk. In accordance with Hanafite procedure,[9] the latter invited them to repent[10] and, when they refused, had them beheaded, after which their bodies were hung on the gibbet set up on the east bank of Baghdad and their heads on the wall of the prison in the west bank.[11] To these names must be added that of one Haykal,[12] possibly Abū 'Abdallāh Shākir Haykalī, who is identical with Shākir Baghdādī, I believe, and not to be identified with his friend A'AA-b-S Qurashī.[13]

This is the way that the real members of the Hallājīya were finally outlawed. At least in Baghdad. Baghdādī,[14] at the end of the century, refers to the Hallājīya, the *"ghulāt-hulūlīya,"* as being among the sects that must suffer the legal treatment accorded apostates, meaning a ban on any subsistence on beasts they raise for slaughter, and on giving their daughters in marriage; a ban on allowing them in Islamic lands for a fee (*jizya*); an obligation[15] to invite them to repent and, should they refuse, to kill them and to confiscate their possessions; as regards the reducing of their women and children to slavery, the matter was subject to discussion.

Some members of [Hallāj's] family escaped. One[16] of [his] sons, it was said, went into hiding in Ahwaz, though his name is not given. The following account given by Ibn Khafīf[17] concerns the fate of his daughter: "The shaykh (= Ibn Khafīf) said: I was speaking to 'Umar ibn Shallūya[18] about Husayn Ibn Mansūr. 'Do you wish to see his daughter?' he asked me. —'Of course,' [I said]. To that end he summoned the young woman. When she entered she covered her face with a veil. But 'Umar

---

[9] Cf. *supra*.   [10] *Rujū'*, the technical word is *"istitāba."*

[11] On both sides of the bridge, cf. *supra*.

[12] According to Harawī; recopied ap. Jāmī, *Nafahat al-uns*, 170 (this passage, giving the deaths of Ibn 'Atā' and Haykal, led 'Attār to believe that there had been two Hallājian martyrs in Balkh?); surnamed *"Shāgird al-Husayn."*

[13] The author of the *Shath al-tawhīd* cited by Kalābādhī, *Ta'arruf* (in chapter V, in which he accepts the *ru'ya* of the divine essence by Muhammad at the time of the *mi'rāj*, over and against the view held by Junayd, Nūrī, and Kharrā'; cf. Arberry tr., p. 27; and in the chapter of the *tawba* in which Haykal is described as Junayd: ms. P. Persian Suppl. 98, f. 152a); cf. Ibn 'Arabī, *Muhādarāt* [bib. no. 421-a] II, 338). Mustawfī, *Guzīda* [bib. no. 1127-b], 794. Sarrāj, *Luma'*, 2255. This A 'AA Haykal Qurashī, cited three times in the *Ta'arruf*, is Haykal Hāshimī, *rāwī* of Ruwaym (Khatīb, VIII, 430).

[14] *Farq*, Badr. ed., pp. 223, 349-350.

[15] *Ibid.*, p. 222.

[16] See this edition, 2, 112.

[17] Ap. Daylamī, *Sīrat ibn Khafīf*: ap. the biography of his seventh shaykh, 'Umar ibn Shallūya (who should be identified with 'Alī ibn Shallūya Istakhrī, whose biography by Baqlī is found in *Mantiq* VII, 62; cf. Ma'sūm 'Alī, *Tarā'iq* II, 221, 219: a friend of Mu'ammal Jassās and of A-M Khaffāf [a disciple of AH Muzā'iya] in Shiraz).

[18] *Mantiq*, f. 62b.

said to her: 'Don't cover your face, for this man is your uncle, whom they call [Abū] 'Abdallāh [ibn] Khafīf.' After this interview, 'Umar explained to him: 'Four years ago[19] her father entrusted her to me. I have raised her and I have given her a husband (= ['Umar's] son).' "

With regard to [Hallāj's] son Hamd, the only biographer of his father's early years, Ibn Bākūyā claimed to have received one account from him in Tustar (Ahwaz) and another in Khujand (Mawara al-Nahr), which specified the rather remote places where he successively lived. Born in 291/903, his death date remains unknown; it seems very unlikely that Ibn Bākūyā (d. 442/1050) could have personally met him.[20] Later, in Bayda, there was a family that claimed Hallāj as an ancestor and founded the Hallājīya tarīqa, as we shall see later.

Following the executions of 312, the Hallājians had to scatter.

Even in Baghdad, M-b-'Alī Qunnā'ī, freed, afterwards a minister in 312, ransomed in 322, seems to have dared do nothing on their behalf.[21] The small group of friends of the Queen Mother Shaghab finally disbanded. Shaghab, betrayed by her Shī'ite secretary, 'Alī ibn 'Abbās Nawbakhtī, who sold her holdings, and tortured by Qāhir, died sheltered by the hājib of Mu'nis, 'Alī-b-Yalbaq (6 Rajab 321); Murtadd died in 325, Umm Mūsā in 327; A. Khasībī in 328,[22] and Shafī' Muqtadirī in the same year. Khafīf helped bring about the new opportunity given his former secretary Ibn Shirzād; and Qāsim, a son of Ibn Abū'l-Hawwārī, became a kātib to Bachkam after Ibn Shirzād (329).

One man, however, seems to have protected them; namely, AH Ahmad-b-Nasr Qushūrī, for wherever he was in command, Hallājism lived on.[23] Ahmad, an assistant hājib at the time of his father's death (in 316), had to watch over the appanage of Nasr, Sus-Jundishapur, under the suzerainty of the new hājib, Yāqūt (316-319, d. end of 321), before ABM-b-Yāqūt (d. 323) was appointed to the position;[24] especially since Ahmad Qushūrī was amīr harb in Ahwaz from 316 to 319 (with authority over the fiscal amīr, Barīdī, 316-321). Appointed afterwards amīr harb of

---

[19] Cf. This edition, 1, 516. Hallāj was put in solitary in Rabī' II 309/922. This occurred, therefore, in 313/926.

[20] Discussion of this in Quatre Textes, pp. 16-17.

[21] Neither Sul-b-H-b. Makhlad, a very fine vizir, nor his sister Maryam, nor the sons 'Alī ibn 'Īsā, Ibrāhīm (d. 350), and 'Īsā (d. 391) (rāwī of Shiblī).

[22] R., p. 143.

[23] Ahmad Qushūrī was not only pro-Hanbalite, but pro-Hāshimite; it was in the palace of his father, in 324, that a Zaynabi, Ibrāhīm-b-'A-Samad Hāshimī (d. Samarra) son and rāwī of naqīb Ibn Tūmār, master of AB-A-b-M ibn Abī Mūsā Ma'badī (315, d. 390), held sessions in hadīth (Khatīb, I, 273; VI, 138; Subkī, IV, 12).

[24] Misk., I, 289.

Basra (319-321), and residing there as a representative of the incumbent, AB M-b-Rāyiq (319-325; named *hājib* at the end of 321), he met 'Alī Barīdī there again as fiscal *wālī*, and fought him on all sides with his chief; Bachkam took him with him afterwards when he replaced Ibn Rāyiq (was briefly imprisoned by him in 327).[25] Playing much the same role that Nasr had played as one of the intimates of the Queen Mother Zalūm[26] (mother of Radī and no doubt also of Hārūn), Ahmad Qushūrī was chosen by the *hājib* Salāma, an old friend of Nasr, of Ibn 'Īsā and his sister Asmā', to be his representative in the Palace when Radī died (in 329). He is the one who arranged for the burial of Barbahārī, the fiery Hanbalite scholar, in the tomb of his father, Nasr, after having undoubtedly defended him (together with the sister of Amīr Tūzūn) against the wrath of Radī and Bachkam. It was in Basra that the Hanbalites found asylum, after having been persecuted in Baghdad in 321,[27] 323, and 327 (the arrest of Barbahārī, executions, and desecration of the Burāthā *masjid*).[28] It was there also that one Hallājian, Abū 'Umāra (around 323), preached again; he had to stop when, after the *amīr harb* M-b-Yazdād (323-325), the Barīdī family gained not only the fiscal, but also the military, control of Basra (*Safar* 325).

b. An Account Concerning Abū 'Umāra (Hāshimī)

We have only one, and very suspect, text dealing with this group by an antagonist. After exposing the charlatan methods used, according to him, by Hallāj in Ahwaz,[29] Abū Hasan Ahmad-b-Yūsuf Tanūkhī adds the following:[30]

And his supporters today believe that the divinity (*lāhūt*) which had infused itself into him has passed into a son whom he left behind—and who is in hiding; and that a Hāshimite man of the tribe of Rabī'a[31] named Muhammad ibn 'Abdallāh and called Abū 'Umāra is infused with the spirit of the Prophet Muhammad (may divine blessings be upon him!); they call him [Abū 'Umāra], "*Sayyidunā*" (Our Lord) and this is the highest rank in their sect.[32]

[25] *R.*, 120.   [26] *R.*, 118.
[27] Against Mu'āwiya [?]; population with the Hanbalites (cf. in 272, Mu'tadid's remark; in 441, *hadhā Mu'āwiya*).
[28] *R.*, 136, 192.
[29] Cf. This edition, 2, 125-126.   [30] *Nishwār*, ff. 57b-58b.
[31] A tribe famous for its jealous rivalry with Mudar, its sister tribe, which gave birth to the Prophet (*Farq*, 285-286).
[32] Could this refer to a reviver of that bastard Hallājism to which Ghazālī alludes (*Fadā'ih al-bātinīya* [bib. no. 280-1], London ms.): "In my own time," he says, "there is a man in the blocks of Basra who has promulgated a religious law and published a Qur'ān, choosing a certain 'Alī ibn Kihlā as his 'prophet' playing the role of Muhammad: he claims sinlessness ('*isma*) for himself" (ed. Goldziher, f. 29).

The following is what I was told by an individual[33] whom one of the Hallājīya had tried to win over to this Abū 'Umāra, who was at that time in Basra, in his reception hall where he was presenting the teachings of Hallāj and preaching them: "I entered and was taken for a neophyte; this individual began to speak in front of me; and squinting, he looked up at the room's ceiling, as if to draw inspiration (khātir) to himself by this pretended ecstasy (hawas). When I was leaving, my introducer said to me: "Do you believe now?" "The greatest argument that I have now against your sect is that this man who assumes the place of the Prophet among you has been unable to cure himself of squinting."[34] "How stupid you are! He appears to squint, but in fact he is letting his eyes wander in the Kingdom (malakūt)."

Now, this Abū 'Umāra had married a woman from Ahwaz, Bint ibn Jānakhsh, who had a brother (Ibn Abī 'Alī) of dissolute character, who played the guitar;[35] the father of both of them,[36] on the other hand, was an eminent shāhid, highly esteemed and rich. The Hallājīya believed that he (this brother) played for them the role of Muhammad ibn Abī Bakr, "the uncle of believers."[37] 'Ubaydal-lāh ibn Muhammad told me with regard to the latter: "We were travelling in Ahwaz one day with a kātib, an intelligent man originally from Siraf named Mubārak ibn Ahmad, when we came upon this man (Ibn Abī 'Alī), who stood up and greeted us. 'Who is this?' asked the kātib. I told him the preceding story but in abridged form. Then he began to kiss the head of the other's mule, and after-wards returned. 'What have you been doing there, O Abū Sa'īd!' I said to him. 'Greeting him and asking him what insults his sister 'Āyisha, the "mother of be-lievers," had said to him at the Battle of the Camel when he took her by the hand to make her let go of her palanquin!' This made me laugh, and I scolded him (for his disrespect for the sahāba)."

The final irony, reminiscent of the ironies of Sūlī, demonstrates rather that one need accept this account only with reservation.

Some indications[38] allow us to think that Hāshimī in editing the six Tawāsin added to them the parable about Hallāj as the disciple of Iblīs and Fir'awn, who were damned through love.[39]

c. The Execution of Mansūr, Son of Hallāj

The moment the Buwayhid army occupied the north of Ahwaz, at the beginning of 326/937, the Hallājians were chased down and the son of

---

[33] 'Ubaydallāh-b-Muhammad, cited below for the "preceding story."

[34] The antichrist will be blind in the right eye (Bukhari [?], 1320 edition, II, 142).

[35] This Ibn Abī 'Alī took the name of Halūz ibn Bā' 'Alī, fitted himself out as a Daylam-ite knight, and in this role cheated Abu Qasim 'AA Baridi, at the time—332 to 336—in Basra (at war with the Daylamites of Ahmad ibn Būya) out of 500 dīnars as the price of his service. The name Halūz still exists in Basra ("Arab legion, 1917").

[36] He was called Abū 'Alī.

[37] Cf. Ibn al-Tiqtaqā, Fakhrī 123. This joke refers to the idea of making the Qutb the successor of Abū Bakr (Qūt II, 78; Taw. I, 4), who had the sakīna in the cave (Qur'ān 9:40).

[38] Cf. Taw. XI.   [39] Taw. VI, f. 20a-f. 20b.

Ḥallāj (Ḥamd) was put to death. Here is what the grammarian and traditionist Najīramī (d. 423/1032)[40] of Basra says about it:

'Alī ibn al-Muhallabī said to me: M-b-Ṭāhir Mūsāwī[41] said: Abū Ṭāhir Ispehdust (d. 338/949)[42] said to me: when Amīr Mu'izz al-Dawla (A Hy A-b-Buwayh) came to Ahwaz, the son of this Ḥallāj who was put to death in your city (in Baghdad) went to find him, and he was preaching what his father had preached. He said (to the amīr): "I will give you back your hand which was cut off,[43] and it will serve you as before; I will give your one-eyed secretary (AHA-b-M Kurdepīr)[44] back the eye which he lost, and he will see; I will walk on water before your very eyes." The Amīr said to me: "What do you make of it?" "Let me take care of him," [I said]. "Agreed," [he said]. Then I grabbed hold of him and ordered someone to cut off his hand. When it was cut off, I said to him, "now restore this hand so we can know you are telling the truth." Then I ordered his eye to be plucked out; when it was done, I said to him: "now bring back this eye." Then I ordered him to be taken to the edge of the water, and I said to him: "now walk on the water, so we can see you do it." But he failed to do it, so we threw him in the water where he ended up drowning.[45]

This ironic and ferocious account of Ispehdust, which he gave in Baghdad after the capture of that city where he was to be put in charge of the arrest of Caliph Muktafī in 334/945, provides us in its way with an interview and an execution which could not have transpired thusly, but which shows us the atmosphere of hatred and contempt in which Qāḍī Tanūkhī, a Shī'ite functionary appointed by the Buwayhids, collected his anti-Ḥallājian anecdotes.

The reference in this account to a one-eyed secretary of the amīr enables us to date the execution of Ḥallāj's son precisely. We know[46] that Kurdepīr, who had betrayed the amīr in 324, joined him again in Ahwaz, coming from Kirman, only around the middle of 326: just when the Sunnite Turk Bachkam, put by Ibn Rāyiq in charge of the military rule of Ahwaz, had removed the Barīdīs[47] from there and held the Buwayhid

---

[40] A Yq Ysf-b-Yq-b-Khurrazādh Najīramī Basrī (345, d. 423), a pupil (indirect) of ḥāfiẓ Zakarīyā-b-Yaḥyā-b-Khallād Sājī Basrī (d. 307), master of Abū Nu'aym (Hilya II, 357) and of Abū'l-Fadl M-b-Ja'far Khuzā'ī (d. 408), and also taught in Cairo.

[41] Abū M-b-Ṭāhir Māsāwī, naqīb of the 'Alids, died in 346 (Kindī [?], 580).

[42] Ispehdust, from 324 in the service of Mu'izz al-Dawla, died imprisoned after the latter in Ramhurmuz in 338 (Misk., 355; II, 84, 114, 121 = Ispehdust-b-M-b-Asfār Daylamī; Yq., Ud. V, 219).

[43] Mu'izz al-Dawla (d. 356) had lost a hand during his defeat at Jirift in 324 (Misk., 355).

[44] Who left him again at the end of 326.

[45] Ap. Ibn Ḥajar 'Asqalānī, Lisān al-mīzān (Hyderabad ed.) [bib. no. 632-b] II, 315.

[46] Misk. I, 382: cf. pp. 378-385.

[47] As fiscal governors of Ahwaz from 322 to Sha'bān 325, they had introduced the Buwayhids into the area. Bachkam at first dislodged them by buying off their underling AB M-b-'Alī ibn Muqātil (an accomplice of Ibn Muqla in 326 [Radī (?), 105], he attached

amīr in siege in 'Askar Mukram. It was then that Ispehdust, aided by
Kurdepīr, succeeded in freeing the amīr to recapture Suq al-Ahwaz,[48]
and, when Bachkam was appointed to the court in Baghdad, to conquer
with a single blow and decisively all of Ahwaz.

We also see that Hallāj's son must have fallen victim to the Buwayhid
reprisals against the Sunnites who had supported Bachkam during his
rule of barely a year (Sha'bān 325-326). Bachkam began with the occupation of Tustar, where he imprisoned Abū'l-Qāsim ibn Abī 'Allān (the
uncle of Qādī AQ Tanūkhī, an emissary between the Barīdīs and the
Buwayhids)[49] and Abū Zak Yahyā-b-Abī Sa'īd Sūsī, an eminent Christian convert (Nishwār) whom he rallied to his side and had handle gently
the Jewish tax collectors of Ahwaz, Isrā'īl-b-Sālih and Sahl-b-Netīra.[50]
After that he occupied Sus and handed the local administration in Tustar
over to the Makhladīya party and entrusted military defense to Abū M
Muhallabī, who barred the river to the Buwayhids.[51] Several of these
names attest to the persistence of parties and local clientage: the Barīdīya,
who, set up by the B. Makhlad whom they betrayed, remained in charge
of fiscal matters in Ahwaz for fifty years; the B. Netīra, Jewish bankers
who had enjoyed the gift of official monopolies for an even longer time;
the Muhallabīya, clients for two centuries of the al-Muhallab family of
Basra, allied with the Karnabā'īya. If Ibn Abī 'Allān is indeed, as we
noted earlier, the main source for the accounts of Qādī Tanūkhī against
Hallāj, whom he must have attacked in person in Ahwaz thirty years earlier, it is easy for us to visualize him putting Hallāj's son on the list of the
Makhladīya to be hunted down.

It is correct to identify this son of Hallāj, who had "taken refuge in
Ahwaz" according to the story about Abū 'Umāra, with the one about
whom Baqlī tells us the following:[52] "Hallāj had a son named Mansūr
ibn Husayn, who used shath, like his father. Thus one day, using shath,
he said: 'God clothed Himself with my father (talabbasa'l-Haqq bi abī) and
my father manifested His personality (fa'zhara nafsahu).' He defined 'ayn
al-jam' like his father. He made his father out to be the mirror of the
transfiguration and the divine word. And he said: 'God called forth the

---

himself after that to Ibn Rāyiq, in Baghdad, and afterwards became vizir of the kharāj in
Egypt, 333-355), then he appeased them by leaving them Basra and by marrying Sāra
Barīdīya (in 328).
[48] Concerning the Barīdīya.
[49] Concerning Ibn Abī 'Allān [Ahwāzī], cf. this edition, 1, 468.
[50] Cf. ibid., p. 265.
[51] Rallied to the side of the Buwayhids, he was to become their vizir.
[52] Mantiq al-asrar, f. 69a-b.

TABLE IV
GENEALOGY OF THE MODERN HALLĀJYA

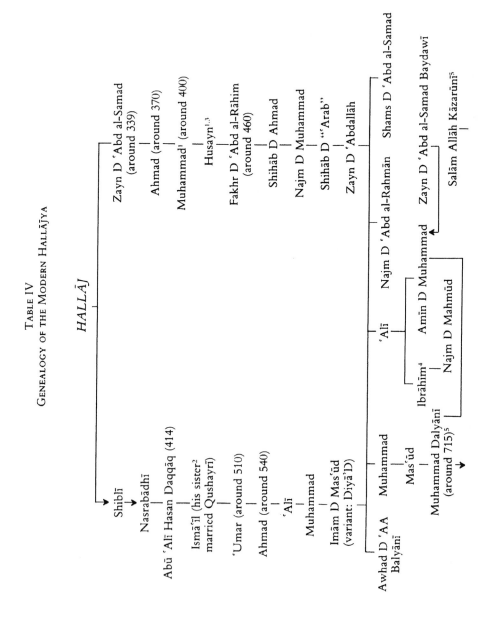

(= Khaṭīb Kāzarūnī)

'Aṭā' Allāh

Hibat Allāh Kāzarūnī

Hibat Allāh Shāh. M
(grandson of the preceding)

Ghaḍanfir

Abū M-b-ʿA = b-ʿA Qds. Shinnāwī (idrākāt), d. 1028/1619

A-b-M Dajjānī Madanī, d. 1071/1660

Ḥasan ʿUjaymī (risāla), d. 1113/1702

Sanūsī

Hibat Allāh Kāzarūnī

Banjarmah ʿAdanī[6]

Sayyid Murtaḍā Zabīdī[3] d. 1205/1791

ABBREVIATIONS:

| = natural descendance
→ = mystical descendance
D = al-Dīn

---

[1] *Itḥāf.*

[2] Fāṭima, d. around 480.

[3] Zabīdī, 'Iqd al-Jumān.

[4] Ibn Junayd, *Shadd*, p. 54.

[5] Is this the *nisba* of the village called Kazerun on the outskirts of Shiraz where the people of Kazerun live, or is it an expression for a member of the Kāzer-ūniya order? [Cf. Brock., s.f.; *Shadd*, p. 34.]

[6] The real intermediary for Zabīdī might be in this instance Majd D Abū'l-Ṭāhir M-b-Yaq-b-M-b-Ibrāhīm Sidīqi Kāzarūnī Firūzābādī, born in Shiraz in 729/1329, died in 817/1414, expressly in Zabīd in Yemen; the author of the *qāmūs* consulted by Zabīdī; defender of Ibn ʿArabī (*Daw'* [?], IX, 84) over his liking for Bukārī, whereas his uncle, Ibrāhīm-b-M wrote about Rifīʿī. [Or also] ʿAA-b-Abū Makhrama (born in 833 in Hajuran, died in 903), followed by Afīf D Abū Harmūz Hadrami (*Daw'* II, 8), followed by ʿAA-b-A Himyari and Shaybāni Hajurāni.

light of His beauty from this mirror, and He spoke through this mirror, just as He called forth and spoke from the [Burning] Bush for Moses on Mt. Sinai and from the star [= the Pleiades] for Abraham (Qur'ān 20:9, 10, 14; 6:76).' " Baqlī also said about him:[53] "he had a persuasive tongue, performed miracles, and had an *isnād*."

II. THE TRANSMISSION IN BAGHDAD AND IN BASRA

Because the recognized *muhaddithīn* had with them a *warrāq* (Ibn 'Asākir [bib. no. 334-a] II, 249) at their group sessions of dictation, the interdiction given the *warrāqīn*[1] in 309 led to the banning in Baghdad of any authenticated transmission of texts concerning Hallāj. Apart from the circle of Ibn Surayj's disciples (Waqf Da'laj) and that of Shiblī's disciples (Husrī-Zawzanī: Ribāt Zawzanī), in which we find signs of a clandestine transmission,[2] and apart from the example of Abū 'Amr Anmātī, who had to break off rather quickly,[3] only those Khurasanian shaykhs passing through Baghdad on their way to the pilgrimage dared dictate in passing some texts concerning Hallāj: In 366, Nasrābadhī, at the home of his aged host, the great *muhaddith* AB-b-Mālik Qatī'ī (d. 368), before a hostile witness, the Qādī and *muqri'* Abū'l-'Alā' Wāsitī; and around 372, Ibn Shādhān Rāzī (d. 376), passing through Baghdad with a patron from Nishapur, A Ishāq Ibrāhīm-b-M Muzakkī (d. 362) (where the young Abū Nu'aym Isfahānī [d. 430] heard him during a brief stay). Between 341 and 378, Mansūr Harawī (d. 402), establishing his authority on a basis of his princely rank, held, when he went to Baghdad, a series of bold sessions at which AB M-b-Ishāq Qatī'ī (d. 378), AQ 'AA-b-M Thallāj (d. 387), and Abū Ya'lā Ishāq-b-'AR Sabūnī were the *rāwīs*.

And this is all, for we do not know if Ibn Shādhān in 361, 'Abdawī in 389, AN Sarrāj, Khargūshī in 396, Salāmī, Nasawī[4] and Naqqāsh dared read in Baghdad their references to Hallāj.

In 423, while stopping over in Baghdad, Ismā'īl-b-A Hīrī[5] read several

---

[53] *Ibid.*, f. 7b. Excerpt ap. Witrī [bib. no. 739A-a], f. 23a.

[1] Shiblī was attacked, Ibn Khafīf also.
[2] Q. 181 Junayd (*samā' mīthāq*); Q. 119 Junayd (*hurrīya*) informs Ibn Shādhān; Q. 12 Sarī' never consoled (Junayd) at age 92; Q. 22 Junayd (visit by the Arit) [Q. = *Qissat*].
[3] We know that this Anmatī, the heir of Ibn 'Atā', supported Fāris by documentary evidence and perhaps also AB Bajalī (when he came to Baghdad in the Harbīya), but Mansūr Harawī, regardless of what he said, could only have given his testimony through Fāris or Bajalī.
[4] In Mecca, Sh. al-Haram before Ibn Jahdam.
[5] Khatīb VIII, 114, 120 (2), 121 (2), 128, 131 (4), 132.

important texts concerning Hallāj[6] drawn from Sulamī (the miracle at
Wasit, Indian magic, Ibn Shaybān, Ibn Abī Sa'dān, and 'Amr Makkī, Ibn
'Atā"s altercation with the vizir, four testimonies concerning the execution [and the dream] taken down three days after it): which Khatīb noted
at the time, with *ijāza* from Hīrī. About the same year, AB M-
b-Ibrāhīm-b-A Ardastānī (d. 427),[7] on his way from Isfahan to Mecca on
the hajj, dictated in Baghdad two texts concerning Hallāj, also from the
Sulamī collection (Qannād; an account of the execution according to
Razzāz), which Khatīb compiled. The interdiction must have been re-
laxed in high places since the coming of Qāyim, because one Hanbalite
Baghdadian shaykh, Abū Tālib 'Ushshārī (d. 451), began to transmit
Hallājian texts in Baghdad: texts preserved by Khatīb and surely known
from Ibn 'Aqīl.[8]

a. Shākir

After Hallāj's execution there were decrees of clemency given to imprisoned Hallājians, possibly even an amnesty, since his daughter and M-
b-'Alī Qunnā'ī were set free. And one important incident showed the in-
defectible loyalty that he had been able to inspire in some and the early
survival of his teaching.

During the course of the trial, the vizir, Hāmid, had tried in vain to get
the Sāmānid government to extradite Shākir, a Baghdadian and one of
the two leading spokesmen for the Hallājian propaganda in Khurasan
(based at Talaqan). This [refusal to extradite], as relayed by the Sāmānid.
ambassador in Baghdad, 'Imrān Marzubānī, indicated that the new
Sāmānid vizir in Bukhara, a master in 317 of the amīr and Hanafite mufti
of Nishapur, A Sahl M-b-Sulayman Su'lūkī (296, d. 369) (*ra'īs* in
337)—who transmitted from Murta'ish to 'Abdawī (*Hilya* X, 335; *Talbīs*); namely, AF M-b- 'UA Bal'amī (308, d. 329), a Shāfi'ite canonist and

---

[6] And concerning Shiblī (Kh.).

[7] Kh. VIII, 117, 131; *Talbīs*, 200.

[8] The following are the Sālimīya, *expatriated* from Basra to Khurasan, who dared:
—Ibn Sālim → Fāris → Wajīhī → Sarrāj;
—before 362: Ibn Shādhān (AB Bajālī: lice + Ibn 'Atā' + synthetic account by Razzāz +
dream);
—accepts 'A Wāhid-b-Zayd;
—before 362: A Nasr Sarrāj Tamīmī (7):*faqīr, bitr, yā' sirra sirrī, hasb, hasharī, hasb, yā' sirra
sirrī*;
—before 370: Mansūr Harawī (*Manhaj*, Shiblī);
—in 392: Ma'rūf Zinjānī (*Urīduka*).
—Then (since 356?) M-b-A-b-Hamdān Hīrī on the death of Ibn 'Atā' (d. 375 in Baghdad)
(like Ibn Sam'ūn);
—(in 396) 'Alī Ahwāzī?

disciple of M-b-Nasr Marwazī (d. 294, mufti of Samarqand), intended to continue to apply the *fatwā* of Ibn Surayj and was refusing to hunt down Hallājians (Hallāj's son Sulayman remained free in Nishapur). Khurasan had been and would remain the place of sanctuary for pro-Hallāj Sūfīs (Ibn Abī'l-Khayr, whose arrest was demanded by the Karrāmīya, was later released). [These measures] would not be applied in Egypt and Syria.

The news of Hallāj's execution, which had produced a kind of riot in Talaqan, convinced Shākir to return to Baghdad. "Fearless (*shahiman*)[9] like Hallāj," as Sulamī remarks, "he was (the first) to publish his words."[10] Which must be taken to mean, we surmise, [his words] from the first group of *Akhbār al-Hallāj* as follows. Shākir, upon arriving in Baghdad, was not arrested at once, and therefore finished out what he knew of the last period of his master's teaching in Baghdad by collecting the accounts of Ibn Fātik, particularly concerning his final moments. One such treatise, focusing on the idea of [Hallāj as] a holy man who had died an anathema for the Muslim Law, was both a bold resumption of the apostolate of a man condemned and an early attempt at [his] rehabilitation. Distributed in Suwayqat Ghālib among the Shāfi'ite disciples of Ibn Surayj, copies were made of them, including the one taken from the Egyptian canonist Ibn al-Haddād (numbers [2 and 5] of the *Akhbār*). The attempt was premature and short-lived. Vizir Hāmid at that time put a new pressure upon the Sāmānid government by sending it Hallāj's head to be borne around Khurasan from district to district; the head was taken from the Caliphal "museum of heads" on 26 *Qa'da* 310, exactly one year after the execution. It was then that Shākir must have been thrown into prison. He was executed in 311—we do not know the precise date, though it was probably after *Rabī'* II—on orders from the new vizirate (of Ibn al-Furāt, who held this position for the third time and who began again the actions against Hallājians), since three [Hallājians] who refused to recant, Haydara (already sought in 309), Sha'rānī, and Ibn Mansūr, were executed by the police commissioner Nāzūk on *Muharram* 23, 312. The accusation of Hallājism must have also contributed to the execution of two other victims of the Banū al-Furāt, the two state secretaries, A-b-Hammād and Nu'mān-b-'AA.

---

[9] This has also been read as "*muttahiman*" (slandered).
[10] Sulamī, *Ta'rīkh al-sūfīya*, excerpt ap. Safadī, *Wāfī* [bib. no. 540-a], ms. P. 2065, f. 137b "*akhraja kalāmahu li'l-nās*" (comm. Jawād-*Akhbar*, no. 47). Ibn Taghrībirdī, *Nujūm* [bib. no. 660-a] II, 218-219 (year 311); to paraphrase: "he gave accounts (concerning Hallāj), so well that he was put to death."

b. Abū Bakr Sūlī

Born in Baghdad around 260,[11] raised there in an environment of grammarians (Mubarrad Tha'lab), men of letters ('AA-b-Hy Qutrubbulī, Buhturī from 276, Abū'l-'Aynā), and traditionists (Abū Dāwūd Sijistānī), he broke away from there, together with a certain Ibn Tāhir Hāshimī, to make brief visits to Basra (after 275: when still very young "*sabī*") in Hāshimite circles ('Atik and B. Himmān districts) and was acquainted at that time with M-b-H-b. Sahl (= Shaylama). It was in this way that he gained his literary formation, studying the "classes of poets" with Qādī Abū Khalīfa Fadl Jumahī (d. 305).[12] He was closely associated with A M-b-A-b-Bishr Marthadī,[13] the personal secretary of the regent Muwaffaq, from 251 (he plagiarized his *Kitāb al-shi'r* in his *Awrāq*), with Shī'ites such as Abū 'Alī Shalmaghānī, and with the learned Shī'ite historian Ghullānī (father of Qādī Abū Umayya, born in Basra in 300, a client of Ibn al-Furāt, satirized by Tanūkhī). He also knew Sunnites (A Mādharā'ī, the pro-'Alid fiscal *wālī* of Basra in 277), but he attached himself particularly to Shī'ites like two of the Banū Nawbakht, the critic 'Alī-b-'Abbās (d. 325) and the theologian Abū Sahl, and like the state secretary Hy Bāqatā'ī. He was well acquainted with the jurisconsult AB ibn Dāwūd, the anti-Hallājian (*Akhbār A. T.*), and with his *Kitāb al-zahra*.

Resettled in Baghdad, he dedicated an anti-Qarmathian *qasīda* to Vizir 'Abbās-b-Hasan in 294 and became a client of the Shī'ite vizir, 'Alī-b-Furāt, who granted him a pension (of seventy dīnārs a month?). Completely devoted to this great state financier, whom he treated as a saint in his biography of him (*Manāqib Ibn al-Furāt*), Sūlī, after his first fall from power, attached himself (as did another friend of the B. al-Furāt, Ibn Muqla) to the chamberlain, Nasr, the guardian of the imperial prince Hārūn. Nasr commissioned him to write occasional verse (306, 308, Sūlī was connected with his son, M-b-Nasr, in 312) and arranged for him to become the private tutor of Prince Hārūn and also of his uterine brother, Rādī (2 lessons a week; he had previously been tutor of Qādī Abū 'Umar). In 318 Sūlī preferred Rādī to Hārūn. Appointed tutor (at first, assistant to Zajjāj and Yazīdī) to the heir apparent Prince Rādī (probably around 305), he gave shelter in his home to the son of his benefactor, Muhassin, who had been pursued from 306 to 311, and was on intimate

---

[11] *Fihrist*, 129, 151; *Khatīb* III, 427; Yāqūt, *Ud.* VII, 136; *Aghānī* (2) IX, 22, 24-26, 29; Jahshīyārī [bib. no. 127-a], 87; *Awrāq* [?], 166, 207; *Akhbār Rādī*, 216.

[12] An enemy of Ibn al-Mu'tazz (*Awlād*, p. 139, line 12).

[13] *Fihrist*, 129: Tabarī III, 1557; Sūlī, *Adāb*, 160; Ibn al-Rūmī I, 314 (his son A).

terms with his servants (particularly Murīb, who was connected with a Qunnā'ī). Sūlī must have known of Muhassin's secret plot[14] with the Shī'ite heretic Shalmaghānī (he omitted mention of his trial and execution in his *Akhbār Rādī*, s.a. 322), and tried to help some victims of his savagery to escape, among others a Shī'ite moneylender named AB A-b-M-b-Qarāba (a friend of Mu'nis and of Ibn al-Hawwarī, and an enemy of the Barīdīs), in 311. Which explains the rancor of Muhassin that led Sūlī to dedicate a laudatory *qasīda* in the form of affectionate scoldings (*tashbīb*)[15] to his father, who had once again become vizir. As Rādī's private tutor, Sūlī enjoyed close relations with the *hājib*, Nasr (and with his son Muhammad). He therefore must have followed the Hallāj proceedings very closely, and indeed he has told us elsewhere that he spoke with him.[16] Nasr was the guardian of Prince Hārūn, the uterine brother of Rādī;[17] in 318, when the empire was divided between Rādī and Hārūn, the latter asked Sūlī to join him,[18] but Sūlī chose to remain with Rādī. He found himself once again in rather the position of an underling, for, though his mastery of chess had earned him the honor prior to 295 of being a *nadīm* (eating companion) of Muktafī, Muqtadir invited him only once to be a *nadīm* (in 306, when he wrote his *qasīda* against the rival Fātimid Caliph), and the Queen Mother curtailed the scholarly lessons that he gave to Rādī.[19]

During the seven-year period of Rādī's reign (322-329), he was the *nadīm* and confidant of the sovereign, whose power was very limited, and who kept him out of important matters in the role of director of activities for his leisure hours. In his history of this reign he withheld his deepest thoughts and gives us little more than mention of its pleasureful literary affairs and princely entertainments. At the end of Rādī's reign he joined the Barīdī faction, which since 325 had been in control of Basra, where he had property and no doubt some family. After trying to remain in the Court (three times he gave advice, which no one followed),[20] through the help of Ibn Shirzād, whom he admired, he retired to Basra under the patronage of the Barīdīs. An imprudent statement about 'Alī forced him to go into hiding, and he died in obscurity in *Ramadān* of 335.[21] It would be interesting to know what text he used for the tradition

---

[14] He shielded Ibn Rāwī (Rent. [?], 104).

[15] 'Arīb, 114; *Akhbār Rādī*, Heyworth Dunne ed., 47 (= 'Arīb, 115).

[16] Kratchkovsky, ap. *Inst. Arch. Russe* (X) 1913, XXI, 137-141.

[17] 'Arīb, 183.   [18] *Ibid.*, 155.

[19] *Akhbār Rādī*, 26.   [20] *Ibid.*, 229.

[21] Y. Sarkū (variant: *I'tidāl* VI-6, pp. 456 ff.; 7, pp. 498 ff.).

on 'Alī that led to his being threatened with death both by Sunnites (Mu'tazilites and Sālimīya) and Shī'ites (supporters of the dissident Imāmite *wakīl*, 'Amrī III, supported by the Barīdīs). Could it have been an 'Azāqirī extremist text (there were some 'Azāqirīya in Basra as early as 311 and in 340)? Or was it the deluded statement about 'Alī that he related without disavowing (ap. *Kitāb awlād al-khulafā'*, 303: "if the Imāmite had been established as a legacy by the Prophet, 'Alī would not have let anyone precede him in it" (which does not mean merely, as Wāsil said, that no one knows which of the two pretenders sinned; but that if 'Alī held back for twenty-five years, it was because the Prophet betrayed him by not designating him: which was the view held by the 'Azāqirīya).[22]

It should be noted, with regard to this, that Sūlī must have been closely connected with Hamza Isfahānī, who reworked his editions of such classical poets as Abū Nuwās. Hamza, in his turn, was a disciple of Shalmaghānī, whose *Kitāb al-'asā* he quotes in his *Tanbīh* (cf. P. Kraus, ap. *Thaqāfa*, Cairo, no. 276, M. 4 [1944], p. 16).

Two well-known men of letters, Abū'l-Faraj Isfahānī (d. 3 [56]) and particularly A 'AA M-b-'Imrān Marzubānī (297, d. 378), transmitted the works of Sūlī, as did the father of Qādī Muhassin Tanūkhī, with whom he conversed in Basra and who was his executor (*I'tidal*, 500).

Sabī[23] considered Sūlī a learned man of letters, but one lacking inspiration and vision, given to writing long-winded moral duties in verse and inserting them in his books along with trifling tidbits. He was laughed at for a rather harmless blunder (*Shay'an* for *Sittan min Shawwāl* in a hadīth). He had a splendid and well-catalogued poetry library, but he remained caught in the grips of a rather disgusting sexual perversion that the malicious tongue of Tanūkhī insisted on revealing.[24]

Sūlī's earliest Muslim ancestor, Abū 'Umāra M-b-Sūl, son of a Turkish nobleman from Jurjān, a client of the Muhallabids (Azd) and great uncle of a *kātib* of Ma'mūn (A Fadl 'Amr-b-Mas'ada-b-Sa'īd-b-Sūl, vizir in 203, d. 217),[25] had been the eleventh of the twelve *naqībs* of the 'Abbāsid propaganda and later, in 132, was *wālī* of Mosul. One of his grandsons, Ibrāhīm-b-'Abbās-b-M Sūlī (176, d. 243), *kātib* of Qā'id 'A 'Azīz-

---

[22] Sūlī had been tutor briefly to the Hamdanid amīr of Aleppo, Sayf al-Dawla, an extremist Shī'ite (*Akhbār Radī*, 218).
[23] Sābī, p. 2, line 4 from the bottom.
[24] Ms. P. 3402, f. 147a (omitted ap. *Nishwār*, Margoliouth edition I, 218, lines 4-5).
[25] Khatīb XII, 203; ms. P. Turkish Suppl. 1125; or *Dīwān al-Rasā'il* with A-b-Yūsuf and Thābit Rāzī (Yq., *Ud.* II, 157).

b-'Imrān (d. 202), then head of the *Dīwān al-rasā'il* (under Ma'mūn, with Jāhiz as his assistant), *wālī* of Ahwaz (before 234), and finally head of the *Dīwān zimām al-diyāʿ* (234, d. 243: with Hasan-b-Makhlad as his assistant); he was a poet, and he wrote the *Kitāb al-dawlat al-ʿAbbāsīya*: his Shīʿite *qasīda* in honor of Imām 'Alī Ridā' was often quoted. Another grandson, Abū Hishām ʿAA, the father of three scholars, Ahmad Tammās, Hasan, and Yahyā, was the grandfather of our AB M-b-Yahyā Sūlī.[26]

A man of old stock, a skilled courtier, an unequaled chess player, a careful collector of ancient and modern poetry, Sūlī classified according to their rhymes the dīwāns of a score of poets: Ibn al-Rūmī, Abū Tammām (with biography), Buhturī (with an interesting preface), Abū Nuwās, ʿAbbās-b-Ahnaf, ʿAlī-b-Jahm, Ibn Tabātabā, Ibrāhīm-b-ʿAbbās Sūlī, M-b-Abī ʿUyayna, Sawwār-b-Abī Shurāʿa, AB Sūlī (himself), Ibrāhīm-b-ʿAlī ibn Harma (with biography, *Akhbār A.T.* [Cairo, 1357]), Muslim-b-Walīd, Diʿbil, Abū'l-Shīs, AB Sanawbarī, Nasr Khubzuruzzī; he wrote monographs on the poets Farazdaq, Sayyid Himyarī, Abū'l-Najm Ijlī,[27] Abū ʿAmr-b-ʿAlā'. He wrote about the Qarmathians (= *Akhbār Abī Saʿīd Jannābī*: corr. Jubbā'ī, *Fihrist*, 151) and about the vizirs (up to 291). His *Kitāb al-awrāq*, a collection of literary and historical documents of mixed interest, has been edited almost completely by Heyworth Dunne, and B Atharī published his *Adab al-kuttāb* dealing with the proper utilization of government secretaries and scribes.[28]

c. AH Ahmad-b-Yūsuf ibn al-Azraq

The son (297, d. 377) of a traditionist who was also a brilliant secretary of the court (secretary of Amīr Badr Lānī under Muwaffaq and Muʿtadid, d. before 296), responsibility for his education was entrusted at first to the historian Ibn al-Mutawwaq, a secretary at the *Dīwān al-zimām*, where he was employed from 313-314 (*Nishw.*, 156); he studied Hanafite law with AH ʿAA Karkhī (260, d. 340); in Qur'ān he became a *hāfiz* and an exponent of the *qirā'a* of Abū ʿAmr-b-ʿAlā' (under the guidance of Ibn Mujāhid), and he studied grammar with Ibn al-Sarrāj. He devoted himself especially, however, to the study of Muʿtazilite theology and forsook rather quickly the Baghdad school (of Ibn al-Ikhshīdh, 270, d. 326) for the Bahshamī school (of Abū Hāshim, d. 321?). He was the master of the father of Qādī Muhassin and dictated to Muhassin most of his anti-Hallāj accounts, probably in Baghdad after 349.

---

[26] A third grandson was the grandfather of a Shīʿite, d. 352.

[27] Compare *Fihrist*, 151, with *Adab al-kuttāb*, 62.

[28] He also wrote *al-Shāmil fī ʿilm al-Qur'ān*, *al-Shukrān wa'l-nawādir* (*Akhbār A.T.*).

There were eight such accounts (*Nishw.* I, 81-87).[29] They had to be redacted before 326 (since the son of Hallāj [Mansūr], who was executed in Ahwaz by Ispehdust in 326, is said in them to be alive; and because Abū 'Umāra Hāshimī is shown as still being allowed to preach in Basra: which possibility ended with the departure of *walī* A-b-Nasr Qushūrī in 324). Two of the accounts (coming from AS Nawbakhtī, who is named here only in the first) are found in Imāmite literature (but emanating from a man of letters having Zaydite, and therefore Mu'tazilite, leanings): Ibn Nūh (A-b-'Alī, *Akhbār*, circa 375); one other portrays Abū 'Umāra Hāshimī as being specifically *hulūlī*, which is typically Mu'tazilite (and in this joins Ibn Rawh Nawbakhti).[30]

A friend of the Bahshamī Mu'tazilite theologian A 'AA Hy-b-'Alī Basrī, who was an advisor of Amīr 'Adud al-Dawla, Ibn al-Azraq was also one of the masters of the famous Mu'tazilite scholar 'Abd al-Jabbār-b-A Hamadhānī (d. 415), a former Ash'arite. He was a Shāfi'ite in law, a friend of Vizir Ismā'īl ibn 'Abbād, who made him grand qādī of Rayy from 367 to 385, and the master of Saymarī and AY Qazwīnī (393, d. 488), who was to polemicize against Hallāj.

Muhassin seems to be giving us only a resumé of Ibn al-Azraq's accounts in his *Nishwār* I (he was to give others of them subsequently). It is difficult to fix the date when Ibn al-Azraq composed them; he could not have written in 309 his thoughts about Hallāj's fasts (on p. 81). The answer depends on the relation of priority between the accounts of Ibn al-Azraq and those of Ibn 'Ayyāsh, which are combined in *Nishwār* I. Ibn 'Ayyāsh, who was still inexperienced in 318, could not have recorded his uncle Abū Muhammad's recollections of Hallāj's trial before 325; which was the time when, coming to Ahwaz as an assistant of Qādī 'Alī, the father of Muhassin, he could have related them to him together with what Ibn al-Azraq had said to him in Baghdad. But if it was Ibn 'Ayyāsh who furnished the early core of these accounts to Ibn al-Azraq, the latter had to have recorded them well before 349 (the date of their transmission to Muhassin) and also before 324-325 (for the abovementioned reasons).[31]

We have inadequate knowledge of the relationship between Ibn 'Ayyāsh and Ibn al-Azraq. Both were Mu'tazilites (*ashābinā*, p. 8, says one was; *mashā'ikhunā*, *Passion* [1st edition], pp. 44, 261, says the other was) with contacts in the court (Ibn 'Ayyāsh, a favorite of Vizir Sulaymān-b-Hasan-b-Makhlad, had a cousin by marriage who was daughter of Grand Qādī Abū 'Umar: the wife of the qādī who gave him

---

[29] They are Ikhshidīyans.   [30] *Ghayba*, 261-262.
[31] The account dealing with Hulūz is *after* 331.

information about the trial of 309). Ibn 'Ayyāsh showed some leaning toward the Shī'ite secret lamentation sessions and hobnobbed with musicians like Gahza Barmakī. Ibn al-Azraq, who was both a renowned theologian, and thus had connections with Yahyā ibn al-Munajjim, leader of the Mu'tazilites in the court and a friend of Ibn al-Ikhshīdh, as well as an heir to a great real estate fortune, appears to be more reserved.

d. Muhassin Tanūkhī

Muhassin Tanūkhī[32] tells us about Hallāj as early as the first volume of his *Nishwār*, hence as early as 360.[33] Some accounts seem almost entirely[34] borrowed from his brother-in-law, the Bahshamī Mu'tazilite theologian, AH ibn al-Azraq (297, d. 377), at whose home he had collected them upon his arrival in Baghdad: in 349. It appears that he also owes to him the accounts of Ibn 'Ayyāsh concerning Hallāj; Ibn 'Ayyāsh could have related them to his father when he was his assistant as qādī of Ahwaz around 325-329 (before the birth of Muhassin) and repeated them to him after 349 (according to *Nishwār* VIII; it was "in the beginning" that Ibn 'Ayyāsh gave accounts to Muhassin, who had them repeated by AHy-b-Hishām). *Nishwār* I contains thirty accounts by Ibn al-Azraq and twenty by Ibn 'Ayyāsh; *Faraj* contains five accounts by Ibn al-Azraq and one by Ibn 'Ayyāsh.

In his home, Muhassin gave hospitality (after 377) to Tāhira, the daughter of Ibn al-Azraq, whose first cousin, AH 'Alī-b-M Tanūkhī (301, d. 358), qādī of Anbar and, later, of Kufa, was also his brother-in-law.

His father, AQ 'Alī Tanūkhī, born in 278, died in 342, a Hanafite and a Mu'tazilite, the author of a collection of poems, learned in astrology, served in his capacity as a resident qādī in Ahwaz, as the representative of his relatives, the two Ibn Buhlūl qādīs (AJ, d. 316; AT, d. 348), for twenty-three years (311-334). His mother must have been an extremist Shī'ite, since she was the sister of an important local fiscal bureaucrat, AQ 'AA-b-M-b-Mihrawayh, so Ibn Abī 'Allān tells us. As an assistant to the fiscal *wālī* until 307, a resident tax farmer of the Queen Mother in Ahwaz (for Abū Yūsuf Barīdī), 307-309, and supervisor of currency in the Suq al-Ahwaz, AQ 'Alī Tanūkhī, a Mu'tazilite and disciple of A 'Alī Jubbā'ī, quickly played a political role. A supporter of Ibn Muqla (in 322), an arbitrator between Yāqūt and the Barīdīs (in 324), he readily

---

[32] The name *ghālī* given him by his mother.
[33] He had written *Faraj* before 351 (*ibid*. II, 184, 187).
[34] Except for that of the qādī of Basra, Ibn Nasrawayh, who was qādī in 332 (Miskawayh II, 54).

won over, through Shī'ism, to the Buwayhids (he was close friends with Muhallabī, their future vizir and his former secretary after 315), H-b-'Alī Munajjim (governor of Ahwaz until 342). He was ordered by the Caliph to sell his land holdings in Ahwaz (in 317), which he did with his mother's brother, Ibn Abī 'Allān; and upon their arrival in Baghdad, he became qādī of Karkh, Wasit, and Kufa. He died in Basra.

Muhassin must have been taken in from 342 to 349 by his maternal great-uncle, Ibn Abī 'Allān, whose grandson, Abū Ahmad 'AA (321, d. 409), a Bahshamī theologian, was also to become qādī of Ahwaz.

In 349, Muhassin had just been approved as a *shāhid* under AB ibn Quray'a (the successor of AB ibn Sayyār as qādī of Ahwaz, d. 350) when Vizir Muhallabī brought him to Baghdad, where Qādī Abū'l-Sa'ib appointed him Qādī of Saqy al-Furāt. A deputy (*nā'ib*) of the qādī of Ahwaz and qādī of Wasit (in 363), Muhassin, after being received in the Court of 'Adud al-Dawla, became the latter's *nadīm* at his drinking bouts. In 367 he delivered the *khutba* for the marriage of the amīr's daughter, Shāhbānū, to Caliph Tāyī; but failing to persuade Tāyī to consummate this marriage, Muhassin was confined in his house by the amīr for five years (367-372).

A friend of the grammarian Abū 'Alī Fasawī (an Ikhshīdhī Mu'tazilite) admired by the free-thinking poet Ibn al-Hajjāj, *muhtasib* of Baghdad, Muhassin seems to have written about Hallāj what was believed about him in the period of 350-360 in the entourages of Vizir Abū'l-Fadl Shīrāzī and Vizir Abū'l-Faraj ibn Fusānjus fifty years after the drama itself. The viewpoint is both Mu'tazilite and Zāhirite, in line with the dual preference of Amīr 'Adud al-Dawla. Emphasis is put on the dangerous charlatanism of this Sunnite pseudo saint, leaving out the accusation that Hallāj was a deserter from Shī'ism (for Muhassin himself was a Mu'tazilite).

His son was AQ 'Alī (365, d. 447), born in Basra, a *shāhid* under the qādī of Baghdad starting in 384, and successor to his father as qādī of Mada'in, as well as supervisor of currency, and friend of the Banū 'Abd al-Rahīm and enemy of the Hallājian vizir, Ibn al-Muslima, who transmitted all of the anti-Hallāj accounts of his father, an esteemed Mu'tazilite author but a qādī not very esteemed for his morals (he was flogged on one occasion).

e. Qannād[35]

This is the author of the earliest collection of *hikāyāt* about Sūfis in which there is a biography of Hallāj: in the company of Bistāmī, Nūrī, Junayd,

---

[35] A Hy 'Alī-b-A Rahīm Wāsitī Qannād (Sam'ānī, s.v. Ibn Yazdanyār, *Rawda*, Cairo ms.).

Ruwaym, and Sumnūn, Qannād, a cultured mind, who had studied the *dīwān* of Abū Tammām,[36] inclined in his theology towards Mu'tazilism.[37] He lived as a wandering Sūfī off by himself, not becoming involved with those he met on his travels. Sulamī, at first, accepted him in his *Ta'rīkh*, but other authors rejected him for being a Mu 'tazilite.[38]

We know from himself that he met Abū'l-Azhar Baydāwī in Qirqīsā in 325; he must have died shortly afterwards, for one of his disciples, 'Alī-b-Tarkān Baghdādī, who retired to Ramlah, had known Junayd and Ibn 'Atā' personally.[39]

His *hikāyāt* are a series of short anecdotes, very skillfully stylized, which draw picturesque outlines of their subjects. His "three meetings"[40] with Hallāj have come down to us in two different recensions,[41] one via A ibn al-'Alā' 'Amirī (= after 352) in Khatīb, the other via AH 'Alī-b-'A 'Azīz Jurjānī, who died in 392, grand qādī of Rayy, a friend of Ibn 'Abbād, and a Mu'tazilite; the beginning of each recension exists in a synthetic account of Hallāj from Qannād transmitted by Silafī (publ. Kinānī).[42] Three other testimonies from Qannād depict Hallāj quoting profane poems in a mystical sense (*Wa badā lahu, Mā lī jafayta, Dalālun*).[43]

Quite unusually, two Sūfī authors, Warthānī and Ibn Bākūyā, accepted Qannād[44] as a source for Bistāmī.[45]

---

[36] Marzubānī, *Muwashsh* [?], 326. Sulamī, ap. Baqlī, *Tafsīr* II, 190; and ap. *Haqā'iq*, concerning [Qur'ān] 57:3: al-Awwal; A Hy Wadinī.

[37] Baghdādī, *Usūl* [bib. no. 201-d], 316.

[38] His *qasīda* against Ibn Yazdanyār.   [39] Khatib IX, 108, and s.v.

[40] Qushayrī [?], 115, 150, 162; *Hilya* X, 251, 253, 254; Sahlajī, *Nūr* [bib. no. 2199-a], 14, 86, 99, 107, 146.

[41] Perhaps Sālimī: for he is cited with Ibn Sālim by Sabī (ms. P. 1369, f. 179a).

[42] *Recueil*, p. 71.   [43] In the present volume, p. 344.]

[44] Sarrāj, *Masāri'* [bib. no. 278-a], 160; Kinānī, *Qāmūs* [?]. Qannād attributes the following poems to Hallāj:

—"*mālijafayta*," attributed to Junayd by Khuldī (*Luma'*, 248);

—'*la'in amsaytu*," attributed to Sumnūn by Naysaburī (IF [?]) (Kutubī [?], 10);

—"*arsalta tas'al*," attributed to Sumnūn by Naysaburī (IF [?]) (Kutubī [?], p. 1);

—"*wabadā lahu*."

[45] Transmission since Qannād:

—Qannād > Amir (the 3 pieces) > Urmawī

—Qannād > A Fadl M-b-Ishāq Sijzī > Sulamī > Ardastānī > Sarrāj (*Man.* [?], 160: *wabadalūhu* concerning Moses)

—Qannād > A Fath Isk > Bazzāz (d. 430). Fadl-b-Hafs > Ardastānī

—Qannād > 'Alī-b-Muwaffaq > Silafī via Habbāl (d. 482)

—Qannād > M-b-Fadl > AN Sarrāj (*Qissa* 150) > Ibn Bākūyā

—Qannād > 'AA Bylgānī (*Nūr*, 99)

—Qannād > AN Barnadhā'ī (*Nūr*, 14, 99, 146) > Ibn Bākūyā (*Qissa* 162).

—Qannād > 'Alī-b-M Qazwīnī (d. 403) > Ibn Bākūyā (*Qissa* 162)?

—Qannād > AF Warthānī > A Nu'aym (*Talbīs*, 377), *Hilya* X, 251) (*Nūr*, 86).

Accounts from Qannād. Qannād recounted the following to Ahmad ibn al-'Alī Sūfī:[46]

I saw Hallāj three times over a period of three years. The first time was when I went to ask him to allow me to accompany him. I was told he was living in Isfahan. I asked there for his house and was told that he had been living there but had already set off again.

I left immediately and resumed my way. It was on the slope of one of the mountains near Isfahan that I met him dressed in a *muraqq'a* holding a beggar's bag and a crooked stick in his hand.[47] When he saw me, he called me, . . . and then he recited the following (verse by Sumnūn al-Muhibb):

Though you have met me this evening dressed in the clothes of Poverty, —I want you to know that I am already closer to the fullest Liberty! Do not grieve to see me—in a state that is so different from my former condition. For I have a soul, and it shall have to die in harness, or carry me along step by step up to the highest destiny![48]

Then he left me, saying: we shall meet again, if God so wills! and he filled my hand with little dīnārs.[49]

A year had gone by after that meeting, when I asked his disciples in Baghdad for news of him. They told me: He is in Jabbana.[50] I went there and asked for him. I was told: he is in the *khān*. I went there and saw him dressed in white wool. When he saw me, he said to me: "We meet again." Yes, I said, and added: [I want] to be your disciple! your disciple! He recited the following:[51]

The worldly life cajoled me as though I were ignorant of its worth. The King forbids us to take what it offers of the forbidden, —but I push away even what it offers that is lawful.[52] It seemed to me it was in need; —Therefore I gave it everything I had.[53]

—Qannād > Jurjānī > Ibn al-Najjār.
—Qannād > Naysabūrī, '*Uqalā*', 137, 144.
—Qannād > 'A Wāhid-b-Bakr (*Hilya* X, 253).
—Qannād > A-b-Hy > 'Uthmīnī (*Hilya* X, 253).
—Qannād > AB-b-M > 'AA Rāzī > Sulamī (*Hilya* X, 254).
—Qannād > Ibn Bākūyā: via AN Barnadhā'ī (*Nūr*, 14, 146), and via 'AA Bīlqūsī (*Nūr*, 99).
—Qannād > Dā'ī al-Mahdī 'Alawī (*Nūr*, 107).

[46] Cf. Khatīb, copied ap. Jildakī. Cf. Sh. *Tab.* I, 108. Cf. Sam'ani, s.v. Another recension ap. Safadī, *Wāfī* [bib. no. 540-a], Tunis ms., based on Ibn al-Najjār (*isnād* going back to Qādī AH 'Ali-b-'A 'Azīz Jurjānī)—*Kashkūl*: the last two meetings.

[47] *Rakwa* (cf. Tālaqānī, *Amthal* [bib. no. 2226-a], 11) *wa 'ukāz.*

[48] Cf. Bāk., 8. These lines are repeated ap. Khatīb, based on another *isnād*, via Abū'l-Fadl ibn Hafs; cf. in the present volume, chapter XIV, III c., for a discussion of their alchemistic meaning.

[49] Dunaynīrāt.

[50] The "cemetery" district. Is this near the *maqābir Quraysh*?

[51] Cf. Khatīb, Rāghib Isfahānī, *Muhadarat*, attributes them to "Naqqād" (*sic*).

[52] Here the text ap. Bustānī superimposes two verses: "it offered me its right hand, —I gave it back together with its left, —when did I seek it in marriage, —in order to desire to be united with it?"

[53] "All of its goods: in order to free myself of it. . . ."

Then he took me by the hand and we left the *khān*. And he said to me: I have to go to the home of some people whom you don't know and who don't know you. But we shall meet again! —And he filled my hand with some little *dīnārs*, then he left me.

I was told by someone: he will be in Baghdad the next year. I went to look for him there, but someone told me: the sultan has ordered his capture. . . .

Now, on one very hot day I was in Karkh between the two surrounding walls[54] when I saw him in the distance covered with a *fūta ramalīya* in which he was trying to disguise himself. When he saw me, he wept and recited these lines of verse (*Tawīl*):

If my eye should keep vigil or weep for another than You,
May it never obtain the Good that it has and will always have desired!
And if my soul should conceive without You, may it never come to graze in the
  meadows of Desire by Your side in Paradise![55]

Then he said to me: O 'Alī! save yourself! I pray that God will reunite us, if that is His will!

f. The Sālimīya[56] Mutakallimūn of Basra[57]

At the very time when the majority of *mutakallimūn*, who were as much Mu'tazilite as Ash'arite in leaning, was counting Hallāj among the *hulūlīya* heretics, "a group of Sālimīya *mutakallimūn* in Basra accepted his orthodoxy and were of the opinion that he had fulfilled the ideal of Sūfism." To whom does this sentence in Baghdādī, written around 375, refer? We believe that it refers, not to AN Sarrāj (*Luma'* transmitted by H-b-M Khabūshanī), the third head of the Sālimīya, but rather to Ibn Jahdam (d. 414), who was the first among them to quote Hallāj (citing Ibn Rufayl). For, neither A-b-M ibn Sālim[58] (d. 356: whose hostility towards Bisṭāmī[59] may conceal a preference for Hallāj), nor AT Makkī (d. 380: whose *Qūt* is possibly expurgated with respect to this matter in the printed edition), seem to have cited him (though a text by Suhrawardī Halabī quotes side by side two sentences associated with Ibn Sālim and with Hallāj concerning the substantial spirituality of the soul; and the 'aqīda of the Sālimīya agrees with Hallājism on too many points for them not to have noted it [*tajallī*]).

[54] *Bayn al-sūrayn* (name of the district, cf. in Cairo). Yāq. I, 799.
[55] These verses are found ap. Khatīb via Abū'l-Fath Iskandarī.
[56] A Hy Basrī (*Luma'*, 316: Qushayrī, 192); Qush., 63 (→ 'Alī-b-A-b-'Abdān Ahwazī, d. 415).
[57] The *tawaqquf* of Ash'arī concerning the *ghulāt al-sūfīya* (Sh., *Mawāzin*).
[58] Unless it might be A Hy Basrī, the informant of Ibn al-Haddād and *rāwī* of Ibn Fātik (*Akhbār*, no. 5) and of Ibn 'Atā' (Khatīb V, 29: one of Sulamī's sources via Abū Nasr Isfahānī: cf. Qush., 100). —Who were his *rāwīs*? Sarrāj, Daraqutnī (*Talbīs*, 212), M-b-H-b-'Alī-b-Mu'ādh of Isfahan.
[59] Born in 266: cf. *Nūr*, 42, against Sahl.

Ibn Jahdam transmitted both to Azajī and to Zawzanī ('Alī-b-Mahmūd, d. 451) Hallāj's celebrated letter to Ibn 'Atā' (ms. 2131, f. 106a: via 'Umar-b-'AR Baghdādī): reproduced on his authority by Khatīb, Sarrāj,[60] and Ibn Khamīs. Several disciples of Ibn Jahdam, Azajī (d. 444: ms. 1384, f. 102b and 130a: for Silafī via Tuyūrī, Yq. 2, 22), and 'Abdawī (d. 417: *ibid*., 132b: for the same ones, via Mas'ūd-b-Nāsir Sijistānī) took part in the transmission of Hallāj texts. One of his disciples, the *hāfiz* A-b-'Umar 'Udhrī ibn Dalāyī (d. 478), returned to Andalusia (Almeria). Much admired by Qushayrī (Q. 36), Ibn Jahdam was the master of 'AR-b-Manda (d. 470). The best known of the *rāwīs* of Ibn Jahdam are the following:[61] 'Abd al-Ghanī-b-Sa'īd, a *muhaddith* from Cairo (d. 409); Abū Tālib 'Ushshārī, a Baghdadian Hanbalite (d. 451); M-b-Salāma Qudā'ī (d. 454), a Shafi'ite qādī of Cairo; the *qārī'* Abū 'Alī M-b-'Alī Ahwāzī (362-446); Shīrawayh (445, d. 509), a Shāfi'ite, the historian of Hamadhan; and Abū Nu'aym (*Hilya* X, 206), a Hanbalite (d. 430) from Isfahan.[62]

---

[60] The master of 'Umar-b-Zafar, d. 542: *Talbīs*, 222.

[61] *Lisān al-Mīzān* IV, 238. 'Alī-b-'AA ibn Jahdam is quoted ap. *Talbīs* II, 221, 222, 252, 263, 305, 317, 326, 328, 329, 333, 334, 344, 353, 354, 374, 378.

[62] Ibn Jahdam A 'Alī-b-Ibrāhīm Naysabūrī > Sahlajī (*Talbīs*, 343 = *Nūr*, 58). Ibn Jahdam > AM Dā'ī-b-Mahdī 'Alawī (*Nūr*, 105).

Rāwīs of A-b-M Salīm (d. at age 90 around 360 —Dh. ms. 1581, f. 292b):

—A-b-Mansūr Shīrāzī Mh Mudhakkir (Yq., *Ud*. II, 118 for a story about AB ibn Mujāhid)

—A Tālib Makkī — AB-b-Shādhān Rāzī, d. 376

—A Muslim M-b'Alī M-b-'Awf Burjī Isfahānī (Dedering [?] II, 304), *rāwī* of Ibn Abī Hātim

—A Nasr Sarrāj Tūsī, Sūfī (d. 377) (*Qissa* 64, 78: "Tamīmī")

—Mansūr-b-'AA, Sūfī, d. 402

—Ma'rūf Zinjānī, d. after 392: quoted by Abū Nu'aym (*Hilya*) and Sulamī (*Ta'rīkh*). Naqqāsh refused *riwāya* from him in 350

—*Rāwī* of Sahl in Baghdad (hence Sālimī): A Fath Yf Kawwān (300, d. 385), one of the *abdāl*, a master of AR 'Ushshārī (hence pro-Hallāj) from 328 (quoted by Ibn Jamīl, d. 374, the disciple of Shiblī, and of Dāraqutnī, friend of Ibn Sam'ūn, and *adl*, d. 385 (*Talbīs*, 212)

—A 'AA M-b-H-b-'Alī-b-Mu'ādh Isfahānī (d. after 350), close to Abū Nu'aym (Dedering II, 293)

The thousand questions (Köpr. 727) directed by AH. A-b-M-b-Sālim to Sahl:

Transmission of the *Luma'*:

Sarrāj > 'Ayyār (d. 457) > M-b-'AA Nihawandī (Qayrawān) > AQ 'AR-b-M-b-'AA Saqallī

—Sarrāj > M-b-M-Khabushnānī, an ancestor of the father of Sahdin: Subkī IV, 190 > A-b-A Nasr Kūfānī (d. 469) > A Waqt (copied it in 553), Karīma Dimishqīya, 'Alī-b-IJ (550, d. 630) (cf. *Talbīs*, 338, 359)

—*Haqā'iq ma'ānī al-sūfīya*, I

g. The Years 334-381

If the three small Baghdadian circles in which Hallāj's memory was kept alive—the Hanbalite friends of Ibn 'Atā' and Anmātī (in Harbiya), Shiblī's friends (near the mosque of Mansūr), and the Shāfi'ite friends of Ibn Surayj (in the Suwayqat Ghālib, in the middle of Karkh district, the fief of Rabī', West Bank)—were already forced to keep silent from 312 onward, pressure became even greater beginning in 334 under the Buwayhid occupation. [This was due to the fact that the Buwayhid aim was] not only to render the Sunnite Caliphate powerless, but also to impose Shī'ism on all sections of Baghdad. Meetings held by Sunnite traditionists were forbidden; the Shī'ite naqīb was put in charge of the pilgrimage (in 354); the Black Stone was returned [to Mecca] in 339[63] and assumed a political importance of the first order through such energetic figures as Ibn al-Dā'ī (348-353), a Hasanid, and Abū Ahmad Mūsāwī (354, d. 396), a Husaynid and father of two shārifs, Radī and Murtadā, who succeeded him.[64]

Sunnite resistance became organized through an alliance of two very different social classes: the 'Abbāsid Hāshimite nobles and the professional demonstrators, the 'ayyārīn, all of whom were Hanbalites. The Hāshimite naqībs, who were either corrupt like M-b-H-b-'Abd al-'Azīz, or won over to the Buwayhid vizirs through marriage alliances like Abū Tammām Zaynabī (naqīb from 341-363 and in 364, died in 372),[65] would have capitulated if the leader of the Sunnite resistance had not been an indefatigible Ma'badī, A-'AA-M-ibn Abī Mūsā Hāshimī, a Mālikite, who died in 351, the grandfather of the famous Hanbalite and a disciple of Ibn Sam'ūn and master of Ibn al-Muslima.[66] After the quelling of the

---

—Talbīs: sirr Anā'l-Haqq (Luma', 354: with commentary by "y-a sirra")
—Taqdīs (Farq, 248, line 8): hasb al-wājid (Luma', 303: said when [Hallāj was] taken from prison to be executed [the same place in Razzāz], and they were his last words; all of the Baghdad mashā'iq admired him ['Isā Qassār]. [Luma', 348, says: "among some of the words said at the time of his execution"]).
—Farq, 249: said at the time of his intercision. Qassār therefore knew the Razzāz account, but denied it afterwards; or Sajjāj knew both. Shiblī: at the moment of his beheading: with XIII, 17 (only said in Razzāz, denied by Zubūr).
[This long footnote contains the author's intended plan for expanding discussion of the subject in this chapter II f.]
[63] 10 Hijja by M-b-M-b-'Azīz until 1641—Bachkam had paid 50,000 dīnārs for that (zīj).
[64] Rabī' II 351: [the] sabb Mu'awīya arose in 353: the instituting of the 'Ashūrā' produced a riot in the Qatī'a. Capture of Antioch in 359.
[65] The riots of Muharram 345, 349, 350, 351 (rabī' II: Sabb Mu'āwiya) (zīj), 353 ('Ashūrā').
[66] Arrested on 8 Jumāda II 334 by the Buwayhids (Misk. II, 85-86): not to be confused with his homonym, the blind Hanafite qādī killed on 27 Rabī' I 335 (Kh. II, 404), who was not a shārif. This Hāshimite had a son, also a Mālikite, AB A, qādī of Mada'in and Samarra,

riot of 350, it was he who argued with the state over the succession in 351 to the *shāhid muhaddith* Daʿlaj Sijzī (born in 260, d. 351), founder of a series of Sunnite *waqfs* in Mecca and in Iraq,[67] who resided in the Qatiʿat Umm Jaʿfar (Darb Abī Khalaf), which the Shīʿites wished to take over.

Caliph Mutīʿ (334-362),[68] whose *kātibs* (A-H-Tāzād 334-335, Fadl-b-Ah Shīrāzī, Ibrāhīm-b-ʿAlī-ʿĪsā [347-350], Saʿīd-b-ʿAmr-b-Sangalā [born 280? d. 363?]) had no authority, and for whom the *khutba* was not sounded in 361 because of his refusal to order a would-be tax for the jihād, tried to erect a tomb for Ibn Hanbal.[69]

Caliph Tāʾī (363-381), whose first *kātib* was ʿĪsā, son of Vizir ʿAlī-b-ʿĪsā (302, d. 391: from 363 to 374), and afterwards ʿAlī ibn Hājib al-Nuʿmān (born in 340, d. 423), lost his throne because he tried to subdue a Buwayhid princely favorite.[70] The entire élite of Baghdad was won over to the Buwayhids, including the grand qāḍīs, Ibn Umm Shaybān (363-364, d. 369) and Ibn Umm Maʿrūf (360-363, 364-369, 372, d. 381), even the Ashʿarite theologian Bāqillānī, under the prodding of determined men like the sharif AH M-b-ʿUmar of Kufa (the prince's *nāʾib* for Baghdad in 372).[71]

The persecution of Sunnism was intensified: a revolt during 361-364 (in Qaʿda 363), both *naqībs* were dismissed; the riot by the Nubuwīya, quelled by the pro-Sunnite *hājib* Sabuktakin (337, d. 364) (co-ruler of Baghdad with the Caliph: Qaʿda 363-Muharram 364) and in the period 369-372 (the Zāhirite grand qāḍī, Bishr-b-Husayn; the Shīʿite *naqīb*, A-H-ʿAlī-b-A ʿUmarī 364-372); Amīr ʿAdud tried at that time to rebuild Baghdad by himself.

It was precisely at that time that the memory of Hallāj was rekindled (he was viewed as a victim of the Rāfidites) among the Sunnite mystics of Baghdad, and this, added to the political coalition of Hāshimites[72] and *ʿayyārīn* (among whom the initiatory organization of the Nubuwīya gave the signal for the riots in *Jumāda* II 360-361), was a precursory sign of a Sunnite revival. Husrī (d. 371), Shiblī's favorite disciple, founded around 365 the first *ribāt* (monastery) opposite the mosque of Mansūr, and we

---

who was for a long time *khatīb* in the Mansūr mosque (315, d. 390; Kh V, 64) following his friend Ibn Burya (d. 350).

[67] Kh. VIII, 290; Ibn ʿAsākir [?] V, 242; Tagr. II, 362-363.

[68] Who made, through a protocol link with the Sāmānids, Abū Ishāq Sabr his secretary in 354 (*zīj*).

[69] Farrā' [bib. no. 2066-b?], 403.

[70] Tanūkhī, a paranymph of the daughter of ʿAdūd forced on the caliph in 369 (who did not want to consummate the marriage: *SIJ*; *Yīq.*, s.v.).

[71] 353: governor of Kufa, d. 390.   [72] *Tawallī Muʿāwiya.*

know that Hallāj was the subject of *riwāyāt* there. The soul of Sūfī opposition to official Shī'ism at that time in Baghdad was another of Shiblī's disciples, a preacher, Ibn Sam'ūn (300, d. 387), who, at the most crucial moments, when the Buwayhid prince 'Adud al-Dawla was entering the capital, in 364 and 367, was able to stand up against its intimidations. Now, Ibn Sam'ūn, in a passage from his *majālis*, without saying so used the *Tawāsīn* for information about Ismā'īl A'zanī—a passage referred to by Ibn Babawayh. And Vizir Ibn al-Muslima, who undertook an official rehabilitation of Hallāj in 437,[73] was connected with his direct disciples,[74] the Hanbalites Abū 'Alī ibn Abī Mūsā Hāshimī, 'A 'Azīz Azajī, and the Shāfi'ite mystics 'Allāf and Qazwīnī.

h. Ibn Sam'ūn

Abū'l-Hy M-b-A-b-Ismā'īl ibn Sam'ūn (300, d. 387),[75] who was both a Hanbalite and a mystic, played a major role in the Baghdadian Sunnites' resistance to Shī'ite domination. Of humble background, he married— thanks to Shaghab—a concubine of Caliph Muqtadir, whose princely dower of repudiation brought him into prominence (Ibn 'Asakir, p. 203). He stood up to the Buwayhid prince 'Adud al-Dawla in 367, continuing to preach in the mosque of Mansūr despite the banning of the *Qussās*. A pupil of Shiblī and of Husrī (d. 371) in mysticism, he was the *rāwī* for Ibn 'Atā''s ideas on suffering[76] and for a Hallājian theory about the Divine Name, which was particularly challenged in this period by a Shī'ite, Ibn Bābawayh.

Of the works of this man, whose eloquence was praised by Harīrī,[77] only fragments have been preserved, published by AH Qazwīnī, and some *amālī* (= 30 *majālis*) transmitted by Fātima Bint ibn Fadlawayh down to Ibn Hajar 'Asqalānī[78] (Damascus ms., *Zah.* 2, *Majm.* 17).

The names of his disciples show us that Ibn Sam'ūn was the source of the Baghdadian Hanbalite mystical movement whose two characteristics were the following: the establishment of convents for women and the cult of Hallāj's memory.

His main Hanbalite disciples were the following: the Hanbalite ascetic 'Ushsharī (366, d. 451), Qādī Abū 'Alī ibn Abī Mūsā (345, d. 428), AM H-b-A-Tālib Khallāl (352, d. 439), from Bab Basra, master of Tuyūrī

---

[73] Ibn Hajar.
[74] [I]bn [S]am'ūn, his works: *amālī* (*Zah.* [2] *maj.* 17).
[75] Jāmī, 260; Farrā', *Tab. Hanab.*, 351; Ma'sūm 'Alī, *Tarā'iq* [bib. no. 1228-a] II, 245; *SIJ*, [ms.] 5866, f. 161a.
[76] Hazm IV, 226.   [77] *Maqāmāt* XXI.
[78] Ibn Hajar, *Lisān al-mīzān* [bib. no. 632-b], v. 60 (via Kindī).

and Harawī, A ʿAzīz Azajī (355, d. 444), *rāwī* of, among others, Ibn Jahdam concerning Hallāj; then Khadīja Shāhjahānīya (376, d. 460, buried at his feet), AB A-b-M-b-A ibn Hamdūya Bazzāz, *muqriʾ* (381, d. 470), AHy A-b-M ibn al-Nuqūr, buried near him (380, d. 470), master of Fātima, the daughter of Hy-b-G ibn Fadlawayh Rāzī, who died in 514, prior of the first *ribāt*[79] or convent for women established in Islam and in Baghdad (probably the famous Dār al-Falak, near the Musannā = the present-day Qumriya on the west bank; where Ibn ʿArabī tells us that in 611 his "Beatrice," Nizām, lived)[80] and *rāwīya* of his *majālis*: A Fadl ʿA Wāhid-b-A ʿAzīz Tamīmī, pro-Ashʿarite (d. 410), *wāʿiz*, who buried him; A Hy M-b-ʿAlī ibn al-Muhtadī, *khatīb* of the mosque of Mansūr (374, d. 565; from 417 to 451); A Fadl M-b-ʿA ʿAzīz-b-ʿAbbās ibn al-Mahdī (380, d. 444), *khatīb* of the Harbīya. His last *rāwī* was ʿAlī-b-M ibn Hamdūya (d. 470).

His leading mystical disciples, Shāfiʿites, were the following: Abū Tāhir M-b-ʿAlī ʿAllāf (born around 358, d. 442, *rāwī* of AB Qatīʿī = 368) called *"sāhib ibn Samʿūn,"* an anti-Sālimīyan[81] and friend of the Hallājian vizir, Ibn al-Muslima; AH ʿAlī-b-ʿUmar Qazwīnī (360, d. 442), a highly respected ascetic who had the confidence of Caliph Qāʾim; AB M-b-M-b-Ismāʿīl Tāhirī (362, d. 442), the *faqīh* AM Sinnī,[82] from Baghdad, also called *"sāhib Ibn Samʿūn."* Tawhīdī preserved a fragment of his work for us, one dealing with Moses and divine love (*Sidq*, 104). He admired the profane singer Ibn Buhlūl (Mez, *Abūʾl-Qāsim* [?], 84).

i. The Years 381-422 (Caliphate of Qādir):
A-H-b-Muhtadī II (380-434), Tammām-b-Hārūn (406-447)

There was a caliph at that time who, taking his responsibility as leader seriously, was able, in spite of the financial impoverishment of his court and the ruinous condition of the country, to break the Shīʿite annexation of the ʿAbbāsid state and to lay the groundwork for a theological and moral restoration of Sunnite Islam. He began with the canonists, by reserving for himself the right to appoint *shūhud* to the religious tribunals[83]

---

[79] Sibt ibn al-Jawzī [bib. no. 440-a] (1907 edition), 78.

[80] *Tarjumān al-ashwāq*, ch. 54, v. 1-12; 61, v. 3; 3, v. 10; 30, v. 35; 52 v. 5; 56 v. 5. Cf. Fuwatī and Goldziher, *Muh. Studien* [bib. no. 1640-a]. He must have seen her there repeatedly from 608 to 610. The story about a saint, Hallāj's sister, must have originated in these convents for women.

[81] ʿAllāf had as *rāwīs* his son, AH ʿAlī, called "Hājib" (406, d. 505), and his grandson, Muhammad, who was an informant of Samʿānī.

[82] Ibn ʿAsākir, *Radd*, 202: cf. AB Sinnī (Yāq. II, 630; IV, 681; V, 248); Subkī III, 207.

[83] Hence, the rather Muʿtazili position of Māwardī (d. 450).

(a battle in 386; aided by one lone qāḍī, Dabbī [d. 398], carried on later by other qāḍīs). As a counter move to the erection by the Shī'ites of the Qaṭī'a cathedral-mosque in 379, he built in 383, quite nearby, the Harbīya cathedral-mosque. He turned next to the *khaṭībs* of the mosques (he chose them from among solid Sunnite Hāshimites, such as A-Hy M-b-'Alī ibn al-Muhtadī II, 418-451, A Faḍl M-b-A 'Azīz ibn al-Mahdī [422, d. 444 in Harbīya]), and after that to the hajj (the annual reception of the pilgrims, especially those from Khurasan, in 383, etc.; an attempt to regain control over the appointment of the *amīr al-hajj*, which had devolved since 354 and 394 to the Shī'ite *naqīb* of the 'Alids: the toll for the hajj caravans was paid each year, since 385, by the Sunnite Kurdish amīr Badr-b-Hasanawayh, d. 405; hajj of 412 org. Mahmūd II).

From the doctrinal point of view, Qādir, who was guided by a non-Ash'arite conservative Shāfi'ite, Abū Hāmid Isfarā'inī (345, d. 406)[84] was able to end once and for all the influence of Mu'tazilism[85] upon the Hanafite jurisconsults (the edict of 408) and to unite Hanbalites[86] and Shāfi'ites in Baghdad against Shī'ism, which was to be the achievement[87] of Grand Qāḍī Ibn Mākūlā (over a period of 30 years [420, d. 447], the master of Ibn al-Muslima).[88] He even envisaged, together with a Hanafite qāḍī, Abū Ja'far Samnānī (d. 444; Hisb. 412-416), the master of Dāmaghānī, the possibility of organizing a real defense of orthodoxy against Mu'tazilism by using Ash'arite scholasticism, an idea that Vizirs Ibn al-Muslima and Niẓām al-Mulk would take up. He used this qāḍī for diplomatic missions (in 416) to Qirwāsh, in 418, with Jalāl al-Dawla. In ethics and asceticism, his friend Abū 'Alī M-A ibn Abī Mūsā Ma'badī (345, d. 428),[89] a disciple of Ibn Sam'ūn, was his guide and the guide also of Qāyim. It is known that he used to pray[90] at the tombs of Ma'rūf Karkhī[91] and Ibn Baghshārī in Najmī.

From the political standpoint, Qādir could rely, externally, on the loyalty given the Caliphate by the powerful ruler of Khurasan, Mahmūd of Ghazna (who put the Mu'tazilite edict into effect in 413) (389, d. 421), and watched closely the growth in the west of the Fāṭimid threat

---

[84] I. T. [Ibn Taymīya], *Tis'īnīya* [?] VIII, 277. The *i'tiqād qādirī*, redacted in 402 from A Hamīd Isfarā'inī by A Qassāf Karajī ('*Ulūw* 307-308-313) *sifatun haqīqatan la majāzan* [a real and not figurative attribute].

[85] For Ibn Hanbal, against Baqillānī.

[86] The Hanbalites were the pillars of the dynasty (Ibn al-Baqqāl, d. 440).

[87] His four *Shuhūd* of 422: Farrā' captured, Tanūkhī hung, Māwardī d. 441.

[88] Cf. also Saymarī, d. 436.

[89] Farrā', 368.

[90] Athīr IX, 283. His dreams: Dīnawarī.

[91] Qaffāl Marwāzī converted him from Hanafism to Shāfi'ism in 413.

(Fātimid riot in Karkh in 396; Fātimid *khutba* in Kufa and Mosul in 401). In 402, he forced the 'Alids of Baghdad to sign a declaration denouncing the Fātimids for having usurped their 'Alid genealogy. He realized that Buwayhid Shī'ism had lost its force as an ideal, and that the Shī'ite threat would come henceforth from the Fātimid propaganda.

The critical moment of the reign was the year 393-394.[92] In 393, Qādir tried to replace the Hanafite and Mu'tazilite Grand Qādī Akfānī (390, d. 405) with a Shāfi'ite grand qādī, Abiwardī, but was stopped.[93] In 394, the Buwayhid amīr and the Shī'ite *naqīb*, instructed by the theologian Mufīd, who was already 'Adud's guide, waged a counterattack against [the Caliph] by enjoining him to take the Shī'ite *naqīb* as the Sunnite grand qādī; but Qādir resisted successfully and, in spite of the Shī'ite riot of 398, of which he took advantage to exile Mufīd, remained lord and master of the land. His best grand qādīs in that period came to him from Basra, where Sunnism was having a revival.

In terms of internal politics, Qādir knew how to take advantage of the character weaknesses of the Buwayhid princes, and was on the best of terms with the governors of Baghdad,[94] Ustādh Hurmuzz (393, d. 401) and Abū Ghālib (d. 409). He had Vizir Ibn Sahlān put an end to the *'ashūrā*, dismissed Vizir Maghribī in 414 for collusion with the Fātimids, and remained on good terms also with the vizirial families of the Banū Fusānjus and the Banū 'Abd al-Rahīm, both ultra-Shī'ite, who, along with the Banū Mākūlā, were sympathetic to his Sunnism despite the Shī'ism of the Buwayhid princes.

For collaborators Qādir had his sons and heirs, Abū'l-Fadl 'Akarī Ghālib (associate in 421), the leading princes of the blood, 'Umar-b-Hārūn-b-Muqtadir (d. 394) and M-b-H-'Isā-b-Muqtadir (born 343, died 432), Hārūn-b-'Isā-b-Muqtadir (346, d. 440), all three of whom were Hanbalites; and particularly his *kātib*, 'Alī ibn Hājib al-Nu'mān,[95] who, beneath a nonchalant exterior and by means of endless protocolary skirmishes, was able to pull off the great schemes to which he was a confidential party. His grandfather Ibrāhīm had been (and hence his name) the *hājib* of a friend of Ibn 'Isā, Nu'mān-b-'Abdallāh, the fiscal *wālī* of Ahwaz, a scrupulously good man who had retired to live the life of an ascetic, and whom Muhassin ordered assassinated in 311 (out of hatred, I

---

[92] Popular Sunnite reaction began in Basra, with the instituting of such anti-Shī'ite festivals as the *ghar* (26 *Hijja* 389) and the *ziyāra* of Mutab-b-Zubayr in Maskī (18 *Muharram* 390); abolished in 393.

[93] Capitulated (letter in Timur).

[94] The excuses by Murtadā in 420 for Khutba Burathā.

[95] *Ghufrān*, 10.

believe, for Hallāj).[96] His father 'Abd al-'Azīz (305, d. 351), who owned a splendid collection of manuscripts of Arab poets, had married the daughter of H-b-A Madhārā'yī, and had been a state secretary (for the Sawād) under the Buwayhid vizir Muhallabī. Born himself in 340 (died in 423), he held the office of vizir of the Caliph almost without interruption[97] from 374 to 421, for a period of 47 years. Qādir bestowed on him the honorific title of Ra'īs al-ru'asā', which Qāyim was later to bestow on Ibn al-Muslima, who continued the same policy.

We have not detected under Qādir any signs of sympathy for Hallājism in official circles, but the renewed outbreak of attacks on Hallāj among Baghdadian Shī'ite authors of the period indicates the increasing degree on the Sunnite side to which his name must have been held up in the battle as a flag.

The three leading Shī'ite theologians of the Karkh district one after another attacked the teaching of Hallāj. Ibn Bābawayh (d. 381/991),[98] in his I'tiqādāt, construed it as an extremist Shī'ite heresy characterized by two contradictory notions: the transfiguration of the soul by means of religious observances, and the abolition of religious obligations: a claim to knowledge to the supreme Names of God and to the branding of a divine seal (intibā' al-Haqq) making the saint, when he has been purified and knows their sect, superior to the prophets; plus a pretended knowledge of alchemy.

After that Mufīd ibn al-Mu'allim (d. 412), the famous theologian who was the policy advisor to the Buwayhids when they tried in 394 to seize control from the Sunnite Caliphate of canonical matters by appointing as qādī of qādīs the naqīb of the 'Alids, Abū Ahmad Mūsawī[99] (who had his I'tiqādāt redacted by the second naqīb, Radī [nā'ib as early as 386, 396, d. 406]), felt obliged to write a long[100] refutation of them, Radd 'alā'l-Hallājīya, which is apparently lost.[101] The following passage, however, taken from another work by Mufīd,[102] indicates that he placed them in it outside the law:

The Hallājīya are a sect of Sūfīs professing ibāha [= abrogation of religious duties] and hulūl; Hallāj himself did not profess Shī'ism exclusively, and he was

[96] Fihrist, 134; Nishwār, 39.
[97] Two and a half months in 388 (Ibn Turayk). A Fadl, his son, the ex-kātib of Ghālib, succeeded him for a year, together with 'Īsā-b-Māsarjis.
[98] A personal friend of the sāhib Ibn 'Abbād (Lisān II, 206).
[99] Appointed naqīb al-Tālibīyīn.
[100] "Kitāb Kabīr" (Zahr al-rabī', 131).
[101] Khuyyī (Sharh manhaj al-barā'a VI, 274; cf. 239, 283, 285, 305) was unable to find it.
[102] Sharh 'aqā'id Ibn Bābawayh, ap. Khuyyī, l.c. VI, 178.

outwardly a Sūfī. They are heretics and *zanādiqa*, who deceive other sects by pretending to imitate them; and they attribute to Hallāj unfounded things, following in that aspect the Mazdaeans who attribute marvels to Zoroaster, and the Christians who attribute convincing miracles to their anchorites. But Christians and Mazdaeans are closer than they to religious observance, and they deviate more from religious duties and their practice than do Mazdaeans and Christians.

With the Sunnite policy of Caliph Qādir asserting itself, Mufīd considered it clever to join the *naqīb* Rādī and his brother, Murtadā I, in signing the anti-Fātimid declaration of 402; for all that troubles once again in the Karkh got him expelled from Baghdad,[103] from 393 to 398.

His successor at the forefront of the Imāmite theologians, Abū Ja'far Tūsī (d. 459/1067), who arrived in Baghdad in 404,[104] renewed the attacks upon Hallāj in two of his works;[105] after the vizir, Ibn al-Muslima, had Ibn Jullāb, head of the cloth merchants of Bab al-Taq, executed in 448 for insulting the first three Caliphs, AJ Tūsī escaped from Karkh,[106] where his house was ransacked the following year during the months of famine, plague, and fires that preceded the coup d'état.[107]

j. The Years 422-451 (the Caliphate of Qāyim down to the End of the Vizirate of Ibn al-Muslima)

During these decisive years, when the Ismā'īli propaganda of the Fātimids of Cairo surrendered and lost the duel for which Qādir had prepared himself, the last three Buwayhid princes of Baghdad—Jalāl al-Dawla, controlled by Murtadā in Basra from 403 to 419 (416-435), Abū Kālijār in Shiraz from 403, in Basra from 419 (435-440), and Malik Rahīm (440-447)—and their vizirs, namely the B. Abd al-Rahīm and the B. Fusānjus[108] alternately, caught between the Turkish guard (Bārastaghūn, Bāsāsīrī) and the 'Uqaylid and Mazyadid Arab amīrs, continued to waver between the temporal support of a Sunnite Caliphate which they detested and the desire to curb the increasingly revolutionary coloration that the Fātimid agents gave to Shī'ite teaching in Iraq. Although for ten years (421-431), the *wālī* of Abū Kālijār AQ Zahir al-Dīn left the administration in Basra in the hands of two Druze vizirs, AH Shābāsh and his son, Salīl al-Barakāt, Abū Kālijār decided not to grant the Fātimid *dā'ī* Mu'ayyad Shīrāzī, during his ten-year secret mission, his support of Ismā'īlism (429-439), and the latter, hunted down by Ibn al-Muslima, had to return to Cairo.

---

[103] Ibn al-Athīr.
[105] *Ibid.*, 261-263; *Iqtisād.*
[107] *Ibid.*, f. 22b.

[104] *Ghayba*, 232.
[106] Sibt ibn al-Jawzī, ms. P. 1506, f. 18b.
[108] Vocal. vouched for (Māmuqānī).

From 422 to 437, Qāyim's *kātib*, Abū Tāhir, exposed to the hatred of the B. Fusānjus,[109] became absorbed in an attempt at regroupment of Sunnite forces. Following objections raised by the book by the Hanbalite Farrā' concerning the concrete nature of the divine attributes (428), the Caliph ordered in 432[110] a text drawn up by Farrā' (d. 458), Tabarī, and the Shāfi'ite 'Alī Qazwīnī (d. 442), a mystic and disciple of Ibn Sam'ūn, dealing with the *balkafīya*.[111] And in 436, he ordered work begun on the monumental tomb of Abū Hanīfa. The leaders of the Turkish guard, the *isfahsalarīya*, Bārīstughān (428) followed by Basāsīrī, who for twenty years had been in command of the Caliphal troops tolerated by the Buwayhids, were posing a threat to the latter:[112] they were named in the *khutba* in Baghdad and in Ahwaz, and were aspiring to play a role.

In 437, at the request of the B. Fusānjus, Abū Tāhir was given an assistant (in *Jumāda* I) who was destined to replace him (in Sha'ban). This man was a professional jurist, a *shāhid* of the Baghdad court, 'Alī ibn al-Muslima. He managed to be given the title of vizir,[113] a title abolished since 334, and assumed power with the fixed purpose of waging a struggle unto death against Shī'ism, and especially Ismā'īlī Shī'ism, and of carrying out the reconstruction of Sunnite Islam undertaken by Qādir. He was a Hallājian and was determined to dedicate his work from the outset publicly to a martyr.

The thirteen years of Ibn al-Muslima's vizirate unfolded in a steady rhythm quickened by the catastrophe of a tragedy.

Externally, two dangers intersected: the Ismā'īlī propaganda of the Fātimids of Cairo, and the Turkish invasion by the Saljūq Ghuzz from the East. Here and there the accomplices of Ismā'īlism abolished the Sunnite *khutba*, among the Mazyadid Arabs of Hilla (in 433) and the 'Uqaylids of Kufa and Wasit (in 448). One after the other of the great Persian Muslim cities fell, laid waste by the Ghuzz, from Nishapur (in 432) to Isfahan (in 442) and Fars (in 442).

Internally, the famine and plague that had decimated Bukhara[114] as well as Cairo[115] moved on to Baghdad, forcing the population, after committing desperate acts, abandonment of hospitals[116] and cannibalism, to a kind of public repentance, whose sincerity was underscored by the *tawqī'* of Caliph Qāyim (447-449).

---

[109] 426: a strike by the qādīs.
[110] Cf. the *'aqīda* of Ibn Abī Mūsā ('Akarī).
[111] *Ibtāl al-ta'wīlāt* (*Tabaqāt*, 380).
[112] Jalīl chased (in 431) from Baghdad.
[113] "*Nā'ib bi'l-dīwān*" (Basāsīrī)—first vizir at Taylasan.
[115] No hajj in 437, 440, and 443.

[114] 'Akarī.
[116] 'Adud [?], 449.

A man like Ibn al-Muslima, who had dedicated his vizirate to Hallāj, that is, to one condemned by the canonical courts, would have been apt to try to win over the body of 'ayyārīn, of Baghdadian Hanbalite outlaws, to his district plan of war against the Shī'ites. And, after the 'ayyārīn riots of Burjumī in 422, 424, and 426, we find them collaborating with the vizir's police, who were sometimes outlaws themselves (for example, Nashwī, the police commissioner against whom, in 442, in common cause, despite these efforts, bourgeois Shī'ites and Sunnites agreed on a truce,[117] and whom the vizir was forced to remove from office when the jurist Abū'l-Tayīb Tabarī, his friend, delivered a final judgment against his misdeeds). The main leaders of the Hanbalite bands in Karkh at that time were the qāss Ibn al-Mudhahhab and Zuhayrī, disciples of the zāhid 'Abd al-Samad (d. 391). It should be noted that Ibn al-Muslima armed them only after he was provoked into doing it by Basāsīrī.

Besides, here is a brief chronological survey of his activities: 1) externally, the vizir began by choking off the advance movement of the Fātimid propagandists, going personally in 438-439 to Basra and Shiraz to prevent the Buwayhid prince Abū Kālijār from joining forces there. In 440, he succeeded in getting the khutba voiced in Qayrawan for Qāyim, which cut off the Fātimids from their supplies of Berber troops. Their dā'ī Mu'ayyad noted with bitterness that this vizir was "the magnet who gathers all of our wrongdoings."

At this time, the Buwayhids,[118] who had pretended like Basāsīrī to ignore the Caliphal court,[119] became uneasy in 436 and after over the vizir's underhanded dealings with the Hanbalites (in 442). The vizir, however, got Basāsīrī to help him subdue Basra (in 444), which he left to the control of 'Izz al-Mulūk Abū 'Alī Kaykhusrū, son of Abū Kālijār. But upon his return to Baghdad he came to a decision. He began negotiations for the Ghuzz Turks and their leader, Tughrīl Beg, to enter the capital to save the Sunnite Caliphate. He got an 'amīd al-'Irāq, Abū Nasr Ahmad ibn 'Alī, dispatched and invested in this position with some objections from Qāyim, who very quickly made him not only his ally, but also his confidant in all of his projects[120] for Sunnite restoration (he was a

---

[117] After Shī'ites and Sunnites together erected fortified walls in 441, Nasāwī was appointed to destroy them in 442.

[118] Basāsīrī captured Anbār (in 441). Tughrīl controlled Shahrizur 'Annāz (in 443): an exchange of letters with the caliph (in 443).

[119] The arrival of Abū Kālijār: four tablkhaviz with five prayers (instead of three previously given in 368).

[120] The first ribāt prior to 441.

Shāfiʿite like himself, and not a Hanafite like Tughrīl) (in 444).[121] The arrival on the scene of this rival military officer precipitated the betrayal that Basāsīrī was harboring[122] and brought him into the service of the Fāṭimids. The vizir, as a second military prop to use against him, had a Kurdish nobleman, Abū'l-Ghanā'im ibn Mahlabān, brought from his castle near Takrit (not without difficulties: Basāsīrī held him prisoner briefly in Anbar; then the ʿamīd, Ahmad, being jealous, entered into battle with him in Wasit; Ibn Mahlabān, annoyed, returned to his castle, where the vizir had to go and find him; henceforth devoted personally to the vizir, it would be he who would save his family and the heir to the Caliphate in 450) (446). The years 447–448 marked the disappearance of the Buwayhid amīrate from Baghdad, and concluding of the accords with Tughrīl (who relinquished Basra to Hāzar Isp-b-Bankīr, the son and grandson of men who had been governors of Ahwaz for fifty years), and the final break with Basāsīrī, one of whose accomplices, Ibn Fusānjus, attempted to kidnap the Caliph (in 446), seize control of Kufa (in 448), and fight Qutlamīhī at Sinjar.

A Ghanā'im, Saʿīd-b-M-b-Jaʿfar ibn Fusānjus, the former Buwayhid vizir in Shiraz (until 447; replaced by Nasawī in 448), who, together with A Talib Nāfūr-b-A-Kālijār) had joined Basāsīrī, who had occupied Wasit and set up the Fāṭimid *khutba* there, was later captured by the future ʿamīd al-ʿIrāq, Abū'l-Fadl Hamadhānī, taken to Baghdad and brutally executed (in 449).[123]

The poet Sarr Durr (ʿAlī-b-M, d. 465) dedicated three *qasīdas* to Vizir Ibn al-Muslima and a funeral eulogy to Abū Mansūr-b-Yūsuf (*Dīwān* [Cairo ed., 1934], nos. 7, 15, 22, 135).

Internally also, the vizir was personally in charge of all ceremonial formalities, including the circumcision (in 440) and investiture of the heir to the throne, Dhakhīrat al-Dīn (born in 431, died in 447), in 441; of the official mourning for the wife of Qāyim (sister of Abū Nasr-b-Buwayh = Mālik Rahīm) and the first prince of the blood, Hārūn, in 440, and for Dhakhīra and Fātima, sister of Qāyim, in 448; and of official protocol for Tughrīl's entry [into Baghdad], in which [he sought] to control the latter's uncouth passions by exposing him to the moral influence of a refined culture. It was he who delivered the *khutbat al-nikāh* in 448 for Qāyim's marriage with Tughrīl's sister, Arslān Khātūn (Khadīja), a jeal-

---

[121] In 445 Tughrīl persecuted Shāfiʿites and Ashʿarites.
[122] Dubays married Basāsīrī's daughter in 444; his brother Thābit was with him from 430 on.
[123] A quarrel between Shāfiʿites and Hanbalites in 447.

ous and brutal woman who tried to do away with the young heir apparent, Prince 'Uddat al-Dīn (the future Muqtadī), Dkakhīra's posthumous child born in 448 of his concubine 'Urjuwān.

He was the one whom Qāyim made suffer for the excesses committed by the Baghdad garrison, which was led in 448 by Tughrīl's vizir, the 'amīd al-mulk, Abū Nasr M-b-Mansūr Kundurī. He had had to promise the latter 300,000 dīnārs, could collect only 180,000, and was quickly blamed by the Caliph for this promise made at the expense of people he kept at bay. The violent protests that Ibn al-Muslima made at that time to Kundurī ended in a slight appeasement,[124] but Qāyim upbraided his vizir for having allowed the 'amīd, Ahmad-b-'Alī, to arrest one of his main servants, Sandal. However, Qāyim protected his vizir in all of the actions that he took against Shī'ites in 441 (abolishing the 'ashūrā), in 443 when he used force against them in Karkh (the tombs of Kazimen were burned, as was the khān al-Hanafīya in retaliation), in 444, the Fātimid nasab, in 447 when the Turkish guard arrested and ransomed Zuhra from Basāsīrī's harem (who had made him ransack his house and put a price on his head in 446), and when he executed AH 'Ubayd-b-Sa'īd, a Christian kātib of Basāsīrī. The Fātimid dā'ī Mu'ayyad, in his dīwān, heaps the same insults upon the vizir and the sovereign, the "grandson of Dimna." In 449, the Shī'ite adhān was forbidden entry into Karkh; a syndic of the Shī'ite craftsmen, Ibn Jullāb, was put on the gibbet; and the leading Shī'ite mujtahid, Abū Ja'far Tūsī, fled: Kazimen was destroyed.

We have some indication that Qāyim did more than just tolerate the Hallājism of his vizir. [Qāyim] had as a confidant a wealthy and learned Hanbalite named Abū Mansūr 'Abd al-Malik ibn Yūsuf,[125] the patron of the young Ibn 'Aqīl, who wrote under his patronage his apologia for Hallāj. When this patron died (in 460) [leaving a son-in-law, Ibn Janda (d. 476)], and when actions were taken against Ibn 'Aqīl,[126] Qāyim hid the latter in his palace for four years (461-465). Undoubtedly Ibn 'Aqīl's being forced to retract, and Qāyim's designating in his will Abū Ja'far, an enemy of Ibn 'Aqīl, to wash his body, were political postures, not personal shifts in attitude.

The extraordinary vicissitudes undergone at the start of his reign were accepted by 'AA-b-A Qāyim (b. 391, d. 467) with a religious presence of mind whose character was noted by historians. And it was certainly with

---

[124] Tughrīl had a dream that settled it.

[125] The father-in-law of AQ ibn Ridwān, 397, d. 460.

[126] Ibn 'Aqīl, a friend of the Hanafite M-b-Wanbān Daylamī, master of the historian Hamadhānī (favorable to the vizir-patron of 'Attār).

his personal consent that Ibn al-Muslima and, later, Ibn Mahlabān[127] founded Sūfī *ribāts* in Baghdad, underwritten by Urjuwān Qurrat (d. 512). Qāyim's leading collaborators were the following: after Abū Mansūr came Abū 'AA Hy-b-'Alī Mardūshānī (b. 383, d. 478), *hājib* Bāb al-Būbī (428-460), and Sā'id-b-Mansūr ibn al-Mawsalāyā, head of the *dīwān al-inshā'* (b. 417; 432 to 497: Christian, converted in 482). Next to Ibn al-Muslima, his closest advisor, there was the Shāfi'ite Abū Ishāq Ibrāhīm-b-'Alī Shīrāzī, a pupil of Ibn Abī Mūsā (*Tabaqāt* I, 47) (b. 393 Firazābād, in Baghdad 415, d. 476), the ascetic AT 'Allāf (b. before 360, d. 442), the historian of Baghdad AB Khatīb (392, d. 463), and the qādīs Abū'l-Tayib Tabarī (d. 450) and AY Farrā' (d. 458).

k. The Hallājian Inspiration of Vizir Ibn al-Muslima

In what sense was Ibn al-Muslima[128] a Hallājian? This is the question that the deliberate and public gesture made by him in dedicating the inauguration of his vizirate to Hallāj prompts us to investigate.

It is possible that in making that gesture he was following the popular tradition of Baghdadian mystical Sunnism: that is, of venerating Hallāj as a Sūfī victim of Shī'ite acts of treachery. In fact, we know that Ibn al-Muslima, with his ties to the disciples of Shiblī, was a friend of AT ibn al-'Allāf, the leading disciple of Ibn Sam'ūn; however, he seems to have shared with Ibn 'Aqīl an aversion to the devotional excesses of the Sūfīs.

Ibn al-Muslima was above all a Shāfi'ite statesman.[129] His vizirate was not merely an anti-Shī'ite reaction using the Hanbalite Sūfism of Baghdad's lower classes, but rather it was first and foremost an enlarged and systematic continuation of the Shāfi'ite theologico-political work sketched out as early as 393 by Abū Hāmid Isfarā'inī (d. 406), advisor to Caliph Qādir, and resumed in the period of 428-432 by the preacher 'Alī Qazwīnī (d. 442; a disciple also of Ibn Sam'ūn) with AT M-b-Ayyūb (d. 442), a secretary of Caliph Qāyim; a work which the famous Saljūq vizir, Nizām al-Mulk (d. 485),[130] was to complete in a grandiose way. It was a

---

[127] Zambaur's errors: Ibn Mahlabān is different from Ibn Fusānjus; and Tughrīl did not have a cousin of IMRR [(Ibn al-Muslima?)] as vizir.

[128] Ibn al-Muslima, a pupil of Ibn Mākūlā and disciple of Ibn Mānda, was a Hanbalite (d. 395); through Shāfi'ism he must have seen Mas'ūd Sijistānī (*rāwī* of Ibn Bākūyā, a friend of Nizām al-Mulk, the vizir of Dāwūd).

[129] Possible motives: Turkish policy? Qushayrian Ash'arism (AT Shirāzī), Surayjian Shāfi'ism? popular devotion? anti-Shī'ism?

[130] Because the Turks had a tendency to keep their customary civil courts (*yarghūjīya*) separate from canonical courts (*shar'īya*), Nizām al-Mulk, the Saljūq subjects and representatives, were much more preoccupied with the restoration of the 'Abbāsid Caliphate (eaten away by Buwayhid encroachments) than with the canonical legitimation (impossible, cf.

work of theoretical and practical reconstruction of caliphal authority. And this is why Māwardī (d. 450), the author of the famous "rules of sovereignty," also dedicated his "proper behavior for a vizir" to a vizir who was none other than Ibn al-Muslima.[131]

The question of that time, in the minds of both Qādir and Qāyim, was how to exercise the basic canonical prerogatives of the Sunnite Caliphate concerning the preservation of dogma (edicts of 402, 408, 432), wa'z, and the right of moral censure,[132] despite the usurpation of temporal power by the Shī'ite Buwayhid "palace mayors."

Ibn al Muslima was a Hallājian, therefore, because in his public life Hallāj had attacked Mu'tazilite theology and preached moral reform. These are the same reasons for which the great Shāfi'ite jurisconsult Ibn Surayj had decided to defend Hallāj, the author of a treatise on polity and of an "ethics of the vizirate." And I believe it was in the Dār Ibn Surayj, situated in Karkh,[133] and used for more than one hundred fifty years for teaching Shāfi'ite law (directed when Nizām al-Mulk visited it by the father of the pro-Hallāj historian Hamadhānī), that Ibn al-Muslima gained his double attachment: to Surayjian Shāfi'ism and to Hallāj. His position would therefore have been exactly the same as that of his friend AB Khatīb, of Ibn 'Aqīl, of Qushayrī, and of Ghazālī: of regarding Hallāj only for the example of his social action: for the good, "salāh"[134] of the Muslim Community, without examining his mystical teaching apart from the social effect of his wa'z (with 'ilm).

1. The Political Theory of Ibn al-Muslima

When the title of vizir, which had been abolished since 334/945, was restored in 437/1045 for Ibn al-Muslima, it marked the beginning of the gradual reestablishment of caliphal authority, which was accomplished, despite the century-old oppression of Buwayhid amīrs, by the im-

---

AH Ghazālī's *Mustazhirī* with his *Tibr Masbūk* dedicated to Sultan Mahmūd II) of the Saljūq Sultanate, which was to forego residing in Baghdad.

131 *Adab al-wazīr*, preface. Māwardī carried out political missions in 429 and 443 (the latter under Ibn al-Muslima).

132 To regain control over the appointment to assigned positions of: *qādi shāhid, imām-khatīb, amīr al-hajj, muhtasib*; and to do away with the 'Alid *naqībs* (cf. Māwardī, *Ahkām*, [bib. no. 2159-a] ch. VIII).

133 In the Suwayqat Ghālib (Hamadhānī, ms. 1469, f. 116b = *waqf* founded by Da'laj Sijzī, d. 351).

134 This word *salāh* appears in Māwardī's preface (*Adab al-wazīr* II, 56, 57), in Hallāj's *wa'z* to Muqtadir preserved in the same legendary Hallājian text (in which the execution *fatwā* signed by Muqtadir revives the expression "*salāh al-muslimīn*") that Ghazālī was to use, ap. *Mustazhirī* [bib. no. 280-g], 30.

plementation under Qādir and Qāyim of a theory of caliphal rights worked out systematically by a series of Shāfi'ite canonists, from A Hāmid Isfarā'inī (d. 406) to Abiwardī and to Ibn al-Muslima; that theory being the same that another Shāfi'ite, AH Māwardī (d. 450), was to set forth in his *Ahkām sultānīya* and to dedicate in his *Adab al-wazīr* to the vizir in office, Ibn al-Muslima, *Ra'īs al-ru'asā* II.

With Shāfi'i emphasizing the idea of continuity in the Muslim Community, and being the only founder of a Sunnite rite that was *Hāshimite* in origin, his disciples agreed little by little, indeed much more slowly than did the Hanafites, to furnish qādīs for the de facto power, for the 'Abbāsid state, which, born out of an extremist Shī'ite sect, was consumed, as in the case of its most vigorous rulers, with a particular affliction, that of having usurped legitimate authority from their cousins, the 'Alids. The Shāfi'ite rite, emphasizing the common Sunnite idea of the *mubāya'a*, the canonical investiture of authority delegated to the sovereign by the Community (which could withdraw it from him: the *fatwā* by a Shāfi'ite qādī of Damascus, Abū Zur'a, calling for the deposing of Caliph Muwaffaq in 272; and the attempt to depose Muqtadir by the *ijmā'* of the Sunnite qādīs of Baghdad in 296),[135] was the only one of the four Sunnite rites even to consider a theory of legitimate authority for safekeeping with the 'Abbāsid dynasty when the capture of Baghdad by the Shī'ites imperiled the very existence of such authority (in 334).

Stripped of their control over finances and the army, over the police and the vizirate, the Caliphs clung to their protocolary formalities (the *khutba*, abolished for two months in 368; *tablkhāne*, shared after 368); they kept high command of the jihad (an incident in 361) and of the hajj (an amīrate representative of the Shī'ite *naqīb* of the 'Alids, d. 354; but the Caliph received visiting pilgrims as volunteers for the faith), and retained the investiture of qādīs (a struggle in 393); they grasped the importance then of their moral obligation to the Community and reserved for themselves the *tazkiya* of the *shuhūd* (Muktafī, before 334 had claimed it back, Qādir put them on strike in 416), the supervision of *waqfs*, and the appointment of *kātibs* in the Baghdad mosques (chosen from among the loyal Hāshimites), struggling step by step, advised by a state secretary, who was a cautious and accomplished diplomat, the *Ra'īs al-ru'asā* I (Ibn Hājib al-Nu'mān, *kātib* of the Caliphate from 374 to 388 and 388 to 421). But it was necessary to give this reviving authority a dogmatic cohesiveness as well as a diplomatic base of operations; and this is where Shāfi'ism

---

[135] Qalānīsī against Ash'arī: *fatwā* calling for the execution of Amīr Khumarūya in 282.

came into the picture,[136] through A Hāmid Isfarā'īnī (345, d. 406); a condemnation of Mu'tazilism, imposed on the Hanafites of Baghdad who moved on to Ash'arism, and enforced by the Ghaznavid prince, Mahmūd II, who was persuaded to shift from Hanafism to Shāfi'ism (408-413), and afterwards through AH Qazwīnī (the 'aqīda of 432). The support of the secular arm, which the 'Abbāsids had achieved with the Tāhirids (237-272) and the Saffārids (266-272, 276; attempts during 296-301 with the Sāmānids) by giving them the shurta of Baghdad, which they had held again briefly (for the hajj) in the person of the Kurd prince (Badr-b-Hasanawayh, 385, d. 405) and afterwards through Mahmūd II (d. 421), had to be firmly established, now that the Shī'ite propaganda of the Fātimids of Cairo was closing in on Baghdad, capturing Basra (421-431: the extremist vizir, AH Shābāsh), attempting to take control of Fars, Mosul, Hilla, and even of Transoxiana (in 435). And the proliferation of its missionaries sent to these areas would eventually force the Sunnite Caliphate in its counterattack movements to take charge of the work of the madrasas, the canonical universities, which the semi-Ash'arite Shafi'ites specifically were the only ones to have instituted, through private funds.

Through thirteen years of unparalleled difficulties, riots, famines, and epidemics, Ibn al-Muslima pursued his plan with relentless determination: to restore the Islamic Caliphate according to Shāfi'ite teaching; to reconcile the different rites, Shāfi'ite and Hanbalite,[137] by setting forth a formula concerning the divine attributes that retained the traditional balkafīya together with incipient theological argumentation that was prudent but positive (certain Hanbalites ventured into kalām, and the majority of Baghdadian Shāfi'ites concentrated on Ash'arism and were joined in this by several Hanafites turning away from Mu'tazilism: Saymarī, Dāmaghānī); and to establish the teaching of this Sunnite dogmatic theology in the universities organized by the state along the lines of the private Shāfi'ite madrasas of Khurasan (established to combat the Hanafite-Karrāmīya converts) by combining a Sūfī waqf for preaching (wa'z) with a school of dogmatic theology studies, the one benefiting the other (e.g., the madrasa of Būshanjī ibn Fūrak, Sūfī-Shāfi'ite [Ash'arite], founded between 372 and 377 in Nishapur). Ibn al-Muslima founded the Sūfī waqf in the ribāt Shaykh al-shuyūkh and dared to receive in Baghdad the Ash'arite

[136] Qādir, in 393, tried to give him control over the qādīs.

[137] Useful in terms of their popularity with the common people, "pillars of the dynastic tent" (Ibn al-Baqqāl, ap. Farrā')—obstinate: beaten in 448, they attacked the Shāfi'ites (cf. Tabarī in 309, Athīr IX, 442).

Shāfiʿite professors who had been driven out of Khurasan during the Hanafite persecution of the Saljūq vizir Kundarī (in 447). These professors were the ones who would later teach in the Nizāmīya university, erected thanks to the above-mentioned Sūfī *waqf*, when the Shāfiʿite rite would reign triumphant in the Saljūq Court with Vizir Nizām al-Mulk, and remain so for nearly a century down to the time of Sinjār.

With regard to the material base of operations capable of protecting the Sunnite Caliphate from the onslaughts of the Fāṭimid offensive, Ibn al-Muslima, who had been successful in reestablishing valuable friendly relations nearby (such as with the Zīrid dynasty in Tunis, in 443, and even with the Shāfiʿites in Cairo; also, in Takrit, with a chivalrous Kurdish amīr, Ibn Mahlabān, who would one day be able to save the families of both vizir and Caliph from disaster), settled on a maneuver that proved decisive: to enter into diplomatic parlies with the Ghuzz, those Turks newly arrived in Khurasan from the steppes, and to substitute their Saljūq chiefs and their bands, which were barbarous and cruel but under control, and also Sunnite, for the degenerate Turkish mercenaries of the Baghdad garrison who had sold out to the Fāṭimids of Cairo.[138]

In terms of historical importance, one might compare the decision by Ibn al-Muslima, in appealing to Tughrīl Beg[139] to save the Caliphate of Qāyim, with St. Boniface's (d. 755) carefully weighed choice, in persuading Pope Stephen II to crown the first of the Carolingians, Pepin the Short, king. The Saljūq model of social structure, which a few years later was winning all of Asia Minor from Baghdad, the same as that which the Ottoman Empire, heir of the Ayyūbids and the Mamlūks, would perpetuate down to our present day,[140] is based on the Shāfiʿite political theory conceived in this period by Isfarāʾinī, Māwardī, Abū Ishāq Shīrāzī, and the two Ghazālīs, but carried out above all by Ibn al-Muslima.

It was fitting to speak of this theory in detail here, because this vizir, on the very day of his investiture, insisted on going to pray at the *maslib* of Hallāj, considering him to be the precursor and inspirer of his Muslim policy.[141]

---

[138] Ibn al-Maʾmūn's embassy for some years (with Nizām al-Mulk).

[139] The pressures brought by Tughrīl on Qāyim must not be compared to those of the Buwayhids on Mutīʿ, Tāyī, or Qādir, for the Buwayhids, who were Shīʿites, were attempting to destroy the Sunnite Caliph.

[140] Not Hanafite originally, though the Hanafite rite was the Turcoman rite.

[141] As if in the ʿAbbāsid court and among Shāfiʿites, this victim of Shīʿite hatred was looked upon as having defended by his writings the legitimacy of the dynasty.

m. The Cortege of Vizir Ibn al-Muslima

We know, from Ibn al-Jawzī,[142] that the *mawkib* (= protocolary escort) of the vizir on the day of his investiture (*yawm khuli'a 'alayhi*), 8 Jumāda I 437/Thursday, November 21, 1045, consisted of "the *khadam, hujjāb, ashrāf, qudāt,* and *shuhūd,*" hence:

(1) Some mamlūks of the sovereign (*ghilmān, hawāshī*), like Sandal, Sāfī (d. 478), and Khumāratakīn; some Turkish *ispahsalārīya* (if not Basāsīrī himself, at least his *kātib,* 'Ubayd); the associates of his predecessor, whom he had dealt with closely (as *kātib* of the sovereign) since November 7: the police commissioner, AM H-b-A Fadl Nawawī (421-449, d. 452; suspended in 422, 425, 438, 442); the *nā'ib* of the vizir, Hasan-b-'Alī-b-'Īsā Rab'ī (d. 447) and the secretary of the *Dīwān al-inshā'* (the Christian 'Alī-b-H ibn al-Mawsalāyā, born in 412, 432, d. 497; next to the *sāhib al-rasā'il,* 'Alī-b-M, d. 437); his friend the Kurd amīr, Ibn al-Mahlabān (Abū'l-Ghanā'im M-b-'Alī); ambassador in 464, founder of a *ribāt*;

(2) The Court chamberlains: Grand Chamberlain Abū 'Alī Nizām-b-'Alī Bakrān (d. 457), the *hājib* Bāb al-Nūbī, Hy Mardūshanī (383, d. 478), the diplomat Hibatullāh ibn al-Ma'mūn; the Buwayhid vizir Ibn Fisānjas VI (436-441);

(3) The *naqīb al-ashrāf*: the Hāshimite Abū Tammān II Zaynabī (428, d. 445), the 'Alawite *naqīb* 'Adnān (436, d. 450: simultaneously *amīr al-hajj*), the Ansārite *naqīb* 'Abd al-Salām-b-Ahmad (d. 467);

(4) Grand Qādī Hy ibn Mākūlā Dulafī (414, d. 447; a Shāfi'ite), Ibn al-Muhtadī, a Hanbalite *qādī* (428-450), Khatīb, *wāsī* of the first prince of the blood (thus *wajh* of the *shuhūd* in 422), director of the Madīnat al-Mansūr, and the *qādīs* of the three other districts, Tāhir Tabarī (of the Karkh), Bāy-b-J Jīlī (of the Tāq-Harīm), Muwaqqir (d. 437: of the 'Askar Mahdī), the *qādī* who was canonical advisor of the Caliph, namely AH Māwardī (from 429 to 443); all Shāfi'ites; and their assistants, the Shāfi'ite Baydāwī, the Hanafites Semnānī, Dāmaghānī, and Muhassin Tanūkhī (an enemy of the vizir and anti-Hallāj);

(5) The *shuhūd* (canonical witnesses in the capital for the Community), including, apart from the vizir himself (*sh.* in 414) and Qādī T. Tabarī (*sh.* in 422), the personal advisor of the caliph, Abū Mansūr 'Abd al-Malik ibn Yūsuf (*sh.* in 437: a Hanbalite; patron of the Hallājian Ibn 'Aqīl; heir to the Shāfi'ite *zāhid*[143] AH ibn al-Qazwīnī in 442, director of the

---

[142] Ibn al-Jawzī, *Muntazam* VIII, 127: more than fifty people.
[143] A pupil of Dārikī and thus a Surayjian.

Māristān 'Adudī), two *khaṭībs* (at least) from mosques, M-b-'Alī ibn al-Muhtadī al-Ghārīq, called the "*rāhib* Banī Hāshim" (*sh.* in 422; *wāsī* of the first prince of blood, H-b-'Isā [d. 440], director of the Māristān 'Adudī; qāḍī in 441 of the Mansūr Mosque and of the Jāmi' al-Qasr, dismissed in 451, d. 465), and M-b-'A 'Azīz ibn al-Mahdī (*sh.* in 422); Kh. mosq. Harbīya[144] Rizqallāh Tamīmī ibn Ukayna (*sh.* in 430, d. 488; a Hanbalite), 'Abd al-Wahhāb-b-AH Māwardī (*sh.* in 431, d. 441), M ibn al-Harrānī (d. 438), AJ M ibn al-Muslima, cousin of the vizir (d. 475); the *wukalā' al-quḍāt*, including Ibn al-Wāthiq and Ibn al-Muhassin.[145] In addition to these there was undoubtedly the Sūfī shaykh 'Alī Zawzanī (d. 451: prior of the *ribāt* in the Round City, and a Shāfi'ite), perhaps Shaykh Abū'l-Barakāt-b-Dūst (the first Sūfī grand shaykh of Baghdad, d. 441), and Shaykh Ibn al-'Allāf, a disciple of Ibn Sam'ūn. For in 433 Caliph Qāyim had summoned the *zuhhād* to testify with the *fuqahā'* (at the time of the promulgation of the theological *i'tiqād* drawn up for his father by the hermit AH ibn al-Qazwīnī); and it seems impossible that the new vizir could have undertaken this unusual step toward the rehabilitation of Hallāj on the very day of his investiture, with the cortege that was obliged to escort him from the Mosque of al-Mansūr to the vizirial Dīwān, without the consent of the sovereign. This step must have announced to Shī'ites like the Buwayhid vizir and the 'Alawid *naqīb* the result of a willful act of emancipation by the Caliphate, not only physical, but also spiritual: outside their tutelage.

n. The Prayer and Death of Vizir Ibn al-Muslima (437/1045)

The historian Muhammad 'Abd al-Malik Hamadhānī, an eyewitness to the tragic death of Vizir Ibn al-Muslima, concluded his account of it, which we shall examine further, with the following lines:[146]

And by a strange coincidence, it so happened that, when Ibn al-Muslima was invested with the office of vizir, as he was riding on horseback to the Mosque of al-Mansūr, after having received the robes of honor, he came with his retinue to a tell and said: "this is a holy place; this is the place where al-Hallāj was crucified."[147] Now, Hamadhānī remarks, it had already been a place of worship [long before this event].[148] The vizir got off his horse, performed two *rak'a*, after

---

[144] There were two other *khaṭībs* from the cathedral-mosques of Rusāfa (Tammām-b-Hārūn, 426, d. 447) and of Burāthā.

[145] Ibn al-Jawzī, *Muntazam* VIII, 214.

[146] *Kitāb 'uyūn al-tawārīkh*, excerpt ap. Sibt ibn al-Jawzī, *Mir'āt*, ms. P. 1506, f. 54b. I owe this valuable reference to M. Jawād.

[147] *Maslib al-Hallāj*; on its location, see this edition, 1, 230-231.

[148] An ironic reflection if indeed, as M. Jawād believes, he is referring here to the ancient Mazdaean fire temple of Qatī'at Umm Ja'far called Istanūs.

which he trembled violently. And this led people to say "he is Hallājian in rite."
He remained vizir for twelve years, at the end of which time he was crucified at
this very site. And people said, "now we understand why he had trembled so [a
warning].

We have here the first step leading to a public rehabilitation of Hallāj in
Baghdad. And it must be noted that the vizir who made it had been by
profession a *shāhid*, which is to say one of the officially accredited professional witnesses close to the qāḍī of qāḍīs of the ʿAbbāsid capital.

It is fitting to examine Ibn al-Muslima's religious polity here, in light
of the fact that he was also the only statesman of the Hallājian rite known
to history and because his vizirate was of crucial importance to the
Caliphate. From the standpoint of dogmatics, he guided the anti-
Muʿtazilite reaction begun[149] by Caliph Qādir (*iʿtiqād qādirī* from 408 to
432) toward an official establishment of Ashʿarite theological teaching
reconciled with the mysticism that was to gain approval by the founding
of the Niẓāmīya in Baghdad nine years after his death. From the political
standpoint, he carried out the anti-Shīʿite struggle, also begun by Qādir,
to its conclusion by freeing the Caliphate from the protectorship of the
Buwayhids, and by calling on the military power of the Ghuzz Turks,[150]
the Saljūqs, to rescue it from the menacing propaganda of the Fātimids.

Ibn al-Muslima succeeded in giving to this Sunnite reaction to Shīʿite
propaganda a structure that was to last for two centuries: by officially and
permanently instating the first time in Baghdad two collective modes of
life, the monasteries (of the Sūfīs) and the school of theology (of the
Ashʿarite Shāfiʿites). What he did was to carry out successfully, with the
help of his close friend Abū Ishāq Shīrāzī, the effort outlined vainly by
the Karrāmīya in Khurasan forty years earlier in trying to get Sultan
Mahmūd II to support both their *ribāṭs* (monasteries), whose prior, Abū
Bakr ibn Mamshādh, was spiritual director for a short time at the Ghaz-
navid Court, and their *madrasas* (schools of theology), in which
Muhammad ibn al-Haysam was renovating their dogmatic terminology.
Ibn al-Muslima was a Shāfiʿite. The Shāfiʿites had not yet captured the

149 *Khaṭīb* IV, 37.
150 A Shāfiʿite like AM Qazwīnī, who for the renovation of the anti-Muʿtazilite formula
in 432 had allied himself with the Hanbalite A Yaʿla Farrāʾ, Ibn al-Muslima allied himself
with Hanbalites to bring the Shīʿite suburb of Karkh under control. He created the post of
shaykh al-shuyūkh before 441. He received in Baghdad the Shāfiʿites driven from Khurasan
(*SIJ*, f. 7b: in 445); he lost the support of the Saljūq vizir, Kundurī, a Hanafite and perse-
cutor of Ashʿarism; in 447 he named as *nāzir al-mazālim* (Subkī III, 99) his close friend, the
Ashʿarite Abū Ishāq Shīrāzī (d. 476), his commensal, who would be buried in his family
home in Barb Salīm (East Bank, in Rusāfa), after having served as the first vice chancellor
of the Niẓāmīya (*IJOG* [?], f. 234b).

majority in Baghdad, and the very recent supremacy that they had gained in Khurasan at the expense of the Karrāmīya had just suddenly collapsed, together with their newly formed *madrasas* in Nishapur, stripped of conventual *waqfs*, during the political persecution that the Hanafites (Mu'tazilites), since 429, had been able to instigate with the Saljūq conquerors against Ash'arism.

At the very time that this persecution was being intensified, Ibn al-Muslima, who was compelled to shelter the state under the protection of Tughrīl's Saljūq archers, boldly granted asylum in Baghdad to all of those Shāfi'ite jurisconsults and Ash'arite theologians whom Tughrīl was expelling from Khurasan. In 447, in order to please the Saljūq vizir, Kundurī, he was obliged to appoint a Hanafite, M Damaghānī, qāḍī of qāḍīs; however, this Hanafite had been won over in dogmatics to Ash'arism, and Ibn al-Muslima made him as *nāzir al-mazālim* an assistant to his friend, the Shāfi'ite Abū Isḥāq Shīrāzī.[151]

With regard to the monasteries, Ibn al-Muslima, prior to 440/1049, thought of creating a *shaykh al-shuyūkh*, a kind of general superior of the monasteries (*khawānik*) representing them vis-à-vis the state, due to whom religious communal life was to become regularized and normalized. This office of general superior, destined to give the Shī'ite *naqīb al-tālibīyīn* a more serious Sunnite antagonist than had the 'Abbāsid *naqīb al-nuqabā'*, became very soon the equal of the qāḍī of qāḍīs and remained so for two centuries. After the premature death of its first incumbent, Abū'l-Barakāt Ismā'īl-b-A-b-M-b-Dūst Nīshāpūrī (d. 441/1050), his brother, Abū Sa'd A-b-A-b-M (407, d. 479), who had studied hadīth with him in Damascus in the *khānqāh* of 'Alī Sumaysāṭī (377, d. 453), succeeded him. Housed at first in the small *zāwiya* of AB A-b-Zuhayr Turaythīthī, Abū Sa'd obtained a *waqf* from an associate and friend of Ibn al-Muslima, the 'Amīd al-'Irāq Abū Naṣr Ahmad-b-'Alī, to build the *ribāṭ shaykh al-shuyūkh*. The latter was rebuilt after the 467 flood, thanks to the powerful friendship of Vizir Nizām al-Mulk, whom he had guided in the establishment of the Nizāmīya *waqf*. The *ribat* was erected on the Nahr al-Mu'allā near the Mashra'a.

Linked together in the mind of Vizir Ibn al-Muslima, as well as in the fiscal structure that the political influence of Abū Sa'd was able to devise

---

[151] In 441, he abolished the feast of the 'Ashūrā' in the Karkh (authorized from 334 to 382 and from 389 to 406); in 444, he revived the denunciations of 363 and 402 that accused the Fāṭimids of falsifying their 'Alid genealogy; in 447, he installed the Saljūq Tughrīl in Baghdad.

for them, the *ribāt* and the Nizāmīya *madrasa* provided shelter both for monastic life and Ash'arite theology. Abū Sa'd, who arranged to have himself buried near his friend Abū Ishāq Shīrāzī at Bab Abraz, continually exerted his influence as rector of the Nizāmīya. When he died, the role played by his successors in the position of *shaykh al-shuyūkh* was even greater: an arbitral, political, and even diplomatic role, played by his son, Abū'l-Barakāt Ismā'īl (465, named as early as 479, d. 541), and his grandsons, 'Abd al-Latīf-b-Ismā'īl (513), d. 596: whose son, Abū'l-Barakāt 'Abd al-Rahīm, became *naqīb al-futuwwa*); by those in the office of *shaykh al-shuyūkh* who were descended from Ismā'īl (d. 541) through his daughter Sukayna: 'Abd al-Wahhāb-b-'Alī (519, d. 607), Ibn Sukayna, 'Abd al-Razzāq-b-'Abd al-Wahhāb (d. 625), and M-b-'Abd al-Razzāq (604, d. 644): who was replaced by a foreigner, 'Alī al-Nayyār (643, d. 656), who was the last *shaykh al-shuyūkh* of Baghdad.[152, 153]

This innovation by Ibn al-Muslima was imitated in Khurasan further west: around 549 in Damascus, the son of a disciple of Fārmadhī was appointed *shaykh al-shuyūkh*: Abū'l-Fath 'Umar-b-M-b-Hammūya (513, d. 577), enthroned in Cairo in 569; he held his see in the *ribāt* known as *Khānqāh Sa'īd al-Su'adā'*. He founded a dynasty, the Āl-Hammūya: M-b-'Umar (*sh.* in 577, d. 617), 'Umar-b-M (581, d. 636), 'AA-b-'Umar (d. 642), 'AA-b-M-b-'Umar (d. 678: whose nephew, Ibrāhīm-b-M, son of a famous mystical author, d. 650, converted the Mongol king Ghazan in 694); the office of *shaykh al-shuyūkh* fell then in Cairo to a foreigner, Shams al-Dīn M-b-A Bakr-b-M Ikī (from 678 to 686, d. 697), who dared to have the *dīwān* of Ibn al-Fārid taught and welcomed 'Afīf Tilimsānī; after that the office was taken over by the qādi of qādis, 'Abd al-Rahmān ibn Bint al-'Izz (686, d. 695): before passing in 725 into the hands of the superior of the Siryāqūs *khānqāh*, much diminished from its earlier splendor. Finally, since the sixteenth century, it has become a hereditary office in the Bayt al-Bakrī (first: AB Zaynal Shams D Bakrī, d. 994).

On the Sunnite side, we have four detailed accounts[154] of the death of Ibn al-Muslima: those of Khatīb (d. 463) and Sābī (d. 480), both eyewit-

---

[152] His friends A Ishāq Shīrāzī (*Talbīs*, 404) and A Tayyib Tabarī (*ibid.*, 245-286) were against *samā'* and *hulūl* (*ahdāth*); 'Allāf was against pietism (*ibid.*, 409) and opposed to AT Makkī [no footnote reference given].

[153] It should be noted that Hallāj was, as we have seen, the first apostle of Islam in Turkish lands; and, in another connection, that his dogmatic *'aqīda* has some points in common with the *i'tiqād qādirī* (Shafi'ite: Subkī II, 3) [no footnote reference given].

[154] Khatīb IX, 400-403; Subkī, II, f. 48b and 54a and b; Ibn al-Athīr [bib. no. 420-a] IX, 223-225; Subkī III, 292-296; Yāqūt I, 608 and III, 595.

nesses, the historian Ibn al-Athīr, and the canonist Subkī; and on the Shī'ite side, some hostile notices from his enemy, the *dā'ī* Mu'ayyad Shīrāzī. The following can be extracted from them.

Before he became vizir, Ibn al-Muslima knew that the relentless war of propaganda waged by the Fātimids threatened the very existence of the Sunnite Caliphate, and was able to uncover its leading agent, Mu'ayyad Shīrāzī, whose autobiography gives us all the details of the conspiracy. When this agent briefly won the support of the Buwayhid prince Abū Kālījār, Ibn al-Muslima went in person to Basra and succeeded in getting him driven out and forced back to Cairo (in 439); and, in terms of his own offensive, he paved the way for the return of the Zīrīds of Qayra-wān to allegiance with the 'Abbāsids. This vizir was "the coherer magnet of all our wrongdoings," as Mu'ayyad noted, who, as head of the Fātimid chancellery of Cairo and as grand *dā'ī* of the initiation, engaged him in a merciless duel. Beginning in 443 with Vizir Yazūrī, the Fātimid state made a considerable effort financially to settle the matter of the Baghdad Caliphate once and for all. He secured the complicity of the old *isfahsalar*, Abū'l-Hārith Arslān Basāsīrī, commander-in-chief of the Baghdadian forces since 416 and a personal enemy of Ibn al-Muslima. A first coup d'état, attempted in 446, failed; Basāsīrī, having escaped, took up a position in Rahba with a few loyal troops and within reach of the Fātimid garrisons of Syria. All this while Ibn al-Muslima, putting an end to the Buwayhid sultanate, was ushering in Tughrīl Beg and his Ghuzz archers to Baghdad (447). In 448 (*Safar*), the *dā'ī* Mu'ayyad returned to Rahba from Cairo with the purpose of putting Basāsīrī in command of the final attack. It began with the revolt of a leading accomplice in Wasit, the Buwayhid vizir, Ibn Fusānjus, whom Ibn al-Muslima succeeded in capturing, and executed pitilessly in 449. A second rebel, Quraysh, the 'Uqaylid prince of Mosul, revolted in the north. Finally, the *dā'ī* Mu'ayyad gained the cooperation of a third accomplice, Tughrīl's own brother, Ināl, who promised to revolt at the right moment. But suddenly a palace revolution erupted in Cairo: the Fātimid vizir, Bābilī, who had tried to continue the military and economic effort for which his predecessor, Yazūrī, had become unpopular (*Muharram* 450/March 1053), in his turn fell (on 25 *Rabī'* II 450/June 21, 1058). And, to the great despair of the *dā'ī* Mu'ayyad, the new vizir, Maghribī IV, a Sunnite, who was perhaps secretly won over by Ibn al-Muslima, officially ordered the *dā'ī* to return to Cairo, thus stopping all payment of subsidies to Basāsīrī. Quraysh, defeated by Tughrīl Beg, evacuated Mosul; and Basāsīrī, dis-couraged, was preparing to flee Rahba for Damascus through the desert when suddenly Inal declared himself on the side of the Fatimids (*Shawwal* 450/November 1058) and entered the campaign. Tughril was forced to leave Baghdad in pursuit of Inal, who succeeded in besieging him in Hamadhan. The Khatun, the wife of Tughril, led what remained of the Ghuzz troops in Baghdad to raise the blockade from her husband, whom his vizir, Kundari, was abandoning, leaving Baghdad and fleeing to Ahwaz. Ibn al-Muslima had no one left to defend Baghdad and Caliph Qayim[155] against a sudden attack by Basasiri, who, with a handful of men, entered Karkh during 6-8 *Qa'da*, and had the Fatimid *khutba* pronounced in the Mosque of al-Mansur on Friday the thirteenth and, also in the Mosque of Rusafa, 20 *Qa'da*. With the palace surrounded, Basasiri ordered the bridge of boats at Bab al-Taq rebuilt; and following a foolhardy sortie, with surrender becoming inevitable, Ibn al-Muslima got Basasiri's ally Quraysh, the 'Uqaylid prince of Mosul who was camped to the west (at Bab Basra), to accept his and the Caliph's surrender (on 1 *Hijja* 450/January 19, 1959). But while the Caliph, taken prisoner on 9 *Hijja* in Anbar and afterwards Haditha (from 'Ana), ended up unscathed[156] by the catastrophe, his vizir was immediately demanded back by Basasiri from Quraysh, and even though he had received his command baton from Quraysh as a guarantee of safety, the vizir was handed over to him. Basasiri, leading his enemy away by the sleeve and uttering such ironic greetings at him as "welcome, O destroyer of Empires. . . . O Ajall, forgive us, it was fate—you were a merchant, wearing the *taylasan*, why have you not remained with the women, children, and flocks: how can I, a man of the sword, forgive you [Basasiri had to avenge the pillage of his palace and his harem carried out in reprisal in 446],"[157] protected him from the crowd, giving him a mount, and led him to his tent, from which he had him transferred to the prison of Harim Tahiri. Once there he beat him brutally with his fists, so much that to stop the swelling in his legs, Ibn al-Muslima had to be unchained. On Monday, 28 *Hijja* 450/February 15, 1059, the vizir, in chains again, was led out of Basasiri's prison at Harim Tahiri dressed in a woolen robe,

---

[155] The Hashimites reproached him harshly "*qamarta fi'l-Dawla*', you have played with the Empire like a gambler" (Sabi, f. 50a).

[156] Basasiri, deprived of subsidies, in vain sent an elephant to Cairo with the turban and *shabbak* of Caliph Qayim (Maqrizi [bib. no. 2157A-a] II, 416), whom he "pawned" with a bedouin from Haditha, where the Fatimids should have bought him "for two sous," Mu'ayyad remarked. But the coffers of the Fatimid state were empty, and the bedouin was forced to make a deal with Tughril Beg, to whom Qayim was given.

[157] Basasiri had at that time issued a decree declaring anyone who would not assist in the capture of Ibn al-Muslima an outlaw (*halal al-damm*) (Sabi, f. 8a).

wearing a pointed red felt cap on his head, and around his neck a collar with leather strips serving as amulets, hoisted up on a camel, with a man seated behind him who was beating him with a leather whip; and Ibn al-Muslima was reciting the following (Qur'ān 3:25): "Say: God is the Lord of power. He gives it to whomsoever He wishes. He takes it away from whomsoever He wishes." Then he was paraded around Baghdad and through Karkh, where the crowd hurled rubbish, curses, and obscenities at him. The procession halted briefly in front of the Caliphal palace on the west bank (where the vizir had had Ibn Fusānjus crucified the year before);[158] then it returned to the campsite in the Sūq al-Maristān (al-'Adudī) where a gibbet had been erected, at Bab Khurasan opposite the turba of Gharīb al-Khāl.[159] There, the vizir was taken down from the camel and sewn inside the hide of a bull[160] that had just been skinned; its horns were fitted on his head, and two iron butcher's hooks were run through the two corners of his jaw. When he was hoisted up onto the post,[161] he said: "say to the Ajall: you have done as you wished with me: give me a task to do, and you will see how I served you; if you kill me, tomorrow the Sultan of Khurasan (= Tughrīl) will return, but he will be the end of the people and the country."[162] They defiled him, but gave him drink.[163] Now, Basāsīrī had ordered two hooks to be driven in under the collar-bone so that he would stay alive for several days to suffer in this way, but he would be forced each day to swallow a biscuit as nourishment. However, the officials in charge of the execution were afraid that Basāsīrī might grant the vizir a pardon, and this is why the two hooks were driven into a fatal spot.[164] Before he died, Ibn al-Muslima said "Glory be to God Who let me live in happiness and die in martyrdom." He continued to stir until the hour of the 'asr prayer, when he expired.[165]

[158] On 19 *Safar* 449, in the Najmī garden, he was hoisted onto a camel, dressed in a red robe, with a red cap on his head and, over his forehead, a diadem consisting of some coins struck in the name of the Fātimid Caliph, which had been seized from among his possessions. While he was being paraded around the city, a man seated behind him [on the camel] beat him, saying "this is the reward for the ungrateful one who behaved badly towards his benefactor." On the gibbet, his head was tied between his legs; when the head was cut off, the trunk was thrown to the dogs, who devoured it (Sābī, ap. Sibt ibn al-Jawzī, f. 22b).

[159] Khatīb says "facing turbas."

[160] Cf. the skin of a cow (sacrifice: Qur'ān 2:68-71: cf. 'Āyisha).

[161] "On a high post"; Ibn Ma'mūn, his messenger in the service of Tughrīl, was hung on another post.

[162] Only Sābī mentions this.   [163] *Istaqawhu.*

[164] In the heart, Subkī says. This punishment (*qunnāra*) was restored around 680 by the Juwaynīs (Fuwatī, 410).

[165] Basāsīrī had M Hibatallāh-b-H ibn al-Ma'mūn, Qāyim's envoy in the service of

The savagery of this personal act of vengeance did not reconcile Basāsīrī with the Fātimids' new vizir, Ibn al-Maghribī,[166] who disavowed him in writing and refused him reinforcements. Consequently, at the end of a year, on 6 Qa'da 451/December 14, 1059,[167] Basāsīrī was defeated and killed by the army of Tughrīl, who reestablished once and for all Caliph Qāyim and the 'Abbāsid khutba in Baghdad. Ibn al-Muslima's heirs held the office of Major Domo (ustādh al-dār) in the Palace for a century.

o. The Apologia and the Retraction of Ibn 'Aqīl (465/1072)

A second attempt to rehabilitate Hallāj was the composition by a famous Hanbalite canonist, 'Alī ibn 'Aqīl[168] of an apologia, *juz' fī nusrat al-Hallāj*, a work kept secret until 461/1067, when it was disclosed. During a sickness, Ibn 'Aqīl, who at the time was thirty years old, had entrusted to a certain Ma'ālā al-Hā'ik some papers to be burned in the event of his death. Hā'ik found among them, together with some notes on Mu'tazilism[169] "an early work in which Ibn 'Aqīl had interpreted the discourses (aqwāl) and poetical works (ash'ār) of Hallāj": to vindicate him, and he decided to turn them over to the head of the Hanbalites, Abū Ja'far 'Abd al-Khāliq-b-'Īsā-b-A ibn Abī Mūsā (d. 470),[170] who, as it happened, had just had Qādir's anti-Mu'tazilite edict read again from the pulpit. After remaining in hiding for five years in the Palace (at Bab al-Maratib), Ibn 'Aqīl had to resign himself to writing and to signing, by order of the head of his rite, an official statement of retraction, in which the following paragraph was included: "I believed that Hallāj was a good Muslim, an ascetic, and that he performed miracles; I even maintained that in a treatise that I wrote. I ask God to forgive me for this; I realize

---

Tughrīl, crucified alongside him, while his ally Quraysh was having Abū Nasr A-b-'Alī, the 'amid al-'Irāq, drowned near Takrit (ms. BN 2145, f. 6a and f. 12b).

[166] Who turned out to be, quite unusually, not a Shī'ite, but a Shāfi'ite Sunnite, and had had to complain about Basāsīrī.

[167] Or 14 Hijja 451/January 21, 1060, according to Khatīb, who detailed his crucifixion *post mortem* at a gate of the palace (Bāb al-Nūbī): perhaps in reparation for the execution of his friend, the vizir (XI, 392).

[168] Sibt Ibn al-Jawzī, f. 117a: born Jumāda II 431; died 12 Jumāda I 513/August 21, 1119; his house was in the Zafarīya quarter. He owed his exceptional culture to the ten-year support of a powerful and generous patron, Shaykh Abū Mansūr 'Abd al-Malik-b-M ibn Yūsuf (d. 460: *Funūn*, f. 235); his master in Hanbalism was Abū Ya'lā ibn al-Farrā' (*ibid.*, f. 18b). Cf. also Alūsī, *Jalā*, 99.

[169] Based on Ibn al-Walīd, who was also a protégé of Abū Mansūr, *SIJ*, *loc. cit.*, f. 112a.

[170] A Hāshimite, nephew of the Hanbalite qādī Ibn Abī Mūsā (d. 428: Khatīb I, 354; V, 65, cf. 'Akarī III, 339, 239), and great-grandson of the *naqab* of the Hāshimites (Khatīb II, 405).

that he was executed by decision of the *ijmā'* of the *'ulamā'* of his time, that they were right, and that he was a sinner." He signed it on Wednesday, 10 *Muharram* 465/1072, and read it in public the next day.[171]

The intolerance toward Ibn 'Aqīl on the part of the Hanbalites stemmed from the fact that he had undertaken to delve into speculative theology and had studied Mu'tazilism with M-b-A ibn al-Walīd (d. 478).[172] But to accuse him of being both a Hallājian and a Mu'tazilite was ridiculous. In dogmatics, Ibn 'Aqīl leaned strongly toward Ash'arism; he had signed, around 455, the *fatwā* protesting against its persecution,[173] and it was he who, in 476, performed the ablutions on the body of his friend, Abū Ishāq Shīrāzī, the Ash'arite rector of the Nizāmīya.[174] His forced retraction represents one episode in the struggle carried on by conservative Hanbalites against Ash'arite Shāfi'ites, who got back at them five years later when Abū Ishāq Shīrāzī succeeded in getting Abū Ja'far ibn Abī Mūsā[175] arrested.

Ibn 'Aqīl, who occupies a unique place in the history of Hanbalism, is also the author of a *Kitāb al-funūn*, a huge collection of anecdotes about the attitudes and customs of his times, in one hundred volumes. Ibn al-Jawzī has preserved for us in his *Talbīs Iblīs* and elsewhere only a tiny portion in the ten volumes of extracts he had chosen.[176] In these Ibn 'Aqīl is shown as being severe about the life style and behavioral excesses of Sūfīs, warning his contemporaries especially of the dangers to their common rule of life of allowing women and young people into their monasteries, affiliations, and recitals. However, he took from them a

[171] Ibn Rajab (d. 795), *Tabaqāt* [bib. no. 570-a] (Leipzig ms.), f. 32a (Goldziher's commentary, *ZDMG*, LXII (1908), 18-21).

[172] Cf. Sibt ibn al-Jawzī, *loc. cit.*, ms. P. 1506, f. 190b: pupil of Abū'l-Husayn Basrī. Ibn 'Aqīl had in no way adopted the ideas of Ibn al-Walīd; he even left us a summary (ms. P. 1506, f. 191a = Suyūtī, ms. P. 3068, f. 21a-b = [. . .] *Yahuda* ms.) of his attitude about putting *liwāt* [pederasty] among the joys allowed in Paradise; with a refutation of it made by the Zaydite Abū Yūsuf Qazwīnī (d. 488). It is interesting that the latter had specifically written a collection of *Akhbār al-Hallāj*, some ironic and hostile fragments of which have come down to us, a work opposing the apologia of Ibn 'Aqīl.

[173] Subkī IV, 260.

[174] Subkī III, 96; prior to his burial in Vizir al-Muslima's family home.

[175] Subkī III, 99.

[176] Mustaphā Jawād, in the course of his studies of the period of Caliph al-Nāsir li-Dīn Allāh, rediscovered a volume of *Kitāb al-funūn* (= ms. P. 787), and it is to him that we owe many of the references included here. A complete copy of it (*waqf* from 528: 'Akarī IV, 85) was kept in a *ribāt* called the Ma'mūnīya, founded by Zumurrud Khātūn, the mother of Nāsir (Sibt Ibn al-Jawzī, ms. P. 1506, f. 117a), who had acquired Ibn 'Aqīl's library, purchased and "*waqf*ed" by the Hanbalite jurisconsult 'AA-b-Mubārak ibn Ināl 'Ukbarī (d. 528) and by the historian A-b-Sālih ibn Shāfi' (d. 465): its *wakīl* was Abū'l-Sa'ādāt Diyā' D ibn al-Nāqid. Ibn al-Jawzī had seen only 157 of its 200 volumes (*Manāqib Ibn Hanbal*, 527).

method of prayer, in which he claimed to be the disciple of three of their masters: Abū Bakr Dīnawārī[177] and Abū'l-Husayn Qazwīnī (d. 442) in *zuhd*, and Ibn al-'Allāf in *wa'z* (for the sermons that he himself preached until the incident in 461/1067). Since the latter two were trained by Ibn Sam'ūn, we base the *isnād* of 'Aqīl's "Hallājism" there.[178]

He retracted it, but only in a forced manner, and did not destroy his *nusra*[179] *intisār*, since a hundred years later it was refuted by Abū'l-Baqā' Azajī (d. 591: *Radd 'alā Abī'l-Wafā' ibn 'Aqīl*), and later adapted by Ibn al-Ghazzāl.[180] It appears to be lost, although we should not exclude the possibility of its being identical with the strange recension of the *Akhbār al-Hallāj* that includes the *ta'rīkh* ms. 1291 of the Taymūr collection,[181] in which excerpts from Ibn Bākūyā (*Bidāya*), deliberately changed, are inserted[182] to vindicate Hallāj. Ibn 'Aqīl undoubtedly relied on this collection of prose and verse (*aqwāl, ash'ar = ash'ar, munājāt*), which we attribute to Fāris[183] and which forms the nucleus of the *Akhbār al-Hallāj*. And this gives special weight to the following indication from Hujwīrī concerning a Sūfī "very fond of Hallāj" who died before 469.[184] "In Iraq I saw Abū Ja'far (Ibn al-Misbāh) Saydalānī and four thousand others calling themselves Hallājīya, who were all excommunicating Fāris" for his *hulūlī* interpretation of Hallāj's teaching. The collection of Fāris, a Hanafite (and thus hated by the Shāfi'ites), assembled a century earlier in Khurasan, and possibly denounced in Baghdad by some Shāfi'ite[185] refugee, had just had attention drawn to it, and by whom other than Ibn 'Aqīl?

---

[177] Sibt ibn al-Jawzī, ms. [P.] 1506, f. 295a; Sam'ānī, f. 238a; *Funūn* 6, f. 247b.

[178] Cf. *isnād*, ap. Ibn al-Jawzī, *Talbīs*, 273.

[179] Whose exact title, in the opinion of Mustaphā M Jawād, should be *Risālat al-intisār*: the *risāla* transmitted to the learned Hanbalite from Damascus, 'Āyisha-bt-M-b-'Abd al-Hādī Maqdisīya (723, d. 816), by A Nasr M ibn al-Sharāzī (d. 682), *rāwī* of 'Alī-b-'AR ibn al-Jawzī (d. 630), *rāwī* of A Fath M-b-Yahyā ibn Marāhib-b-Isrā'īl Baradānī, born in 499, died in 583 (Rūdānī, *Silat* [bib. no. 834-a], ms. P. 4470, f. 76a).

[180] Dhahabī, *Ta'rīkh*, s.a. 591. For Ibn al-Ghazzāl, cf. this edition, 2, 478.

[181] In Cairo. Analyzed ap. our 1936 edition, pp. 9-10.

[182] The following is a list of parallelisms (between AT = *Akhbār*, T. ms., and IB = *Bidāya*): AT 21 abridges IB 9, Part 2; AT 19 turns the conclusion of IB II around in favor of Hallāj; AT 68 reproduces IB 12; AT 69 abridges IB 15; AT 18 (seventh indented line) relates to IB 7; lastly, AT 71-72, concerning Ibn Surayj, and AT 61, where Junayd is refuted, have a distinct apologetic tone; and the long commentary in paragraph 19 concerning the verses found in *Dīwān*, p. 103 (at the bottom of the page), published App. 4 in the 1936 edition, is connected with a text of Ibn Abī'l-Khayr (d. 440) given in the *tafsīr* of Fakhr Rāzī (I, 53) via Salmān Ansārī. All of that seems rather to belong to the period of Ibn 'Aqīl.

[183] This edition, 2, 198.   [184] *Kashf*.

[185] They left Nishapur in 427, Rayy in 429; and the persecution of the Ash'arites (which overtook them) began in 446.

The Hallājian revival brought about among the Shāfiʿites and Ashʿarites of Baghdad because of the position taken by Vizir Ibn al-Muslima and the apologia of Ibn ʿAqīl[186] explains the scruple behind Ghazālī's feeling that it was necessary to devise a formula of reconciliation for readmitting Hallāj into the Islamic Community.

p. The Hallājian Revival in Baghdad Following the Death of Ibn al-Muslima. The Saljūq Influence. The Ashʿarite Offensive of the Khurasanians, and the Hostile Reaction of the Hanbalites

Ibn al-Muslima, a Shāfiʿite, had had the constant support of the Hanbalites against the Shīʿite threat, politically speaking; but in theology, his advisors and friends increasingly advocated the teaching of Ashʿarism to use against the infiltrations of Ismāʿīlī propaganda. Despite the prejudices of his rite against scholasticism, a Hanbalite like Ibn ʿAqīl realized the need for a metaphysics to defend Sunnite Islam. The coordination of the Sūfī pious foundations, instituted by Ibn al-Muslima under a single head, the *shaykh al-shuyūkh*, and intended, in his mind, to give the masses of Sunnite faithful a mystical ideal capable of countering the Shīʿite devotion to the Imāms, had been suggested to him by his Hallājism; and it was going to be used to finance (through its *waqfs*) and to vitalize (through a Hallājian mysticism) the first orthodox university of Islam, the Nizāmīya.

Thanks to Ibn al-Muslima, the memory of Hallāj came to inspire a movement of spiritual renewal in Baghdad. The movement, curiously enough, was the work almost exclusively of foreigners, of Khurasanians.[187] Certainly the old Hanbalite milieu of Baghdad was not without its secret admirers of Hallāj, but periodically it rose up in rebellion against these foreign Ashʿarite supporters of theological innovations and against disreputable admirers of Hallāj.

The revival took two officially authorized forms: the founding of Sūfī monasteries, and the organizing of sermons by preachers; most of the priors of monasteries and sermon writers happened to be in Khurasan.

Ibn al-Muslima (together with his friend Abū Nasr) had founded the *ribāt shaykh al-shuyūkh*; its second prior, Abū Saʿd (441, d. 479), succeeded in 459, under the prompting of the Saljūq vizir, Nizām al-Mulk,

---

[186] [See George Makdisi, *Ibn ʿAqīl et la résurgence de l'Islam traditionaliste au XIe siècle*, Damascus, 1963, for a thorough study of this important figure.—H.M.]

[187] Official representation of the Saljūqs, who *named* the rector of the Nizāmīya (cf. Sanjar in 517, then Bāqarhī, then Asʿad Meghanī: Subkī IV, 268).

in founding the Nizāmīya, whose first rector was the friend of Ibn al-Muslima, Abū Ishāq Shīrāzī,[188] whose body at his death would be washed by Ibn 'Aqīl.[189]

Abū'l-Ghanā'im ibn Mahlabān,[190] a nobleman from Jazira and *nā'ib* for the citadel of Takrit for the 'Uqaylids since 448 (he defended it magnificently at the time of the catastrophe of 450), devoted himself in a chivalric way to the protection of the wife and children of his friend Ibn al-Muslima, and succeeded in saving along with them in Mayafariqin (in the care of the Kurd amīr A-b-Marwān [401, d. 453] close to the learned Shāfi'ite M-b-Kāzarūnī [d. 455], a friend of Abū Ishāq Shīrāzī), the widow of the heir to the Caliphate, the Armenian Urjuwān Qurrat al-'Ayn and her child, the future Caliph Muqtadī, the *qaharmāna* Wisāl and Abū Mansūr-b-Yūsuf, the friend of Qāyim under whose protection Ibn 'Aqīl wrote his apologia of Hallāj. He brought them back to Baghdad in 452, and founded there the Ibn Mahlabān (or Bistāmī) *ribāt*, whose priors would be AH Bistāmī (d. 493), followed by the grandson Tāhir-b-Sa'īd (d. 542), of Ibn Abī'l-Khayr, the great pro-Hallāj mystic.[191] The very devout Urjuwān (d. 512)[192] in his turn, founded his own *ribāt* (= *jadīd*), which I believe was identical with the Ikhlātīya *ribāt* (= of the Armenian)[193] or the *turba* of Saljūqa Khātūn (eponym Nāsir 583, d. 584: for his paranymph was the prior of the Ribāt Urjuwānī,[194] the future monastery of the Bektashīs). It must also have been she who founded the first convent for women in Islam in Baghdad, with the prioress being Fātima (d. 521), the daughter of Ibn Fadlawayh, from Rayy,[195] an admirer of Ibn Sam'ūn; it must have been the famous Dār al-Falak, which was surely patronized also by the Saljūq princesses.[196] In this period, in fact, women played an important role in the dynastic story and in the pious foundations (because of their dowries); indeed around Qāyim there were his

---

[188] Subkī III, 96.

[189] The B. al-Muslima family founded a *ribāt* (Ibn Ra'ys al-Ru'asā', in the Palace) (Ibn al-Najjār, ms. P. 2131, f. 86a; Bundārī, ms. P. 6152, f. 71b—Dubaythī, ms. P. 5922, f. 6a, 7a; Ibn al-Dā'ī, 56), and undertook to found the Zawzanī *ribāt* where it had a *turba* (after its *turba* at Bāb Abraz).

[190] Athīr IX, 417, 432; X, 205, 289-290. The account (truncated in the Tornberg edition) by Ibn al-Athīr of the rebellion led by Abū'l-Ghanā'im ibn Fusānjus (d. 449) in Wasit forced Zambaur (s.v.) to combine both "Abū'l-Ghanā'ims."

[191] Athīr X, 205; 'Akarī, s.a.; *tarā'iq*.

[192] It was in his *turba* in the Qasr 'Īsā that Caliphs Muqtadī' and Mustadī were interred (Harawī, ms. P. 5975, f. 67a).

[193] Ibn al-Sā'ī, 189 n. = Yāqūt, *Udabā'*, VI, 231. His alms to Sūfis (ms. P. 1570, f. 24b).

[194] Ms. P. 2064, f. 153a.

[195] Rāwiya of A-J M-b-al-Muslima, and of Khatīb, d. 465.

[196] Sibt ibn al-Jawzī, 78.

mother, Qatr al-Nadā (362, d. 452); his sister, Fāṭima (d. 448); his daughter, Sayyida Khātūn (d. 496);[197] the widow of Tughrīl; his own Saljūq widow, Khadīja Arslān Khātūn-bt-Chaghrī Dāwūd (who withdrew in 474 to the court of Isfahan).[198] Then in the Saljūq court itself, whose ambitious princesses, coming from Isfahan, had close ties with Baghdad, there were the old Khātūn, Tughrīl's first wife; Shāh Khātūn-bt-Qadrkhān I, wife of Alp Arslān (widow of the Ghaznavid Mas'ūd, d. 433);[199] and the three wives of Malikshāh (447, sultan in 465, d. 485). The first of these three wives was Zubayda Khātūn-bt-Yāqūtī-b-Chaghrī Dāwūd, mother of Ahmad, of Barqiyāruq (487, d. 498), and of three daughters, one of whom was married to the Ghaznavid Ibrāhīm (d. 492),[200] the other to the Ilekkhan Ahmad II (d. 488), the third, Mahemulk: in 474 her mother came to Baghdad to marry her off to Caliph Muqtadī (d. 482; repudiated in 480).[201] The second wife of Malikshāh, Khātūn Jalālīya-bt-'Īsā[202] (d. 487), the mother of Mahmūd (485, d. 487), tried to gain the upper hand in Baghdad, and seized control of Takrit. The third, Tārkān Khātūn Safariya, the mother of Sanjar[203] (reigned 491-552) and of Muhammad (498-511), the grandmother of Mas'ūd[204] (527-547), was married in 471, died in 515; she was a benefactress of the Holy Places, and also managed to get Caliph Mustazhir (d. 512), who had married her daughter 'Ismat Khātūn (in 502), to build a ribāt for the Sūfī 'Alī-b-Hy Ghaznawī (d. 551). Ahmad Ghazālī was the one who delivered her funeral oration,[205] and she must have patronized him, enabling him to reside both in the palace of her grandson, Mahmūd II (511-525), and in the Behrūz ribāt, where he read portions of the Tawāsīn from the pulpit.

It should be noted that three of these Saljūq sultanas were daughters of Ilekkhans; that the Uyghur dynasty was fervent in its Sunnism and very partial to writers of mystical sermons; that Hallāj at that time (as the dīwāns of Ahmad Yasawī and 'Attār prove) was the main subject of mystical sermons in Transoxiana; and that it was immediately after Hallāj's mission to their lands, two centuries earlier, that the first Ilekkhan had converted to Islam. One can therefore say that Tārkān Khātūn encouraged the diffusion of Hallājian sermons in Baghdad.

---

[197] Ibid., 6.   [198] Athīr, s.v.
[199] Ilekkhanid, d. 412; her daughter was therefore older than Alp Arslān, born in 420, who must have married her for her superior breeding (Rāwandī, s.v.).
[200] Rāwandī, Rāhat, s.v.   [201] Athīr, s.v.   [202] Athīr X, 419.
[203] Sanjar married the Ilekkhanid Tarkan Khātūn-bt-M Arslān (Rāwandī, s.v.).
[204] Mas'ūd married 'Arab Khātūn (Rāwandī, s.v.) Tagr., ms. P. 1780, f. 27a.
[205] Sibt ibn al-Jawzī (1907 ed.), 61.

The movement of pro-Hallāj and Ash'arite mystical Khurasanian preachers formed in opposition to the Ismā'īlīs started in Baghdad in 447 with Vizir ibn al-Muslima and AQ Qushayrī, who had fled Saljūq persecution (Tughrīl's Hanafism made him anti-Ash'arite) and published his famous *risāla*, which affirms Hallāj's orthodoxy in the introduction to a synthesis of Sūfism and Ash'arism.

In 469 the latter's son, Abū Nasr 'A Rahīm Qushayrī (d. 514), carried on the same work, while residing in the *ribāt shaykh al-shuyūkh* and teaching at the Nizāmīya; it met strong resistance from the Hanbalites, including a riot, for which Nizām al-Mulk held the 'Abbāsid vizir, Ibn Juhayr, responsible (in 471).[206]

Next are three sermonizers, Shaydhalā' Jīlī (d. 494),[207] 'Abbādī Ardashīr[208] (485, d. 496) and 'Īsā-b-'UA Ghaznawī[209] (former *kātib* of the vizir in Ghazna), driven out (493, d. 497). The first preached on Hallāj at Bab Azaj, as an Ash'arite and as an assistant of the grand qādī; the second, a friend of AH Ghazālī; and the third *r*esided in the *ribāt shaykh al-shuyūkh*. Riots in 493.

Then came the following: Ahmad Ghazālī (d. 520), whose Hallājism will be examined shortly, his friends and disciples: Abū'l-Fath Harbī[210] (d. 514), Abū'l-Fath M-b-Fadl Isfarā'inī (474, d. 538;[211] preached from 515 to 521, 530 to 537; expelled in the years between), Muzaffar-b-Ardashīr ibn al-'Abbādī[212] (491, d. 547: official envoy of Sanjar), Shibāb M-b-Mahmūd Sanabadhi Tūsī[213] (522, d. 597; preached from 547 to 574). The Ash'arite sermonizer movement declined after 540 with the decline of the Saljūqs, and due to a growing reaction from the Hanbalite conservative party, buttressed by two preachers in the foreground: 'Abd al-Qādir Bushtīrī[214] Kīlānī (d. 561; after 520), and Ibn al-Jawzī (510, d. 597; after 545). Kīlānī, who personally was pro-Hallāj (in the earlier manner of Harawī), made only brief references to Hallāj in his genuine homilies; and these long poetic parables glorifying his martyrdom, and published later, could only have been sketched out in a select gathering before being orchestrated by a stylist[215] like Ibn al-Ghazzāl or Ibn al-Mansūrī. As for Ibn al-Jawzī, Kīlānī's rival and enemy, he did not conceal his hatred of Hallāj, but he was alone in this. Indeed, he himself ac-

[206] Cf. Subkī IV, 251. In 476, the preacher AB Bakrī, *muqri'*, also a representative.
[207] Cf. his *Lawāmi'*, studied by S. Pines.
[208] Sibt ibn al-Jawzī, 4.
[209] *Ibid.*, 6, 9.   [210] *Ibid.*, 4.   [211] *Ibid.*, 58.
[212] *Ibid.*, 77.   [213] *Ibid.*, 307; Dubaythī, ms. P. 5921, f. 137a.
[214] [See 2, 356 in this edition.]
[215] Abū Shāma, *Dhayl*, ms. P. 5852, f. 20b-26a.

knowledged that the majority of sermonizers were pro-Hallāj.[216] Sixty years after his death, at the time of the Mongol sacking of Baghdad, Ash'arite scholasticism had conquered the Sunnite world thanks to the professors of the Nizāmīya;[217] the institution of *shaykh al-shuyūkh* had been duplicated in Syria, Egypt, and Khurasan, where *ribāts* for men and for women had multiplied, in which the Hallājian mystical experience increasingly became the object of study and discussion; moving beyond, penetrating far into India and Turkestan, bordering on the Saljūq empire, it continued its emphasis on apologetics and its inter-religious efficiency in infidel lands.

q. Ahmad Ghazālī

We are able to evaluate the teaching of Ahmad Ghazālī[218] thanks to excerpts of sermons[219] he delivered in Baghdad in the *ribāt* that the *shīhna* Behrūz had been ordered by the Saljūq sultan to build for him. He exhibited in these an unusual literary boldness in preaching a universalistic monotheism that ran the risk of divulging the secret mystical teaching that at times tempted his brother; the same teaching, before him, of their joint masters Abū Bakr Nassāj, Fārmadhī, Jurjānī: thus going back, in Khurasan, to Abū Sa'īd.[220] And it is this teaching that Ahmad Ghazālī's favorite disciple, 'Ayn al-Qudāt Hamadhānī, will finally make known.

According to this teaching, God moves all creatures to love Him, the chosen as well as the damned, each in his own way; confessional denominations are empty appearances; beyond faith and infidelity, there is *ikhlās*, the saints' purity of intention towards the Beloved.[221] Ahmad judges the prophets in a sarcastic, off-handed way as follows: Abraham, according to him, was sick with the jaundice of love, imagining he saw God successively in the light of a star (= the damned, as 'AQ Hamadhānī[222] was to specify), of the moon (= Iblīs, 'AQH), and of the sun (= Muhammad, 'AQH),[223] because the lover believes he sees the Be-

---

[216] *Talbīs*, 183.

[217] At the end of the sixth century, Mosul was won over by Ash'arism over the opposition of the Hanbalites (and the 'Adawīya, the future Yezidis) (Safadī, ms. P. 2064, f. 160a).

[218] Corresponded with Sanjār (*SIJ* [Sibt ibn al-Jawzī], 73).

[219] Collected by Sā'id-b-Fāris Labbānī (*Majālis Baghdādīya*, Subkī IV, 54).

[220] Also to Qushayrī; and even to Husrī, saying *"min al-shaytān al-rajīm"* without *isti'ādha* (Sha'rāwī, *Lawāq* I, 123).

[221] 'AQ Hamadhānī, *Maktūbāt*, f. 345a = *Kanz*, f. 12a = *Tamhīdāt*, ms. [P., Persian supplement] 1356, f. 39a. This theory has the advantage of avoiding any hint of divine *hulūl* in the saints.

[222] Ibn Hamdūn, *Tadhk.*, ms. P. 3324, f. 54b; 'AQ Hamadhānī, *Kanz*, f. 33b-34a.

[223] In the pseudo Kīlānī (*Fusūl*), star = *nafs*, moon = *qalb*, sun is *sirr*.

loved everywhere. Jesus was unable to practice complete abandon; he had a sewing needle in his pocket.[224] Even Muhammad himself is not shielded from the criticism of Ash'arite sermonizers formed by Ahmad Ghazālī. A Fath Isfarā'inī has [the Prophet] say: "I am a blind man among the blind, a lost man (cf. Qur'ān 93:7) among the lost." A Fath Harbī has him reproached by Gabriel with a repudiation on grounds of sickness.[225] Ahmad Ghazālī himself shows Muhammad out of jealousy refusing to accept keys from God which God does not need.[226] Iblīs, on the other hand, has Ahmad's complete sympathy: it was through love that he was damned, the love of hearing God speak the final $y\bar{a}$ of his damnation (la'natī), just as Muhammad loved His delivering the kāf ('alayk) of his election.[227] Ahmad Ghazālī pities [Iblīs], for the martyrdom of love in which he is imprisoned out of a subtle jealousy; a martyrdom that will last only for awhile, for Iblīs is holy. And this is the point where Ahmad Ghazālī lights upon the Tawāsīn of Hallāj, using what Iblīs says in it to Moses[228] to illustrate his teaching from the pulpit, but without daring to cite his source, which 'AQ Hamadhānī would later be the first to cite by name.[229]

If we compare this closely with the original dialogue between Iblīs and Moses found in the Tawāsīn, that is, Ahmad Ghazālī's highly colored version, embellished with personal reflection: "he who does not learn tawhīd in the school of Iblīs is only a zindīq," and "when Iblīs was damned, nothing was taken away from him in terms of his service, his love, or his memento of God," we see that Ahmad opted for the "satanic" interpretation of the Tawāsīn, setting up as his model the extreme insolence of Iblīs's loving despair. His master Jurjānī, who had called himself a "disciple (murīd) of Iblīs," called Iblīs "the Master of masters, the Prince of the forsaken (Khāja-i khājagān, server-i mahjūran)."[230] The interpolation in Tawāsīn, chapter VI, 20-25, of the famous parable in which Hallāj is supposed to combine his "I (am the Truth)" with two blasphemies, the "I (am worth more than Adam)" of Iblīs and the "I (am

---

[224] Recueil, p. 97.
[225] Sibt ibn al-Jawzī (1907 ed.), 58, 77.
[226] Recueil, p. 97.
[227] 'Ishqīya, ms. P., Persian suppl. 1851, f. 144a; Sawānih, f. 35a. 'AQ Hamadhānī, Maktūbāt, f. 282b; Kanz, f. 34b; Tamhīdāt, ms. P. Persian suppl. 1356, f. 42a, 71b; Qur'ān 38:78; hadith.
[228] Tawāsīn VI, 13-17 = Ahmad Ghazālī, ap. Ibn al-Jawzī, Qussās, f. 117a, ap. Ibn Abī'l-Hadīd, Sharh al-nahj, ap. Sha'rāwī, Lawāqih (1343 ed.), 57 (Recueil, p. 96).
[229] Maktūbāt, f. 126b.
[230] Recueil, p. 102; 'AQ Hamadhānī, Maktūbāt, f. 42b, 53b.

your supreme Lord)" of Fir'awn, must therefore date prior to Jurjānī.[231]

In his *Intuitions of Lovers*[232] published in Persian by 'AQ Hamadhānī, Ahmad recalls two well-known[233] Sūfī anecdotes to present Hallāj: first, as the thief who suffers without flinching a flagellation consisting of a thousand blows, and afterwards says "my Beloved was with me; the power of His contemplation enabled me to endure"; and secondly, as the bandit (*'ayyār*)[234] who, while his hands and feet were being cut off, smiled: "what are you [smiling at]?" "Don't be astonished at my joy: my Beloved is with me, my Father[235] looks down at me with grace; the power of His contemplation overcomes me; the violence of His appearance distracts me from myself:

> He, He is going to kill me, —and I, I am enraptured in Him;
> In the thrust of His sword, —there is such beauty."[236]

Two other Baghdad mystics whose Hallājism was more penetrating objected to this aesthetics of despair, this paradoxical eulogy of a sadistic victimal devotion. Yūsuf Hamadhānī, in 505/1111, singling out one of Ahmad Ghazālī's sermons, discussed his "satanic" inspiration; and his disciple 'Abd al-Qādir Kīlānī, battling on this terrain later against the disciples of Ahmad Ghazālī, was to repudiate, in two celebrated parables, any effort to assimilate the tender and self-renunciatory "I" of Hallāj with the aggressive and jealous "I" that caused Iblīs to be damned.[237]

r. 'Ayn al-Qudāt Hamadhānī

'Abdallāh-b-M Miyānajī of Hamadhan, a pupil of M-b-Hammūya Juwaynī, became the favorite disciple, the "spiritual son," of Ahmad Ghazālī immediately following his sojourn in Hamadhan. A Shāfi'ite qādī, trained also in mathematics and in Avicennian philosophy, 'Ayn al-Qudāt was hanged in his thirty-third year in Hamadhan: on 23 *Jumāda* II 525/May 23, 1131, by order of Sultan Mahmūd, along with several

---

[231] It dates back possibly to AB Wāsitī (the theory about the "fermentation" of the divine "I," ap. Baqlī, *Tafsīr* I, 245; P., p. 936), although it already includes *futuwwa*.

[232] *Sawānih*, ap. *Recueil*, p. 95 = French tr., ap. *Commerce* VI (1925), 161-163.

[233] AH Ghazālī, *Kimiyā*, ap. Ritter, *Elixir*, p. 171, and *Philologika* VII, 94-95.

[234] Hallāj here is the patron saint of the *futuwwa* of the *'ayyārīn*; he repeats the words of Khālid, an *'ayyār* who was admired by Ibn Hanbal (*Talbīs*, 421; cf. also Kattānī, Qush., 91).

[235] 'AQ Hamadhānī alluded to that.

[236] A.G. repeats these verses, f. 79b (cf. 68b), as having been uttered by Hallāj at the moment when the Beloved had the leather execution mat spread out, and when the lover, on the verge of being put to death, felt himself in an ecstasy of love. The reference to Qur'ān 20:72 is found ap. *Ikhwān* IV, 146, and ap. Ibn al-Fārid.

[237] 'Attār (ap. *Tadhk.*), R Baqlī (*Sharh al-tawāsin*), J Rūmī, Semnānī will maintain this opposition, against assimilation, advocated by the school of Ibn 'Arabī.

high officials with whom he had close ties, notably the atabeg Shīrgīr of Abhar.[238] He had been imprisoned in Baghdad for several months (which is where he wrote in Arabic the *Shakwa*, the moving epistle in which he tried to explain some of the mystical ideas that had incriminated him).[239]

The 'Ayn al-Qudāt case is an important one. Less of an aesthetician, more fervent and more sincere than Ahmad Ghazālī, he published[240] and wrote a commentary in Persian on the works of his master. In an authentic collection of his letters, *maktūbāt*,[241] he uses select quotations to stress certain basic themes; such themes and quotations appear in the posthumous collections, *Kanz al-haqā'iq*, *Zubdat al-haqā'iq*, *Tamhīdāt*, which his disciples compiled.[242] Quotations from the Qur'ān, hadīths, maxims, especially those of mystics from Ma'rūf, Sahl, Junayd, and Bayezid down to Khurraqānī, Qassāb, and Harawī; Shiblī is quoted often and, more than any other, Husayn-i Mansūr (= Hallāj), the "prince of Lovers," seven of whose maxims had not been quoted previously by anyone; he was the first to quote from the *Tawāsīn*, giving the famous verse "*baynī wa baynaka*. . . ." The Persian work of 'Ayn al-Qudāt presents a series of classical love themes: Yūsuf, Layla, Ayāz; in it he dares to quote skeptical verses by Ma'arrī, he discusses in Aristotelian terms the problem of transcendent unity, as distinct from numerical unity,[243] and accepts as genuine one of the "letters" exchanged between Abū Sa'īd and the philosopher Ibn Sīnā.[244]

In the works of 'AQ Hamadhānī, the quietistic theory of pure love, fusing the example of Hallāj with that of Iblīs, becomes less ticklish; if Iblīs refused, it was in order to comply with a secret command from God.[245] This is how he changes the well-known dream of Shiblī making his *istikhāra* after the execution of Hallāj: "on the day when this prince of lovers was crucified, Shiblī in a dream asked God: 'Why do You put Your lovers to death?' 'So that they will receive the *diya* (= blood

---

[238] 'Imad Isfahānī, *Nusra*, ms. P. 2145, ff. 165-176. He was protected by the treasurer 'Azīz-b-Rajā, hated by Vizir Qiwām Darguzīnī (whom the Supreme Sultan, Sanjar, a friend of Ahmad Ghazālī, would have executed in Sapurkhwast in 527).

[239] Critical edition by M-b-'Abd al-Jalīl, ap. *JAP*, 1930, pp. 1 ff., 193 ff.

[240] *Sawānih* (= *lawā'ih*).

[241] Ms. P., Persian a. f. 35: two letters, ff. 359a, 361a, are from A Ghazālī.

[242] The *Kanz*, known in a Turkish translation, was, according to a dream cited at the end, supposed to have been redacted by Abū 'Alī Amulī in 531 (f. 41a; f. 35a, another disciple, Shaykh Siyāwūsh, learned details of his death through an appearance of the Prophet). The *Tamhīdāt* (app. also *Zubda*) are filled with interpolations.

[243] He is, on this point, more firm than Ibn Sīnā.

[244] *Recueil*, p. 189.   [245] *Maktūbāt*, f. 283a.

money) from Me.' 'Lord, what is Your blood money?' 'My meeting and
my beauty, that is my lovers' ransom.' "[246]
'AQ Hamadhānī, like Ghazālī, accepts the bodily death of Jesus on the
cross in terms of ecstasy: the Qur'ānic *raf*', according to him, is rapture of
the soul, not bodily ascension (*Tamhīdāt*, ms. P. s. p. 1356, f. 78b; cf. the
Hallājian *mi'rāj* according to 'Attār, who must have been influenced by
'AQ Hamadhānī).[247]
    A recent Shī'ite critic,[248] commenting on 'AQ Hamadhānī, has said
that he was *'isawī-i-mashrab, mansūrī-i-maslak*. If his interest in Jesus is
characterized particularly by his theory about the death on the cross and
the charisms that he also was supposed to have had, his admiration for
Mansūr Hallāj is not demonstrated only by his original quotations; it
seems to have gone as far as the desire to imitate his martyrdom. The text
that Husayn Bāyqara attributes to him on this subject must be authentic,[249] and Sārī 'Abdallāh Çelebī indeed felt the spiritual kinship between
'Ayn al-Qudāt and Hallāj.[250]
    The thought of 'Ayn al-Qudāt, awakened in mysticism by the power-
ful romanticism of Ahmad Ghazālī, led to a stronger spirituality than that
of the two Ghazālī brothers. He believed above all in the things of the
spirit, and may very well have given his life for them, like the two Hallājians whom 'Attār cites in the same era in Balkh, and like Suhrawardī
Maqtūl a little later in Aleppo. In any event, it was out of a desire to imitate him that Mas'ūdī Bāk was to get himself killed in Delhi in 800/1397.
    'Ayn al-Qudāt describes Hallāj as a kind of knight-errant of divine
love, an insurgent of sanctity, a rebel against legal formalism, a herald of

[246] *Tamhīdāt*, ms. P. Pers. Suppl. 1356, f. 74b: this text, linked to a saying of Ahmad
Ghazālī (Subkī IV, 54), became a hadīth. The origin of it seems to be the response made by
the Sūfī Jallā concerning the death of pilgrims who set out deliberately without provisions
across the Arabian desert: "*al-diya 'alā'l-qātil*" (*Talbīs*, 320; cf. 'Attār, Pavet tr. of *Tadhk.*,
92). A response that 'AQ H incorporated boldly into the framework of the dream.
    [247] On the problem of the real crucifixion of Jesus in the opinion of certain Muslims, cf.
Recueil, pp. 193, 257; and our references ap. *Revue des études islamiques*, 1932, pp. 533-536.
This is the opinion of the Qarmathians Abū Hātim Rāzī (*A'lam al-nubuwwa*, verse 322),
Ikhwān al-Safā' (*Rasā'il*, 1st ed., IV, 86, 115-117), Mu'ayyad Shīrāzī (d. 470: ap. 520 m.
majlis); of Abū Hāmid Ghazālī (*Mustazhirī*, 30, line 13), of his brother, of 'AQ Hamadhānī,
of one of the authors of the Hallājian *hikāya* (*Recueil*, p. 62, cf. *Mustazhirī* cited *supra*), of
Fakhr Rāzī (*Tafsīr*, ms. P. 613, f. 559a); of the Turkish mystics Badr Simā'una Oghlu
(*Wāridāt*, Cairo ms. II, 43, cf. 'Alī Dede, *Khaw* [?], 248), Muhammad Nūr the Bayrāmī
(born 1228 Mahallat Kubra, d. 1305 Strumitza; cf. Abd al-Baki, *Melamiler* [1931], 225; the
jasad 'unsurī of Jesus did die in the crucifixion); Shaykh Ahmad Lahsā'i, the master of the
Bāb, also believed in the death of the *jasad 'unsurī*.
    [248] Ma'sūm 'Alī Shāh, *Tarā'iq*.
    [249] *Majālis al-'ushshāq*, ms. P. Pers. Suppl., 776, f. 86.
    [250] *Thamarāt*.

love's paradise. As a precursor, in this view, of the Indian Calenders, the Shattārīya and the Shāhmadārīya, 'Ayn al-Qudāt emphasized, more than 'Attār did, this aspect of Hallāj's character.

'Ayn al-Qudāt extends the self-denial that one must practice in mysticism, with respect to all choices and specific observances, to confessional differences; and he connects an Arabic verse ("In Qādisīya there are people who know what dishonors him, —and who, moreover, are neither Muslims, Mazdaeans, Jews, nor Christians") with the audacious response made by Hallāj (to the question "and what *madhhab* do you belong to?"): "I am in the *madhhab* of my Lord."[251]

Hallāj had said, in Arabic: "between me and You there lingers an 'it is I' which torments me, —ah, remove my 'it is I' from between us with Your 'it is I.' " 'AQ Hamadhānī, also in verse, though Persian, comments as follows:[252]

> Raise the cup of wine, and ravish my soul
> Inebriate me in both these worlds, ravish me.
> As long as I am sober, "it is I" exists which either wins or loses.
> Out of this concern of mine, profit or loss, ravish me.

Ibn Abī'l-Hadīd (d. 643), a Zaydite, quotes the following apocryphal lines of Hallāj, which are Shī'ite-inspired:

> Of course, I conceal the jewels of my knowledge, —lest the ignorant, beholding it, should be tempted. —AH (= 'Alī) did the same before me, —and he transmitted it to Husayn and Hasan. —And the devout should approve my execution, —they who admire what they consider worse.[253]

t. Shaydhalā'[254] and His "Lawāmi'"

This is a collection of maxims dealing with mystical "states" (*ahwāl*), written down in the manner of Qushayrī; an Ash'arite like him, this *wā'iz* appeals more often to sentiment and puts more emphasis on love, using mainly the maxims of Hallāj, which he comments on one after

---

[251] *Maktūbāt*, f. 345a (= *Kanz*, f. 12a): "*bi'l-Qādisīyati fi'atun, mā an yarawna'l-'āra 'āran lā muslimūna wa lā majūsa, wa lā yahuda, wa lā nasāra.*" Only the *Kanz* gives Hallāj's response (*Tamhīdāt*, I.O. ms. 445, f. 6b). 'AQ Hamadhānī was also the first to give Hallāj's verse "*kafartu bi dīn Allāh . . .*" (*Tamhīdāt*, ms. P. Pers. Suppl. 1356, f. 68a).

[252] *Tamhīdāt*, ms. P. Pers. Suppl. 1356, f. 80a. It should be noted that 'AQ H overemphasized this trait and limited the perspective: Hallāj does not ask to be chloroformed during the transforming union operation. 'AQ H seems to believe that it is not compatible with mental lucidity (*sahw*).

[253] The last two verses are now attributed to 'Alī ('Ayyāshī [?] I, 421); cf. *Sharh Nahj* [?] III, 73.

[254] A pupil of Sābūnī, Ibn Ghaylān, Ibrāhīm-b-'Umar Barmakī, and AT Tabarī (Subkī III, 287).

another, juxtaposing them with lines of verse. Several of the groupings are assigned to Shiblī, but are also found in the *Hikāyat Ibn Khafīf*, representing the early part of the latter, thus a Hallājian tradition transmitted privately in the Zawzanī ribāt and which Shaydhalā' was one of the first who dared disseminate.

His *rāwīs* were AH M-b-Mubārak ibn al-Khall (d. 552), A-b-Tarīq Karkī Lubnānī (529, d. 592), and Abū 'Alī-b-Sukkara; his *rāwiya*, Shuhda Dīnawarīya (d. 554), for the *Hikāya*.

u. *The Historian AH M-b-Abū'l-Fadl 'Abd al-Malik-b-Ibrāhīm-b-A Faradī ibn al-Maqdisī Hamadhānī (d. 521)*[255]

A disciple, like his friend Vizir Rūdhrāwarī,[256] of Abū Ishāq Shīrāzī, whose *Tabaqāt al-fuqahā'* he continued, this historian, who lived at court, was the first who called attention in his works to sympathy for Hallāj. It was he who signaled the fact that Vizir Ibn al-Muslima was a Hallājian (ap. *Kitāb al-wuzarā'*; cit. ap. 'Aynī). And in his *'Unwān al-siyar* (or *Ma'ārif muta'akhkhara*), he gives us the following, after a very careful abridgment of the "account by Ibn Zanjī" of the trial of 309 (f. 18a–21a), ending with "and Hājib Nasr said that [Hallāj] was unjustly killed": (1) four poems attributed to Hallāj, but which, I believe, must be restored to Abū'l-'Atāhīya, a friend of 'Īsā Ghaznawī (against Vizir Ibn Juhayr); (2) a verse proving, according to the Sūfīs, that Hallāj had penetrated the supreme mystery, and a quatrain, known to be by the Qādirī Ibrāhīm A'zab; (3) an excerpt from the *Hikāya*; (4) the account of Nasr's son's apple; (5) a second excerpt from the *Hikāya*; (6) etymologies of the name *"Hallāj"*; and a review of the controversies about him among Sūfīs; (7) a third excerpt from the *Hikāya* (with a reflection on the poem *"Tajāsartu,"* to be restored to Khalī'); (8) a distich "written by a Sūfī about the gibbet of Hallāj" to proclaim his divulging of the secret a disgrace. It is very significant that the three excerpts from the *Hikāya* are found again based on the same recension in our manuscripts of the *Hikāya* (1. = *Ilahiya innaka tatawaddad + Nazarī badw 'illatī* = L. ms. 330b; 2. = Shiblī's first

---

[255] His grandfather, Abū'l-Fadā'il, was a friend of A Ishāq Shīrāzī and of Ibn Bayān Kāzarūnī (Subkī III, 91). His father (409, d. 489), a respected Shāfi'ite and ascetic, was a disciple of Māwardī and a friend of Ibn 'Aqīl (Subkī III, 248), also a friend of 'Allāf and Ibn al-Muslima (*Talbīs*, 409).

[256] Three of whose works he completed. The Rūdhrāwarī vizirial family from Hamadhan, four times in power in Baghdad and once in Isfahan, must have been pro-Hallāj; for Vizir Abū Shujā' Zāhir M-b-Hy Rūdhrāwarī II (b. 437, d. 488 in Medina: vizir in 471, 478–484) was a patron of this historian, his associate; and his son Nizām Rabīb Rūdhrāwarī III (Saljūq vizir 511–513) was a patron of 'Attār (cf. Ibn Khallikān s.v.; and ms. P. 1570, f. 29b).

visit = L. ms. 325a, K 73-74; 3. = Fātima's bearing + the poem "*Wahur-mat al-wadd*" = L. ms. 324b, and Tūzarī, + L. ms. 331a, K 88). Hamadhānī, who completed his *'Unwān* around 511, would not have hesitated using (in the absence of the *Akhbār*, put under interdict by the condemnation of Ibn 'Aqīl in 465) the Hallājian compilation just finished by Ibn al-Qassās in Shirwan. And the other excerpts that the historian Tūzarī a little later included in his *Iktifā'* came possibly from a more complete manuscript of Hamadhānī and, in any case, imitate his model.

v. Abū Hāmid Ghazālī and His Four Years of Lecturing in Baghdad (484-488)

AH Ghazālī came to Baghdad on a quasi-official mission for the great Sal-jūq vizir Nizām al-Mulk, who died a few months later. He was thirty-four years old at the time. After having become interested for a brief period in mysticism with his brother Ahmad under the tutelage of Fārmadhī, he had studied Shāfi'ite law and Ash'arite dogmatics thoroughly in Nishapur with Juwaynī. He was known as a jurisconsult, and had already delivered, as early as 485, a *fatwā* of political significance. In Baghdad he studied Avicennism in secret, and was instructed by Caliph Mustazhir to write a refutation of the Ismā'īlīs. It was only after the spiritual crisis which led him to resign from his position in order to experiment with mysticism that he seems to have been interested in Hallāj.

w. The Literary Emergence of the Hallājian Legend and the Fatwā of Shihāb Tūsī (569/1174) Concerning the Testimony of Blood. The Case of Ibn al-Ghazzāl

In the beginning of our twelfth century, bits of popular legend crop up in a historian's notice dealing with Hallāj: in AF Hamadhānī (d. 521/1127).[257] No individual variations on a theme for meditation, as with Shaydhalā'; but rather many traces of one and the same written source, of which the historian Tūzarī (d. 580/1184) gives us a rather long excerpt enabling us to identify it with the *Hikāyat Ibn Khafīf*, that fictionalized account, still unpublished,[258] in which manuscripts *L*, *K* and *T* capsulize the *Akhbār al-Hallāj* like the pit inside a fruit's pulp.[259] There was undoubtedly one author who conceived this unique literary amalgam,

---

[257] M-b-Abī'l-Fadl Hamadhānī, *Dhayl* (written in 487/1094), making use perhaps also of both Ibn 'Aqīl and Abū Yūsuf Qazwīnī.

[258] Ap. *Recueil*, pp. 63-64. It will be analyzed in this edition, 2, 442-444.

[259] Ap. Jamāl D A Hamīd M-b-'Alī-b-Mahmūd ibn al-Sābūnī, *Takmīlat al-ikmāl*, Evkaf ms. Baghdad, 852, p. 118 (commentary by M. Jawād).

which was intended perhaps to "encase" this condemned collection in the harmless framework of a story freely imposed on Ibn Khafif's account. Our suspicions are concentrated for the moment on a Caucasian preacher, 'Alī ibn al-Qaṣṣāṣ Shirwānī, a "despicable liar," in Dhahabī's words,[260] "the author of the *Akhbār al-Hallāj* that Abū Ṭāhir Silafī (d. 576/1180) knew first" as being by another Shirwānī,[261] and afterwards arranged to have read by the author himself[262] in Shirwan: and with regard to which he acknowledged "that most of the *isnāds* derived from a work lacking in authority, '*lā aṣla lahu*.' " Given the fact that Silafī passed through Shirwan just prior to 509/1115, [the period] when he was settled in Alexandria,[263] we arrive at a date for the composition of the book which fits in approximately with our hypothesis.

With regard to the *Hikāyat Ibn Khafīf*, let us keep in mind at this point simply this fictionalized text accomplished in a popular form the elaboration of Hallāj's martyrdom by the preachers, *wu"āz*, who had meditated on its meaning for two centuries. In spite of the classic presupposition that God could abandon neither His prophets nor His saints to an ignominious death, they preached that Hallāj's punishment was truly undergone in his own body, that he desired this suffering out of love; that he suffered it in a state of union with God; and that God granted him that, because "when his hands were cut off, his blood, when it spilled on the ground, wrote "*Allāh, Allāh*":[264] the Pure Name, "God, God."

This theme of the testimony of blood, arising apart from any historicity, met an objection, among Muslim canonists, based on principle: blood is impure (*al-dam najas*). This explains Hasan Basrī's statement, praised by Sunnites, that when it comes to testimony, "the ink of the learned takes precedence over the blood of martyrs,"[265] and the age-old obstinacy of the Shī'ites, who, dismayed by repeated disasters and by the cruel fate given their Imāms, convinced themselves that God, through a miracle of unexpected substitution, exempted them from physical suffering while materializing the previously damned soul of one of their

---

[260] *Mīzān al-i'tidāl* II, 218 (commentary by Lammens).

[261] This elliptical statement refers more to the *Akhbār* than the *Hikāya*.

[262] Whom Silafī depicts in his *Mu'jam al-safar* as an "old shaykh, renowned in the cities of Shirwan and neighboring regions, a good preacher respected (*hurma*) in court circles in the capital, Yazdiya, of Shirwan."

[263] Subkī IV, 43.   [264] Ms. I [?].

[265] Cf. *Essai*, p. 127. E. Psichari was quick to become angry against this saying: in which "martyrs" stands figuratively for the "Muslims killed in action." According to Shī'ites, it was the impure blood of Shamir, the murderer of Husayn, which wrote on the ground, when he was put to death, his condemnation "*ayya munqalab*" (Qur'ān 26:227; Tunakabuni, *Mawā'iz* [?] XVII).

enemies[266] within the same garments rent and blood spilt by execution-ers. We encountered the same state of mind among the early Hallājīya,[267] and it ceases only with the transposition on the mystical plane of the theme, so dear to profane poets, of the "death through love."[268]

In this instance, the spilling of the blood of a saint is presented to us in prose as a sacrifice of atonement accepted by God; just as Kīlānī was later to point out, around 545/1150, in a kind of sermon in rhymed prose.[269]

The question was posed and settled affirmatively in a juridical way in a *fatwā* given by a Shāfi'ite who was an Ash'arite in dogmatics and a dis-ciple of the Sūfī Abū'l-Waqt Sijzī (d. 553/1158), namely Shihāb al-Dīn M Tūsī (b. 522/1128, d. 597/1200), a clever and irreverent wit, who was a preacher in the Tājīya Saljūq *madrasa* of Baghdad (from 547 to 569).[270] According to Abū Shāma, the *istiftā'* was: "which blood was the purest, that of Husayn (the martyred Imām of the Shī'ites killed at Karbala), or that of Hallāj?" Feigning astonishment, Tūsī asked: "how can one say such a thing, given the fact that a single drop of the blood of Husayn is worth more than a hundred thousand drops of the blood of Hallāj?" and resuming the *istiftā'*: "did not the blood of Hallāj write '*Allāh, Allāh*' on the ground, which the blood of Husayn did not do?" Here is the *fatwā*: "only the state of the accused requires rehabilitation (*tazkiya*)."[271]

Tūsī thus, like a good humorist, accomplished his dual aim: of annoy-ing the conservative Hanbalites[272] by reaffirming, after Ibn 'Aqīl, the sanctity of Hallāj, and of provoking the Shī'ites, among whom he caused a riot by affirming from his pulpit that Ibn Muljam was not necessarily damned for killing 'Alī. For that, Tūsī was obliged to appear before the *naqīb* of *naqībs* (568-582), Ibn al-Zawwāl. Banished as a disturber of the peace in the pay of the Saljūqs, he left for Cairo[273] to direct the Manāzil al-'Izz *madrasa*, founded in 566 for Shāfi'ites by the nephew of Saladin.

It was at that time that another Baghdad preacher, a Hanbalite, Ibn al-Jawzī (d. 597/1200), wrote a pamphlet "of a little more than two *kurrās*

---

[266] This edition, 1, 322 ff.; *damm* = 'Umar.

[267] This edition, 2, 109 (?).

[268] This edition, 1, 468 ff.

[269] This edition, 2, 356.

[270] Sibt ibn al-Jawzī, *Mir'āt*, s.a. 596, f. 307; Munāwī (d. 1031/1622), in abridging it, plagiarized this *fatwā*, which M M Jawād uncovered again.

[271] S[ibt] i[bn al-] J[awzi] comments as follows: "this response presupposes that Hallāj's blood actually did write "*Allāh, Allāh*," which is not a proven fact (this was the argument of his grandfather); Dhahabī comments: "a splendid retort, but it was not necessary to di-rect it at Hallāj."

[272] Zayd ibn Najīya, in 564 in Baghdad; d. 599 in Quds; a friend of Saladin.

[273] Abū Shāma, *Rawdatayn* [bib. no. 445-a] I, 191; II, 240. Maqrīzī II, 364.

(= 32 pages)[274] entitled *al-Qāti'*:[275] "to refute the notion of Hallāj's sanctity and particularly the argument based on the [supposed] fact that his blood, when spilt on the ground, could have written the Declaration of the (Divine) Majesty" (= *Allāh*). He said in this work that "blood is a canonically impure liquid, therefore how could it write the Pure Name?"—a view repeated later by Ibn Taymīya and Dhahabī. He also presented the deceptions and tricks used by Hallāj and the consultations of the *'ulamā'* who condemned him.[276] We also have some short ironic quips by him on the subject: "Hallāj? Who cares about the carder, other than the weaver (*hā'ik*)."[277] And "the spindle of Rābi'a gave out, but we still have the cotton of Hallāj."[278]

Ibn 'Arabī continued the testimony of blood theme:[279] "just as it is told of Zulaykhā, that after he was wounded by an arrow, when his blood spilt on the ground, it wrote 'Joseph, Joseph' in many places, wherever the blood had spilt, because of his continual commemoration of this name, which flowed like blood through his arteries, so also is it said of Hallāj, that when his four extremities were amputated, his blood wrote '*Allāh, Allāh*' on the ground where it had spilt." And this is why he said:

> No limb nor joint of mine has been cut off
> In which I have not commemorated Your Name.[280]

Due to Ibn 'Arabī's influence, this theme, propagated in Arabic,[281] of the testimony of blood writing on the ground, finally made its way into Islam through Persian, in which, to vindicate Hallāj, the other theme was introduced, that of the testimony of ashes writing "*Anā'l-Haqq*" on the waters of the Tigris. Thus we find a fusion of the two themes in Chapter V of the *Qawā'im al-anwār* of Abū'l-Qāsim Bābā, called al-Qutb, founder of the Imāmite order of the Dhahabīya (around 1076/1653):[282] where it is the ashes that write "*Allāh, Allāh*" on the bubbles of the Tigris' waves,[283]

---

[274] According to the manuscript in the library of Sibt ibn al-'Ajamī in Cairo, described by Ibn Khalīl (*Minhāj al-Hunafā'*).

[275] Cf. our bibliography, no. 370-c.

[276] Ibn al-Jawzī, *Talbīs*, 183.

[277] Among others, the *Hā'ik* who betrayed Ibn 'Aqīl (this edition, 2, 157).

[278] "We have no more good yarn," meaning "there are no more true mystics." On Rābi'a, cf. *Essai*, p. 215.

[279] *Futūhat* II, 375; *Tāj al-rasā'il*, 578.

[280] This edition, 2, 395 ff.

[281] Dāwūd Qaysarī summarizes Ibn 'Arabī; Ibn al-Sā'ī (*Mukhtasar*), Ibn Abī Sharīf (*Sharh al-shifā'*) and 'Alī Qāri' were acquainted with the theme.

[282] Ap. Khuyyī, *Sharh minhāj al-barā'a* [bib. no. 1236-a] VI, 263.

[283] The ashes are canonically pure (for the fire produced *istihāla*).

and where it is the blood whose drops write "*Anā'l-Haqq*" on the ground.

Another disciple of Abū'l-Waqt Sijzī, Ibn al-Ghazzāl, undertook, a little after the banishment of Tūsī, the preparation of a new defense of Hallāj; he was a highly respected *muhaddith* of the Hanbalite rite. Ibn Rajab[284] tells us, "I saw a short treatise written in his own hand entitled *Akhbār al-Hallāj*, which seems to have been composed by him. In it he gives an account, with their *isnāds*, of traditions received from his masters;[285] he tends to eulogize Hallāj (the very minutiae uncovered in his inquiry proved indeed that he was praising him from the bottom of his heart)[286] and to exalt him (*ta'zīm*); he even gives excerpts in it from the work that Ibn 'Aqīl had previously composed on him, which he retracted; which is an error (on the part of Ibn al-Ghazzāl)." It was apparently on account of this error, that another Hanbalite, the *hāfiz* Abū'l-Futūh Nasr Husurī (d. 619/1222), waged a campaign to assure that no *rāwī* would transmit from any *samā'* traceable to Ibn al-Ghazzāl.[287] This theme of the "blood that bears witness" appears to derive from the *hadīth al-maklūm*, quoted twice by Bukharī:[288] "No one wounded for the cause of God whose wound, at the Judgment, does not bleed again, its color the color of blood, its scent the scent of musk."[289]

x. The Rifā'īya

It was in the marshlands, the *batā'ih*, of Wasit that this Iraqi order was born; in that region where, around A.H. 520, a local Sūfi, Mansūr Batā'ihī Ansārī (d. 540),[290] the maternal uncle of the founder, specified four dis-

---

[284] *Tabaqāt al-Hanābila* [bib. no. 570-a], s.v. (commentary by Goldziher).

[285] His father, 'Umar, was connected with Kīlanī (Shattanawfī, *Bahja* [bib. no. 502-a], 30, 31, 107).

[286] (Addenda of the Damascus ms.)

[287] Ibn al-Dubaythī, ms. P. 5922, f. 121a (reference and commentary owed to M. Jawād).

[288] Chapter on jihād, *Manāqib*; cited seventeen times in Ibn Hanbal.

[289] The source of R Baqlī's dreams about the blood of the *abdāl*, "*fard* which streaks the dawn of eternity" (*Kashf*, f. 18a).

[290] Mansūr, who lived and died at Nahr Dajla, came from an old Wasit family, the B. Matt—whose eponymous ancestor, who came there in A.H. 180, was said to be the grandson of the standard bearer of the Prophet, Abū Ayyūb Khālid-b-Zayd Ansārī (d. A.H. 52), and would have had as his fifth descendant AB M-b-Mūsā Wāsitī ibn al-Farghānī (d. 326), a well-known pro-Hallāj mystic who died in exile in Marw. It is interesting that the great Hanbalite Harawī (d, 481) had also belonged, like Sultan Injū of Baghdad (Hanbalite, 742, d. 745) (catalogue IO, II, 914), to a branch of the B. Matt, whose eponym also was said to descend from Abū Ayyūb (Dhahabī, *Ta'rīkh*, London ms. Or. 50, f. 176a: he vocalizes it *Matt*, not *Mutt*). The B. Matt seem to go back to Turkish origins, for the B. Matt were princes of Isfijab (two known amirs, M-b-Hy-b-Matt, d. 309, and Abū Mansūr M-b-Hy-b-Matt, d. 387, according to Barthold, *Turkestan*, Eng. tr., [H.A.R. Gibb, London,

tinct mystical affiliations according to their original features:[291] "the disciples of Hallāj love to speak of unification (wahda), those of Abū Yazīd (Bistāmī) love the esoteric and subtle arguments, the disciples of Junayd love to connect mystical and canonical terms, those of Salamābādhī[292] love the pomp associated with social status, and those of Abū'l-Fadl ('Alī Wāsitī Qāri')[293] love to speak of unification with God, but in humility vis-à-vis Him and His creatures." It was under Abū'l-Fadl's tutelage that Ahmad Rifā'ī (b. around 510, d. in 580 at Umm 'Abida) was formed.

The Banū Rifā'a were an Arab clan, from the Maghrib about sixty years back and endowed with an 'Alid genealogy,[294] which gained the successors of Ahmad Rifā'ī, during the period of the Mongol domination,[295] the position of power, through the niqāba of the shurafā' of Basra, which they maintained until 1920. Ahmad Rifā'ī, who had studied a little of Shāfi'ite law, required his disciples first to follow strictly the rule of their juridical rite,[296] and to keep on the purely private level their more spirited devotional exercises (wazā'if)[297] combined with tricks (swallowing serpents, eating fire, and the like) that appeal to the masses. The order forbids any doctrinal incursion into theological terminology. Its founder, moreover, motivated by a certain jealousy of the Baghdad Qādirīya order, uttered several hostile opinions of Hallāj.

1. This first is a text of the Wazā'if Ahmadīya of Ahmad Sayyād (d. 670):[298]

The shaykh and 'adl Mufarrij-b-Nabhān Shaybānī told me: I was in the reception hall of Shaykh 'Abd al-Qādir Jīlī when Shaykh 'Alī Hītī and Shaykh 'Alī-b-Idrīs Ba'qūbī were also present; now a man of the Batā'ih entered, greeted Shaykh 'Abd al-Qādir and greeted us, and then sat down; the shaykh asked him about Shaykh Ahmad Rifā'ī, and he replied that he was well and, at the request of the shaykh, gave an account of his ecstasies and miracles, in considerable detail, for this Batā'ihī had verve and a good memory; then the conversation came to

1928], pp. 241, 264; and one Shāfi'ite jurisconsult, A B M-b-A-b-Matt, d. around 350, Subkī II, 125). We know that Hallāj was considered by some as having descended from Abū Ayyūb (this edition, 2, 30). Witrī [bib. no. 739A-a], f. 151a.
[291] Witrī, f. 15b, 50a = Rifā'ī, Burhān [bib. no. 361-b], 58.
[292] 'Uthmān Salamābādhī and his son 'Alī (Abū'l-Hudā, Qilāba, 199, 193, 189).
[293] Whose initiatory isnād begins with unknowns (whose names are foreign: Abū'l-Fadl-b-Kāmikh, 'Alī Ghulām ibn Tarkān, 'Iqd, 53) and goes back to Shiblī.
[294] Rejected by the genealogists Ibn Tabataba and Ibn Ma'yī (Witrī, f. 112a, 117b, 296a).
[295] The tawqī' of A.H. 451 is a forgery (Witrī, f. 85a).
[296] Ap. Burhān, 55: "do not say: Hārith (= Muhāsibī) said, or Abū Yazīd, or Hallāj; but Shāfi'ī said, or Mālik, or Ahmad, or Nu'mān: first concentrate on external behavior, then amuse yourself with nonessential words."
[297] The riyādāt marbūta stipulates that at certain times, depending on rank, one must recite, for example, the invocation "yā Wahhāb" five thousand times a day (Witrī, f. 274b ff.).
[298] Witrī, f. 161b-162a.

Hallāj. Shaykh 'Abd al-Qādir asked him what SA Rifā'ī thought of him, and the Batā'ihī asked him to give his opinion first, which he did: "He was a sage (*'ārif*) whose mind flew like a bird out of the nest of his body up to heaven, where he entered the ranks of the angels; he found there none of the light he had been seeking, [instead] 'I see my Lord'; and so he came away and redescended, increasingly bedazzled; when he finally came back to earth again, he uttered, in his ecstatic way of speaking, the famous words (*Anā'l-Haqq*); after that he became an exile among other strange persons, and his visible being became truly reabsorbed in God."[299] Then the Batā'ihī spoke: there is disagreement between the two masters; Shaykh Ahmad (Rifā'ī) says concerning Hallāj, "in my opinion, he was not a sage; in my opinion he neither imbibed nor perceived anything; I believe that he heard only a murmuring, a tinkling, and that his imagination then carried him away from state to state"; anyone who claims to be increasingly close [to God] and does not appear increasingly filled with fear, is only deluded; it is said of him that he uttered "I am the Truth"; his imagination led him astray; if he had indeed been truthful, he would not have said "*Anā'l-Haqq.*" Ibn al-Warrāq[300] became indignant at these words of the Batā'ihī and stood up: "How can Shaykh Ahmad say that when Shaykh 'Abd al-Qādir has said what you have just heard?" But Shaykh 'Abd al-Qādir, irritated, said "Sit down, Ibn al-Warrāq; God knows that Shaykh Ahmad is His witness before the saints of today and presides over this reception." Ibn al-Warrāq, overcome with weakness, was unable to remain standing. Those present interceded on his behalf with the shaykh, who gave him his hand and he stood up cured. Then, turning to those present, Shaykh 'Abd al-Qādir declared, "God is great Who has given us such a man," referring to Shaykh Ahmad; and he recited the following: "He is the one who walks ahead of the early saints, and when you see him, you should say: there goes the last of the men."

2. Another recension of Ahmad Rifā'ī's opinion [of Hallāj] was inserted in a very unusual anecdote about Shaykh 'Azāz saving Hallāj from a lion at Wadi Arzan before he was even born: an anecdote plagiarized from a Shī'ite account showing 'Alī, not yet born, saving Salmān from a lion at Deshti Arjan near Kazerun.[301]

Ibrāhīm al-A'zab, a disciple [of Rifā'ī], related[302] that a *faqīr* said in his presence one day, "O Shaykh! the people of Baghdad[303] claim that there

---

[299] ". . . *fa'staghrab li'l-aghyār, fa'ntawā mazharuhu bi'l-Haqq 'alā'l-Haqq.*" This noteworthy and daring statement is not included in the Qādirīyan recension given earlier here.

[300] This name perhaps stands for Makārim-b-Khalīl al-Basrī (*Bahja*, 137).

[301] Tabarsī Nūrī, *Nafas al-Rahmān fī . . . Salmān*, Tehran Lith. 13 . . . , p. 28. The Bektāshīs add that Salmān recognized 'Alī by an aroma of hyacinths ('Abd al-Bakī, *Melāmīler*, p. 60, n. 1).

[302] There are two different recensions: I have used that of Qāsim ibn al-Hajj found in his *Umm al-barāhin* (Shahīd 'Alī Pāshā ms. 1127, end of second third) collected with the Arabic translation of the Persian recension of al-Kāzarūnī according to Abū'l-Hudā (*Qilāda*, 200), based on Ibn Jalāl.

[303] Meaning the "Qādirīya" in contradistinction to the shaykhs of the Batā'ih = the Rifā'īya.

was no shaykh among the Batā'ih[304] before the time of Hallāj: when his body was burned and his ashes thrown on the waters of the Tigris, they drank them, and this was the way they became shaykhs. The Baghdadians express this in a verse attributed to Hallāj:

The lovers have drunk only my remains, and they have known the source of love only by drawing from my gourd.[305]

Hearing these words, Rifā'ī (excited), exclaimed: "May their mother bear their mourning! Who gave them the right to speak thus? Such ignoramuses should be put to the sword! One believes he has discovered the source, another that he has drunk from it, another that he has seen it, another that he has heard it. But he has not heard, for if he had heard, he would have drunk! Hallāj passed along outside the enclosure where the presence of the Holy resides. He overheard a song, he listened to a wail, a jingle, a sigh in union;[306] that was enough to intoxicate him without his having seen or drunk anything. [Let them answer me only] where was Hallāj in the clearing of Wadi Arzan!" "What is Wadi Arzan?" someone asked him. "A region in the valley of Damascus,[307] which Hallāj passed through one day. He saw some gnawed bones there. He spoke the 'Supreme Name' that he had learned over them. Now, they were the bones of a lion, whom God then brought back to life;[308] he sprang up at Hallāj, who fled screaming. His cry made Shaykh 'Azāz shudder in the loins of his father;[309] 'Azāz with a word made the lion return to his earlier state of dried bones, and thereby saved Hallāj. How can one claim, after hearing that, that it was the ashes of Hallāj's burned body that made masters of the Batā'ih shaykhs?"

Rifā'ī pursued that further: "There is nothing about this story of the lion that should surprise us, but what is surprising is that the first thing that Shaykh 'Azāz did when he came into the world was to tell this story and to declare:[310] "Tomorrow (= on Judgment Day) 'Azāz ibn Mustawdi' will be admitted to the court of the Glorious God with twelve thousand horsemen on his right and twelve thousand on his left, none of whom would wish to think about Hallāj; and their eyes will turn neither right nor left, for each of them will have only God in their thoughts; and

---

[304] Text of Ibn al-Hājj; Abū'l-Hudā corrects "shaykhs of the 'Irāq" (= Baghdad): so that the anger of Rifā'ī is no longer explainable.

[305] *Wird* (= *mashrab*), perhaps already an initiation.

[306] A reference to Kīlānī (*Bahja*, 71).

[307] Arzūnā (Yāqūt I, 206): more simply, Urdun (Jordan).

[308] A well-known folkloric theme: see *Mélanges Basset*.

[309] Meaning "yet to be born": a century later.

[310] Cf. the Qur'ān on Jesus: "*al-salām 'alayya yawma wulidtu. . . .*"

from His eyes a light will shine, seventy times brighter than the sun. Even the servant entrusted to carry His ewer would refuse to be reduced to the rank of Hallāj. Tomorrow, Hallāj will be incapable of saying what I say at this moment, I, 'Azāz ibn Mustawdi'. And if he wanted to say it, I would beat him on all sides with a sword until he understood, and until he no longer understood!"[311]

This anecdote is very interesting. It shows 'Azāz fighting against the dying Hallājian madhhab, represented by a magical Hallāj, who reminds us of the Talmudic representation of Jesus, thief of the "Ineffable Name."

3. We find in a sermon of A Rifā'ī[312] a condemnation ex cathedra of the Hallājian Anā'l-Haqq: to which the two previously cited texts belong: "Take care, do not lie when it comes to God. Among the worst offenses made to God, in lying, is the statement that Hallāj is reported to have said: Anā'l-Haqq. His imagination led him astray; if he had been truthful, he would not have said 'Anā'l-Haqq.' People refer to poems of his in which he deludes himself with the notion of having arrived at unification, but all of that, and anything like it, is false. In my opinion, this man did not reach his objective (wāsil), ever; in my opinion, he imbibed and perceived nothing; I believe that he heard only a murmur, a tinkle, and that his imagination then carried him away from one state to the next; anyone who claims to be increasingly close [to God], and does not appear to be increasingly filled with fear, is only deluded. You must never repeat such sentences which are mere falsehoods. Only the ignorant know no bounds (tajāwuz al-hadd), only the blind step into the pit in spite of Him. . . . Sanctity does not imitate Pharaoh."

The vehemence of this judgment is toned down somewhat in a letter (riqa')[313] written by A Rifā'ī to Shārif 'Abd al-Samī' 'Abbāsī Wāsitī that 'Alī-b-M (d. 620), the grandson of Abū'l-Fadl Wāsitī, had seen in the library of this shārif: ". . . if I had lived in the time of Hallāj, I would have signed the fatwā of those who condemned him to death, after verification of the incriminating words; then I would have moved for a figurative interpretation of the verdict to have him avoid the death penalty, being satisfied with his retraction and his return to God; for the door of mercy must not be closed." Even today, outside his orders, which consider him the seal of the saints, Ahmad Rifā'ī is regarded as the presiding officer of the Hadra Rabbānīya who, above the "poles," decides the fate of the living every night.

---

311 'Azāz was buried near Aleppo (in a town of this name). He also has a maqām in Egypt, at Bayda (in Cherqiya) ('Alī Pāshā Mubārak, Khidat X, 64).
312 Witrī, f. 14b = Burhān, 28.   313 Witrī, f. 220b.

4. Following his example, the authors affiliated with his order have systematically minimized the character and teaching of Hallāj. In his *Tiryāq al-muhibbīn*, the historian of the *khirqa*, Taqī D 'AR-b-'A Muhsin Wāsitī (d. 744), remarks[314] that Hallāj, a true disciple of Junayd, had the misfortune to utter words espousing unification; it was proven that he retracted them all, but the caliph's vizir was hell bent against him, and forced the qādī to sign his death warrant without canonical cause (*mujib shar'ī*). As regards the statements attributed to him, if he had upheld them, it would unquestionably have been necessary to put him to death, for such statements have led many people into error . . . trusting in would-be shaykhs. . . . *Shath* (= theopathic locution) is defined as an overstepping of one's limits, a building of distance that changes perspective, or indeed as a hoarseness in which one's words overstep canonical bounds; it is an internal malady of the soul, which betrays a looseness of the tongue that the heart cannot control; it is an imperfection, in any case; when one has entered the stage of sanctity, one must avoid such a thing; one gains mastery over it by submitting to obedience. Likewise Sirāj D Makhzūmī (d. 885), who had influence in Baghdad, where he had married the daughter of a rich jeweler (after having saved her young brother, whose beauty enraptured him, from drowning), and who went to Cairo to join the jurisconsult Sirāj Sālih Bulqīnī (d. 868) in Rifā'ism (he went as far as Yemen), reissued what S A Rifā'ī had said against Hallāj and against Kīlānī.[315] His leading disciple, M-b-A Witrī (born in Witrīya near Mosul in 820, died in Baghdad in 901),[316] had a son A-b-M Witrī Kīnānī, a noted Shāfi'ite writer (d. 970), author of a famous collection of *qasīdas* in honor of the Prophet (*Witriyāt*), who dealt with the case of Hallāj several times in his *Manāqib al-Sālihīn* (d. 945), a work that was otherwise dedicated to the glory of Ahmad Rifā'ī. We find in it, first of all, a detailed critique of the notion of *shath* similar to the one given by Baqlī in his *Mantiq al-asrār*, with quotations to support it,[317] including the two Hallāj poems "*Baynī wa baynaka*" and "*Subhāna man azhara*," "in which his feet slipped from under him"; next, after a lively polemic against the *Bahja* of the extreme Qādirīyan Shattanawfī, Witrī takes up, among other references, the majority of the Rifā'ian ones touching on Hallāj. This book, finished in 945 after the first Ottoman conquest of Baghdad, seems to have been aimed at Turkish canonists.[318]

---

[314] Witrī, in the biographical notice of 'Amr Makkī: ap. Witrī, f. 78a, 11a, 44a.
[315] Witrī, f. 329b-340a.   [316] *Ibid.*, f. 359b.
[317] *Ibid.*, f. 23a-33a. He calls it "*Muntawī al-Asrār*."
[318] *Ibid.*, f. 325b. Eflakī, the Mewlewlī historian, gives a scabrous anecdote about him

From the independent branches of the order, such as the Kāzarūnīya of Wasit and the Sayyādīya of Aleppo, we note the *Shifā' al-asqām* (in Persian) of Muhammad Kāzarūnī (d. 790) and the *Qilāda* (in Arabic) of Abū'l-Hudā (d. 1326), chaplain of Abd al-Hamīd II, as repositories of Rifā'ian references to Hallāj among others.

5. Though it is quite separate from the others, we must call attention to the *Rifā'īya Harīrīya* sect founded by Abū Muhammad 'Alī Harīrī,[319] who, after suffering persecution by the authorities, died in Basra (Hawran) in 645/1247. A notebook written by an adept of the sect and containing, among other things, different texts of Hallāj commented on in the monist sense of Ibn 'Arabī, fell into the hands of Ibn Taymīya, who published it with a refutation.[320]

6. Lastly, we can link to the tradition of the Rifā'īya order, and especially to the alphabetical symbolism of prayers attributed to Rifā'ī,[321] the following interesting legend concerning the execution of Hallāj:

It is reported, according to Shīrāzī (= Ibn Khafīf): that when Hallāj was hung (on the cross), he remained there for three days without dying. Then they took him down and searched him; in his pocket they found a sheet of paper on which was written in his own hand the verse of the Throne (Qur'ān 2:256), followed by this prayer (*du'ā'*): "O God, inure my heart to submit to You, cut away from my spirit all that is not You, teach me Your Supreme Name (*ism a'zam*), grant me whatever You permit and deprive me of whatever You forbid, give me what no one cares about, through the truth of *H.M.'.S.Q.*,[322] and make me die a martyr of *K.H.I.'.S.*"[323] They confiscated this paper, and then he was beheaded. The trunk remained erect for two hours and the head fell between his two legs, repeating a single phrase "Only One! O Only One!" And when people drew near him, they saw that his blood spilling on the ground had written "God! God! God!" in *thirty-five* places. Then they threw him in the fire, may God make him happy![324]

(Huart tr. [bib. no. 1665-h] II, 137). He forsook for a time his shaykh, 'Alī-b-A Muhsin Rifā'ī Harīrī (d. 620; whom his homonymy has made identify with him), to follow 'Alī Mugharbil, a disciple of Raslān Turkumanī (from Damascus); afterwards he joined his former shaykh's son, Yahyā-b-'Alī Rifā'ī.

[319] A historical work in manuscript by his nephew, ap. St. Joseph mss., Beirut.

[320] Cf. Jawbarī (Sauvaire, *JAP*, 1895, p. 387); and ap. *Quatre Textes*, pp. 77, 81.

[321] Cf. Abū'l-Hudā, *Qilāda*, 260, lines 4-7; and Būnī. The two Qur'ānic sigils which are included in it form the basis of the *hizb al-bahr* of Shādhilī (*RMM*, XIV, 116): this would therefore be a Shādhilite legend [a later footnote].

[322] Sūra 42 initials (cf. verse 17. According to Ibn al-Khashshāb, ms. P., 643, f. 31. This is the "revelation to Muhammad." Cf. Tabarī, *Tafsīr*; Khatīb I, 40: in a hadīth concerning the foundation of Baghdad, city of the Eyram, which will be destroyed by the Sufyānī (a [hadīth] series studied by Khatīb I, 29 iqd [?]).

[323] Sūra 19 initials (Mary): cf. Ibn 'Arabī, *Futūhāt* IV, 167. This is the "mission given to Jesus in Mary."

[324] Borgian ms. 3; London ms. 888, f. 328a.

7. There were a few exceptions among the Rifāʿīya who showed their sympathy for the memory of Hallāj.[325] First of all, ʿAlī Harīrī (d. 645), son of a man from Marw settled in Damascus and of a daughter of the Arab amīr Qirwāsh-b-Musayyib, founder of an eccentric semi-monistic school and of a zāwiya in Hauran; his son and successor, Hasan (d. 699), was at loggerheads with Ibn Taymīya. We have some fine verses on the funeral of ʿAlī Harīrī by his disciple Najm ibn Isrāyil (d. 677).[326] Next, Qāsim ibn al-Hājj (d. 680) whose Umm al-barāhīn contains, not only the legend of ʿAzāz, but an account of the appearance of Hallāj before Muqtadir, where he is cleared of the accusation of magic, gives proof of knowledge in mysticism and in law, pardons his accusers, "they have not seen what I have seen, nor contemplated what I contemplated," and ends by the verse "Wa humati'l-wadd." Finally, a Rifāʿī of Egypt, Dulunjāwī (d. 1123/1711) expressed with vehemence his devotion for Hallāj in comments in the margins of the Ta'rīkh of al-Khatīb: "The cream of the Sūfīs, their realizer, the one immersed in adorations of divine illumination, the contemplater with the naked eye of the emanations of holiness, the crown placed on the heads of those of mystic realization (tahqīq), is Husayn Hallāj . . . may God redouble, for us and for all Muslims, the benedictions He has brought us, and the benedictions attached to his knowledge, may He abandon whomever criticizes Hallāj in any manner whatsoever, may He hate him with his strongest hate and take vengeance with his harshest vengeance, for the honor of Muhammad, the lord of creatures!"

III. The Survival of Hallāj in Fars

a. Ibn Khafīf[1]

The oldest cemetery in Shiraz, rawda kabīrīya, bears the surname (shaykh kabīr) of Ibn Khafīf (268, d. 371). Abū ʿAA M-b-Khafīf-b-Isfikshādh,

---

[325] On Hallāj: cit. ap. Ibn Taymīya, Majm. ras. wa masā'il (Cairo 1341), 64, 105.

[326] There was a white frost on the ground the night before his funeral; and hence these verses: "The firmament wept over him at the hour of his burial; tears like scattered pearls. / Tears, I think, of joy, when the ascension of his soul to its apogee surrounded him with light. / Should not the rain also crystallize this way when it weeps? Such indeed are tears of joy" ('Akarī [bib. no. 830-a] V, 232). His Dīwān has been preserved (Aya Sofia ms. 1644); it includes some monistic verses that got him excommunicated. When very young (he was born in 603), he had a debate with Ibn al-Fārid (d. 632) on the subject of a qasīda of Ibn al-Khaymī (Ibn Hajar, Lisān al-mīzān V, 195-197).

---

[1] Ibn Junayd, Shadd al-izār [bib. no. 591-a], pp. 23-27 (only pp. 1-58 printed); Maʿsūm ʿAlī, Tarā'iq [bib. no. 1228-a] II, 212-226; Hujwīrī, 247, 158; ʿAttār [see bib. no. 1101] II, 124-131; Subkī II, 150-159; Ibn ʿAsākir, Tabyīn [?], 190-192; Jāmī, 262.

member of a very distinguished and wealthy Persian family from Shiraz, a client from Dabba (his mother, Umm Muhammad,[2] interred near him, was from Nishapur), had an early vocation to the life of a wandering mystic and a discipline of strict fasting. Returning from the hajj, around 290, he became acquainted with Junayd in Baghdad and received the khirqa from Ruwaym. He also saw Ibn 'Atā' and questioned Shiblī,[3] but did not see Hallāj.[4] Then, when he was about thirty, he began to study Shāfi'ite law in the school of Ibn Surayj, who at that time was qādī of Shiraz (296-301). During his second journey to Cairo, when he went to visit Rūdhabārī, another Persian nobleman who had become a mystic, in a ribāt at Ramlah, he was maltreated when falsely suspected of larceny in Jerusalem (whose governor turned out to be a former mamlūk of his father), and passed through Sur. In 309, he returned to Baghdad and paid a still famous visit to Hallāj prior to his execution. He resumed contact at that time, not only with Ibn 'Atā', but also with the friends of Ibn Surayj. It was then that his other, equally famous, visit to Ash'arī[5] in Basra must be placed. And if it is true, as Fīrūzābādhī thought, that Ibn Khafīf had a hand in his return to orthodoxy, this event would have had to have occurred a decade later.[6]

His visit to Ash'arī completes the character of Ibn Khafīf; still a fervent mystic, but having become a respected Shāfi'ite jurisconsult, he is now a militant Ash'arite theologian. The second half century of this unusually long life was to be marked by the redaction of some thirty mystical works, juridical and theological, coupled with long excursions, which ceased after 338, when the Buwayhid amīr, 'Adud al-Dawla, embarked on an all-out campaign against Sunnites and mystics, in which Ibn Khafīf was personally singled out and persecuted, as much by the prince[7] as by the Zāhirite qādī, Bishr-b-H [. . .]. It was at this very moment that Tanūkhī was peddling his vulgar anecdote about Ibn Khafīf bringing Sūfīs together one night of mourning for a sexual orgy.[8] In actual fact, of the many marriages (four hundred, it was said) contracted by him, at the request of his admirers, only one seems to have been consummated, from which he had a son, 'Abd al-Salām. Despite local persecution, Ibn Khafīf was for Sunnites, both traditionists and mystics, the object of a veneration that Sulamī conveyed, around 370, in an important way by

[2] Tarā'iq II, 224.   [3] Subkī II, 155.
[4] A protest by him then against Junayd (Akhbār, no. 61) was apocryphal.
[5] Subkī II, 155, 27.
[6] Shadd [bib. no. 591-a], London ms. 5677, f. 26a.
[7] His friend! (according to Ghanī, Hāfiz [bib. no. 1242-a] I, 12).
[8] Talbīs, 396; that parodied the notion of 'irs, ibid., 362.

entering his name as the thousandth and last shaykh in his *Ta'rīkh al-sūfīya* though he was still alive, because for them he had become the highest authority. He died on Tuesday, 23 *Ramadān* 371, a few days after he had recounted, with tears in his eyes, in a sermon (preached seated, because of his frailness) in the Tolstoian manner a theophany in the thatched hut of a charitable family at the very moment when a poor young man whom they had taken in to care for died.[9]

A *rāwī* of many hadīths, he transmitted to Nasawī, Abū Nu'aym, Qushayrī, the *qāri'* A Fadl M-b-Jafr Khuzā'ī (d. after 834), H-b-Hafs Andalūsī,[10] and Ibn Bākūyā.

In Shāfi'ite law, he wrote the following: *Kitāb manhaj, al-Istidrāj wa'l-indirāj, al-Mu'taqad (saghīr, kabīr), Ma'rifat al-zawāl.*

In parenetics: *Kitāb al-mi'rāj, Kitāb asāmī al-mashāyikh, al-Jaw' wa tark al-shahwāt, al-Istidhkār, al-Munqati'īn, al-Ighāna, al-Iqtisād, al-Mafarrāt, al-Radd wa'l-ulfa, Balwā'l-anbiyā', Sharaf al-fadā'il.*

In mysticism: *Kitāb sharaf al-fuqarā',*[11] *Lawāmi', Labs al-muraqqa'āt, Fadl al-tasawwuf, al-Jam' wa'l-tafriqa.*

In *usūl* and in dogmatics: *Kitāb al-fusūl fi'l-usūl, Ikhtilāf al-nās fi'l-Rūh, Masā'il 'Alī-b-Sahl* (Isfahānī), *Radd 'alā Ibn Ruzmān* (= Yazdānyār?), *Radd 'alā Ibn Sālim.*[12]

Examination of these titles helps us determine the intellectual position of Ibn Khafīf. An ascetic rather than a mystic, he preferred *hudūr* to ecstasy, putting emphasis on the practice of strict moral virtues; a jurisconsult and prudent theologian, he was perhaps the first in Ash'arism clearly to condemn two dangerous ideas: that of the eternity of the *Rūh* (espoused by the Hallājian Fāris), and that espoused by Ibn Sālim depicting God as creating *ab aeterno.*[13] His steadfast public defense of Hallāj's orthodoxy is much more significant and interesting to study. This was against Bundār (d. 353), like him an Ash'arite and a mystic; against a Tayfūrīyan, 'Īsā-b-Yazūl Qazwīnī; against Ibn Yazdānyār; against Abū Zur'a Tabarī, who had collected statements made by early mystics hostile to Hallāj.

In his *Mashyakha*, redacted by his disciple Daylamī, nine testimonies concerning Hallāj are assembled together, collected by Ibn Khafīf: three are from hostile sources (*Halwā* of Nahrajūrī, visit to Isfahan ['Alī-b-

---

[9] *Shadd*, f. 26. His tomb is today in the meidan Na'lbandan (*FNN* II, 158).
[10] Subkī II, 51.
[11] List ap. Ibn Junayd, *Shadd*, f. 24.
[12] He preferred *faqr* to *ghinā*.
[13] Harawī considers this attack exaggerated (*Tarā'iq* II).

Sahl], departure for India), but four others in which Ibn Khafif figures personally are intentionally favorable (fast in the *sahn* of the Ka'ba: "God was his only food"; debate over the tercet "*Subhāna*," objected to indignantly (two texts); visit to 'Umar (*sic*: 'Alī-b-Shallūya, ap. Jāmī-b-Shālūya, who had saved Hallāj's daughter; account of his own visit in prison, dream of AY Wāsitī).[14]

This *Mashyakha* consists of notices with anecdotes on 34 [. . .] Sūfis from Fars and from Iraq who had personal contacts with Ibn Khafif; their list is given in the *Tarā'iq*:[15] beginning with his first master, Abū Tālib Khazraj-b-'Alī Shīrāzī; Baqlī gives excerpts from it in his *Mantiq*.

Harawī refers, via Daqqāq, to other pro-Hallāj texts of Ibn Khafif.[16]

Ibn Khafif has been cited[17] by traditionists, Shāfi'ite jurisconsults, and Ash'arite theologians (AB A-b-Ibrāhīm Ismā'īlī Jurjānī, d. 371, Bāqillānī), but we know best his disciples in mysticism. First, his two *khādims*, Abū A (Fadl-b-M) Kabīr (d. 377), and Abū A (H-b-'Alī) Saghīr (315, d. 385; with him since 350), the real source of Ibn Bākūyā (d. 428)[18] for the *riwāyāt* that he tells us he received directly from Ibn Khafif. Next, his biographer, 'Alī-b-M? Daylamī (352, d. around 415), author, in Arabic, of the first book on divine love, *Kitāb al-alif al-ma'lūf* (title repeated from Hallāj); Abū'l-'Abbās Nahāwandī, master of Akh Faraj Zinjānī (d. 457), to whom is traced the *isnād* of a later congreganistic affiliation, the Kabīrīya,[19] whose ascetic rule may have been preserved for us in a *wasāyā* name.[20] But his true heir in mysticism was, per Abū 'Alī Hy-b-M-b-'Akkār, Abū Ishāq Ibrāhīm-b-Shāhryār Kāzerūnī (d. 426) called al-Murshid, founder of an order that was very prevalent among sailors of the

[14] To which Ibn Bākūyā was to give a series of almost identical pat answers in numbers 11, 12, 9b, 13, 14, 10, and 18 of his *Bidāya*; Baqlī reproduced the last five in the Arabic original (*Mantiq*).

[15] *Tarā'iq* II, 213 ff.

[16] Harawī: the two recensions of the *Wahhidnī* (ap. *Tabaqāt*).

[17] His *rāwīs*: Nasawī (according to Subkī).

[18] *Talbīs*, 223.

[19] Zabīdī, *'Iqd* [bib. no. 862-b], 88; this *isnād* ap. *Suhrawardīya* (the first was formed by Zinjānī in his monastery): IK > Nahāwandī > AF Zinjānī > Pīr Sīdāb > Bābā Husayn > Bābā A Shādābādhī > Sadr D Sā'igh > Hājj M > his grandson > Khāja M > M Shāh >Bahā' D Sijistānī (nephew of the previous one) AF Tāwūrī Muhyī D Qasrkinārī > Nahrawālī > Qutb Hanafī (his son) > A Wafā'-b-'Ajīl > A Bannā > 'Umar-b-A 'Alawī.

Murshidīya ('*Iqd*, 91): IK > Hy 'Akkār > Ibrāhīm-b-Shahryār K >A Fath Nasr-b-Khalifa Baydawī > Ibrāhīm Fārisī > M-b-Ibrāhīm Fārisī (Najm D) > Muhyī D 'AR-b-A Mun'im-b-Khalaf Damīrī > Fath D A Haram M Qalānisī > Zayn 'Irāqī > Shams D M ibn al-Jazawī (751, d. 833) > 'A Rahīm 'Izz-b-Furāt > A Khazr Sukhāwī > 'AR Shaybānī > Tābir-b-H-Ahdal > M Battāh > Yf Battāh > Yahyā-b-'Umar Zubayrī > 'A Khāliq Zubayrī.

[20] Shahīd 'Alī ms. 1388; Blochet tr., *Études esoteriques*, 1910, p. 175, n.1.

Indian Ocean, which spread the fame of the saint of Shiraz, Ibn Khafīf, "*shaykh kabīr*," all the way to those Hindu parents who gave to their son, Kabīr,[21] that ideal poetic summit of an Islamo-Hindu reconciliation, the name that he immortalized.[22]

Ibn Khafīf plays a considerable role in the legend of Hallāj. In the great Persian poems of 'Attār and, consequently, in Turkish and Urdu poetry, "*Shaykh Kabīr*" is the classic interlocutor who unfolds his doctrine in long-winded dialogues. In Arabic, the "visit of Ibn Khafīf" becomes the narrative frame in which the poems of Hallāj's *dīwān* are set.

b. The Ribāt of Bayda and the Kāzerūnīya

It is beyond doubt[23] that the *ribāt* founded in Bayda itself immediately after Hallāj's death kept alive the veneration of his memory, thereby preparing the way for the future birth in Bayda of the *dhikr* of the Hallājīya in the thirteenth century.

After the death of Ibn Khafīf (d. 371/982), the communal life of Sunnite mystics in Fars became organized under the direction of an authentic religious order, the Kāzerūnīya (or 'Ishāqīya), founded by Abū Ishāq Ibrāhīm Murshid ibn Shāhryār (b. 352, on hajj 388, d. 426),[24] member of an old Kazerun family, the B. Farrūkh, which had been permitted for a long time to remain Mazdaean, because of its descent from the brother of Salmān. Murshid, the founder, acknowledged three masters, Muhāsibī, Ibn Khafīf, and Abū 'Amr 'Abd al-Malik-b-'Alī Nūrdī (d. 358),[25] but he had received the *khirqa* from Ibn Khafīf via Husayn Akkār Bāzyār Fīrūzābādhī Jūrī (d. 391), a *khirqa* that he claimed dated back to Salmān via Shaqīq Balkhī (and also to Uways).[26] Murshid is the source of the Salmānī *isnād* in Sūfism.[27]

The fourth director of the order, Khatīb Imām Abū Bakr M-b-'Abd al-Karīm, who died in 502, was the author of *Firdaws al-Murshidīya*, published by Meier in a Persian translation. He was the successor to his

[21] Born in 1398, died in 1480 of our era, in Mahgar near Gorakhpur (U. P.).

[22] The *Kabirpanthis*, his disciples.

[23] In view of the reports of Murshid's friendly relations with his religious, especially with Abū'l-Azhar, Būlbūl, and the B. Sālbih.

[24] Mahmūd-b-'Uthmān (d. 745: disciple of Amīn D Balyānī), *Firdaws al-Murshidīya fī Asrār al-Samadīya*, edited by Fr. Meier, Istanbul, 1943. (Vol. XIV of the Bibl. Isl.) = the Persian translation of *Firdaws* by Khatīb Imām Abū Bakr (d. 502), a source used by 'Attār II, 291-304; cf. Köpr. M. Fuat, *Abū Ishāq, Ishaqī in-Anatolien*, ap. DI, 1930, pp. 18-26.

[25] *Firdaws*, 17.

[26] *Ibid.*, 25°.

[27] FNN II, 249; our *Salmān Pāk*, p. 10, n. 4; the cemetery of Kazerun (old name: Nūrd) is called "*Salmānī*"; Dasht Arjan was nearby.

brother, Abū Saʿd (d. 458), and his father, ʿAbd al-Karīm-b-ʿAlī-b-Saʿd (d. 442), and directed sixty-seven *ribāts* of the order, which was spread by Persian sailors from Siraf to Aden (where they implanted the Mundhirīya dynasty),[28] to India and China, in the sixteenth century, and later to Turkish Anatolia.

Murshid, who was fond of Hallājians like Shiblī and ʿAlī Daylamī,[29] and welcomed the visit of Daqqāq, and also sent back a long *wasīya* to Abū'l-Fath ʿAA ibn Sālbih, from Bayda, declared himself publicly for Hallāj (which may have been the reason for the brief persecution he suffered at the hands of Vizir Fakhr al-Mulk [d. 407], for which the father of Ibn Sālbih, ʿAbd al-Salām ibn Sālbih, came to console him in Bayda). Here is the text:[30]

Shaykh Murshid was sitting one day with a group of novices in his charge. He was beginning to speak in a moment of high and fruitful inspiration when one of those present said to him: "O shaykh, tell us something of the fragrance of Shaykh Husayn Mansūr's states." And the shaykh answered: "Since I do not know the states of this Sultan of Religion with any certainty, how can I tell you about them? You yourselves have heard him described, but, as for myself, I have not yet heard him (described by God) in such a way as to be able to tell you what I have actually seen of them." When night came, Shaykh Murshid uttered a prayer to God (*munājāt*), saying: "O Glorious, O Provident One, show me the state of this servant of Yours who gave You his soul, so that I may truly see his states." (A kind of *istikhāra*.) And a heavenly voice (*hātif*) rose up: "O noble servant, think of the gibbet, and behold"; and Murshid said: "while I was looking, a veil was lifted in front of me: I saw the Lord of Glory like a hanging curtain (*āwīkhte*), white with light; and I said: 'O my God, what is this white curtain of light?' And the voice said: 'O Abū Ishāq, this white curtain is the spirit of our Mansūr (Hallāj), for he is our "*manzūr*" (= Our Visible Form): because he gave his soul to Our way, he was crucified and burned because of Us, his spirit faced Our Presence without a veil. [We reveal this] so that you may know that whosoever will give his own soul to Our way will hold the same place as he in Our Presence.' " The next day, the shaykh recounted these states to his disciples, and this beautiful inspired moment became manifest to all (followed by a fervent eulogy of the author).

The Kāzerūnīya had recourse to a collection dealing with the miracles of Hallāj of which we made use above, and which ʿAttār seems to have used. Murshid accepts the idea of saints being able to transform material substances (*Firdaws*, 73), basing his view on the instance of Mary (Qur'ān 19:25: the dates), Dhū'l-Nūn, Hallāj (the dates, *Firdaws*, 74), and AN Sarrāj. He had as a disciple ʿAW Kashkānī, a pupil of Qādī Ibn Kajj (who

[28] *Firdaws*; s.v. index.
[29] Around 500-550 Hijra (Paris ms. 6021, ff. 60a-73a).
[30] *Firdaws*, 312.

had published a miracle of Hallāj). It must also be noted that the Kāzerūnī Abū Shujāʿ M-b-Saʿdān Maqārīdī (d. 509), author of a *mashyakha* and of a *Shīrāznāma* (Tehran ed., A.H. 1310), was, in the field of philosophy, a disciple of Abū Hayyān Tawhīdī and edited the ʿ*Atf* of Daylamī.

Two Suhrawardian branches were established in Fars after the death of Baqlī: that of ʿAlī Buzghush (d. 678; and of his son ʿAR, d. 716) in Shiraz, and that of Awhad D ʿAA-b-Masʿūd Bālyānī (d. 686) in Kazerun. Buzghush venerated Baqlī; his disciples, Natanzī and the two Kāshī, adopted the monist teaching of Ibn ʿArabī.[31] The branch of Awhad Bālyānī is doubly interesting: in the familial sense, he claimed to go back through seven generations to Abū ʿAlī Daqqāq (d. 414; which actually is nine, not seven, generations), the master and father-in-law of Qushayrī; and in the spiritual sense, his *isnād* includes, before his father, Imām D Masʿūd, already two Shirazians.[32] It is in connection with the nephew of Awhad Bālyānī, Amīn D M-b-ʿAlī-b-Masʿūd Bālyānī (d. 740), himself affiliated with the Kāzerūnīya order,[33] that we encounter the first known branch of the *tarīqa hallājīya* which had been founded a century earlier in Bayda. In view of the fact that Awhad Bālyānī was a well-known Sūfī writer (*Risāla al-wahda*), should we attribute to him this artificial creation that would have brought him to insert the name of Hallāj into the *isnād* of the Sabʿīnīya school? But the disdainful manner in which Awhad Bālyanī speaks of Mansūr leads us away from this hypothesis.

In fact, it was a member of the Kāzerūnīya order (or as it preferred at that time to be called, the Murshidīya),[34] Amīn Bālyānī (d. 740), who transmitted to Tāwūsī in Shiraz, the initiation in the *tarīqa hallājīya* which came to him from Zayn D ʿAbd al-Samad-b-ʿAR Baydawī.[35] The latter claimed (around 710) to be a tenth generation descendant of Hallāj (d. 309: actually thirteen generations). Zabīdī clearly states that Tāwūsī (d. 871) received this initiation through "M-b-Bahāʾ D Khabbāz Kāzerūnī." This individual is hard to identify: he seems to be the son of Bahāʾ D Abū Bakr-b-Hassām (*sic* = Khabbāz) Kāzerūnī, another master of Tāwūsī, according to Zabīdī;[36] and it would be tantalizing to imagine his son to be Qiwām D M-b-Ghiyāth D Ibrāhīm-b-M-Yahyā-b-Ibrāhīm Husaynī

---

[31] ʿAttār II, 291-304; Köpr. MF. *Abū Ishāq, Ishaqī en Anatolie* (DI, 1930, pp. 18-26).
[32] Jāmī, 291.
[33] Shaykh al-shuyūkh: *FNN* II, 249; *Salmān*, p. 10, n.4.
[34] A cousin, Saʿīd D M, d. 758, figures in *musalsalāt*: concerning Hallāj, cf. *Durar* IV, 255; *Shadd*, 34, 35; from another Bālyānī Kāzerūnīya branch, ʿAfīf Junayd (746, d. 811). Cf. *Daw'* III, 79, *muʿabbir* in Shiraz, master of Ibn al-Jazarī.
[35] Disciple of *Qādī'l-qudāt* Baydawī, commentary on the Qurʾān (Z[abīdī], 38).
[36] Cf. Z[abīdī], 65.

Kāzerūnī, whom Sakhāwī expressly tells us was "born in Gaza in 743, a disciple of Amīn Balyānī, a *rāwī* of Sa'īd D Kāzerūnī (d. 758); he gave the *ijāza* to Tāwūsī in 829."

In Bayda itself, a *ribāt* was founded about thirty years after the death of Hallāj by Abū'l-Azhar A Wāhid-b-M-b-Hayyān Istakhrī Baydāwī, *rāwī* of Abū Hamza, according to Kattānī,[37] whom Qannād had met in 325 in Qirqisa in the company of four hundred disciples. We do not know if the Sūfīs of this monastery were pro-Hallāj or not; we only have their names: Abū'l-'Abbās Hāshimī, whom Ibn Bākūyā came to see, 'Alī-b-Hy Kurdī Baydāwī, Yūsuf-b-'Alī-b-'AA (*muqri'*, and Sūfī),[38] and particularly AB A-b-M ibn Bunhūr Būlbūl, a disciple (indirect) of Abū'l-Azhar, who died in Shiraz in 455, but whose body was taken back to Bayda.

A religious of Bayda, A Hy Shihāb D A-b-M-b-Ibrāhīm ibn Sābih (b. 388, d. 473),[39] came to found a *khānqāh* in Shiraz in 443, endowed with a special rule, that of the Siddīqīya[40] (in honor of Abū Bakr; cf. the same feature among the early Hallājians), which it took from its master, Mu'ammal-b-'AA Bannā;[41] he was appointed *shaykh al-shuyūkh* of Fars; his son 'Abd al-Salām, and his grandson A Fath Nasr-b-Khalīfa-b-A Baydāwī, directed the monastery, where his other grandson was to confer the *khirqa* of the order, then connected with the Kāzerūnīya, on Rūzbihān Baqlī,[42] around 550. The latter does not tell us the source of his Hallājian documentation, but it is reasonable to suppose that he obtained it, if not from the *ribāt* of Bayda, at least from the Siddīqīya *khānqāh* of Shiraz, through his master, Sirāj D Mahmūd-b-Khalīfa-b-'A Salām-b-A ibn Sālbih Baydāwī Murshidī.

Around 620, a prominent man (*bayt riyāsa wa jalāl*) in Bayda, of Arab descent and language ('*arab ya'rub*), named Shihāb A-b-M-b-A-b-'Abd al-Rahīm, claimed to be an eighth generation (*sic*: for eleventh) descendant of Hallāj. Zabīdī, noting that fact, states that this family still existed in his time.[43] A later grandson of this Shihāb Ahmad, Zayn D 'Abd al-Samad-b-Najm D 'AR-b-Rukn D 'AA-b-Shihāb D Ahmad Baydāwī, a direct disciple of the grand qādī of Fars, 'AA-b-'Umar-b-Baydāwī (d. 685), passed on two congreganistic affiliations, around 710 in Shiraz: that

[37] Sarrāj, *Luma'*, 325; *Hilya* X, 275, 321; Ibn Yazdanyār, Cairo ms., n.p.; Sam'ānī, 99.
[38] Yāqūt I, 792.
[39] Cf. Ibn al-Jazarī [bib. no. 2104-a], no. 3012. Jāmī, 314; Ibn Junayd, *Shadd*, 29: Tawhīdī post mortem absolution.
[40] Whose founder was Khafājī (Sigla 30).
[41] Zabīdī, 94, s.v. Mu'ammalīya; *Salsabīl*, s.v. Siddīqīya, 29.
[42] "*Rūzbihānīya, shu'ba min al-Murshidīya*" (Zabīdī, s.v.); Jāmī, 288.
[43] *Sic*: Zabīdī, *Ithāf* I, 250: "his time" = the time of Abū Makhrama? or of Tawūsī?

of the Baydāwīya, which his master had received from Khadir,[44] and handed on to his son, Nizām D 'Abd al-Karīm; and that of the Hallājīya, which he had inherited from his father, passed on to Amīn Balānī Kāzerūnī (d. 740). Nizām D 'Abd al-Karīm Baydāwī, the last known descendant of Hallāj, transmitted the *isnād* of the Baydāwīya to Safī D Mardastī, master of Tāwūsī, around 740.[45]

c. Tāwūsī

Tāwūsī, whose full name was Nūr al-Dīn Abū'l-Futūh Ahmad-b-Jalāl D A Karam 'AA-b-Abī'l-Futūh 'A Qādir-b-Abī'l-Khayr 'Abd al-Haqq ibn 'AQ-b-'A Salām Tāwūsī, born in 790, died in 871,[46] came from a very old scholarly family from Aberquh, settled in Shiraz for two generations. A disciple of his grandfather and of his two paternal uncles Zahīr D A Nasr 'AR, *shaykh al-shuyūkh* of Shiraz (755, d. 831), and A Fadl Muhammad, Tāwūsī, a Shāfi'ite, is a certain type of *muhaddith* worthy of being described as representative of the aspirations of an important class of traditionists.[47] Disheartened by the fall of the Caliphate, these men, being fervent Muslims, tried to rebuild the unity of the Community on a mental plane: through the systematic memorization of certain hadīths, whose chains of *isnāds* linked to the Prophet were multiplied, trying to have the fewest number of possible intermediaries, thanks to several long-lived persons, and linking them to certain important collective acts, as follows: "X told me that Y had conferred the accolade on him, telling me: Z conferred the accolade on me, telling me . . . in this way did the Prophet confer the accolade on me"; or as follows: "X gave me a morsel to swallow, telling me . . . in this way did the Prophet. . . ." The whole body of *musalsalāt* literature is devoted, with touching care, to this kind of hadīth.[48] On the same mental plane, a similar amalgamating and coordinating effort was made to connect the principal supererogatory prayers, especially the *dhikr* and the *tahlīl*, with a certain posture and ap-

---

[44] Zabīdī, s.v., 38, 45 (cf. *Salsabīl*, 43). See his *Tafsīr*, XVIII.

[45] And via Tāwūsī, 'Atallāh Kāzerūnī, his son Nasīm D Hibatallāh Kāzerūnī, called Shāh Mīr (d. 904), in Medina to Amīr Kilān Rakhawī, 177. Kilān, son of the Naqishbandī M Islām Jawbyadī Bukhārī (d. 971), then to Ghadanfir, the former *caziaskar* of Emperor Akbar.

One has an inkling of some unexplainable interferences in this "family of Hallāj," which claimed to be Ansārian (via Abū Ayyūb), made by Ibn Salība and the grand qādī, both Baydāwīs. By 1937, M. Gaulmier met a descendant of Hallāj in the Ma'rif of Aleppo.

[46] *Daw'* I, 360; Kattānī II, 274, 300; Zabīdī; *Sharh al-qāmūs* IV, 182. In 819 in Mecca.

[47] Tāwūs al-Harawīya A Khayr Iqbāl, a disciple of Junayd via A H Sīrwānī (Zabīdī, s.v. Tāwūsīya).

[48] Cf. *Daw'* IV, 117; VIII, 166; VI, 326.

propriate gestures; hence, another series of works grouping together with the various religious orders their initiation *isnāds* going back to the Companions of the Prophet. Lastly, the pilgrimage, the sojourn in Mecca, where for more than a century members of the Kāzerūnīya (750-867)[49] were the chief muezzins of the Ka'ba, was looked upon as the means of spreading and of unifying the branches of the congreganist *dhikr* and of coming into contact with the spiritual hierarchy distributing the gifts of God to the world, for it was increasingly believed that its mysterious leader, who was called the Khadir, the Ghawth, or the Qutb, should reside in Mecca and Medina, at least for certain annual festivals.

Tāwūsī most certainly, Sakhāwī stresses, was a qualified master in grammar, in Qur'ān (a *hāfiz* pupil of Ibn al-Jazarī for the *qirā'a* of Āsim), in hadīth, in law (received the *iftā'* from M-b-M Kāzerūnī), and in theology, but his main effort went into the threefold mental plane examined above. He was given the *khirqa* by Zayn D AB M-b-M Khwāfī (757, d. 838),[50] because he believed in him and called him the Ghawth of the age, the disciple of the previous Ghawth ('AR Shibrīsī), and because he was the *rāwī* of the hadīth "X gave me the accolade . . . as did the Prophet. . . ." In hadīth, he wrote the *Khizānat al-la'ālī* about the *isnāds* that go back the furthest (= the macrobiotics), and he himself plays a role in one of the most famous of them, in the transmission of the *Sahīh* of Bukhārī, studied at length by Kittānī in his *Fihrist* (II, 302-313). Lastly, for the branches of the congreganist *dhikr*, he wrote a basic treatise, *Jam' al-firaq li-raf' al-firaq*, in two parts: a list of eight *wasā'it* connected with the Prophet (Khadir, Ilyās, Abū Bakr, 'Umar, 'Alī, 'AA ibn 'Abbās, Abū'l-Dardā', the *qutb* Abū'l-Bayān Nabāb-b-M-b Mahfūz Qurashī, d. 616 in Damascus); and a list of twenty-six *khirqas*. Since this manual formed the basis for subsequent manuals ('Ujaymī, etc.), it is appropriate here to give the names of the twenty-six orders chosen by Tāwūsī.[51] Six go back directly to the Prophet, through *suhba* or *kashf*: Uwaysīya (via M Asyābī Harawī), Bayānīya (via Nasrallāh ibn Jamā'a in Jerusalem), Dardā'īya (A Habīb Dihlawī), Shurayhīya (via Bahā' Kāzerūnī), Kardawīya (via 'Arabshāh Husaynī), Mu'ammarīya (by "the accolade," via Ibrāhīm Adham). Four go back to macrobiotics (*mu'ammarīn*): Bākharzīya (Ibr. Kubrawī: via Khiyādānī), Jāmīya (via Yf Harawī), Haydarīya (via 'Īsā Zāwajī and Chishtīya), Kubrawīya (via Yf Harawī).

[49] *Daw'* V, 34; *IX*, 26.   [50] Jāmī, 569; *Daw'* IX, 260; *Simt*, 145, 147.
[51] Zabīdī, *'Iqd*, s.v.; *Salsabīl* refers to Tāwūsī only for the following: Mu'ammarīya, Kardawīya, Hallājīya, Nūrīya, Ruknīya (based on Shinnāwī), Shanbakīya, and Mewlewīya (39, 40, 43, 106, 112, 169, 141).

Six are mere revivals of extinct schools: Bistāmīya (via AB Khwāfī), Junaydīya (via Sharaf Abarqūhī), Kharrāzīya (via M Khwānī), Saī'dīya (= of Ibn Abī'l-Khayr, via Sa'd D Bāba), Shanbakīya (= of Sahl Tustarī, via Yūnus Shanbakī in Huwayza), Adhamīya (= Adhamī monastery of Jerusalem, via Ni'matallāh Kirmānī).

The other ten are unusual local survivals (or resurgences): Bukhārīya (India, via Makhdūm Jahāniyān), Baydāwīya (= Qādī of Qādīs M Baydāwī, d. 685, via Zayn D 'Abd al-Samad, a descendant of Hallāj), Hallājīya (via the previous *rāwī*), Elyāsīya-Hammawayhīya (= the *shaykh al-shuyūkh* M-b-M ibn Hammūya Juwaynī, via M. Derguzīnī), Murshidīya-Rūzbahānīya (= Baqlī, d. 606, via Ghiyāth D M Kāzerūnī), Sādiqīya (M-b-Muzaffar 'Umarī, via Ibrāhīm Kāzerūnī and the Jāmīya monastery in Shiraz, *Shadd*, 55), Qāsimīya (= Abū'l-Qāsim-b-Ramadān, via 'A 'Azīz Qirshawī, Mu'ayyad Janādī, 'Attār and Ibn Abī'l-Khayr), Kabīrīya (= Khafīfīya, via Bahā' D Sijistānī), Mewlewīya (via Ayyūb-b-M Tūsī), Nūrīya (= Kasirqī, via Tāhir Kāzerūnī).

We know, moreover, that Tāwūsī had been initiated into the Ruknīya (via Yahyā Sijistānī), and the Naqishbandīya (via S. Jurjānī),[52] but these two orders must not have been included in the manual, from which the early great orders are missing.[53] Tāwūsī did not dare merge them (as Sanūsī would later) with this assemblage and local constriction of Shirazian Sunnite Islam's spiritual ties with the Prophet, around a Tāwūsīya *tarīqa*[54] skeleton plan. Six out of the twenty-six orders chosen were from around Shiraz, and, in the case of four, Tāwūsī was initiated by a member of the Kāzerūnīya.

Two of Tāwūsī's grandsons used his manual, informing[55] Indian pilgrims in the Hijaz about it: Shāh Mīr (d. 904), in his *Musalsalāt* used by Qushāshī;[56] Tāj 'AR Kāzerūnī, in his *Riwāyāt* transmitted to Shinnāwī (by Ghadanfir), and inserted into his commentary on the Shattārian *jawāhir*, thereby accrediting initiation into the Hallājian order for pilgrims coming from all parts of the Muslim world.

In Fars itself and in Shiraz, after Tāwūsī,[57] with the decline of Sunnism

---

[52] Kattanī II, 275.
[53] Qādirīya, etc.
[54] Zabīdī, s.v.
[55] *Simt*, 145-146.
[56] Nasīm D Hibatallāh-b-'Atallāh-b-Lutfallāh-b-Salāmallāh-b-Rūhallāh Kāzerūnī Shāh Mīr came from a Shīrāzī line that played an important religious role for two centuries; the first, Rūhallāh, was initiated before 719 into the Nūrīya order, which he transmitted, through his son Salāmallāh and his grandson Safī D Tāhir, to Tāwūsī, whose daughter married another grandson (Zabīdī, s.v.).
[57] Concerning his disciple Muhyī' D A Yazīd M-b-M-b-Mahmūd Qasr Kinārī, cf. Zabīdī, s.v. Adhanīya Kabīrīya.

and the Kāzerūnīya order, it is in three religious orders converted to Imāmism that we find the memory of Hallāj revived.

d. Imāmite Religious Orders[58-62]

1. Ni'matallāhīya

The founder of this order, Ni'matallāh-b-'AA Husaynī, who died in Kirman in 834/1431, was the murīd of the Sunnite Yāfi'ī (d. 768), in the Adhamīya order into which he initiated Tāwūsī. He quoted Hallāj's interview with Khawwā in his Rasā'il (Calc. ms. 1239, f. 409).

A contemporary Ni'matallāhī, Ma'sūm 'Alī Shāh (d. A.H. 1337), reproduced in his Tarā'iq the account of Ibn Khafīf's visit to Hallāj in prison, and noted that "numberless are the quotations concerning his states in prose and verse in the books of Sūfīs."

2. Nūrbakhshīya

The Ruknīya, a branch of the Kubrawīya founded by 'Alā"l-Dawla Semnānī (d. 736) and directed after him by Mahmūd Mazdaqānī (or Sharaf Ghawrī) and by 'Alī Hamadhānī (d. 736), were split under his successor, Ishāq Khuttalānī, into two rival branches, both Shī'ite: the Dhahabīya and the Nūrbakhshīya, from M Nūrbakhsh (d. 869). The writer Nūrallāh Shūshtarī, who upheld the memory of Hallāj, belonged to this order, which was quite powerful in Fars.

3. Dhahabīya

The Dhahabīya, dissidents of the Ruknīya, founded around 830 by 'AA Barzashābādī Mashhadī, have continued for five centuries to have many members among eminent Shī'ites of Fars and Tehran; and they have been especially interested in Hallāj. One of their writers, Kamāl Hy Khwārizmī (d. around 839), was the author[63] of a Persian dīwān attributed to Hallāj.[64]

---

[58] Tarā'iq II, 146 [no footnote reference].
[59] Ivanow, Calcutta ASB catalogue [no footnote reference].
[60] Tarā'iq II, 214 [no footnote reference].
[61] Ibid., 143; Salsabīl, 104, 107 [no footnote reference].
[62] Tarā'iq II, 154 [no footnote reference].
[63] An attribution pointed out by M. Ghazvinī of Qasīda I, ap. Riyād al-'arifīn, 68, and Habīb al-siyar, 93.
[64] This attribution of the dīwān does not seem to be ascribable to the author, but rather to a modern Indian editor. Hallāj is extolled in it in four places, but as distinct from the author (p. 12 where it is formal; p. 25 Anā'l-Haqq; p. 37 his heroism; p. 80 the greats predestined to love: Moses, Ahmad, 'Alī, Mansūr).

Their leader at the beginning of the seventeenth century, Qutb al-Dīn Nīrīzī Dhahabī,[65] analyzing the mystical stages, stated that in order to go beyond the fifth (qurb, hadrat al-ahadīya) only a special grace can bring the holy soul into the walāya ʿalawīya without its being conscious of it. Similarly, Bistāmī, having been the saqqā of Jaʿfar Sādiq, said "in my jubba, there is only God; like Husayn ibn Mansūr Hallāj, who, having prostrated himself on the threshold of the mahdī, declared passively "Anāʾl-Haqq"; killed and burned, his ashes wrote on the waves of the Tigris "Allāh, Allāh" and his blood "Anāʾl-Haqq" on the ground to vindicate him of his seeming impiety. When the Prophet reproached him, "why did you cause this breach in my law?" [He said:] "Let me be your ransom; my head will fill it, so that no one may pass through it after me."[66]

e. Husayn ibn A Rāzī[67]

Originally from Rayy, he lived for a time in Baghdad[68] under Shiblī's (d. 334) direction, and afterwards settled in Nishapur to become a disciple of Ibn al-Farghānī, son of the great AJ M-b-ʿAA. In Baghdad before 328, he must have died in Nishapur around 360.[69]

He must have written the account of Rūdhabārī's death,[70] for it was said specifically to have been by him. His great interest to us rests on the fact that he was the only one to accept the two Sūfī masters excluded for hulūl, Abū Hulmān and Hallāj. He implies that Ibn Hanbal (according to his son, Qādī Sālih) allowed dancing.[71]

Husayn Rāzī became acquainted with Abū Hulmān via Farghānī through an original mind, a Hāshimite, ʿAbbās-b-Muhtadī, who followed Kharrāz from Baghdad to Egypt, traveled around Syria, and finally settled in Mecca, where he died in 317.[72] Like Ibn ʿAtāʾ, he meditated on suffering. He saw Abū Hulmān, withdrawn in Ramlah, spend a whole night prostrate and weeping "before someone" (bayn yaday shakhs).[73]

---

[65] The Tarāʾiq have a Dhahabī of the fourth generation as leader (II, 154, lines 13-15), thus deceased around 990, just when Mahmūd Ghujdwānī wrote his biography.

[66] Qawāʾim al-anwār, ap. Khuyyī, Sharh minhāj al-barāʾa, VI, 263.

[67] Abū ʿAA Hy-b-A-b-Jaʿfar Rāzī (Qushayrī, 28, 63, 112, 127, 130, 147, 151, 181 (= Lumaʿ, 316), 192, Hilya X, 324, 354.

[68] Cf. AN Sarrāj, Lumaʿ, 316.

[69] Since he was the rāwī of Murtaʿish (Qushayrī, 147), Kattānī, and Khuldī (Qissa, 110).

[70] Kh. VII, 2482.   [71] Talbīs, 259.

[72] Died in 299, according to Ibn al-Jawzī. The very same account of the dream enables us to identify him with his homonym, Abūʾl-Dadl ʿAbbās-b-Samura Hāshimī, but Sulamī gives him as two persons: Ibn ʿAsākir VII, 268, 223. Cf. Taʿarruf, 117.

[73] This "someone" was undoubtedly a handsome-faced novice selected as a shāhid = a

[As far as Hallāj is concerned], Husayn Rāzī seems to have been the first to call attention[74] to certain contradictions in the accounts of his execution. We take from him the two versions of his flagellation published by Sulamī (*Ta'rīkh*, nos. 19-20), that of AB 'Atūfī (d. 343), and that of Abū'l-'Abbās [A-b-M]-b-'Abd al-'Azīz.[75] Finally, since he was the only direct *rāwī* of AB ibn Mamshādh,[76] he had to be the one who gave AQ J-b-A Rāzī (d. 378, Nishapur) the decisive account by Ibn Mamshādh of the *'ayn al-jam'* incident at the trial of 309, published by Abū'l-'Abbās Muqri' A-b-M-b-Z Nasawī (d. 396) in his *Ta'rīkh* and transmitted at the same time to Sulamī by Nasrabādhī.[77] Commonly called "*Abū 'Abdallāh*," he was also perhaps the one who received from Shiblī the "*Anā'l-Ḥaqq*" account containing the verse "*Yā sirra sirrī*," published as early as 355, based on "*Abū 'Abdallāh*" by Maqdisī in the *Kitāb al-bad' wa'l-ta'rīkh*.[78]

f. Abū Bakr ibn Ghālib [79]

This Hallājian *rāwī*, an "unknown, whose testimony is therefore lacking in authority" (Khatīb), was a disciple of Ibn Khafīf, on whom Kalābādhī published, through his go-between, an interesting notice concerning Kattānī's method of oniromantics (of seeing the Prophet in a dream on the twenty-fifth of each month, for purposes of solving questions of law; a noncanonical method based on *istikhāra*, like that which was condemned much later in Ibn Abī Jamra).[80]

---

manifestation of divine beauty, for Mihrijān used to do this (*Masāri'*, 142 = *Talbīs*, 287). Cf. the quatrain of Jalāl D Rūmī "*qawl bi'l-shāhid*" (= "*badāliya*" with Badawīya Maraziqa; Mutāwi'a, *Salsabīl*, 7 = reference ap. Ibn al-Fārid, *Ta'iya*).

[74] Ms. P. 2137, f. 122b (Ibn 'Asākir).

[75] *Talbīs*, 362: *rāwī* of Shiblī in Bāk. Also, concerning 'Atūfī, Kh. VII, 248 (pupil of A-b-H-b-'Abd al-Jabbār of Bāb Harb, d. 306).

[76] Qushayrī, 181.

[77] Sulamī, *Ta'rīkh*, no. 11; cf. Qushayrī, 192; and *Lawaq*. I, 124 (AQ Rāzī).

[78] A comparison is just drawn in it between Hallāj and Abū Hulmān (*Qawl bi'l-Shāhid*). Huart read "Ibn 'AA," which would indicate Mansūr-b-'AA (*rāwī* as early as 341). There is still a problem to be resolved about other *riwāyāt* of Ja'far Rāzī (concerning Ibn Abī Sa'dān, Kh. IV, 361, his master according to Qushayrī, p. 79) and Ibn 'Atā' (*Lawaq*. I, 124), in relation to Abū Zur'a Tabarī or to Husayn Rāzī.
[Transmission:] From Farghānī (and Khuldī) to Harawī up to Sarrāj (Q. 192: *Luma'*, 316), to Sulamī, to J. Rāzī.
From Shiblī to Abū Ishāq Zajjāj up to Ibn 'AA (surname of the Mu'tazilite grammarian Sirāfī, d. 368, pupil of Zajjāj via AB M-b-Sarī' ibn al-Sarrāj, d. 315, and AB M-b-'Alī Mabramān) and up to Fasawī, d. 377 (*rāwī* of Zajjāj: *Fihrist*, 64).
Ibn al-Farghānī introduced the *samā'* in Nishapur around 361 (before individual *qawwāl*): cf. Qushayrī, 177; *Talbīs*, 264 (Su'lukī converted).

[79] AB M-b-M ibn Ghālib, d. around 375. Khatīb VIII.

[80] *Ta'arruf*, 119. Ibn Abī Jamra: ms. P.

Sulamī received four important texts dealing with Hallāj from him: in his *Ta'rīkh*, an explanation of the condemnation of Hallāj toning down the idea of *shāhid*;[81] a version (via Isfījānī) of his *'aqīda* in theodicy which would be preferred by Ash'arites (Qushayrī) to the one edited by Kalābādhī, for it condemns the words *"imtizāj"* and *"hulūl"*;[82] a statement about the acme of fasting,[83] less elaborate than his recension given in the *Tafsīr* of Sulamī;[84] and, in his *Tabaqāt*, eleven maxims by Hallāj (nos. 10-20: nos. 12 and 13 are found also in *Tafsīr* 55, 58; and no. 21 is related to *Tafsīr* 193; nos. 13, 20, and 21 are pro-Ash'arite;[85] no. 17 gives the verses found in *Akhbār* 36).[86]

This source of Sulamī's shares the Ash'arite tendency of Ibn Khafīf and defines the Hallāj texts in this sense.

IV. THE SURVIVAL IN KHURASAN

Hallājians sprang up immediately in Nishapur, where Hallāj must have spent some time, and where his son Sulaymān had settled. In 311, when Vizir Hāmid, who had had Ibn 'Atā' killed for being a Hallājian, in his turn died, it was said among Sūfīs in Nishapur that the curse of Ibn 'Atā' had fallen upon Hāmid.[1] This version came from Abū 'Amr-M-b-A-b-Hamdān,[2] son of a noted *muqri'* and disciple of Abū 'Uthmān Hīrī (d. 298), who had been present in 298 at the funeral of this master (who had implanted Baghdadian Sūfism in Nishapur, though being himself originally from Rayy). The father of Abū 'Amr, A-b-Hamdān-b-'Alī-b-Sinān (d. 311, Mecca),[3] was a Malāmatī and disciple of Abū Hafs Haddād (d. 264, master of Hīrī).

From the leading disciple of Hīrī, AM 'AA-b-M-b-'AR Sha'rānī Rāzī (d. 353;[4] he lived in Nishapur and went to Iraq), we have one of the oldest versions of Hallāj's interview in Kufa with Khawwās,[5] which Sulamī

---

[81] *Shāhid* ceased to signify a person and became again, as in grammar, an argument.
[82] Qushayrī, 8 = *Akhbār*, no. 13.   [83] Qushayrī.   [84] No. 182.
[85] No. 13: *masmūd* (cf. Rāzī, *Asas*, 23); no. 20, against Jubbā'ī; no. 21, "neither distinct nor combined" (thus immaterial: F. Rāzī, *Asas*, 82).
[86] Which shows that this number from *Akhbār* is earlier than Ibn Ghālib.

---

[1] Sulamī, *Ta'rīkh* (ap. Dhahabī, cf. Amedroz).
[2] *Hilya* X, 229, 230, 240; Qushayrī, 23, 107 (hadīth). Abū 'Amr M-b-A-b-Hamdan-b-'Alī-b-Sunān Hīrī, d. 338, a pupil of Baghawī, master of Ibn al-Bayyī' (Sam'ānī): Sibt ibn al-Jawzi, ms. P. 5866, f. 113b, gives 376.
[3] *Hilya* X, 230; Sh., *Lawaq*. I, 102-103.
[4] *Lawaq*. I, 119; *Hilya* X, 253; Qushayrī, 71, 82, 91, 104, 106, 122, 169, 174, 178, 183.
[5] Qushayrī, 111, 51.

received from him, no doubt through his grandfather, Ibn Nujayd, the last *rāwī* of Abū 'Uthmān Hīrī.

Hīrī and his school (his son Muhammad, d. 325, his grandson Ahmad, d. 353) sympathized with Hallāj in the same way, without considering the excommunication issued against him by 'Amr Makkī. The Sāmānid government, both in Khurasan and in Transoxiana, undoubtedly refused, in 309 and after 309, to track down Hallājians outlawed in 'Abbāsid cities.[6] AB Wāsitī (d. 331), plagued by A 'Uthmān Maghribī, settled in Marw, and Fāris went off to die in Bukhara. The *ra'īs* and qādīs of Nishapur were sympathetic towards Sūfīs; that is, until 393.[7] Then persecution erupted under Mahmūd II with the *ra'īs* Abū Bakr ibn Mamshādh (398-410 and 421-430), a member of the Karrāmīya sect, and with the Hanafite qādīs Sā'id Ustuwā'ī (393-398 and 421, d. 431), 'Utba-b-Khaythama (398, d. 406), Ismā'īl-b-Sā'id (431, d. 443), and A-b-M-b-Sā'id (443, d. 482). The persecution, which at first was anti-Shāfi'ite (the Shāfi'ites recaptured the office of qādī in 413 and held it— until 421?), began in 445 against the Ash'arites.[8] The line of the Awlād Sa'id Ustuwā'ī, hereditary grand qādīs of Nishapur from 393 to 554, was hostile to Hallājians like Ibn Abī'-Khayr,[9] but the Hanafite qādī M-b-'AA Nāsihī (d. 484) had been a pupil of the son (Ismā'īl) of the Hallājian Nasrābādhī; and, for the most part, West Khurasan was hospitable to Hallājians (the Karrāmīyans were broken up in 488). The position of *shaykh al-shuyūkh* (inspector general of monasteries) of Khurasan,[10] created by the Saljūqs in imitation of Baghdad (440-686), had the following as incumbents: Sahlajī (455, d. 476), Jurjānī (465? d. 469), Fārmadhī

---

[6] Vizir Bal'amī (307, d. 329) was a Shāfi'ite and pro-Sūfī (cf. Dh[ahabī] ms. 1581, f. 100a).

[7] The year 393 also marked a defeat for Shāfi'ism in Baghdad in its struggle against the Mu'tazilism of the Hanafites, supported there by Shī'ism.

[8] The coalition of Ash'arites and Sūfīs, establishing theological *madrasas* thanks to the *waqfs* of mystical *khānqāhs*, was founded in Nishapur under the auspices of the *ra'īs* 'AA-b-Ismā'īl Mīkālī (360, d. 379) and the amīr AH M-b-Ibrāhīm-b-Simjūr (372-377), when the Ash'arite *madrasa* of Ibn Fūrak (d. 406) was installed in the *khānqāh* of Bushānjī (d. 348). Isfarā'inī (340, d. 418) also taught there. He was a pupil of Da'laj (d. 351), and the initial idea of the Ash'arite *madrasa* probably went back to the Shāfi'ite *waqf* founded by Da'laj in Baghdad. Ibn al-Muslima took from it the idea of the Nizāmīya university, which Nizām al-Mulk made a reality.

For the association between Shāfi'ism and the *ribāt* (*waqf* of the Da'laj sort): 'Amrī became a Shāfi'ite and founded a *ribāt* in M al-Mansūr around 360; Isfarā'inī made sure that no one was for Bāqillānī there.

The (*madrasa*) of Ibn Surayj: those who were buried there "close to Ibn Surayj": Abīwardī, 'Umar Zinjānī (Subkī IV, 18), d. 459; M-b-Hy. Shāmī, 478-488 (Subkī III, 84).

[9] In [?] the *khānqāh* of Nishapur was in Bāgh al-bazzāzīn (Sam'ānī, f. 80b).

[10] Athīr XI, 115.

(469, d. 477), AB Nassāj Tūsī (d. 487), M-b-Hammūya Juwaynī (449, d. 530, head of the Banū Hammūya line of *shaykh al-shuyūkh* office holders of Damascus and Cairo, 563-678), Abū'l-Asad 'AR Qushayrī (d. 547); Jurjānī and Fārmadhī were openly Hallājian.[11] But at the time of the sacking of Nishapur (in 554), the duties of *ra'īs* passed to the Husaynid Shī'ite anti-Shāfi'ite *naqīb al-nuqabā'*.

In Herat, the B. Dhuhl amīrs supported Sūfīs and Hallājians. In Balkh, the qādīs remained Mu'tazilite Hanafites until 378 and 421; but the amīrs supported Sūfīs, from the B. Māhān (136-230) down to the B. Bānījūr (233-340), who granted asylum to the Hallājians of Talaqan (Iskāf, who found refuge with an 'Aqīlī sharīf of Balkh around 400); and the Farighūn (279-401).

In Bukhara, the Al-Saffār, who through the sixth century controlled the supervision of the *ribāt* and the position of *ra'īs* of the city, appear to have curtailed Hallājians' devotional practices.[12]

We shall study in a separate section later in the present work the main witnesses of the Hallājian tradition in Khurasan: Fāris Dīnawārī, Ibrāhīm Nasrabadhī, Warthānī, Ibn Shādhān, Mansūr Harawī, Sulamī, Ibn Bākūyā, Abū Ismā'īl Harawī. The testimony of 'Attār will be studied elsewhere, as will the Hallājian infiltration into the court of the Mongol Khans.

a. *Fāris Dīnawārī (= AQ Baghdādī)*

Fāris, of Dinawar stock, was born in Baghdad around 285 and spent the early part of his life there in the Sūfī atmosphere surrounding Junayd, Nūrī, Yf-b-Hy Rāzī, and especially Ibn 'Atā'.[13] He was not present at Hallāj's execution, but became attached to his teaching after his death, kept his memory alive, and must have then left his own homeland. First settling in Nishapur, he went further north to preach, to Marw (in 340), and afterwards to Samarqand, where he died around 345. People visited his tomb in the cemetery of the citadel near the tomb of his friend, the

---

[11] The death of the mystic Akkāf in 549 (pupil of AN Qushayrī) should be studied carefully (Sam'ānī).

[12] An irony, ap. 'Attār, *Tadhk.*

[13] Abū'l-Qāsim (= Abū'l-Tayī-b-Abī'l-Fawāris) Fāris-b-'Īsā Dīnawārī Baghdādī: biography ap. Ibn al-Bayyī', *Ta'rīkh Nīsābūr*, ms. abridged [by Dhahabī: Subkī V, 217], *Brousse*, f. 47a (commentary by Viqar A Hamdanī, 6, II, 1938); Khatīb XII, 390; XIV, 316; VII, 246; VIII, 114, I, . . .; Jāmī, 174. Possibly the son of 'Īsā Qassār Dīnawārī, a disciple of Shiblī (*Luma'*, 148) and of Hallāj (*ibid.*, 303), *rāwī* of Ruwaym (*ibid.*, 303), *rāwī* of Ruwaym (*ibid.*, 189, Q[*isse*] [?] 155). A Dīnawār, the *Luma'* then cites eight Sūfīs, RMM XIV, 318, not counting Mamshādh.

Hanafite qāḍī Ḥakīm AQ Ishāq-b-M Samarqandī (d. 342),[14] patronized, it can be assumed, as was he by the Hanafite qāḍī of Bukhara, M-b-Sulamī (d. when vizir, in 334) (*Tab. Hanaf.* II, 113), and the local amīr (Mansūr-b-Qaratagīn, d. 340, or rather Ibrāhīm-b-Sīmjūr), who was the patron of AB Qaffāl (d. 338).

A highly cultivated mind, writing in a fine *saj'* style,[15] Fāris, in the manner of, but much more profoundly than, Qannād, extracted from Hallāj's life, and especially from his death, a theme for aesthetic and amatory contemplation which he developed in his works. We do not know the titles [of these works] but do have excerpts, thanks to the *Ta'arruf* of Kalābādhī and especially to the *Tafsīr* of Sulamī, in which they served as a critique of the Qur'ānic interpretation that one of his elders, AB Wāsiṭī (d. 320, like him a refugee in Khurasan), had attempted of Hallāj's thought.[16]

Deeply enamored of Hallāj, and adhering fully to all of his passionate vocabulary of divine love, Fāris saw him as a *shāhid*, like the Biblical and Qur'ānic Joseph (Ibn 'Atā''s idea), who transcends practical law and reason; that is to say, a chosen being through whom divine beauty radiates to win hearts. He therefore accepts daring theological ideas, such as that of *shāhid*, *hulūl* (divine infusion into the saint), and *imtizāj* (the fusion of two natures). He asserts that, in the state of *fanā'*, far from being annihilated, the *shāhid* continues to perceive his own form, but wholly tinted by the One Who has carried him away, and his carnal self (*bashariya*) is not destroyed but enclosed in a sheath of joy and aroused at the sight of suffering, like the onlookers enthralled by Joseph's beauty.[17]

We are indebted to Fāris for having preserved Hallāj's most beautiful lines of verse: the distich "*Anā man ahwā*" (whose second verse is "we are two spirits infused into one body"), the quatrain "*Anta bayn al-shaghāf*" (whose second verse is "and You infuse my heart with consciousness, as You infuse bodies with souls"), the distich "*hammaltum*" ("the weight You have given our hearts to bear . . . "; cf. *Akhbār*, no. 11); and proba-

---

[14] *Der Çāker Dīz* (Dārā Shikūh, *Safīna*, f. 89a; *Tab. Hanaf.* I, 139, s.v. Ḥakīm Ishāq).

[15] Excerpt in Kal., no. 33.

[16] Fāris' quotations ap. Sulamī's *Tafsīr* (two-thirds of those relating to Qur'ān 2:2 are missing), preserved in Baqlī's *Tafsīr* (printed edition, Vol. I, 24, 49, 66, 79, 87, 128, 218, 236, 328, 383, 520, 556, 566 (2), 592 (2), 593; Vol. II, 20, 26, 27, 31, 58, 76, 106, 162, 203, 211, 314, 355, 368, 383. The following quotations from "Husayn" (= Hallāj) in Sulamī's *Tafsīr* must have come from Fāris' works: no. 5 (= Baqlī, *Tafsīr* I, 24), 64, 75, 90 (cf. "*aw-jab*" at the end of Kh., 114, and "*wahdānī*" in Q [*isse*] 150), 130-131 (surely), 146, 201 (to be completed by Baqlī II, 383).

[17] *Ta'arruf*, 95.

bly also the distichs on the *imtizāj* reported by A Hātim Tabarī (based on Shiblī), the poem *"Tāha'l-khalā'iq"* (or *"muhill,"* as corrected by the Ismā'īlī Mu'ayyad Shīrāzī), the poem *"haykali'l-jism"* (in which *"samadiyu'l-rūhi"* was corrected by the Nusayrī Khasībī to read *"jawharīyu'l-nafsi"*). All are *hulūlī* texts.[18]

The fragmentary pieces by Fāris on Hallāj (Kal., nos. 23, 26b, 32 [*dhikr*], 33, 51; Sulamī, *Tafsīr*, nos. 75, 130; cf. 19 on *dhikr*; Khwīshāgī [is-*tīlā'*]; Sayyārī [thirteen chains; face not ashen]; Warthānī [*murīd*]; and AHy Fārisī) seem like commentaries, tending to systematize (*wasīya*, Kh., 114).

Fāris quoted other masters; here, too, his *isnāds* show that he left Baghdad without having their direct *ijāza*: for Nūrī he based himself on Anmātī (Kal. 112) and on Dūrī (Kal. 67); for Ibrāhīm Khawwās, on AH 'Alawī (of Kufa: cf. the poem *"man sārarūhu"*); for Summūn, on AB Qahtabī.[19] For Junayd and Hallāj, Fāris undoubtedly made use of Ibrāhīm-b-Fātik (perhaps via Anmātī), but he omitted his name, for this *rāwī* was at that time "excluded," or refers to him merely as *"rajulun"* (= someone; for the famous *wasīya* of Hallāj, which he gives in a form already commented on); and the *isnād*, in the *Tabaqāt* of Sulamī, for the quatrain *"Anta bayn al-shaghāf"* must be completed as follows: Sulamī A Hy (M-b-Ibrāhīm) Fārisī + AB A-b-'Alī-b-J Wajīhī + Fāris + Anmātī + Ibrāhīm-b-Fātik.[20]

The leading *rāwīs* of Fāris were:

—AB A-b-'Alī Wajīhī (Ped. 29, 31, 45), a friend of Rūdhabarī, *rāwī* of Khuldī; who was an informant of the Sālimīyan AN Sarrāj Tamīmī and AHy Fārisī (*ibid.*).

—Abū'l-'Abbās M-b-H Mukharrimī Baghdādī Khashshāb (d. 362) (Ped. 29), the *rāwī* of Shiblī, Sulamī's source.

—AN Sarrāj (Q. 121; missing in *Luma'*).

—Abū Bakr Rāzī Bajalī (Ped. *Mumshādh*).

—Abū'l-Husayn M-b-A-b-Ibrāhīm Fārisī, *rāwī* of Wajīhī, also took his *ijāza* directly from Fāris (Q. 104; Ped. 31, 32) and transmitted it to Kalābādhī (Kal. 123) and Sulamī (Q. 104; *Hilya* X, 3); this is the only extant *isnād* for Fāris.

[18] Kalābādhī, *Akhbār*, ms. P., f. 264a; Sulamī, *Tab.*, no. 7 (AHy Fārisī, from Ibn Fātik via Fāris and Wajīhī, left out); *Dīwān*, nos. 62, 41–47, 12 (cf. Mu'ayyad Shīrāzī, *Dīwān*, London ms. SOS), 53 (cf. Khasībī, *Dīwān*, Manch ms., f. 120a). The beautiful fragmentary pieces by Fāris on sūra 12 (Joseph), ap. *Ta'arruf*, 95 (= tr. p. 125); those of Ibn 'Atā', ap. Baqlī, *'Arā'is* I, 413–449; on *"hashasa,"* cf. Ismā'il Haqqī IV, 272 (and IV, 247, on Joseph = *shāhid*).

[19] Kalābādhī, *Ta'arruf*, pp. 112, 67, 122, 70; cf. 40, 63, 68, 95, 103, 106, 114, 122, 126. Cf. *'Awārif* IV, 278. (Q. 176 = on the *ghibta* of the *mustāqīn*, cf. Mājid Kurdī, Sh. *Tab*, 147; and 'A Wd[Wāhid?]-b-Zayd).

[20] Following Sulamī, *Tab.*, Pedersen edition (in preparation: friendly commentary).

—A Faraj ʿA Wāhid-b-Bakr Warthānī Shīrāzī (Sulamī, *Tab*. nos. 8-9).[21]

—A Hy ʿA Wāhid-b-ʿAlī Sayyārī Nīsābūrī (Kh. 131), a disciple through his uncle, the Jabarite mystic Qāsim-b-Q Sayyārī Marwazī (d. 342), of AB Wāsitī.

—AB A-b-AN-b-Salāma Marwazī, who was an informant of Ibn Fadāla (via Nahāwandī), and the great historian Hākim M-b-Nuʿaym Dabbī ibn al-Bayyī (d. 405)[22] associated with Fāris in his youth (*Talbīs*, 258, concerning the *samāʿ*), whose biography he wrote in his *Taʾrīkh Nīshāpūr* (except Khatīb; Brusa abridged ms.; Azhar ms., according to Frye).

—AB M-b-Ish Kalābādhī (d. 380), a master in hadīth and in mysticism, a Hanafite, who wrote the *Taʿarruf* and the *Akhbār*.

Fāris' aesthetic tendency is indicated by the fact that he attended the *samāʿ* (spiritual concert) given by a respected lady, Hezare, with Ibn al-Bayyāʿ, in the home of the wealthy AB Ibrisamī;[23] an extralegal activity that Ibn al-Bayyīʿ got approved by his two disciples A ʿUthmān Ism-b-ʿAR Sābūnī (373), d. 449: *khatīb* of the Nishapur *Jāmiʿ* mosque) and AB A-b-H Bayhaqī (382, d. 468: a Shāfiʿite): to the great consternation of Ibn al-Jawzī (*Talbīs*, 258, 207).

The name of Fāris, included in the list of early defenders of Hallāj found in Baghdādī (and his son-in-law, Isfarāʾinī), is removed from it in Sulamī (*Tab*, no. LIV), Khatīb (who inadvertently included his biographical notice, XII, 390), and Qushayrī (who cites him by accident, Q. 104, 121, 160, 176). Fāris is deliberately ignored by Hallājians like Ibn Khafīf and Ibn Bākūyā, and even Baqlī. Only Harawī mentions him in his *Tabaqāt*, written in Balkh in a milieu of mystics in which AB M-b-ʿUmar Warrāq (d. 290) had converted the Hanafite qādī Hakīm Samarqandī (Fāris' friend) to Sūfism. The Hanafite Jāmī, republishing Harawī, inserted a rehabilitation of Fāris, from the Māturidīyan point of view, five centuries later.

It is true that Fāris was excommunicated and the Hallājian Fārisīya classified, along with the Sālimīya Hulmānīya, among the Hulūlīya heretics. But when? There were direct disciples of Ashʿarī—Ibn Khafīf against the Sālimīya, Bundār Shīrāzī (and AB ibn Yazdānyār) against the Hallājīya—who took the initiative in mystic circles of forcing authors

---

21 No. 8. It should be read "Shīrāzī" (Berlin ms. 9972, f. 73b), not "Sayyārī" (Pedersen ed.) and not "Nīsābūrī" (Berlin ms. 3492, f. 43a).

22 Ibn al-Bayyīʿ, *rāwī* of Qāsim Sayyārī (Kh. X, 167, 153, 166); cf. *Talbīs*, 325, Khatib's source for the biography of ʿAA ibn al-Mubārak. (Kh. X, 153-169); accepted Shīʿite hadīths (*Lisān* V, 233).

23 Whose son AN died in Baghdad in 371 (Samʿānī, f. 16b).

like Sarrāj (*Luma'*, 426) and Sulamī (*Ghalatāt*) to break their ties with *hulūl* (cf. previously Sahl, ap. Q. 160; and Hallāj; ap. *'aqīda* and *ghalatāt* of Sulamī) and with *qawl bi'l-shāhid* (Q. 52, 217). Prior to 350, in Iraq and in Fars, and about 360 in Khurasan at the time of their rapprochement with Sūfis, the Ash'arites called upon Hallājian Sūfis (like Nasrabādhī) to renounce Hallāj's idea of the uncreated Spirit infusing itself into saints, an idea that they then abandoned, imputing it to Fāris, who in turn was excommunicated as the head of the Fārisīya, the extremist Hallājians (*ghulāt* = divinizing Hallāj by attributing to him this *hulūl*, which neither the prophets, nor the angels, nor Iblīs had known).[24]

This excommunication was repeated around 440 in Iraq, under the vizirate of the Hallājian Ibn al-Muslima, when the *mutasawwif* AJ M-b-Sabbāh Saydalānī, "speaking on behalf of the four thousand (moderate) Hallājīya of Iraq," publicly cursed the memory of Fāris (as *hulūlī*)— believing thereby to be facilitating a posthumous rehabilitation of Hallāj. At the same time, the Shāfi'ite and Ash'arite author A Fath Nasr-b-Ibrāhīm Maqdisī (405, d. 490) recondemned the Sālimīya Hulmānīya as *hulūlīya*.[25] In actuality, it was Fāris who propagated Hallājism in Transoxiana among Turks who were becoming converted [to Islam], and Anatolian and Indian authors still revere his memory.

Fāris may have commented on all of the basic texts relating to Hallāj (Sarrāj, ap. *Luma'*, 348, 232, 384, 346, may have derived from Fāris via Wajīhī, "*hasb al-wājid*" "*yā sirrī*" (with "*Anā'l-Haqq*"), and "*Anā man ahwā*" "*hashasnī sayyidī*": in which case we should look for traces in the *Akhbār al-Hallāj* of a transmission by the Fārisīya prior to Ibn 'Aqīl).

b. Abū'l-Husayn Fārisī

Abū'l-Husayn Fārisī, who resided at times in his place of origin (in Istakhr: Pedersen; biography of Shāh Kirmānī), but lived principally in Khurasan, was the direct master of AB Kalābādhī (d. 380), to whom he taught the ten foundations of Sūfism (much older: to renew *tawhīd*, to be ready for any hint of the divine, to be a good comrade, to practice abandonment and self-sacrifice, to be quick to enter the state of ecstasy, to perceive inmost thoughts, to travel a great deal, not to work for personal gain, not to set up reserves) (Kal. 61).[26]

Sulamī refers to him at least twenty-five times in his *Tabaqāt* and eight

[24] Hujwīrī, *Kashf*, 214, 334 (= tr., pp. 131, 260; cf. p. 152); 'Attār II, 135; Khatīb VIII, 112; M ibn al-Haysam Karrāmī (d. around 420), *Maqālāt*, excerpts ap. Ibn Abī'l-Hadīd, *Sharh al-nahj* [bib. no. 431-a] I, 297.
[25] On this Maqdisī, see Ibn 'Asākir (*Radd*, 262, 286), Ibn Taymīya (*Fat*. IV, 302).
[26] It is quoted in Sulamī's *Tafsīr* (Baqlī, *Tafsīr* I, 169, 257, 507).

times in the *Hilya* of AN, and with no more than an isolated statement or series of statements with verses, particularly in the case of Ibn 'Atā' and Hallāj (the beautiful quatrain *"Anta bayn al-shaghāf"*).

In most cases, AHy Fārisī, whom Sulamī lists as his direct informant (he quotes him in his *Ta'rīkh*, in the notice on Shiblī, recopied by Ibn 'Asākir, ms. P. 2137, f. 97a, via 'AA-b-'Alī Sarrāj, though Sarrāj never refers to him in his *Luma'*), claims that he was either directly informed by the great masters, Ibn 'Atā', Jurayrī, Kattānī, or that he was separated from them by only one intermediary (H-b-'Alawīya, in the case of the Khurasanian shaykhs; various *rāwīs*, in the case of the Iraqis). Was this indeed true? Let us take Nahrajūrī, for example (d. 330: Ped., biographical notice, 69); hadīth numbers 1-3 of AHy F go back to him directly, numbers 4-6 (ff.?) via Ibrāhīm-b-Fātik. Similarly, in the notice on Ibn 'Atā', alongside a direct hadīth of AHy F, we find another that comes via A-b-'Alī Wajīhī (*ibid.*, ap. biography of Ibn al-Jallā, Pedersen, notice 24 = *Talbīs*, 320). And it is unusual to find Sulamī going back to 'Abbās-b-'Āsim (*rāwī* of Ibn al-Jallā; Ped., notice 24) via Wajīhī alone, though Sulamī does go back to the same 'Abbās-b-'Assām (Ped., notice on Sahl = *Hilya* X 198), via AHy Fārisī alone.

It is necessary to set up comparative tables as follows for the Hallājian *rāwīs* with whom we are concerned:

Sulamī gives: (no. of times; *isnād*; source; AHy F = Fārisī; IF = Ibrāhīm-b-Fātik; W = Wajīhī; FS = Fāris Baghdādī; Kh. = Mukharrimī):

Five times: AHy F — IF:[27] ap. *Stb* (notices: Nūrī, Ruwaym, Hallāj, Nahrajūrī), *Sta* (Junayd = Q. 6).

Six times: W — IF:[28] ap. *Stb* (notices: Ibn 'Atā', Rūdhbārī), *Sta* (Junayd Q. 67, 82, 99; Sumnūn Q. 172).

Three times: AHy F — W: ap. *Stb* (notices: Bistamī, Ibn Jallā, A 'Amr Dimishqī) (Q = 0).

Four times: AHy F — FS:[29] ap. *Stb* (notices Yf-b-Hy.; Ped. 31, 32); *Sta* (*Hilya* X, 3).

Two times: W — FS: ap. *Stb* (Ped. 29, 31).

Two times: A Hy F — Kh.: ap. *Stb* (notice: Ibn 'Atā').

One time: Kh. — FS: ap. *Stb* (Ped. 29).

One time: Abū Bakr Rāzī — FS: ap. *Stb* (notice: Mamshādh).

Kalābādhī gives, similarly [ap. *Ta'arruf* = TK):

Three times: Kal. — AHy F: ap. TK 61, 117 (on Muzayin), 123.

---

[27] [W omitted.]
[29] [W omitted?]

[28] [FS omitted?]

Ten times: Kal. — FS: ap. TK 63, 67 (on Dūrī), 70, 74, 112 (on An-mātī), 114, 122, 126, 127.

One time: Kal. — W: ap. TK 118.

We can draw the following conclusions, with a rather high degree of accuracy, from these two tables: that the accounts of AHy Fārisī are independent of AB Rāzī; that his main Iraqi source (therefore for Hallāj) is Ibrāhīm-b-Fātik, and that he knew him through Wajīhī; that Wajīhī himself could have known Ibrāhīm-b-Fātik only through Fāris Baghdādī (who referred to him only as *"rajul"*; Wajīhī should have restored the name). For the previously mentioned quatrain by Hallāj, the complete *isnād* of *Stb* no. [. . .] should be: Sulamī + A Hy (M-b-A-b-Ibrāhīm Fārisī + A-b-'Alī Wajīhī + Fāris Baghdādī + Ibrāhīm-b-Fātik.

Abū'l-Husayn Fārisī appears to have been a Fārisian Hallājian. His full name, Abū'l-Husayn Muhammad-b-A-b-Ibrāhīm Fārisī, is verified by Kal. 61 and *Stb* (Ped. 31, 45).

c. Qaffāl Kabīr

After Qādī Ibn al-Haddād, the first chain of transmission for Hallāj's last prayer was AB M-b-'Alī-b-Ismā'īl Qaffāl Shāshī Kabīr (291, d. 365), who like him was a Shāfi'ite canonist and a supporter of Ibn Surayj. He lived in Bukhara and held great prestige in Transoxiana as a dialectician in *usūl* and as a critic in hadīth. A pupil in Nishapur of Ibn Khuzayma, afterwards in Baghdad (beginning in 307) of the Surayjian *usūlī* AB M-b-'AA Sayrafī (d. 330)[30] of Tabarī and of the traditionist AQ Baghawī, his main *rāwīs* were Hākim Ibn al-Bayyī' (d. 405), A 'AA Hy-b-H Jurjānī Halīmī (338, d. 403), a Shāfi'ite qādī of Bukhara, A 'AA M-b-Ishāq ibn Manda (d. 395: a Hanbalite from Isfahan), Abū Nasr 'Umar-b-A 'Azīz-b-Qatāda and Abū 'Āsim M-b-A 'Abbādī (375, d. 458; born in Herat, died in Marw).

Qaffāl wrote a *Tafsīr* referred to by Sulamī[31] and said to have both mystical and Mu'tazilite tendencies, according to Abū Sahl Su'lūkī (d. 369), who reproached him for the latter. The matter in question was the *shukr al-Mun'im wājib 'aqlan* according to Ibn Surayj and Hallāj, and his idea of the *mīthāq* lasting until the Last Judgment: *istidlāl 'aqlī* given to men (Māturīdī approved it; also Baydawī) (*Khilāfiyāt*, 31). In 355 he led the famous Khurasanian expedition of Holy War fighters that wanted to capture Byzantium but got itself decimated by the Muslim princes whose territories it passed through under arms (cf. his bellicose *qasīda* published

---

[30] Preferable to Ibn Khuzayma, page D.
[31] Baqlī, *Tafsīr* I, 478.

by Subkī). He also wrote *Dalā'il al-nubuwwa* and *Jawāmi' al-kilam*, our source for the mystic Firiyābī (Arles ms.).

Born in Shash (Tashkent), to which he later returned, Qaffāl resided mostly in Bukhara. To Hanafite Turkish Transoxiana he brought a Shāfi'ism with mystical and Ash'arite leanings whose importance was pointed out by the geographer Muqaddasī. Pro-Hallāj, he was supported by various Sāmānid amīrs, notably Ibrāhīm-b-Sīmjūr (d. 338) "known from Rayy all the way to the Turks," *walī* of Nishapur (310-314, 320; d. 338), Bukhara, Marw, and Herat, the same amīrs who enabled Fāris Dīnawārī to preach a complete Hallājism in Samarqand. "Without Ibn Sīmjūr," said Qaffāl, "I would not have been able to keep my roots in Shash."

It was no doubt Qaffāl who was responsible for Ibn Sīmjūr's son AH M-b-Ibrāhīm Nāsir al-Dawla's[32] being given *muhaddithīn* masters with mystical leanings (founders of a *madrasa*: the *madrasa* of Ibn Fūrak, as much a *mutakallim* disciple of Qalānisī as of Ash'arī;[33] he enjoyed reread-ing the saying of Dhū'l-Nūn, "*qulūb al-ahrār, qubūr al-asrār*," found in the Hallāj legend); pro-Sūfī leanings that were even more explicit in the grandson, Abū 'Alī Muzaffar ibn M. Sīmjūrī,[34] who collected the "*zuhhād wa mutasawwifa*," and was buried in Qayim, in his hereditary fief of Quhistan (d. 388).[35] One might even imagine that the head of this lineage, Abū 'Imrān Sīmjūr Dawātī (d. 310), the Sāmānid governor of Herat from 287 and after 306 (both times replacing the allied amīr of Marrudh), the governor of Sijistan, and the military cohort of Vizir Bal'amī in 309, was one of the Sāmānid amīrs who knew and supported Hallāj.

d. Ibrāhīm Nasrābādhī[36]

Nasrābādhī (*circa* 295, d. 367) represents the point at which the Hallājian traditions become inserted into the Sunnite milieu of the *ahl al-hadīth* of Khurasan. He was born and raised in Nishapur, close to the famous *muhaddith* Ibn Khuzayma Sulamī (223, d. 311), who must not previously

---

[32] Amīr of Nishapur, 344-374, and of Herat.
[33] In the *khānqāh* of AH Būshanjī, *Muftarī*, 282.
[34] Amīr of Nishapur, 374-377, 384.
[35] Cf. Subkī II, 176; Dhahabī [ms. P.] 1581, f. 309a; Sam'ānī, 323.
[36] AQ Ibrāhīm-b-M-b-Mahmawayh Nasrābādhī: Khatīb VI, 169; Sam'ānī, s.v.; Ibn 'Asākir II, 246-250; Qushayrī, 6, 35, 42, 56, 66, 74, 109, 124, 137, 140, 156, 158, 175, 186; references to Nasrābādhī, ap. *Tafsīr* of Sulamī preserved in the *Tafsīr* of Baqlī, printed ed., Vol. I, 63, 82, 97 (2), 109, 127, 148, 228, 231, 276, 292, 318, 342, 345, 356, 371, 383, 393, 426, 460, 510, 526, 535, 540, 551; Vol. II, 86, 109, 167, 168, 262, 291 (2), 315, 351.

have been hostile to Hallāj, given the fact that his editor, Da'laj Sijzī (260, d. 351), had defended against the Shī'ites the quarter in Baghdad (Qatī'at Umm Ja'far) where Hallāj had preached; that his leading pupil, Abū 'Alī Thaqafī (244, d. 328), a Shāfi'ite anti-Mu'tazilite and a mystic, whose evolution to *kalām* he accepted, was associated with Shiblī and Su'lūkī; and that his friend Abū 'Uthmān Hīrī (d. 298) trained Ibn Nujayd Sulamī (272, d. 365), the grandfather and master of A 'AR M-b-Hy Sulamī (330, d. 412), who was later to defend Hallāj. Nasrābādhī also knew in Nishapur the *muhaddith* M-b-Ishāq (d. 313).

Next there is a period of twenty years (320-340) during which time he was on *rihla*, hearing hadīth from masters: in Rayy, 'AR-b-A Hātim M Rāzī (d. 327);[37] in Damascus, A-b-'Umayr-b-Hawsa (d. 330) and Makhūl (= M-b-'AA-b-A Salām Bayrūtī) (d. 321); in Ramlah, Rūdhabārī (d. 322); in Damietta, Zak-b-Yahyā Dimyātī; in Cairo, AJ Tahāwī (d. 321) and A-b-A Wārith 'Assāl Aswānī (d. 321). Finally, in Baghdad, where he remained for fifteen years (325-340),[38] he was *rāwī* of Yahyā-b-Sā'id (d. 318), and a steady visitor to AB A-b-J-b-Hamdān ibn Mālik Qatī'ī (274, d. 368), a renowned Hanbalite traditionist and nephew of the banker Ibn al-Jassās, who lived in the Qatī'at D Daqīq. Perhaps it was through this Qatī'ī, who was favorably disposed to mystics, that Nasrābādhī knew Shiblī (d. 334), whose *murīd* he became in Sūfism.[39]

Nasrābādhī, in renouncing beautiful clothes, "became converted" thus prior to 330 in Baghdad. He appears to have continued for a brief time his profession as a *warrāq* (a bookseller, the manager of a dictation shop making copies of hadīth collections).[40]

Shiblī seems to have been his only direct master in mysticism;[41] for he cites Murta'ish (d. 328) after AB Bajalī and Rūdhabārī (via Wajīhī) after the Hanafite canonist A Sahl M-b-Sul Su'lūkī (d. 369).[42] He was interested in Antakī.[43]

From 340 to 364, Nasrābādhī, having returned to Nishapur, taught traditions and mysticism there as a much admired master. During that time he collected texts of Hallāj (*dawwana kalāmahu*)[44] probably reediting

---

[37] Cf. Qushayrī, 74: for Antakī.

[38] Ibn 'Asākir [bib. no. 334-a], II, 249.

[39] In this respect, he is included in the classical *isnād* of Muslim congregations, from Qushayrī via Dāqqāq (Qushayrī, 158).

[40] He is the first known Hallājian *warrāq*; this is important for verifying the survival of a condemned man's unburned manuscripts.

[41] Nasrābādhī knew Ibrāhīm-b-Shaybān (d. 337): cf. *Hilya* X, 43; two B. Wāsitī (d. 331), Abū 'Alī H-b-A-ibn al-Kātib and AB-b-Tāhir Abharī (d. 330).

[42] Cf. *Hilya* X, 355.   [43] Qushayrī, 74.   [44] Khatīb VIII.

the *Akhbār al-Hallāj* of Shākir. Accused of *hulūl* because of this, he was supposed to have steadfastly maintained his attachment to Hallāj: "if there is any believer in the One God who ranks right after the Prophets and the Siddīqīn, it is Hallāj";[45] and it is to him we owe the transmission of the account of the incident at the trial concerning the essential union (*'ayn al-jam'*).[46]

On the other hand, when pressed by the young *usūlī* theologian Abū Ishāq Isfarā'inī (b. 338, d. 418), founder of the first Ash'arite *madrasa* in Nishapur (around 363), Nasrābādhī supposedly abandoned the *hulūlī* notion of the uncreated *Rūh* (Spirit), in the presence of the Sūfī M-b-A-b-M Farrā' (d. 370).[47]

His main disciples were his son Ismā'īl (d. 428), an ordinary *muhaddith*; his *murīd* in mysticism, the historian Sulamī; and a noted traditionist, Abū Hāzim 'Umar-b-A 'Abdawī (d. 417).

Nasrābādhī departed for a spiritual retreat in Mecca (in 366) to prepare himself for death, taking Sulamī with him for the hajj. His friend Hākim Ibn al-Bayyī', the historian of Nishapur, accompanying his wife and son on hajj, told how their party entered Mecca seven days after his death. He was buried in Batha near the tomb of Fudayl-b-'Iyād; and his books, "which revealed his inner thought" (his daring in mysticism),[48] were sold.

Nasrābādhī follows Hallāj closely (*fanā"l-dhikr*, Baqlī II, 109); (Hadra [?] I, 526; *Tajallī* II, 315; *Ru'ya* II, 351; *Najāt* II, 393 is copied from II, 15). Two Hallājian passages from Sulamī (*Tafsīr*), no. 37, in which Nasrābādhī quotes a distich by Hallāj ("*tala'at shamsan*"), and no. 80, in which he repeats one of his maxims (*ahl al-kahf* = 'Attār II, 316), pose the question of Nasrābādhī's affinities with various collections of Hallāj pieces.

Our text of the *Akhbār al-Hallāj* is probably Nasrābādhī's own Hallāj collection. It was he who must have attached a prologue to number 1, the account of the preparations for the execution, in which he prefaced these in such a way as to minimize Shiblī's moral weakness that led him to deny his friend; he is portrayed as giving his own *sajāda* [prayer rug] to Hallāj for his final prayer. Nasrābādhī transmitted some pieces by Hallāj (*Tafsīr* of Sulamī on Qur'ān 6:76 and 18:8 = 'Attār II, 316); and the quiet tone of loving shyness on the part of the redactor of *Akhbār al-Hallāj* is

---

[45] Sulamī, *Ta'rīkh*, no. 7.
[46] *Ibid*., no. 11.
[47] A friend of 'Abdawī: Subkī III, 112; Yāfi'ī, *Kashf*, f. 43a = Qushayrī, 6.
[48] A discreet reference to suspect (Hallājian?) texts.

very characteristic of the style of some of Nasrābādhī's sentences. For example, "God is jealous, and one sign of His jealousy is that He does not clear any way through to Himself other than Himself";[49] "the ascetic is exiled in this world, the wise man in the next"; "someone said to him: you have nothing of a true lover. —That is true [he replied]; I have nothing that they have, except their tears; and I am consumed [with desire] for that"; "the blood of lovers beats and boils"; "though there is a (fraternal) love that forbids (Muslims) to shed (Muslim) blood, there is a (divine) Love that commands (the Muslim) to spill (his own blood) with swords of love, and this is the highest Love (ajall)."[50]

AQ Nasrābādhī happened to be within the walls of the Ka'ba at a time when the northern wind sprang up and made the hanging drapes flutter to and fro, so much so that AQ stood up and held them, saying to them: "you foolish things, keep calm, instead of strutting about like this; if He said to you once 'clean out my house,' He said to me in seventy places [you are] 'my servant.' "[51]

When AQ Nasrābādhī had completed his pilgrimage,[52] he went to the Mawqif (of 'Arafāt, where in fact laborers are hired), sold his pilgrimage for two biscuits, fed them to a dog, and then returned to the Ka'ba, where he grasped the ring on the gate, and cried out "O my God, if I have pretended up to now to possess anything, now I am bankrupt; pity my bankruptcy, forgive my sins"; he remained there and died.[53]

e. Abū Bakr M ibn Shādhān Bajalī Rāzī

Born before 300 in Rayy into an Arab family (he tried at the end of his life to improve upon his genealogy; his son kept the nisba "Bajalī"),[54] Abū Bakr (d. 376) was the disciple of Abū Bakr Paykandī (Q. 67) and of Abū 'Amr Paykandī, the author of a history of Sufism. He himself wrote a ta'rīkh, which, according to Harawī, formed the basis of Sulamī's great

---

[49] Ibn Khamīs.   [50] Baqlī, Tafsīr on Qur'ān 3:29.

[51] Umar-b-Hy Naysābūrī, Rawnaq al-qulūb, ms. P. 6674, f. 61b (= ms. P. 4929, f. 67b).

[52] There is a blank followed by a plural; but, in the similar anecdote concerning A S Muqaffa' (Talbīs), we find "seventy hajj" (AQ N made only one).

[53] 'Umar-b-Hy Naysābūrī, ms. P. 6674, f. 61b (= ms. P. 4929, f. 67a); this author belonged to the school of Ibn Karrām and wrote under the Mazyadite amīr, Sadaqa I (d. 501) (ms. P. 5039, f. 87b: corr. Brockelmann, S. II, 262, 285); cf. Akhbār al-Hallāj, no. [66] and p. 75. He points out that Ibn Nujayd criticized Nasrābādhī's penchant for samā' (ms. P. 4591, f. 21b).

[54] AB M-b-'AA-b-'A 'Azīz-b-'Amr-b-Shādhān Bajalī Rāzī: Khatīb V, 464; I'tidāl III, 85; Lisān V, 230; Jāmī, 257; Shadharāt, s.a. 376. His son, Abū Mas'ūd A-b-M-b-'AA Bajalī (362, d. 449), was a noted hāfiz in Bukhara and a rāwī of 'Amr-b-Hamdān (283, d. 370) (Sam'ānī, f. 66a).

ta'rīkh al-Sūfīya. Khatīb also notes the unusual number of quotations from AB Rāzī in Sulamī (in fact, Qushayrī kept sixty-two of them).[55] AB Rāzī refers directly to Jurayrī, Ibn 'Atā', Kattānī, Shiblī,[56] but, at least in the case of Ibn 'Atā', he relies on Anmātī (Qush., 12, 57, 60, 84, 119, 181; Ped., p. 47; *Hilya* X, 123), whom he must have questioned in Baghdad when he came to consult AB Harbī in the Harbīya (Khatīb V, 310; Qush. 12, 77, 143).

After 340, AB Rāzī, who had become a renowned *mudhakkir*, settled in Nishapur; he also gave readings from his history in Samarqand and Bukhara. He was the protégé of a very prominent man, the *muzakkī al-shuhūd* (supervisor of the list of professional witnesses) of Nishapur, appointed in 326, no doubt, by Qādī Yahyā-b-Mansūr (who was both a Shāfi'ite and a disciple of the [Hanafite] mystic Tirmīdhī): A Ishāq Ibrāhīm-b-M-b-Yahyā (285, d. 362), who took him on hajj and to Baghdad (where AB Rāzī gave courses in 361).

AB Rāzī, who appears to have consulted Yf-b-Hy Rāzī (d. 303)[57] directly, had adopted his syneisaktism, according to Baqlī; and this ticklish way of practicing purity caused AB Rāzī to be slandered in connection with a young novice (Harawī's account). AB Rāzī had Sālimīyan tendencies (he was one of Ibn Sālim's *rāwīs*) and enjoyed referring to eccentric accounts (by Sārī concerning the miracles of the cave, in Lebanon; by Kattānī about the quantity of the lice in Hallāj's robe); he had the qualifications of a historian, and his account of the death of Ibn 'Atā' (*Sta*, no. 12) is a restatement, recorded no doubt under Anmātī's influence (the final "punishment" of the vizir, which apart from being inaccurate, is written very much in the style of Anmātī), of the Khurasanian account of Abū 'Amr ibn Hamdān.

Rejected as a *muhaddith*, according to 'AR Idrīsī, the historian of Samarqand, AB Rāzī nevertheless had the following *rāwīs*: in Rayy, 'AR

---

[55] Qushayrī, 4, 6, 7, 11, 12 (2), 13 (2), 21, 25 (2), 31, 32, 33, 55, 57, 58 (2), 60, 61 (3), 64, 67-69, 72, 77, 82, 84, 85, 93, 100, 101 (2), 103, 108 (2), 109, 110 (3), 114, 116, 118, 119, 121, 124, 125, 130, 136, 146, 160 (2), 166, 168, 169, 181, 183, 186, 204, 214. *Rāwī* of A 'U Adamī (*Talbīs*, 222, 305, 308); Ibn 'Arabī (*Stb*), AJ Farghānī, Ibn Yazdanyār (*Hilya* X, 208; Sul., *'Uyub.*, f. 2a).
A Sa'īd H-b-'Alī 'Adawī (d. 317 in Basra). Warthānī may have been referring to him in "M-b-'A," *Stb*, biography of Shiblī; "M-b-A 'Azīz": *Hilya* X, 123, 321; *Mas.*, 375). Harawī also (*Dhamm.*, f. 112b).
[56] But he then had to draw from Khuldī, whose *hikāyat* he used to advantage (Qushayrī 33, 60; *Stf* on Qur'ān 51:1; 112:4; *Hilya* X, 214; *Stb* (biographies of Junayd, Nūrī, Ibn Masrūq, Ibn 'Atā', Shiblī); and also in Qannād (*Hilya* X, 254; Kh. V, 133; *Stb*, biography of Nūrī).
[57] Qushayrī, 58, 160, 168, 204.

ibn Fadāla (Kh. VIII, 117); in Nishapur, Warthānī and, after Sulamī, A Hāzim 'Abdawī (d. 417) (Kh. III, 75); in Isfahan, Abū Nu'aym (*Hilya* X, 123, 232).

It seems very much as if the account of A 'Abbās Razzāz concerning Hallāj's execution, which is the oldest synthetic Sūfī document, was tacitly recopied by Sulamī in his *Ta'rīkh* from AB Rāzī (*Sta*, no. 12; but, since AB Rāzī is referred to in *Sta* no. 24 in connection with the *wasīya* of Abū'l-Fātik, some doubt remains).

f. Sulamī[58]

Sulamī (330, d. 412) is our main source for knowledge of the Sufism of the first three centuries; only publication of his *Tabaqāt* [bib. no. 170-a] and his still unedited *Tafsīr* will enable us to know its history in detail. In the case of Hallāj, three-quarters of the isolated pieces (282 out of the 375) that were saved when his works were destroyed were preserved for us by Sulamī.

Of pure Arab[59] stock, "Azdī" on his father's side, "Sulamī" on his mother's, Sulamī belonged to the wealthy and powerful Arab aristocracy of the important cities of Khurasan. His father (d. 348) had known Shiblī, and his maternal grandfather, Ibn Nujayd Sulamī (272, d. 364), who adopted him, was an eminent Sūfī, a disciple of Abū 'Uthmān Hīrī, a benefactor of Sūfīs and owner of a library that he bequeathed to him. Sulamī made it into the "unrivaled" library of the small monastery (*duwayra*) that he founded for Sūfīs in his home, *sikkat al-Nūnd*, in Nishapur.[60] He made several long journeys, apart from the pilgrimage he made in 366 (with Nasrabādhī), which enabled him to visit Baghdad. Sulamī spent the last part of his life, studious and sedentary, in Nishapur, where, over a period of forty years (368-408), he taught hadīth (*imlā'*, *qirā'a*). Khatīb, who came there to study with him, emphasizes the renown and respect accorded him in Khurasan.

His main masters were his grandfather Ismā'īl ibn Nujayd, Amīr Abū Sahl M-b-Sulaymān Su'lūkī (296, d. 369), *ra'īs* of Nishapur from 337, a Hanafite canonist, and AQ Nasrabādhī, a mystic and *muhaddith*. According to Subkī, he was the *rāwī* in hadīth of Asamm (d. 346) and of his school. He was a Shāfi'ite in canon law.

---

[58] Khatīb II, 248; *I'tidāl* III, 46; Ibn Hajar, *Lisān al-mīzān* V, 140, 307; *Hilya* II, 25; Subkī III, 60. He died on 3 *Sha'ban* 412.
[59] Like AB ibn Khuzayma Sulamī, Mansūr-b-'AA Harawī Dhuhlī, Abū Hāzim 'Umar 'Abdawī Hanzalī (d. 417).
[60] Sam'ānī, 14.

His main disciples were his two sons, AQ Zāhir and AB Wajīh, his *rāwī* Abū Mansūr 'Umar-b-A Jūrī (d. 469: Sam 'anī, f. 141b) his *rāwī* AB Ahmad-b-Khalaf (*Talbīs*, 202; cf. Rūdānī); his friend Ibn al-Bayyī' (d. 405), Abū Nu'aym, Ibn Bākūyā, Qushayrī (376, d. 465), and AB Bayhaqī (d. 448).

A compatriot, M-b-Yūsuf Qattān (d. 422), accused him of having knowingly fabricated pro-Sūfī hadīths;[61] but this accusation seems unfair. Sulamī, whose honesty as a historian and whose commitment to Muslim orthodoxy are beyond question, can only be faulted for having included in his huge body of documentation some accounts that were inadequately guaranteed by overly imaginative *rāwīs*.

The catalogue of his works (*Fihrist al-tasānīf*)[62] includes a hundred items. Their diffusion was organized in a noteworthy way by his *khādim* and bookseller (*warrāq*) Abū Sa'd M-b-'Alī Hassāb Saffār (381, d. 456), who, as *bundār kutub al-hadīth* (trustee of the books of hadīth), based the publication of traditions in Nishapur. Sulamī wrote on the history of Sūfism, on Qur'ānic exegesis, and on monastic customs and practices.

Sulamī's major historical work, the *Ta'rīkh al-sūfīya*, which he wrote before 371, is lost (excerpts have survived in Khatīb and Abū Nu'aym). He compiled biographical notices of a thousand Sūfis in it, only three of whom were suspected of heresy: Hallāj, Qannād, and Abū Hulmān.[63] He continued it and abridged it later[64] in his *Tabaqāt al-Sūfīya*, whose edition was undertaken by Pedersen[65] and whose accepted text, approved even by the Hanbalites, was transmitted by AB A-b-'Alī Shīrāzī.[66] Abū Nu'aym gave high praise to the *Ta'rīkh*, which is the documentary source of the *risāla* of Qushayrī.

In the field of Qur'ānic exegesis, his is a monumental *tafsīr*, *haqā'iq al-tafsīr*, based, he asserts, on the *tafsīr* attributed to Ja'far Sādiq via AB Malatī and especially on the *Kitāb fahm al-Qur'ān* of Ibn 'Ata'. However, it has other unacknowledged sources, particularly the Hallājian works of AB Wāsitī and Fāris. This very original *tafsīr* is the only one that gives us the analogical meaning of the Qur'ān ascribed to it by Muslim thinkers

---

[61] Khatīb, II, 248. And of claiming to be the direct *rāwī* of Hātim Asamm after the death of Ibn al-Bayyī' (*Talbīs*, 174).

[62] 'A. Ghāfir Fārisī, *Ta'rīkh Nīshāpūr* (and *Siyāq*), ap. *Lisān al-mīzān* V, 307.

[63] Baghdādī (pupil of Ibn Nujayd and Ibn Fūrak), *Usūl* [bib. no. 201-d], 316.

[64] After 387, compiling notices of only a hundred and five Sūfis (and adding maxims).

[65] [*Kitāb tabaqāt al-sūfīya*, edited with introduction and index by J. Pedersen, Leiden, 1960. —H.M.]

[66] Rūdānī, *Sila* [bib. no. 834-a], 4470, f. 91b; and by M-b-A Nasr Tālaqānī (d. 460: *Lisān*, s.v.).

(which the *tafsīr* of Sahl Tustarī had barely outlined), which Ghazālī stressed in the beginnings of his *Ladunnīya*. It was also intensely criticized by literalistic exegetes from Wāhidī (d. 468)[67] to Ibn al-Jawzī,[68] from Dhahabī[69] to Ibn Hajar 'Asqalānī.

In the study of monastic customs, Sulamī's *Sunan al-Sūfīya*, we have only two works: *Jawāmī' adāb al-sūfīya*[70] and *Usūl al-malāmatīya wa ghalatāt al-sūfīya*. The latter, an argument for the defense, refutes certain accusations (as Sarrāj had done in his *Luma'*), and concludes his refutation of *hulūl* with a quotation from Hallāj.

On the whole, Sulamī's historical sources are of two kinds (the example of his master Nasrabādhī, a former *warrāq*, must have been his guide): (1) works actually composed, like the *Tabaqāt al-Nussāk* of Ibn al-'Arābī (d. 341), the *Ta'rīkh al-Sūfīya* of 'Abd al-Wāhid-b-Bakr Warthāmī Shīrāzī, the *Luma'* of AN 'AA-b-'Alī Sarrāj Tamīmī Tūsī (d. 378: text edited by Nicholson);[71] and (2) collections of accounts, *hikāyat*, peddled by itinerant traditionists (making free use of the strictly speaking historical works), like AB M-b-'AA ibn Shādhān Bajalī Rāzī (d. 376) (his main source, according to Harawī), and Mansūr-b-'AA Dhuhlī Harawī (*circa* 320, d. 405): the latter two were sharply criticized for the improbability of their anecdotes, which Sulamī accepted too easily.

Particularly in the case of Hallāj, we shall give later the critical list of Sulamī's Hallājian *rāwīs*: authors of works (Ibn 'Atā' published by Anmatī, Qannād, Abū Zur'a Tabarī published by AQ Rāzī, Ja'far Khuldī, 'AW Warthānī Shīrāzī; Fāris Dīnawarī and his school), and sermonizers (AB ibn Shādhān Rāzī Bajalī, Mansūr-b-'AA Harawī).

Transmission: his *Tabaqāt* was transmitted (Rūdānī, ms. 4470, f. 91b): by AB A-b-'Alī Shīrāzī (400, d. 487) > A Zur'a Tāhir-b-A Fadl-b-Tāhir (481, d. 576) > AR-b-'Alī Bakrī > A Nasr Shīrāzī (629, d. 723) > 'Āyīsha: his *Tafsīr* was transmitted by AB-b-'Alī-b-Khalaf (400, d. 487 in Nishapur) to Wajīh Shahhāmī (455, d. 541): > Tāhir-b-M-b-Tāhir Maqdisī (481, d. 576) > 'Uthmān-b-M Shahrazūrī > A Nasr M ibn al-Shīrāzī (629, d. 723) > 'Āyīsha Maqdisīya (723, d. 816); and by A 'AA-M-b-A

---

[67] Subkī II, 290.   [68] *Talbīs*, 353-356.

[69] Dhahabī, *I'tidāl*, *loc. cit.*; and *Ta'rīkh al-Islām*, ms. P. 1581.

[70] Excerpt published ap. *Essai*, appendix pp. 427-429.

[71] For the same account of Sarrāj (*Luma'*, 210 = *Talbīs*, 283 = Qushayrī, 164 = Kh. XIV, 396; and Qushayrī, 185 = *Luma'*, 293). Qushayrī enables us to reconstitute the *isnād*; example: Qushayrī, 164, Shiblī + Bakrān Dīnawarī + Ja'far Khuldī = AN Sarrāj Tamīmī Tūsī. Example: *Hilya* X, 211 and 208 complete the *isnād* of Sarrāj's accounts of Sahl via A-b-M. Ibn Sālim as follows: Sahl + Ibn Sālim + M-b-H-b-'Alī + A-b-'Atā' (Rūdhabārī, d. 369) + Sarrāj + Sulamī.

Nasr Tālaqānī[72] to AT Ibrāhīm-b-Shaybān Nufaylī Dimishqī (d. 529: alive in 534, according to Köpr. ms. 91). [According to] *Talbīs*, 300, the *Tafsīr* of Sulamī [was transmitted] to AB A-b-Khalaf > M-b-Nāsir (467, d. 550: master of I J [= Ibn al-Jawzi; see *Muntazam* X, 24]); according to *Nūr*, 25, 85, to AH M-b-Q Fārisī and Sahlajī; according to *Nūr*, 32, 34, to Tayīb-b-M [. . .] and Sahlajī; according to *Nūr*, 89, to AM Dārī-b-Mahdī 'Alawī Astarābādhī and Sahlajī (cf. also Rūdānī, f. 66a).

g. 'Abd al-Wāhid-b-Bakr Warthānī Shīrāzī

Warthānī, who died in the Hijaz in 372, traveled about collecting traditions and anecdotes. Born in Warthan near Shiraz, a disciple in Damascus of the *hāfiz* and *mudhakkir* Ahmad-b-Mansūr Shīrāzī[73] and of Khuldī in Tarsus (Q. 200), he came to Jurjan in 365.[74]

He composed a large collection of anecdotes, which Sulamī made use of, and which Ibn Jahdam and Ibn Bākūyā[75] later imitated.

Anecdotes drawn in some cases from earlier collections (Qannād about Nūrī, Abū Zur'a to Tabarī about Bistāmī), and dealing mostly with Sūfī masters, particularly with Bistāmī[76] and Rūdhabarī, whose sister, Fātima,[77] he interviewed.

One of his informants, Ahmad-b-Fāris, provided him with six maxims of Hallāj, which Sulamī put at the beginning of the notice in his *Tabaqāt* (numbers 1-6).[78] Who was this Ahmad-b-Fāris? Ibn Jahdam, omitting the name of Warthānī,[79] lists as *rāwīs* for Kattānī, Ruwaym, and Yūsuf ibn Hy Rāzī. He may be the AB Ahmad-b-Fāris Jalājilī who knew Ibn Khafīf.[80]

Ahmad-b-Fāris was the *rāwī* of the *Akhbār al-Hallāj*, which would make Warthānī one of the possible authors of this basic text.

---

[72] D. 466 in Sur (Yāqūt III, 492): originally from Talaqan, from Marrudh.

[73] Abū'l-Faraj 'AW-b-Bakr Warthānī (Hamza-b-Yūsuf, *Ta'rīkh Jurjān*, ap. Sam'ānī, f. 580b; *Hilya* X, 123, 251, 321, 329, 342, 343. Qushayrī, 6, 24, 80, 90, 116, 145, 147, 182, 199, 200, 201, 205. Cf. *Nūr*, 86; Bākūyā, 80, 199, 200; *Talbīs*, 358.

[74] Cf. ms. 2012, f. 241a; Qushayrī, 201, 80; Yāqūt, *Ud*. II, 118.

[75] Compare the *isnād* found in *Nūr*, 99: Bāk., Qādi Qūmisī (d. 367, friend of AB Ismā'īl), A-b-Fadl (= Abū Zur'a Tabarī, a disciple of AB ibn Yazdanyār), with those in *Nūr*, 85, 89: A Wāhid-b-M-b-Shāh Fārisī, A Faraj (= 'AW-b-Bakr Warthanī), A-b-Fadl, AB ibn Yazdanyār (cf. *Talbīs*, 358).

[76] *Nūr*, 40, 85, 89, 101, 127.

[77] Qushayrī, 147, 6; *Masāri'*, 375.

[78] Khatīb III, 76; *Bahja* VI, f. 3a, 10b, 25a; cf. *Hilya* X, 297.

[79] Daylamī, concerning Baqlī, *Mantiq*, f. 16b; *Tarā'iq*, one problem: Ibn Jahdam calls him "A-b-Fāris-b-M," and the Berlin ms. of the *Tabaqāt* calls him "A-b-Fāris-b-Khusrī (?)."

[80] *Tarā'iq*.

'Abd al-Wāhid Shīrāzī[81] received two of Hallāj's maxims[82] from Fāris Dīnawarī.

h. Ibn Bākūyā Shīrāzī[83]

Abū 'AA M-b-'AA-b-'UA Shīrāzī (350? d. 428) spent the largest part of his life traveling far and wide[84] to collect hadīths and, especially, anecdotes (hikāyāt) about famous mystics; he assembled 3,000 in each category, according to Harawī. His collection quickly superseded the previous ones of Qannād,[85] Ibn Farrūkhān Dūrī (used by him),[86] Khuldī, M-b-'AA ibn Shādhān Rāzī, and Mansūr-b-'AA Dhuhlī. He was highly regarded for his concern for orthodoxy and for his great personal piety.[87] Sulamī, who revered him, kept him close to him in Nishapur, and at his death (in 412) bequeathed to him the supervision of his small monastery whose collection of mystical books was famous. Ibn Bākūyā stayed about twenty years in Nishapur, assembling his hikāyāt there. It was there, in Sha'bān 419, that he transmitted those anecdotes dealing with mystics from Bistāmī to Sahlajī,[88] and there where, in 426, he dictated his Bidāyat al-Hallāj to Ibn Nāsir Sijzī. He died in Nishapur in Qa'da 428;[89] his body was said to have been taken back to Shiraz and buried in a mountain cave, one which is still today known as the hermitage of "Bābā Kūhī."

His masters were M-b-Khafīf (268, d. 371), Abū B A-b-Ja'far Qatī'ī (270, d. 368), Abū A 'AA-b-'Adī, 'Alī-b-'AR Kattānī, and Abū B M-b-Ibrāhīm Muqri' Isfahānī. His rāwīs were Abū Sa'd 'Alī-b-M-b-A-Sādiq Hīrī,[90] Qushayrī,[91] and his sons, Abū B-b-Khālid, Mas'ūd-b-Nāsir Sijzī

---

[81] Sayyārī (Pedersen). A mistake in the Akhbār edition puts Naysābūrī there. A disciple of AB Rāzī (Hilya X, 123). Cf. Stb, 1-6; master of Ibn Bākūyā (Talbīs, 209, 358, 383; Q. 199; Sahlajī, Nūr, 40, 74, 85-86, 88-89, 99, 101, 102; AH M-b-Q Fārisī, Nūr, 86; Abū Nu'aym, Nūr, 127); source for Sulamī (Nūr, 86).

[82] Numbers 8 and 9 of Sulamī's Tabaqāt.

[83] Jāmī, 363 (calls him 'Alī-b-M); Ibn Hajar, Lisān al-mīzān V, 230; M. 'Alī, Tarā'iq II, 222. Not to be confused with his homonym, d. 379 ('Akarī).

[84] In 375 in Baghdad (Najjār, ms. 2131, f. 180a).

[85] Used by him: Sahlajī, f. 146b; Qushayrī, 177.

[86] Qushayrī, 177. Baqlī Yamanī refers to his Kitāb hikāyāt al-sālihīn (Q 'AM Çelebi ms. 331).

[87] Warthanī (Qushayrī, 199).

[88] Nūr, 135.

[89] According to Abū 'Alī-b-Jahandār (Bidāya Zah. ms., f. 98a). Ibn Hajar. Others have him dying in 425 (Tagrib, s.a.); 442 (Dhahabī), and even 467 (Mustawfī), "after 420" (Sam'ānī, s.v. Bākūwī).

[90] Who was supposed to have received the ijāza for transmitting others' hikāyāt: M-b-'AA-b-Habīb > Ibn Jawzī > [Ibn Qudāma] Tawwabīn (f. 102a, 106b, 107a, 114a). Ibn Jawzī refers to Ibn Bākūyā (via Abū Sa'd Hīrī) ap. Talbīs, 124, 184, 200, 202, 209, 220, 221,

(d. 377), Khadīja Shāhahānīya (376, d. 460), AB A-b-M Zinjānī, *muqri'*,[92] Harawī Ansārī (d. 481), Farmadhī,[93] Abū 'AA Hy-b-Ismā'īl Qatī'ī Karkhī (d. 538: *sic*), 'Abd al-Ghaffār Shirawī (414, d. 510).

Though his *hikāyāt* were accepted, Ibn Bākūyā was regarded as suspect because of his hadīths, whose *isnāds* were severely criticized by the historians 'Abd al-Ghāfir Fārisī (*Siyāq*) and Abū 'AA (? = A Salīh A Malik) Mu'adhdhin (d. 470). He claimed that he had known Mutanabbī[94] personally, or, at least, that his grandfather, father, and brothers in 354 had had *samā'* in Shiraz with this poet. Even with regard to this we called attention to the inaccuracy of the *isnād* of his Hallājian *hikāyāt*.

The Persian poems in the *Dīwān Bābā Kūhī*, which are very interesting in dialectical terms, are later than he.[95]

The fact remains that Ibn Bākūyā was accepted in Nishapur as an authority in the mystical tradition by Abū'l-'Abbās A-b-M-b-Fadl Nahāwandī[96] (a disciple of Khuldī), Sulamī, Ibn Abī'l-Khayr,[97] and Qushayrī; and that he was able, through the prudent stylistic techniques of his *Bidāya*, to get some basic Hallāj texts accepted and transmitted in Hanbalite traditionist circles.

i. Mansūr-b-'Abdallāh Harawī

This personage (d. 402) was an Arab amīr of Herat of old stock,[98] the author of a collection of controversial anecdotes about Sūfī masters. He seems to have been the first to publish the *"subhānī"* of Bistāmī and the *"Anā'l-Haqq"* of Hallāj. Taking advantage of the exterritorial status

---

223, 263, 272, 321, 331, 333, 335, 348, 352, 358, 360, 361, 365, 370, 371, 372, 375, 380, 383, 412—without *isnād*, except 344, 362, 367, 368 (via Sahlajī).

[91] Qushayrī, whose source it was, refers to him 47 times (*risāla*): 13, 15, 23, 27, 34 (3: from Mansūr-b-'AA Isf), 57, 71, 78 (2), 79 (2), 80 (3: Warthānī), 89 (Dūrī), 94, 110, 147, 148, 149, 153, 154, 156, 161, 165, 176, 194, 195, 196 (3), 197, 198, 199 (2), 200, 201, 202 (2), 203 (3), 205, 206, 217.

[92] Cf. *Musalsalāt* of S. Kāzerūnī, ff. 48b, 49a; the link between Ibn Bākūyā and Silafī is AB A-b-M Zinjanī (Ibn Zinjawayh).

[93] Cf. Subkī IV, 9, and Sam'ānī.

[94] Blachère [bib. no. 2035], p. 227.

[95] The legend of his love for a princess seems to be groundless. M. Berthels has made a study of this *dīwān*.

[96] *Masāri'*, 175[?].

[97] Ibn Abī'l-Khayr, d. 440; his son, Abū Tāhir, was associated with Nizām al-Mulk, who must have helped him establish his son in Baghdad ('Attār, *Tadhk.*).

[98] Abū 'Alī Mansūr-b-'AA-b-Khālid Khālidī Sadūsī Dhuhlī Bakrī, of the family of the princes of Herat (Khatīb XIII, 85; Dhahabī, *I'tidāl* III, 202; Sam'ānī, s.v. Khālidī (not to be confused with Khuldī), f. 186a, *Lisān* VI, 96. Qushayrī refers to him twenty-four times: 5, 8, 9, 19, 22 (Anmātī), 31 (Rūdhabarī), 32, 41, 55 (Khuldī), 58, 60, 95, 100 (Nahrajūrī), 115, 126, 139, 140, 147, 148, 160, 165, 173, 186, 199.

granted the Khurasanian pilgrimage by the authorities of Baghdad, he read his collection in public when passing through Baghdad on his way to the hajj, which caused a sensation among the traditionists of the capital. This was around the year 355.

An exact contemporary of Ibn al-Bayyi' (321, d. 405), the historian of Nishapur, who was his *rāwī* from the year 341 on, his life span can be placed between 320 and 405; for Sam'ānī asserts that he was the direct *rāwī* of M-b-Yq Asamm (d. 346), of Abū Sa'īd A'rābī (d. 341), of Khalaf-b-M Bukhārī (d. 361), of the first Banū Saffār of Bukhara, Ismā'īl-b-M and of Ibn Sālim.

Mansūr-b-'AA had several *rāwīs*: the Baghdadians who had heard him, particularly the Hanbalite M-b-Ishāq Qatī'ī (d. 378), A Ya'lā Sābūnī and 'AQ 'AA-b-M Thallāj (d. 387);[99] and among the Khurasanians, Sulamī, from before 371 (for he is referred to ap. *Ta'rīkh* and *Tafsīr*),[100] 'AR-b-M Dāwūdī, a friend of Daqqāq and Sulamī, 'AR-b-'AA Qaffāl, Abū Hāzim 'Abdawī (d. 417), Mujīb-b-Maymūn Wāsitī.

Then, the scandal caused by his accounts among the orthodox brought about a reversal: 'AR-b-M Idrīsī (d. 405), the historian of Samarqand, put him, so to speak, on the blacklist of the *muhaddithūn*, declaring him to be guilty of interpolations, and Mālinī and 'Abdawī followed him.[101] Abū Nu'aym, however, accepted him.

The many quotations by Mansūr-b-'AA concerning Bistāmī contained in the *Hilya* of Abū Nu'aym and the *Nūr* of Sahlajī[102] enable us to establish the *isnād* connecting him with Bistāmī: through Abū 'Amr 'Uthmān-b-Juhdūrāmihr Kāzarūnī, A-b-H-b-Sahl Misrī ibn al-Himsī[103] and Abū Mūsa Dubaylī; or through the familial *isnād* of H-b-'Alī-b-Hasanawayh (his *'amm* Abū 'Imrān Mūsā-b-'Īsā born in 239, a son of Bistāmī's brother); or through Yq-b-Ishāq and Ibrāhīm Harawī Setenbih. As for the *isnād* linking him to Hallāj through Shiblī (d. 334), it is impossible that Mansūr-b-'AA could have directly interviewed Shiblī; however, we know that he was the *rāwī*, through Abū 'Amr Anmātī (the friend of Ibn 'Atā'), of a question asked Junayd by a *"rajul"* (*rāwī* put on blacklist = Ibn Fātik?),[104] and that he gave (prior to 360 to AB Bajalī?) the Hallājian account from the same source, whom Sulamī's account (be-

---

[99] Khatīb, XIII, 85; Jāmī, 222.
[100] Baqlī I, 32, 61.
[101] He is left out of the *Luma'* (of Sarrāj) and of the *Kashf* (of Hujwīrī).
[102] *Hilya* X, 34-40; *Nūr*, 25, 50, 83, 90, 107, 128-135.
[103] Criticized by Abū Nu'aym (*Hilya* X, 41). Cf. *Talbīs*, 369.
[104] Subkī II, 36, line 2: cf. Qushayrī, 22 (Anmātī).

fore 371), number 8b, describes prudently as "one of our own" (= Ibn Fātik).[105]

j. Abū Ismā'īl Harawī Ansārī

For the Hallājian survival, Harawī (396, d. 481) is a witness of very major importance.

Abū Ismā'īl 'AA-b-Abī Mansūr M-b-'Alī ibn Matt, born in Quhandiz (inner city of Herat),[106] belonged to the Banū Matt family, which claimed descendence from Abū Ayyūb Khālid-b-Zayd Mālikī Ansārī, the Prophet's standard bearer. A noted traditionist, an earnest Hanbalite in law, deeply devout in spirit, Harawī demonstrated throughout his life the most courageous independence vis-à-vis the powerful of his day. Threatened five times with the blade, he was forced to appear before the court in Rayy; he was chased out of Herat three times: in 438 by Sūfīs, in 458 and 478[107] by order of the pro-Ash'arite vizir, Nizām al-Mulk; the first time, he took refuge in Marrudh, the other two times in Balkh, where it appears he spent his youth (except for the hajj); via Baghdad,[108] until the death of his father (in 430). In 474, Caliph Muqtadī bestowed on him the honorific title of "shaykh al-Islām" on the advice of the naqīb of the Ansār. He died in 481 and his descendents remained in Quhandiz.[109]

He was trained in hadīth by a wā'iz, Yahyā-b-'Ammār Shaybānī Sijis-tānī (332, d. 422),[110] who had succeeded Abū 'Alī Hāmid Raffā', a disciple of 'Uthmān Dārīmī Sijzī (d. 280), as preacher in Herat. Yahyā instilled a permanent hatred in him of the Jahmite theology, and therefore against the Kullābīya and the Ash'arites. He also attended in Nishapur the instructions in hadīth given by the disciples of A 'Abbās M-b-Yq Umawī Asamm (247, d. 346),[111] particularly those given by a Hanbalite close to Isfijāb named 'Alī-b-M Tarāzī (d. 430), and in Baghdad those given by AM Khallāl (d. 439), a preacher who was a disciple of Ibn Sam'ūn.

His principal master in Hanbalite law was A 'AA M-b-Fadl Tāqī

---

[105] His account of Nahrajūrī (Hilya X, 40; Qushayrī, 173) must be from the same source. Also on Abū 'Amr Dimishqī (Hilya X, 346).

[106] Dhahabī, Ta'rīkh, London ms. Or. 50, f. 176 to 178b; Jamī, 376-380. He preferred the sahīh of Tirmidhī to the others.

[107] He came to Nishapur before 428 (Ibn Bākūyā).

[108] Following the controversy with the Shāfi'ite 'Alī-b-A Ya'lā Dabbūsī 'Alawī, d. 482.

[109] His son, 'Abd al-Hādī, killed by Isma'īlīs (cf. JAP, 1860, II, 479), was interred with him and with Gāzurgāh.

[110] Jamī, 380.

[111] Dhahabī, Ta'rīkh, f. 176 to 178b.

Sijistānī (d. 416),[112] of Herat, to whom he owed his attachment to Ibn Hanbal.[113]

In the field of mysticism, his book of *tabaqāt* gives us the names of about fifty of his masters, three of whom he himself puts in a separate category: Tāqī, cited previously, Khurqānī (d. 425), and A Hy Bisrī Sijzī, a pupil of Ibn Khafīf, Ibn Jahdam, and Husrī.[114] He is referring here to the masters who gave courses of instruction and readings, whereas in mysticism the important thing is direction, which Harawī actually received from his father, who was a *qāri'* and, in mysticism, the *murīd* of Sharīf Hamza 'Aqīlī from Balkh,[115] in whose house he had been buried. The Tālibite, probably a descendent from the 'Aqīlids of Busht and Turshiz,[116] was not only a member of the school of Hakīm Tirmidhī.[117] His *dār* in Balkh was the center for a little mystical group of Malāmatīya comprising, as Harawī tells us, apart from his father, Pīr (A Muslim) Fārisī, 'Abd al-Malik Iskāf, 'AQ Hannūna, AH Tabarī and 'Arīf (Mansūr) 'Ayyār.[118] This little group included at least one Hallājian of note, who I believe was a survival of the Hallājīya of Talaqan, one who had taken refuge in Balkh, namely, 'Abd al-Malik Iskāf (= the cobbler; a powerful guild at that time).[119]

Among Harawī's other masters in mysticism in Herat we call attention again to 'Amū (A-b-M, d. 441), who taught him Sūfī propriety; Qurbanj, who died in the state prison of Qilāt (northeast of Tus); M-b-'AA Jāzir and A Layth Fūshanjī,[120] friends of the Banū Dhuhl, hereditary princes of Herat; one of these amīrs had bestowed generous gifts on Shiblī.[121]

---

[112] Jāmī, 383, 147.

[113] The Banū Manda: he venerated above all A 'AA M-b-Ishāq-b-Zak-b-Yahyā ibn Manda 'Abdi Isfahānī (310, d. 395), *rāwī* of A S ibn 'Arabī (d. 341), master of Ibn Mākūlā, who was attacked by Abū Nu'aym (Ash'arite); his son, 'AR-b-M ibn Manda, was a friend of Harawī and a disciple of ibn Jahdam (388, d. 470); his second son, 'A Wahhāb (d. 475), had a son, Yahyā-b-'A Wahhāb (d. 511), who was the master of Silafī (cf. Kazarūnī, f. 7b).

[114] Jāmī, 384. Harawī came to appreciate the doctrine of suffering through Husrī, a Hanbalite (Jāmī, 260, 258, 326, 384, 392).

[115] Jāmī, 385.

[116] Sam'ānī, ff. 395a-b, 370b.

[117] Jāmī, 312, *isnād*: A Muzaffar Tirmidhī, a Hanbalite; M-b-Hāmid Wāshgirdī; AB Warrāq.

[118] Jāmī, 170, 313-314.

[119] By an undoubtedly deliberate mistake, a *tarīqa Harawīya* was conceived later as going back through Harawī to another sharīf, Hamza (-b-M AA Husaynī) of Tus, and through him to AQ [Hannūna], even though this sharīf Hamza Husaynī is the source indicated by Harawī for chapter 7 of no. VIII (*Ghurba*) of his *Manāzil* (his preface, p. 3).

[120] Jāmī, 391, 398, 399.

[121] *Ibid.*, 399; cf. Mansūr-b-'AA Dhuhlī.

Among mystical authors, Harawī particularly admired Yahyā-b-Mu'adh Rāzī (as did Husrī), AB Wāsitī and Nasrābādhī (whose son he knew).[122]

Finally to place Harawī, mention must be made of his disciples. First of all, his *khādim*, Abū'l-Waqt 'Abd al-Lawwāl Sijzī (458, d. 553), famous among *muhaddithūn* as a link in the chain of *mu'ammarīn*,[123] the "macrobiotic" transmitters of Bukhārī's *Sahīh*; he was also a mystic, associated with Kīlānī. Next, his *mawlā*, the *hāfiz* 'AA-b-Marzūq Harawī (441, d. 508), Mu'tamin-b-A Sājī (445, c. 507), the master of Silafī, M-b-Tāhir Maqdisī (447, d. 507), who tried to combine hadīth with Sūfism in his book *Safwat al-tasawwuf*: a learned man and a Zāhirite *hāfiz* accused of laxity;[124] 'Atā-b-Sa'īd Fuqā'ī (454, d. 534), who carried on debates (*majālis wa hikāyāt*)[125] with Vizir Nizām al-Mulk; and lastly, Yūsuf Hamadhānī (441, d. 535), who apparently was the heir to his thought (through him, Harawī reached Yesewī); for we owe to him, not only the publication (with commentary), but also the arrangement of his final testament in mysticism, *Kitāb manāzil al-sā'irīn* (518). This is a major work, which *wujūdīya* monists of the Ibn 'Arabī school tried to treat as a precursor, even though according to Ibn Rajab's cogent remark, Harawī was not *wujūdī* (an advocate of existential monism), but *shuhūdī* (an advocate of testimonial monism).[126]

It is rather ironic that, at a time when important Shāfi'ites, from Qushayrī (and Ibn al-Muslima) to Ghazālī, were trying to justify Hallāj on a basis of Ash'arite theology, there should appear a Hanbalite (and not a Hanbalite influenced, like Ibn 'Aqīl, by theology, but a pure anti-Ash'arite traditionist like Harawī) who was undertaking publicly the defense of Hallāj.

Before examining this defense, it is essential to analyze the anti-Ash'arite position of Harawī. He formulated it in his *Dhamm al-kalām*.[127] What makes him indignant about Ash'arism are its unswerving oc-

---

[122] Jāmī; we cite A Chishtī again, the founder of an order (*ibid.*, 386), and A Jāmī (447, d. 536), a disciple of Ibn Abī'l-Khayr ("Zende," 135), an ancestor of the poet (Jāmī, 405) and pīr of Sanjar (*Bayqarā'*, ms. P., 317).

[123] 'Akarī, s.a.   [124] *Talbīs*.

[125] Sam'ānī, s.v.   [126] *Tarā'iq* II, 247.

[127] *Dhamm al-kalām*, London ms. 27520, Add.: f. 109b, 114b, 118a; cf. Subkī III, 117. Excerpts ap. Ibn Taymīya, *Tis'īnīya*, concerning volume V of the 1329 edition, pp. 239, 274-278; cf. Najdī, *Tanbīh al-nabīh* [bib. no. 976-a], concerning *Majm. Mushtamal* . . . of 1329, 481-497. Cf. Qādir's edict of 408 [cited by Lālakā'ī (AQ Nibatallāh-b-M, d. 418) ap. *Sharh usūl i'tiqād ahl al-sunna*] promulgated in 413 throughout the domains of Mahmūd II; cf. the Shāfi'ite AH M-b-A Malik Karajī, (d. 532), *Kitāb usūl al-fusūl*, the *qasīda* on the *'aqīda* of Harawī (Dhahabī, *'Ulūw*, 337). Subkī IV, 83.

casionalistic principles. Ibn Kullāb and Ash'arī, in reacting against
Mu'tazilite "liberalism" which stripped human acts of their actualization
in God, lost sight of the permanence of God's distinct created living substances; so much so that in contempt for the notion of God's transcendent holiness, Ash'arite occasionalism ended up by construing divine
power as the universal substance, amorphous and neutral, of all phenomena and of all actions, good and bad. By weakening the nominalistic doctrine that confused divine attributes with divine essence, these "female
Jahmites," the Ash'arites, took away from believers their potential for
becoming imbued with the life-giving reality of these attributes when
meditating on the Qur'ānic verses that describe them. They put God in
everything, even in the belly of a dog or a pig, for fear of affirming Him
and dread at the thought of realizing Him. Deep down they really believed, as Ibn 'Ammār said, that "God is no longer in Heaven, the
Prophet is no longer in his tomb (rawda), the Qur'ān no longer on earth.
To affirm Him," according to them, "would be to liken [Him] (tashbīh)
to His creation. The Qur'ān is no longer honored, nor hadīth respected;
they have destroyed piety, the tenderness of the heart, the blessing associated with worship, the importance of humility."

The Ash'arite interpretation of Hallāj, both the nominalistic and the
occasionalistic, leads logically, in the case of Ahmad Ghazālī, to a comparison with Satan, a monist Satan; whereas the realistic and finalistic interpretation of Hallāj leads, in the cases of Harawī, Yf Hamadhānī,
Kīlānī, and Simnānī, to the presentation of his "I" as the antithesis of the
sin of Satan.

At a very young age in Balkh Harawī had heard people speak about
Hallāj. His father, who was living with Shārif Hamza-b-M-b-'AA
'Aqīlī, his master in mysticism (like AB Warrāq, he claimed to have seen
apparitions of Khadir), heard an account there one evening given by a
centenarian, the last direct disciple of Hallāj still living, 'Abd al-Malik
Iskāf: "one day, I asked Hallāj: 'master, who is the adept ('arif)?' [He
said,] 'the one who (on Tuesday 24 Qa'da 309) will be taken to Baghdad's
Bab al-Taq, will have his feet and hands cut off, his eyes put out, will be
hanged upside down, will have his body burned, his ashes thrown to the
wind.' " Iskāf added: "I saw him dealt with in this very way. Everything
that he said was done to him." Harawī commented as follows: "I do not
know if he knew beforehand what would happen to him, or even if it
happened just as he said. He had a disciple whose name was Haykal, who
was killed with him; he was called 'shājird al-Husayn' (the pupil of Hallāj);
and A 'Abbās (b.) 'Atā', it was because of him that he was killed."

This text of Harawī is very interesting. Iskāf suggests that to be initiated one must suffer the same death as Hallāj—in accordance with the teaching of voluntary sacrifice clearly stated by Hallāj in his final sermon, and repeated in the statement that ʿAttār attributes to Shiblī: "give me your hand, help me; it will be necessary to put me to death." It is also ʿAttār who recalls for us that this was carried out literally in Balkh by two mystics. [128-130] It would appear therefore that in Khurasan, in Balkh as early as Harawī's time, some mystical circles (arising from the Hallājīya of Talaqan) regarded the execution of Hallāj as the symbol of mystical union, and its acceptance by the novice as the sign of his initiation. [We are reminded again of the fact that] the Turkish order of Bektāshīs commemorates this execution even in our own time with the Dāre Mansūr, the "gibbet of Mansūr," which is the point in the center of the initiation cell where the novice must prostrate himself with the cord around his neck when he asks to be admitted.

Harawī's tone, in any case, when dealing with Hallāj, introduces us to a milieu in which Hallāj is not only held in honor, but survives through desire to share in his supreme sacrifice in a quasi-sacramental sense. And after having shared the common view that every *grievous* punishment has the character of a divine punishment, and therefore that the punished one has sinned, Harawī, in a personally written document, claimed to be convinced that Hallāj (being a saint) must not have suffered on the gibbet, but that God at that moment had raised him to Himself (like ʿĪsā). To imitate Hallāj is therefore to be initiated into the triumph in God over the (apparent) horrors of the worst death.

Harawī does not mention Hallāj by name in his works. Furthermore, along with *Dhamm al-kalām*, neither *Fārūq fī ithbāt al-sifāt* nor *Kitāb al-arbaʿīn* afforded an opportunity for this. However, in *Manāzil al-sāʾirīn*, a basic treatise on mysticism, the last chapter is aimed at the Hallāj case; and Ibn Taymīya, as we shall see, was aware of this.

In Persian, along with his *munājāt*, a form of short ejaculatory prayers much admired in India, in which Hallāj is referred to by name, he left us the *Tabaqāt al-Sūfīya*, [131] a collection of biographies of saints, a complement to Sulamī's *Tabaqāt* in Arabic, because he adds a valuable introspec-

---

128 *Tisʿīnīya*, 275 [no footnote reference].
129 Harawī, *Tab.*; reproduced ap. Jāmī 170 [no footnote reference].
130 ʿAttār, *Tadhk.* II, 135, line 24; 136, line 1. ʿAttār pretends to be indignant at this stated condition (*shart*): the requirement for being an ʿārif, to be crucified and burned like Hallāj. However, all of these Hallājian poems orchestrate this theme.
131 Nūrī ʿUthmānīya ms. 2500; Calc. ASB ms. D232, ff. 85b-87 (Ivanow). Schaeder corrigenda *DI*, 1916, p. 126.

tive documentation to their technical definitions. Written in the archaistic dialect of Herat (it has been studied by Ivanow),[132] the *Nafahāt* of Jāmī is only an abridgment of it.

Given the fact that this collection is still unedited, we present here a summary with excerpts of its notices on Hallāj (67, out of 120). In the manner of Sulamī, [Harawī] summarizes his education, his masters, his travels, and opinions held of him. He gives in two recensions the tercet "*Wahhidnī Wāhidī*," based on the version of Ibn Khafīf (according to Ibn Bākūyā[133] and Daqqāq). He accepts him as a master, but notes that his public statements exposed him to legal sanctions. He notes his thousand *rak'a* performed in a twenty-four hour period (five hundred the night before his execution). [Hallāj] was condemned to death because of private revelation (*ilhām*) which was interpreted as an attempt to claim prophethood for himself, as his judge (Qādī Abū 'Umar) said to Shiblī when delivering his scathing reprimand of him.[134] Harawī was the first to report the words spoken by Hallāj when he knocked at Junayd's door ("it is *Haqq*")—Junayd, who foretold his punishment, Makkī's curse (hands and feet cut off, eyes put out).[135] He gives the account taken from his father of 'Abd al-Malik Iskāf and Ibn Fātik's dream (he includes his given names, his father, his black-listing, *mahjūran*, by the Sūfī brotherhood). He then presents his own opinion in the following terms:

The fact that Hallāj was executed shows that there was an imperfection in him; his death was a punishment, not a miracle of grace, since each miracle is a source of life. If he had been perfect, not overstepping his proper place as a creature, nothing would have happened to him. His sin was conversing with garrulous people; also his secret was not safeguarded. "Do not tell it to them; you give them a burden; and this is damaging for you." To have spoken thus proves that he was not perfect; perfect, these words characterizing his spiritual rank (*maqām nafs*) should have renewed him, and no one could have failed to recognize him. But the moment had not (yet) come for him to speak; he was not inviolable (*muhram*). As for myself, I use the same words as he, but secretly, so that no uninitiated person may get hold of them.[136] There is light in these words of mine, but does the one who hears me and gains access to it believe that it is mine as such? Indeed no. For this light is the (divine) Word which makes life flow through me. Hallāj was speaking in a state of essential union ('*ayn al-jam'*); he was in it most of the time. Now, this state is delicate and difficult to grasp; essential

---

[132] Ivanow, *JRAS*, 1923, pp. 1 ff., 337 ff.; cf. *JRASB*, 1922, pp. 385-402.

[133] Who, like Ibn Khafīf, quotes it in a response to the question "what do you think of Hallāj?"

[134] The *Tarā'iq* appears to attribute this quotation to Husrī.

[135] Cf. Iskāf, also 'Attār; this punishment comes from the hadīth of the B. 'Urayna.

[136] Cf. *Bayqarā'*. See, this edition, 2, Figure 15, the Persian text translated in this edition (2, 43).

union is part of the ocean of *Tawḥīd*. In this state it is God Who expresses Himself, no longer I; it announces the annihilation of myself and the present permanence of God.

And this comes from one of the signed notebooks of the *Shaykh al-Islām* (= Harawī), from his "journal":[137] chapter: "How would Hallāj have made the drum resound (*tabl*.: hailing the Sovereign)[138] unless he had been forewarned of the secrets of God by Him? Hallāj,[139] when he was on the gibbet, was alive in God, while the Law, out of jealousy, was putting his form (*bahre*)[140] to death.

There was a spring whose owner wanted to keep hidden; Hallāj made it gush forth. But what spring would churn, what drum proclaim the glory (of the Sovereign Lord) from the bottom of a well? He (Hallāj) was not the one whom they crucified, for God gave him new life; people's eyes were deceived by that [crucifixion], for God had consumed his form (*bahre*: vital part) in Himself. He (Hallāj)[141] had said: "the sun does not rise without My permission"; he was right. A powerless man may not reach the Omnipotent One, which is not surprising, since He Who has His foot placed on the sun[142] bows the head of the enemy. Hallāj looked within himself and saw the Unique One there and was bound to Him."[143]

Harawī then recalls four miracles: the parrot (*tūtlī*)[144] resuscitated, the cotton carded in a single stroke, the candles lit "in Syria" (in the Holy Sepulchre), the table cloth in prison. He observes that, in the opinion of the masters, Hallāj's miracles were genuine though combined with tricks (*nīran [ji]yāt*). He quotes Hallāj as saying "the *tawḥīd* of Sūfīs is *ifrād al-qidam wa iqāmat al-azal*,"[145] comparing it to another by Habashī-b-Dāwūd. He follows that with the quatrain "*Mawājīd Haqq*" (Sulamī, no. 17) and with maxims, from numbers 18, 19, 21, 3, 8, 9, and 11 of Sulamī (*Tabaqāt*). He says that many people lied about Hallāj, attributing incomprehensible or absurd statements to him as well as apocryphal writings and charlatan tricks, which tricks served as a pretext for accusations leveled against him by theologians, well-founded accusations, for people saw him do them. To show examples of [Hallāj's] poetic style "*fasīḥ*," Harawī gives first a quatrain in Persian, which poses a problem,[146] fol-

---

137 *Rūznāmeha*, Ivanow reads and connects: *būd nāma hā Fasl*.

138 The *tablkhāneh* is the daily fivefold drumroll hailing the sovereign (granted the Buwayhids by the caliph once a day in 368, three and, later, five times a day in 408, 418 and 436) Tagrīb. ms. BN 1778, s.a.; 'Akarī, s.a.; 'Attār, s.a.

139 D. ms. a: *salāh*.

140 *Bahre* literally means the portion, the personal fate, assigned to the soul in life.

141 Harawī is quoting here a statement that he claims is by Hallāj, which Hilāl repeated to him, not in Arabic, which he claimed was by Husrī (Jāmī, 392).

142 *Bāftāba*, which Ivanow interprets as "leggings"; the meaning then becomes "he who continues to journey."

143 According to Ivanow, who reads *nihād bend*: the MU[?] ms. has only *nihād*.

144 *Sic*: for *tūtī*.   145 Cf. Junayd.

146 Published in *Essai*, appendix p. 436; is this a sextain? six rhymes are found: -*dī*, -*dī*,

lowed by the Arabic quatrain *"Anta bayn al-shaghāfi."* He adds the following:

The idea that Hallāj was a charlatan is repugnant, especially since charlatanism is a substitute for mysticism and the two were combined in him. As far as I am concerned, I accept his mystical state and his life. With regard to his death, I do not consider it a *karāma* (= a divine wonder); but I do not reject it. Among the shaykhs of mysticism, he was great. As Murtaʿish said, the story of his external life is public knowledge known to all, but his inner life remains a personal mystery to the initiated.

Harawī concludes by quoting the *wasīya* of Hallāj to his son (*pesar*), according to the version of Ibn Bākūyā, to whom it had been delivered by Ahmad Chishtī in Khujand: to concern his soul with the search for *maʿrifa*.[147]

Hallāj is cited in other biographical notices in the *Tabaqāt*: in the biographies of Bistāmī (a/s. Nibājī: Yak Kāmest),[148] AS Karrāz,[149] Junayd (second verse of the *naʿī: ʾan ʾī ilayka qulūban . . .* then verse 1), ʿAli Hallāj Isfahānī (he was not a carder like Hy-b-Mansūr Hallāj), Ibn ʿAtāʾ (the cause of his death), and AB ʿAtūfī (who quotes a statement by Junayd comparable to a statement by Sīrwānī and to what "Hallāj says at the end of his book:[150] whosoever believes in these words of mine and savors them will receive my *salām*"); finally, in the last chapter (*fīʾl-maʿrifa waʾl-tawhīd*), Harawī quotes a distich by Hallāj (*fīʾl-jamʿ* = *Dīwān*, 116, no. 3; from Junayd).

The anonymous disciple of Harawī who recorded this book from his

---

-khīsh, -dī, -khīsh, -dī, in that order. Or are these simple prose assonances? Daylamī asserts that Hallāj did not know Persian; did Harawī believe this?

[147] Corr. Jāmī thus, 174, line 17. The given name of Hallāj's son is not included. Ahmad Chistī was an ancestor of the founder of the Chishtīya order (Jāmī, 386), in actuality older than Harawī.

[148] "What do you say about Hallāj?" "And you, what do you think about what you have not paid? Pay people their money." "You defy me?" The vizir gave an order: his teeth were pulled out and hammered into his skull until he died.

[149] The Persian translation of Sulamī's number 19, followed by a piece on *tanzīh*.

[150] *Kitābeh khūd*; Jāmī designates, without source, the *Kitāb ʿayn al-jamʿ*, which seems to be wrongly deduced from a passage in Harawī (this edition, 2, 219, lines 17-18); but Ivanow reads this title in f. 103b of the Calcutta ms.; *JASB*, 1922, p. 393. Here is how Jāmī (*Nafahāt*, 168-174) recast this biography of Hallāj, by reviving the language; (masters): Fuwatī is omitted; (travels): "they say that he went secretly to Khurasan and that he was seen in Marw" (omitted); (opinions): Ibn Surayj (excerpts Baqlī), Hujwīrī, Ibn Abīʾl-Khayr (added material); "*wahhidnī*" tercet (omitted); Ibn Fātik (his father's name omitted); Harawī's opinion (the last five indented lines omitted); (miracles): candles (substitute Baqlī text), prison (substitute Daylamī text), tricks (omitted); Habashī (omitted); statements taken from Sulamī (omitted), except for the Fāris version of the one about the *murīd*; Jāmī adds to it a biography of Fāris; (*wasīya*); Jāmī confuses Ahmad (Chishtī) with the son (Hamd) of Hallāj, after leaving out Murtaʿish's judgment.

dictation must have been one of his close friends: either Abū'l-Waqt Sijzī, or, more likely, Kurūkhī, who also spoke the dialect of Herat.

In his *Makātīb* (referred to by Nūr Shūshtarī as being authentic, though not dialectal), Harawī excuses Hallāj as follows: "When love contemplates the face of its Only One and rejoices in it, this rejoicing suspends self-restraint and propriety and is wrong. Reverential fear, which is the opposite of love—love being the contemplation of beauty, and fear the submission to majesty, must be united with this criticizable rejoicing in order to achieve the desired balance. The masters have also said: he who adores God out of admiration is *zindīq*, he who adores Him out of fear is *hashwī*, and he who adores Him both out of love and fear is a true believer (Qur'ān: *khawfan wa tama'an*, 7:56, etc.). And, as in the case of Hy.-b-Mansūr, domination by amorous thought erases any sign of fear; but lest he rejoice to the point of claiming to be the Only One, the whip of majesty must be raised against him and his head must roll where heads roll. However, God is satisfied when the love one shows for Him does not obliterate one's self-restraint."

The *Manāzil al-sā'irīn* sets forth the mystic's route to God by defining very briefly a hundred steps arranged in ten sections of ten each, preceded by a short preface; at the very end we find the famous tercet "*mā wahhada'l-Wāhida min wāhidin,*" which indicates very well the central position of Harawī, both in the opposition to existential monism and to the scholastic occasionalism of Ash'arī. Its form as a collection of definitions makes us suspect that it was one of his pupils[151,152] who assembled it after his death. There are no authors quoted except in the preface; one statement about the *ghurba* goes back via Nasrabādhī to Hallāj.[153]

Ibn Taymīya, who revered Harawī for his avowed Hanbalism, was very affected by the use that the monists, especially 'Afīf Tilimsānī, made of the *Manāzil* to defend their theories. And as with Hallāj's verse, a large body of which they had made great use, he left the *Manāzil* to them and then attacked the *Manāzil* in order to refute them, the monists, more effectively. He aimed his attack at two points: the tercet "*Mā wahhada'l-Wāhida min wāhidin,*" and the last paragraph of the hundredth *manzil*, which defines the highest *tawhīd* as attainable by certain intimate friends of God through the immediate intervention of a divine light, *lā'ih*, a kind of uncreated and life-giving inspiration (*rūh*).[154] Harawī was repeating

---

[151] *Majālis al-mu'minīn* [no footnote reference].
[152] Is this Yf Hamadhānī? is it M-b-A-b-A Nasr Hāzim (*Tarā'iq* II, 163)?
[153] Nasrabādhī: *gharīb* . . . ; Hallāj: Fārigh . . . (Sulamī, no. 5) = *Manāzil*, no. 78, p. 27.
[154] Ibn Taymīya's objection, ap. *Jawāb sahīh* [bib. no. 512-i], II, 167, 199; cf. *Madārij* III, 162.

here an idea already mentioned in the seventy-fifth *manzil* (*sirr*);[155] his text reads as follows:[156] "the third and highest degree of *tawhīd* is the one that God has chosen for Himself, the one of which He alone is worthy; and He radiates from it a ray of light (*alāha minhu la'īhan*) in the consciousness of a group of His chosen ones, while causing them to be silent about defining it and helpless to transmit it. . . . This is what the scholastics call '*ayn al-jam*'."

Ibn Taymīya objects[157] on the grounds that this is the *hulūl khāss* heresy of which Christians were accused (God's infusing Himself into certain chosen beings, *khāssa*; not into the totality of beings, as in the position of existential monism). He notes that the author of this statement (Harawī) had declared that the execution of Hallāj had been necessary because he had revealed this (not-to-be-divulged) secret;[158] which explains precisely the reason for the very elaborate redaction of the statement in question. Ibn Taymīya observes that this statement does injury to the primacy of the prophets, that it renders their public teaching of *tawhīd* meaningless. That it implies God's infusing Himself into the heart of Hallāj, just as people imagine that a demon enters the heart of a person possessed. Now, first of all, the demon possesses all parts of the possessed one's body; whereas God, Whose transcendence remains remote from creatures, could not infuse Himself into a circumscribed heart; furthermore, the heart is essentially a spirit, thus an accident, and not a substance; and God could not become an accident of a material accident. In conclusion, Ibn Taymīya expresses regret that Harawī, who had been so forceful against the occasionalistic Jahmīya (and Ash'arīya) who fused divine action with everything, had accepted the possibility of a certain divine presence in certain chosen hearts. He also minimizes the *hadīth* of Abū Dharr, accepted by Ibn Hanbal, relating that the Prophet saw God "in his heart."

Ibn Qayīm al-Jawzīya, a direct disciple of Ibn Taymīya, tried in his lengthy *Manāzil* commentaries to bring their text in line with the *fatwā* in which Ibn Taymīya, besides following the threefold classification of Harawī, tries, apropos of Hallāj's verse, to define the term *fanā*', "the annihilation of the self in God," in an orthodox way.[159]

[155] *Manāzil* (Cairo ed., 1328), 26; Ibn Q al-Jawzīya, *Madārij* III, 15.
[156] *Manāzil*, 34; Ibn Q al-Jawzīya, *Madārij*, 333 ff.
[157] *Minhāj al-sunna* [bib. no. 512-k], III, 93-95.
[158] *QT*.; Ibn Taymīya, *Majm. ras. kub.* [bib. no. 512-j], II, 98.
[159] Ibn Q al-Jawzīya, *Madārij*, I, 79; III, 242; Ibn Taymīya, *Majm. ras. wa masā'il* (Cairo 1341), 82.

k. The Kubrawīya

The Khurasanian order of the Kubrawīya claimed to go back to Junayd through Abū 'Uthmān Maghribī (d. 373/984), Abū 'Alī Kātib and Abū 'Alī Rūdhbārī (d. 321/933).[160] But its two founders were Abū'l-Qāsim 'Alī Jurjānī (d. 469/1075) and Najm al-Dīn Ahmad al-Khīwaqī, surnamed Kubrā (d. 618/1221), who bequeathed to it his name. Its leading representatives from Jurjani to Kubrā were Abū Bakr al-Nassāj, Ahmad Ghazālī (d. 517/1123), Abū'l-Najīb Suhrawardī (d. 563/1167), and 'Ammār ibn Yāsir.

After Kubrā, Majd al-Dīn Baghdādī (d. 616/1219), 'Alī Lā'lā', and Ahmad Jūrjānī (d. 669/1270) lead us to Nūr al-Dīn Kasirqī (d. 690/1291) and 'Alā' Dawla Simnānī (d. 736/1336), leaders of the Baghdad branch, represented after them by Farāhī and Bahā"l-Dīn 'Umar (d. 857/1453). Jalāl al-Dīn Rūmī (d. 672/1273), founder of the Mevleviya, was connected with the Khurasanian branch.

Among the Kubrawīya who declared themselves in favor of Hallāj, we call attention, after Jurjānī, to Kubrā in his Tarīqat nāme, Majd al-Dīn al-Baghdādī in his Risālat al-safar, Najm Rāzī "Dāyah" in his Mirsād al-'ibād, Kasirqī in his Tafsīr, and 'Alā' Dawla Simnānī.

Another Kubrawī, 'Abdullāh Balyānī (d. 686/1287),[161] has left us an account that is very characteristic of his era's approach to the personality of Hallāj (referred to as Mansūr).[162] He was living for a certain time in solitude, he tells us, high on a mountain in the company of his master, Abū Bakr Zāhid Hamadhānī. At one moment, when he declared: "I am no longer anything but God!" his master admonished him, saying: "Are you talking like Mansūr?" — "By a single 'ah!' that I utter, I can create a thousand such like Mansūr!" "I went on. And as I was saying that, Zāhid took his stick and threw it at me. I jumped out of the way . . . and he reviled me, saying: 'They crucified Mansūr, and he did not run away from it; but you, you jump out of the way of an ordinary stick!' — 'That proves that Mansūr was not perfect,' I retorted; 'otherwise he would have fled, for, in the sight of God, it is all one and the same!' (After making me sit down), Zāhid continued: 'You have said to me that it was because Mansūr was not perfect that he did not flee and that he was crucified; how can you prove that?' — 'The proof is that a horseman who

---

[160] Or through Abū 'Amr Zajjājī (d. 348/959): cf. the certification of the Kubrawīya khirqa given in Damascus in 625/1227 by the grandson of Sa'd al-Dīn ibn Hammūya: published by Ibn Abī Usaybi'a in his 'Uyūn al-anbā' [bib. no. 2092-a] (1299 ed.), II, 250. Cf. Jāmī, 652.

[161] From Balyan near Dusht Arjan (Fars): Fārsnāma Nacin II, 249.

[162] Jāmī, Nafahāt, 292-293.

claims to be a horseman is not going to lose his reins when his horse runs; if he succeeds in getting his horse to go the other way, he is a skillful horseman, if not he is not a good horseman.' — 'You are right,' Zāhid answered me.''

This dialogue reveals the ingenuous arrogance of monistic mysticism and its incomprehension of the meaning of martyrdom.

1. The Naqishbandīya

The early nucleus of the Naqishbandīya was formed in Khurasan by Abū Hasan Khurqānī (d. 425/1033), who declared himself to be the direct spiritual heir of Abū Yazīd Bistāmī, who had died a hundred years before (261/875).[163] Kremer believed that Khurqānī had repeated Hallāj's "Anā'l-Haqq"; however, he based that belief on a wrong translation made by Tholuck of a passage in 'Attār in which Khurqānī says merely "God is my waqt (instant)."[164]

After Khurqānī's death, his disciples were directed by Sahlajī [and by] Abū 'Alī al-Fadl Fārmadhī (d. 477/1084), who was also a disciple of Jurjānī (d. 469) and who was Ghazālī's master in mysticism; then by Yūsuf Hamadhānī (d. Marv, 535/1140).[165] Both, as we know,[166] upheld the memory of Hallāj. A pupil of Yūsuf Hamadhānī, Ahmad Yesewī, the first poet of the Turkish language, extolled Hallāj. After 'Abd al-Khāliq Ghujdawānī, Riwajīrrī, Mahmūd Anjīr, Rāmaytanī, Muhammad Bābā, Amīr Kulāl and Bahā' al-Dīn Naqishband,[167] the second founder of the order, who claimed to be the direct spiritual heir of Uways Qaranī (d. 37/657)[168] and of Ghujdawānī, we find Pārsā (d. 822/1419), who, after examining the life of Hallāj in his Fasl al-khitāb, avoids giving his opinion.[169]

Via 'Alā' al-Dīn 'Attār, Nizām al-Dīn Khāmush and Sa'd al-Dīn

---

[163] It appears that it actually recruited its members from among those of the Tayfūrīya school, founded in fact by Abū Yazīd (Hujwīrī, Kashf, 184) and whose last head was Abū 'Abdallāh Dāsitānī (b. 358/968, d. 417/1026) (Jāmī, 338).

[164] 'Attār II, 211. Meaning: God is the measure of my intuition of time. Cf. with regard to the word waqt, infra, Chapter XI.

[165] Harawī's commentator, the master of Hakīm Sanā'ī (Tarā'iq II, 262).

[166] 'Attār II, 135.

[167] There exists a miniature of him in Persian Cairo ms., 208, no. 41, f. 79.

[168] Cf. Jurjānī's cry "Uways! Uways!" ('Attār I, 23).

[169] Khwīshagī (Tahqīq al-muhaqqiqīn, written in 1170/1756) says, on the contrary, that he says the following in it: "Ijmā' was formed among Shaykhs of old, who are the imāms of the learned and of Shaykhs, regarding (sic: one would expect to read: against) the fact that Husayn-b-Mansūr died a martyr. And it is this later ijmā' which, by right, settles the question of the earlier dissent, even though this dissent was based on the normal exercise of ijtihād, which is not the case."

Kāshgharī, Naqishbandism found its way to Jāmī and his disciples, Lārī and Kāshif Jāmī, and carried on the ideas of Harawī (d. 481/1088) with regard to Hallāj. The movement seems to have looked upon him, in addition, as a precursor of Ibn 'Arabī, whose monism (*wahdat al-wujūd*) it adopted.

Kāshifī has preserved for us a beautiful passage by Rashīd al-Dīn Maybūdhī on the ecstasies of Hallāj dealing with the "incandescent fire of God" (Qur'ān 104:6).

The fire that kindles our hearts is the fire of loving admiration (for God).[170] And Husayn Mansūr Hallāj (God's blessings be upon him!) said: "For *seventy* years[171] the incandescent fire of God has filled us within to the point of consuming us entirely. Suddenly a spark struck from a flint 'I am the Truth' (*Anā'l-Haqq*) has fallen on our lifeless ashes (to revive them). And now may he come, the one who is burned, to tell us what our burning is!" Kāshifī sums this up as follows:

O Torch, come, that you and I may moan together
For the states of a burned heart, which he who burns from the same fire knows!

Beha Naqishband relates the following: "Twice in Bukhara, I yearned for *sifa Mansūr*: as I was going to echo his words (*Ana'l-Haqq*) before a gibbet, a voice said to me *jāyi tū īnsar Dār ast*, then grace turned me from doing it."[172]

In this regard, Khāja 'Azīzān said (previously to the B. Naqishband) "if one of the children (*farzandun*) of 'Abd al-Khāliq (= Ghujdawānī) had been there, Mansūr would not have been hanged."

In the last century, Diyā"l-Dīn Khālid, who preached in Baghdad[173] and in Syria, extolled the "*Anā'l-Haqq*" of Hallāj in one of the poems of his *dīwān*.

m. Fakhr al-Dīn Rāzī

Fakhr Rāzī (b. 544, d. 606/1209 in Herat), a student through his father, Diyā', of 'Umar-b-Husayn and Salmān Ansārī, a theologian of the Shafi'ite rite and founder of classical neo-Ash'arite scholasticism, had no hesitation making use of Hellenistic philosophy and Mu'tazilism. Very rigid when it came to the vocabulary of the *via remotionis* in theodicy, he brought about the overthrow of the Karrāmīya in Afghanistan. But he

---

[170] Cf. Najm Rāzī (this volume, p. 424).   [171] Cf. Hulwānī, *supra* [?].

[172] Ap. *Anis al-tālibīn*, a biography of Beha Naqishband compiled by a pupil of 'Alā' 'l-Dīn 'Attār. Marian Molé believes that Beha Naqishband is thinking of an initiation hall, Dāre Mansūr, of the Bektashī sort (cf. this volume, pp. 268-271; Yf Hamadhānī in the two Naqishbandīya *isnāds*).

[173] On his *tekke*, cf. *Mém. Inst. Fr. Archéol. Or.* (Cairo, 1912), XXXI, 64, n. 2; Alūsī, *Gharā'ib al-ightirab* [bib. no. 910-b], 17.

accepts mysticism, in which his father transmitted to him maxims received from Ibn Abī'l-Khayr via Salmān-b-Nāsir Ansārī (d. 512).[174] He put the name of Hallāj after the *tarahhum* in the *fatwā* after his "I am the Truth."[175]

His response consisted of five points:

(1) It is absurd to consider this a question of *ittihād* (unification): for if two things are united, either they continue to exist, which makes two of them, or they disappear and a third comes into being that is different, replacing them; or indeed one continues to exist and the other disappears, which is not union.[176] It therefore remains, "in view of the perfection (*kamāl*) of this man," to interpret these words in one of the following senses (*ta'wīl*):

a) (*fanā'*) = (*hulūl*). Only God is truly living. Hallāj, annihilated, sees only God, and, in this intoxicated state, it is God Who says, with his tongue, "Anā," "I." Hallāj was unable then to correct it to "*Anā bi'l-Haqq*," as (Junayd) had asked him to do: "It is *by* the Truth that I am," which would have had him harking back to himself;[177]

b) (*inqilāb*) = (*tajawhur*). Just as the elixir changes lead into gold, the elixir of *ma'rifa* (= divine wisdom) had changed the spirit of Hallāj from "nothingness" into "reality" and, having become pure gold, he said "I am the Truth";[178]

c) (*ghalaba*). Of the one who is consumed by an object, we say metaphorically that he *is* that object (he "is" generosity). It is through *mubālagha* that the believer who is immersed in the divine glory (*mustaghriq*) says, without sinning (*lā jaram*), "I am the Truth." It is he, not God, who says it, as in interpretation (a);[179]

d) (*tajallī*) = (*wahdat al-wujūd*). Divine radiance removes the veils of one's charnal nature (*basharīya*), and one's spirit becomes Haqq, "Truth" (cf. Qur'ān 8:8);[180] one is therefore right to say "I am the Truth," for the real "Truth" is a more general (Idea) than "the real Truth by itself" or the "real Truth expressed in terms of another." One can object that, in this view, the whole (universe) is "Truth";[181] why specify it in this way (*takhsīs*)? Fakhr Rāzī concludes: because divine radiance, which illuminated his spirit without introducing him into the world of divinity (*ilāhīya*), conferred this perfection (*kamāl*) on him, Hallāj mentioned this unusual privilege granted him (by saying "I").

---

[174] Sam'ānī, f. 550a, *Tafs. kab.* I.   [175] Taymūr Majm. ms. 193, f. 85.
[176] Ibn Sīnā's argument (ap. *Ishārāt*, which Fakhr had summarized).
[177] Harawī's thesis.   [178] Ibn Sab'īn's thesis.   [179] Ghazālī's thesis.
[180] Cf. Qur'ān 21:18, a verse quoted by Hallāj himself—*Akhbār*, nos. 7 and 37.
[181] Ibn 'Arabī's thesis, which Fakhr is trying here to free from monism.

v. The Legend of Hallāce Mansūr in Turkish Lands

The Hallājian legend held a very high place in the Islamicization of Turkish peoples; it not only presented them with a moving literary leitmotiv, it also provided for them an ideal model of sanctity.[1] It was not by chance that the establishment of the Saljūqs' Turkish sultanate in Baghdad, the capital of the 'Abbāsid caliphate, was conceived and carried out by a Shāfi'ite Muslim jurisconsult, the only one to be vizir, and, in fact, a Hallājian vizir: Ibn al-Muslima (like St. Boniface, the archbishop of Mayence, anointing the first of the Carolingians).[2]

Therefore, I did not want to wait for the appearance of critical editions of the prose and verse texts that will be quoted in this section, in part, from unedited manuscripts, which makes the analysis incomplete and the translation often approximate. I hope that the present study, representing a preliminary clearing of almost virgin ground, will lead Turkologists to focus attention on and examine in depth one of the spiritual sources of Turkish cultural history.

a. In Eastern Turkish

1. The *Hikam* of Ahmed Yesewī

The supereminent importance assigned in Turkish literature from its earliest beginnings to the Hallājian theme as expressed in the most sublime form (the martyrdom of love) indicates an initiation linking the first Turkish poets in Turkestan together with a mystical group of specifically Hallājian adepts.

We are concerned here, most probably, with a group from Talaqan and Balkh, exemplified in Persian by 'Attār and reorganized somewhat earlier by a *lūr* Kurd, Yūsuf Hamadhānī Burūjirdī (441, d. 535),[3] the direct master of Ahmed Yesewī (d. 561), who was the first and greatest of the eastern Turkish poets. In this group, which survives today with the Bektāshīs, the "gibbet of Mansūr" is an integral part of the initiation rite complete with a symbolism of dedication unto death, one which the Shī'ite alterations undergone by this rite in the sixteenth century did not dare suppress.[4]

The *hikam* of Ahmed Yesewī are far from being wholly genuine; there are retouches dating from the fifteenth century (Nesīmī, as we shall see,

---

[1] Koprülüzāde M Fuat, in a footnote, recalled the existence of Turkish "old *Mansūrnāmac*," (cf. my "*Recueil*" of 1929, pp. 152-154).

[2] Cf. my February 1940 lecture at the University of Istanbul on Ibn al-Muslima and Tughril Beg.

[3] A Shāfi'ite; died in Marw.   [4] See here, *in fine*.

is cited), but all of them belong to the same collection of poems used in the monasteries of religious orders in Turkestan.

Among the *hikam*, numbers X, XXI, and LXXXIII of the Kazan edition (1311/1893) are devoted to Shāh Mansūr (= Hallāj), who is also referred to in numbers V, LXXIII, LXXXI, and CVIII.

Number V contains an interesting chronological chart (from age 22 to 29) of the mystical evolution of Ahmed Yesewī: annihilation (*fanā'*) at age 22, preaching of the precepts (*tā'a*) at 23, of the future life at 24; *dhikr* (*subhān*) at 25; vision of God "like Mansūr" at 26, spiritual guidance at 27, persecution (*mihna*) at 28, resulting in destruction (*kharāb*)[5] and burning at age 29.

Yesewī, *hikam* no. X (pp. 38-42):

O friends! I am dedicated to the service of pure love, —with the enemy capturing this world, I have left.

Holding the back of my neck, I have come to find shelter in the Presence, —and, like Mansūr, I am at the door of love.

—On the route of love, Mansūr passed by, as a lover, girding his loins; from God he received love.

The Malāmīya, the voluntary despised ones, have done much; —O believers, I am with Mansūr.

—In love, Mansūr uttered with his tongue "*Anā'l-Haqq*," —and arriving unexpectedly, Jibrīl said "*Anā'l-Haqq*" with him.

Jibrīl in coming said to him "offer your head" (= become a martyr),[6] and Mansūr threw it (as an offering) on the Way, —hung on the gibbet, the (divine) vision, I saw it, I myself.

—When Mansūr arrived, the gibbet, groaning, received him—and those whose inner eyes were open went into ecstasies,

For in diffusing His light God Himself cast a glance, —and, in saying "O desire," the divine vision, I saw it, I myself.

—A voice was raised from this gibbet, "do not be choked too much, remain steadfast (in your faith) and do not glance to any side on rising, —

"Do not concern yourself with what I have to do apart (from you)";[7] —I saw that, I myself, on the plank, the Lawh Mahfūz.

—These three hundred assembled mullas[8] have written many *riwāyet* (traditions); —this is the Law; but I too will write a *riwāyet*: "God is our safeguard on the Way and in the Reality"; —and by giving my head, I myself have found the secret of God.

—"*Anā'l-Haqq*" has a hidden meaning which escapes the ignorant, —there must be learned and pure men [to guide us] along these Ways.

The illuminated believers remembered God in their soul (*can-nan*); —When I renounce my soul because of this lover, I do love Him, I.

[5] Cf. 'Attār's meaning of this (*Jawhar al-dhāt* [bib. no. 1101-d], Book I, chapter 72: "to be destroyed = loss of reputation").

[6] This role played by Jibrīl is shared by the Prophet, ap. Rūmī, Ahmadī, Murīdī.

[7] This advice from the gibbet is found ap. Bukharian *Qisse*.

[8] Three hundred. The number of mullas is 380, ap. *Waslatnāma*.

—I made a sign, and if there is a wise man, he will understand its meaning, —I discussed the knowledge of *qāl* (letter) so that this might be a clue.

Our words have pearls and precious stones within, so he may find them there, —I have given the experiences of the *hāl* (spiritual state) to those who love.

—Mansūr, alas (*isiz*), humbled himself deliberately, and thereby paid his debt; —with a single utterance he became isolated from his friends;

None of those who are ignorant of the heart's *hāl* are witnesses of God; —through a pact of blood (drunk up) I stand also as a witness, I.

—The "*Anā'l-Haqq*" of Shāh Mansūr is not untimely;

—Standing apart from the people of the Way, our fellow men, straying, lose all sense of where they are;

None of these people without relations understand these words; —understanding that, I seized upon the scent of God, I.

—At the end of one night, at dawn, Gharīb Mansūr[9] was deeply moaning; —and God Himself, spreading His light, forgave him; —

After which, the Forty, pondering over him, gave him some wine. —I say these words to wise men.

—But to the ignorant my words are madness, my wisdom injustice.

Yesewī, *Hikam* no. XXI (pp. 58-59):

The lovers untiringly (*tinmay*) say "*Huwa*"[10] when they implore God.

—They walk night and day, growing increasingly pale. My Lord "*Khudāyim*" makes the lover moan under the hand of love, —and blame, according to God, is very fitting for the lover on love's way.

One day Mansūr emitted this moan, and the adepts cried mercy (interceding on his behalf), —and the Forty (*chilten*) gave Mansūr the love-giving wine to drink.

Mansūr said "*Anā'l-Haqq*," the adept's only concern is God alone, —but the mullas retort, opening their unjust heart to evil.

"Do not say '*Anā'l-Haqq*';[11] you are speaking blasphemy, Mansūr," —Then, saying: this is in the Qur'ān, they, having come together, put him to death.

These mullas were unable to understand "*Anā'l-Haqq*," —God did not judge it proper to give knowledge of the mystical state (*hāl*) to these people of the letter (*qāl*), —traditions (*riwāyet*) were redacted for them, but they did not discern this state.

They placed a saint like Mansūr hung on a gibbet, —the epos (*afsāne*) is the Law, the judicious is the Way, the single pearl is the Reality, which are prepared for all of the lovers.

All of the people in this world gathered and wept, saying "Mansūr" —and the friends of Mansūr have remained there (*onda*), together.[12]

---

[9] "*Gharīb*" is a much more meaningful surname than "*Shāh*," for it refers to the *Tawāsīn*.

[10] "He" instead of the canonical name "*Allāh*," the only one allowed in public.

[11] *Anā'l-Haqq* = *bātil*; cf. the *fatwā* of Ibn Dāwūd; the idea was used again by the poet Gevherī (154) and by the Osmanli theologian Mehmet 'Arīf Ketkhudāzāde (*Manāqib*, Supplement, 9: how would Hallāj have been able to respond, when united with God, "Anā'l-bātil").

[12] An allusion to *Dār-i Mansūr*, the central place of the Bektāshī initiation hall, where the

Do penance, Khaja Ahmed, and you will receive God's grace, —a hundred thousand saints already have gone beyond, who linked their mysteries to mysteries.

Yesewī, *Hikam* no. LXXXIII (pp. 153-157):

Those who have knowledge of love, the lovers, —if they say "Allāh," the nine heavens burn; —on the Throne, if the just utter a moan, the angels heap kindness on them out of their beloved soul.

Be loving, you will find light shines for the lovers; raising the curtain, glory comes to the just; —God shows His vision to those who are worthy of it (*lāyiq*), —He is the Lover of those who are worthy of it.

(Couplets 3-6 counsel the invocations "*Allāh, labbayk*"; they mention a *murīd* of Bayezid.)

To lovers, their own self, without the one God, is something forbidden; —let a drop of His mercy fall, and the act is perfect; —those who do not seek their daily means of life are in complete *tawakkul*; —to remember God repeatedly satisfies.

—The lovers out of fear of God, remain heedful; —loving the reality, their thought is vision; to the one who gives his head, his soul and his faith take wing; —he who renounces his soul in the Way of God becomes *avlār* (= a hunter).

By repeating (the *dhikr*) *lā lā*,[13] you become wise, but you declare yourself blasphemous; —calling yourself blasphemous, you hang like Mansūr on the gibbet; —by giving your head, you reveal (to others) the vision of God; —he who has given his head enjoys the vision of God.

Hanging high above the great gate, you see the whole town; —which seeing, you become a symbol for all of its inhabitants; —you pass through showing both the great and the small how to walk on the Route; —he who says "*Anā'l-Haqq*," secretly loved, smiles.

The head of the mullas assembled before the king (*shāh*) continued his attacks; —the king opened the session saying "Mansūr is not a blasphemer—saying that the law of the Prophet does not ordain it so; —and those who understood the external side (of the law) gave their consent to the king.

"This is the Law," said the *'ulamā'* on handing down the order (for execution); —even though (the king) had said "Mansūr is not a blasphemer," they had him burned; —sparks flew this way and that skyward, while the ashes, remaining, were saying "*Anā'l-Haqq*."

Those who burned from the same desire ascended to heaven; —the angels wept before God; —within paradise, the *hūri* and the *ghilmān* closed the gates; —those who are mad (for love), crying "*yā Mansūr*," burst into flame.

Beginning to rise, the river left its bed; in midwinter, the river, overflowing, emitted cries; the townspeople, having run to see, scattered in all directions; —they were moaning, fearful for their lives.

---

professed must take the oath (cf. 'Attār, *Tadhk.* II, 135, lines 24 ff.; and Harawī, ap. Jāmī, *Naf.*, 170, lines 10-18).
[13] This is also the name that Ibn Abī'l-Khayr (*Talbīs*, 363) gives to the *shahāda*.

Now, Shaykh Dhū'l-Nūn was the *pīr* of Shāh Mansūr; —the sovereign had hastened to forewarn the group of saints; —the saints, questioning God, complained to Him; —Shaykh Dhū'l-Nūn, who had set out in secret, arrived.

Gharīb Mansūr had said one thing to a disciple: "take a handful of my ashes, and make an offering of them to me; —if you throw them into the river while saying "*yā Mansūr*," as he said to do it, —if God so wills, the river that overflowed will return (to its bed)."

The sovereign decided to summon the *pīr*, —to throw the ashes into the river; —the disciple of Gharīb, —to collect (the ashes); —the sovereign's vizir ordered them collected with reverence.

Shaykh Dhū'l-Nūn rose from the ground saying "all right!"; —the vizirs and the sovereign, in haste worshipped the ground he walked on; —Shaykh Dhū'l-Nūn, walking off, came to the river, —and he threw the ashes into the river.

He threw the ashes into the water while saying "*ya Mansūr*"; —through the *qudra* the river, obeying, was calmed; —the khojas and mullas, seeing this, thanked the shaykh; —opening their hands, they prayed for the shaykh, we are told.

(The sovereign offers the shaykh his town, the hand of his daughter, and all that is his if he will serve him. Dhū'l-Nūn refuses.

Dhū'l-Nūn has nothing to do in this world with an outward sovereignty, being himself internally the "king of kings"; and as for a wife, he is divorced from both worlds.)

(Couplets 20-25 contain an exhortation to those who are careless about hell; calling them to die of love):

Like Nesīmī for saying "*Haqq*," you will be skinned alive; —while you are being hanged, the head of the mullas will be objecting to the reason; —the one whose skin (flayed) is stuffed with straw repeats "*Haqq*."

(In the last couplet, 27, Khāja Ahmed [= Yesewī] recalls the *mīthāq*.)

The other Hallājian references in the *hikam* of Ahmed Yesewī are quite brief:

In number LXXIII (p. 136, 7th couplet): between Majnūn, who searched throughout the world for Layla, and Bishr Hāfī, who in love found a vision [of God], "Shaykh Mansūr saying '*Anā'l-Haqq*' instigated a riot."

In number LXXXI (p. 152, 11th couplet): "The calling to love is something easily accomplished; it means giving one's head; —like Mansūr renouncing himself, it means giving one's soul; —the hadīth 'die before you die' means to share in the dust."

In number CVIII (p. 203, 5th couplet): a list of prophets (Zakariyā, Ayyūb, Mūsā, Yūnus, Yūsuf, Ya'qūb) and saints (Shiblī [his *samā'*], Bayezid [and the Ka'ba], Ma'rūf and Mansūr) ends thus:

"Like Ma'rūf therefore, I will walk always in the Way; —like Mansūr, renouncing my soul, I will be put on the gibbet, through desire I will be God."

2. The Disciples of Yesewī: the *Qisse-i Mansūr Shaykh*

One of the Bukhara manuscripts of the *hikam* of Yesewī[14] contains in an appendix some later poems of the same style, two of which are signed Qul Sulaymān Gharīb and Shams Gharīb, a "descendant of Mustafā (= the Prophet)," the probable author of the *Qisse*.

This *Qisse*, written in literary eastern Turkish but in a popular style (and at times uneven orthography), with traces of the dialect of Awliya Ata,[15] narrates in 358 lines the legend of Hallāj. It is closely related to the oral legend noted by Sidikov among the Qirghiz of 'Osh, though the poet tells in the colophon that his Turkish verse version was based on an original Persian prose text.

He begins, following the *hamdala*, by recalling that God created the Nūr Muhammadī before anything else; then He let seven drops of sweat[16] fall, which produced the four *rāshidīn* caliphs, the Red Rose (Qyzyl Gul = Hallāj,[17] Kūrūnj [? = Qurbanj]),[18] and (7th), all of the Faithful. To make the religion even purer, Islam was built up with the Imām A'zam (= A Hanīfa), Shāfi'ī, Abū Yūsuf, and Mālik. After burning away the heart's impurities, here follows a tale—it was written in prose, I have put it into verse—*Hikāyet-i Mansūr*, a ruby, a marvelous thing:

(Line 12) In the city of Cairo, on the banks of the wide river, there lived a believer named Mansūr, who wept in his devotions and spoke the name of God in fear. He also used to say *"Anā'l-Haqq,"* thereby revealing the mystery in part. There was also a girl there (his sister), her head covered with a *tarboosh*,[19] who was superior to others and who also said *"Allāh."* Like the houris of Paradise, she visited the Forty (*chilten*) to drink with them the *"sharāb tuhūr"* reserved for saints to drink at night; they come out only after dawn. She tied her hair up. People had suspicions about her behavior; an old woman came to Mansūr and said: your sister is a good girl, but she does things that are reprehensible. A man named 'Āshiq also came to Mansūr, advising him to keep a close eye on his sister. Mansūr was aware that his sister Anāl had become Haqq,[20] that she had been slandered, for

[14] Paris ms., Turkish Supplement 1191, ff. 70a, 76b; 83b-93b (= *Qisse*).
[15] Usually *nī* (for *nink*). I owe this provisional analysis to the general help of J. Deny.
[16] Cf. Mughīra.   [17] Cf. *infra* [?].
[18] A Khurasanian Sūfī who died around 375 (Jāmī, 399) in the Kilāt prison (LS, 395); a friend of Gādhir Harawī, a pupil of Shiblī.
[19] To give herself the appearance of a man.
[20] A restructuring of the sentence *"Anā'l-Haqq"* resulting from a faulty knowledge of Arabic.

the secret of the saints remains misunderstood. One evening, he went out immediately after she had gone, following her shadow, without her knowing, to a cave; the door was opened; she entered alone; Mansūr stayed outside, for the Forty stood guard at the door. They drank with Anāl; intoxicated, they shouted Anālhaqq. Then they bid Mansūr enter and he also drank and also became intoxicated; his eyes became bloodshot, his face reddened (like the girl's), they kept shouting Anālhaqq. The mullas, informed, scolded Mansūr, who paid no attention to them. The padishah, when it was his turn to reprimand, summoned Mansūr before him, [but Mansūr only] repeated Anālhaqq and wept. The mullas analyzed the meaning of these words and declared him a kāfir; the mufti and the qādī condemned him to be hanged. Hung on the gibbet, he continued to say Anālhaqq; the gibbet leaned forward and a celestial voice (nidā') said to it "do not clasp him too tightly"; Mansūr stayed on the gibbet for seven nights uttering Anālhaqq. Everyone heard him where they were standing near the high gate.

Then Dhū'l-Nūn, the Pole of poles, arrived; in this garden, like a nightingale, he drifted into the corolla of this fully bloomed Red Rose (ācheqlīb 'irdī Qyzyl gul = Mansūr in ecstasy on the gibbet). Since the padishah had ordered everyone with stones to hurl them at him, Dhū'l-Nūn said, yes, let them strike him. Then they burned his body and threw the ashes into the river.

Three days later the river swelled and threatened to engulf the city. Dhū'l-Nūn, seeing the terror in the hearts of the mullas and the people, decided to throw Mansūr's ashes into the river. He did this himself, and the waves were calmed; the city was saved by a miracle of Mansūr (Mansūrdīn karāmet). The waters of the river wailed, saying "O God, reveal Your face to the lovers." The Nile receded, the ashes condensed into foam, and then, several days later, having carried across the gulf, they came again to a river, flowing toward Aleppo (Halab), and passing along a ditch through a garden arrived at a basin (hawd).

Now a beloved and obedient daughter of the king of Aleppo, who was walking in the garden, leaned over the water and said to her slaves "draw some water"; one came forward. Now, on the surface of the water in the basin there was some foam which was uttering Anālhaqq. When she drew the water, she also took the foam. Opening her mouth to drink, she swallowed the foam. After a short time her mother saw that she was pregnant; the daughter, in desolation ("I would like to become earth"), told her the tale, which made her mother weep. Shaykh Mansūre Hallāc said to her, he the Crown of the saints, the only cure is found in what is predestined. Nine months later the birth pangs began. The mother and the king were deeply dismayed; they deliberated together: if anyone finds out, it will be a scandal; however, it would be a sin to kill her. They hit upon the idea of [putting her in] a gold and ivory chest that they would seal with wax. When night came, they put their daughter in the chest, sealed its lid tight, and threw it into the water. Satisfied, they returned to their palace to weep.

No one knew their secret except God, and the daughter repeated ceaselessly the word "Allāh." The chest floated away without stopping, half on the water and half beneath it; the daughter did not know if she was floating, nor if the sun had risen, the only thing that shone to her was the wax substance. After floating for many days, to and fro, the chest arrived at the outskirts of a city named Baghdad, and there a fisherman, using his hook (qarmāq) to harpoon, halted it in the reeds. His own wife had bore him no child, but she would have one that night when he returned. Now, inside the chest the daughter had given birth to a son, by the power of God; as the foam had entered her through her mouth, so the child had come out of her mouth. When he returned home, the fisherman struck open the chest, saw the child and the daughter, and was overjoyed. The child was later adopted, and the king of Baghdad gave him the name *Nesīmī*.

When he was seven years old, Nesīmī was entrusted to a mulla. Following his period in school, his witty retorts led him to be taken for a madman. Finally, as he desired, he was condemned by the mullas and skinned alive (in lines 11-14, f. 91b, a *ghazal* by Nesīmī in Ottoman Turkish was inserted into the account).

In the colophon, the poet tells how, after having been touched in his heart by this tale, he wanted to translate it from Persian prose into Turkish verse. One Thursday evening, he made *istikāra*; and he had formed the *niya*, and while waiting for the answer (from God, *khabar*), began to write, when suddenly Mansūr entered his dream, holding a rose in his hand, which he gave to him; and this hero (*yigīt* = *fatā*), in this apparition, said to him: "O *tālib*, it is I, Mansūr; do not arouse my heart to anger; take paper and pen, and write."

This unique *Qisse* poses various problems. Hallāj is described in it as a "Red Rose" in ecstasy on the gibbet: probably because of the hadīth published by his disciple Abū Bakr Wāsitī, "the one who wants to see the glory of God (*bahā'u'llāh*), let him contemplate the red rose";[21] and this is why Lāmi'ī began his long *qasīda* on the Rose by comparing it when it leans over to Mansūr on the gibbet. 'Attār had already pointed out that Hallāj, mutilated, smeared his stumps with his blood, for they could not appear pale from fear, and "red rose (*gulgūne*) is the color of the blood of heroes";[22] Ibn Abī'l-Khayr had also said that the gibbet is for heroes.[23]

The site of his execution was shifted from Baghdad to Cairo, due to the role assigned to the Egyptian Sūfī Dhū'l-Nūn, in the time of Yesewī,[24] as the spiritual director of Hallāj. Such a shift was possible to make only among very ignorant Turks cut off geographically from Baghdad, in the time of Baghdad's fall, after our fifteenth century, in the era of Nesīmī's martyrdom.

The application of the theme of Hallāj's virginal reincarnation to Nesīmī, who was executed in Aleppo in 820/1417 for having repeated his "*Anā'l-Haqq*,"[25] is very unusual, representing a naive actualization of a claim of spiritual filiation. It should also be noted that the mention of Aleppo proves that the author, since the beginning of the *Qisse*, believed

---

[21] This edition, 3, 168, n. 198; and 269, n. 36.
[22] 'Attār, *Tadhk.* II, 144.
[23] Ibn al-Munawwar.
[24] This edition, 3, 229.
[25] Ap. Hifzi Tewfik, *Türk Edebiyatı*, I, ...

he was speaking in it of Nesīmī, though he had him die at the end of the tale in Baghdad, not in Aleppo.

Yesewī's 83rd *hikam* had already connected the names of Mansūr, Dhū'l-Nūn, and Nesīmī. To express his gratitude to Dhū'l-Nūn for having saved Baghdad (and not Cairo) from the flood by throwing Hallāj's ashes into the water, the king offered him his kingdom and the hand of his daughter, but Dhū'l-Nūn refused, saying that he was already the King of Kings, and that he had divorced himself from this world. It was only by accident that Nesīmī came on the scene subsequently, following exhortations of a general nature made to believers oblivious to *ikhlās*: "O *Faqīr*, you must know, like Nesīmī, how to speak the Truth, and to let yourself be flayed and then, stuffed with straw, to be hung; Nesīmī's flesh repeated "*Anālhaqq*."[26] The *Qisse* was apparently not influenced by this *hikam* when it was constructed.

3. Among the Qaraqirghiz of 'Osh

These are the real Qirghiz (in contrast to the Qazaq Qirghiz of the west = Uzbegs). Coming from the High Yenisei, they ruled from 840 to 917 of our era over the Uyghur of Mongolia, sending forth some tribes ever since that time to their present location (South Semirechye, East Ferghana), which the bulk of them rejoined only in 1703, after having fought in the name of Islam against the Buddhist Kalmouk; vassals of the Uzbegs, Russia conquered them in 1864.[27]

The Qaraqirghiz were divided into two clans, the right wing *on* and the left wing *sol*, and said to comprise forty tribes, hence their name (Qirq qiz = forty daughters). Thirty tribes of clan *on* called themselves *otuz-ogul*, the "thirty sons"; the ten of clan *sol* (and not *on*), *on-ogul*, the "ten sons" (subdivided in two; Adigne to the northeast of 'Osh, and Tagai in Karakol (= east of Lake Issyk Kul) and to the east of Pichpek.[28]

Here is how these names are explained in the legend assembled by Sidikov among the Qirghiz of 'Osh to the east of Khokand:[29]

Two pious believers, Shāh Mansūr and his sister Anāl,[30] were living in Pshevir.[31] One evening the brother took note of the fact that his sister had gone out; he looked for her and found her in a cave in a nearby mountain seated in the

---

[26] 3rd ed., Qazan, pp. 156-157.   [27] Barthold, ap. *Enc. Isl.* s.v.

[28] Aristov (quoting Sidikov).

[29] A. S. Sidikov, *Rodovoe delenie Kirgiz*, ap. V. V. Barthold, *'Iqd al-juman* (= anthology of verse presented to Barthold), Tashkent, 1927, p. 275. Sidikov did not realize that the subject was Hallāj (J. Deny's friendly comment).

[30] The legend presumed that "*Anā*" was a proper name and read it as "*Anāl*."

[31] Toponym (Pechaver is unlikely).

midst of a group of intoxicated young people who were imbibing an unknown drink. Outraged, he went in and, invited to drink, he refused. Then, yielding to entreaties, he drank and felt that this strong drink was inebriating him. All those who were present then went out, and Shāh Mansūr, completely intoxicated, shouted "Anā'l-Haqq, menam Haqq," which is to say, "Anāl is the Truth, and I am the Truth."[32] Some mullas who were nearby heard this shout and considered it blasphemous and decided there and then that the brother and sister should be put to death. The verdict was sent to the Khan, who approved it: the brother and sister were strangled. But their lifeless bodies continued to cry out their blasphemy; they were burned, and their ashes were thrown into a river basin (hawd) on the banks of which forty little girls were playing, the daughters of the Khan. Now, it so happened, as stated on authority, that they saw the surface of the water was covered with a foam which uttered the words "Anā'l-Haqq, menam Haqq." Following their curiosity, they drew near the basin and put some of the foam in their mouths. The foam proved to be miraculous, and, some time later, the forty girls had forty sons.[33] The Khan, informed of these developments, and seething with rage, drove them out from under his roof. Thirty came to Turkestan, settling in 'Osh; it was the Qirghiz branch of the Otuz-ogul that descended from these sons. The remainder, the other ten, came at a later time, and it was the On-ogul who descended from them.

b. In Anatolian Turkish

1. Yūnus Emre

Yūnus Emre was without doubt the earliest poet in Anatolian Turkish. His mystical Dīwān is still praised and, in the tekkē, his melodies (ilāhi)[34] still sung.

Recent studies have removed any doubt concerning the direct connection of his initiation isnād with the Bābā'īs-Bektāshīs through Tapdūq Emre, Barāq Qrimī (d. 707, Aleppo), Sāry Sāltūq (d. after 663).[35] We therefore must shift his death date forward from the year 707 to around 740, which makes him the exact contemporary of 'Ashīq Pāsha (d. 733), the author of the gharīb nāma and a statesman who was also initiated into the Bābā'īs.[36]

Yūnus, like his contemporary, the Andalusian Shushtarī, wrote short

---

[32] The Russian tradition gives "istina" = truth.

[33] It is very strange that this feature of the Hallāj legend is found near Mosul (Yazīdīs) and in Java. Cf. the toponyms Cihil Dukhteran near Badghis (Jap, 1860, II, 500) and near Qandahar (seen on April 29, 1945).

[34] Burhān Toprak (ex-Umit) to whom we owe the edition of Yūnus' Dīwān (3 vols., 1933-1934); another of his poems about Mansūr, ap. Köprülü M. Fu'at, Ilk [bib. no. 1378-a], 350.

[35] Abdülbaki Gölpinarli, Yūnus Emre [bib. no. 1383-c], 1936.

[36] Raif Yelkenci considers "Yūnus Emre" a "nom de plume" for 'Ashīq Pāsha (Cumhuriyet, nos. 3-4, February 1940).

poems, which were both popular and studded with the vocabulary of initiation, in which he celebrated the joys of his soul, finding God in everything, in a perpetual theopathic ecstasy whose latent doctrinal pantheism
exhausts neither its spontaneity nor its freshness but does begin to
undermine its moral discipline. Yūnus established for all time the classical refrains of Ottoman religious poetry; only Niyāzī Misrī would be
able to give new life to its themes. In the midst of his *Dīwān's* poetic
themes, Qur'ānic themes exhorting men to repent (Fir'awn, Qārūn), and
Persian (Ferīdūn, Rustem, Shīrīn) or Persianized (Majnūn, Layla) symbols of profane love, Yūnus mentions, along with his contemporary
Bābā'ī shaykhs and Jalāl Rūmī and their predecessors, Ahmad Kabīr (=
Rifā'ī) and Abū'l-Wafā' Tāj al-'Arifīn (d. 501), three great Sūfīs: Bayezid,
Junayd, and Mansūr, the latter considered without peer. We must be
ready to distinguish between the two *isnāds* of the Bābā'īs, the Bukharan
(Ahmad Yesewī) and the Baghdadian (Abū'l-Wafā', via Bābā' Ilyās
Khurasānī), the latter being the one that provided Yūnus with his cult of
Mansūr. This cult, centered around the gibbet, reminds us, in any case,
of the arrangement of the Bektāshī initiation hall, which places the *Dār-i
Mansūr* in the center, without the present-day Shī'ite additions about
which Yūnus' *Dīwān*, though considerably retouched, says nothing.

I have said this "Anā'l-Haqq" with Hallāce Mansūr, —attaching the cord again
to his neck myself (I, 220).
I have been trampled down with Girgīs,[37] I have been hanged with Mansūr,
—like the cotton of the Carder (= Hallāj), I have been pulverized (I, 171).
I have been Joseph paraded at the slave market. I have been Mansūr led to the
gibbet (I, 158).
Mansūr, I have come to the gibbet, I have been reduced to ashes (I, 197).

The above lines seem to allude to an initiation rite that likens the professed to a divinized martyr. The following lines merely remind us of the
doctrinal importance of the saying "*Anā'l-Haqq*":

To Yūnus taking the cup that made anyone say "Anā'l-Haqq,"—I drank it all
in a single gulp, and was not aroused by it (I, 195).
I. (I, 119): I drank wine given me by a Cupbearer, —whose tavern is higher
than the Throne . . .
Those who become intoxicated there utter the words "Anā'l-Haqq," and the
least of these madmen is one Hallāce Mansūr . . .
The intoxicated in this hall are like Shāh Edhem, and its corners hold the ruins
of a hundred thousand towns of Balkh.
And one hundred thousand Bayezids play music there, —"*utruk nafsak ta'āl*"
(abandon your soul, come) is their song's refrain . . .
II. (I, 157): My single pearl is one that no ocean has seen:

[37] Girgīs (St. George) is mentioned in 'Attār.

I am only a drop, it makes me an ocean for the ocean;
Come, see this wondrous wave which conceals the ocean;
The sea is hidden by this infinite drop.
Mansūr did not claim the *tawhīd* of Anā'l-Haqq in vain;
On the gibbet of love, it was the belt of the Beloved that hung me naked. . . .

III. (II, 248): "If all the seas were a single cup, my thirst would not be quenched by it. . . .
So many times the cup of Mansūr has been put in my hand by the Beloved,
The fire has been set all around me, no one knows my state.
Burning, burning, in order to become ashes in the Way of the Beloved.
IV. (II, 252): This fire of love was pre-eternal in my soul. . . .
My mind has commemorated Anā'l-Haqq from pre-eternity;
When this Mansūr Baghdādī [translated from Rūmī][38] had not yet been born,
the soul, entering love's battle, was reproached;
That is why the name of poor Yūnus is held in disrepute.
V. (II, 340): Neither my body nor my soul has yet understood the meaning of Anā'l-Haqq.
If, up to the present, they have not understood, henceforth I shall go to Him.
VI. (II, 348): If you are a true lover, what does it matter (to you) that [you wear] around your neck a (written divine reprieve = *manshūr* [Qur'ān 17:14])?
If you are sincere in the way of God, what effect have lies and falsehood on you? . . .
If you are believing, come hither, may this old *burj* totter; the separation of good people will occur and bad ones will be recognized as such.
All those who have said "yes" here, will be perfect over there; to those who ask for a sign, what does this Hallāce Mansūr matter?
VII. (II, 361): I have journeyed internally, I have found a wondrous secret, my brother (? *akhī*). . . .
The Beloved is with us, He is not set apart from us, hair close to hair.
Let the distant journey (*irāq*: allusion to Iraq?) happen without me.
I have found the Friend right near me;
What difference does it make where my route is? I shall not waste my time over any route.
This journey has been a happy one for me, I have a good resting place, my brother (*akhī*).
I was Mansūr in his time, and I returned here because of him;
Scatter my burned ashes to heaven, I have become Anā'l-Haqq, my brother;
I no longer care about which fire consumed me or on which gibbet I was hanged. —Reaching the end of my action, I am here to enjoy the spectacle, my brother (*akhī*).

Four poets who allude to Hallāj are directly connected with the school of Yūnus Emre:

Sa'īd Emre (after evoking Moses and Bayezid):[39] " 'Anā'l-Haqq' inebriated me with love, the knowledge that makes us see, —fear came into

---

[38] Cf. Eflakī [bib. no. 1131-a], I, p. 111.   [39] Gölpinarli, p. 241.

my heart, I became Mansūr, I was on the gibbet, —I drank from the cup
of Mansūr; becoming Majnūn, I plunged into the lake."

Mulla Qāsim: "For us love of God is both the sickness and the cure.
. . . For us becoming Mansūr is love of God (*'ishqe Khudādur*)."[40]

"Today the *'Anā'l-Haqq'* mystery was born a hundred thousand times
in my heart; show me the buckle of the Beloved so that I may climb onto
the gibbet with Mansūr."[41]

Shaykhoghlu Satu: "Poor Hallāce Mansūr was crying out *'Anā'l-Haqq'*
while they were taking him down from the gibbet and while I was burning him, I."[42]

Ismā'īl Ummī (enumerating his successive theophanies): "I have been
Husayn; I have been Mansūr; He suddenly considered this form his own,
and, having commended himself to God, He alone incited the riot in
Baghdad, —

"He was Yūnus our leader, 'Ashīq Pāshā our master, —on this occasion He is poor Ismā'īl Ummī."[43]

"I have said *'Anā'l-Haqq'* with this Hallāce Mansūr, —and I have tied
the noose with sorrow around his neck" (Gölpinarli, p. 143); an echo of
the Yūnus refrain I, 202: "The chain was fastened on my neck with love
by my Friend, and is still fastened" (*'ishq zencīrin Dūst buyūnma taqageldi
taqagider*).

The long poem attributed to Yūnus in which the narrator identifies
with all creation, like Ibn Isrā'īl, shares the same pantheistic accents as
this poetry:

> I am the gibbet, I am the act (of hanging), I am the hanged, I am Mansūr, —I
> am the soul and also the body, also this, also that.[44]

The famous *qasīda* of Qayghūsuz Abdāl (line 1030) in which Hallāj is
named[45] can also be connected with the school of Yūnus:

> Do not say absurd things like children;
> You will not become Mansūr by using false words.

2. The Qastamunian Husayn Mansūr *Hikāya*

An appendix to the Halawīyāt of the last Qyzyl-Ahmadli dynasty of
Qastamunī, probably derived from the entourage of Qādī Mahmūd

[40] *Ibid.*, p. 248. [41] *Ibid.*, p. 251.
[42] *Ibid.*, p. 145.
[43] *Ibid.*, p. 143. (Cf. Yūnus, *Dīwān* [bib. no. 1311-a], I, 220.)
[44] Gölpinarli, p. 23.
[45] Hammer, *GOD* III, 357; Gölpinarli, p. 124; Atalay [?], 109.

Mīnās Oghlu (d. around 840), provides us with an archaic version of the Hallājian tradition of Anatolia:[46]

How did Husayn Mansūr say "*Anā'l-Haqq*": when he said it, people explained it in two ways:

(1) Some (*birnecheler*) say the following: God said to Mansūr: "Ask me what you want." —Mansūr said: "what have You in Yourself that I can ask of You?" —God said: "O Mansūr, do I not have everything that you can ask of me?" —Mansūr said: "O my Lord (*chelepem*), what should I ask of You? I am disgusted with this world and with the next life, and I shall enter paradise (*uchmāq*)[47] only in order to see You." —"O Mansūr, do I not have everything that can please you?" —"O my God, would it therefore suit You to have me become You (come to You)?" —Once again the Despot of this world said: Ask me for whatever you desire." —"O my Lord, give me Your personality in my language." —God said: "O Mansūr, in this world the great who have a treasure also have faithful servants who stand rigid watch over it; they cut off the hands and hang those who try to steal it. I too, in this world, I have a treasure; and as soon as you say "I am God" (*bin Tangriyim* = "*Anā'l-Haqq* = *bin gercheyim*), which is my treasure, I have my honest and faithful servants who hear it, seize the thief, impose the canonical penalties on him, imprison him, cut off his hands, hang him on the gibbet, and burn him in the fire, scattering his ashes to the winds." Mansūr said: "O my just Lord, after You have given me Your personality, let them do with my life according to Your will." After Mansūr said that, God gave him His permission (*dustūr*),[48] and this is the reason Mansūr said "*Anā'l-Haqq*." That is the first explanation.

(2) Some said the following: Mansūr was sitting with the Forty . . .[49] and said to them: "If Muhammad Mustafā were to return now to the palace of this world, I would ask him one question which he could not answer. —What question is there that the glory of this world and the guide of the prophets could not answer? —I would say to him: O prophet of God, if a king of this world ordered some persons to hang, you would not gain for their countries freedom for them from the rope by demanding only one of them be freed; similarly, in the presence of God, Whose mercy is so great, you could say only 'my community'; if you had been able to say 'both,' God willing, you would have saved them (all) from Hell; how could he answer that? —And they said nothing further to him. . . . That night the Prophet appeared to Mansūr and said to him: Rise, I must speak to you: listen to my answer to your question. —O Lord Prophet, these formidable words . . . what question? —*You know it* —O Mansūr, at that moment I was in the presence of God . . . in His light . . . listen . . . on the Throne, I performed four *rak'a*, at the third light . . . six hours of *sajda*, at the *salām* of the third *rak'a*, I said: my God, is this prayer of mine a sin? —'No, O Muhammad, when your community concludes its five times of (canonical) prayer, let it do two (additional) *rak'a*; and when hands are raised for the third *rak'a*, the curtains of heaven will open at their

---

[46] Paris ms., a. f. Turc 13, ff. 242b-243b, before the *fatwās* of Mīnās Oghlū.

[47] A Soghdian word.

[48] The word *dustūr* is corporate. Murīdī will say "*pāzār*."

[49] The Forty (= the first Muslims = the saints who come to see Salmān = the *chilten* who make forty-day retreats). Cf. *Dīwān*, p. 146.

prayer; this prayer shall be called "*witr*" and shall be "*wājib*." '[50] At that moment I did not know where I was, and this was when you said to me '*you know it*'; now, a little bit of this secret remains hidden to you; open your mouth, O Mansūr!" He opened it, and when the Prophet had spit into it, Mansūr exclaimed "*Anā'l-Haqq*." —The Prophet then said to him: "you will not be able to live assuming such a role; by saying '*Anā'l-Haqq*,' if you become His presence, you will bring about your own ruin"; and then the Prophet vanished. —Hallāj then said "*Anā'l-Haqq*"; the Caliph and Shiblī beseeched him to forego this cry. . . . Imprisonment.

Once there, he was observed closely for seven days. In the prison there was a tower (*burghūs* = *pyrgos*). On the first day, the tower was seen melting, like paste on a tray (in the oven), for it could not contain Mansūr. On the second day, Mansūr and the tower disappeared. On the third day, only the tower was seen again. On the fourth day, Mansūr was there as well, but shrunken almost to the size of a rat (*gibīche*). On the fifth day, Mansūr resumed the size of a man. The caliph and Shiblī visited him. Mansūr, responding to Shiblī's questions about these transformations, said the following: on the first day, you are only able to understand this: if even the sun that you see, from east to west, cannot contain the light of the Prophet, and I the one in whom God shines forth His majesty, it follows necessarily that the Seven Heavens and the Seven Earths cannot contain me, and this tower is nothing; —on the second day, I had gone to see God, and this tower was with me; —on the third day, the tower had not been admitted into the divine light, also it was visible; —on the fourth day, I was plunged into fear and hope of God; —on the fifth day, I was delivered from forty cares.[51]

Mansūr repeated "*Anā'l-Haqq*." Shiblī verified the fact that Mansūr stole the role of God, and therefore one of his hands had to be cut off. Mansūr went further: since in this world a thief gets one of his hands cut off for stealing ten silver dirhams,[52] I must have both hands cut off for having stolen God.

First they cut off his right hand, and then his left. He repeated "*Anā'l-Haqq*." The Caliph ordered him to be hung on the gibbet; then his two hands, spilling their blood on the ground, both wrote the *shahāda* there. Mansūr smeared his face (?) looking up at the sky with his hands (stumps). —Why did he do that? —In this way I purify myself for prayer. —O shaykh, it is not lawful for one who has lain in his own spilled blood on the ground to perform the prayer; how can you pray with your hands bleeding this way? —O unknowing ones, for the lover in the house of the Beloved, two *rak'a* are sufficient, but ablution is not lawful with anything but the blood of the lover.

Shiblī asked him: who is the lover? the beloved? —O Shaykh Shiblī, I will tell you when you make me put the gibbet cord around my neck. —Answer me. —The Beloved is the One who allows His lovers to assume His identity; the lover is the one who first is flagellated, who secondly is imprisoned, who thirdly has his hands cut off, ablutes himself with his blood and prays two *rak'a*, then is hung on the gibbet, burned on the fire, his ashes scattered to the winds.

[50] The origin of the nocturnal *witr*?

[51] This seems to be more than an amplification of the very brief, similar passage found in the *Tadhk.* of 'Attār (II, 141, lines 10-17) which it explains; could they have had a common source? (*Waslatnāma*)?

[52] A Hanafite rule.

He repeated: "*Anā'l-Haqq.*" They drew the cord, they hanged him: the lover found union in going to the Beloved.[53]

3. The *Dāsitān-i Mansūr* of Ahmadī and the
Mansūrnāma-i Hallāj of Murīdī

Ahmadī, who died in 815, preceded Murīdī, who died around 1004, by nearly two centuries, but their two Hallājian poems relate so directly to each other that they must be looked at together.

I refer to my *Recueil* of 1929, pp. 152-154, for identification of the lithographed texts of these two poems, both published under the name of Niyāzī Misrī, one in 1288/1871, the other in 1261/1845, in Istanbul (sigils: *Ad., Br.,*).

The one by Ahmadī has 557 lines, the one by Murīdī 970. Murīdī borrowed, though shifted around the order of, at least 30 percent of the hemistichs of the *Dāsitān*, while still following its structural plan step by step.

The following is the structural plan common to both the *Dāsitān* and the *Mansūrnāma* (alias: *Manzūme Mansūr*): twenty-two pericopes: no. 1, *dībāja* (*Ad.*, p. 2, lines 1-5; *Br.*, p. 2, 6 lines); no. 2, the theory of *'ishq* (*Ad.*, p. 2, line 6; p. 4, line 1; *Br.*, p. 2; p. 4, line 4); no. 3, Mansūr Baghdādī was a saint (*Ad.*, p. 4, lines 2-4; *Br.*, p. 4; p. 6, line 2, adds the dialogue between Mansūr and God); no. 4, his dialogue with the Prophet, who confirms for him that he must, through love of God, offer himself in martyrdom[54] (*Ad.*, p. 4, line 2; p. 5, line 10; *Br.*, p. 6, line 3; p. 7, line 17); no. 5, Mansūr summoned before the caliph, asks him to be put to death (*Ad.*, p. 5, lines 11-24; *Br.*, p. 7; p. 8, line 13); no. 6, miracle of the ink pot (*Ad.*, p. 5, line 25; p. 6, line 27; *Br.*, p. 8; p. 9, line 21); no. 7, the imprisonment (*Ad.*, p. 7, lines 1-13; *Br.*, p. 10, line 1; p. 12, line 7, adds the address to the muezzin at the beginning); no. 8, the miraculous escape of the prisoners (*Ad.*, p. 7, line 14; p. 8, line 11; *Br.*, p. 12, line 8; p. 13, line 19); no. 9, the beginning of Mansūr's offertory prayer (*Ad.*, p. 8, lines 12-13, combined with the rest; *Br.*, p. 13, line 20; p. 14, line 3, isolated); no. 10, the conclusion of this prayer (*Ad.*, p. 8, line 14; p. 9,

[53] The second explanation refers to the dreams of Ibn 'Arabī and Jalāl Rūmī in a popular form—so much so that one might ask if the theme of these dreams is not Anatolian in origin, and if Ibn 'Arabī did not collect it by coming to Konya himself (someone foredated it by placing it in Cordova; Ibn 'Arabī said in it himself: "more than 300 years after the death of Hallāj [309]." Now, he had left Cordova around 596, and he was in Konya from 607 to 611. It may have been Ismā'īl Haqqī who foredated it or even attributed it to Ibn 'Arabī. Khafājī attributed it to Shādhilī).

[54] And spat *Anā'l-Haqq* into his mouth (*B.*, p. 4 *ad calcem*, p. 12, line 22; p. 14).

line 15; *Br.*, p. 14, line 4; p. 15, line 11); no. 11, the opinions of Shiblī and Junayd concerning the condemnation *fatwā* (*Ad.*, p. 9, line 16; p. 11, line 25; *Br.*, p. 15, line 12; p. 19, line 11); no. 12, Mansūr debates the definition of his deification; he announces that Kabīr (= Ibn Khafīf) "will come tomorrow from Shiraz to explain it" (*Ad.*, p. 11, line 26; p. 13, line 24; *Br.*, p. 19, line 12; p. 21, line 18, omits Shiraz and Kabīr); no. 13, after sunrise the deification and condemnation of Mansūr are proclaimed (by a revered shaykh) before everyone (*Ad.*, p. 13, line 24-p. 14, line 22; *Br.*, p. 21, line 19-p. 24, line 7); no. 14, Mansūr thanks this revered shaykh, praises him, and claims deification again (*Ad.*, p. 14, line 23-p. 16, line 2; *Br.*, p. 24, line 8-p. 26, line 17); no. 15, Mansūr, condemned to death, leaves the prison joyous, and in total loving self-annihilation claims deification (*Ad.*, p. 16, line 3-p. 17, line 5; *Br.*, p. 26, line 18-p. 28, line 19); no. 16, Mansūr, joyous, arrives at the gibbet for his *mi'rāj*, beats the drum to "I am the Truth"; both of his hands are cut off, he says that they have been spiritually restored to him (*Ad.*, p. 17, line 6-p. 18, line 2; *Br.*, p. 28, line 20-p. 31, line 18, specifies, following the *Waslatnāma* [?], "*yad al-qudra*"); no. 17, Mansūr smears his face with blood, he explains to Shiblī why he washes his stumps with his blood (*Ad.*, p. 18, lines 3-14; *Br.*, p. 31, line 19-p. 33, line 6); no. 18, the executioner cuts off his feet, puts out his eyes; at the beginning of his last prayer, he entreats God on behalf of his enemies (*Ad.*, p. 18, line 15-p. 20, line 1; *Br.*, p. 33, line 7-p. 38, line 16); no. 19, the body of Mansūr is burned; his ashes cry out "*Anā'l-Haqq*"; the Tigris, into which they are thrown, floods, threatening Baghdad and its inhabitants (*Ad.*, p. 20, lines 2-19; *Br.*, p. 38, line 17-p. 41, line 1); no. 20 Mansūr had foretold this to a disciple suggesting that he throw his robe in to calm the Tigris (*Ad.*, p. 20, line 20-p. 21, line 4; *Br.*, p. 41, line 2-p. 43, line 2); no. 21, which is done in the presence of Shiblī and Junayd; the recognition of the people (*Ad.*, p. 21, lines 5-14; *Br.*, p. 43, line 3-p. 44, line 10); no. 22 (addition added onto *Ad.*, built into *Br.*) conclusion placing love above intellect (*'aql*) (*Ad.*, p. 21, line 15-p. 23, line 3; *Br.*, p. 44, line 11-p. 49, line 10).

The *Dāsitān* of Ahmadī, who followed closely the *Waslatnāma* of 'Attār, nearly doubling the size of the latter, did not subdivide his account distinctly. It is with Murīdī that the twenty-two pericopes become clearly distinguished, usually introduced by the preface "listen, O brother." Murīdī's language, which is less archaic and more diffuse than that of Ahmadī, omits certain words (e.g., the important technical term *mazhar* [*al-dhāt*] used by Ahmadī, p. 12, line 11, which derived from the school of Ibn al-Farīd) and is fond of certain others (e.g., *bakhtly*).

The originality of the two poets, in terms of themes, is very slight. Ahmadī added (in no. 4) a dialogue with the Prophet, which appears in outline form in Kīlānī and Rūmī. Murīdī retains it, but precedes it with a much more important dialogue with God (which is bold) (no. 3). Ahmadī also added (and Murīdī kept) an account whose source is unknown of the miracle of the ink pot whose ink wrote "I am the Truth" on the terrace ground. Murīdī adds the one about the muezzin.[55] Both neglect the person of Ibn Khafīf (nos. 12-13). Murīdī develops the antithesis of the terms *'ishq 'aql*, outlined in an appendix by Ahmadī (no. 22), and adds (in no. 21) a ceremony of thanksgiving lasting "for three days and three nights." In his conclusion, Murīdī stresses the symbolism of the "gibbet of Mansūr (*Dār-i Mansūr*)," the site of his Ascension (*mi'rāj*), and the divine light that surrounds it:

Behold now what the witness of lovers is, —and how lovers give their lives through love.

Grasp this secret, which is the site of the gibbet (*dār-i maqāmī nīche der*), —contemplate this fact with the eyes of your soul, see that it is a wonderful thing (*yūje*),

The gibbet of Mansūr, this thing, is the *Mi'rāj*, —and the light of God above the gibbet forms a perfect halo.

These lines (no. 22, lines 2-3) make allusion to the symbolism of the "gibbet of Mansūr" in the initiation ceremony of the Bektāshis.

The two poems mainly orchestrate two themes: God wants His lovers to give themselves in martyrdom; and the cry "I am the Truth," an affirmation of the highest reality, is echoed by the whole of creation.

The following is a chapter from Murīdī (p. 4) [no. 3]:

In the world of the dream, this soul of the world (= Hallāj) had a vision of God:

In which he said to Him: "O You Who welcome the complaints of the poor, —my soul is a wing of a gnat in Your presence; —here I am in need, I have nothing, I beg, —I have a need, grant it, O God. —I say to You in my heart, be my Guest, —be merciful to me, become my soul's soul, —refresh my bondage with a breath of air, and rebuild this devastated heart."

"O Mansūr," said God the Eternal One, "your soul is well disposed for Me to take My place in you; —but if you wish to be at your home to receive the Guest, what hospitality will you offer the Beloved?"

"O God," said Mansūr, "You see what is hidden. —I am only a poor slave at the entrance to Your guardianship, but I have removed my hand from everyone else (but You). —If I make You the Guest of my heart, I will sacrifice my head

---

[55] This seems to have been devised to replace the miracle of the blood (which is impure) writing "*Anā'l-Haqq*" on the ground: in harmony with the *hadīth* about the ink of scholars being superior to the blood of martyrs.

and my soul on Your way. —There is nothing else in my soul, O God; —be merciful, receive me, O King."

God said to Mansūr: "If you do this, offer your head and your soul, —I will be the Guest in the dwelling-place of your heart; —I will become the Soul in the depths of your soul. —If you give hospitality to this Soul, you will surely satisfy your Guest, —for whosoever loves Me must give his soul; I put him who loves Me to death; —I make him contemptible to all; —but I will resurrect his body; — I will destroy his form and his body, —then, I will be his reward, —for he will attain his reward in my Presence (for his sacrifice). —And you, if you are loving, I will treat you this way. —No one fathoms My wisdom, only I."

Mansūr said: "O God, I obey You! —cut my body into a hundred pieces. —You forbid me to turn my face away from You; —I must bend my head to everything You desire; —I will put my soul and my head on the Way, —they will spill my blood, O Truth, on the ground."

God said to Mansūr: "Just as you have come to Me, so too will I be your Guest in Your heart—and as you have stolen My Being, —I, surely within You, will be near. —To your health: I will inebriate you with this mouthful; —from the well 'of nothingness.' I will save you, and will fashion your 'existence'; my friend Mustafā will join you; —under his guidance you will find peace; with his help you will drink from the mouth of the Friend. —I am your self, forget [all else]; —I am you and you are I, this time; —you are one, both being and non-being, —with God since the transaction is completed, —listen to the words of love, good man!"

What did the Omnipotence then say in the attentive ear of the soul? In the attentive Mansūr He said "Anā'l-Haqq."

4. 'Imād Nesīmī and the Poets of the Janissaries

'Imād al-Dīn Nesīmī,[56] whose real name was Nesīm al-Dīn Tabrīzī, set forth in very beautiful Turkish verse the ideas of an extremist mystical sect, one that had been founded among the Turcomans of the Black Sheep Dynasty in their capital of Tabriz by Fadlallāh-b-Abī M Tabrīzī, who had been captured, condemned (by a synod in Samarqand) and executed by the Timūrids (in 804, not 796). This sect bore the name of Hurūfīya, because of its alphabetical cabala, barely perceptible in the verse of Nesīmī, which affirms the deification of Fadl-Allāh but is almost silent regarding his cult of the twelve Shī'ite Imāms. Nesīmī, who went from Tabriz to Aleppo, developed many adepts in the latter. Denounced by the 'ulamā' to the Mamlūk Sultan Mu'ayyad, the latter had him executed in 820 at the time of his arrival in Aleppo for military operations against the Turcomans (Yashbak Yūsufī, d. 824, had just replaced Qajasār Qirdī as governor of Aleppo; however, it was probably the in-

---

[56] Cf. Raghib Tabbākh, Ta'rīkh Halab (which I have been unable to consult); I published his epitaph (Recueil, p. 151).

dependent amīr of the citadel of Aleppo, Shāhīn Duwaydār, who initiated the execution of Nesīmī). Nesīmī was beheaded, after which his trunk was flayed and the skin exposed on the gibbet.[57]

The Turcoman sect of the Hurūfīya, persecuted simultaneously among the Timūrids (it got its revenge by assassinating Shāh Rukh, d. 850), the Osmanlis (the execution of the poet Temennai), and the Mamlūks of Egypt (proceedings in 841, in Antioch and in Cairo, during which an intimate of Sultan Ashraf Barsbay was forced to a retraction), survived among the Turks of Egypt and Anatolia thanks to the poetry of Nesīmī, which Sultan Qānsūh Ghawrī admired, and to the ʿIshq-nāma of Firishte-Oghlu (d. 874; written in 833).

According to Fadl-Allāh, and according to ʿAlī al-Aʿlā (d. 822), his khalīfa, the Hurūfīya adepts were supposed not only to desire martyrdom, but also to provoke their execution. This extreme characteristic is so apparent in Nesīmī that one might wonder if he, who names almost no one in his poetry but Shiblī and especially Hallāce Mansūr, in more than twenty passages in which he shows himself to be as convinced a Hallājian as ʿAttār, is not the one who incorporates in this new Hurūfīya sect the old Hallājian extremist party that ʿAttār criticized in his Tadhkira for its provocative desire for martyrdom, in a time when the initiation rite preserved by Bektāshism was presenting the "Dāre Mansūr" (= the gibbet of Mansūr) only as a symbol of the mystical death of the professed. Sārī ʿAA Çelebi, in his Thamarāt al-fuwād [?] (pp. 196, 198, 199, 200), gives us four of Nesīmī's Hallājian poetical passages missing from the Dīwān.

There are indications in his poems of a sustained personal reflection on the drama of Hallāj. Certainly, at the outset, his evocation of the name of Mansūr, inspired perhaps by some reminder of his native Baghdad, provides above all a way of declaring himself, as did the poets of the Yūnus school, to be one with all saints and all creation:

I am the everlastingness of the perdurable world, and also the delight of its felicity, —I am also the decrepitude of this perishable world, and the gibbet of Mansūr (37).

I am Baghdad's river and its caliph, and in this era now I too say "Anā'l-Haqq," thus am I the gibbet and Mansūr (38).

I am the word of God, I who, with His essence, alone without partner, am His attributes (109).

Listen, I am telling you the whole secret,[58] —without Him, do not utter the

---

[57] Was he executed for being Hurūfī or Hallājī?

[58] This piece, falling between two other entirely Hurūfī ones, views the statement "Anā'l-Haqq" only in a static way.

"*Anā'l-Haqq*," —because you know where your limitation is, —(there) where the moonlight is, and the hue of mercury. —You know that Fadl[59] is surely God, the Creator of the earth and of the silvery vault . . . (6: in Persian).

I am Isrāfīl and here I am, his trumpet, —consider in the "*Anā'l-Haqq*" the Mansūr that I am. —I am the *salsabīl*, here I am Paradise and houri, devoid of riches and fruitful in love, here I am (176).

A Mansūr does not want to sit on the throne nor speak from the *minbar*,[60] —He who is Mansūr is elevated to king on the gibbet of love (137).

Nesīmī here and there, however, tries to elaborate on the meaning of "*Anā'l-Haqq*":

Moses and Sinai, what do they mean? Shiblī and Mansūr, what do they mean? —And this monstrous[61] tree trunk, which was the gibbet (of Mansūr) with its cord, what does it mean? (87).

Always I am saying "*Anā'l-Haqq*"; like Mansūr I exist by order of God, —who leads me to the gibbet and makes me famous by this desire (for death). —I am the *qibla* of the true-hearted, the Beloved of lovers, —the Mansūr of the elect, here I am the Bayt Ma'mūr (52).

God makes me "*Anā'l-Haqq*"; behold what Mansūr I am; —I am the word of the Holy Spirit;[62] from head to toe, I am the light (53).

Do not ask, dear one, what it is I desire, —for, but for the Beloved, nothing is ground for complaint by lovers; —while a Mansūr desires the gibbet of "*Anā'l-Haqq*" he who is not Mansūr desires neither the "*Anā'l-Haqq*" nor the "*Laysa fī'l-dār*"[63] (95).

O heart, God is within you, God is within you;[64] —tell the truth, that "*Anā'l-Haqq*" is within you; —the absolute reality, the absolute essence is within you, —the true text of the Qur'ān is within you (166).

God has appeared, come, behold God,[65] —distinguish the true from the false, perceive the difference between them; —see the crack in the face of this Moon of mine; —God is not confined (*saghmaz*) in this (perishable) world: behold the "*Anā'l-Haqq*" (172).

I have found God, I say "*Anā'l-Haqq*"; —I am God, God is within me, I speak the truth; —behold the dark mystery I reveal, —my words are honest, I speak openly (177).

In everything I see, I see God.[66] —My sight is God, it is I, *Anā'l-Haqq*, who sees. —Because God is absolute, it is I, God the absolute, who sees; —surely I am God, who really sees (179).

Nesīmī honestly believes that such an apparently blasphemous doctrinal claim is justified only by desire and hope rooted in martyrdom, as in

---

[59] This is Fadl-Allāh.   [60] When he comes to the gibbet of Mansūr.

[61] *Ajdehā* = *tinnīn*, a specifically Hallājian term.

[62] = Jesus; Niyāzī repeats that (*Dīwān*, 52, 54).

[63] "There is no longer anyone else in my house (but God)" (a play on the word "*dār*," which also means "gibbet").

[64] Imitated by Niyāzī (*Dīwān*, 22, 45).

[65] Qur'ān 54:1.   [66] Cf. Hallāj, *Akhbār*, no. 4, note.

the case of Hallāj; and he declares his determination to court it (we know he died beheaded):

I have disclosed the enigma of "Anā'l-Haqq" to the world, —I am therefore rightly forewarned that I shall end my life on the gibbet (57).

Mansūr said "Anā'l-Haqq"; it is true, he spoke the truth; —there was no pain in his punishment, which was imposed on a man in ecstasy (who felt nothing) (99).

If I have said "Anā'l-Haqq" like Mansūr, —O faqīh, do not blame me, for I have found my gibbet (111).

Do not ask what one feels on the gibbet during this auction from the *minbar* where sermons are sold; —he who will not go to the gibbet when he has said "Anā'l-Haqq" has only told a lie (144).

If the "Anā'l-Haqq" is spoken one day by me, O lover, —declare me a saint ('ārif) only when I have become Mansūr on the gibbet (28).[67]

O you who at the end of your *sajāda* prostrate your *tasbīh*, listen to—this groan of "Anā'l-Haqq" strangled in the ring of this (divine) buckle (22, in Persian).

Know that in this world the one inebriated with love says "Anā'l-Haqq," —meaning that the loving Mansūr was inebriated on the gibbet (40).

Like Mansūr, the completely sincere lover, who made away (with the wine) of the Tavern, became excited and cried out "Anā'l-Haqq" (62).

Because I drank from the "Saqāhum" cup (Qur'ān 76:21) in pre-eternity, I am constantly saying "Anā'l-Haqq" (102).

Come, receive the secret of "Anā'l-Haqq" from the tavern and the wine, —O you inclined to deny, why do you deny the tavern now? (116).

Your face, Anā'l-Haqq, hung me on the gibbet by Your hair, —a Mansūr hanged in this world on the gibbet of Your love (138).

It is right for Mansūr to depart this perishable world by the gibbet, —but one who is ignorant of "Anā'l-Haqq" will be unaware of this vocation (71).

What difference does it make if, by saying "Anā'l-Haqq," I am hanged on the gibbet? —see how the head of Mansūr was hanging on the gibbet (73).

What difference did it make to Mansūr to be on the gibbet for having said "Anā'l-Haqq," since he knew that the divine Command would end his suffering with his eternal reward (74).

Though Mansūr, by order of God, was exposed to public scorn in the pillory, —what difference could that make to the One Who, He too, is exposed to the world (85).

Are you seeking, like Mansūr, a high rank? —do not make the gibbet your eternal abode, do not become attached to the fleeting world (143).

O wise one, I am this Mansūr who found salvation in God, —saying always "Anā'l-Haqq," as long as life endures (*pāydār*)[68] (146).

Go burn on the gibbet, saying "Anā'l-Haqq," —O Mansūr, —if you desire the place of salvation in the next life (154).

Ask this Nesīmī, who is still so far from Anā'l-Haqq. —Who can remain heroic when afire on the gibbet with this (divine) lament? (51).

---

[67] Cf. Iskāf, ap. Harawī.
[68] This word also means "at the foot of the gibbet."

Why does Nesīmī not burn with the fire of Fir'awn (= *Anā rabbukum*), when he arises from the flame of "*Anā'l-Haqq*" (76).

Mansūr said ('*īder*) "*Anā'l-Haqq*," meaning "I am God, really" —while God is visible, behold Him Who is invisible (155).

The speech of God is light, —he who sees it not is far from Him; —when Mansūr says "*Anā'l-Haqq*," —Isrāfīl is there with the Trumpet in his hand (166-167).[69]

Nesīmī was the first to mix the Hallājian theme with symbols of profane love, particularly with *zulf*, the black hair of his beloved, which to him and his imitators stands for the Dark Night in which God blinds the reason of His lovers:

Your seduction is so great that everything from one end of the universe to the other explodes because of You; —voice, drum, flute, all things chant "*Anā'l-Haqq*," —the lying "*Lā ilāha*" collides with "*illā*"[70] (100).

You alone, ravishing Being, suffice me; let no others be the Intimate One; —let there by only one Friend, not two; and never two Beloveds; — . . . Mansūr was hanged on the gibbet with Your divine hair, O King; —let no one who has not become Mansūr[71] be hanged with Your hair (126).

The following fourteen-line poem deals further with this theme:

He coated His locks of hair with amber, —and perfumed with musk, He let it hang loosely. —Why should my heart and soul not play polo every moment, —when my gaze is struck by His hair as by a mallet? —Now the Adored One spreads His hair over His face (to conceal it). —By arousing me to infidelity, this cruel One endangers my faith;[72] —He soaks His hands in the blood of His lovers; —see how great is His treason, the treason that He commits; —with His eyes (raising) His eyebrows, He calls out "*Anā'l-Haqq*"; —think about this mystery, and the one in whom He conceals it. —Heaven has not seen such beauty as his, —he who causes so many revolutions by revolving in this way; —today is the '*Īd Akbar* for Nesīmī; —he offers up his soul now to this divine Crescent as a sacrifice (*qurbān*) (99).[73]

The deeper than merely poetical feeling of these amorous lines, which contributed to Nesīmī's being condemned to death, helps us to understand why popular legend saw Hallāj come to life again in him.[74] He had admirers as far away as Egypt: Sultan Qānsūh Ghawrī venerated

---

[69] [Julius Theodor] Zenker, *Dict. Turc* [*Türkisch-Arabisch-Persisches Handwörterbuch* (Leipzig, 1866-76)], p. 481, col. 1.

[70] Negation of the canonical *shahāda*.

[71] A possible allusion to the Bektāshi initiation ceremony.

[72] In an invisible God.

[73] An allegory of the Feast of sacrifices. Imitated by Nedīm.

[74] Cf. here the Bukhara *Qisse*.

his memory,[75] and Sha'rāwī praised his cheerful attitude before the executioner, chanting *muwashshahāt*.[76] A legend still alive among the Armenians of Aleppo depicts Nesīmī as the son-in-law of a priest, becoming converted when he sees him celebrating mass.[77] The *madfan* of Nesīmī stands in the Farafira quarter at the foot of the citadel,[78] and preserves in a stone at Bab al-Nasr the imprint of three of his fingers.

Nesīmī had some disciples: first, Rafī'ī (around 811), the author of the *Bashārat nāma*; later, Temennā'ī and Usūlī. Sārī 'Abdallāh Çelebī admired him.[79]

We owe to Nesīmī, even more than to Yūnus Emre, the constant references made by later Turkish poets to the "gibbet of Mansūr." Especially those made by poets belonging to the Bektāshī initiatory circles affiliated with the Janissary imperial militia.

As Mordtmann[80] noted, the popular poems of the Janissaries (*dūdmāne Bektāshiyān*) have a special fondness for Hallāj and Nesīmī. Is this to be explained by the Christian origin of the recruits of this militia, levied by means of the tithe of male children (*devshirme* = *paidomazōma*)? These poems, whose metrics have been studied by M. Fuat Köprülü (poets writing in *sāz*), expand Nesīmī's tendency to mix symbols of profane love with the agony of Hallāj; [for example, those] by Quyūn Oghlu (ap. *Wārsaghi*) and Kātibī, a portion of whose *ghazal*[81] is given here:

> Why do you flee, you, my blue eyes: my fickle heart is yours.
> Mansūr, who is still hanging from the (divine) Hair,
> Is not the slightest bit ashamed of it.
> As for me, the Friend who makes me weep,
> Makes only those who spy on me smile.

Mustafā Gevheri (d. 1127?), a protégé of the Crimean Khān, says in a similar vein the following:

[75] Ibn Iyās, Kahle ed. [?], p. 80 (commentary by Sauvaget).
[76] *Yawāqīt*, 14.
[77] Yūsufian, ap. *al-Machriq*, September 1920, p. 706.
[78] Cf. *Recueil*, p. 151 (the epitaph).
[79] *Jawāhir* I, 442; II, 453; V, 136.
[80] *Literatur Denkmäler aus Ungarus Türkenzeit* [Berlin], 1927, p. 136. See Nesim Atalay, *Bektāshīlik* (poems of the *nefes* genre): pp. 65 (anonymous), 73 (Perūshān), 109 (Qāyghūsuz), 113 (Seyyid Nizām Oghlu). It should be noted that the *tekkē* of the Bektāshīs of Baghdad (in Karkh) inherited directly the *waqf* of Seljūqa Khātūn (d.584), the daughter of Qilij Arslān II (d. 588), the ruler of Konya. MM Jawād has shown that the initial lacuna in the dedicatory inscription copied by Niebuhr should be completed as follows: "[*hadhā qabr Seljūqe Khātūn-bint-*] *al-Malik....*" This *tekkē* must have been the propagation center of this later Hallājism (see my *Mission en Mésopotamie* II, 50): Ibn al-'Adīm visited this *waqf*.
[81] Fuat Köprülü, *Türk Sazsairleri Antolojisi* [bib. no. 1378-b], III, 97.

Fleeing His friend, the Beloved proves faithless; —at the end His eye no longer loves the one He had intoxicated; —as with Nesīmī, one's skin must be flayed, —as with Mansūr, the divine Hair must become one's gibbet.[82]

O gardener, I have a question for you: —how do these thorns grow so near these roses? . . . since he had authority and respect with his tongue, —since he was causing the friend to converse with the Beloved, —whom, refusing to say "Anā'l-bātil" (= I am the liar), he said "Anā'l-Haqq." (= I am the Truth), how did the gibbet come to Hallāce Mansūr? . . . With regard to the rose, union, —how does the lament "ah" come to the nightingale?[83]

It has come, the heaven of my life: "the dawn will come," he said; —
"I cauterized their sighs with fire," he said; —
Here I am, Mansūr, let Him come; "I am going to reveal myself," he said; —
And He has raised this gibbet with His hair close by (170).

I was walking in the garden of beauty; —the nightingale, bud, and rose were like voices; —and my ear, coming upon them, listened to the gifts: the voices (fruit raised to be eaten) of the quince, the orange, and the pomegranate; —how great was Your beauty, face of Peri; —each one, seeing You, lost his heart to You; —and from Your locks, at every moment, there reached my ear, like voices, the words: chains, Mansūr, gibbet . . . (161).

A friend of Gevheri, Feizi Mustafā Çelebi Topqapulizāde, inspector general of the Janissaries, also spoke of Hallāj in a *ghazal*:

Love, which the chest conceals, will be divulged one day; —
The heart will be martyred again like Mansūr one day.[84]

And here are some *nefes*, undated, sung in the Bektāshi *tekkēs* and published by Nesīm Atalay:[85]

Since He fashioned us all from His being, —I have come forth with Mansūr to be hanged on the gibbet (p. 65).

My form of pledge (*iqrār*) is "*Anā'l-Haqq*," —and this pledge of mine is my true "yes" (of the *Mīthāq, balā'*); —beauty is the clear light of God; —the truth of the identity of Muhammad-'Alī is God Himself;[86] —Hājjī Bektāsh *weli* is God (p. 73).

In inebriating me, make me spin around, —and here I am, inebriated with You; —I am Mansūr on the gibbet of love, where I manifest the divine appearance (p. 113).

---

[82] *Ibid.*, IV, 143.

[83] *Ibid.*, IV, 154.

[84] Taken from Hammer, GOD, III, 548.

[85] *Bektāshīlik*, 1340.

[86] The divine identity of Muhammad and 'Alī is a very old extremist Shī'ite concept. It forms the basis of the Khattābīya initiation (in *jafr*, the numerical value of these two names added together is equal to *Rabb* (Lord; = 202).

5. The Long Ode by Lāmi'ī and the Evoking of Hallāce Mansūr
by Poets of the Classical Tradition

Lāmi'ī (d. 958)[87] extols Hallāce Mansūr at the beginning of his great third *qasīda*, rhymed in *"gul* = the rose," "offered to our gracious sovereign S. H. Sultan Sulaymān, son of Selīm Khān":[88] *(ramal* meter):[89]

Since it was the secret of *Anā'l-Haqq* (I am the Truth) that made bloom, like the bursting flame in the burning bush[90] of Moses (in his full-bloomed heart), the Rose—

Why should we be surprised if it hangs its head down,[91] like Mansūr on the gibbet, the Rose?

In the fire of the crucible, intact, like pure gold, —In the world, it appears, miraculously saved, like Abraham from the furnace, the Rose.

Torn like Joseph's shirt by its thorns, —this is why, in the prison of this world, night and day, it weeps, the Rose.

For a century it has given sweet fragrance to the soul, like the breath that quickened Jesus, —like the narcissus, it captures the eye of discerning people, the Rose.

At one moment, like Sālih, it splits the substance of the rock, —at another, like David (with his cuirasses), it forges the tips of its points from iron, [the Rose].

At one moment, like Solomon, it surrenders its sovereign throne to the wind, —at another, owing to its seal, it submits to the spirit of the water, the Rose.

At one moment, like Moses, it bows down before the rod of Khadir, —at another, like Aaron, it covers its head with a white turban, the Rose.

Must we be surprised if it lights its flame in the Light of Ahmad, —since in the moon's orbit, as in full daylight, it is Chosroes shining, the Rose.

It could even blot out the gleam from the candelabra of the Throne, —since it is a reflection of the beauty of the Chosen Ahmad, [the Rose].

Its heart burned like a candle, with the (flame of the) nightingale's sigh, —and it smeared its arms all over with blood, like the lover (= Hallāj),[92] the Rose.

So that neither wind nor trampling feet, nor churls might touch it, it surrounded its sanctuary on all sides with a cluster of thorns, the Rose. . . .

Lāmi'ī, who was able to translate the statements of mystics collected by Jāmī into a forceful, spare Turkish prose, must have devoted one im-

---

[87] See his tomb and his son's tomb, this edition, II, Plates XXV and XXVI.

[88] Page 59 of the excellent copy of the *Dīwān* which I owe to a learned Turkish friend (609 plus XVII pages, including variants).

[89] Rhymed in *rā'*; its hundred distichs have been paraphrased in German by Hammer, *GOD* II, 40; the suggestions of J. Deny have enabled me to grasp more of this.

[90] On the symbolic connection between Hallāj and the Burning Bush, cf. Najm Rāzī, according to 'Attār *Tadhk.* II, 136; and Beha' 'Amilī. For the surname "Red Rose" given to Hallāj, cf. the Bukhara *Qisse.*

[91] *Ser-niqūn* = the head down; did Lāmi'ī believe, with Iskāf and Harawī, that Hallāj was crucified upside down like St. Peter and the "hanging" of the Tarot? I believe instead that he was thinking of the rose's leaning on its stalk, which droops its head when it withers.

[92] Cf. 'Attār, *Tadhkira* II, 143.

portant section of his *Munshā'āt* to Hallāj, according to Hammer. It is significant that Lāmi'ī, in the *qasīda* just cited, goes back to the prose *tadhkira* of 'Attār for the inspiration in distichs 1 and 10 about Hallāj.

Usūlī (d. 945), a contemporary of Lāmi'ī, also cites the *Anā'l-Haqq*. He was a disciple of Nesīmī. Wasīfī of Kastoria (around 970) also reiterated one of Nesīmī's ideas:

Until my heart is hanging in Your hair, —
I shall be unable to attain, with Mansūr, the crown of love.[93]

Next come the poets who were affiliated with a new secret religious order, the Bayrāmīya-Hamzawīya: Dūkaginzāde Ahmed Bey, a member of an aristocratic Albanian family, Osmān Hāshim, and Oghlān Shaykh Ibrāhīm. The following is a line of verse by Dūkaginzāde (which was reiterated by Sārī 'Abdallāh Çelebī):

On earth and in heaven there is only one single absolute light, —and every atom diffuses the light of *"Anā'l-Haqq.*"[94]

And the following is one by Osmān Hāshim:

We have beaten the drum with *"Anā'l-Haqq,"* —we have seized the leadership of the Kingdom.[95]

And the following is by Oghlān Shaykh Ibrāhīm:

We have divulged the mystery of *Anā'l-Haqq* to the world; — now let Mansūr come, —and Our rope execute him.[96]

Zuhūrī Qaraçelebīzāde (d. 1042) in a very strange *ghazal* (*hazaj* meter):

This Ant would become a true male lion in the den of independence if you could make it speak (= reveal the mystery of its real identity); —this Sparrow soaring would become a phoenix at the height of detachment [from the world], if you could make it speak; —
How great is the delicious sweetness which the honey offers to our palates, —which you would seize in its plaintive buzzing; the (sterile) Wasp, if you could make it speak, would tell you; —
If a true Carder could tell you by what rollers (of fate) (*chenberlerde*) his consummate skill has been laminated, —you would understand by his account, O my heart, by Mansūr on the gibbet, if you could make him speak.

Zuhūrī seems to be suggesting here that Mansūr, like the Ant, the Sparrow, and the Wasp, is right in speaking of a sublime state that he has not experienced outwardly: the state of a true Carder (= Hallāj, which

---

[93] Hammer, *GOD* II, 221, 557.
[94] 'Abd al-Bākī, *Kaygusuz* [?], 133, 145.
[95] *Ibid.*, 145.   [96] *Ibid.*

happened to be his surname) *laminated* by wheels (*chenberler* = *mihlāj* in Arabic, *chirchir* in Turkish, *chūbek* in Persian = a rolling mill made of two rollers turning in opposite directions; it is also called *dawlāb* [in Arabic = *charkh* in Persian and Turkish], hence "wheel"); "rollers" referring here to the Wheel of Fate (*charkh-i falak*).

This passage by Zuhūrī has a direct connection with one of Wehbī's lines of verse, which describes a sūq (cf. Evliyā I, 589 [bib. no. 1340]): "There are too many carder's mallets (*toqmaq*) in here, see for yourself— remember the carder's roller by which Hallāj was laminated." (Wehbī, *Suwar-nāma*, ap. *Mecelle umūr belediye*, [bib. no. 2177-a], I, by Usman Nūrī, p. 590. —*Topmaq* = the "notch" with which one beats on the [fel- ter's] bow [*qaws* in Arabic, *yay* in Turkish]. I owe most of the preceding explanations to J. Deny).[97]

Riyāzī (d. 1054), also in a *ghazal*, wishes the morning breeze to blow where Mansūr was killed and to honor this martyr of love, by kissing his gibbet.[98]

The historian Mustafā Na'īma (d. 1127) of Aleppo said in verse:

Thousands die like Mansūr, blinded, —hanged in the hair (of the Idol), and from the gibbet his heart said: —beware of enemy thorns (enemies of Beauty), —the nightingale ceaselessly laments the thorn pricks of the rose; —Learn how to love, Na'īma, like the butterfly who, seeing the light, considers neither the part- ing nor the burning in order to lament it.[99]

The poet Munīf Mustafā Eff. Antakiewī (d. 1156) said the following: "To listen too much to the crowd's telling you the pros and cons of love multiplies your problems needlessly; —therefore seek God on your own, like Mansūr."[100]

The Mewlewi Abū Bakr Kānī (d. 1206), recalling Hallāj and Nesīmī said, "the heart yearns to know who Mansūr is and what is the (divine) hair on the gibbet."[101]

Ghālib Dede (d. 1210), "likening the rose in the rose garden to Man- sūr,"[102] says, not without irony, "a thousand people have dared to lay claim to 'Anā'l-Haqq,' basing their claim to that only on a few sentences of Mewlānā (= Rūmī)."[103]

Esrār Dede, a Mewlewi of the *tekkē* of Galata (d. 1211), evokes the

---

[97] Bursālī M Tāhir Bey, *Osmanli Mu'ellefleri* [bib. no. 1371-a], II, 302; translation re- viewed by M. Necaty.
[98] Gibb, *HOP* [?] III, 286.
[99] Hammer, *GOD* IV, 25.
[100] Bursālī M Tāhir Bey, *Osmanli Mu'ellefleri*, II, 419.
[101] Gibb, *HOP* IV, 168.
[102] Hammer, *GOD* IV, 395. [103] Abd al-Bākī, *Kaygusuz*, 52, note.

memory of Mansūr's drops of blood spilling on the ground, the martyr
of "*Anā'l-Haqq.*"[104]

In the *Terjī'bend* of 'Abd al-Hamīd Ziyā Pāshā (d. 1297), another reference to Mansūr's "I am the Truth" occurs.[105]

The poet laureate of Mahmūd II, Hilmī Hasan Eff. Qibrīslī (d. 1264),
declared the case of Mansūr to be a ticklish one:

> Opinion is divided on Hazret Mansūr; —one concentrates on the truthfulness of
> his response, —another on the way he laid claim to it.[106]
> The cry of "*Anā'l-Haqq*" reveals unity to you, —absolute light shone forth in
> the guise of Mansūr.[107]

The renown of the Hallājian theme in Istanbul is underscored by the
fact that, in the Eyub Cemetery, passersby can read on the gravestone of
the Rumelian *caziasker* Hasan Tahsīn Bey, who died in 1278, the following epitaph rendered in verse by his friend Mehmet Jān, a *Naqshī* in fact:
"This friend, who takes with him our heart and soul, —is accorded a renown in conversations like that of Mansūr."[108]

The flutists of the Mewlewi spiritual recitals still had, as of fifty years
ago, a special flute called *ney-i Mansūr* (syn: *ney-i Shāh*) dedicated to Hallāce
Mansūr, as shown by the following lines of Shems 'Uthmān, a Qādirī
religious buried in Scutari on the Asian side in 1311:

> The decanter of wine is passed round, —the mysterious inebriety overflows,
> from heart to heart—
> The melodious speech, accompanied by the Shāh flute, turns to Mansūr, —the
> conversation between initiates joins in: from heart to heart.[109]

We have shown that Hallāj's memory is still alive today in modern
Turkey, particularly in the popular folklore of Istanbul.[110] We noted the

[104] Gibb, *HOP* IV, 210.   [105] *Ibid.*, V, 93, n.6.

[106] Bursālī M Tāhir Bey, *Osmanli Mu'ellefleri*, II, 146.

[107] *Ibid.*, II, 150.

[108] *Ibid.*, II, 145.

[109] *Ibid.*, II, 271; witnessed by Pr. Sherefettin in Istanbul on February 14, 1940. With re-
gard to this "flute of Mansūr," J. Deny kindly sent me the following references: *Burhāne
Qāti'* [?], Turkish tr., p. 514 (s.v. Shāhney); Villoteau, ap. *Descr. Égypte* XIII, 442; Raouf
Yekta, ap. *Encycl. Music. de Lavignac*, V, 3018-3019 (an analysis of basic tonalities).

[110] An invocation made by mothers to quiet their crying babies (observed by Sabri Essad
in Istanbul on February 7, 1940). An article by Valā Nurettin in *Aqshām* (May 17, 1940, p.
7, col. 1) reporting the following comment made by a woman on the street: (This war) is
punishment sent to men for having rebelled against the wishes of God, for having dug tun-
nels underground, for going to the bottom of the sea . . . and look at the result! the carder
(Hallāce) Mansūr is going to pulverize the world as if it was cotton to be carded" (cf.
Qur'ān 101:4; and Lescot, *Yézidis*, 66: the following is the Kurdish text (unpublished,
commentary by Lescot): "*Pashva, rabe Mansūre* (sic) *Hellac. Masūre dine bijene, dine, hemri
dūz bike.*"

newspaper accounts of October 1927 concerning the giving of the name of "Ḥallāj Street," "Hallāce Mansūr sūqāghi," to a street in the Shāhzāde section by the commission in charge of numbering streets in the municipality of Istanbul (*Recueil*, pp. 171-172). We also analyzed the neo-Hallājian philosophical theory of the revolution conceived by Nurettin Topçu (1934), and the drama written by S. Z. Aktay (1944).

6. Sārī 'Abdallāh Çelebī and Ismā'īl Ḥaqqī

When an intellectual élite was formed in Istanbul, the capital of the empire, its most enlightened members adopted a mystical philosophy; and, whereas in Persia it was the illuminative (*ishrāq*) school of Suhrawardī Maqtūl that predominated, in Turkey it was the monist school of Ibn 'Arabī, especially important among adherents of the Mewlewis of Konya.

Hallāj was therefore known by the Ottoman intellectual élite mostly through what Ibn 'Arabī and Rūmī had written about him.

There were some men, however, who were specifically interested in Hallāj; they were members of a secret religious order, the Bayramīya Melāmiler (founded by Hamza Bālī Bosnalī, executed in 969). In 942, the first conquest of Baghdad had attracted attention to his tomb, mentioned (with a miniature) by Silāhlī Matrāqī.[111] A high official for foreign affairs participated in the second capture of Baghdad, in 1048; he was the *ra'is al-kuttāb*, Sārī 'Abdallāh Çelebi (d. 1071),[112] a highly cultured man, a Bayrāmī[113] in secret, who was drawn to the character of Hallāj. Not only was he successful in obtaining the *Kitāb al-tawāsīn*, he also dared include excerpts of it (chapters I-III) in his famous commentary on the Methnewī,[114] in which we also find other texts of Hallāj, drawn from the *Tafsīr* of Sulamī and the *Tamhīdāt* of 'AQ Hamadhānī: in particular the lines "baynī wabaynaka . . . ,"[115] the word "uqtulūnī" ("said by the gleaner of grain on the millstone of the munificent Friend, the crown on the head of lovers, Hy-b-Mansūr Hallāj"),[116] and finally, anticipating the notice on "Hallāj" in his *Thamarāt al-fu'ād*,[117] two important tributes:

[111] Cf. this edition, 2, Figures 17 and 18. Yildiz ms. 2295, f. 54a. Paris ms. also by him.
[112] 'Abd al-Bākī (Gölpinarlī, *Melāmilik ve melāmiler* [bib. no. 1383-a], 1931, 72).
[113] *Ibid.*, 137.
[114] *Jawāhire Bawāhire Methnewī*, 1287, V., 112-113, 118-120 (noted by our friend Hasan Fehmi Bey, d. 1928, in Ankara, who was a Mewlewī but was fond of the Bayramīs).
[115] *Ibid.*, IV, 102.   [116] *Ibid.*, p. 149.
[117] This notice should be studied very closely, together with the eight poems that it contains on Hallāj's ecstasy and punishment; the four Arabic poems on pages 177-178 imitate the *Sharh hāl al-awliyā'* of 'Izz Maqdisī; and the final comparison between Hallāj and 'AQ Hammadhānī is personal.

O you who seek the love of the Friend, as Mansūr to explain desire and the [mystical] states of the lover, and meditate on the three days (of his punishment)[118] when he regarded the highest love and final state of the lover as actually foregoing asking anything for one's self. The first day, Mansūr on the gibbet; the second day, he was burned in the fire; the third day, his ashes were mingled with the waters of the Tigris, like sugar dissolved, to make them invisible. But lo! each particle of ash becomes a bright sun, and each drop looms as an ocean, proclaiming such is Love, and they reveal openly in their response the reality of its state.[119]

Suffering caused by God's drawing near is only a trial; —and the saint, passing through the trial, attains sovereignty; —therefore endure the trial and have patience with God, —for He puts salve on the heart's wound; —therefore gamble your head, like Mansūr Hallāj; renunciation is a presage of the [martyr's] crown; —it is your execution that invites you into eternal life, —while it orders the damned to leave it; —you poor unfortunate one, you do not know what I am speaking of here; —what may I tell you, as long as you do not realize that even here you see God; —reflect, O careless one, do not lose the game when you are on the threshold; —go in the care of a perfect *pīr*, hurry.[120]

His grandson La'līzāde 'Abd al-Bāqī (d. 1159), the author of the *Sergüzesht*, the history of the Bayrāmīya (Shattārīya), initiated into this order the grand vizir, Shehīd Dāmād 'Alī Pāshā (1125, d. 1128 in Petervaradin), whose very interesting library contained Baqlī's monograph on Hallāj.[121] One of the last of the Bayramīya, the scholar Bursali Tāhir Bey (1278, d. 1341),[122] was very kind in helping me with my research in Istanbul.

The master of Sārī 'Abdallāh, Mahmūd Hudā (d. 1038), had disciples in another order, the Jelwetīya. Among others was the indirect disciple Ismā'īl Haqqī of Brusa (d. 1137), who continued the anagogical exegesis of Simnānī in his great Qur'ān commentary, *Rūh al-bayān*; he spoke of Hallāj in this work;[123] and elsewhere, in his commentary on Yūnus Emre, he interpreted his punishment as follows (in relation to a verse of Rūmī):[124]

Compared with a verse of Yūnus: "They have thrown a stone from Mt. Qāf at me, —but it fell at noon on the way, grazing me in the face":

[118] Cf. the response to a dervish in 'Attār (II, 142, lines 1-10). And ap. *Hik.*
[119] *Jawāhir* I, 107.   [120] *Ibid.*, V, 438.
[121] Ms. no. 1342, risāla no. 19; the other known ms. of the *Shathiyāt* was "waqfed" in the Dār al-Mathnawī of the Mewlewis of Fanār by the *caziaskar* Dāmādzāde Murat Molla (no. 1271).
[122] Abd al-Bākī [bib. no. 1383-a], 328; his father, Rif'at Bey, killed in Plevna.
[123] In reproducing the text of Ibn 'Arabī's *Tajallīyat* previously referred to by Sārī 'Abdallāh (*Jawāhir* IV, 487 = *Rūh al-bayān*).
[124] *Sherhi Rümuzati Yūnus Emre*, edited by Burhan Toprak, ap. edited *Dīwān* of Yūnus Emre, III, 92-93. See his tomb, this volume, Figures 26 and 27.

which he interprets as follows: the *'ulamā'* of the Law stone the saints and lower their heads; but the stone that they have thrown, falling on the Way, at the Friend, did not hurt me. If it had struck me, it might have destroyed the entire reality of my face, and would have forced me to turn back on the Way of God, and my disciples would have lost the Way. But the strong, even if they are struck, do not turn from the *qibla* of the Way; and even if they suffer, do not alter their mental state. Thus, when they put Hallāce Mansūr on the gibbet, he did not retract; because the lover progresses only through suffering. And it may be that this "retouching (God's blotting out, and then marking) of my face," this trace, is borne with steadfastness. Be assured of this. As for "noon on the Way," this stands for this world below, which is half way to the next life as noon is the middle of the day. And the suffering of this world does not injure the future life of men of God. It may be sweet to the spirit to be here below;[125] but to worldly people the sweetness of this life is changed to punishment in the next and becomes suffering. Thus calumniators must be stoned, since unjust hostility bears grief as its fruit. This is also why no enemy of Hallāj has been admitted into bliss, even though Hallāj had not been hostile to them and had even prayed for their good fortune."[126]

7. The Khelwetīya and Niyāzī Misrī

This eastern Turkish order, which claimed to have originated with Suhrawardī via Ibrāhīm Zāhid Kīlānī, was formed in Kharezm (the tombs at Serpol Gazergah were noted by Jāmī at the end of our fourteenth century)[127] and spread to the principalities of the Black Sheep Turcoman rulers, whence it swarmed over Anatolia.[128]

Hallāj is continually alluded to by poets of the order, so much so that one wonders if, when their center was in Tabriz, which Nesīmī left for Aleppo, there wasn't also among the Khelwetīya a kind of ritual commemoration of the "gibbet of Mansūr" such as existed among the Bektāshīya. In any case, although the Khelwetī *dhikr*, which mentions ten of the divine names[129] by choice, avoids in the recitation of the *shahāda* the break between "*lā*" and "*ilāha*," indicated as dangerous in meditation by the Naqshīya.[130] One of the disciples of the Khelwetī Dede 'Umar Rūshenī of Tabriz (d. 891), Shāh Mīr (d. 904), the author of *Musalsalāt*[131]

---

[125] "Dareynde" also means "on the gibbet."
[126] Cf. Najm Rāzī, also Shams Kīshī (on *Akhbār*, no. 1).
[127] Jāmī, 582. [128] *Isnād*. [129] *Salsabīl*, 94.
[130] Qushāshī, *Simt*, 154-155; 'Ayyāshī, *Rihla* I, 214.
[131] Shāh Mīr Hibatallāh-b-'Atallāh-Lutfallāh-b-Salāmallāh Kāzarūnī, the grandson

accepted the Ruknī *dhikr* and even the Hallājī *dhikr*, because he transmitted it to Abū Makhrama 'Adanī (833, d. 903); he received it from Balyānī via his paternal grandfather, Lutfallāh Kāzarūnī.[132]

Two disciples of Dede 'Umar Rūshenī, arriving in Egypt, became heads of the order established in the Turkish quarters of Cairo: M Demirdāsh (d. 930) and Ibrāhīm Gulshanī (d. 933). M Demirdāsh, when dealing with Hallāj, was fond of quoting the passage from the *Futūhāt* of Ibn 'Arabī that compares his writing the name of the Beloved on the ground with the blood of Zalīkhā.[133] We have this prudent advice versified by the Ghulshanian Turkish poet Wālihī Qūrtzāde Edirnewī (d. 1018):

> If you are initiated, do not divulge the secret of Reality; —for the word *"Haqq"* caused Hallāj to lose his head.[134]

In Anatolia, after the Bayrāmīya,[135] other branches of the Khelwetīya became autonomous: the Sha'bānīya, Shamsīya, Niyāzīya, Jelwetīya, to name a few, preserved the memory of Hallāj.

The following is a verse by the Sha'bānī Dhakā'ī Must. Eff. (§ 1227):[136]

> You hold the cry *"Anā'l-Haqq"* with your soul, with your ear, in everything; —perceive when contemplating: each atom is a Mansūr.

A descendant of another Sha'bānī, Nessūhī (d. 1130: commented on Niyāzī Misrī), 'Alī Haydar (d. 1321), a Hanafite juridical advisor to the grand vizirate (Bursali [bib. no. 1371-a], I, 389), wrote this distich:

> One must not draw the (bow) string of (divine) Unity as Mansūr did (= must not say *"Anā'l-Haqq"*);
> On the contrary, the name of Hallāj is enough (to say) in order to enter the (divine) Abode.

From Shams A Sīwāsī (d. 1006), the founder of the Shamsīya (d. 1006), we have the following:[137]

> How could anyone who (has) not (become) Mansūr say *"Anā'l-Haqq"*?

---

through his mother of Nūr Tāwāsī (d. 871: cf. *Salsabil*, 39; *Simt*, 145, 154, 157); he first received the Pirjamālīya *khirqa* from Jamāl A Ardistānī, d. 879: *Tarā'iq* II, 159.

[132] Zabīdī, *'Iqd*.

[133] Munāwī, Paris ms. 6490, f. 339b; cf. *Futūhāt* II, 375. Concerning his *zāwiya* in the Abbasiya of Cairo, cf. Sha'rāwī, *Law*. [bib. no. 741-f] II, 149.

[134] Bursali M Tāhir Bey, *Osmanli Mu'ellefleri* [bib. no. 1371-a], II, 476.

[135] This volume, p. 274.

[136] Bursali M Tāhir Bey [bib. no. 1371-a], I, 74.

[137] *Ibid.*, I, 96.

From Naqshī Aqkermānī (d. 1062), a Khelwetī:[138]

What rank is there that *"Anā'l-Haqq"* cannot attain, since this saying (when spoken) makes one king of the world;—as it did with Mansūr, the vision of love comes through the heart (f. 80b).

If my intellect is dazzled today by Your radiance, —it is because another has not kept secret the mystery of *"Anā'l-Haqq"* (f. 77b).

How shall I know when one who says *"Anā'l-Haqq"* is put to death, since everything in all things utters these words? (f. 81b).

When you divulge the secret of *"Anā'l-Haqq,"* you become like Mansūr in everything you say (f. 84b).

O ascetic, he who does not perceive the secret of *"Anā'l-Haqq"* in everything, —[will find that] whoever is Mansūr will not enter his company in this world (f. 88a).

As it is with the intoxicated who have lost their speech, —so is it with the loving; he who says *"Anā'l-Haqq"* is the Royal Spirit (f. 89b).

I educated myself in this secret *"Anā'l-Haqq,"* —when the words of Mansūr burned my heart (f. 91a). *Tawhīd* is *"Anā'l-Haqq,"* this pre-eternal engraver of the destiny of the ascetic, —Naqshī, having become Mansūr, acquires knowledge every moment because of that (f. 91b).

Why would I not perish at death, when I, like Mansūr, am following the Way of love, —as long as I remain ignorant of this secret, my idle thought plunges me into denial (f. 97a).

The divine hair enveloped the friend, who did not draw it back with the hand of his goal, —giving, like Mansūr, his soul to God today (f. 97b).

Niyāzī Misrī, a mystical poet who wrote in a melancholy and sensitive style, and who was the founder of a new branch of the Khalwatīya order, was disturbed by the moral breakdown of the court and wanted to reform it. Banished the first time in 1088, he returned to Adrianople during the reign of Ahmad II, whom he was unable to convert. He died in exile in 1105 at Limni Kal'e (Kastro) on the Isle of Lemnos; I visited his tomb there in 1916 (the *waqf* placed it at that time in the hands of Field-Marshall Fevzi Çakmak).[139]

The *Mansūr-nāma* of Murīdī and the *Dāsitāne Mansūr* of Ahmadī[140] were published under his name in Istanbul. The following are the only authentic passages in which Niyāzī Misrī (ap. *Dīwān*) speaks of Hallāj:

Here is the call (of the muezzin)! today Mansūr dies on the gibbet of *"Anā'l-Haqq"*! —Surrendering his soul and his head on the gibbet out of love; this is the call (of the muezzin)! (9).

Those who (at the *Mithāq*) steadied their gaze on the (divine) Face, come into this world—faithfully adhering to the covenant, and profess it—

---

[138] Pagination of the Metzger ms., with commentary by G. Vajda.

[139] See this volume, Figure 22. Text of his epitaph, ap. *Recueil*, pp. 164-167 (with poems *"Dermān arārdem"* and *"Devr idüpgeldim"*; tr. ap. *Commerce*, 1925, pp. 167-168).

[140] Cf. *Recueil*, pp. 152-154.

Whereas those who, pre-eternally, looked every which way, —understanding nothing here below, are deniers; —

Drinking from the cup of the eye, the divine *Abdāl*— come into this shaky world with this Love"; —

Whosoever has his heart entangled in the locks of the (divine) hair,[141] —like Mansūr entering the arena, ascends the gibbet (23).

The riddles of the prophets? Who reads consciences, ask them? —The mystery of "*Anā'l-Haqq*"? He Who surrenders his soul on the gibbet, ask him! (32).

In my body is my soul, in my soul is my God, when I say "Allāh Huwa."[142]

The cry of "*Anā'l-Haqq*" rises from all of my limbs, —and my lament wails in my body when I say "*Allāh Huwa*" (56);

I have gained ipseity, and my ipseity is in the divine Ipseity; —I am only a tool used for completing the word of the Essence (62);

Beating the "*Anā'l-Haqq*" drum of the honor guard,[143] like Mansūr, —let me enter the arena ascending the gibbet once again (65).

Preaching by example, let me enter the arena of love, —let me be Mansūr on the gibbet of Love (69).

The following verse comes from the master of Niyāzī Misrī, M Sinān Ummī (d. 1075):

Contemplating "*Anā'l-Haqq*," Sinān Ummī attains the vision in love; —having reached the vision, nothing more needs to be seen.[144]

Among the Jelwetīya (Uftāde), we have already examined Ismā'īl Haqqī;[145] the following is from a *ghazal* by his disciple Dhātī Sulaymān Eff. (d. 1151): "Seek not, Dhātī, the secret of '*Anā'l-Haqq*' among the ambitious; —rather ask it of the loving on the gibbet who have become Mansūr on this day."[146] And from another Jalwatī, Fakhrī A Eff. (d. 1214), this verse: "Drinking from the cup of '*Anā'l-Haqq*,' you drink deeply of the wine of '*Huwa'l-Haqq*';[147] —O heart, authority on saints, desire the secret (of the hadīth) 'I was a treasure. . . .' "[148]

Sayyid Sayfallāh Qāsim Eff. (d. 1010), a disciple of Ibrāhīm Ummī Sinān, founder of the Khelwetīya Sinānīya (d. 958), in a famous *ilāhī*: "in this area, no questions are asked, the heads are cut off . . . of those who are on the Way of the Beloved; the blood price is not paid in gold pieces—look what happened to Mansūr, —the way the people mobbed him; —on the deathbed of '*Anā'l-Haqq*' (= the gibbet), those who succumb are not cared for (literally: receive no pension).[149]

---

[141] The *zulf* theme (Nesīmī).
[142] Cry of the conventual *dhikr*: "God! He!"
[143] The *tablkhāneh* theme (already in Harawī).
[144] Bursali M Tāhir Bey [bib. no. 1371-a], I, 85.
[145] This volume, p. 261.
[146] Bursali I, 73: "On this day" = the day of initiation?
[147] *Ibid.*, I, 141: "*Anā*" = I; "*Huwa*" = he.
[148] *Kuntu kanzan*.
[149] Bursali I, 82; Köprülü M Fuat, *Ilk* [bib. no. 1378-a], 383.

8. The Mewlewīya: Jalāl Rūmī and Shams Tabrīzī; Ahmad Rūmī

A continuous Hallājian tradition can be reconstructed for the Turkish Mewlewīya order similar to that within the Khelwetīya tradition, with the difference being that the members of this [Mewlewīya] order, for the most part, seem to prefer to approach Hallāce Mansūr only through passages (which we present below) from the work of their founder, Jalāl Rūmī, even though they were written in Persian.

On the other hand, the manuscript collections of the order's monasteries must contain Hallājian documents (their *tekkē* in Baghdad had fallen heir to a *Qalandarkhāne* dating from our sixteenth century, around 1535); it was in their Dār el-Methnewī (in Istanbul, near the Fanār) that I discovered in 1911 the very rare commentary on the Hallājian corpus by R Baqlī, the *Shathīyāt*; in the manuscript (dating around A.H. 900) "waqfed" by Dāmādzāde Murād Mulla (1130, d. 1191), who was twice *caziasker* from Rumelia, *re'ys el-ulema* and qādī of Medina.

The influence of Jalāl Rūmī on Persian literature and, more profoundly, on the whole of Iranian Muslim culture, has been considerable. He remains the one spiritual guide taken seriously by a secular Turkish élite cognizant always of his great gifts as an artist; and, overlooking his Sunnism, some highly educated Persians have been undertaking for some years, in Tehran itself, an Islamic renewal heralded by Jalāl Rūmī.

Rūmī (b. 604, d. 673) spoke often of Hallāj in terms that many Turkish poets have piously imitated. We should be able to distinguish the origins of Rūmī's interest in the Hallājian theme. Brought at age twenty to Konya in Anatolia by his father, a well-known mystic originally from Balkh, Jalāl Rūmī himself realized that his two masters in poetry were Sanā'ī[150] and 'Attār, both famous in Balkh; he maintained that 'Attār had the soul of Hallāj as his posthumous spiritual guide (which is the idea behind 'Attār's *"Haylāj-nāma"*). It would seem that the inspiration for Rūmī's Hallājian passages came more from his memory of the Balkh milieu in which he lived as a young man. Rūmī was thirty years old when, through contact with Shams Tabrīzī (d. in Konya, A.H. 645), he underwent the profound psychic change that plunged him into the fierce pursuit and the paradoxical aesthetics to which the cyclic dances and the conscious eccentricities of his spiritual counsels bear witness. Now, as we shall see, Shams Tabrīzī regards the Hallājian ecstasy as imperfect;[151]

---

[150] His *Hadīqe* (Bombay ed., p. 44) [bib. no. 1083-a] contains a *qasīda* "*fī sulūk tarīq āl al-ākhira*," in which Hallāj's death is placed at the zenith of his sanctity: "his (bodily = *sūret*) form fell by fate to the gibbet, but his living form (*sīret*) fell by fate to the Friend" (*nesībe Yār āmed*). I visited his tomb in Ghazna (in 1945).

[151] In his *Risāla* discovered in 1945 by M. Furuzanfar, he criticizes the Hallājian "*Anā man ahwā.*"

which is not the view of Rūmī. And the two masters of Shams Tabrīzī, Radī 'Alī-b-Sa'īd-b-'Abd al-Jalīl and his father, belonged to that Bukhara line of the Āl-Saffār that did not have much admiration for Hallāj.[152]

Rūmī was captivated by some of Hallāj's verses, which he inserted, though in Arabic, into his Persian methnewī and which he imitated in his ghazal.[153] Rūmī wrote the following in the Methnewī (III, 3839) concerning a vizir under Sadr of Bukhara, who after having taken flight, returned voluntarily to be executed in Bukhara:

If this friendly face can shed my blood, I shall strew his path with my life dancing for joy;[154] —I have truly felt "my death will be my life,"[155] to forsake this life is [to enter] eternity; —Murder me now, my faithful friends; my death will be my life.[156] —O radiant cheek, O immortalizing spirit, draw my spirit [to Yours] and enable it to meet [Yours]; —this Friend of mine, whose love is in my heart, if He so wills, let Him trample on my cheek;

[His spirit is my spirit, and my spirit is His spirit; Whatever He desires, I desire; whatever I desire, He desires].[157]

Rūmī, first of all, supports without reservations the thesis that the doctors of the Law (he will later even say the Law, even the Prophet) were guilty in condemning Hallāj:

When authority is in the hands of profligates, it wouldn't be surprising if Dhū'l-Nūn were put in prison . . . —when authority's pen is in the hand of a traitor, it wouldn't be surprising if Mansūr were put on the gibbet; —when the state is run by fools, it necessarily follows that prophets will be killed (II, 1398).[158]

Mansūr Hallāj, who said "Anā'l-Haqq," had swept the dust of all roads with the points of his eyelashes; —it was after he plunged into the Red Sea of his nothingness, after that, that he found the pearl of Anā'l-Haqq (Rubā'īyāt, no. 65).[159]

As for me, I am the servant of those who say "Anā'l-Haqq" and who keep their hearts free of any fault; —they have written a book on their essence and their attributes, and they called its index "Anā'l-Haqq" (Rubā'īyāt, no. 224).[160]

Blessed are those who have moved away from self —and are liberated from it like Mansūr.[161]

A hypocrite is one who has drunk curdled milk and not the wine of God; become a Mansūr and you will set the cotton of your friends aflame (Methnewī III, 692).

The brightness of Dawn shines forth and, thanks to Your light, we are here drinking the wine of Your Mansūr for breakfast (I, 1809).

[152] Zabīdī, 'Iqd, s.v. Mewlewīya.
[153] Cf. Anqirawī.
[154] Cf. Akhbār, no. 16, 5.
[155] Hallāj, Dīwān, p. 32.
[156] Ibid.
[157] Ibid., p. 69.
[158] Qur'ān 5:74.
[159] Asaf Hālet Çelebī, Mevlānanin Rubaileri (1939), cf. lith. Isfahan, 1320 (and the Bogdanov project).
[160] Ibid.
[161] Five verses dealing with Paris ms., Persian suppl. 115, f. 58b.

Like Kīlānī, ʿAṭṭār, and Simnānī, and in opposition to Ibn ʿArabī, Rūmī contrasts the "I" of Firʿawn with the "I" of Hallāj:

"*Anā'l-Haqq*" on the lips of Mansūr was light, and on the lips of Firʿawn false-hood (II, 305).

The midwife says that the woman giving birth does not suffer; oh yes, one must suffer to give birth to a child. —He who does not suffer is a villain, —like the one who says "*Anā'l-Haqq*" without suffering. —The "I" of Mansūr was surely a grace, and the "I" of Firʿawn surely a curse. —Must one also cut off the head of every hasty cock as a warning? —And what does it mean to cut off the head?[162] It means killing his self in holy war, it means renouncing one's self (II, 2523).

(When the dark and opaque stone is transformed into a [transparent] ruby, it possesses the attributes of the sun—) Firʿawn said "I am God" and was damned, Mansūr said "*Anā'l-Haqq*" and was saved. —The first "I" was cursed by God and the other blessed, O lover; —for the first (Firʿawn) was a dark stone, and the other (Mansūr) a ruby; —the first was an enemy of light, the other an impas-sioned lover. . . . His "I" was He (God) inwardly, O presumptuous one, —through the light of union (*ittihād*), not by means of infusion (*hulūl*) (V, 2035).

On the subject of the Qur'ānic expression "*sibghat Allāh*" = the bap-tism of God (2:132), literally the "dyeing of God," Rūmī speaks of the "dyeing pot '*Huwa*' (= ipseity) of the Creator":

"The one who falls into it cries out in joy (for having found his true 'self ' ") "I am this pot (= *anā huwa* = I am He)"; this is what the words "*Anā'l-Haqq*" mean —(similarly, on the forge), he changed to the color of fire (in which he is burn-ing), he who is only iron—but the color of iron is destroyed by that of fire . . . he says "I am fire" . . . just as when Adam received light from God, the angels adored him because of this election. . . . —What is fire? What is iron now? Seal your lips. . . . (II, 1348)

The following is a *ghazal* rhymed in *rā'* ("*ay sāqiye jān* . . ."):

"That wine, from grapes (*ān bādei augūrī*), is the wine of the Community of Jesus (*ummete 'Īsārā*), —whereas this wine, from Mansūr ('*īn bādei Mansūrī*) is the wine of the Religion of Yāsīn (*millete Yāsīnrā*); —that wine, from Jesus, does not cure sorrow and gives only a fleeting joy, —whereas this wine, from Mansūr, makes sorrow give way to joy. . . .

Later, no doubt under Shams Tabrīzī's influence, Rūmī limited his admiration to the pre-eternal aspect of "*Anā'l-Haqq*":

Mansūr, revealing this allusion, went to the gibbet; —it is I who, through one of the buds of my mysteries, inspired Hallāj to speak.[163]

We, in the Baghdad of the spiritual world, we have said "*Anā'l-Haqq*," even before this gibbet, this uproar, and this saying of Mansūr's existed.[164]

---

[162] Cf. *Basarnāma*.   [163] ʿAbd al-Bāqī, *Kaygusuz* [bib. no. 1383-b], 145.

[164] Aflākī (d.754), *Kāshif al-asrār*, Paris ms., Persian Catalogue 114, [line 3: coined by

O divine drink from the cup of *"Anā'l-Haqq,"* —each round that they drink of it comes from the vase of my instant.[165]

Rūmī then limits *"Anā'l-Haqq"* to the pre-eternal identity of God with His elect, as it was proclaimed in the *Mīthāq.*

This is, in fact, what he says to Shams Tabrīzī in his famous *Ode on the Appearance of Absolute Holiness:*[166]

At every blink of the eye, the Beloved comes secretly in a different form—to enrapture the heart and disappear.

In every instant, the Friend arrives in another garb, sometimes old, sometimes young.

Behold him who immersed himself in clay (= Adam), —the Spirit Who plunged into it.

Then, when this mud was modeled and baked, —He rose up and appeared in the world.

He was Noah, who when His prayer deluged the world, went into the Arc.

He was Abraham, who was cast into the fire, —from which arose all the flames of the Magi (1).

He was Joseph, whose shirt was sent from Egypt, —and whose beauty illumined the world.

It was He who appeared to Jacob in the form of lights, —so many that he regained his sight.

In truth, it was also He (Moses) whose white hand was that of a shepherd.

And He was in his staff which changed into a serpent, —before the glory of Kings.

He wandered many times on earth, —to please his fancy.

He was Jesus, whose ascension, to the moving dome (of heaven) gave Him glory.

In sum, He was all of those who have come and gone in every century you have known.

Until the appointed time, when He came forth as an Arab, —and was the Darius of this world (= Muhammad).

What form is annulled? where is the transmigration of souls? Reality[167] —is that ravishing object, Beauty.

He was lastly the sword in the hand of the duelist ('Alī)—who battled time.

L. M.: "Porte-idées."]; French tr. by Huart, *Saints des derviches tourneurs,* Paris, 1918, I, 111 (this volume, p. 288).

[165] 'Abd al-Bākī, *Kaygusuz,* 133.

[166] *Qasīdat al-mustazād fī zuhūr al-wilāya al-mutlaqa al-'alawīya (Dīwān Shams al-Haqā'iq,* Tabriz, 1280, 199); cf. Nicholson tr. in *JRAS,* January 1913. [Nicholson, *Rūmī, Poet and Mystic, 1207-1273* (New York, 1974), p. 142: "The Universal Spirit Revealed in Prophets and Saints.] See miniatures of Rūmī with his friend Tabrīzī, Cairo Persian ms., 208, n. 41, before the last folio and f. 53: cf. Aflākī, Huart tr. I, 70.

[167] A kind of metempsychosis; cf. the transmigration of the germ of the *nūr muhammadīya* (this volume, p. 376).

No! No! It was He again who said "*Anā'l-Haqq*"—in the form of a living person.

But Mansūr (= Hallāj) was not the One who ascended the cross: —only an idiot would think he was.

Rūmī has not uttered blasphemy nor will he ever; do not be one who does.

(20) "The blasphemer is one who denies (that God is everything); —and such a one is damned.[168]

He also said: "Our forefathers reached the heart by breaking their bodies, and they truly freed it through the utterance of '*Anā'l-Haqq*.' "[169] However, later on, he remarked that there were some illusionists who imagined themselves transported to a higher spiritual world (why, therefore, did they come back down from it?); and that *Anā'l-Haqq* is proof that Mansūr had not plunged into this spiritual world. For what relation is there between God, the pronoun (*Anā*), and the consonants (', *A*, *n*).[170]

It is reported that one day, when Hazret Mawlānā (= Jalāl Rūmī) was passionately discoursing on mystical ideas and unfolding the secrets of grace, and was giving part of the biography of Mansūr Hallāj, he ended by saying: "The reason for Mansūr's crucifixion was his saying one day: 'if I had met Muhammad (during his lifetime), I would have demanded payment of a debt (*gherāmet*).' "[171] Why, on the night of his Ascent, when he was admitted into the presence of His Glorious Majesty, did he only ask Him for (the salvation of) the faithful[172] members of His community? Why did he not ask for (the salvation of) all men? Why did he not say "give them all to me" instead of "only these faithful"? Immediately NS Mustafā (may God's mercy be upon him), assuming a form and a body, walked through the doorway, saying: "here I am, if you have a debt to hold against me, claim it." Then he added: "it is by order of God that we demanded (on the night of the Ascent) what we demanded; our heart is the dwelling place of His command, it has been purified of and preserved from everything which is not His decree or His command. If he had said: 'ask that all be brought to Me,' I would have asked for 'all'; but He did not say 'all,' He said 'these faithful.' "

Mansūr then lifted up his turban (*destār*),[173] signifying by that gesture that "I

---

[168] Jalāl Rūmī repeats the theme of the dialogue between Muhammad and Hallāj (Aflākī, Huart tr. I, 254); he says that the "clarity of Hallāj" was 'Attār's spiritual guide (*ibid.* II, 89); he praises his spiritual presence in an assembly (*ibid.* II, 210). His distich (*ibid.* I, 111: third verse after Köprülüzāde; 176). "We declaimed this saying *Anā'l-Haqq* in the pre-eternal Baghdad. Nothing existed before this world, our acts, and Mansūr's subtle statement." Sultān Walad approves of *Anā'l-Haqq* (*ibid.* I, 368): Shams Tabrīzī, who quotes it (*ibid.* II, 159), criticizes the affirmation in this expression of a survival of the "self" after union (*ibid.* II, 167).

[169] Aflākī, Huart tr. II, 159.   [170] *Ibid.*, II, 167.

[171] Ap. Aflākī, Persian cat. 114, f. 83a (published in *Recueil* II, 140-141), Huart tr. I, 254 (reworked), and our "Folklore de la mystique musulmane," *Mélange R. Basset*, 1923, p. 10.

[172] This refers to his right of intercession (*shafā'a*) at the Judgment on behalf of the great sinners (*ahl al-kabā'ir*) of the Islamic Community. Bistāmī and Shiblī had also criticized its narrowness.

[173] To throw one's turban on the ground means to assert a claim for justice (cf. Ibn 'Īsā's "*anā makshūf al-ra's*," ap. Sābī, 93). The gesture made by the "*fatā*" in defending his honor.

keep my trust in you." —And the Prophet replied: "I accept the turban only with the head."[174]

So much so that a day later the sentence was carried out to which this dialogue had given rise. And he, Mansūr, from high on the gibbet, said: "I know very well what has brought this upon me, and at whose demand; but I do not frown at this demand." And this was the way he gambled his head (= offered his head).[175]

Indeed, no true lover frowns at decisions made by the leaders of religion who know the hidden certitude (of God). One such learned man is a treasure house of divine knowledge; his soul nourishes the spirits of novices, his spirit contains leaves of the revelation given by the Lord of the worlds; even if he be an uncultivated bedouin, he is a treasure house of right thinking and correctness (toward God).[176]

In the *Sherh-ī arba'īn* of Ahmad Rūmī, whose author was the Mewlewī Ahmad Pāshā (d. circa 740), grandson of Sultan Weled (d. 712), rather than the Hanafite Ahmad Rūmī (d. 717), the thirty-three verses of Chapter XI are devoted to "Shaykh Mansūr."

He tells us how he was at first the *khādim* of great masters—Shiblī, Junayd, Sarī' Saqatī—who, mistrustful of his indescretion, expelled him from their *khalwa* when they wished to unburden their consciences. However, he felt, at that moment, that all of his limbs had become "listening ears," ringing with *tawhīd*, attentive to the theopathic expressions of his three masters: "if you want to see God, look at me, you will unite (with Him)"; and "By God, verily it is through the Merciful, the Compassionate, that I speak"; and "In my *jubba* there is only God; all the more so in heaven and on earth (i.e., I have become the divine attributes, my unextended speech reverberates on six sides of space)." At this point the author remarks as follows: "When a peri takes hold of a man, the tongue of this man no longer belongs to him; everything he says, it says; and whatever comes from him comes from it; therefore whatever is spoken with the breath and at the command of the peri, brings us that other Peri (= God)."

Listen to a short tale, my friends: that of Mansūr the truthful; whatever Mansūr had listened to came from within him; —the Friend of "I am the Truth" who entered him was God saying "*Anā'l-Haqq*" with his tongue, —making (within him) his hand move by His power to fulfill the needs of men. Mansūr in this way obtained the following one after another: a dish of roast meat (with loaves of bread), a bunch of ripe yellow grapes, a piece of varicolored sugared cake for anybody asking for it, by simply thrusting his hand in his pocket (*kurībān*).

---

[174] He recognized, in short, the claim put forward by Hallāj, on the condition that he let himself be put to death (in order for God to pardon all men). Cf. this volume, p. 244.

[175] An expression typical of 'Attār.

[176] This last sentence, in Arabic, is a gesture of courtesy made to the Prophet; but Rūmī, in his universalism, approves of Hallāj deep down.

The motive for citing these examples, O hearts, is to show that the self is one of the veils along the way; —and that the one who washes his hands of "us" and of "me" by the same means tears away these veils.[177]

c. The "Gibbet of Mansūr" (Dār-i Mansūr) in Bektāshī Ritual

The collections of mystical poetry (nefes) used in its recitals are not the only means by which the Turkish order of Bektāshīs has preserved the memory of Hallāj. The "gibbet of Mansūr" (= Hallāj) indicates in its ritual the center of the initiation hall, or meydān, between the entrance and the steps up to the Throne topped with candles set behind it, between the "foyer of Fātima" (on the right side) and the four (or twelve) pūst, "hides of lamb," on which the religious sit (on the left side).

Once a year the members of the hall who have guilty consciences accuse themselves publicly of having "offended the soul of one of their brothers." This is the "maghfiret zūnūp." They perform the following ritual prayer: "O God, God, here I am in the Dār, face down, on the gibbet of Mansūr, before Muhammad-'Alī,[178] my soul the presence of al-Haqq." During the initiation ceremony, one must place oneself on the Dāre Mansūr thirteen times: first, the meydanci with a bow (niyāz) when one lights the censer, then during the invocation over the asperges (gülabdan), then at the time of one's own aspersion (followed by a niyāz). After that comes the chiraghci, in which one girds one's loins with the ghayret kushaghi (= tīghbent) done with a bow, then one blesses the candles, before and after they are used, and after that one recites the gülbenk (with a niyāz). Then, at the invitation of the prior (murshit), the sponsor (rehber) of the professed (talip) bows down in the Dār before girding the professed with the tīghbent, and also after, when the professed, his "head uncovered, feet bare, rope around his neck, crawling head down" (like the male lamb offered sacrificially), asks for his admission. Once admitted, the professed, having received the cap (tāc) and the girdle (tīghbent: which his sponsor ties in three knots), offers his prayer of thanksgiving in the Dār. His sponsor then describes to him the four pūst and the throne, then leads him to bow down in the Dār and says to him: "This is what we call the gibbet of Mansūr. If one does not come here, one does not take a step: it is here that one reaches God." Then, after having guided

---

[177] Paris ms., Persian Supplement, 115, f. 57b–58b.
[178] Birge, The Bektashi Order [bib. no. 1797-a], 1937, p. 170. We know that the Bektāshīs, like the Khattābīya, esoterically combine the two distinct personalities of Muhammad and 'Alī (their two numerical values added together = 202 = Rabb).

him to the *meidān* of Muhammad-'Alī (the place of the Ascent), he leads him back to the *Dār*, where he bows down and prays. Thus finally the *chiraghci*: after having offered the cup of *sharāb* to those present, one returns to the *Dār* to drink and to recite a prayer.[179]

Contemporary texts of prayers accompanying these thirteen visits to the "gibbet of Mansūr" during the initiation ceremony make no reference to Hallāj, and extol the twelve Shī'ite imāms. We shall see that there were some changes made in the ritual, either by the Hurūfīs or by Bālim Sultan (d. A.H. 922).

The culminating point of the initiation ceremony is the *shadd*, as it is with the *futuwwa* of craftsmen and the *shāṭir*: the putting on of the girdle, the girding on of the *tīghbent*, the waist-belt tied with the arrow-knot, then the sword-knot (and razor-knot, in memory of Salmān). According to Bektāshī teaching, this ceremony, of the girding on of the *tīghbent*, stands for "the acceptance of the gibbet of Mansūr, the proclamation of the unity of the Ternary Name (*ism muthallathī*),[180] the affirmation within oneself of [the divine] Existence (*wujūd*), deliverance from the onus of canonical prohibitions. The triple binding of the hand, of the tongue, and of the loins represents the confirmation and upholding of the Covenant (pre-eternal *Mīthāq*)."[181] The first to gird himself with the *tīghbent* "with the astonishing effect of love" was Rizāyī, the brother of a Shī'ite martyr, Mu'min 'Ayyār,[182] who, in order to save Imām Bāqir from being hanged, made a noose (*tīghbent*) out of the wool of a ram about to be sacrificed and tied it in three knots, first garroting the ram with it and afterwards putting it around his own neck. "And going to the door of the holy cell in which the imām (Bāqir) was imprisoned, he hung himself on the gibbet of Mansūr, delivering his soul up to God. The Yazīdīs (servants of the Umayyad Caliph Hishām), believing it was true (a noose capable of hanging Bāqir), removed this *tīghbent* from the neck of

---

[179] *Ibid.*, pp. 184-196. Brown-Rose, *Dervishes* [bib. no. 2038-a], pp. 195-197, analyzes a Bektāshī collection of 75 prayers whose numbers 13, 14, 15, and 52 relate to the *Dār-i Mansūr* and should be studied.

[180] This refers to the "three holy names."

[181] Ahmad Rif'at, *Mir'āt al-maqāsid* [bib. no. 1369-b] (Istanbul, 1293), 268 (*der bayāne tīghbent*).

[182] A symbolic name, in contrast to that of *"nadīm kāfir."* A hadīth by Ja'far tells how Hishām had tried in vain to have Bāqir strangled in his cell with lamb's gut. Each of the three times it was tried a knot appeared (when Bāqir was saying the Three Names: Allāh, Muhammad, 'Alī). Then Mu'min 'Ayyār took it upon himself to construct a noose that would work (Ahmad Rif'at, *Mir'āt*, 269).

The Yazīdī *feqīrān*, though anti-Shī'ite, wear, like the Bektāshīs, a *tīghbent* which they call a *qenberbest* (a Shī'ite name) and a collar (*meftūl*; Lescot, *Yézidis* [bib. no. 1798-a], 1938, p. 93). This raises the question of Turco-Kurdish affinities with regard to Hallāj.

Mu'min 'Ayyār and went to the door of the imām's cell to hang him, only to find that he was already setting out for Paradise. "Give me the *tīghbent* of my brother." They threw it to him. Taking the *tīghbent*, he spoke the three holy names, girded his waist with the noose and was gone."[183]

This text is quite remarkable. Mu'min 'Ayyār, whose symbolic name refers to the 'Ayyārīn,[184] offers himself and is accepted as a substitute for Bāqir, who ascends to Heaven at the very moment when 'Ayyār made *"fidā'"* for him, just like Hanzala Shibāmī, who, according to the Nusayrīs, made *"fidā'"* for Husayn.[185] 'Ayyār hanged himself on the "gibbet of Mansūr." This Shī'ite *tīghbent* ritual thus presupposes a previous ritualization of the "gibbet of Mansūr" on which it was superimposed. The enemies of Bāqir, in this instance, are called "Yazīdīs," which would lead us to believe that this Shī'ite ritual originated with the Qyzylbash Kurds, neighbors and enemies of the Yazīdī Kurds (who, as we know, also venerated Hallāj) and that it began in Kurdistan in a milieu that had been pro-Hallājian too long for the substratum of the "gibbet" to be eliminated from the altered ritual. In fact, it may have been this *tīghbent* ritual, which, interacting with "the gibbet of Mansūr," little by little transformed in the popular imagination the *taslīb* of Hallāj, the exposure on the gibbet," into the "hanging on a gibbet."[186]

The present-day Bektāshī ritual, with its Ithnā'asharī Shī'ite emphasis, goes back rather to our fifteenth century (Hurūfīs), though it has some older elements. The *shadd al-mihzam*, of the *futuwwa*, with its four knots, corresponds to the *tīghbent* with its three; its *shirb* to the Bektāshī *sharāb*; both have the *meydān* '*Alī*, but I suspect that the *Dār-i Mansūr* was originally the complete *meydān* of the Hallājian initiation as it existed in the period of Yūsuf Hamadhānī and Ahmed Yesewī, the forefathers of Bektāshism. And one might raise the question of a direct parentage between the initiatory *meydān*, the *bayt khalwa* of the Druzes (and Mehdevīs) and Nusayrīs, and the symbolic *harām* of Ibn Masarra[187] and of Hallāj himself.[188]

---

[183] *Ibid.*, p. 269.

[184] Cf. this volume, p. 32; J. Deny, who has studied them [the 'Ayyārīn] in detail, aided me in my examination of this difficult text.

[185] *REI*, 1932, p. 35.

[186] One might also imagine that hanging *without* intercision was substituted for exposure *after* intercision to avoid any contradiction over spilled blood, *masfūh*, which is legally impure, given the fact that it is shed lawfully in the case of a martyr.

[187] *Recueil*, p. 70.

[188] This edition, 1, 539 ff.; cf. also the *Durāh* (= Bayt Ma'mūr; Ka'ba venerated by angels in the fourth heaven).

VI. THE SURVIVAL OF HALLĀJ IN INDIA

Although the conversion of two small casts in Gujrat[1] (the contemporary "Mansūrīya") did not actually originate with the apostolate of Hallāj, it was in Gujrat that his influence in the process of Islamization first appeared: around A.H. 744, with a disciple of 'Ayn Mahrū, apropos of the "Anā'l-Haqq" dhikr. Then we find in Bengal a cult of "the master of truth" (Satya Pir) identified with Hallāj—around A.H. 900. We can verify, parallel to these in time, the existence of an outright Hallājism among Indian Muslim mystics, who were disciples of 'AQ Hamadhānī, like Sh. Munyārī (782: in Bihar), Mas'ūde Bāk (800: in Delhi), Gīsūdirāz (d. 822: Gulbarga), and with the Chisti Jalāl Bukhārī (= Makhdūm Jahāniyān, d. 784), founder of the Jalālīya. Increasingly the two laws, the Islamic and the Hindu, shar' and kufr, proved, by the experimental route of mysticism, that they lead in a parallel direction to mystical union. Now, 'AQ Hamadhānī had derived this idea particularly from Hallāj. Around 928, again in Gujrat, the head of the Shattārīya, Ghawth, produced a Hallājian dhikr, which was to spread to other parts.

The two principal advisors of Emperor Akbar, concerned with his attempt at an Islamo-Hindu religious syncretism, were two brothers—Feizi and Abū'l-Fadl—who were sons of a Mehdewī shaykh named Mubārak (concentrating still on Gujrat and on a mystical mahdism). They surely did not exclude Hallāj from among the Sūfī masters whom they venerated and whose doctrine they wanted to make Akbar, after 982/1574, establish as a state religion (dīn Ilāhī). When Feizi, in explaining his plan in Persian verse, writes:

I am wine which intoxicates the mind,
—it is not my fault if I ferment;
there are a hundred melodies that the drunken nightingale creates, —just so the rose of Iraq may flower in the soil of India,

the "rose of Iraq" seems to be an allusion to the teaching, and even to the person, of Hallāj, who had been defended by the great Hanafite jurisconsult Ahmad Sirhindī (d. 1031), a shuhūdī in metaphysics like Semnānī and Jīlī.[2] A little later, Prince Dārā Shīkūh, whose syncretism is even more pronounced, praised Hallāj by name; and when his friend, the poet and philosopher Sermed Qāshānī, was executed in Delhi for blasphemy, in

---

[1] Referred to by Nājūrī, a friend of S Qutbadhin Bakhtiar, d. a Mehrawli, pīr of Iltutmish, who was just toward both Muslims and Hindus (cf. Gandhi, 1/24/48).

[2] Y. H., p. 164 [Yūsuf Husain, L'Inde mystique (1929)].

1071/1660, he went to his martyrdom as an avowed disciple of Mansūr Hallāj.[3]

It was not only in the literary Persian of the conquering Muslim élite that Hallāj came to be associated with this serious movement of mystical syncretism, but also in the Indian dialects, in Dakhni and Urdu. The cases of the *caziaskar* Ghadanfir, of Qādī Gūgīde Bijapūr, and of the Hindustani writer Shīvrājpūrī are important examples.

The existence of the *madfan* of Hallāj at Porto-Novo (Muhammad Bandar) in a center of *Tamil*-speaking *Marakkayar* Shāfi'ite Muslim sailors (mixed with *Tamil Labbai* Muslims in Nagore) must certainly be connected with the apostolate of Nathan Shah Mazhar al-Dīn (d. 411 Trichinopoly), one of whose disciples, Bābā Fakhr al-Dīn Sijistānī, buried in Penukondah (in the district of Anantapur, the present-day Sūfī center of the Presidency of Madras), is the patron saint there of "cotton carders" (*Pinjaras*).[4]

a. The Appearance of the Utterance "Anā'l-Haqq" around A.H. 754

One of the leading amīrs of Sultan Fīrūz Shāh of Delhi (752, d. 780), 'Ayn al-Dawla 'AA-b-M Māhrū, governor of Sindh and later of Deogarh, rebelled against him briefly around 754, which is probably the date on which the following incident, recounted by Fīrūz Shāh himself in his recollections (*Futūhāt*),[5] should be placed.

One of the followers of 'Ayn Māhrū (*ez melāzādegān 'Ayn Māhrū*)[6] went to Gujrat. This shaykh gathered together some disciples and began to speak the formula "*Anā'l-Haqq*," to which his disciples had then to respond "it is You."[7] Afterwards he declared, "I am the King who does not die," and wrote a book containing his words (*Kalimāt*). The Sultan, informed of this, had him brought to him in chains, condemned him, and ordered the book burned to remove the contagion of evil (*fasād*).

This may have been merely the implantation in Gujrat of the *tarīqa Hallājīya*, whose first transmission in Shiraz we noted as being in 710; but his *dhikr*, according to 'Ujaymī, specifically omitted any open anticipation of *Anā'l-Haqq*. We are dealing here therefore with an attempt

---

[3] Sermed: cf. Hāshimī, *Islamic Culture*, 1933, p. 663; Yūsuf Husain [*loc. cit.*].

[4] Khāja Khān, *Studies* [bib. no. 2133-b], p. 153.

[5] In Persian, Thomas ms., tr. by Elliot, *History of India*, 1871, III [bib. no. 2062-a], 379-380.

[6] Elliot puts "one of the disciples"; 'Ayn Māhrū was a very learned amīr, not a scholar; 124 of his letters have been preserved (Ivanow cat. [bib. no. 1771-b], Calcutta, I, 145 (no. 338); but *āzād* = an ascetic freed from religious observances by his vows.

[7] Cf. "*anta*" of the Zutt for 'Alī; and Bīrūnī.

made by one convinced mystic to carry out the poet 'Attār's theory about the famous Hallājian theopathic expression. In Gujrat, where precisely a descendant of 'Attār, the sixth ancestor of the famous Shattārī shaykh Ghawth (d. 960), must have already been settled. And we know that Ghawth, at the end of a long retreat in Gujrat, made public the first Hallājian *dhikr*, mentioning specifically that he obtained it as "fruit" resulting from his uttering "*Anā'l-Haqq.*"

To the Shattārīya, "Haqq" is actually the Essential Name. Now, since the end of our thirteenth century, the prevailing opinion among mystical scholars, being especially careful to avoid condemning Hallāj, teaches, as Qāshānī says in his *tafsīr*, that *Haqq* is merely the fourth in the ascending sequence of Seven Divine Names, corresponding to the fourth layer of the soul (*sirr = nafs mutma'inna*);[8] the introduction of "*Anā'l-Haqq*" as *dhikr* in India occurred at least prior to 'Abd al-Razzāq Kāshī Qāshānī (d. A.H. 730), as in Turkestan.

b. The Shattārīya

This order, founded by 'Abdallāh Shattārī around 810 in India, claims to have an *isnād*[9] going back to Kharqānī. In actual fact, its founder was a disciple of the third head of the Ruknīya, 'Alī Hamadhānī, buried in Khuttalan. The order flaunts this name "*shattār*" (bold) brazenly, and claims as its distinction election to the paradisiacal cup of the pure brew (*sharāb tuhūr*) that intoxicated the Prophet, making him say "I am Ahmad, without *mīm* (= *Anā-Ahad* = I am the One God)."[10]

Its fifth head, M-b-Khatīr al-Dīn called Ghawth (906, d. 960 in Gwalior), a descendant of Farīd al-Dīn 'Attār, wrote in Gujrat (in the hermitage of Qal'at al-Khayyār) the *Jawāhir al-khamsa*, a very interesting manual of mysticism, the first to reveal the *dhikr* formula for the *tahlīl* according to Hallāj,[11] including a description of the position to be taken when uttering it, which brings one thereby to the state in which the words "*Anā'l-Haqq*" come to one's lips.

The well-known Arabic recension of the *Jawāhir* was made by Sib-

---

[8] First Name: *shahāda* (*nafs, nafs ammāra*); —second: *Allāh* (*qalb, nafs lawwāma*); —third: *Huwa* (*rūh, nafs mulhima*); —fifth: *Hayy* (*sirr al-sirr, nafs rādīya*); —sixth: *Qayyūm* (*sirr khafī, nafs murdīya*); —seventh: *Qahhār* (*sirr akhfā, nafs sāfīya*). Cf. *Recueil*, p. 143; in which, according to Semnānī, *Haqq* (*latīfa haqqīya*) is again the seventh Name, the Highest Name; perhaps the Indian attempt in question derived from him.

[9] Ghawth Hajj Hudūr—Hidāyatallāh Sarmast—Fathallāh Qādī Ansārī (d. 862)—'AA Shattārī (d. 832) (Zabīdī, s.v.: *Salsabīl*, 107, 155, 159). F Qādī Ansārī was also a disciple of Shāhmadār, whose *Jawāhir* extols him (ms. 1197, f. 163a) though he was a Hinduist.

[10] *Jawāhir*, ms. 1197, f. 2a.   [11] *Ibid.*, f. 126b.

ghatallāh, a disciple of Ghawth via Wajīh al-Dīn ʿAlawī Ahmadābādī (d. 998).[12] Sibghatallāh-b-Rūhallāh-b-Jamālallāh Bārūchī, who made the hajj in 1005, stayed and died in Medina (d. 1025). The main disciple (buried in Baqir, at his side) to whom he transmitted,[13] among other dhikr, the Hallājian dhikr, Abū'l-Mawāhib A-b-Shinnāwī (d. 1028/ 1619),[14] a Shāfiʿite and author of a commentary on the Jawāhir, was, on the one hand, through his disciple Ahmad Qushāshī Dajjānī (d. 1070),[15] the master of H ʿUjaymī (d. 1113)[16] a Hanafite and author of the risāla recopied by Sanūsī (d. 1260) in his Maghribian Salsabīl, and, on the other hand, the master of Ibrāhīm-b-H Kawrānī (d. 1101), who sent ʿAbd al-Raʾūf-b-ʿAlī forth to preach Shattārism in Malaysia. In the latter, this order expanded greatly thanks to such adherents as the prince of Tjeribon, Raden M Nūrallāh Habību'l-Dīn; its head in 1905 was Ahmad Saliha-ing-Pati-maring.[17]

In his Makhzane-daʿwat, the Shattārī Ismāʿīl-b-Mahmūd Sindihī (in 1037) includes an incantational formula[18] in which the seven leaders of the jinn, the jān, the saints, and the prophets are called upon. This is the qasam Hallājī, also called the "qasam-i pahlawī" and the "Sikandar Rūhānī," practiced by thousands of masters in sīmīya, the science whose guardian (muwakkil) was Hallāj and whose divulgence, according to the Kitāb zubdat al-daʿwa, caused his downfall.

In the Deccan, where this order flourished, the Shattārī is often called "Anāʾl-Haqq-walla." In the words of Gāzure Ilāhī (ap. Irshādāt al-ʿārifīn),[19] "the Shattārī order is unacquainted with fanāʾ, and contains nothing more than the divine 'I' (innī Anā)"; its dhikr is therefore the dhikr al-Dhāt (= Anāʾl-Haqq).[20]

c. The Naqishbandīya at the Court of the Mughal Emperors of Delhi

It was the Turkish and Hanafite empire of the Mughals that introduced the Naqishbandīya into India.

[12] Ibid., f. 120a; ms. 5359, f. 99b: in which Sibghatallāh signs as "al-haqīr, gharīb Allāh fī ardih"; cf. Cousens, Bijapur [bib. no. 2049-a], 1916, p. 20.

[13] Sometimes through an intermediary, Fudayl-b-Diyāʾ D Mindī (Salsabīl, 87).

[14] His son: Habībullāh (Kattānī [?] I, 145: Wali Dihlawī).

[15] Dajjānī, a Meccan and a Mālikite who became a Shāfiʿite, author of Simt Majīd (Hyderabad, 1327).

[16] Actually a pupil of Kawrānī (Kattānī I, 372).

[17] Rinkes, ʿAbderraoef, 1909, pp. 48, 95 ff.

[18] Calcutta ms. I, 916, f. 259, 297b (commentary made by V. Ivanow): "basmala; diʿyum (twice) mahīn (twice), hāsūlī (twice), kubrā, hidrīsh, uhdurū, Alshīgh, yaʿū, bīh, bih, tinkif, birkif, birkifāl (all of these words repeated), then: Qurʾān 36:82-83."

[19] Khaja Khan, The Secret of Anāʾl-Haqq (Madras, 1926), pp. 1, 4.

[20] Ibid., pp. 157-158, 178.

Under Akbar (Jalāl al-Dīn, b. 963/1556 d. 1014/1605), the spiritual advisor of the emperor and his *caziaskar* until 983 (that is, before the period of Feizi's syncretistic influence), was a Naqishbandī named Ghadanfir-b-Ja'far Husaynī Nahrawālī Sīrāwī,[21] a disciple of M Amīn, son of a daughter of Jāmī. After 983, Ghadanfir retired to Medina and drew around him there a circle of disciples: the Bosnian Hanafite Hasan Kāfī Aqhisārī, author of a *Tabaqāt al-'ulamā';*[22] and an Egyptian, AM A-b-'Alī-b-'A Quddūs Shinnāwī (975, d. 1028), who wrote a commentary on the Shattarian *Jawāhir* in which he included (and thereby transmitted) the Hallājian *dhikr*. Ghadanfir also accepted the Hallājian *dhikr*, which he received[23] from Tāj 'AR-b-Mas'ūd Kāzarūnī, a member of the Murshidīya order and a disciple of Nūr Tāwūsī (d. 871),[24] the transmitter of the *tarīqa Hallājīya* and *ruknīya* and, through Amīr Kilān, of Shāh Mīr.[25]

d. The Fatwās of Ahmad Sirhindī

Ahmad Sirhindī (d. 1031), both an eminent Hanafite canonist and leader of the Naqishbandīs of northern India, a disciple of Semnānī (*wahdat al-shuhūd*; the scale of colors visualized in ecstasy),[26] and a victim of persecution at the end of his life by certain Shī'ite advisors of Emperor Jahāngīr, left two juridical counsels' opinions in favor of Hallāj:
1. (II, 72: the response to Muhammad Sādiq-b-Hajj Muhammad Mu'min = the 44th letter):

In saying "*Anā'l-Haqq*," Husayn ibn Mansūr Hallāj did not mean to say "*Anā Haqq*" (= I am God), as one with God, a blasphemy which would have deserved death; the true meaning of his words is "I am nothingness (*ma'dūm*) and He Who is (*mawjūd*) is God . . . the silhouette of the shadow cast no longer appears outside the divine person who cast it," his love being so great for this person. . . . Things, according to the Sūfis, are reflections of divine appearances, and not His essence. . . . The world is not a mere figment of the imagination: a comparison with the image reflected in a mirror; with the circle traced by a moving point; —objected to by Qādī Jalāl Agrī: is reality one, or multiple? one, according to Sūfis; multiple, according to the Law. —answer: this is not a problem; it is the coexisting contrast between the literal meaning and the metaphor (which is multiple).

---

[21] *Salsabīl*, 117; Kattanī, *Fihrist* II, 320.
[22] Edition prepared by M. T. Okid of Serajevo.
[23] Via a third unnamed: Qushāshī, *Simt*, 157; 'Ayyāshī, *Rihla* I, 207; *Salsabīl* (111, 141; Kattānī II, 310).
[24] And also his grandson ('Ayyāshī, *Rihla* I, 207).
[25] Zabīdī [see bib. no. 862], 38; cf. 42, 97.
[26] Khāja Khān, *Studies* [bib. no. 2133-b], pp. 81, 189.

2. (III, 166-167: = the 118th letter, written to Shaykh Mawdūd Muhammad):

Shaykh Suhrawardī, in Chapter IX of the '*Awārif*, refuted the advocates of *hulūl* who believed it lawful to fix one's gaze on beautiful things and to place one's reliance on certain words uttered by ecstatics who are implicitly "*hulūlī*," words that they lay claim to, such as the statement of Hallāj, "*Anā'l-Haqq*," and the words attributed to Abū Yazīd Subhānī. But we must not believe that Abū Yazīd had said them in any other way than in indirect speech (*hikāya*; in a kind of narrative quotation). We must also explain the statement of Hallāj in a similar way, for if we had learned that he uttered it as a way of promoting *hulūl*, we should have condemned him with these heretics. —Heavens! What can it mean "to quote words of God" and to reduce the masters of divine intoxication "to speaking in a kind of narrative quotation." Lord! Unless Suhrawardī (may God sanctify his soul) had intended to assert in this way that the subject speaking is the believer, as is the prevailing opinion. However, the subject speaking in this case is, in fact, the Lord (to Him be all glory) and the tongue of the believer plays the role of Moses' Burning Bush without there being any grounds for incriminating Hallāj. . . . In this intoxication of Unity, in this occultation of everything which is not the witnessed Only One, in this brilliant light of Witnessing without any stain of *hulūl* or *ittihād*; the meaning of his words "*Anā'l-Haqq*," since he is withdrawn from his own gaze, is "my self is nothing, surely; what exists is God. . . ." Apropos of Suhrawardī's words, "the gaze on beautiful things," it is unusual of him to identify *hulūl* (infusion within a thing) with *zuhūr* (reflection outside a thing). The possibility of Witnessing divine perfections revealed in the mirrors of the contingent thing does not imply the possibility of infusion of these perfections into mirrors. . . .

Sirhindī was *shuhūdī*, not *wujūdī*.

e. The Ode of Qādī Mahmūd Bahrī Gūgī

Mahmūd Bahrī (d. around 1117/1705), a Sūfī from the Deccan,[27] lived in Gugi, near Bijapur. Gugi was where the Adilshāhīs, the rulers of Bijapur, were interred from 916/1510 onwards. A disciple of Hadrat Hādī (= Miyān Shāh), a descendant of the Chistī saint, Gīsūdirāz of Golburga (d. 825), he expressed lyrically one day his desire to go and get himself condemned to death and executed in imitation of Hallāj:[28] we do not know if this transpired. The following is a portion of a work on this subject preserved for us in the Persian abridgement of his Persian and Dakhānī works:[29]

[27] The author of *Maulagān Mathnawī* in Dakkani and of *Dastūr al-'amal* (Ethé cat. 1.O.11, 197); H. Cousans, *Bijapur*, pp. 3, 7 (2 photos).

[28] 'Attār, Ibn 'Arabī, Rūmī (Ivanow): against.

[29] *Arūs'i 'Irfān*, Calcutta ms. E 129, f. 26 (V. Ivanow's commentary); in the chapter on light (*nūr*: from God, contrasted with Satan). The manuscript is dedicated to Tīpū Sultān (d. 1213/1799), the *nawāb* of Mysore. Includes ten chapters.

"A friend (Bahrī) asked Hadrat Hādī (may God illumine his grave) what final state he believed he would reach. —[The state of] the (divine) Self, he said, Who destroyed polytheism and pluralism, Who vivifies unity and moneity; this Self then (when I die) will be mine." Another time he said: "in Gugi people say evil things about me, but they do not kill me. I want to go to the capital, to Bijapur, to restore the time of Mansūr, and to realize (in myself, through death) his personality (deified: innīya):

O merciful intention towards every creature,
Like the crown for Caesar, O (divine) personality!
The origin is this personality, how sweet a root of this bitter tree of the world!
This knowledge and its vision comes from it
The soul, heart, spirit come from it.
From it all meaning and all form come.
And if there is something clear in what is murky, it comes from it.
The radiance of the sun, and also of the stars,
The straight path for angels, and also for men;
The adept finds his joy in this personality,
Even on the gibbet, like Husayn Mansūr.
Polytheism, which is a night lacking ardor,
Opposes this personality as if it were a sun.
Bahrī! In this personality rejoice!
Let the sun shine forth, it is enough.

The 'Adilshāhī kingdom was conquered by the Mughal empire in 1097/1686; the ode, therefore, was written prior to that date.

f. Ahmad 'Alī Shīvrājpūrī

This Hindustani man of letters, born in a village west of Lucknow (Oudh), versified two popular legends, probably at the end of the eighteenth century: the *Qissa-i jumjuma* ("the legend of the skull," which recounts the fate of its possessor? in which the miracles performed by Jesus are assigned to the Hindu king, Jamjama?) and the *Qissa-i Mansūr*, about Hallāj.

His *Qissa-i Mansūr*, written in sixteen rather short chapters (314 verses in all), copies closely the *Waslatnāma* of 'Attār, to which chapters 1-3 of the prologue and chapters 8-9 are added; chapters 7 and 16 are watered down. After the eulogy at the beginning, and some thoughts about real love (*'ishq haqīqī*; divine) as opposed to symbolic love (*majāzī*; profane), we are told that Hallāj had attained perfection, both exoteric and esoteric; intoxicated with the cup of union, he revealed its secret: "*Anā'l-Haqq*" (chapter 4); the *'ulamā'* demand of the Caliph that he be put to death (chapter 5), he is imprisoned, frees his fellow prisoners by helping them escape, while he himself remains in prison, which fills his jailor with respect for him (chapter 6); Mansūr then addresses a long prayer to God (munājāt; chapter 7). At this point, Shīvrājpūrī, using an unknown source, reports the criticism of an adversary, who asks why Mansūr ablutes himself (what good is a drop of water over against a sea) and prays, if he is truly deified (chapter 8: cf. perhaps 'Attār). In a second addition, the real motive behind Hallāj's being put to death is explained by the account of a vision "of one of the mystics" (chapter 9): he sees a splendid lighted tent; through a slit he recognizes inside the Prophet, the Elect, surrounded by all the saints (awliyā') and the pure (asfiyā'), whom he asks the following: who wants to offer himself in sacrifice? Mansūr offers himself as fidā' (ransom) of the beloved (God), at the request of the Friend (= the Prophet): who tells him to declare "Anā'l-Haqq," which will get him condemned to death. At this point the text once again follows the Waslatnāma: Junayd, followed by Shiblī, comes to reproach Mansūr for his utterance; against the Law (shar', dustūr; chapter 10); Mansūr retorts (quoting the same hadīth as the one included in the Waslatnāma; chapter 11); after six days, Junayd in his capacity as a jurisconsult, signs the fatwā calling for his death (chapter 12); Mansūr explains to Shiblī why he cannot renounce his saying "Anā'l-Haqq" and looks forward to the coming of Shaykh Kabīr (= Ibn Khafīf) (chapter 13); Shaykh Kabīr arrives from Shiraz, asks Mansūr why he revealed the secret, and recognizes the divine presence in him; Mansūr agrees that he must be killed (chapter 14); Shaykh Kabīr signs the fatwā; Hallāj is stoned after having thus disturbed the universe and innumerable spectators by repeating his cry; Shiblī throws him a flower bud (ipek, phūl); with each drop crying "I am the Truth," Mansūr washes his arms and face with blood; Shiblī asks him why; because ablution in blood is obligatory for the prayers of lovers; Shiblī asks him "what is Sūfism?" and also "what is love?" (chapter 15); after he is burned and his ashes are scattered, in the last chapter (number 16) entitled "ishāret-banafse serkesh," "a hint for the disobedient soul": an exhortation to the love of God: "Mansūr did his ablution in the blood of his heart; you, do it in the water of your eyes."

g. AQ Bīdīl

Chagatai in origin, 'Abd al-Qādir-b-'Abd al-Khāliq Bīdīl (d. 1133/ 1720)[30] lived first in Bukhara, then in the Indies, in the ruling circles of the Mughal empire, where his Sunnism, hostile to Shī'ite mental reservations, and his intense mysticism, an activity in which he was always

[30] See his tomb, this volume, Figures 30 and 31.

ready to abandon himself, exposed him to the hostility of the leading financiers and tax farmers of the empire, who in Delhi as in the time of the Banū al-Furāt in Baghdad, were extremist crypto-Shī'ites.

A poet and writer of prose in Persian, Bīdil forged for himself a lavish, overelaborate, difficult style. In the present day there has been a revival of his influence in certain Indo-Persian centers, in Tadjikistan, Bukhara, and especially Afghanistan, among writers such as Saljūqī, M Ibrāhīm Khalīl, Haīrat and Hāshim-Shāyeq.

A disciple of the mystic Shāh Sāhib Kābulī, Bīdil left some important texts on Hallāj; and critical analysis of them,—here too—has been made possible by the studies of M Ibrāhīm Khalīl and the translations of M Ferhadi, by which we are guided.

Bīdil is *shuhūdī* and his *'aqīda* is the very *'aqīda* of Hallāj. Like Hallāj, he sets his course on Union via a route that is fraught with dangers, which he is not hesitant to acknowledge as rash; but he does affirm, and in a sharply clear way, that Hallāj did indeed reach the highest goal of the discipline, and in union with the Truth.

I. How is the "I" of Mansūr (Hallāj) different from the "I" of Pharaoh?

In this poetic piece from his *Ghazalīyāt*, Bīdil takes up this famous theme inserted in the *Tā' Sīn al-Azal* which likens these two "I"s with the "I" of Satan. The first to oppose (versus Ahmad Ghazālī) this very old *wujūdī* notion (held by Qushayrī and continued down to 'Attār and Ibn 'Arabī) was Yūsuf Hamadhānī, followed by 'AQ Kīlānī, Rūmī, Baqlī, Semnānī, 'Alī Hamadhānī, Gīsūdirāz, and Sirhindī. Like these latter, Bīdil was *shuhūdī*.

What perfection makes the "I" murmured by Mansūr praiseworthy? And what imperfection makes the "I" shouted by Pharaoh a dissonance banished from the harmony of the Supreme Musician? Since both sang in the same world, each emitting the same note. . . .

Mansūr, subjected to the very exigencies of indiscriminant Poverty, became intimate with the secrets of *Yaqīn*; and in no state did he release the protective orthogonal frame; —up to the drops of his blood keeping the color of the Only One crimson—up to the dust of his ashes radiating the melody of the Only One.
. . .

II. Dialogue between the spirits of Mansūr and Desire (*Tamannī*):

In this ocean full of protective coverings of "me and you"
Our tongues are like complaining waves.
As long as the Mansūrian Desire does not arouse you
What can you reach with the (unexpressed) vitality of your "Secret"?
Which is grasped in the full Glory of this Single Flame (Qurbanīyān).

This is the final Gaze, the opening of the eyes of those who have sacrificed themselves voluntarily.

III. My symbolic cup of Desire brought on the intoxication of Fulfillment.

In the little blood I had, the image of Majnūn became Mansūr.

IV. In the palm grove of judgments and feelings, a whole crowd goes about plucking useless and deceiving fruits. —Surely it is not easy to pluck the flowers of the consciences of the True, —see the purple one in this garden, it is a pool of Mansūr's blood.

V. Say "I" before the display in the ready-sale shop of "self," what a useless word. And such was the folly of that brazenness which came into the head of Mansūr.

h. The Madfan of Mansūr Hallāj at Porto-Novo

In 1938, Professor Hamidullāh called attention to the existence of a cenotaph of Mansūr Hallāj in Muhammad Bandar (= Porto-Novo), on the southeastern coast of India, south of Madras, in the Tamil region, where there is only a tiny minority of converts to Islam forming two casts, the Marakkayar in Porto-Novo, Nagore, and Kayalpatnam, the Labbai in Nagore and Trichinopoly.[31] This madfan could be attributed to the Sūfīs of this region, who, in the present day, are divided into four orders: the Banava (= Qādirīya of Ghulām 'Alī Shāh Dihlawī), the Rifā'īya, the Shāhmadārīya (and Malang), and the Jalālīya Chishtīya (of Jalāl Bukhārī = Makhdūme Jahanīyān), subject to the supreme authority of a "sirguru," a hereditary position belonging to the family of Bābā Fakhr al-Dīn, interred in Penukondah (in northwestern Arcot). This Fakhr al-Dīn Sijistānī, a direct disciple of Natharn Shāh Mazhar al-Dīn (d. 411/1020), the saint of Trichinopoly, is the patron saint of the Panjuris cast (= Pinjaras) or "carders of cotton"; this is because Mansūr Hallāj Qattān was in the Ottoman empire. This madfan should be attributed to one Pinjara Labbai,[32] converted by some member of the Shirazian order of the Kāzerūnīya.

i. The Hallājian Cult of the "Master of Truth" in East Bengal

Hindu tradition did not wait for Islam to propagate the cult of truth, even in Bengal. Concerning the love of truth (satya), we know of the Siva legends (the mystery of Raja Harischandra who always spoke the truth; King Viśvamitra forces him to have to execute his wife; Siva saves

---

[31] Cf. REI, 1938, pp. [101-111].
[32] Khāja Khān, Studies [bib. no. 2133-b], p. 153.

him),[33] the Vishnu legends (the cult of Satya Narāyana), Buddhist legends (the cult of Dharma,[34] which has survived Brahmanic persecutions since the eleventh century, and is identified with the Muslim Khuda, ap. Sat-Dharma, cf. *satyavakya*), some common survivals (Prahlad),[35] and some Hindu-Muslim syncretist efforts (the Kibirpanthis[36] identify Satya Purusa with the God of Islam [= *Sāhib*, *Haqq*], and the *Satyaloka* with the Islamic Paradise). But in two limited areas, that of Dacca-Fenny-Chittagong in East Bengal and that of Murbhanj in Orissa, we find a peasant cult of the "master of truth," *Satya Pir*, whose Muslim and Hallājian origins are as indisputable as they are strange.

In Orissa, Satya Pir is identified with Satya Narayāna (= Vishnu) and, despite the Brahmans, the offering of flour and milk mixed with bananas and sugar is called, not *bhoga* (the term used in the Hindu temple), but *shinni* (a Muslim term).[37] In East Bengal, Satya Pir is above all the tutelary patron of woodsmen against wild beasts of the jungle, and icons depict him astride a tiger;[38] this being the view held by Muslims. But among Hindus, in their weekly *pūja* in Satya Narāyana, which no Muslim may participate in, it is the Hallājian legend of Satya Pir that is told in popular Bengali poems in every village.

There is a considerable body of literature about him that has been studied by Munshi 'Abdul Karīm, the former principal of Anwārā College in Chittagong, from the standpoint of the Muslim sources,[39] and appraised by Dinesh Chandra Sen in terms of the Bengali national and religious reaction to the Muslim conquest, which gives all the more value to his admission to the Muslim origin of Satya Pir.[40]

This literature comprises, first of all, Bengali poems by Muslim or Islamized authors who, in many cases, still had Hindu names and whose works dated from the beginning of the seventeenth century: 'Arif, Krishnharī Dās (1645), Nāyek Mayāj Gājī, Śankarāchārya (between 1636 and 1662), the poems entitled "*Satya Pir*." This is also true in the case of the "*Satya Pir*" of Rāmānanda, and of the "*Satya Pirer Panchāli*" written

---

[33] Dinesh Chandra Sen (from Tipperah), *A History of Bengali Language and Literature* (Calcutta, 1911), p. 168; cf. P. Meile and Gandhi, ap. *Harijan*, February [?] p. 38.

[34] *Ibid.*, p. 30; [Jean] Przyluski, *Le Concile de Rājagṛha* [Paris, 1926], pp. 260-269.

[35] Cf. Gandhi, who compared his "*satyagraha*" (upholding the truth); cf. *RMM*, XLIV (1921), 55-63.

[36] Yūsuf Husain, *L'Inde mystique* (1929), pp. 81, 96, 122.

[37] Dinesh Chandra Sen, *The Folk Literature of Bengal* (Calcutta, 1920), p. 100.

[38] The direct communication of Mr. Suhrawardy in Paris, May 1940; Husain, *L'Inde mystique*, p. 26. Ibn al-Athir already pointed this out; cf. Z Qazwīnī.

[39] Sen, *Hist. Beng. Lang.*, pp. 803-804.

[40] *Ibid.*, appendix, p. 7.

by Fakir Chānd, who lived in Chuchiā and Chittagong (1734). A Hindu poet, Fakir Rāma Kavibhusana, was the first in that period to identify "Satya Pir" with Nārayān in his popular poems written in an elegant Bengali style. His legend is also incorporated into the poems about S. Narayana by Bharatachandra (1722, d. 1760), by Jayanarayana Sen ("Hari Līlā," written in 1763), and by his niece, Ananda Mayī (alive in 1761).[41]

D. C. Sen, our only available present-day source, has the following to say about the "Satya Pir" of Śankarāchārya, a long poem consisting of fifteen chants, rediscovered by Babu Nagendra Nath Vasu in Murbhanj (= Mayurbhanja, Orissa): "this book reveals an interesting fact about the origin of the god "Satya Pir." Couched in a legendary form, but elucidated by comparison with the plot of another work on "Satya Pir" attributed to Nāyek Mayāj Gājī, it reveals to us that it was Emperor Husayn Shāh of Gauda who, in his efforts to draw the sympathy of his Hindu subjects to himself, created the cult of Satya Pir, so that Hindus and Muslims would come together in the common worship of a single God." "One legend," he says elsewhere, "describes Satya Pir as the son of a princess, probably the daughter of Hushen Shāh, the Emperor of Gaur,[42] hence the grandson of Hushen Shāh."[43]

D. C. Sen, together with the accounts of the miracles of Satya Pir (for Sundara, in Chandernagore) as chanted by Wazīr ʿAli and by Ananda Mayī,[44] in which the Muslim influence is not discernible, analyzes the poem by Krishnaharī Dās, [the influence] strong on 8 of its 250 pages,[45] versified by a semi-Islamized Kayastha who invoked Allāh at the beginning of it. According to a prediction known in Paradise (= vehest, Persian: behesht), Satya Pir will come into the world to stop the injustices of Kaliyuga and the persecution of the faqīrs carried out by Rāja Maya-Dānava and indicated by the archangel Jibrīl. A houri, Chāndbibi, is sent from Paradise to the world to be "sandhyā-vati," the "virgin mother," and to give birth to Satya Pir. This child, conceived by divine will, is raised in the beginning by a tortoise, and exhibits superhuman powers; he performs many heroic exploits, notably in an encounter with (Rāja) Mān Singh, Emperor Akbar's governor general of Bengal from 996/1587

[41] Sen, Folk Lit., pp. 100-103; Hist. Beng. Lang., pp. 796-798.
[42] Sen, Hist. Beng. Lang., p. 797; and Folk Lit., p. 99, adapted from "the Viśva Kośa" XVIII, 159.
[43] Sen, Folk. Lit., p. 103.
[44] Analyzed by Sen, ibid., pp. 103-113, and Hist. Beng. Lang., pp. 683-687.
[45] Published by Garanhata Bengal Roy Press. (Sen, Folk. Lit., pp. 102-103); Yf Husain, L'Inde mystique, p. 26.

to 1015/1606. Krishnahari Dās dresses his hero as a *yogi*, staff in hand, hair tied in a knot, with the sandalwood mark on his forehead, the brown cordon over his shoulder (gold threads on his chest), a flute in his left hand, and around his ocher-colored attire a chain (the only Muslim feature) serving as a belt.

Glasenapp, who gathered more infomation from people about Satya Pir, asserts that local Muslim tradition originally saw in him the figure of Mansūr Hallāj with his cry "I am the Truth," his execution, and his ashes scattered in the river."[46] The "*Satya Pir*" sung by Bengali poets should be considered one of his reincarnations, the Hallājian identity of which can be established by a simple internal investigation. The "virgin mother," a former houri, is the sister of Mansūr Hallāj, the houri who poured for him the intoxicating wine of "I am the Truth" (a Persian legend); it is she who becomes pregnant by him after having drunk water from the river in which his ashes had been thrown (a Yazīdī and a Turkish legend). She is also a princess (of Aleppo) and after drinking the ashes of Hallāj, she gives birth to Nesīmī, the Turkish poet, who will die a martyr also for crying out "I am the Truth." That holds true in western India for the sources of the "master of truth" theme in Bengal. But in eastern India the canvas of the Javanese legend of Siti Jenar contains, along with other Hallājian features, those which we have just emphasized in the figure of Satya Pir. Therefore it is correct to infer from this that the Hallājian theme, after having arrived in Bengal (either by sea or by the Khilji conquest), was carried by sea from Kalinga to Java in a form of popular drama for *wayang*.

D. C. Sen sees the cult of Satya Pir as a governmental creation, a deliberate attempt at syncretism, aimed at a Hindu-Muslim religious reconciliation; and he attributes it to Emperor Husayn Shāh.

Indeed, already in the seventh century of the Hijra a qāḍī of Gaur had identified, through syncreticism, Brahma and Vishnu with Abraham and Moses.[47] And the Bengali *Sunya Purana* of Rāmai Pandit (in its Chapter 56, tacked on by Sahadeva Chakravarti, after our twelfth century),[48] had presented Brahma = Muhammad, Vishnu = Payghambar, Siva = Adam, *rishi* = *faqīr*, etc. Husayn Shāh, whose full name was Sayyid Abū'l-Muzaffar 'Alā"l-Dīn Husayn-b-Ashraf Makkī, was a Khurasanian

---

[46] H. von Glasenapp, *Hinduismus* [bib. no. 1770-a], p. 102; Zoetmulder, *Panth. Soeloek-Lit.* [bib. no. 1796-a], p. 344, n. 8.

[47] *Recueil*, p. 119, n. 2. —Mr. Enamudha states that prior to the sixteenth century Narayāna had not been linked by anyone to Satya.

[48] Sen, *Hist. Beng. Lang.*, pp. 30, 36.

from Tirmidh, who claimed to come from Meccan stock, went to settle near Sunargaon (near Dacca),[49] the capital of Bengal since 1351, married the daughter of a qāḍī there, and reigned from 899/1493 to 925/1519.[50] Though he had the beginning of the *Bhagavata Purana* and the *Mahabharata* translated into Bengali (the translation dedicated to Paragāl Khan), he mistreated and desacralized the Brahmans of Nawadwipa in 1509 (= Nadia; the famous family of Tagore) because of a disturbing prophesy (Chaitanya Dēva, d. 1534, then left it for Orissa; he converted two of Husayn Shāh's officials and the Sūfī Hari Dās to Hinduism).[51] His many inscriptions dedicating mosques[52] demonstrates to us his respect for mystics; for example, Nūr Qutb al-'Alam (d. 808 or 851/1447) buried in Pandua near Gaur (= Lakhnawti).[53] It is doubtful if Husayn Shāh was the one who had officially Islamized the local cult of Satya Pir by identifying him with Hallāj. For it was his son, Nusrat Shāh, who methodically organized the Islamization of Chittagong (1518-1538)[54] with the help of his Afghan vassal, the Amīr of Fenny[55] (1. Rasti Khan, 1466; 2. his son Parāgal Khan and his grandson Chhuti Khan, 1518-1538, the first governors of Chittagong). Hallāj should have already been venerated there, like Bistāmī and Kīlānī, who have cenotaphs there, because of the presence of Baghdadi immigrants (one of whom, the wealthy Alfa Husaynī, married the daughter of Nusrat Shāh).[56] However, it is possible that the cult of Hallāj was introduced by a local Muslim saint: perhaps Badr al-Dīn Badre 'Alam, patron saint of Chittagong and a friend of the pro-

---

[49] A. Chandpur, the Rarah district south of Dacca.

[50] H. Blochmann, *A History of Bengal* (*JASB*, XLI, 1872).

[51] Sen, *Hist. Beng. Lang.*, pp. 12, 222, 474, 503.

[52] *Épigraphie Indo-Moslemica* (G. Yazdani, Calcuta), 1915-1916 (pp. 10-14), 1929-1930 (p. 12), 1933-1934 (pp. 2-7, 23).

[53] Ghulām Husayn Salīm, *Riyād al-Salātīn*, in translation [?], pp. 133, 46; Abū'l-Fazl, *Ayn-i Akbari*, [?ed.], 11, 371.

[54] Chittagong = Chatgaon. Cf. O'Malley, Chittagong, ap. *East Bengal Districts Gazetteer*. The Muslim name is "Islāmabad." The city was fought over by Buddhist rais of Arakan (ninth century—1243, 1516-1518, 1538-1638) and Vaisnava anti-Muslim rajas of Tipperah (1243-1345, 1512-1516), and occupied by Muslims (1345-1512, 1518-1538, and since 1638 and 1666-1760).

[55] Fenny is in the district of Noakhali (D. C. Sen, *Hist. Beng. Lang.*, pp. 202-205); the palace of the amīrs was in Paragalpur. Cf. Mawl. Hamīdullāh Bahādur, *Ahādīth al-khawānīn*, Calcutta, 441 pages, a documented history of Chittagong (Blochmann, ap. *JASB*, 1872, p. 336).

[56] Blochmann, *JASB*, 1879, p. 109. In 1901 in Chittagong: 968, 054 Muslims (Sunnites and Faraizis: a cast of shaykhs), in contrast to 185,000 Hindus (especially of the Kayastha caste), and some Buddhists; Noakhali: 866,290 Muslims and 274,474 Hindus (same distribution). Many weavers in Noakhali. Sunnargaon was a center of cotton workers.

Hallājian Sharaf Munyarī (d. 844/1440),[57] or Nūr Qutb al-'Alam whose *isnād* goes back, via 'Alā"l-Dīn 'Alā"l-Haqq (a curious name), to both the pro-Hallājian Hāmid Nāgurī of Jodhpur and Nizām Awliyā' of Delhi (via Akhī Sirāj al-Dīn 'Uthmān, d. 758).[58]

VII. THE INFLUENCE OF THE MARTYRDOM OF HALLĀJ
ON THE ISLAMIZATION OF JAVA

The Muslim mystical circles of Malaysia, from the beginning, knew and argued over Hallāj's "I am the Truth." Quotations will be given further on in which the Qādirī poet Hamza Fānsūrī (d. around 1040/1630) extolled Mansūr's "Anā'l-Haqq."[1] Hamza was from Baroes (Sumatra) like his disciple and commentator Shams Samatrānī (from Pasei). A jurisconsult from Atjeh, Nūr Ranīrī (d. 1040), had signed a *fatwā* condemning Hamza for being *wujūdī* (= monist). This *fatwā*, adopted by the sultan of Atjeh, Iskandar II, in 1052/1642, led to the works of Hamza being burned. But sixty years later, the Javanese sultan of Banten, Zaynal (d. 1146/1734), had copies made of them.[2] At this very time, it should be added, a sudden change of attitude took place, even in Sumatra, in favor of Hallāj under the prompting of Shattārīya missionaries implanted in Oelakan (on the west coast) by 'Abd al-Ra'ūf of Singkel. Later, in the last century, Naqishbandīya missionaries, whom Ismā'īl Simaboer had introduced into Minangkabau, combatted there, as well as in India, the extreme positions of the Shattārīya, among others the importance given by them to the Hallājian "Anā'l-Haqq."[3]

The Hallājian theme, however, not only served to add fresh fuel, in Malaysia and elsewhere, to the unceasing debate between canonists and mystics. We have proof that the account of Hallāj's martyrdom was one of the main apologetical means used by all of the early pioneers of Islam to convert the Hindu circles of Java, in which Brahmanic and Buddhistic asceticism had already inculcated an ideal of self-sacrifice. Four similar accounts of the martyrdom dating from the early years of Java's Islamization are replete with details borrowed from an account of Hallāj's martyrdom whose origin is not yet firmly established, but seem to go back

---

[57] *JASB*, XLII, 302.   [58] *Ibid.*, p. 260, n. 1.

[1] Ed. Doorenbos [?], pp. 41, 47-48, 50, 55, 57, 105 (*Shā'ir*); 170 (*Asrār al-'ārifīn*); 203 (*Sharāb al-'āshiqīn*).
[2] Kramers, *Een Javansche primbon* [?], pp. 26, 46.
[3] *Ibid.*, pp. 33, 49.

to the *tadhkira* of 'Attār brought to the Archipelago by Indo-Persian missionaries, either from Fars (Kāzerūnīya) or from Khurasan, by way of the Deccan or Chittagong.

a. The Martyrdom of Siti Jenar, the Saint of Giri, in 893/1488

The figure of Siti Jenar (= Lemah Abang)[4] is extremely popular in Java. He is the protomartyr of Javanese mystical Islam. Just when the Buddhist empire of Majapahit was collapsing under the first sultan of the new Muslim state of Demak, this shaykh, from whom the *sasahidan* mystical school derives (= *shāhidīya* = *shuhūdīya*),[5] became suspect to the other local holy men because of its excesses. Invited to appear before them to vindicate himself, and having a presentiment of his fate, he dressed in white, and put intoxicating *soelasih* flowers in his ears (= *ocimum basilicum*). On the way there, he refuted in a friendly way the *hulūlī* mysticism of a Buddhist, Kebo Kenanga, who believed it possible for God to "remain mingled" (*soeksma*) with us. In his appearance before the synod of holy men, a canonical tribunal as yet nonexistent,[6] Siti Jenar made a public disclosure (*miak werana*) of the arcana of "*Anā'l-Kak*" (= *Anā'l-Haqq* = "I am the Truth"), and was condemned to death. The prince of Tjeribon, S. Bajat, ordered his execution on 22 *Jumāda* II of the year *Śaka* 1410 (= 893/1488). The executioners' swords at first became blunted when used on Siti Jenar, who then spit out some saliva, a drop of which fell on a dry betel leaf. This leaf was soon to be eaten by Princess Mandapa of Pajajaran, who was then on ascetical retreat; and from it she conceived a daughter, Tandoeran Gagang.[7] The soul of Siti Jenar thus was in his saliva; his body was no more than a cadaver in the hands of the executioners. His blood poured out, but white, not red,[8] and then yellow and black. It smelled of musk and patchouli, and talked.[9] Moved by this miracle, one disciple, Ki Lontang Semarang, submitted to the execution-

---

[4] Siti Jenar (in the Krama dialect) = Lemah Abang (in the Ngoko dialect = the red earth, an allusion to the blood spilled?). Three versions of his *Sīra* are extant: "Babad Poerwareja" (Rinkes ed., *TBG* [?], LV, 1913, 106 ff.); the Widya Poestaka ed., Weltevreden, 1917; and the Tan Khoen Swie, Kediri, 1922 and 1932.

[5] The school of Semnānī.

[6] Among their ten names, we find at least four of the nine holy apostles of Javanese Islam represented: S. Maghrabī (I, d. 1419), P. Bonang (III, d. 1525), S. Giri (IV), and S. Kalijaga (IX).

[7] Who, in the beginning, was incapable of bearing children, was later taken to Holland, where she was cured (= the legitimization of the future Dutch invasion, Pajajaran's revenge against Mataram).

[8] White blood (*darah poetih*) = (*diri poetih*) = the last covering layer of the soul.

[9] Cf. the good repute of Sri Tandjoens.

ers. Only the holy S. Kali Jaga, who had beheaded the martyr, dared bear his body to the mosque, though it spoke, and afterwards only grudgingly let him be buried in the Kemlaten Cemetery near Tjeribon. The next day, when the tomb was reopened, only two luminous buds of *melati* (= sambuc jasmin) were found in it. The holy men, in burying him there, substituted a mangy dog for him which they claimed to be the only remains of Siti Jenar.

As early as 1913 Rinkes identified Hallāj's cry of *"Anā'l-Haqq"* with Siti Jenar and spotted three other Hallājian features in the latter's legend: that a substitute (a dog) had died in place of him; that his blood spoke; and that his soul had been reincarnated in the womb of a virgin. The latter two did not stem from 'Attār.

b. The Martyrdom of Soenan Panggoeng, the Saint of Tegal, in 907/1501

According to his legend, which is included in the *wayang* (the shadow theatre) repertory, S. Panggoeng, brother of the third sultan of Demak, Bintara Tranggāna II (1500-1537), was mad with divine love. Among his other extralegal eccentricities, he had two dogs as pets, one black, the other reddish brown, whom he named *Imān* (faith) and *Tawhīd* (Divine Unity). They were the embodiments of his two tamed carnal souls, *nafs lawwāma* and *nafs ammāra*.[10] And these dogs accompanied him into the mosque. Summoned before the synod of the holies and the sultan in 1501, S. Panggoeng, on the basis of the *fatwā* of S. Bonang, was sentenced to be burned alive. He greeted the judgment with laughter, and got someone to feed rice to his dogs while the fire was being fanned. The dogs, fighting, extinguished it, which led the sultan to ask his brother to assist the executioners. S. Panggoeng agreed, and asked only for ink and paper. Then, following a friendly exchange of greetings with his brother and his judges, he threw himself into the fire with his dogs, the ink, and the paper. When the fire had died down, the only thing found in the ashes was a manuscript by a mystic, Soeloek Malang Soemirang, drawn from a work of S. Panggoeng, *"Dakapanalalpana."*[11]

In 1927, Drewes[12] showed that the metamorphosis of the two souls into dogs derived, via 'Attār, from Turughbadhī's account of Hallāj's

---

[10] The first two coverings of the soul (the theory of the seven *latīfa*).

[11] A bizarre feature: Malang Soemirang is the brother of Amīr Hamza.

[12] *TBG*, LIV (1913), 139 ff. There are a dozen dogs in the Tjabolek legend; Drewes, ap. *Djawa*, 7th year, pp. 98-103.

return from Qashmir. The rest seemed to him to be a duplication of Siti Jenar.

c. The Martyrs of Ki Baghdād in Pajang and of Shaykh Among Raga in Mataram

Rinkes and Drewes are inclined to see in these two legends, as in the preceding ones, the survival of the Hindu theme of Ajar Wisrawa, who, in the novel of Arjūna, arouses the wrath of gods for having "raised the curtain" and revealed the *sastra* to Prince Soemali. Let us note that we are not excluding the impossibility that the four martyrdoms really occurred, and that, in any case, the coloration of the early theme was heightened by the Muslim addition of Hallājian details.

d. Hamza Fānsūrī

In a Malaysian prose tract, Hamza interprets "*Anā'l-Haqq*" as having been uttered in a state of rapture (*ghalaba*):[13]

(P. 203) This is the utterance of a man intoxicated, not at all an expression of personal egoism: thus did Mansūr Hallāj say "*Anā'l-Haqq.*" Now, this utterance need not be imitated, for we are not ruled by ecstasy (*maghlūb al-hāl*), except when we are in love or intoxicated, no longer having control of our judgement; —when (therefore) these words are uttered, they are not false; they must be interpreted.

In his poems he leans toward the monism of Ibn 'Arabī:

(P. 107) Be assured that once one finds adequate such words as the "*laysa fī'l-jubba*" of Junayd Baghdādī, the "*subhānī*" of Abū Yazīd, or the "*Anā'l-Haqq*" of Mansūr Hallāj, seeing that all of these people of magnificent wisdom can no longer distinguish (material) density from what is (spiritually) fine, but see Essence equally in all things, everything that these people say about it is correct.

(P. 55) Do not be afraid to say "*Anā'l-Haqq*"! —this wave becomes the sea! —outside [you are] a simple branch of humanity, —within you are always at your Origin; —we would like to see the face, —but Mansūr is beyond view;[14] —your soul must fight the "self," —Mansūr is right, he, the leader in this war; —this battle, O soul, do not regret it.

(Pp. 47-48) To transgress the "*liya ma'a*"[15] completely; the slave becomes the Master; thus does this wise one assume the name of "knowledge"; and Abū Yazīd, very exalted, annihilated in this sublime knowledge, says "*subhāni*," which becomes in this very place the pilgrimage to the Creator; like Mansūr, the leader of lovers, also says "*Anā'l-Khāliq*"; he too has this right of utterance; whosoever here is qualified for it, let him utter his *aleh*.[16] O Perfect Man! —we

[13] Attempted translation (assisted by Miss Sokolov).
[14] Literally, interval (= *bayn* in Arabic?).
[15] Hadīth: "I have moments with God that are inaccessible to Angels."
[16] " '*Alayhi'l-salām.*"

must not seek useless knowledge nor what the uneducated know —"*Anā'l-Haqq*"! Mansūr, in saying this, reached his goal (= *wāsil*).

(P. 50) Magnificent drink, received from the hands of the Creator, —Who gives it to all of His lovers to drink; —whosoever says "*Anā'l-Haqq*" is very honest; this draught is indeed such a cure giving health to the whole body that in drinking it one forgets one's companions—Mansūr became a noncombatant—drinking this does not enlighten.

(P. 57) Asceticism leads to Paradise, —while desiring this world leads to death. —'Abd al-Wāhid is the origin of his name,[17] —he says "*Anā'l-Haqq*" constantly, his calling is to be intoxicated and in love, —a knowledge glorious and exalted.

(P. 105) The divine Name "*Wāhid*" (One) means being simultaneously visible and hidden—which is the end of knowledge—your branch and its trunk, —within full power, outside mutilation—you are still the cup-bearer, and the one who thanks him, —now Mansūr has (also) become "*nāsir*"[18] —the eye put out, the clothing (of his body) burned; —one must affirm God, and deny idolatry.

(P. 41) After that one attains a very high knowledge, like Abū Yazīd and Mansūr Baghdādī, by saying "*Anā'l-Haqq*" and "*Subhānī*"; —this is the method of those who are outwardly children, —according to the triumphant sages; —thus does the ship (?) of *tawhīd* arrive at its destination (?).

VIII. The Survival in Arabia

a. Ahmad ibn 'Ulwān Yamanī[1]

Kratchkovsky discovered in the *Kitāb al-futūh* of this Ahmadī shaykh from Yemen (d. 665/1266) an interesting *dhikr al-Hallāj* (the name is connected with the *tarahhum*) explaining "how the sincere lover bears witness to his veracious beloved on the most direct route to knowledge of the compassionate Companion (= God?)."

Hallāj, having submitted to the divine light, realized by his *'aql* and by his intuition that it is indeed the divine will which, in entering his will and his purpose (*himma*), desires in his stead and speaks in his stead ("*lā yantiq 'an al-hawā*' [Qur'ān]"). This is what the philosophers (*hukamā'*) tell us in connection with a ray of sunlight entering a recess in a wall like fresh water in a glass, consuming its substance; the house sparkles with this glory, and this is the light that expressed itself in Hallāj when he said "I"; we have proof of it to hold up to the ignorant: it is that the effusion of this light, vibrant and limitless, in the niche of Hallāj, that broke his glass and lit his torch, plunging his paths and mountain passes into darkness; then he was confused, had a foreboding of his death, shuddered; his power of discernment and argument failed, every sign of a right way for his perception to follow sank in the ocean of these splashing waves. He had to make his way through the night of nonbeing without a torch, he cried out, while Being had lain in ambush to capture his reason, making all else but God vanish, "I am

---

[17] Meaning a saint.   [18] A play on words.

[1] Brockelmann I, 449.

God." No reference was made to his corporal substance, nor to his spiritual soul, but because of his annihilated identity, to his Sovereign identity. His eye no longer saw any sign of light but that. Through a Merciful power he expressed a real and fervent ecstasy, unlike that of Pharaoh, Satan, Nimrod, and Kan'ān, through the disappearance of his human dimension and his incorporation of an Eternal dimension; and when the light of this incorporation flashed forth, shaking his heart and disrupting his heavens and his earth, he formed these words on his tongue.

There follows a poem "excusing" Hallāj and expressing his ardent acceptance of punishment, then a commentary on the hadīth "*kuntu sam'hu.* . . ." Ibn 'Ulwān then explains how he himself, after rejecting the robe of ignorance to "run naked in search" of God, he felt himself reclothed in the robe of knowledge, which made him perceive the divined secret flowing (*sārī*) into all of his sensations and engraving his name under the name of God, his impersonal knowledge under the knowledge of God, wavering between saying "I" (through *baqā'*) or "He" (through *fanā'*). "And since I chose (to say 'I'), the witness of *Baqā'* told me, 'You are going to fall from the sun into dust, and from holiness into prison.' And I said to him, shaking my finger, 'Do you intend to kill me as you killed that soul yesterday?'[2] And he smiled thinking of this debate with Hallāj, for he had failed, as was my choice, to nail me on the gibbet of Hallāj, and said 'now add an epithet.' And I wrote (beneath the engraving of our two names) 'servant of God.' "

God explained to him how it was the very Name of "*Allāh*" which was the instrument of Hallāj's execution. The A was the gibbet, the gap between the A and the L was the knife; the two Witnesses, *fanā'* and *baqā'*, were disagreed as to whether he should die or not; and since every man must have his vindication, his blood ran with his sighs toward his beloved in asking him for it; and God wanted to exonerate him from the ignorant accusations, and his blood wrote "*Anā Allāh*" "It is I, God, his murderer." Executed, though innocent of *shirk*, to show his beloved his patient endurance, and so that no one coming after him would dare to be so bold as he.

b. Yāfi'ī

Yāfi'ī (d. 768/1367)[3] supported his theory of Hallāj's sanctity with the textual testimonies of Kīlānī, Suhrawardī of Baghdad, and Ghazālī, and with the names of Ibn 'Atā', Nasrābādhī, and Ibn Khafīf. He condensed his opinion into verses 4 to 7 of his *qasīda* entitled *al-Durr al-munaddad*,[4] or "Collected Pearls," consisting of forty-seven verses:

---

[2] Qur'ān 28:19.   [3] Ash'arite, who died in Mecca; an opponent of Ibn Taymīya.
[4] The full title is "pearls strung around the neck of beautiful women—in order to explain

(1) Hail to this group, suns of the straight path, for whom—love like ecstasy increases on the horizon up to their resurrection, tomorrow! . . .

(4) One of them (Bistāmī) disappeared among the people, but the other, pushing ecstasy to the extreme, ended up in riot.

(5) Also the Law drew the sword against him in defense of its precepts, —and we saw Hallāj die executed.

(6) He died a martyr, according to you, having accomplished his plan. How many others, alas, leave your ranks to become heretics!

(7) Whereas the man from Bistām, curbing his ecstasy, —avoided difficulties, and died respected and esteemed. . . .

The following commentary is added: "I have indicated by these latter verses that Hallāj was arrested by the authority of the literal law, whereas Abū Yazīd assumed the armor of a 'state' which protected him against the seizure of power by force." No one expressed better than one of the masters[5] the dangerous situation in which Hallāj perished and which Bistāmī avoided: "Hallāj, in order to be brought out of the ocean of Reality onto the shore[6] had to be arrested and imprisoned to suffer his sentence [of death]; but Abū Yazīd did not emerge from the ocean of reality and realization; there was also no way to arrest him."

IX. The Survival in Egypt and Syria

a. The Testimony of Ibn al-Haddād[1]

That there happened to be, prior to *Shawwāl* 310,[2] less than a year after the execution of Hallāj, a Shāfi'ite canonist courageous enough to dare to collect and transmit on his own professional authority the text of the last

---

how to excuse the words uttered by the masters of beautiful ecstasies—and what Hallāj said; which the letter of the law judged lawful (*mustabāh*) and the fact that the shaykhs made a martyr out of him, —for one who is enraptured in ecstasy cannot be accused of sin."

[5] Who is this? (Ibn Fadl Allāh alluded to this: Nājurī [*Tawālī' al-badūr*, 211] says in commenting on the verse "while Bayazid . . . in the ocean . . . , we, ill prepared, on the shore of desire we have not reached . . ."). Cf. Rūmī, *Mathnawī* II, 50, 22. An analogous image in Hallāj (verse: *khidtu bahran* . . .) and Ibn al-Fārid (*Nazm al-sulūk* [bib. no. 403-a], verse 288). Cf. *Ibrīz* [?] II, 168; Bistāmī according to Haytamī, *Fat. Had.* [bib. no. 742-a], 95; in Ibn 'Arabī according to Dawwānī, Alexandria cat. *Fun. Mutan.* [?], 126.

[6] *Bahja*, 70.

---

[1] Abū Bakr (and Abū'l-Hadīd) M-b-A-b-Ja'far ibn al-Haddād Kinānī Misrī, born in 264, died in 344 (Subkī II, 112, 302; Kindī, *Qudāt*, s.v.). Not to be confused with the Sūfī Abū Bakr M-b-Ism Misrī (d. 345). On the other hand, I believe him to be identical with Abū'l-Hadīd, who wrote on the mystic A 'AA M-b-Sa'īd Qurashī (Sarrāj), *Luma'*, 255, not to be confused with an Abū'l-Hadīd of minor importance, who was a pupil of Ibn Yūnus (254, d. 332, Dhahabī, ms. P. 1581, f. 119a). His "testimony" is reproduced here in Chapter IV.

[2] The date of his visit to A 'Alī Hy-b-Khayrān (Dhahabī, ms. P. 1581, f. 95b).

prayer of this condemned man, is indeed a very significant fact. The collaborator and confidant of the grand qāḍī of Cairo,[3] (Ibn Harbawayh), Ibn al-Haddād came to Baghdad on a mission, to get the deputy vizir, 'Alī ibn 'Īsā, to accept the resignation of his superior, being dissatisfied with the walī, Hilāl-b-Badr (6 Rabī' II 309 to 1 Jumāda I 311);[4] Ibn 'Īsā was unable to satisfy him by appointing as walī A-b-Kayaghlagh (1 Jumāda I 311 to 3 Qa'da 311), and it was the new vizir, Ibn al-Furāt (21 Rabī' II 311), an enemy of Ibn Harbawayh, who was eager to accept his resignation. Ibn al-Haddād returned in haste to Cairo, where he found his

[3] A list of the grand qāḍīs of Cairo: Bakkār-b-Qutayba, 8 Jumāda II 246-Hijja 270; (vacancy of 7 years); 'UA. M-b-'Abda ibn Harb 277-Jumāda II 283; Abū Zur'a-b-'Uthmān Thaqafī 284-292; 'UA ibn Harb 7 Rabī' I to 19 Jumāda II 292; Abū 'Ubayd 'Alī-b-Hy ibn Harbawayh 19 Jumāda II 292-Hijja 311 (b. 237, d. 319; arrived in Baghdad 4 Sha'bān 293); Abū Yahyā 'AA-b-Ibrāhīm-b-M-ibn Mukram, Hijja 311-19 Rabī' I 313 (with khalīfa: Abū Dhikr M-b-Yahya Tammār, followed by Ibrāhīm-b-M Kurayzī, 12 Safar 312); Hārūn-b-Ibrāhīm Hammādī 19 Rabī' I 313 to 16 Hijja 316 (with khalīfa: 'AR-b-Ish-b-M-b-Mi'mar Jawharī, followed by Ahmad-b-Ibrāhīm Hammādī 22 Rabī' II 314); 'AA-b-A ibn Zabr (resident titular) 15 Muharram 317 to 2 Jumāda II 317; Hārūn Hammādī (with khalīfa: his brother Ahmad, followed by 'Alī-b-M-b-'Alī 'Askarī, 7 Rabī' II 320), 2 Jumāda II 317-19 Rabī' II 320; Ibn Zabr 19 Rabī' II 320-10 Safar 321 (with khalīfa Abū Hāshim Ism-b-'A Wāhid Maqdisī, until 15 Rabī' I); M-b-H ibn Abī'l-Shawārib (titular; khalīfa: AQ 'AA-b-Muslim-b-Qutayba (son of the great writer), followed by Abū'l-Dhikr Tammār (29 Jumāda II 321) 15 Rabī' 321-7 Ramadān 321; Ahmad Hammādī (res. tit.) 4 Ramadān 321-22 Safar 322 (followed by khalīfa: AHy M-b-'Alī-b-Abī'l-Hadīd 22 Safar to 24 Jumāda II 322); M-b-Mūsa Sarakhsī (interim) 24 Jumāda II 322-5 Shawwāl 322; M ibn Abī'l-Shawārib (tit.) 5 Shawwāl 322-3 Rabī' II 329 (with khalīfa: M-b-Badr Sayrafī, 5 Shawwāl 322-25 Shawwāl 324, with kātib: Ibn al-Haddād 322-23; followed by khalīfa: Ibn Zabr 25 Shawwāl to 15 Qa'da 324, with Ibn al-Haddād nā'ib; followed by khalīfa: Ibn al-Haddād (interim; regime of Ibn Tughj: 16 Qa'da-end of Rabī' II 325), A 'AA Hy-b-Abī Zur'a Thaqafī (end of Rabī' II 325, d. 10 Hijja 327: retained his friend Ibn al-Haddād as nā'ib), M-b-Badr Sayrafī (18 Hijja 327-1 Safar 329); Ibn Zabr (tit.) 1 Rabī' I 329, d. 3 Rabī' II 329; A-b-'AA Khiraqī (tit.), Rabī' II 329-Muharram 334 (with khalīfa Hy.-b-'Īsā-b-Harawān Ramlī) who appointed himself deputy to 'AA-b-A-b-Shu'ayb ibn Ukht Walīd with Ibn al-Haddād as walī (Rabī' II-Shawwāl 329), M-b-Badr Sayrafī (Shawwāl 329, d. 27 Sha'bān 330), Abū'l-Dhikr Tammār (1-7 Ramadān 330), H-b-'AR Jawharī (7 Ramadān-Rabī' II 331), A-b-'AA Kishshī (Rabī' II-Rajab 331), 'AA-b-A-b-Shu'ayb ibn Ukht Walīd (Rajab 331-Jumāda I 333), H-b-'AR Jawharī (Jumāda 333), Ibn al-Haddad (Jumāda 333-23 Muharram 334); Abū Tāhir M-b-A Dhuhlī (tit.), Muharram 334-Rajab 336, retained as khalīfa Hy-b-'Īsā-b-Harawān Ramlī (d. 336), who appointed himself deputy to 'AA-b-A-b-Shu'ayb ibn Ukht Walīd, with Ibn al-Haddād as walī; M-b-H-b-'A 'Azīz Hāshimī (tit.) Rajab 336-15 Hijja 339 (with khalīfa Ibn al-Walīd, followed by 'Umar-b-H Hāshimī [brother of the tit.] with Ibn al-Haddād as walī); M-b-Sālih ibn Umm Shaybān Hāshimī (tit.) 15 Hijja 339-Rabī' II 348 (with khalīfa 'AA-b-M-ibn al-Khasīb, 1 Muharram 348, followed by his son, M-b-'AA, d. Rabī' I 348; Abū Tāhir M-b-A Dhuhlī (res. tit.), 15 Rabī' II 348-2 Safar 366 (Fātimid conquest).

List based on Kindī; cf. for Ibn Zabr, Lisān III, 263; for Ibn Ukht Walīd (qāḍī of Damascus 348, d. 369), Lisān III, 251; for Ibn Mukram, Lisān III, 248.

[4] He must have arrived a few months before the death of Tabarī (26 Shawwāl 310), given the fact that he heard him, and before the death of Ibn Khayrān, since he found him forced to remain in his house by order of Ibn 'Īsā (d. 17 Hijja 310).

superior in the clutches of Abū'l-Dhikr Aswānī, the *nā'ib* (*Qa'da* 311-312, *Safar* 312) of his successor, the Mālikite Ibn Mukram; Ibn Harbawayh finally was able to return to Baghdad (in 313), where he died in 319; Ibn al-Haddād, who remained after that in Cairo, had taken advantage of his prolonged stay in Baghdad to work closely with a Shāfi'ite group of disciples of Ibn Surayj, "whom he regretted deeply not having met during his lifetime."

It was therefore as a disciple of Ibn Surayj that he took up the cause of Hallāj, and we owe to him a text of great importance.

The juridical career of Ibn al-Haddād[5] may be summarized as follows: persecuted from 311 to 322 by Mālikite *qāḍī*s, which kept him from becoming head of the *shuhūd* in the Cairo court; held the position of deputy to a Shāfi'ite *qāḍī* of bad reputation, Ibn Zabr (19 *Rabī'* II 320 to 10 *Safar* 321); recommended as *khalīfa* of the *nā'ib* (29 *Jumāda* II 321); appointed *kātib* of the *nā'ib* (5 *Shawwāl* 322), *khalīfa* of the *nā'ib* (= his friend Husayn-b-Abī Zur'a, 15 *Qa'da* 324, by order of Amīr Ibn Tughj; retained in that capacity from *Rabī'* II 325 until 18 *Hijja* 327); he held that position again under Ibn Zabr (1 *Rabī'* I 329, d. 3 *Rabī'* II 329).[6] The new *nā'ib*, Hy-b-'Īsā ibn Harawān (329, d. 336), who held him in esteem and tried to keep him as *kātib* to his *khulafā'* (particularly to Ibn Ukht Walīd, a Mu'tazilī Zāhirite who claimed to have descended from Malik-b-Dīnār, the ascetic), and took him as his own *khalīfa* for eight months (*Jumāda* I 333-23 *Muharram* 334). Ibn al-Haddād became *nā'ib* again to the *khalīfa* 'Umar-b-H-b-'Abd al-'Azīz Hāshimī, son of the former 'Abbāsid *naqīb* of Baghdad (d. 333, and brother of the titular *qāḍī*, Muhammad), from *Rajab* 336 to 15 *Hijja* 339;[7] next, though still the respected head of the *shuhūd*, he found himself dismissed in the change of regimes by the new titular *qāḍī*, the Mālikite Ibn Umm Shaybān (the son-in-law of Grand Qāḍī Abū 'Umar, who had condemned Hallāj), and by his *khalīfa* in Cairo, the Shāfi'ite 'AA ibn al-Khasīb (339, d. 348); he died there after returning from the hajj, in Jubba Yūsuf, on 26 *Muharram* 344; the sovereign and the entire court attended his funeral.

He had been able to command the respect of his adversaries, Mālikite as well as Hanafite; and although the Ikhshīdhīd dynasty was Hanafite, it was Amīr Ibn Tughj himself who sent for him in 324. Like his master Ibn Harbawayh, Ibn al-Haddād lived in close association with the powerful Mādharā'iyūn family of financiers, whom he also had to enjoin on sev-

---

[5] Kindī.
[6] In the Rūdhbārī circle, Ibn al-Khashshāb; in the Mādharā'ī circle, Ibn Abī Zur'a.
[7] He went at that time to receive the black stone (13 *Hijja* 339).

eral occasions to respect the law. His friend Ibn Abī Zurʿa was their grandson; they shared the same rivals to power, particularly from 310 to 318, from 323 to 328 (inspectorship and vizirate of Fadl-b-J-b-Furāt) and from 333 to 336 (vizirate of Ibn Muqātil,[8] the friend of Awārijī); and he was their *rāwī* in hadīth.

Two of his collaborators, Sulaymān-b-M-b-Rustum and Husayn-b-Kihmish, served as head of the *shuhūd* after him, the former in 336, the latter under the Fātimids, whom he held out against.[9]

A man of extremely broad Islamic knowledge, extending to the juridical, Qurʾānic (*hāfiz* and *qāriʾ*), traditionist, and grammatical plains, to include, "in the manner of Asmaʿī," the history and poetry of the whole Arab past, Ibn al-Haddād practiced severe asceticism (facilitated, it was said, by the fact of his monorchism) and a strict life of prayer. A pupil in hadīth of M-b-ʿAqīl Firyābī, he was first and foremost a disciple of Ibn Harbawayh in Shāfiʿite law and a convinced partisan of Ibn Surayj, whose *masʾala surayjīya* he adopted and transmitted. Ibn Harbawayh, in 300 in Cairo, welcomed with him the great *muhaddith* Nasāʾī, who shared with them, *in petto*, his thesis of the *tafdīl* of ʿAlī over Abū Bakr.

His main pupils were the following: the traditionists Abū Mansūr M-b-Saʿīd Bāwardī and Dāraqutnī, the historians M-b-Yūsuf Kindī (d. 350) and H-b-Ibrāhīm ibn Zūlaq (d. 386), the jurisconsults M-b-ʿAlī Qaffāl Kabīr (d. 365),[10] the *rāwī* of his account of Hallāj (he transmitted it to Sulamī), and his son Qāsim. They might have met together, either in Mecca (hajj) or in Syria (Ramlah), around 330.

Among his important works on law, there was one, the *Kitāb mukhtasar fīʾl-furūʿ al-muwallada*, which merited commentaries being written on it on three different occasions: by Abū ʿAlī Husayn-b-Saʿīd Sinjī (d. 430, buried at Sinjdān in Marw, his homeland, near his master ʿAA-b-A Qaffāl Saghīr, d. 417), by his fellow student Husayn-b-M-Marrūdhī (d. 462, whose *sharh* has been attributed to their master Qaffāl), and by Abūʾl-Tayyib Tabarī (d. 450).[11]

Through his master Ibn Harbawayh,[12] Ibn al-Haddād became affiliated with an autonomous branch of Shāfiʿism, that of Abū Thawr Kalbī, as had Junayd.[13]

---

[8] And of Ibn Muqbal (in 326; Rādī [bib. no. 122-a], 105); Athīr [bib. no. 420-a], VII, 312-313 (in 332).

[9] Dhahabī, *Huffāz* [?], III, 108.

[10] Subkī II, 176. [11] Cf. Ghazālī, *Jawāhir*, 51.

[12] Whom he revered for his independent character (even toward the powerful, like Muʾnis: Subkī II, 305).

[13] *Isnād*: (Qushayrī, 202) Abūʾl-Hadīd, a contemporary of M-b-ʿAA Farghānī, Khuldī→

b. Fakhr Fārisī Khabrī

Fakhr Fārisī (528, d. 622) was a great *muhaddith*, the leading disciple of Silafī of Alexandria, whose *isnād* he popularized in Cairo. Born near Kazarun, he came around 557 to the Ibn Sallār *madrasa* with two other Persians, AN Suhrawardī and Rūzbehan Baqlī, who were soon to depart, however, whereas Fakhr remained.[14]

Though initiated in Fars into the Murshidīya order (like Baqlī),[15] it seems that only in Egypt, under Silafī, did he study Hallāj and become a Hallājian. For all of his references to Hallāj come from the Chirvanian edition of the *Akhbār*, to which the authority of Fakhr after Silafī, lent authority in Egypt.

This edition included the superimposed dramatic exhortative themes used to stir hearts to love of God; and, thanks to Fakhr, they affected some of the Madyanīya (Ibn Ghānim Maqdisī), Shādhilīya (Mursī), and neo-Junaydīya (Ghamrī). And even some simple Hanbalites.

Fakhr Fārisī also belonged to the Siddīqīya[16] order (born in Bayda, Hallāj's birthplace) whose fervent Sunnism held Abū Bakr without equal among the Companions of the Prophet; in this his transmitters were 'Abd al-Rahīm Damīrī (d. 695, master of Ibn al-Raf'a, d. 710) and the Hanbalite Qalānisī (d. 765).

His last direct *rāwī*, 'Īsā b. Sul-Tha'labī, died in 710.

Following a vision of AB Tīnātī, Fakhr built himself a small monastery in the Qarāfa of Cairo, where his tomb still stands, near that of Dhū'l-Nūn,[17] with a very interesting epitaph, which was the starting point of a monograph by Yūsuf Ahmad on the huge necropolis of Cairo, called "Imām Shāfi'ī," as a place of religious meditations.[18]

Fakhr went around Cairo preaching (he was at Qus, in Sa'id, in 604);[19] esteemed and consulted by the Ayyūbid ruler Mālik Kāmil; the story of his relationship with Mālik Kāmil, which arose apropos of the *Rāhib* ("monk") is famous, "*mashhūra*." Mālik Kāmil was quite conciliatory towards the Latin Christians, as we know from his treaty with Frederick II; and I believe that this "monk" was none other than St. Francis of As-

---

'Abbās M-b-Hy ibn al-Khashshāb Mukharrimī Baghdādī, *rāwī* of Shiblī's *Hikāyāt* (→ A Hy Fārisī [Qush., 113] → Sulamī).

[14] Ibn Junayd, *Fakk* [?], 243-244.

[15] Zabidī, *'Iqd*, 91.   [16] Sānūsī, *Salsabil*, 29.

[17] Ibn al-Zayyāt, *Kaw. Sayy.* [bib. no. 2105-a], pp. 83, 108 ff., 225; Sakhāwī, *Tuhfa*, 238 ff.

[18] *Turbat al-Fakhr al-Fārisī*, written in 1913, published in 1922, 96 pages; the epitaph on pp. 6-7 with 2 photographs.

[19] J-b-Th Adfūwī, *Tāli'*, 1332 ed. [?], 121.

sisi, and the "story" his appearance near Damietta before Mālik Kāmil (in 618).[20] Up to now I have found no details about the role that might have been played by Fakhr, a nonogenerian advisor (carried in a litter), in this encounter, he an old Hallājian, with the future stigmatized saint from the Alvern. Born near Kazarun, the "Persian Damietta," Fakhr was anti-Sālimīyan in theology, with Ash'arite leanings, and he must have advised Mālik Kāmil to refuse the ordeal by fire proposed by Francis. Mālik Kāmil had been rather patient during the trial of the Coptic martyr John of Phanidjoit (April 29, 1209), and it must have been Fakhr who, at the time of the restoration of Shāfi'ī's tomb in Qarāfa by Queen Mother Shamsa, had the body of the Hanbalite Ibn al-Kayzānī (d. 562) disinterred by Sultanian order because of his *hulūl* heresy.[21]

A Shāfi'ite polemicist like Shibāb Tūsī, Fakhr Fārisī attacked the "Dahrīya philosophers and the Ismā'īlīs," surviving the recent expulsion of the Fātimids, and he denounced the "Nusayrīya" (Talā'i had been one), Hulūlīya, Kayzānīya, and Marzūqīya[22] as heretics who considered dogs and pigs clean. He was attacked in turn by antimystical *muhaddithūn* with regard to his *isnāds*: by Ibn Nuqta (d. 629) and Ibn al-Hājib (d. 630), whom Dhahabī would echo later. Ibn Hajar, though suspicious, would be less hostile (ap. *Lisān al-mīzān* V, 29-31); and Ibn al-Qayīm and Ibn Qādī Shuhba (d. 851) would defend him.

The number of tombs grouped around his and that of his son Ahmad, including that of a shaykh of the Sa'īd al-Su'adā' Khānqāh, Karīm al-Dīn 'Ajamī (= Amūlī, d. 710), attested further to his renown down to the fifteenth century.

A traditionist with anti-Sālimīyan Ash'arite leanings, his main opponents were either "*Hulūlīya*" Hanbalites like Ibn al-Kayzānī (d. 562) and Ibn Marzūq (d. 1564), who were Qādirīyans and thus pro-Hallāj; or non-*Hulūlīya* like Ibn Najīya (d. 599); their amusing altercation in Qarāfa is recounted. Fakhr was a popular orator able to stir his audience to give full vent to its emotion, according to the testimony of such learned men as 'Alī-b-Zarzūr, who had the Mashhad Husaynī (built in 544) restored. Being rather credulous, he accepted accounts of the bizarre charisms of his master Rūzbahan Kāzarunī, the father-in-law of Najm Kubrā. He had some directed dreams, communication with the beyond, like his son. The Madyanī mystic Safīl Dīn-b-Abī Mansūr Ansārī, who died in 682, the son of a pious vizir of Mālik Kāmil, includes him among his masters in his *risāla*. And Yāfi'ī considered him a saint.

---

[20] *Kaw. Sayy.* [bib. no. 2105-a], 110; *Tuhfa*, p. 240; Yf. Ahmad, *Turbat*, p. 18, n.1.
[21] See Diyaīya ms., f. 127a-138a.   [22] Welieddin ms., 1828, f. 60a.

That Fakhr Fārisī was a conscious and deliberate Hallājian on the philosophical level, leaving out his moving sermons, is shown by an examination of the commentaries he wrote on the more crucial statements of Hallāj.

1. *Labbayka*

Verse 2: "I call You, no it is You Who call me to Yourself—how can I whisper to You 'it is You,' if You have whispered to me 'it is I'."

The commentary by Fakhr Fārisī (*Salwa*, f. 142b):

The saint finds himself (all at once) immobile, kept in the world by his duty of obedience (*'ubūdīya*), and standing high in the heaven of *His Affirmation* (of the One God) from beginning to end; also, he is allowed to confuse the two kinds of states; he is caught between his status of "desiring," which holds him back, and his status of "desired," which attracts him.

He defined mystical union, then, as a testimonial monism (*wahdat al-shuhūd*), uniting the *shāhid* with the *Mashhūd*.

2. *Na'y*

Verse 2: "I cry to You my 'sorrow' for those hearts so long refreshed in vain by clouds of Revelation."

The commentary by Fakhr Fārisī (*Nasl*, f. 68a)

The true *dhikr* is found only in the heart which is *unconscious* of the realities of the nearness of expatriation, a heart in which there are only *"signs attesting to the Lord"* (Hallāj's allusions emphasized).

3. *Fardānī'ldhāt*

"The Sūfī is unified as to essence, he receives no one [into himself] and no one receives him, given his aloneness in God for God."

The commentary by Fakhr Fārisī (*Jamha*, f. 46b):

The Sūfī is one whose meaning is deified by divine meaning, whose own meaning is annihilated by divine meaning, who is *divested of his carnal aspects and becomes like the moon* burned from the impact of the sun's meanings, as a smell is burned away by the scent of musk, as the eye's and the heart's own light is turned by their perception of the essence of the beloved.

4. *Uqtulūnī*

"Murder me now, my faithful friends . . ." (*Akhbar*, no. 1).

The commentary by Fakhr Fārisī (*Jamha*, f. 48b):

It is said "let them stop the shedding of blood?" —but I say "no, this is *true generosity*: let my blood be lawful for them [to shed], as long as there be blood in my veins. (Hallāj's allusions emphasized)

5. *Lā yajūz*

"A person who still perceives someone, or still remembers someone, is not allowed to say: I know Who this One is apart from whom the monads appeared" (*Stb*, no. [?]).

The commentary by Fakhr Fārisī, *Mustabhij*, excerpt ap. Ghamrī, *Intisār*, f. 41b:[23]

The aim of this allegory is to present the hidden meaning of the verse (Qur'ān 24:36) "in these abodes that God permitted to be built . . .": above all that He is not; in order that he who has access to them enters the mystery of realizing the meaning of creatures, "of you who are the Uppermost" (al-A'lawnā: Qur'ān 47:35); "that is to say, in 'Illiyīn (= the Highest Paradise): whose height is limitless, being enclosed in the meaning of His attributes and His names: so that He may raise them up to the Abode beyond eternity. Yes, they are the Uppermost, marked by the union in which they will know intimately the secrets of the King and the disclosures of the Sovereign. In which they will know the ecstasy of contemplating the Divinity in His perfection. These Uppermost are men destined by God to have access to the knowledge of the attributes and names, and to see the source of Existence in the mystery of *Tawhīd*: so that the one who might wish to unveil this mysterty dies, and the one who has delved into it so as to be enraptured by it in Him lives again, —He Who shielded His splendor from any likeness and His glory from unveiling. Did he (Hallāj) also not say in his prayer: "O my God, You know my powerlessness to give You thanks; I thank You, Yourself." —Then Hallāj said in an(other) invocation (*Akhbār*, no. 9): "O our God, You are the One Who, by Your very nature, cannot be completed by any deficient number. . . ."[24] The man capable of expressing himself in this way is as worthy of receiving the grace of praise as the proscription described."[25]

[23] This passage from Fakhr Fārisī repeats the famous passage from *Qūt* (2, 76) by the Sālimīyan AT Makkī concerning Qur'ān 47:35, "*al-A'lawnā*"; having reached the summit of love in al-Ridā' (the state of grace). Fakhr suppresses the semi-Pelagian duality in which Makkī combines *maqām* and *hāl*, *wasf* and *sifa*, in the soul that God raises up to the Friend undergoing a transfiguration in the understanding of His attributes (*tajallī maʿānī al-sifāt*). Fakhr Fārisī suppresses here the word *tajallī* (because of his Ashʿarism?) and corrects, in a dynamic and Hallājian way, this static explanation by showing the soul gaining access (*wusūl*) to *takhallul* (intimacy; a word already foreseen by Makkī but weakened by him in *khulla*), the sign of union (*maʿīya*; Makkī said only "*maʿahum*"). —And the emphasis put here by Fakhr in terms of a purer experience of transcendence, is all the more significant given the fact that Fakhr Fārisī, because of his Shirazian origins, expresses himself, like Rūzbehān Baqlī, in an Arabic that is often too laden with metaphors resulting from a labored aestheticism, as in the famous prologue of his treatise "*Barq al-baqā' wa Shams al-naqā',*" which aroused the indignation of Dhahabī and Ibn Hajar.

[24] A "deficient number," *ʿadad nāqis*, is one whose sum is *less* than all of its parts. Eg., the number 10, in which (10/2) + (10/5) + (10/10) = 8, a sum less than 10.

[25] [A commentary on] Qur'ān 24:36:
"*Al-a'lāwna*" = the elect of 'Illiyīn (cf. Semnānī): those elevated by the meanings of His attributes and names, —by the sign of being with (*maʿīya*) [God], which engenders "*takhallul al-asrār al-malakūtīya*" (a sensitivity to the secrets of the Kingdom) = the attaining of knowledge of the attributes and names, of the *sirr al-tawhīd*—the last two words come from

c. Ibn al-Fārid

Certain specific borrowings, at least one of which was pointed out by Farghānī,[26] show that Ibn al-Fārid, in his *Dīwān* and particularly in the *Nazm al-sulūk*, had explicitly taken Hallāj's texts into account in his writing. He even developed in his own way some Hallājian ideas, such as the *Khal' al-idhār*, the *nāsūt*, and the spiritual hajj.[27] In fact, in two places in the *Nazm*, he gave his own explanation of Hallāj's *"Anā'l-Haqq,"* seeing it as a desire to die. The sumptuous beauty of these verses and their metaphysical quality, which is aesthetic rather than transcendental, has to be regarded with care. Ascetical enthusiasm induces one to say in theopathic locution: "how can I forego saying: I am He (the Divinity), but how could I say, God forbid, that He has infused Himself in me?" (verse 277). It must therefore be God Himself Who says "I" through my mouth, disguising Himself in my appearance, like the angel Jibrīl visiting the Prophet in the form of Dihya. It is a simple disguise (*talabbus*), one that does not suggest union, but only an actor playing his reciting role (*'alā'l-hikāya*; cf. Suhrawardī). That from the standpoint of God. But in terms of the person speaking, of the actor chosen by God as a masked spokesman, what is his inner state? Ibn al-Fārid deals with this in the second passage. Love brings the lover to realize that outside himself his beloved appears in everything and, correlatively, to declare, within himself, as in a microcosm, that everything praises Him within: "If He were to open my body, He would see that I am all essence within, that my heart is given wholly to Him, that it is filled with love" (verse 387). So much so that it is normal for the lover, when not in my state of ecstasy, to speak "the language of sober union" (*lisān sahw al-jam'*, as Farghānī says): to say "I" in the name of God. But from the standpoint of the scandal caused by that among those strict adherers to the law who hear

---

Sahl (Sālimīyan). But Makkī (cf. the preceding page, n. 935) gives a different commentary (*Qūt* 2, 76) "*al-a'lawunā*": *wasf* (not *sifa*), God is "with them" (*ma'ahum*: not *ma'īya*); *tajallī ma'anī al-sifāt* (not the attaining of the knowledge of the attributes). F.F. is Ash'arite. *Tajallī* is Sālimīyan. *Lā'ih* is Hanbalite. F.F. does not use them. Makkī says "*takhallul asrār al-ghayb.*" —In this passage F.F. tries to alter the famous passage by Makkī (imitated already by Ghazālī?) in an Ash'arite way (cf. also Fakhr Rāzī).

It is because of his Ash'arism that Fakhr is so violent against the Hanbalites Ibn al-Kayzānī and Ibn Marzūq (*Rūh qadīma*, which runs the danger of leading to *wahdat al-wujūd*, to static existential monism. [See also his commentary on the sentence "*ya sirra sirrī.*"]

[26] "*Ilā fi'yati fī ghayrihi'l-'umra afnati*" (verse 301) is extracted from Hallāj's retort made to Khawwās (Farghānī, *Muntahā* [bib. no. 508-a] I, 310). Cf. "*yuzāhimuni*" in verse 208; cf. *Dīwān*, pp. 15, 68, 85, 89, and "*ya'dhubu 'adhābī,*" verse 72 = *Dīwān*, p. 123. The role of Īkī (d. 697).

[27] Verse 76 (= *Dīwān*, p. 62; and Jīlī, *Recueil*, p. 149); verse 455; verse 449.

him and who are insufficiently initiated, the lover should see himself as unworthy of the state of communicating Prophet[28] that he involuntarily avowed, and ask to be put to death.[29] This was what happened in the case of Hallāj, Farghānī notes; but, to Ibn al-Fārid, the one who has clearly realized that the Qur'ān and tradition confirm his certainty that God is in everything, and that everything is within him to bear witness to God in a lasting way, is prevented by this certain knowledge from exposing himself to be killed: "One whose blood God has not made it lawful to shed cannot be blamed for that, and the allusion[30] (to theopathic locution) contains a meaning whose definition is (of necessity) restricted" (verse 394).

This explanation is not completely candid; there is a hiatus between the outward role that the lover is entrusted to play and the inner state that would be conferred upon him, since, according to Farghānī, this state is an exclusive Ahmadian privilege (the "aw adnā" stage).[31] The notion that one must be conscious of the whole of creation in order to have the right to say the Creator's "I," is one of Ibn 'Arabī's ideas; and by adopting it, Ibn al-Fārid moved away from Hallāj, especially when he said that his "I" was the same as that of all profane lovers, including Jamīl, Buthayna, etc.[32]

d. Mursī

Abū'l-'Abbās Mursī came to the city of Qus and went into the 'Izzīya madrasa on the bank (of the Nile), which originally was a ribāt. Many people gathered around him; he did a great deal of good for the fuqarā', many of whom, from the Maghrib and elsewhere, entered the Way under his guidance, may God keep him in His Mercy. I met him once in the home of Shaykh Nāsir al-Dīn (-b-'Abd al-Qawī)[33] in Qus, and derived much good from the experience. It was Shaykh Jalāl al-Dīn (Dashnāwī), may God keep him in His Mercy, who said to me: "Come with me to see Shaykh Abū'l-'Abbās (Mursī). The fuqarā' do not go to see him at just any hour, I objected. But he forced me (or pledged an oath that he would oblige me) to go with him. Which I did. I found the shaykh (Mursī) seated on his heels in a trance, his eyes bloodshot, his teeth chattering, his beard dancing on his chest. I did not greet him nor did I speak, since that would have been inappropriate for us at such a moment; I moved away and sat down some distance from him. But Shaykh Jalāl approached him and sat down very close to him after greeting him.

[28] Istihqāq tab'an, cf. Akhbār, p. 50.
[29] Ishāra, cf. Shushtarī.
[30] Verses 276-285 and 382-396; cf. also verses 99-102 concerning voluntary death.
[31] In actual fact, Ibn al-Fārid considered himself raised to the rank of "insān kāmil."
[32] Verses 240-261. See his tomb, in this edition, 3, Figure 33.
[33] This account of 'Abd al-Ghaffār Qūsī (Wahīd, ms. P. 3525, f. 86a) is remarkable because of its degree of accuracy: it is an official report. ([On Qūsī, see] Zabīdī, 'Iqd., 194.)

And the shaykh (Mursī): "By God, the One of whom there is no other, we hate only two things among the *fuqahā*': the fact that they excommunicate Hallāj and that they insist Khidr is no longer alive.[34] What do you say about it?" —"Master, people are divided with regard to Khidr: some say that he is dead, because of Qur'ān 21:34-35: 'No one before you has been given immortality by Us; should you die, and they be immortal? (No), each soul will taste death'; others say no, for Khidr would then have appeared at the funeral of the Prophet."

Mursī resumed: "I saw Ibn Abī Shāma[35] in a dream (or upon waking), he shook my hand[36] and said to me: 'I shook the hand of the Prophet in this way,' then he taught me the (fourfold) deprecation of Khidr, which is: 'O God, be merciful to the Community of Muhammad, forgive it, calm it (*aslih*), protect it (*ajir*)[37] those who recite it became *abdāl*.'[38] —I awoke and I was going to see (or, visit the home of) my shaykh (Shādhilī): now, I found him reciting this same prayer. Going afterwards into the *sūq*, I saw three men, and I had a sense inwardly that one of them was Khidr; I went back to see my shaykh, who raised his head: 'Ahmad?' —Yes, at your service! (*labbayka*).'[39] 'It was indeed he, you have divined him.' After this, while I was mending my cord (*rifās*), Khidr appeared to me: he told me his name, and enabled me to detect the spirits of those who believe in the divine mystery. And, by God, the One of Whom there is no other, I saw your spirit among those spirits." And Shaykh Jalāl turned to me to take me to testify to that before the shaykh. Now, Mursī, when he spoke, he turned toward me, staring at me, which made a great impression on me. Then the shaykh (Mursī) added: "And what do you think about Hallāj?" —"Master (responded Jalāl), I used to love and admire him; then I learned that he had said:[40] 'It is in the confession (*dīn*) of the Cross that I shall die' and that did something to me (or a word I cannot now recall)." —Mursī resumed: "So, what is this? Confession (*dīn*) is the instant (of avowal), the climax: according to the verse (Qur'ān 1): O Lord of the Day of *Dīn*." This was therefore an allusion to the fact that he would die on a cross: which actually happened. Then Mursī began to recite a *qasīda*[41] by one of the sages, a part of which I remember:

Come, let us enter the cave (*hānā*), we shall drink there as I please.
Let us break the pulpit of the mosque, we shall make my flutes out of it.
Let us yank the qādī's beard, we shall make my (lute) strings out of it.

[34] Statement attributed by Sha'rāwī to Shādhilī. Shaykh Jalāl was a *faqīh*.
[35] Son of the historian, d. 665.
[36] A kind of initiation. In 646, Ibn Abū Shāma was already dead and buried in Alexandria (Abū Shāma, *Dhayl*, ms. P. 5852, f. 201b).
[37] Cf. the prayer of Ma'rūf Karkhī.
[38] That is, the apotropaic saints, universal intercessors.
[39] The word of sacralization uttered on hajj. In fact, in line with the general teaching of later Sūfīs, formulated by 'Alī-b-M Wafā' (ap. Sha'rāwī, *Tab.*, II, 28), the disciple who contemplates the spiritual perfection of his shaykh sees the Divine Presence (*Hadrat al-Haqq*) in it encircled by the spirits of all the masters of the Way including the prophets; to forsake his shaykh to go to Mecca would be to forsake the real place of God's appearance, where He shows him these spirits, to go look for their mere physical traces (the commentary prudently adds: this does not refer to the obligatory hajj).
[40] This edition, 3, 220-221.
[41] In dialectal Arabic.

And Mursī commented on these lines with wit, saying: the "mosque" is the court room of the heart (or perhaps something else), the "pulpit" is the devil's own, the "qādī" is Iblīs, and some other explanations: God give him good fortune. I remembered this meeting (*majlis*) by heart from beginning to end; the moment (that we lived through) was a moment of trance and intuition (*waqt hāl wa wijdān*). Mursī himself explained himself, which is not to be overlooked.[42]

e. Ghamrī Wāsitī and His Intisār

M-b-'Umar Ghamrī (d. 849/1445), from Miyat Ghamr,[43] devoted a special chapter to Hallāj on a defense[44] "of mystical Reality, of *tasawwuf*, of the miracles of saints, and of the sanctity of Hallāj." This chapter must have been a response to the attack against the Qussās (popular mystical preachers) published by Zayn 'AR 'Irāqī (d. 804) and his son Ahmad (d. 821), an attack also refuted by 'Alī Wafā' in which we know that Muhāsibī and Ghazālī themselves had been maligned. Hallāj being the most exposed of these early mystics, Ghamrī defended him, not on the philosophical level on which he was condemned as a precursor of the existential monism of Ibn 'Arabī, but on the strict ethical level of the early masters of fervent prayer, of which the Sunnite traditionists since Silafī, especially in Egypt (with Alexandria as the center), considered Hallāj a model. Ghamrī based himself in this instance on a famous traditionist, Fakhr Fārisī, and we have seen above the arguments used.[45]

Was it solely through traditionists of the school of Fakhr Fārisī (Damirī, Qalanisī d. 765) that Ghamrī felt obliged to defend Hallāj? It is possible, since Ghamrī's fervor expressed itself in the reconstruction of mosques (among others a Ghamrī mosque in Cairo in which he appointed a certain 'Alī Ghamrī [817, d. 890] as *khatīb*[46] and tutor of his son; the latter was a disciple of Damirī). But it seems that he owed his initiation into mysticism, not to the two orders to which Fakhr Fārisī had belonged, but to the Junaydīya order restored by Ibn Buzghush Shīrāzī (d. 678) or rather created and directed in Egypt by a Kurd from Guran, Yf 'Ajamī (d. 768, a disciple of Shamshīrī), Hasan Tustarī (d. 797: tomb

---

[42] [Mursī was] buried, like Ibn 'Atallāh, in Alexandria, a Shadhilī center.

[43] *Daw'* VIII, 238.

[44] *Kitāb al-intisār fī'l-dhabb 'an tarīq al-akhyār*, Brusa ms., Ulu Cami 169, ff. 13b-84a; Hallāj fills ff. 38b-42a; I verified that the manuscript was transferred on September 14, 1951, to the mosque adjacent to number 4 in the Qaysariya alley (noted by H. Ritter); photographs given by Professor Suhayl Unver and Father Anawati.

[45] His *Bayān al-'unwān* (Samannādī [?], 85) criticized previously by Shirāwī (*Tawīl* [?], p. 189) for being excessive.

[46] *Lawāq*.

in Mousky), and Ahmad-b-Sul Zāhid (d. 419),[47] a passionate preacher, who moved men as well as women, and who retired for fifteen years to Ghamrī and chose Madyan Ushmūnī (d. 862) as his main executor for it from among his close associates. The latter succeeded the great Shams Hanafī, the Shādhilī, who died in 847 and passed the Khudayrī *isnād* to Zakk.

Ghamrī lived out his last years in Mahallat Kubra, of which he is the patron "saint" (it is the leading industrial city of the Delta). His work was continued there for about a century by his son Ahmad (d. 905), who founded the Tawba mosque there (in a red-light district), and by his grandson, Abū'l-Hasan (d. 939). Ghamrī continued to be venerated in Cairo in the area of his Ghamrī mosque[48] thanks to two brothers, 'Alī and Ahmad, rich merchants who were *khatībs* in it and bore his *nisba*, down to the time of Sha'rāwī (connected with Ghamrī through his master M Shinnāwī [d. 932],[49] who had organized the meetings of his budding congregation in the Ghamrī mosque).[50]

f. Sayyid Murtadā Zabīdī

Sayyid Murtadā Zabīdī (d. 1205/1791), whose great commentary on the *Ihyā'* of Ghazālī was the starting point for an important intellectual movement in Islam, adopted all of the master's ideas about the sanctity of Hallāj.[51] Furthermore, he seems to have been initiated into the *tarīqa hallājīya*. He concluded, with respect to the Hallājian *Anā'l-Haqq*, that "this statement was uttered in a state of intoxication, of rapture, which means that no one should condemn him for saying it. The one who should be criticized is the one who takes such words at their face value." Suyūtī[52] said the following in this regard: "We are obliged not to think badly of a Muslim, especially when tradition affirms that he is regarded as a saint; popular testimony on that is an honest witness, as the Prophet said to 'Umar: 'Do not think badly of your brother for any word he said and which you can take in a good sense.' "[53]

---

[47] Zāhid: ap. *Daw'*.

[48] *Daw'* II, 74; p. 118; V, 308. This mosque is in the Bulaybil *sūq* near Bāb al-Sha'rīya (Amīr al-Juyūsh). Hurayfish was a pupil of Ghamrī.

[49] Ghamrī appears in the *isnād* of the Shinnāwīya, according to Zabīdī (d. 69: between Ahmad Zāhid and M Shinnāwī). Attacks in A.H. 1105 at al-Azhar (Ishbīlī, *Hujjat al-dhākirīn* [?], 46).

[50] *Tawfīq tawīl*, 186: [?].   [51] Reaction to Wahhābism.

[52] Cf. his *Tanzīh al-i'tiqād* based on the *Mi'yār al-murīdīn*.

[53] *Ithāf al-sādah* 1, 250-252.

x. THE SURVIVAL IN ANDALUSIA, THE MAGHRIB, AND THE SUDAN

*a. Ibn Sab'īn, Shushtarī, and the "Hallājian Conspiracy"
in Andalusia in the Thirteenth Century*

It was barely yesterday that great souls expressed the desire for an ecumenical unity of mankind, of which the economic and pedagogic anthem in which we are swept along by the progress of secular techniques often presents only a dreadful caricature.

The founder of Islam (as Gaudefroy-Demombynes emphatically showed)[1] was one of those who had called all sects sharing the lineage of Abraham, the father of all believers, to rally absolutely together. But the "administrative" exploitation of the *Umma* was soon to set off local explosions throughout the whole community, which had been wounded in the "virginal point" of its faith in God by either the hypocrisy or self-interested cynicism of its leaders. Thirteenth-century Andalusia was the setting for a crisis of this kind: just when the *Dhimmis* of the *Umma*, the Jews and Christians, gained their freedom from the Muslim political unity that had tricked them with its contemptuous religious toleration. The community as a whole, threatened militarily and economically (by the Christian Crusades and the exodus of Jewish banking), was faced with two courses of action. It either had to take a hard line against the foreign enemy and its possible "accomplices" within, or open its heart further to all men, in accordance with the sacred hospitality of Abraham, including both manual and intellectual workers, craftsmen, physicians, astronomers, logicians, etc. But if it did the latter, it would be exposed to the accusation of forming intellectual societies working to subvert society, an accusation delivered immediately by strict "observants" of the letter and the law, *Qurrā'* and *Muhaddithūn*. The same had three centuries earlier denounced just such a conspiracy [on the part of the] *Ismāʿīlīs*, from which the rival Fātimid Caliphate had collapsed in 567/1171. This time they believed they had uncovered among the *falāsifa* and the *sūfīya* a new conspiracy of this sort, and they [vowed] to turn its members automatically over to the secular arm, and [affirmed] that it was traceable to a heresiarch excommunicated and executed three centuries earlier: Hallāj (d. 309/922).[2]

---

[1] Ap. *Mahomet*, 1957 ed., p. 382.

[2] It was fashionable in the period to regard Hallāj as an "Ismāʿīlī conspirator." The Ismāʿīlis and Druzes themselves wrote that Hallāj was one of their martyred *Dāʿis*. According to the prophesy in the famous "letter of Hasan Sabbāh," it was the "blood of the just sacrificed in Baghdad by the ʿAbbāsid caliphs from the time of the ʿAlid Imāms down to Hallāj" that would bring on the destruction of Baghdad in 656/1258 by Hulagu (cf. Serefettin

From the trial of Ibn Ahlā (d. 645) to that of Ibn al-Khatīb (d. 776), western Muslim "integrism," helped by such easterners as Ibn Taymīya and Ibn Kathīr, pursued in this way some of the great souls of Islam for being "Hallājians."[3]

1. The Denunciation of Qutb ibn al-Qastallānī

Taken from a *risāla* of Qutb (614, d. 686), preserved by Abū Hayyān Jayyānī (d. 745) ap. *Kitāb al-nudār* (= Pure Gold): recopied ap. Sakkāwī; *Qawl Munbī* (Berlin 2849, f. 43b: a friendly commentary by Dr. Osman Yahia):

And Qutb composed a book dealing with the sect (*tā'ifa*) professing absolute monism. He began with Hallāj, including some excerpts about his life, his poems and his execution. He adds: "when his ideas were disseminated, they were adopted by those who believed that Hallāj had truly realized the perfection (*kamāl*, of mysticism). And his profession of faith (*'aqīda*) was taught,[4] except that one part was not explained by the teacher to the adept; it was openly revealed only to intimate friends among the members who entered into it through the discipline of the arcana, with respect to the aims behind their entering. For the pledge of the professed was made in the hall (*dā'ira*) when he accepted the initia-

---

Yattkaya, *Fatimilèr wa H. Sabbāh*, ap. *Ilāh Fak.* [bib. no. 2253-a], Istanbul, November 192[?], p. 27 Turkish translation, and pp. 41-43, Persian text). —It was Nasīr Tūsī, the great philosopher and Shī'ite *usūlī*, the inspector general of the Abrahamic *waqfs* of Iraq for the Mongols, who officially restored at that time the tomb of Hallāj in Karkh.

In terms of his own psychological make-up, the idea of Hallāj being an Ismā'īlī, suggested by his exegis of A.H. 290, by his marriage to a Karnabā'īya (of the pro-Zanj party in Basra), and by the police inscription on his pillory in 301 ("here is a *dā'ī* of the Qarmathians"), is hard to believe. His use of Salmanīyan terms in his sermons, his "evangelizing" of bandits even in prison (not to make them into "*fidā'īs*" or "police spies," but penitents belonging to a mystical *futuwwa*, studied by us in the *Nouvelle Clio* [1952, pp. 187 ff.]), are clarified moreover both by his rejection of the initiatory robe and by the terrible reproach hurled by Shiblī, his *musāhib*, at him on the gibbet concerning the "secret of Sodom" (*Akhbār al-Hallāj*, 3rd ed., pp. 170-172 = Qur'ān 15:70). Concerning his gibbet, cf. the full-page plate included here.

[3] Denounced, not only to the government as subversive, but also to the pious populace as agents of Satan. On the development of the satanic interpretation of Hallāj, fashionable in early Ash'arism, cf. Introduction to *Dīwān d'al-Hallāj, Cahiers du Sud*, p. xliv, n. 1. It grew out of a kind of Promethean Hallājism advocating general salvation for all creatures, angels and men, elect and damned. There was also the notion that Hallāj, the grandson of a Mazdaean (according to AY Qazwīnī), was a secret Zoroastrian bent on destroying Islam. This is an old idea, rather widely held today; it is sketched out in the work of M Mazaheri and in the attack of Bahjat Atharī (*al-Sha'b*, Baghdad, May 1958: in an interview discussing his recollections [?] of our joint teacher Abū'l-Hasan Mahmūd Shukrī Alussy [1924], in which I am an "accomplice of Hallāj" in that); and even in his beautiful play about the martyrdom of Hallace Mansūr, Sālih Zeki Aktay presents Hallāj and his chosen sister Gülfidan as having a "Mazdaean mentality" (a radio play broadcast in Paris on January 19, 1959, in the French translation of Irène Mélikoff).

[4] The manuscript, which is unique, uses a particularly clumsy phrase here.

tion (da'wa), *just the way it occurred among the Ismā'ilīs;*[5] he promised secrecy about the pursued goals, and the oath of the initiated one was accepted. Over the years this teaching, which had become viewed with suspicion, was continued only by isolated (adepts) scattered throughout various countries. There was a certain 'A 'AA Shūdhī who, at that time, presented it publicly in the countries of the Maghrib. (Qutb adds), He lived in Tlemcen but had no known home where he resided; he was knowledgeable in the (religious) sciences, able to use the technique (sun'a) necessary for stirring illusions (awhām) in souls. He was associated with Abū Ishāq Ibrāhīm-b-Yf-b-M-ibn Dihāq, according to Ibn al-Mar'a, who studied the science of *kalām* with him; it was by Shūdhī that he was initiated (talaqqana), it was said ('alā mā qīla), into this teaching, in secret . . . (S. f. 43b).

Qutb's pamphlet, which is given us by Sakhāwī via Abū Hayyān, along with other pieces, seems to have received a kind of official stamp, for political reasons; it was supposed to have been written by Qutb at the time of his appointment by Baybars as head of the *kāmilīya* following his expulsion from Mecca (by Ibn Sab'īn) in 667.[6]

Mālik Kāmil had founded this *Dār al-hadīth*[7] in Cairo at the demand of conservative traditionalism, which had been upset over the influence of

---

[5] Apart from the "Assassins" of Syria and Kuhistan, there were others who practiced this, even in the Maghrib, notably, the *Khātūfīya* (*REI*, 1954, p. 73, n. 2).

[6] In his *Kitāb al-nudār*. Abū Hayyān is much less detailed in his *Tafsīr* (V, 32; cf. on the margin of III, 448 [= *Tafsīr* III, 449] his *Durr madād*), which had a very wide circulation; and he adds to Qutb's list of heretics those whom he had known personally (Sakhāwī, f. 90a): the two Ibn Labbājs, AH Lūrqī, Ibn 'Ayyāsh A Mālaqī, Ibn al-Mu'akhkhar, M-b-Abī Bakr Ikī, AY ibn Mubashshir, 'Abd al-'Azīz Manūfī Hasanī, 'Abd al-Ghaffār Qūsī.

[7] The list of directors of the *Dār al-Hadīth al-Kāmilīya*: 'Umar-b-H ibn Dihya (622, d. 633), the former tutor of Mālik Kāmil, a Valencian émigré, a Zāhirite and *hāfiz*, very learned in hadīth, at times not very scrupulous in the matter of *isnād*. He denounced the falseness of the 'Alī-H Basrī congregationist *isnād*, and attacked Hallāj above all as a satanic anti-Christ (in his *Nibrās*). His tomb is located near that of Dīnawūsī (cf. *Cité des Morts au Caire*, p. 64). Dismissed, 'Umar ibn Dihya was replaced by his brother 'Uthmān (632 and 634), a grammarian. There was a truce in polemics under his successor, 'Abd al-'Azīm Mundhirī (634, d. 656), a Hanbalite turned Shāfi'ite and Ash'arite who was sympathetic to Fakhr Fārisī and to the Qādirīya religious (Kurdish, like the dynasty). Abū Sahl Qasrī. Then the integrist polemic was resumed by AB M-b-M-b-Ibrāhīm ibn Surāqa Shātibī (b. 592, d. 662), an Andalusian refugee inclined toward the Sūfism of AB ibn 'Arabī (d. 543) and even to that of his homonym from Damascus, but initiated early into the *tarīqa* Suhrawardīya, the congregation "politicized" by Caliph Nāsir in Baghdad to enable him quietly to control the mystical circles, in the manner of the shaykhs al-Mashāykh (cf. *WZKM*, 1948, p. 114), which quickly disgusted the young Shustarī. Ibn Surāqa taught in the Kāmilīya the books of his master, 'Umar Suhrawardī, in opposition to the calendar and to Hellenistic philosophy (Fadā'ih al-Yunān). After him came Rashīd Yf-b-'Alī Attār Misrī (660-662; Zabīdī, 'Iqd., 59), head of a little "politicized" congregation, the Saharmīnīya. Next, Tāj 'Alī-b-M ibn al-Qastallānī (b. 588, d. 665), an Andalusian émigré, a Mālikite formed in Mecca, who was succeeded by his brother Qutb AB M-b-A-b-'Alī ibn al-Qastallānī (b. 614; 665-686), the author of the polemical writing examined here. After him came Ibn Daqīq al-'Īd, who lasted until 695 (cf. also, f. 230b).

the Shāfi'ite schools of theology founded by Saladin, the *khānqāh* Sa'īd al-Su'adā' and the Manāzil al-'Izz, in which Shihāb Tūsī (d. 599) and Fakhr Fārisī (d. 622) had been declared Hallājians. Qutb, a Mālikite, in principle was not hostile to Sūfism. He was to be buried near 'Izz Maqdisī, beside AB Turtūshī (d. 520: gave the *khirqa* to Abū Madyan, *'Iqd*, 90-91; cf. *Cité des Morts*, p. 67). Affiliated with two "politicized" *khirqas* through two of his predecessors, Ibn Suraqa (Suhrawardīya) and 'Attār (Sahramīnīya), Qutb accepted neither the philosophy nor the Hallājism dealt with together in his pamphlet. Qutb added two things to Ibn al-Zubayr's basic documentation of the "Hallājian" heresy of Ibn al-Mar'a (as viewed through Ibn Ahlā): first, he focussed his attack on Ibn Sab'īn; then he combined haphazardly the various heads of the mystical school with that of the *Tahqīq*, the only one alluded to by Ibn al-Zubayr, showing by this his ignorance of the philosophical differences that divided them, in contrast to both Ibn Taymīya and Ibn al-Khatīb, who pinpointed them to combat them[8] and to excuse them,[9] respectively.

The intellectual mediocrity of such hunters of sorcerers as Ibn al-Zubayr[10] and Qutb, concentrating on the base police records of independent and recognized thinkers, did not discourage Abū Hayyān Jayyānī from joining in the work of Qutb beginning in 679 in Cairo. Scholars both of them, they wormed their way into the company of many of those whom they intended to disqualify, and one wonders how Abū Hayyān had the gall to be surprised when Ibn Hānī and Najm Jurjānī turned their backs on him.[11]

This is how Qutb constructed his pamphlet, the title of which is still to be stated:[12] concerning a "summary" set forth by A 'AA M-b-M-b-'Umar-b-Rashīd ibn al-Darrāj[13] Ansārī (*qāri'*, a third-degree disciple of M ibn Sharīh Ishbīlī 388 x 476 [?]), entitled *"Imātat al-adhiya al-nāshi'a min sabātāt al-Shūdhīya"* (= a sweeping up of the evils derived from the filth of the Shūdhīya). This *"mukhtasar"* abridged a fragment preserved by Abū Hayyān written by his master, the noted *qāri'* Abū

---

[8] Ibn Taymīya distinguished between Ibn 'Arabī, Sadr Qunawī, 'Afīf, and Ibn Sab'īn ("*ihāta*") (Sab'īnīya, 90 ff.). The *"masāhir"* of Ibn al-Fārid classifies him separately.

[9] An account of the "search" of the Malagueno sorcerer Fazārī: to track down the talisman that prevented the sword from cutting into his neck (*Durar* [?] I, 85).

[10] The so-called "rape" of 'Afīf (S. f. 97b).

[11] Sakhāwī [bib. no. 670], ff. 95a, 97a.

[12] Either *"Irtibātāt"* or *"Nasha sarīha min qarīha sahīha fī'l-man' min al-da'wa wa'l-shath"* (S. f. 43a).

[13] His tomb still existed in Ceuta in the fifteenth century in Rabd Barrānī at the wall by the sea (the "butcher's shop"): according to M-b-Q Ansārī, *Ihtisār al-akhbār*, edited by Lévi-Provençal, ap. *Hespéris*, 1931, p. 147, n. 2 (a friendly commentary by G. S. Colin).

Ja'far A-b-Ibrāhīm Ibn al-Zubayr (627 and 708), of the *"Rad' al-jāhil 'an i'tisāf al-majāhil"* (= to deter the ignorant from deviations in uncharted deserts): A long and wordy factum written in youth against Ibn Ahlā, a disciple of Ibn al-Mar'a, and against his *"Tadhkira"* dealing with the reform of the *Umma*. The author tells us that he resided for several years (*sinīn*) in Lorca with Ibn Ahlā to teach grammar to his son. Ibn al-Zubayr verifies the fairness with which Ibn Ahlā governed Lorca, from the depths of the grand mosque, all the time remaining committed to the secret teaching of Ibn al-Mar'a until his death (in 645). His successor, Ibn Mutarrif (d. 663), did likewise in Murcia (from within the Jāmi'). The *Rad'* must have given some details there, not only related to *fiqh*, but also to *usūl*, concerning the heresy that Ibn al-Mar'a had received from Shūdhī.[14] Taking advantage of his influence gained through close association with the first of the Banū'l-Ahmar of Granada, Ibn al-Zubayr had a certain Saffār[15] stoned in 670 as one of the *Shūdhīya*[16] in the presence of his pupil Abū Hayyān. This early feat encouraged Abū Hayyān and Qutb, to whom he must have sent the "summary" of Ibn al-Darrāj at the time of Qutb's debates with Ibn Sab'īn in Mecca; hence, prior to 667.

2. Its Aims and Its Juridical Results, from the Shūdhīya to Ibn al-Khatīb

Abū Hayyān Jayyānī states in his *Tafsīr* (V, 32) that the pamphlet of Qutb began its list of heretics with Hallāj (summarizing his life, giving some of his verse, and alluding to his punishment) and ended with 'Afīf Tilimsānī (probably because he was the son-in-law of Ibn Sab'īn). The eleven names:

Hy-b-Mansūr Hallāj, A 'AA Shūdhī (from Tlemcen), Ibrāhīm-b-Yf-b-M-b-Dihāq (= Ibn al-Mar'a), A 'AA ibn Ahlā (master from Lorca), AB ibn al-'Arabi Tā'yī, 'Umar-b-'Alī ibn al-Fārid, 'Abd al-Haqq ibn Sab'īn, AH Shushtarī (his disciple), Ibn Mutarrif A'mā (disciple of Ibn Ahlā), al-Sufayfir (*id.*), and 'Afīf Tilimsānī.

"Proving by their behavior, their statements, and their verse their commitment to this teaching" (of the *wahda mutlaqa*).

Qutb, himself a Sūfī, attacked thoroughly only their opinions, not

[14] According to *Durar* I, 85.

[15] In common parlance, "Sufayfir": he had fled Murcia to Almeria in 668 (S. f. 94a); a friend, Nāfih, got himself killed after him.

[16] In the following century, the lists of *Shūdhīya* ("sensu largo") were arranged in an absurd manner, with Hallāj shifted three centuries. In Sakhāwī, f. 33a, in which two lists became all entangled up ('Ayzarī, *Fatāwa*, edited by Tāj Fāsī, *Ta'rīkh Makka*, and the historian 'Aynī), Hallāj appeared twice: once between Shushtarī and Ibn Shadāra ("AH Hallāj"; S. corrects thus: *"sawābuhu"* Hy-b-Mansūr, *"qaf madā"*), another time between Shūdhī and Ibn Mubashshir ("Hallāj": S. corrects: *"huwa Hy-b-Mansūr taqaddama'l-dīwān, wa huwa min ashāb Ibn Sab'īn"* (*sic*).

their congreganist affiliations (sometimes multiple), suggesting that a special discipline of the arcana, of the Ismā'īlī variety, was being practiced among them.

Ibn Taymīya, more blunt, summarized this list of Qutb's (without naming him, for he had had an argument with Abū Hayyān) while treating it (with *isnād*) as *khirqa*: (*Rasā'il kubrā* II, 99): "(the only mystics who have not condemned Hallāj are those who, professing *hulūl* and *ittihād* (absolute or individual), rediscovered in those the doctrine taught and defended by Hallāj. And this is why (the *isnād* of) the *khirqa* of Ibn Sab'īn listed many masters of iniquity (*rijāl al-zulm* or *al-zulūm*? of darkness?)."

This attack was not aimed only at Shūdhī and Ibn al-Mar'a, but at the Greek philosophers from Hermes to Aristotle before Hallāj, who had been claimed previously by Ibn Sab'īn in his *Masā'il* (f. 316-317) and boldly listed in the long *Qasīda* of Shushtarī, "*Arā tāliban minnā . . .*" that Ibn al-Khatīb admired so much:

"I understand, you ask this excess (Union) of us which surpasses the rewards (Qur'ān 10:27), —And your thought shot its arrow beyond Eden. . . . We have scorned the fates (created, *huzūz*) which were offered our glances, —for a nobler goal and a higher purpose. . . . Say: for me there is no other goal than Your essence (*Dhātika*) (verse 17). . . . Now, His three aspects shine (*talūhu*) for us, —as the seer (*rā'ī*), the mirror (*mar'ayy*), and the vision (*ru'ya*) (verse 23). . . . And He has enslaved the *Hermeses* (with His love: *tayyama*) (verse 41)." (N.B.: the discontinuous achromic list of the Muhaqqiqīn begins here in verses 41-67:

Harāmis;[17] Socrates; Plato; Aristotle;[18] Dhū'l-Qarnayn;[19] Hallāj; Shiblī;[20] Niffarī;[21] Habashī;[22] Qadīb al-Bān;[23] Shūdhī;[24] Suhrawardī;[25] 'Umar ibn al-Fārid;[26] Ibn Qasyī;[27] Ibn Masarra;[28] Ibn Sīnā;[29] Tūsī;[30] Ibn Tufayl[31] and Ibn Rushd;[32] Shu'ayb;[33] Tā'yī;[34] Najl al-Harrānī;[35] Umawī;[36] Ghāfiqī.[37]

[17] These are the three Hermeses.

[18] Because of the Plotinian *Uthulūjīya*; cf. on the Plotinian *attraction*, a statement made by Bergson to Maritain: ap. Henri Bars, *Maritain en notre temps* (Paris, 1959), p. 323.

[19] For his role as "guided one" of Khadir-Eliyas in sūra 18.

[20] Shiblī: we know that the classical *isnād* of Sūfism, according to Qushayrī, goes from Junayd to Shiblī and Nasrabādhī, while "leaving out" Hallāj; in this instance, it is Hallāj who resumes his place alone at the beginning of the *isnād*.

[21] The author of the *Mawāqif*, with commentary by 'Afīf.

[22] 'AA-b-Badr Habashī, to whom Ibn 'Arabī dedicated his *Hilyat al-awliyā'* in 599.

[23] The famous Mawsilī.

[24] Cf. *infra*.

[25] The martyr of Aleppo and eponym of a discontinuous *isnād*.

[26] Was Ibn al-Fārid a Hallājian?

[27] Because of his *Khal' al-na'layn*, which is being edited by J.D.G. Domingues.

[28] Died in 319; thus an obvious anachronism here.

[29] Because of his *Ishārāt* and his *Tayr*, which are neither works of gnostic symbolism nor ludic gymnastics.

We have here, in its highest form, a spiritual aspiration that exceeds that of natural religion, a pure desire for the Divine Essence in Its naked truth, a supraconfessional consummation in *Tawhīd*. It is clear that neither the *fuqahā'*, the *Qurrā'*, nor the *muhaddithūn* could tolerate such a thing. Furthermore, since Hallāj, these spiritual men knew that one must die to oneself in order to take part in divine Joy: "be *Mujāhidūn* and I shall be *shahīd*" ("the Law of Muhammad kills Saints," just as the Law of the City State kills Socrates, by his own consent: cf. *Akhbār al-Hallāj*, p. 70, n. 6).

Ibn al-Zubayr had ordered Sufayfir stoned; Qutb, unable to get Ibn Sab'īn executed, succeeded in getting Ikī dismissed and in getting 'Afīf exiled. Less than a hundred years later, 'Imād ibn Kathīr (701, d. 774), the rigid Shafi'ite so revered by the present-day Salafiya and the Wahhābis, repeats the very particulars of Qutb's denunciation in a *fatwā* rendered in Damascus against a preacher using the mystical poems of the same Ittihādīya school. He bases the outlawing of these men expressly on the *ijmā'* that condemned Hallāj to death, an *ijmā'* affirmed by the Mālikite imām, AB Māzarī, and one concurred with, according to Ibn Kathīr, by Ibn Khafīf, and Ibn 'Alā'.[38] The following is the list of these nine "major blasphemers" (S. f. 117b): Ibn 'Arabī, Ibn Sab'īn, Sadr Rūmī (= Qunawī), 'Afīf Tilimsānī, Shushtarī, Ibn Hūd, Harīrī, Ibn Ahlā, Ibn al-Fārid.

With the last being the worst, these poems offer "poison in a crystal cup." On the authority of Ibn Kathīr, Ibn Abī Hajala, the author of the *Dīwān al-sabāba* and of *Sukkardān*, a specialist in profane love, wrote his *Ghayth al-'arīd* against Ibn al-Fārid and the other eight, and was later buried with this text in his shroud (in 776).

The unexpected violence of this poet against Ibn al-Fārid,[39] comparable (almost) to that of Ibn Dāwūd against Hallāj, aroused great emotion among Andalusian scholars. And Ibn al-Khatīb responded to it in his fa-

---

[30] Ghazālī.   [31] For his "Ibn Yaqzān."
[32] For the *Tawhīd al-khāssa*; cf. *Recueil*, 1929, p. 191.
[33] Abū Madyan of Tlemcen.
[34] Ibn 'Arabī.   [35] Hayāt Harrānī: cf. Jāmī, 620.
[36] Shaykh 'Adī, whose Hallājism Shushtarī could have known about only in Egypt, in the *Zāwiya 'Adawiya* of Cairo: cf. our *Cité des morts*, p. 58.
[37] Ibn Sab'īn. Cf. ms. P. 3347, ff. 208a-212a.
[38] Because of the tercet "*Subhāna . . .*"; which is debatable in the case of the first, and false in the case of the second.
[39] Cf. Biqā'ī, *Tanbīh al-ghabī* [bib. no. 661-b], Cairo, 1953, p. 215 (against the lapsus in Brockelmann, *GAL* II, 13). Pages 213-258 of Biqā'ī are against Ibn al-Fārid.

mous "*Rawdat al-ta'rīf fī'l-hubb al-sharīf* (Damascus ms., Zah. tas. 85, ff. 101b-111a): in which he lists in six categories "the seekers of God":
(1) The Greek philosophers; (2) the *Ishrāqīyūn* (Hermes and the Muslim ones); (3) the *falāsifa* (Muslims); (4) the *muntammīn* (Ibn al-Fārid, Ibn 'Arabī, Ibn al-'Arīf, Ibn Barrajān, Ibn Qasyī, Būnī); (5) the extremists, partisans of *Wahda Mutlaqa*: Shūdhī, Ibn Dihāq, Ibn Sab'īn, Shushtarī, Ibn Mutarrif, Ibn Ahlā, al-Hajj Maghribī (variant: 'Uranī), the people of *Wādī* Riqut (near Murcia: cf. E. Lator, *Budd*, ap. *al-Andalus* 1944, p. 373, n. 3 and *Don Quixote* II, 54); (6) the *sūfīya qudamā'* (Nasrabādhī is cited there but not his master, Hallāj, who is cited elsewhere, f. 126).

This list, reproduced by Sakhawī (f. 125) in connection with Ibn Abī Hajala, separates two of the nine "accused" from the latter—namely, Ibn al-Fārid and Ibn 'Arabī—to defend them fundamentally; and three to pardon them: Ibn Sab'īn, Shushtarī, and Ibn Ahlā (with their first two masters, which should be noted).

If we compare the list of Ibn al-Khatīb with that of Ibn Khaldūn found in his *Shifā'* (Tanjī ed. 58, 61), it includes only two numbers: (1) the *Tajallī* school: Ibn al-Fārid, Ibn Barrajān, Ibn Qasyī, Būnī, Hātimī (= Ibn 'Arabī), Ibn Sūdagin; and (2) the *Wahda* school: Ibn Dihāq (Ibn al-'Arīf's commentary), Ibn Sab'īn, Shushtarī. These two numbers of Ibn Khaldūn correspond to numbers (4) and (5) of Ibn al-Khatīb, which indicates that they took this classification from their joint master in Sūfism, Abū Mahdī ibn al-Zayyāt (mentioned as such by Ibn Khaldūn in a manuscript [autographed copy of his *Muqaddama*] with friendly commentary by M. Tanjī).

In this same year, 776, Ibn al-Khatīb was sentenced and executed in Granada.[40]

3. The Early Shūdhīya: Ibn al-Mar'a and Ibn Ahlā of Lorca

We are once again dependent on what Qutb tells us for our knowledge of *Shūdhī*.[41] What he says is probably taken from Ibn al-Mar'a, through whom, according to Qutb (copying here Ibn al-Zubayr, without saying so), Imām A 'AA M-b-'AA-b-A Fadl Sulamī Mursī gives us this tercet by A 'AA Shūdhī:

When the Being (*Wujūd*) has aroused to ecstasy the desire for reform (*islāh*) of certain people (*qawmin*)
By permitting them the same utterance as the Being

[40] It is highly probable that "*Rawdat al-ta'rīf*" contributed to this execution.
[41] Qutb, ap. Sakhawī, *Qawl munbī* [bib. no. 670-c], ff. 33a, 43b, 90a, 125a, 125b; Ibn Taymīya, *Sab'īnīya* [?], 107; *Durar kāmina* [?] I, 85.

Then this utterance is no longer intelligible (*in'ijām*)
And yet it baffles the understanding of the fool
And if we (are quiet), it calls (us) from nearby
For it is not "you" whom we call from afar.

Ibn al-Mar'a depicts Shūdhī as a wandering mendicant intoxicated with God, roaming in Musalla through the *sūqs* of Tlemcen (on the Bab al-Qarmadin side). Ibn Maryam adds that he was buried at Bab 'Ali.[42]

Why did A 'AA Hallawī Shūdhī, qādī of Seville, flee to Tlemcen to follow this unusual vocation? Rather than assume with Qutb that he was using it to cloak a conspiracy, and while granting that he had acted in this way to imitate Hallāj, we connect this "Hallājian" conversion of a Sevillian qādī more with a series of visions in which some Sūfis, Ibn 'Arabī in Cordova and Shādhilī at al-Aqsā, envisioned the Saints interceding with the Prophet in an effort to lift the excommunication of Hallāj in 609, on the three hundredth anniversary of his execution.[43]

The life of Ibn al-Mar'a Awsī is better known.[44] An undisputed *mutakallim*, master of Sulamī Mūrsī, he preached and taught in Malaga. Exiled to Murcia, he died there in 611. There is no doubt that he founded a *madhhab* of *kalām*, the school of *Tahqīq al-Tawhīd*, a "Way of Realization" of the Divine Unity through a flight over intellectual contemplation, a unification of the ninety-nine Names of God reduced to the Hallājian "*al-Haqq*," "the Creative Truth." A way involving the *isqāt al-wasā'it*, the legal observances, and alphabetical talismans (Qādī Ibn al-Murābit, in Malaga, stupidly accused him of cabalistic marvels, like Hallāj, like Itfīhī).[45] Ibn al-Mar'a had probably drawn this *Tahqīq* from the works of Ghazālī and from his Ash'arite *kalām*.[46] I published his refutation of the (Sālimīyan) thesis of Ibn Masarra about the real plurality of the divine attributes. His two main pupils were Ibn Ahlā and Ibn Sab'īn (with 'AR-b-Wasla).

M-b-'Alī Ahlā (580, d. 645) seems also to have been an undisputed *mutakallim*[47] and the police records that Ibn al-Zubayr published to smear him, thereby abusing hospitality, are unreliable. Qutb, following Ibn

[42] Ibn Maryam, *Bustān* [?], 68-70.

[43] Cf. *P.*, pp. 383, 424.

[44] Qutb, ap. Sakhawī, *l.c.* [?], f. 27b, 34a, 151b.

[45] Maqrīzī [see bib. no. 2157A], I, 459-460 (G. Wil [?]) s.a. 516.

[46] He comments on the *Irshād* of Juwaynī (cf. our *Recueil*, 1929, p. 131), the *Mahāsin* of Ibn al-'Arif [bib. no. 287-a]; he must have taken the *Tahqīq* from the *Muhaqqīq* of Ghazālī (*Mustazhirī* [bib. no 280-g], 30; cf. *REI*, 1933, p. 531 (the remark of an Ismā'ilī); *Maqsad Aqsā*. [?], 73-76).

[47] Qutb, ap. Sakhawī, f. 31b, 32b, 33b, 43b, 92b, 93b, 117b, 236b; P. ms. 2156, f. 174b, calls him "Ansarī"; but Sakhawī claims he was the son of wealthy landowning converts.

al-Zubayr, shows he too is incapable of understanding his *"Tadhkira"* concerning the theological and social reform of the *Umma*; he at least recognized the great fairness *(taswiya)* with which he ruled Lorca (f. 92b). The imprisonment he suffered in Malaga, the relentlessness of the attacks against his memory by pamphleteers, and the slander that reached as far as Mecca, thanks to the hatred of Abū Hayyān and Qutb (Ibn Daqīq al-ʿĪd, who succeeded Qutb in the Kāmilīya [*Quraf* (?) IV, 94] debating there on Ibn Sabʿīn, said "this is the [condemned] teaching of Ibn al-Marʾa and of Ibn Ahlā),[48] cost him to be defamed again in 776. Abū Hayyān left us the names of his pupils: the two Ibn Labbāj brothers (AH, Yf), AH Lūrqī, ʿAlī-b-M ibn Mutarrif Aʿmā (d.663),[49] and Sufayfir.

4. Ibn Sabʿīn, His Metaphysical and Political Thought[50]

Examination of the *Kitāb al-ʿatf* of AH Daylamī led me in 1950 to locate the *interférences philosophiques et les percées métaphysiques* that led Hallāj to define Divine Essence as "Essential Desire" (ʿIshq = *Dhāt al-dhāt*); and I expressed the hypothesis (p. 293) that these theological texts preserved by Daylamī must have led Ibn Sabʿīn to believe that Hallāj had been "initiated" into the esotericism of the Greek philosophers. The latter would constitute part of the grounds for the denunciation of Qutb, unless a new problem, that of an authentic Hallājian relationship with the Shūdhīya, were not to force us to link them more to the Qurʾānic *ikhlās*.

It is with Ibn Sabʿīn that the double aim of this neo-Hallājian movement becomes completely clear to us: the *social reform* of the Muslim *Umma*, endowed with an executive, an *Imām* who is a model of fairness, under the spiritual directorship of the head of a *"dīwān al-sālihīn"* endowed with a *rūhānīya ʿīsāwīya*, living in Mecca as head of a brotherhood of itinerant ascetics;[51] and the elaboration of an "Abrahamic" monotheistic *dogmatic theology* of abandonment to God *(islām)*, positing Divine Essence as the supreme goal of scholastics, in the realization within ourselves of His unity, *Tahqīq al-Tawhīd*, not through the vision of intellectual observation, but through the *"fiat"* (*kun*, feminine *kūnī*)[52] of the will's abandonment.

---

[48] *Ibid.*, f. 95b-96b.

[49] A homonym, ap. Shāmī [?], 674.   [50] [See below, p. 416, n. 36.]

[51] The Sabʿīnīya, under the direction of Shushtarī, pursued their ideal of community life, as *mutajarridun* in the form of nomadic brotherhoods of wandering ascetics (cf. the similar effort of the Harīrīya in Hauran), in face of the failure of settled urban communities (accused of allowing more than four simultaneous wives and of drinking wine).

[52] The copula "to be" is without duration in Semitic languages (cf. "o ōn" of the Septuagint, Ex. 3:14); the Ismāʿilis, by deriving the first emanation "*kūnī*" from *KWN* (an ac-

What is original about Ibn Sab'īn is the fact that he attempted to create a metaphysical propaedentics with this renewed mystical effort of Hallāj, whose theory of love had been compared by AH Daylamī to that of the pre-Socratic Greek philosophers Empedocles and Heraclites[53] —by basing it on the Aristotelian theory of hylomorphism,[54] and through a movement in Islam similar to the Thomistic movement, especially of Eckhart, in Christianity.

The scholastic undertaking of Ibn Sab'īn brought about a rectification of the theses of Ibn Sīnā and Ibn Rushd, symmetrical with that undertaken by St. Thomas. It did not have the same success as did Thomism; *falsafa* endured, moreover, only on the fringes of *kalām* with the masters of *ishrāq* (Sadr Shīrāzī).

Like Hallāj, Ibn Sab'īn had wanted to construct a metaphysical way of approach to the transcendent, inaccessible Divine Essence, one that would be for everyone, "enemies and friends"[55] alike, that of the Jewish *Shema' Israel* and that of the Qur'ānic *sūra al-Ikhlās*. He was not trying to dilute the "negative" miracle of an Incomparable Uncreated Word (*I'jāz*) by rationalizing it as the Mu'tazilite school had, but rather to "drink it pure" by conforming to the savor of His inspiration. Ibn Sab'īn, after combining the Hallājian *'aqīda* concerning transcendence[56] with the Ash'arite one (of Juwaynī in *Irshād*)[57] in a form similar to that of Ghaz-

cidental analogy: *ka'anna*), and the Avicennians, by deriving the category *"wujūd"* from WJD (the instant of sorrow or ecstasy in the consciousness), ended up in existential monism.

[53] The edition prepared by J. Cl. Vadet. Cf. my study "Interférences philosophiques . . . dans la mystique hallagienne," which appeared in *Mélanges Joseph Maréchal* (Brussels, 1950), II, 263 and 270, n. 2. Also, the "Hellenizing" commentary on the *Manāzil al-sā'irīn* (of the rigid Hanbalite Ansārī) by 'Afif, corrected by Ibn al-Qayīm.

[54] For *"morphe,"* turning from the sense of "appearance" (physical) to the sense of "apparition" (intelligible). Cf. previously Paul (*Phil.* 2:7). Hallāj (ap. Daylamī), before Ibn Sab'īn, imprints on the word *"sūra"* the same "semantic countenance"—form = immaterial structure = the "divine essence" of beauty (cf. Baudelaire).

[55] Cf. *Akhbār al-Hallāj*, 3rd ed., pp. 133, 162, n. 3; cf. *Mél. W. Marçais* (Shushtarī), p. 261, n. 2. This exalted universalism, so unappreciated, made pardonable the approach of quackish vanity that was so offensive in Ibn Sab'īn (and which shocked Ibn 'Abbād).

[56] The Hallājian *'aqīda* is classical in Sūfism (Qushayrī, Kalābādhī); it derives from as it refines the testimony of Ibn Hanbal on behalf of the transcendence of the Word and of the Spirit expressed in "vulgar" terms. In a parallel way, Hermetism considered Enoch and Idrīs "Sabaeans" (hence, the prophetic revelation of Seth [= Agathodemon]); Thābit-b-Qurra had published the *"Nawāmis"* of Hermes guided by simple ascetic *ilhām* to a realization of the transcendent unity of God, one very close to the Hallājian and the Sab'īnian *'aqīdas* (cf. appendix to Festugière, *Révélation d'Hermès*, 1944, I, 390). Cf. the piece by Ibn Sab'īn, ap. *Recueil*, 1929, p. 134.

[57] Deficient on the *rūh* (*Recueil*, 1929, p. 131), which is the reason for Ibn Taymīya's irony, 103, line 1.

ālī,[58] turned his attention to the *falāsifa* (whereas his predecessor, Ibn 'Arabī, who was not well-acquainted with them, belatedly, like Ghazālī, touched lightly on the agnostic *'aqīda* of the Ismā'īlī *Ikhwān al-safā'*). He realized that the mediating element between man and the Divine Essence could not be an angelic emanation (tainted with matter) like Ibn Sīnā's Unity of Intellect or Ibn Rushd's Unity of the Active Intellect. He discovered that the whole of believing humanity could be philosophically described as being in the process of unification with God, through a supremely enveloping *form* (*ihāta*),[59] the Creative Word (*kalima jāmi'a*) and the personalizing spirituality (*rūhānīya 'īsāwīya*), constituting each of the human Elect as *Muhaqqīq al-Tawhīd*, that is to say, as a witness in time of the Divine Reality (this is an extension of Hallāj's theory of the *shāhid ānī* "standing up erect with the beloved" because "in renouncing his characteristics, his conformation came into conformity with His."[60]

This "conformation with God" occurs through a relentless *via negativa* and is expressed through a linguistic alchemy that reduces the *I'rāb*, trifunctional vocalization of Semitic grammar, to unity. Through a sublimated *jafr*, it sublimates numbers, volatilizes the (28) letters of the alphabet (both numerals and consonants),[61] breaks the magical *"sīmiya"* that imprisons bodies in their *talisman*; it frees souls from it briefly[62] in a supreme, infinitely pure resonance of the three Semitic functional vowels (from Akkadian to Qur'ānic Arabic): *"hū"* (= He, the Adored One, Qur'ān 113:1), *"ah"* (= the supreme Name of consolation for sufferers, according to Sarī' Saqatī), *"īhi"* (= the relation to supreme Truth, the function of the *jarr*, according to Ibn Sab'īn, in folios 453-471 of his *Ihāta*).[63]

Ibn Sab'īn tried to isolate "philosophically" the Hallājian *shahāda*, "*lā Huwa illā Huwa*" (solidified by Ibn Rushd), by means of the famous couple *"Aysa-Laysa"* of Kindī exploited by the Ismā'īlīs, which is identical with the Eckhartian *"ichts-nichts."* His Muslim *shahāda* becomes

---

[58] A passage from *"takhalluq bi asmā' Llāh"* or Jurjani on *Tahqīq*: since Ghazālī (*Mustazhirī*, 30; *Maqsad asnā*, 73), Ibn Barrajān, and Ibn al-Mar'a commenting on the ninety-nine Names of God as a single Name, al-Haqq, for the *Muhaqqiqūn*. See also the al-Mohadin *'Aqīda* of Ibn Tūmart.

[59] Ibn Taymīya, *Sab'īnīya*, 91, 93 (*ba'd al-wahīd, 'umra*), 94, 104, 116.

[60] *Al-ittisāf bi-ittisāfihi*. Thomistic hylomorphism shows how the Divine Essence can be in a single man (God: Christ, the substantial *form* of His existence and his thought), and in other men who are beatified, their intelligible form being accidental (Rp. Joseph Michel de Montmirail, a note concerning Hallāj).

[61] Cf. Ibn Sīnā, *Nayrūzīya*: note *Essai*, 2nd ed., pp. 98-103; and *Arabica*, 1954, I, p. 12.

[62] Ibn Sab'īn believes less clearly in bodily resurrection (denied by the *falāsifa*) than Hallāj and Suhrawardī of Aleppo.

[63] *Recueil*, p. 137; and *Ihāta*, ff. 453, 471.

"*laysa, illā'l-Aysa*," which is to say "there is nothing except this Nothing." Like Hallāj, he was conscious of exceeding in his "*Bustān al-maʿrifa*" the boldness of his most famous predecessors' formulas.[64] One might say that Ibn Sabʿīn put forth in this formula of *Tahqīq al-Tawhīd* the most compressed philosophical formulation of the Hallājian "*Anā'l-Haqq*": a "death of God" in the martyr.

The individual has steps he must climb before he reaches the level of *Muhaqqiq*, which Shushtarī mentions.[65] But did Ibn Sabʿīn teach as Ibn Taymīya, following Qutb, accused him of teaching, that there was a continuous series, an *isnād* of *Muhaqqiqīn*, stretching from age to age, necessary for "achieving the *hikma* presented by the Hermeses and the *ʿilm* taught by the Prophets"?[66] The deliberately interrupted and acronycal *isnād* given by Shushtarī in his *Qasīda*, and the criticisms directed by Ibn Sabʿīn at Ibn Sīnā, Ibn Rushd (he spares only Ibn Bājja and Tufayl[67] among *falāsifa*), and Ghazālī among Sūfīs, dissuades us from thinking so. And the unimportant *isnāds* attributed after him to the *Tarīqa Sabʿīnīya* are only subterfuges.[68]

A hierarchy of simultaneous ranks in the society to be reformed—in the Muslim *Umma* and in the other, Jewish and Christian, communities—corresponds to successive degrees in the individual's ascent. Here

[64] "*Mashraba kulliwārid*" (Ibn Sīnā, *Ishārāt*), "*mā wahhad'l-Wāhida*" (Ansārī, *Manāzil*, end) (*Ihāta*, f. 450).

[65] *Maqālīd* [?], f. 440. In this magnificent Cairo ms., DK, tas. 149, its contents summarized as follows: *K. al-ʿaqd* (with commentary), *K. al-nasīha* (*risāla nūrīya*), two anonymous fragments, *al-anwāʾ*, two anon., *Wasāyā fī anwār al-Mustafā* (in two parts, separated by two fragments 202, 204), *Ral-Faqīrīya*, 205-242 (with a piece cut out, 213), *K. al-ridwānīya* (243-292), *K. hikam wa mawāʾiz*, fragment of an anon. work, *K. al-qawsīya* (I believe by IS) *Kitāb Allāh bi'lisān mūrihī* (ibid.) (no. 16) *juzʾ fī'l-faraj wa'l-ikhlās* (*Hizb al-fath wa'l-nūr*. *Hizb al-hifz wa'l-safawa* (?) *Hikam* (double *supra*). *K. Bayʿat ahl Makka li'l-Shaykh Ibn Sabʿīn* (p. 273 = *al-Ridwānīya*). *Kitāb* by Ibn Hūd (d. 699). *Risāla qudsīya* by Shushtarī, *Sharh al-Fātiha wa marāt* (ibid.) *al-Fāʾizīn*. *Tatimmat al-kullīya* by Ibn Asbāt (277), *R. al-suhba* by Ibn Watīl (282), *Idhāh fī . . . tanāwul al-tayyibat watarkihā* by SʿA ʿAzīz Qustantīnī (293), *Istinbāt al-wasīla* (by him), *al-dharīʿa* (by him), *Mawāʾiz* (by him), *fī jamāʿatin ijtamaʿūʾl-ziyāra* (by him). *Fī sabab iqbāl al-khalq ʿalāʾl-sulahāʾ watarkiʾl-fuqarāʾ*, *murqāt al-zulfā wa* (ʾl)-*mashrab al-asfiyā* (*sic*) by AB ibn Tufayl (323). *Al-Tajrīd* by Shaykh ʿA ʿAzīz, *al-Asbāb* (also by him). Sayings of Shaykh ʿAbd al-Qādir (RD). *Al-Maqālīd al-wujūdīya* by Shushtarī (413-443), *K. al-ihāta* by Ibn Sabʿīn (pp. 444-477). A *qasīda* by Shushtarī (478). A fragment of the work (end). AR Badawī edited three of them in Madrid, ap. *Revista Inst. Est. Isl.* (1956), pp. 1-45 (*Nkhriya*), 1957, pp. 1-103 (ʿAqd), and 1958, pp. 11-34 (*Ihāta*).

[66] Ibn Taymīya, *Sabʿīnīya*, 91.

[67] His "*lā addabathuʾl-maʿārif*," cited ap. *Ihāta*, f. 473.

[68] Probably decided upon by the school of Ibn Qunfud (Constantine): cf. the *isnād* of Zabīdī, *ʿIqd*, 57, with *Budd*, Berlin ms. 1744, f. 127b (*Akhbār*, p. 203): these *isnād*, going back through two "*muhaqqiq*" to Junayd (via AT Makkī) and to Jaʿfar Sādiq, have as known intermediaries only Qadīb al-Bān and AQ Tūsī (= Ghazālī?).

too Ibn Sab'īn tries a method whose approach is philosophical. He too has his utopia of the Ideal City "drawn into conformation" with God through his "rightly guided" leader, "Mahdī." In contrast to the Ismā'īlīs, he does not believe in the blind rule of the discipline of the arcana imposed by a spiritual oligarchy; he no longer believes in the efficacy of an elemental rationalization of the revealed Law, reduced by an external hygiene. The Sab'īnians believe that the suffering masses become increasingly mindful of the Holiness of God through the participating compassion of their leaders at the trial. The *Muhaqqiq* must therefore find leaders for the community who are just. Ibn Sab'īn for this reason found himself involved at Ceuta in a "cultural" reconciliation between the Almohad Rashid and Frederick II, drafting his famous *"Masā'il Siqillīya"*[69] this being the first attempt at a philosophical presentation of *Tahqīq* (in A.H. 641). Two years later, he sent his brother to Pope Gregory IX in Rome to make sure that the word given to the Beni Hūd of Murcia not be broken (in fact, Murcia was captured only in A.H. 668). This was to be inserted into the sequence of very noble efforts at "valid" Islamo-Christian interchanges, begun by the gesture of St. Francis of Assisi toward Mālik Kāmil at Damietta (in A.H. 616), continued by Mālik Kāmil returning Jerusalem to the "Christian" Frederick II, its king (in A.H. 627),[70] and culminating in the arrival of St. Louis at Carthage (in A.H. 668 = 1270 of our era) to "persuade" Mustansir. In fact, R. Brunschvig has shown[71] that the "crusade" of 1270 was influenced by Raimon Marti of the Dominican theological Studium, established since 1243 in Tunis, who was received in Paris by the king.

This Islamo-Christian contact grew out of a long convergence of philosophical preoccupations. The Christian West, going beyond the Greek East, which had never been able (and is still unable in Russia) to develop a scholastic dogmatic theology, had begun to develop one in Toledo around 1130: through a catalysis of the Muslim *kalām* with a minimum dose of the Hellenistic philosophy, which Ghazālī had allowed (in logic and in psychology), and which Israel was getting ready to adopt with Maimonides. Furthermore, it was through Jewish translators, from Latin to Arabic (through Hispanic romance), that Christian theologians constructed the scholastic edifice whose foundation Thomism (more than

---

[69] Studied by Amari (*JAP*, 1853, pp. 239 ff.) and Mehren (*JAP*, 1879, pp. 341 ff.).

[70] Cf. H. Gottschalk, *Al-Malik al-kāmil* ([Wiesbaden], 1958, pp. 152-160: from the perspective of straight political history).

[71] R. Brunschvig, *Berbérie Or. sous les Hafsides* [bib. no. 2039-a], 1940, I, 57, 462, 469; Berthier, cf. *Rev. Afric.*, 1932, p. 2.

Scotism) completed. A scholasticism founded, as we have just seen in the case of the Ghazalian neo-Ash'arite *kalām*, on the negative definition of the transcendence of the Divine Essence, the *Ikhlās al-Tawhīd* expressed in *sūra* 112, (which Manuel Comnenus had forbidden the Byzantine bishops to anathematize in 1182, threatening to call in the pope to settle the matter, which the Lateran Council of 1215 confirmed[72] against the tritheism[73] of Joachim and the emanationism of Amaury of Bena; originating with Avicenna).[74] Thomists, the Dominicans, fortified with the powerful weapon of a sharpened Averroist Aristotelianism,[75] set up permanent contacts in the Islamic world for an intellectual reconciliation through their "Studia." In Tunis they found a group of Murcian refugees, disciples of Ibn Sab'īn who had the favor of Mustansir, to be better partners than the "logicians" whom Frederick II had used in his relations with Mālik Kāmil. In 1269 when St. Louis, in a heroic act, told the ambassadors of Mustansir (October 9, St. Denis) that he would allow himself to be put in the Saracen prison (already known by him at Damietta in 1249) if Mustansir and his people became Christians, Raimon Marti succeeded in diverting the fleet crossing toward the Holy Land for a peaceful stopover in Tunis, where an *entente spirituelle* between St. Louis and Mustansir might have been begun had St. Louis not died shortly after disembarking. There was no further attempt at a *parôle donnée* between Islam and Christian France until the Capitulations of 1536 between François I and Suleyman.

Mustansir had taken the (Almohad) title of Commander of the Faithful in A.H. 651; and in 656/1258, at the time of the capture of Baghdad. Ibn Sab'īn, who was for several years the spiritual advisor of the sharif of Mecca, the Hasanid Abū Numay, made him deliver the *bay'a*[76] on the Night of Destiny (27 *Ramadān* 656) to Mustansir on behalf of Sultan Sayf D Qutūz, who, in the name of Caliph Mustansir and confirmed by the Prophet in a dream, saved Islam from the Mongol invader at the battle of Ayn Jālūt (25 *Ramadān* 658). Ibn Sab'īn during these years acted as the conscience of Islam; he had hopes of inducing Mustansir to make an ex-

---

[72] Cf. Denzinger, *Enchir[idion symbolorum* (Freiburg)], 1908, no. 432: "*una quaedam summa res est . . . Essentia sed Natura Divina: quae sola est universorum principium . . . et illa res non est generans, neque genita, nec procedens, sed. . . .*"

[73] That "tritheism" which calls the tritheistic Christian apostate (Maimonides).

[74] The "amatricien" return of this ideal model to us predestined in the Divine Essence is a kind of satanic refusal of Union.

[75] The suppression of the emanationism of the ten *'Uqūl* (Ibn Sīna), of the *'Aql fa''āl* (Ibn Rushd). Similarly, Shushtarī condemns "*tanāsukh, dawrāt.*"

[76] *Histoire des Berbères*, de Slane, ed., I, 416-428; cf. Cairo ms. Dk. tas. 149, Paris ms. 2065, f. 129b; cf. R. Brunschvig, [bib. no. 2039-a], I, 45-47.

tended truce with the Christian states of the West in order to permit eastern Islam to confront the coalition of Greeks (who had just recaptured Constantinople, in 660/1261) and Mongols.

But Baybars assassinated Qutūz and fabricated a dynasty of fictional 'Abbāsid caliphs in Cairo (a "Mustansir" [sic] 13 Rajab 659, followed by a "Hākim," 8 Muharram 661); still the prestige of Ibn Sab'īn remained such in Mecca that during the hajj in 667, Baybars had to recall Qutb Ibn al-Qastallānī to Cairo from his mission to Mecca to attack Ibn Sab'īn. Ibn Sab'īn died there in a quasi-Stoic act of suicide on 28 Shawwāl 668 (or 2 Shawwāl 669), opening his veins "out of desire for God."

Ibn Khaldūn has preserved for us the text, attributed to Ibn Sab'īn, relating the bay'a of 656. This is a very interesting apocalyptic text built on four Qur'ānic passages (48:1-4; 44:1-6; 28:1-5; 81:1) and two hadīths. It was, I believe, as the confidant of the mysterious "dīwān al-sālihīn," which, according to the Sab'īnian Manūfī,[77] attached itself to the Laylat al-Qadr (on Mt. Hira), that Ibn Sab'īn was to install Mustansir (whose son Wāthiq was to preserve the "caliphate" for two years).

This brilliant and brief political intervention by the Muhaqqīq al-'Asā, followed by his voluntary death, was rather in keeping with the style of total impoverishment ("iftiqār mahd") professed by Ibn Sab'īn: a mysterious philosophical death in imitation of Socrates (Empedocles and Cato), of the satī of the Hindu widow, of the Brahmachari gymnosophist,[78] and even of the rite of "the binding of Isaac," by which rabbis at that time, at the request of their mothers, were strangling circumcised Jewish infants whom dreadful bishops wanted to baptize by force. This testimonial suicide is a supreme appeal to God's justice against the false swearing in the Holy Name committed by His servants. It is only through brief and tragic pulsations that the heart of the Umma can realize its Unity at the sites of the Qurbān and Qurbānīyīn: at its Qibla.

A List of the Early Sab'īnīya (taken from Sakhāwī)

'Abd al-Wāhid b. 'Alī Madījī Gharnātī b. al-Mu'akhkhar, usūlī, imām of the Meharist caravaneers (Mahrānī), retired to Dechna (east of Fao, Sa'īd), f. 29a; M-b-A Aswad Aqta' Mālaqī f. 95a; —M-b-'Ayyāsh Qīnī Malaqī, ibid.; —Zayn D ibn al-Habāb Ermentī of Qus, f. 31b, 95a; master of 'Abd al-Ghaffār Qūsī, author of the Wahīd, f. 93b; —M-b-Abī Tālib Ansārī (d. 727), Durar II, 458, Brock. II, 130, from Hattin (near Tiberias) and Rabwe (near Damascus), f. 31b;—Najm D Jurjānī Isfahānī

---

[77] Durar kāmina I, 273-274.
[78] For whom the body means nothing.

Hattīnī, f. 31b, 33b; —Ibn Abī Duql, *Mujāwir*, Mecca, f. 31b, 95a; —'Abd al-'Azīz Manūfī, d. 707, disciple of Zayn Ermentī, f. 92b; —A 'AA ibn Shadāra Gharnātī, *Mujāwir*, Mecca, f. 33a; —Abū'l-Hukm ibn Hānī Gharnātī, *Mujāwir*, Mecca, *qāri'* trained in the home of Ibn al-Zubayr with Abū Hayyān, f. 95a; AB Qudsī, disciple of Ibn Hānī and Ibn Abī Duql in Mecca, f. 95a; —AH Shushtarī, f. 95b (*vide infra*); —Abū'l-Fadl Raqqām Tūnusī, called to Cairo, reciter with 'Alā' D Qunawī: Ibn al-Lihyānī wanted him in Tunis (in 694), f. 97b; —Muhyī D Isfahānī, also with Qunawī, f. 97b; —Amīr Hasan ibn Hūd (d. 699) of the ruling dynasty of Murcia, head of the Sab'īnīya in Damascus, converted Jews there; buried by Badr D ibn Jamā'a (who listed Hallāj in his *"Qāmūs al-Shu'arā'*," f. 97b; —Nasr Manbijī, the famous opponent of Ibn Taymīya, in Cairo, in his *zāwiya* outside of Bab al-Nasr, f. 103a; —Najm D Jurjānī, studied the *usūl* with Abū Hayyān, f. 98a; —'Alī al-Mugharbil, a friend of Harīrī (with M-b-'A Rahīm Bājirqī, f. 34b) in Damascus, f. 150b; —M-b-'Abd al-Malik Manūfī, first a Madyanī in Egypt,[79] afterwards Sab'īnī, f. 31b.

5. Shushtarī (d. 668)[80] and the Agape in His Nomadic Brotherhoods[81]

Qutb's attack against Ibn Sab'īn was based on a poem by Shushtarī; Shushtarī was passionately devoted to his master, Ibn Sab'īn, and we owe to him our knowledge of the kind of monastic life followed by Ibn Sab'īn with his disciples, a kind of life that his philosophical works do not describe, though they lead to it.

In actual fact, we find the Truth (concerning our ultimate goals) only by practicing a common rule of life with colleagues in work earning a proper living estimated at a just price: their gaining of the bread and wine of (symbolic) Hospitality in the peace of God.

Shushtarī, in his prose works, such as the *Maqālīd*,[82] about the Sab'ī-

---

[79] Cf. *REI*, 1951, p. 86.

[80] Cf. our study ap. *Mél. W. Marçais* (1950, II, 251 ff.; cf. ap. *al-Andalus*, tr. E. Garcia Gomez, 1949, pp. 29 ff.); —'Alī Sāmī Nashar edited the *"dīwān"* ap. *Rev. Inst. D'gipcio Stud. Isl.*, Madrid I-I, 1953, 175 pages; Spanish tr. *ibid.*, 190 pages; and prior to that the English tr., (Cambridge, Great Britain) typed thesis (cf. also the review *Adab*, Beirut, 1944). —Nashar studied seventeen manuscripts (*stemma* not established) and abstracted the technical terms (*Khalīfat al-dayr*, etc., ap. English thesis, pp. 114-115: compared with Hallāj); the metrics of *zajal* and their links with the "romance" are not studied [in this thesis]; it followed 'Abd al-'Azīz Ahwānī (against G. S. Colin) in order to minimize the scabrous side of Shushtarī's dialectalism. Cf. his edition of the *Dīwān al-Shushtarī*, Ma'arif, Cairo, 1960, 488 pages.

[81] [See below, p. 419, n. 49.]

[82] *Kitāb maqālīd wujūdīya* (ff. 413-443 of Cairo ms. Dk tas. 149) describes the mystic route; the Law is regarded as Nature's medication; we find in it the nine steps of "knowl-

nian rule of life, envisages an ascetic tradition going back to Muslim "desert fathers" directly "connected" with Christian ascetics and their "*logia*" of Jesus, breaking like them the bread of hospitality (*hadīth al-talqīm*)[83] and making vows. In his poems, Shushtarī speaks also of the wine reserved for the Elect by *sūra* "*hal atā*" (Qur'ān 76:1); this wine, which is forbidden to the faithful in this world, uncovered in secret by the adepts of the Salmānīyan guilds (Ismā'īlīs, Nusayrīs, Druzes), was desired by Sūfīs at an early time, especially after Hallāj[84] —like the pre-eternal cup of our predestination as men (of flesh and blood) to Divine Love, of which the consecrated wine of Christians is only the prefigure. According to Shushtarī, the Muslim Sūfī "follows" an asymptotic line with the Christian ascetic; he venerates, without sharing in, the Christian Holy Grail in a form of invitation to the final punishment. Hallāj was executed for having "stolen" in broad daylight[85] the Cup set aside for the angels. And his disciples chant, along with Shushtarī, for the Chalice and the Deacon cup-bearer of the heavenly banquet, reduced in this world under the features of equivocating sacristans of the district set aside for Christian minorities and their tavern keepers; for that is where, among the Muslim mountebanks and prostitutes who frequented it that Shushtarī, with Promethean boldness, came to call men to repent, sublimating in his poems the crudest vocabulary and the most provocative rhythmic cadences of the "milieu."

Nabulūsī tells us, not without emotion,[86] of the joy he felt in having located the tomb of Shushtarī[87] in Cairo. After having looked for it (as we did) beside the Qarāfa, he finally found it (for the purpose of meditating there, twice) to the east of Bab Zuwayla, right in the middle of the

---

edge" (f. 430) and the five degrees of initiation; there is even a list of twenty-six heresies (numbers 25-26: *falāsifa, ahl al-tanāsukh wa'l-dawrāt. Usūlī*, he received the *ijāza* of the *mustasfā'* from Ghazālī (Nashar, *l.c.* [?]).

[83] *Akhbār al-Hallāj*, 3rd ed., p. 203.

[84] Before Shustarī, Andalusian literature barely mentions Hallāj, apart from the historian Qurtubī 'Arīb, the Pseudo-Majrītī (*Picatrix*) and the poet AJ A-b-'A Mālik Ansī Ansārī (d. 550, Almeria: in his death-song). [Mediaeval Latin translation of Arabic text published under this title. See Hellmut Ritter in *Studien der Bibliothek Warburg*, XII (Leipzig, 1933); and Henry Corbin, *Man of Light* (Boulder, Colo., 1977).]

[85] Kilānī, ap. our *Passion*, p. 412: *Qissat al-Hallāj*, ap. *Don. Natal. Nyberg*, Stockholm, 1954, pp. 102 ff.; French tr., ap. *Lettres Nouvelles*, Paris, May 20, 1959, pp. 23, 26-28, 34 (no. 36 of the text); *Akhbār al-Hallāj*, 3rd ed., pp. 117, 131, 153.

[86] *Haqīqa wa majāz*, Cairo ms. DK jughr. 344, f. 120b-127b.

[87] After Damietta, we looked for it in Cairo specifically in Musky (corrigenda to the inscription published ap. *Mél. W. Marçais*, 1950, II, 276, can be found in our *Cité des morts au Caire*, 1958, p. 73 n. 2). Nashar did not resolve the problem (the biographies of M Sharqī and Ahmad Bābā' did not help solve it).

Christian tavern district, in Harat al-Nasara, a setting which, as Nabulsī notes, truly conforms to the atmosphere of mystical intoxication found in his poems.

In praising the spiritual rapture of an outlaw like Hallāj, in glorifying his execution by showing the pickaxe of the Law destroying his Kaʿba (his body as a condemned man),[88] Shushtarī was clearly not thinking of an appeal by an Ismāʿīlī conspirator to subversion of the state. And the tactical use made of it in this sense by Qutb was not without hypocrisy. Nor was what Qādī Abū ʿUmar did against Hallāj (with the letter to Shākir about the Kaʿba).

Among the disciples of Shushtarī whom we pointed out in 1950, Abū Yaʿqūb ibn Mubashshir (S: Musattir), the hermit of Bab Zuwayla, who was his true successor, must be singled out as being without peer. He told how Shushtarī snatched him away (aqlaʿ-ahu) when young and brilliant from the home of his father in Tunis to go live with him his life as a wandering mendicant. The tutor of Jāshangir, Saʿd al-Dawla, built him a zāwiya to the east of Bab Zuwayla. If Nabulsī was shown the body of Shushtarī there, it was because it may have been transferred there; but belatedly, since Sakhāwī says that in his time people still visited his tomb in Damietta (S. f. 95b).

6. The Zāwiya of Ibn Sid Bono and Its Present-Day Counterparts (in Mauritania, Albania, and Bengal)

In 1949, in the course of his research on Ibn al-Khatīb, Lévi-Provençal pointed out to me that this acute writer had observed in the Albaycin of Granada, in the zāwiya of Ibn Sid Bono, dances performed (in a regular rhythm, without excess) to poems by Husayn Hallāj and his like. The choice of these poems by a man excommunicated and executed, and the fact that Ibn al-Khatīb was condemned to death a few years later on grounds of mystical heresy, possibly alluding to his "Rawdat al-taʿrīf," lead us to believe that this zāwiya may have been a cover for a "subversive Hallājian propaganda";[89] in Granada, where "Sufayfir"[90] had been executed less than a century before for heretical propaganda.

---

[88] Cf. Dīwān of Hallāj, Journal Asiatique, pp. 135-137, —Ibn Dihya, Nibrās [bib. no. 419-a], 105, —and the third verse ("And he bestowed upon you a robe of honor, 'Kiswa,' for your Kaʿba [fated to be broken]") of an unpublished poem by Shushtarī about Hallāj, my copy of which improved by Dr. ʿIzzet Hasan, I give here for the verse in question: "Qad salakta yā Hallāj / minhāj al-tarīq. —Saddi dhīʾl-dībāj" waʾnsij ghazlaka ʿIrāqīq. —Wāksi min hallāk hullā baytak al-ʿatīq. —Falammaʾntahayt / falammaʾntahayt. —Wawasalt al-Hadrā / waʾntahā mā mashayt. (Damascus ms., Zah. 8835, f. 44b.)

[89] The references, owed mostly to Lévi-Provençal, ap. Akhbār al-Hallāj, 3rd ed., p. 98, n. 3.

[90] Sufayfir = pejorative form of Saffār (Abū Hayyān Jayyānī [bib. no. 514-a]).

Its founder, Ibn Sid Bono (Abū Ahmad J-b-'AA-b-M Khuzā'ī 'Abid, 544, d. 624), a direct disciple of Abū Madyan and Ibn Hirzahim, is ranked with his great younger colleague Shādhilī, among the Shādhilīya. Like them, he must have received the transmission from the east, through Abū Madyan, of the clandestine collection of *"Akhbār al-Hallāj,"* the lively history of which we have already related. This collection contains, of special interest to us now, a particularly "blasphemous" hemistich allowed by the second Egyptian prior of the Shādhilīya, Mursī:[91] "it is in the supreme court of the Cross that I shall die" and the enigmatic *Tā' Sīn al-Azal*. But these two texts were susceptible to Orthodox exegesis; and neither the mother *zāwiya* of Ibn Sid Bono in Cosentayna near Valencia, later in Elche, finally in Granada (under Ghālib, 653, d. 733 and Ja'far-b-A-b-'Alī ibn Sid Bono, 709, d. 765), nor its Egyptian offshoots, offers any instance of extremism. If Ibn Musdī (d. 663), a Zaydite politically, and a direct disciple of Ibn Sid Bono, transmitted the *hadīth al-talqīm*[92] as originating with Hallāj, this auspicious detail shows merely that this Andalusian *Zāwiya* preserved the memory of a mystic who had been a censor of the vices and crimes of the powerful, a posture traditionally antithetical to that of jurisconsults "kept" by the authorities and "unanimous in excommunicating Hallāj" (Shādhilī).

In our own time, looking at other Shādhilīya, in this instance in Mauritania, we find that the *Ghudf*[93] were denounced emphatically for being a secret society, involved in immoral practices, in which Hallāj is particularly revered. Here again, the *odium theologicum* of the jurisconsults gave rise to suspicion.[94]

In Albania, where the *Bektāshīs*, driven out of Turkey for their secret dissolute ways as freethinkers, survive in a cryptic way under the Marxist inquisition, it is difficult to find out if the central ritual of their early initiation, *"Dār-i Mansūr,"* the Gibbet of Mansūr, still exists as it exists among the Qyzylbash of Anatolia.[95] But this Hallājian feature is not the main cause of suspicion in Sunnite orthodoxy's opposition.

To conclude, we would like to examine in some detail the typical case

---

[91] (*Akhbar*, p. 108.) Two "toned down" recensions of this verse (*Dīwān, Cahiers du Sud*, p. 106) are given on the margin of 1st ms. N.O. 2406:

a) f. 96b: *A lā a'lam akhissā'ī bi annanī / rashaytu'l-bahra wa'nhadama'l-safīna / Nafaytu'ikulla tarran bilā mahalin / Walā"l-janāna urīdu, wa lā Hazira.*

b) f. 97a: *A lā nādaytu ilā'l-ushshāqī bi annanī / ghariqtu'l-bahra wa'd mahalā' safīna / Nataytu'l-shirka, wa'l-tawhīda kullan / Walā"l-mahyata urīdu walā"l-sakīna.*

[92] Akhbār, p. 205.

[93] *Ibid.*, p. 98, n. 2.

[94] REI, 1946, pp. 112-115.

[95] Cemal Bardekai, *Kızılbaslık nedir*, Istanbul, 1945; —Beha Saîd, *Qyzylbaslık* (ap. *Türk Yürdü* IV [1926], no. 22, 250-315).

of the *Mansūrīs* of East Bengal, in which the authorities of West Pakistan, behind an appearance of the greatest courteousness, have yet to permit a direct impartial study of the religious practices of this small surviving Hallājian community.

What is involved here is an ancient devotion to Hallāj and to his martyrdom continued by the Qādirīya, Chishtīya, or Shattārīya. It was revived in the sixteenth century by the "reappearance of Hallāj" (of his spirit) in the person of a "Master of Truth,"[96] *Satya Pir*, born of a houri, Chāndbibi, identified with a daughter of Husayn Shāh, emperor of Gaur. One quasi-Islamized poet, Krishnahari-Dās, depicts him as a conqueror, wearing the *yogi*[97] costume of a Hindu, Raja Mān Singh (d. 1015), to whom Akbar had given authority, as *wālī* of Bengal, over the unworthy Muslim lower classes. And these [classes] are the people today who constitute a fervent group of Mansūrīs. It is the Mansūrīs who, since the sixteenth century, have countered the processions and the Hindu "revival" of Shaytaniya Deba (d. 1534) and of his Mahajana with popular dramas (on the lives of martyrs). But the Islam of the jurisconsults was not grateful to the Mansūrīs for contending in this way; it stigmatized them by means of anti-Hallājian *fatwās*: at their two centers of Sureshwara (Faridpur) and Maij Bhandar (Chittagong).[98] H. Sterneberg has recently filmed for us the "dramas" of Maij Bhandar, and we shall be able to see if they have actually remained Hallājian.

Politically, in 1947-1948, these lower classes, though Muslim, formed in opposition to the federation of Pakistan a coalition of the Mu'min Ansār with Gandhi[99] of which the Mansūrīs were a part. The influence of works like "*Maharshi Mansūr*"[100] by Muzammal Haq brought about a revival in East Bengal, as in the Andalusia of Shushtarī, of an enduring aspect of Hallāj's thought among the poor and the oppressed.

---

[96] Dinesh Chandra Sen, *Hist. Beng. Lang.* 1911, pp. 746 ff.; *ibid.*, *Folklore*, Calcutta, 1920, pp. 100-103. —"*Satya* = truth = *Haqq*."

[97] On yogi infiltrations into Indian Islam, cf. Sanūsī (*Salsabil*, 131-136; on the eighty-four *asanas* of the Yūjīya, s.v. Ghawthīya; — ap. 'Ujaymī); and the *risāla Yūjīya* attributed to Mu'īn Chishtī (ms. Inayat Khan).

[98] *Ann. M. de Mus.*, 4th ed., p. 137.

[99] W. Cantwell Smith, *Modern Islam in India*, New York, 1946, p. 229.

[100] The complete title is "*Maharshi Mansūr, Dharma-vīra Mahatma Mansūr Hallajer alaukika jīvāna-kāhinī*," "The Miraculous Love Story of the Holy and Venerable Mansūr Hallāj," with a preface by C. S. Sen, Moslem Publishing House, 3 College Square (East), Calcutta, 128 pages, with eight editions from 1896 to 1948. This is the legend of the virgin made pregnant by drinking either the blood, ashes, or saliva of Hallāj, and the resurrection in the person of a hero, either Shams-i Tabrīz (*REI*, 1955, pp. 69-91), Nesimi, or Siti Jenar. The virgin is sometimes his adopted sister, chosen to pass the cup of initiatory ecstasy (analogous among the Qaraqirghiz to 'Ayinā or among the Ahl-i Haqq to *Rāmzbār*; cf. their "hunting book," Damyar, no. 108; cf. the Yazīdīs) (Mokri's commentary).

b. Ibn 'Abbād Rundī's Opinion of Hallājian Self-Abnegation

A pupil of Ibn 'Ashīr (from Salé), an Andalusian but settled in Morocco, Ibn 'Abbād, whose *Tanbīh* is based explicitly on the *Nasā'ih* of Muhāsibī and the *'Uyūh al-nafs* of Sulamī,[101,102] and whose personality Asin Palacios has recently studied in detail, left us a collection of letters written as spiritual counsel (to the *faqīh* Yahyā Sarrāj,[103] Mu'addib of Fez), in which several cases of ascetic and mystical casuistry are examined. We have presented elsewhere his opinion of the style of Ibn Sab'īn's works.[104] The following is a response to self-abnegation, in which Hallāj's solution is preferred to that of 'Uways Qaranī:

"As for the problem conceived by X, if he did indeed present it in this way, his solution is clear and should elude no one. Be assured that he who, after having fasted for twenty consecutive days, is given food (vegetables) by God, but sees that someone else needs it more than he, and gives it to him, —such a one is superior to one other, who earns his living, restricts his consumption, and gives alms out of his surplus. And this is so for two reasons: (1) because the first is in a state of detachment (*tajrīd*), a state that is superior to the state of the second, in which the giver lives by his trade; and (2) because the first thought of the gift of food to be given before thinking of his own life, whereas the second gave only of his surplus, nothing more. The objection raised by the fact that the second, in his (ceaseless) alms-giving from his surplus, renounced making any choice of his own, whereas the first chose, does not hold up. Neither of the two, Ibn 'Abbād argues, is concerned with making a choice, but rather with a greater divine reward promised to one who has helped another in greater need—not through his own choice (in the case of the first), but to relieve another misery greater than his own. This only seems to be a choice, for the first is in a state of self-abnegation (*zuhd*), and when one achieves this self-abnegation with a gift out of one's hand, it doesn't matter to whom one chooses to give it; in accordance with the saying 'to renounce oneself is to leave the world in a state without saying: build a *ribāt* or construct a mosque'; and in accordance with the saying of 'Alī: 'to renounce oneself is to forget what one eats in this world, to forget whether it comes from one of the faithful or from an infidel' (which would force one to choose). As for the argument that the second, living by his trade, gives alms out of his surplus without choosing, I fail

---

[101] In two *'Urs* (solar: 10 [or 8] *Māgh*, 22 *Chāitra* [or 8 *Açwin*]): dedicated to Shāh Ghulam ar-Rahman and to Shāh Ahmadullāh [footnote without reference].

[102] Zarrūq, *'Umdat al-murīd*, Kattani ms.

[103] The author of *'Arūs al-Awliyā'* (Bencheneb, *Ijāza* [bib. no. 2033-a], 248).

[104] *Recueil*, p. 146; tr., ap. *Mémorial H. Basset*.

to understand it. For the second may have chosen to whom to give alms, and the prayer that is attributed to him (the prayer of 'Uways): 'O my God, if someone passes this night without food or clothing, don't reproach me for it,' such a prayer, I say, implies that there may indeed exist a needy case more worthy (than the one who received the alms), whom he did not succeed in finding; this prayer is also in keeping with the state of the second (= 'Uways), since it is impossible for him to distribute his surplus to every passerby, and since it must be admitted that somewhere there was a man dying of hunger and naked whom he could have found if he had looked for him; on the other hand, this prayer is one of those that is offered only after one had done one's utmost amply, or if one dreads there is still something left to try. And the desire one has, when one goes out to give alms, to give it to the first who comes, does not necessarily imply that one is obliged to forego making any choice, but rather that one does not want to run the risk of changing one's mind before giving to the first who comes (like the one who decides in the public bath to give his clothes as alms, and who gives them before even going out, because he is afraid he may change his mind). It is said that 'generosity must follow its first impulse.' And that is what can be said about this problem if it is presented as you have told me, for it arouses some suspicion in me, and God knows more about that. The fact that the state of the second, which is known to be that of 'Uways, has been considered inferior by me to the state of the first, which is the state of Hallāj, according to what you have told me based on X, does not imply that Hallāj is superior to 'Uways; one could not judge the state in anyone's favor." And Ibn 'Abbād concludes with a remark of Pauline irony about the pretensions of his correspondent to place the mystics of his time higher than these two old masters.[105]

c. The Shādhilīya

We know the reverence that 'Alī Shādhilī (d. 654/1256),[106] their founder, expressed for Hallāj. "I hate two things about the jurisconsults (fuqahā'), he said: they deny that Khidr may be alive,[107] and they excommunicate Hallāj!"[108]

Khafājī has preserved[109] for us the account of a vision that Shādhilī had

---

[105] Rasā'il kubrā, pp. 221-222 (Recueil, p. 148); cf. Akhbār, no. 66.
[106] See his tomb, this volume, Figure 21. A disciple of AH b-Hirzahim of Fez, flagellated in a dream for having wished to burn the Ihyā' of Ghazālī (Yafi'ī, Marham [bib. no. 541-e], I, 12-13).
[107] Cf. Essai, p. 131, n. 2.
[108] Sha'rawī, Mīzān khidrīya [bib. no. 741-c], f. 14.
[109] Taken from the Muhādarāt (sic).

when in Jerusalem: "I was resting in al-Aqsā Mosque in the middle of the *haram*, when I saw a large crowd enter in serried ranks. And I said, 'What is this crowd? —It is the assembly of Prophets and Messengers of God which has gathered to intercede on behalf of Husayn Hallāj before the (Prophet) Muhammad, upon him be prayers and peace! on the matter of a sin against proprieties[110] which he committed. . . .' "[111] We have seen a similar vision, reported of Ibn 'Arabī, that is more detailed.[112]

After him, Ibn 'Atā' Allāh, Hurayfīsh, Wafā', Hanafī, and Abū Mawāhib extolled Hallāj. The popular legend of Hallāj *"al-qawl al-sadīd"* must be of Shādhilīyan origin.

d. The Hallājian Dhikr *in the Maghrib*

In the Maghrib, the name of Hallāj was preserved only by historians, moreover by scholastics, on account of Ghazālī. Silafī, and then the Shādhilīya, had managed to circulate copies of the *Akhbār al-Hallāj* there; but, after Ibn Sab'īn, it was not until the sojourn of Ibn 'Ayyāshī in the Hijaz in 1072-1074, that the personality of Hallāj inspired veneration in congreganistic circles of Maghribin Mālikite Islam.

Abū Sālim 'Ayyāshī ('AA-b-M, b. 1037, d. 1090) was connected, in Mecca as well as in Medina, with the mystical group of Qushāshī, the *ghawth* of the age, particularly with Ibrāhīm Kawrānī, who edited his travel account (*rihla*), whose value as a document is considerable, and with Husayn 'Ujaymī, who sent him, on 19 *Hijja* 1074, the copy, hastily made expressly for him, at the Ka'ba, of the confidential *risāla* that he had finished the previous year on the forty main Muslim brotherhoods, their litanies and postures used in prayer.[113] 'Ayyāshī mentions them, with the Hallājīya being number thirty-eight[114] among them (cf. his abridged edition, *Mā'l-mawā'id*; a reedition by M-b-Madanī Guennūn, d. 1302).[115]

The *risāla* of Hy 'Ujaymī, in which for the first time the spiritual balance of the entire Muslim world was envisioned as being dependent upon these forty brotherhoods, caused permanent reverberations immediately in the Maghrib. As early as 1112 in Fez, the father of M-b-Tayyib Sharajī (d. 1170); aged two at the time, insisted on conferring on him the *ijāza*.[116] Sharajī who also had received the *ijāza* of 'Ayyāshī (d. 1175),

---

[110] In the sequel to the vision, which is not concerned with Hallāj, Muhammad appears on a throne and introduces Ghazālī to Moses as a "Prophet of Israel." Cf. Yafi'ī, *Nashr* [bib. no. 541-c], f. 103a.

[111] In this instance, the respect due the Prophet.

[112] Cf. this volume, p. 398. Cf. Qūsī.

[113] *Rihla*, printed in Fez, 11, 214, 217 (cf. his *qasīda*, Kattānī [?] II, 443).

[114] *Ibid.* II, 217, 220.

[115] *Ibid.* I, 337.   [116] *Ibid.* II, 396.

conferred that of the *risāla* of 'Ujaymī on A-b-'A 'Azīz Hilālī (d. 1175), which passed on to Sultan S Muhammad I (d. 1204) and to his son Sulaymān (d. 1236), both of whom were Shādhilīya. These two sultans, furthermore, had received the *ijāza* of 'Ayyāshī via M-b-'Abbās Sharrādī Zurādī Qudā (and his father)[117] and H-b-Mas'ūd Yūsī (d. 1102).

Hy 'Ujaymī, who profited among the Maghribins from the fact that, although he was a Yemenite, he had had as his principal master Abū Mahdī 'Isā Tha'ālibī the Algerian (d. in Mecca in 1082),[118] was one of the fifteen masters (of the written *ijāza*) of M Saghīr-b-'AR Fāsī (d. 1134: author of the Minah *Bādiya*, which included the *tarīqa Hallājīya*), again along with 'Ayyāshī.[119]

Finally, the *risāla* of 'Ujaymī was recopied in full (with a different classification: the Hallājīya are number five in it) in the *Salsabīl* of M-b-'Alī Sanūsī (1202, d. 1276/1859), the famous founder of the military order of Sanūsīs (his authorization, ap. *Asānīd*).[120] Kattānī noted that four *isnāds* with authorized *ijāzas* connect Sanūsī in that to 'Ujaymī:[121] (1) going back from his last grandson, the qādī of Mecca 'Abd al-Hafīz-b-Darwīsh-b-M-b-Hy 'Ujaymī, to M Tāhir Sūnbul Madanī, M 'Arif Fitanī, as far as Hy 'Ujaymī; (2) from the same qādī via M Hāshim-b-A Ghafūr Sindī, 'AQ Siddī'qī Makkī Jamāl to Hy 'Ujaymī; (3) from 'Umar-b-A Rasūl 'Attār (d. 1249) to his line of descendants through Abū'l-Fath-b-M-b-Hy 'Ujaymī (and his father); (4) from the same 'Attār via Tāj al-Dīn A Dahhān Makkī, a direct pupil of 'Ujaymī, author of the *Kifāyat al-Mustatlī*,[122] a monograph on the *isnāds* of 'Ujaymī. It should be noted that these four *isnāds* of Sanūsī[123] are eastern; their purpose would therefore be to indicate that he could not have known of the *risāla* of 'Ujaymī before going to Mecca. In actual fact Sanūsī had two *isnāds* of Maghribin *talqīn* by which he knew it already: his local *isnād*, of Oranian initiation (of the Banū Sanūs): via Badr al-Dīn-b-'AA Mustaghānimī and A 'AA M-b-'Alī-b-Sharaf Māzūnī (and his father); and the *isnād*, via Abū'l-'Abbās, of Qutb Tāzī ('A Wahhāb Irshidī, who had the *ijāza* of 'Ayyāshī for his *rihla*), a disciple of 'A 'Azīz-b-Mas'ūd Dabbāgh (d. 1129),[124] of Fez, the famous founder of the Khadirīya, of which the Sanūsīs and the Amīrghanis (a branch of the Idrissīs) are only subdivisions.

---

117 *Ibid*. II, 328.
118 *Ustādha* of Ibn al-Mayyid and Quraysh Tabarīya.
119 Kattānī II, 191 and 31; I, 148.
120 Stenciled French translation by Colas.
121 Kattānī II, 195.
122 *Ibid*. II, 237; I, 380.
123 *Ibid*. II, 389 (*Salsabīl*, Persian ms., 43).
124 Dabbāgh.

e. The Survival in Morocco

Around 1135/1722, a chief of Berber bands from the region near Tin-mel,[125] writing the account of the destruction of his father's *zāwiya* in Tasaft,[126] evoked the memory of great Muslims who had been persecuted in a list which, beginning with Ibn Hanbal and Mālik, finished with Hallāj as its twelfth name, "one of the great saints, an illuminee, a miracle worker, an ecstatic, possessing exalted knowledge to a sublime degree, who traveled in the desert. When the divine graces enraptured him, the jurisconsults hated him, attacked him, denounced him to Caliph Muntasir[127] bi'llāh, and drafted a unanimous legal opinion against him 'by eighty-four jurisconsults certifying that Hasan[128] Hallāj is blasphemous.' But when their judgment reached the sovereign, he read the following into it: 'by eighty-four blasphemers certifying that Hasan Hallāj is a just man.' This miracle did not stop them, but increased their hatred and their rage; they killed him and exposed him on the gibbet, after having cut off his hands and feet; and he laughed and smeared blood on his face to remove the pallor of emotion. All such men have borne the trials of this world through desire for the next life; they have denied themselves the sweet things of this life aspiring to a glance at the merciful face of God."[129]

f. 'Abd al-Kader-b-Muhieddin Hasanī Jazā'irī

Amīr 'Abd al-Kader, whose father, head of the Qādirīya *zāwiya*, must have spoken to him of Hallāj in cautious, but favorable, terms, left us his personal opinion of the Hallāj case only in his last book, *Kitāb al-mawāqif*, written in Damascus on the margin of his readings of Ibn 'Arabī (especially *Futūhāt*, *Fusūs*, and *Tajallīyāt*) and published after his death by Nabīh Hanum in Cairo.

His opinions are not always those of a mere disciple of Ibn 'Arabī. Though he reproduces the interesting text of the *Tajallīyāt* (III, 216-217)

---

[125] 8 km. to the south.

[126] Founded in 1007/1598, destroyed in 1127/1715.

[127] *Sic*: for Muqtadir.

[128] *Sic*: for Husayn.

[129] Hājj M-b-Ibrāhīm Idrīsī Zarhūnī, *Rihlat al-wāfid fī hijrat al-wālid*; discovered and published by Justinard, 1939 (passage omitted in the printed translation).

[Footnote without reference:] In Morocco: Ibn Hirzahim (d. 567/1173); (1) a Kurd *isnād* via his paternal uncle, AM Sālih (Suhrawardīya) → A 'Abbās Nahawandī, Ibn Khafif back to Hallāj; (2) an *isnād* via AB ibn 'Arabī (d. 543) → Ghazālī; (3) → Abū Medzen → Ibn Mashīsh → 'A Rahīm Qanawī and Shadhilī, at the time of the persecutions of the Almohad Zāhirite qādīs: Hajjāj-b-Yf (535, d. 572), 'Isā-b-'Imrān (572, d. 578), Ibn Mudā Qurtubī (578, d. 592), Mūsa-b-'Isā-b-'Imrān and 'AQ Fāsī.

and comments on Hallāj's verses as a *wujūdī* (I, 315; II, 384; III, 61), he also conveys to us two personal impressions:

(1) (I, 31-32): God says out of a sense of reality "I" and His servant says out of ignorance "I". . . . God, enrapturing me in myself, has reconciled me with Myself; heaven and earth have disappeared, the Whole and the part are blended together, *ṭūl* and *'arḍ* have ceased, the supererogatory has become the obligatory. . . . Your genealogies have ceased in the presence of Mine;[130] the Hallājian utterance has been given to me, with one difference, that Hallāj said it, and that it was said to me, without my saying it; something that the person who knows understands and accepts, and that the one ruled by ignorance does not know and denies.

(2) (I, 65): God says to one, do you know who you are?—the fairness that you show, and the darkness that you bring light to . . . you are forever contingent . . . do you know who you are? —Yes: *Anā'l-Ḥaqq* in actual fact, and *al-khalq* figuratively and in accord with the Way, I am the contingent form of the Necessary; the Name *"Ḥaqq"* is essentially necessary to me, and the name *"khalq"* is my assumed differentiating sign. —Elaborate on that. —I have two realities in me, of two distinct kinds: in relation to You, "I" is the Absolute (in Your knowledge and Your attributes) and the Necessary (in Your essence) . . . ; in relation to myself, "I" is the Nothingness without the odor of existence, and the private Relative self at the time of its birth; nor was I present in You for You as a being, and You were not absent from You in my me in my private self. . . . You are the Truth, and I am the Truth, and You are Creation (act), and I am creation (action), and You are not truth, and I am not truth, and You are not creation, and I am not creation. —That is enough: you have understood Me: veil me from those who do not understand Me; for "the Divine Omnipotence" has a secret . . . " (Sahl Tustarī's saying).

The amīr had the *tardiya* follow the name of Hallāj.

g. The Sanūsīya

Hallāj is one of forty patron saints of this militant order.[131] Founded in 1837, it constituted,[132] under the leadership of Sīdī Muhammad al-Mahdī (1859, d. 1901 in Gouro), Ahmad ibn al-Sharīf (1901), and Muhammad Idrīs ibn al-Mahdī (1916), a zone of influence that embraced the Cyrenaic, Tibesti, Borkou, Ouadai, Fezzan, and Touareg confederation; and in Mecca itself it had an important *zāwiya* on Mt. Abū Qubays.[133]

---

[130] Ḥadīth qudsī: *"al-yama ada'ū ansābakum wa'rfa'ū nasabī."*

[131] Sanūsī, *Salsabīl*. Cf. this volume, pp. 28 ff.

[132] It grew out of a reaction comparable to that which gave birth to the militant Jazūlīya order in Morocco, with Muhammad Jazūlī (d. 870/1465), the author of the famous *"Dalā'il al-khayrāt."* Cf. Graefe, *Der Islam* III, 141, and Enrico Insabato, ap. *Rassegna contemporanea*, VI-2, Rome, 1913.

[133] Where Hallāj had lived.

h. The Hallājian dhikr in the Two Sudans and in East Africa

In the Nigerian Sudan, manuscripts of the *Jawāhir khamsa* of Ghawth Hindī spread the Hallājian *dhikr*.[134] As 'Ayyāshī tells us in his *rihla* of the *jawāhir*,[135] in their new edition by Sibghatallāh Bharūchī[136] and their gloss (*hāshiya*: "*damā'ir al-sarā'ir*") by Shinnāwī, he was probably the one who initiated it both there and in the Maghrib. No Qādirī or Tījānī reference noted.

The Shadhilīya *ghudf* of Mauritania are Hallājians.

In 988, the future qādī of Timbuctu, Ahmad Bābā (963, d. 1032), arriving in Mecca with a delegation of Takrur to the home of Qutb Nahrawālī (917, d. 990), became initiated by him into the Rūzbehānīya *tarīqa*, founded by the biographer of Hallāj, Rūzbehān Baqlī; he transmitted it during his exile in Fez to 'AQ-b-A Nu'aym Ghassānī (d. 1032), the master of three Fasiyīn.[137]

In the Egyptian Sudan, the order of Amīrghanīs, an offshoot of the Moroccan Khadirīya, accepts the sanctity of Hallāj, but believes he was wrong to "reveal the secret of the King" (which was told me in Cairo, December 16, 1909, by Shaykh Bādī Sannārī, a direct disciple of H-b-M-b-'Uthmān Amīrghanī, who died a centenarian in March 1910). This is also a Mālikite milieu.

As for Chad, no data.

In East Africa, the following distinctions must be made: in the Comoro Islands,[138] following a Shirazian influence that the Kāzerūnīya order must have brought about, we find today the Shādhilīya. In Somaliland and Ethiopia, it is the influence of the Shāfi'ites from South Yemen, with the Khalwatīya-Sālihīya order. For "Swahili" regions (Zanj and Bantus), no data.

The problem of Hallāj's relations with black Islam crops up, first due to the fact that the burial places grouped around his tomb in Baghdad were described to me in 1907 as belonging to black slaves (Abyssinian or Zanj from the Ra's al-Falahat district). Next, because of contacts that he had in his lifetime with Negroes at court (Muflih, Sa'd Nūbī). Lastly, the South Arabian elements of Yemen which, due to the fact of Negro racial

---

[134] Paris ms. 5359 is Nigerian.

[135] *Rihla* I, 375.

[136] *Ibid.* I, 378.

[137] *'Iqd*, 53; Kittānī I, 76; II, 300.

[138] There were also Kāzerūnīya in Aden at the time of the Mundhirīya domination (came from Sīrāf; hunt the Comoro Islands of Aden; tanners and fishermen between 450 and 554); leaders: Sultān Shāh-b-Jamshīd-b-As'ad-b-Qaysar, his brother Hezārasp, his grandson Abū Samsām Ad-b-Shaddād-b-Jamshīd; cf. Ibn al-Mujāwir, ms. P. 6021, f. 60a-b, 72a-73b; ms. P. 6062, f. 7a, wiped out with the Habash by 'Alī-b-Mahdī in 554/1160.

incursions, are particularly sensitive to the affective elements (*dhikr, raqs*: cf. in Egypt also) of congreganistic rules, have played a role in this matter in the propagation of the Hallājian *dhikr*. Bā' Makhrama 'Adanī (d. 903),[139] from whom Zabīdī received it, 'Ujaymī himself, and 'Umar-b-'Aqīl Bā'alawī Saqqāf (d. 1174, from Hadramut, a link between 'Ujaymī and Zabīdī) belonged to this mixed Yemenite element.[140]

[139] 'Umar-b-'AA Bā Makhrama 'Adanī claimed to be a Kazerūnī and Ghazalian (*Nūr sāfir*, 34, line 7) and transmitted the Hallājian *tarīqa*.

[140] [Chapter IX of the present edition is an enlargement of Section I of Chapter VIII (*Hallāj devant l'Islam*) and Section II of Chapter IX (*Hallāj devant le sūfisme*) of the 1922 edition. It was to have begun with a general table of contents, which has not been found.

Studies that the author planned to include have not been found; they were to have been arranged in the following sections of Chapter IX of the present edition:

II. (Baghdad): Ibn Mardawayh.

III. (Fars): Sa'ib.

IV. (Turks): Sihale Qipçaki, Mahmūdī (*basāratnāma*), Muzammalhaq (*maharshi Mansūr*), Lāmi'ī (*munsha'at*), Sidi 'Alī Reyys, Suleyman Çelebi on *nāsūt, lāhūt*, and *hulūl al-Rūh* re *dewriye*.

VI. (India): Mahmūd Bahrī, Hujwirī, Gisudiraz.

IX. (Arabia): Itfayhī, Ikī, Izz-b-Ghanim Makdisī, Khafagī.

X. (Maghrib, Andalusia): Ibn 'Ammār, Maqqarī (*sirr al-'alamayn*), Tasaftī, the Madyanīya.

Finally, other studies intended for this Chapter IX were to deal with AH Sarrāf, A'A Saidzade (on Ibn Bākūyā), Ishkaveri, Ghulam Ahmed (in Pushtu), Wāmiqī, Sarmad, Sana'ī, Zafar Ahmad, Ibn Ayyub, and Biqā'ī, Fakhr Rāzī (*Anā'l-Haqq*), Najm Dāyā, Ibn 'Arabī (analysis of *jadhwa* and *intisār*), Sinjārī, 'Abd al-Jabbār (*mughnī*), and A Ghazālī (analysis of *radd jamīl, mīzān al-'amal*).]

X

~~~~~~

THE HALLĀJIAN LEGEND, ITS ORIGINS,
ITS LITERARY FLOWERING

I. Oneirocriticism of the *"Mu'abbirūn"*
and Its Importance for the Origins of the
Hallājian Legend

The realm of dreams is a sphere of teeming mental activity, much broader than the region controlled during waking by diligent reason and its censure. In logic we know that when awake, normally intelligent beings use, as modes of conclusive reasoning, only ten of the sixty-four possible combinations (four propositions taken three by three), and that of the forty possible syllogisms proceeding from these ten modes (taken two by two), there are only nineteen viable ones. But the play of the imagination with the four other inner senses acts upon many other classifiable mental planes; (the topic of the imagination associates with certain constants all sorts of transformations) by inversion, torsion, intussusception; all of that multiplies in our dreams, and in spite of the inhibitions of logic, upsurges during wakefulness in the form of associations of images, whose beauty is, at times, as real as those beautiful dissonances in music excommunicated by the harmony of the classics.

And it is this numberless mass of paralogical or metalogical images which, by its shifting statistical equilibrium, responds when the incisive word of a man of doctrine and desire raises itself above the continuous noise of self-interested and commercial discourse.

We know what an important place dreams—either spontaneous or directed—occupy in the Semitic tradition. And in Islam in particular, the dream is the preamble, the embryo, of prophecy. Witness Adam's dream of the birth of Eve, Abraham's dream of the sacrifice, and Muhammad's dreams during the pre-Qur'ānic months, and also for the *adhān* and the five prayers.

As early as the first century of the Hijra, we find *mu'abbirūn*:[1] first Ibn

---

[1] Kind of psychic bonesetters, of *mu'azzimūn*; in *'akfa*, the *murshid* must exercise *ta'bīr* of the novice's dreams.

Sīrīn, and then, fifty years after Hallāj, Hasan-b-Hy Khallāl, in his *Tabaqāt al-mu'abbirīn*, enumerated seven thousand five hundred of them, six hundred of whom his abridger, Nasr Dīnawarī, in 397, studied in his *Kitāb al-qādiri*.[2] The latter book is infinitely valuable, because it is an empirical collection giving, as a manual of pathology, numerous concrete examples. They reveal to us the collective mental substratum of the Islamic Community, which in the freedom of its undirected dreams constructs its associations of ideas unconcerned with the censures of the Law that controls it during waking hours. To be sure, one sees in the classification of the subjects and their explanations that the *mu'abbirūn* seek systematically to bring the imagination of the believers within the bounds of orthodoxy—like the canonists in pursuit of noncanonical or folkloric observances (especially among women)—and it is this that immediately renders the dogmatic school of oneirocriticism very artificial and useless.

But Dīnawarī is a more or less conscientious observer, whose concordism is only intermittent; and by checking him against other accounts, one may, by making soundings, take several model specimens of families of idea-associations that Hallāj brought to life in the mental substratum of his hearers as generators of dreams, and sources of legends.[3]

Let us first consider those that Hallāj himself constructed in his works, in unconscious conformity with oneirocritical rules all clearly independent of canonical rules:

(1) The ideas associated with *"safīna*, boat" and *"salīb*, cross," in the distich found in *Dīwān*, no. 56, p. 91. Dīnawarī[4] points out that in dreams *"salīb*," even though it evokes an execution,[5] must be interpreted as a portent of a successful crossing in a *"safīna*," whose keel resembles a cross (the gibbet is also made of wood).[6] He took that from the manual of Artemidores, but affirms, supported by a dream that Shāfi'ī had during imprisonment, that in Islam to dream of being crucified is a good omen, auguring that one will become famous. The meaning of this dream is qualified somewhat if one is a slave, foretelling that one will be freed (the crucified one can no longer be forced to work nor be sold); if one is rich, one will become impoverished (one is crucified naked and one's color changes); if one is poor, the opposite occurs (the gibbet attracts animals). The gibbet is a presage of the revelation of hidden things

---

[2] Dīnawarī, Qādirī, Paris ms. 2745 (ch. I-XI; the end, particularly the important ch. XII [trades], XIII [tools], XXX are missing).

[3] The *ta'bīr* is the source of the *majāz*.

[4] Dīnawarī [?], f. 204b.

[5] Rome: execution of runaway slaves.

[6] Cf. the Seven Sleepers and *safīna* (in view of *taqlīb*).

and the annunciation of displacements (the crucified one is not buried). In a dream the gibbet strap (the hanging rope) forebodes marriage; hence, the insulting jeering at Hallāj on the cross: "he who has repudiated this base world has only the next life left to take as his spouse."[7]

(2) The idea associated with "*bala*'," suffering and its accompanying divine predilection, taught by Hallāj and by Ibn 'Atā', is confirmed by Dīnawarī as a constant in oneirocriticism. If one dreams that God touches us, visits us, clothes us by His own hands, this is a dual annunciation of final beatitude and of a life of suffering—which agrees with the interpretation given by Ibn Sīrīn of a dream had by Farqad before he became paralyzed.[8]

(3) The idea of the *hadīth al-nuzūl* associated with God Who "descends" to a "hallowed" ground, used by Hallāj in his *Riwāya XXII*, agrees with Dīnawarī's explanation of the dream in which God is seen descending with His angels and the *sakīna*, as a promise of fertility and of rectification of wrongs in the place where it was dreamed.

(4) The association of ideas between God and a father, accepted by Hallāj (ap. *Dīwān*, p. 17, verse 10), is justified, as 'AQ Hamadhānī pointed out,[9] in spite of the disapprobation of theologians, by the experience of the *mu'abbirūn*. Dīnawarī teaches that it is normal for God to appear in a dream in the form of a close relative, a brother, father, loving and comforting.[10]

(5) The twin association of ideas, pointed out by the Khalwatīya, distinguishing two drinks taken in a dream, milk (= *sharī'a*) and wine (= *tawhīd*), refer partly to a Hallājian theme. Let us recall, in this connection, the strange encounter with the same image, love's intoxication, compared to the sun's entering the mansion of the Lion, in Hallāj and in Ruysbroek.[11]

From the disciples and hearers of Hallāj, mentioning only dreams in which, on *istikhāra*, God answers the question why[12] He killed him, stating various reasons, a comparative study of which is suggestive; we draw attention here to only three dreams, about which the oneirocritical explanation enlightens us:[13]

[7] Cf. the Nusayrī proverb ('Alī Nā'im, 1934 ms. [?], f. 37a: *uskun al-safīna = Ma'nā, watruk al-madīna = Ism* [live in the boat and leave the city]).

[8] Dīnawarī, f. 46a.

[9] Hamadhānī, *Maktūbāt* [bib. no. 1082-b], f. 317 a-b.

[10] *Salsabīl*, 96.   [11] *Recueil*, p. 65.

[12] Ibn Fātik, AY Wāsitī, Shiblī (3 versions).

[13] A dream of Ibn 'Arabī, taken up by Shādhilī, modified by Rūmī (cf. ap. *Mélanges René Basset*, 1923, *Le Folklore chez les mystiques musulmans*, 10 [bib. no. 1695-r]; and three Qādirīyan recensions of ecstasy).

(1) Baqlī tells us that, after finishing the Persian translation of the *Tawāsīn* (in his *Mantiq al-asrār*), he saw Hallāj in a dream praising him with these words: "you have known what the tiara is (*qurmus = kulāh*), you have crossed the desert of vision (*bādiye-i basar*)."[14] In oneirocriticism, the tiara stands for a "bestowed honor." The symbol, in this instance, derives from the custom of dressing the hair of a man condemned to death with a high headdress (cf. the *san benito* of the Spanish *Autodafé*), a royal tiara, out of derision.[15] A custom quoted by Baqlī, and perhaps by the Naqishbandīya order, to make the peaked cap of the religious a symbol of their voluntary death.

(2) 'Attār points out to us the following: the dream, had by an unknown man, in which Hallāj appeared to him headless with a lighted candle given him to replace his severed head. In oneirocriticism, to dream of a decapitation means to dream of one's release, cure, comfort, or payment of debts; to dream of a severed head that is replaced by something else is to dream of a martyr on *jihād*. The candle signifies knowledge (especially that which illumines the heart), glory, and a wise soul.[16]

This dream served for 'Attār as the starting point of another dream on which he based his *Basarnāma*. Hallāj had appeared to him in a dream, beheaded, with a cup of julep in his hand. He explains to him that God gave it to him to replace his severed head, and that to drink from this cup would make one forget one's head, renounce one's self, and disappear in God. This is *fanā'*,[17] hence, his refrain (*Basarnāma*): "Here I am, God (*repeat*); devoid of name, of pride, and of desire; I have revealed the secret of decapitation; and I search for lovers in the world" (refrain used again in *Waslatnāma*).

(3) In Eastern Turkish poetry, and even in Anatolian Turkish poetry, Hallāj is called "the Rose, the Red Rose" (*Qyzyl gul*). The author of a Hallājian poem of the Bukhara school of Yesewī tells us that he composed it after having made *istikhāra* and been given to see Hallāj in a dream offering him a rose. In oneirocriticism, a red rose signifies "splendor, beauty, gold dīnārs, a kiss snatched from an alluring woman." Its use, in this instance, derives from a saying of Wāsitī which became a hadīth.[18] The paradoxical and engaging use of this symbol in this poem is significant in terms of its paralogical and oneiral origin.

---

[14] *Shathīyāt.*

[15] Nicholson.

[16] Dīnawarī, f. 200b-201b; Nābulusī, *Ta'tīr* [bib. no. 842-e], I, 240-241; Ibn Sīrīn, *Muntakhab*, on the margin of *Ta'tīr* (A.H. 1350), I, 233.

[17] 'Attār, *Asrārnāma* [bib. no. 1101-h], Paris ms., afp. 256, f. 8b.

[18] Nābulusī, *Ta'tīr* II, 328-329, and I, 164 (the meaning of *hallāj* in oneirocriticism).

The Qur'ānic eschatological theme (Qur'ān 101:5) of "when the mountains shall be as tufts of carded wool" (*'ihn manfūsh*)[19] is applied to Hallāj at the end of time by Yazīdī tradition.

II. POPULAR LEGEND

a. The Two Types: "Assemblies" and "Miracles"

In what form did Hallāj's memory survive after his execution? To what extent was it able to resist persecutions? Did it prevail in popular Sunnite circles, especially in Baghdad? We hope to determine the answers to these questions here with the help of the extraordinary documents that have come down to us dealing with these humble but fertile popular traditions, veritable "maternal waters" of later literary crystallizations, and the sources of inspiration for the "*Sharh hāl al-awlīyā'*" of Maqdisī (d. 660/1262) and for the "*Rawd*" of Hurayfīsh (d. 801/1398).

The written documents, in which we believe we find this oral tradition in its "nascent" form, are anonymous collections of accounts, of which two distinct types predominate:

(1) The first, the oldest, tell us the legend of Hallāj in the form of didactic and almost doctrinal "assemblies," written on the model of the highly esteemed "*maqāmāt*" literary genre.[1] They imitate the latter, but in a looser style, with a prose that rarely uses assonances, filled with maxims by Hallāj, interrupted by poetic interpolations among which one recognizes simple variations (in *takhmīs*) of known pieces from the *dīwān* of Hallāj corresponding more or less well to the maxims that they accompany. Various signs[2] make us think that these collections must have actually been used in the assemblies or *majālis* of Sūfīs, that their prose portions were declaimed and their verse pieces chanted accompanied by an instrument in the assemblies of "*samā'*," "spiritual concert"[3] whose program of dramatic readings is intended to arouse its audience to a kind of artificial ecstasy by releasing its senses. And we understand that the subject of Hallāj's execution offered Sūfī circles touched resources that were at least comparable, if not superior, to those that the death of Husayn ibn 'Alī provided the Shī'a.[4]

---

[19] Cf. *Kanadif al-qutni manthūr* (Ibn Qutayba, *Shi'r* [bib. no. 2112-a], the beginning).

[1] Of 'Abd al-Hamīd Asghar (Brockelmann II, 690), Badi' al-Zamān, Harīrī, Ibn Nāqīyā.

[2] We find among them specifically verses that the Qādirīya like to recite in order to enter into ecstasy (Tādhifī, *Qalā'id* [bib. no. 740-a], 94, 99, 101, 125, 131). Cf. Ibn 'Arabī, *Futūhāt* I, 498; II, 375, 388, 403; III, 132, 157; IV, 413.

[3] Oratorios. Cf. this edition, 1, 316.   [4] The *ta'ziya* and *marthīya* literature.

(2) The other documents, which are the more recent, bring the legend a step closer to the uneducated, in the direction of people incapable of grasping the teaching of these long didactic "assemblies" and these strings of maxims. They present it in short complete scenes, a succession of brief dramatic settings, most often of *miracles*—themes with commentaries written in almost childish and nearly unscannable verse—in which here and there we find prolonged the distinct echo of this or that famous poem of which Hallāj was the hero. These accounts were undoubtedly[5] composed, like the popular tales of the Banū Hilāl and of 'Antara, to be declaimed and chanted by the "singers of tales" and popular storytellers.

Among the continuous texts that we still have of the legend of Hallāj, the first type indicated above is rather well represented by the "Tale of a *faqīr*, taken from Ibn Khafīf,"[6] and the second type by the "Authentic Last Word on the Life of the Wise Man and Martyr."[7]

The following is a brief analysis of the subjects dealt with in these legends.

1. Maxims and Verses

They are generally extracted, almost literally, from authentic maxims of Hallāj; and the verses that accompany them represent an attempt at exegesis, meant to tranquilize [the readers], of [the maxims] which had been regarded as suspect. Most of these maxims comment on the following points of doctrine: the ineffable raptures of amorous union,[8] the

---

[5] The clause *"qāla'l-rāwī"* is interpolated there.

[6] *Hikāyat ba'd al-fuqarā' 'an Ibn Khafīf* (London ms. 888, f. 322b-333 [330a]. Berlin ms. 3492, f. 41-43 [bib. no. 141-b]. These are the *Manāqib* quoted ap. Baqlī, giving the date of the execution according to Ibn Khafīf). The thread of the account:
a) The six visits by Ibn Khafīf to Hallāj in prison, and three accounts of the execution, one of which includes special formulas (cf. *P.*, 1st ed., p. 419). The publisher appears to be a Shāfi'ite, Abū 'Abdallāh Husayn ibn Razīn 'Amirī Hamawī (f. 322b), whose son Taqī al-Dīn died in 680/1281 and grandson Badr al-Dīn, in 710/1310 (Subkī V, 19; VI, 130). Ibn Razin had received it via Shaykh Abū Husayn ('AA) Wannī ibn Yūsuf Faradī (Abū Ish, *Tab*. 99) from Abū 'Abdallāh ibn 'Abd Rahmān Kirmanī (d. 451/1060 according to Ibn Khallikān [bib. no. 471-a], Slane tr. I, 421?).
b) The six visits by Shiblī to Hallāj in prison, with the insertion of the full account of Hallāj's interview with the Caliph, of his execution, and of lengthy dialogues between the crucified Hallāj and Nūrī (*sic*) and Fātima (*Shathīyāt*, f. 125, 126, 136 ff.). Excerpts ap. Harawī, Qazwīnī, Hamadhānī, Jildakī, and 'Āmilī. Abbreviation: *Hik*.

[7] *"Al-qawl al-sadīd fī tarjamat al-'ārif al-shahīd"* (Shaykh Ahmad Jumaylī's ms., Baghdad; cf. L. Chebab ms. (499-a) The thread of the account: a) Hallāj's beginnings; b) break with Sūfis; c) first preaching, first arrest, and escape; d) second preaching, summons, second arrest, and execution; e) scenes with his sister (*wasīya*, dream). Cf. Niyāzī, this volume, p. 262.

[8] *Hik*., 119 Qazwīnī, *Qawl.*, 4, 8, 19, 26.

sanctification of prophets through trials (mihan),[9] the excuses for having "revealed divine secrets" (ifshā' al-asrār),[10] the condition of exile (gharīb) in which the saint is condemned in this world.[11] To emphasize their full significance they are put in the mouth of Hallāj in prison or on the cross.

The Visits of Ibn Khafīf: On six different occasions,[12, 13] Ibn Khafīf came to consult Hallāj and to write down, like an amenable pupil, the verse that he dictated, such as the famous poem "Labbaykā . . . ," "Wa hurmat al-wadd . . . ,"[14] and the "Man atla'ūhu. . . ."[15] Ibn Khafīf hears him predict his death.[16] According to legend,[17] Ibn Khafīf is the one who asks the following three questions, whose response becomes renowned as a miracle, like the precept of an example: (I) What is patience (sabr)?[18] —"The prison wall cracks, and here they are at the bank of the Tigris." —[It is to remain in prison when one could leave it.] (II) What is poverty (faqr)? —"Stones are changed into gold and silver before their eyes." —[It is to lack the copper coins to buy oil when miracles are being made.] (III) What is nobility of soul (futuwwa or karam)?[19] —"You will see tomorrow." —And when night fell, Ibn Khafīf, transported in a dream to the Day of Resurrection, hears the munādī cry out "Where is Husayn ibn Mansūr al-Hallāj?" Then Hallāj appears before God, Who says to him: "Whosoever has loved you will enter Paradise, and whosoever has hated you, will enter Hell!" —"Oh, no! forgive them all, Lord!" replies Hallāj; and, turning to Ibn Khafīf, he says: "This is nobility of soul."

Shiblī's Visits: Shiblī also made six[20] visits to Hallāj, the story of which brought together many famous sayings: the response to the question, "What is love?" —"You will behold it tomorrow (the day when his

[9] Hik., 9. Cf. this edition, 1, 610.

[10] "Man zāda hubbuhu dhahaba qalbuhu" (Hik., 119).

[11] Hik., 44 and 103 (Nūrī).

[12] Cf. Baqlī, Shath. [bib. no. 1091-b], f. 17-18.

[13] Hik., 1-5, 55.

[14] Hik., 4-5. Cf. Baqlī, Tafsīr [bib. no. 380-a], Qur'ān 6:70, and Shathīyāt, f. 125; Hamadhānī.

[15] Hik., 6. Baqlī, Tafsīr on Qur'ān 5:101; Ibn 'Arabī, Muhādarāt [bib. no. 421-a], II, 316; Ibn al-Sā'ī, Mukhtasar, [bib. no. 463-c], 76; Tādhifī [bib. no. 740-a], 94. Sulamī (Ghalatāt, f. 67) already cited it, based on this same Muhammad ibn al-Husayn al-' Alawī, in whose home Hallāj had met al-Khawwās (cf. this edition, 1, 114).

[16] Munāwī. Hik., 5.

[17] Nabahānī, Karāmāt al-awliyā', based on Latā'if al-minan of al-Sha'rāwī [bib. no. 741-d] (II, 84), copied from Qūsī, Wahīd, f. 87b (this edition, 3, 220-221).

[18] Cf. Hik., 19. "Qad tasabbartu . . ." (cf. Ibn 'Arabī, Futūhāt [bib. no. 421-b], III, 132). Cf. Baqlī (beginning).

[19] Enlargements of Amīn al-'Umarī, ap. Manhal al-safā' and Manhal al-awliyā'.

[20] Hik., 14-19.

corpse was burned);[21] the statement *"likulli Haqq haqīqa . . ."* (every truth has its reality, every creature his way, every contract its guarantee!);[22] the verses of *"Yā mawdi' al-nazar . . . ,"*[23] the quatrain *"Ahruf arba' . . ."* on the word *"Allāh,"* indicated here as the true "Supreme Name" of God.[24] *Nūrī's Questions:*[25] the verses of *"Arthā al-subb"*[26] and "your soul is your enemy."[27]

Questions posed to Hallāj on the cross[28] *by Fātima and Shiblī or Bundār ibn al-Husayn:*[29] Legend enlarges upon the historical facts about known questions; it gives the famous response, "I have not separated his joy from his suffering for a moment,"[30] and adds the famous verses *"Tajāsartu . . . ,"*[31] *"Yā shams, yā badr, yā nahār . . . ,"*[32] *"lam aslam al-nafs . . . ,"*[33] *"qālūa jafayta . . . ,"*[34] and the distich *"Lam tughīruhu rusūmūn. . . ."*[35]

2. Miracle Themes

These themes form a complete biography of Hallāj and a gallery of symbolic paintings.

a) *Themes dealing with his early beginnings:* his family: descends from Abū Ayyūb, the Prophet's standard-bearer.[36]

Vocation. How his mother, in carrying out a vow, offers him, with his consent at age seven, as a servant to the shaykh of the Sūfīs, Junayd.[37]

Early miracles. He rides a lion and uses a serpent as a whip.[38]

[21] Ghazālī, *Mukāshafāt*, 19; 'Attār.
[22] *Hik.*, 14, Hamadhānī.
[23] *Hik.*, 15, Jildakī.
[24] *Hik.*, 1. Shādhilī (*zahra*), *Qawl.*, 17. In agreement with the theory of Ibn Mubārak (Makkī, *Qūt* [bib. no. 145-a], II) and of Sahl (Ibn al-Khashshāb, Paris ms. 643, f. 63b, Baqlī I, of Kīlānī (Shattanawfī, *Bahja* [bib. no. 502-a] = 48) and Shādhilī.
[25] *Hik.*, 98-112.   [26] *Hik.*, 104, Qazwīnī.   [27] *Hik.*, 107.
[28] *Hik.*, 10, and 112-130, Hamadhānī, Jildakī.
[29] Baqlī, *Shathīyāt*, f. 125-126.
[30] Cf. this edition, 1, 609; Hamadhānī.
[31] *Hik.*, 10, Hamadhānī; by al-Dahhāk, translation this edition, 1, 609-610.
[32] *Hik.*, 13, Genizah.
[33] *Hik.*, 41, 'Āmilī, *Kashkūl* [bib. no. 794-a], 90; Damirī; Subkī VI, 66.
[34] *Hik.*, 46. Borrowed from profane poetry, of rather dubious inspiration (Ibn 'Arabī, *Muhādarāt* II, 338); cf. Baqlī, *Tafsīr*, Qur'ān 7:140, 'Amilī, *Kashkūl*, 90.
[35] *Hik.*, 113-114.
[36] Cf. this volume, p. 30.
[37] *Qawl.*, 2. On the contrary, Rousseau (*Voyage de Bagdad à Alep* [bib. no. 1565-a], p. 11) has him running away from home.
[38] Qazwīnī, *'Ajā'ib al-makhlūqāt* [bib. no. 458-a]. These are the signs of the Messiah (cf. Hammer [see bib. no. 1602], VI, 183 ff. for Sabatai Zevi) [cf. Gershom Scholem, *Sabbatai Şevi: The Mystical Messiah* (Princeton: Princeton University Press, Bollingen Series XCIII, 1976)].

The Larceny. How Hallāj, when still a very young novice, detected the formula of the ·"Very Great Name of God"[39] that his shaykh had lost; which brought upon him the curse delivered by his master against the thief.[40]

Fasts. Hallāj fasted the whole month of *Ramadān*, day and night.[41]

The Philtre. How Hallāj, having seen his sister in a dream[42] drinking wine from the cup of the celestial houris, entreated her to let him drink from it. But a single drop was enough to intoxicate him with God, and he was unable thereafter to keep from crying out constantly *"Anā'l-Haqq!"* until he incurred the extreme penalty.[43]

The Reciprocal Prediction. To Junayd's objurgation to him: "What scaffold will you defile with your blood!"[44] Hallāj retorted: "On that day you will throw off your Sūfī garb and put on the robe of a *faqīh!*"[45]

The Miracle of the Carded Cotton. We have examined the anecdote of al-Sammāk earlier.[46] One commentator of the *hikam* of Ibn 'Atā' Allāh modified it as follows:[47] the proprietor of the shop is a great Sūfī who, after the miracle of the carded cotton, forces Hallāj to return the cotton to its previous state with another miracle—for the purpose of teaching him not to make useless visits to his peers but to seek only God.

The Muezzin Accused of Lying. Hearing the muezzin making his call to prayer, Hallāj exclaimed: "You have lied!"[48] When people became indignant at him, deciding to put him to death, Hallāj spoke again on this matter: "No, you do not say the *shahāda* as it should be said!" And as he was saying it, the minaret collapsed.[49]

---

[39] Cf. Hamadhānī, 'Azzāz.

[40] *Qawl.*, 3. The origin of this story, ap. Harawī; Hallāj steals Makkī's book on *tawhīd* (when he is purifying himself) and publishes it. Cf. Sha'rāwī, I, 15 [bib. 741-a]. 'Attār II, 37; this was the *ganjnāma* in which Makkī explains how Iblīs, after refusing the *sujūd*, sees the *rūh* breathed into Adam.

[41] Amīr Dāmād, *Rawāshih* [bib. no. 805-a], cf. this edition, 1, 71.

[42] 'Alī Khawwās, *al-Jawāhir: zabarjad*: refers only to the cup.

[43] Graham (*Transactions of the Bombay Literary Society*, 1811, I, 119). Where the verse "*Saqawntī . . .*" comes from (Qazwīnī) (imitated ap. Maqdisī, and ap. Hurayfish, the *qasīda* beginning with this oft criticized expletive [Jurjānī, *Wisāta bayn Mutanabbī wa khusūmihi*, pp. 81-82] '*Min dhī alladhī . . .*"). Cf. the theory of *ittihād* according to Jāmī (Probst-Biraben).

[44] A historic statement (Hadramī, ap. Ibn Bākūyā: translated this edition, 1, 105.

[45] 'Attār; or a widow's robe, *Qawl.*, 7, 36. Contamination as a result of the so-called trial of Ghulām Khalīl (cf. this edition, 1, 79-80).

[46] Cf. this edition, 1, 101.

[47] As'ad ms. 1764, s.f.

[48] Compare Bistāmī hearing the *takbīr* (*Essai*, p. 247).

[49] *Qawl.*, 28, Khafajī, Niyāzī, Bādī Sannāri (cf. this volume, p. 335 and bib. no. 982), *Qasīda "al-khamr dīnī . . . ";* verse 12: "I am the one who said to the muezzin, 'Do not make

The Meeting With the Caliph Prior to the Trial. We have two different versions of this.[50] One in which Hallāj in the presence of the Caliph avowed to give himself up completely to the Will of God, and to assent in advance to the judgment handed down by the legal authority. The other in which Hallāj, pressed to say something in his own defense, answered simply with the following verse:

Through the holy sanctity of this love. . . .

The Legal Ordeal. Before the Caliph's tribunal, Hallāj challenges his calumniators to a "judgment of God." All of them decline; he comes forward alone and sits down in a boiling caldron set over a pit filled with hot coals and is not touched by the fire.[51]

His Change of Size at Will (tatawwur, the power to change completely). Hallāj had become capable of enlarging his body until it filled the width of a street and of reducing it until it assumed the size of a new-born baby.[52]

He had a room known as "*bayt al-'azama*" because he could fill it entirely with his person.[53] He did this when they came there to take him to his execution; and they would not have been able to extract him from it had Junayd not come to urge him, in the name of God, to give himself up by resuming his normal size, which he did.[54]

The Transferring of the Towel (Mandīl); or of the Cowl (Khirqa). This material, hung on a line forty cubits away, alights in his hand when he had finished his ablutions.[55]

The Pomegranate Tree. In prison, at the request of a visitor, he makes a pomegranate tree spring from the ground, covered with fruit.[56]

The Omnipresence. He shows a visitor that he is only a voluntary pris-

---

your call to prayer'; I did not come when I heard it, I regarded the (white) Cock beneath the Throne with my eyes." This is the famous white cock responsible for the *adhān* in Paradise (cf. Ibn al-Jawzī, *Mawdū'āt* [bib. no. 370-1] and the Cock of the Jewish Temple; this edition, 3, 334, n. 69). Its origin: an authentic statement about the *shahāda bi'l-haqīqa*, *tafsīr* on Qur'ān 3:18; 27:29.

[50] *Hik.*, 87, and Ibn al-Hajj (*Umm al-barāhīn*).

[51] *Qawl.*, 29, Khafājī.

[52] "*Mawlūd,*" *Qawl.*, 9.

[53] Ibn 'Arabī, *Fut.* IV, 90, 265.

[54] Sha'rawī, *Kibrīt* [bib. no. 741-b], 251-252; as in the case of the preceding passage, this account grows out of a historical detail of the trial (cf. this edition, 1, 504-505).

[55] *Qawl.*, 24. Qazwīnī, Berlin ms. 3492, f. 41b. Its origin: the account of Ibn Khafīf (cf. this edition, 1, 509). Munāwī, *Rawākih* [bib. no. 795-a].

[56] He gives ten of them to Ibn Khafīf, then makes the tree disappear, and says: it is a poppy which I play with and which I can't weed out (T. ms. 1b). Cf. the classical mango trees of Hindu fakirs. *Hik.*, 56 (sixth visit of Ibn Khafīf). *Qawl.*, 13. Munāwī, *Rawākih*.

oner, by taking him in a vision to Nishapur (or to Baghdad on the banks of the Tigris).[57]

The Visit to the Absolute. For the first two nights of his imprisonment, he remains invisible; he explains this afterwards by saying that on the first night he had paid a visit to the Absolute, and that during the second night the Absolute had paid him a visit in return.[58]

The Escape and the Ship of the Elect. In the oldest recension, he helps all of his companions escape from bondage, and remains in prison alone, voluntarily.[59] In the most recent, he persuades the prisoners to pray with him; he draws an outline of a ship on the wall, and embarks in it with all of those who abandon themselves to God; "the ship of the Elect"[60] helps them all escape.[61]

Divine Confirmation and Condemnation. The legend presents this in two different forms:

(1) The Prophet appears, recognizes the sanctity of Hallāj, but persuades him to sacrifice himself out of respect for the established law;[62]

(2) Hallāj writes to God, Who answers him in a miraculous missive warning him to sacrifice himself, for "our law must kill the 'self.' "[63]

3. The Execution

The fullest account is given by 'Attār (*Tadhkirat al-awliyā'* [bib. no. 1101-c] II, 141-145), but the dramatic sequence in which he presents it to us seems to be of his own creation.

The Testament. His testament is his cowl (*jubba, khirqa*),[64] meaning that Hallāj announces before his execution that it will be sufficient to throw his cowl into the river to save Baghdad from the flooding of the Tigris

---

[57] Cf. this volume, p. 343. *Hik.*, 5. Qazwīnī. Its origin: the deposition of the daughter of al-Sāmarrī at the trial (cf. this edition, 1, 513).

[58] 'Attār (the Hadra). Qazwīnī, *Ziyarāt al-qadīm* [?].

[59] A historical fact (in *Hijja* 308). 'Attār. His relations with the other prisoners is referred to ap. Ibn Khafif (this edition, 1, 501-505); Nājūrī [bib. no. 2170-a], f. 98a.

[60] *Markab al-nujāt*: cf. the fresco in the Sinī mosque (Girgeh).

[61] Khafājī, *Qawl.*, 14, 15.

[62] Najm Rāzī. J. W. Graham [bib. no. 1570-a]. Its origin: the commentary by al-Kīlānī on "*Hasb al-wājid* . . ." (this volume, p. 356. Cf. this volume, p. 263).

[63] *Qawl.*, 32. Cf. the verse "Murder me . . ." (*Qawl.*, 33). Cf. the statement of Ibn Taymīya stigmatizing the Sūfī proverb, "the law of Muhammad puts saints to death" (cf. this volume, p. 45). Qur'ān 2:54.

[64] It is the *silsilat al-khirqa* which is broken off: Maqdisī (*Sharh hāl awliyā'*). One must look there for the source of the attribution of Ibn Abī al-Khayr's saying, *Laysa fī jubbatī illa'-llāh*, to Hallāj (cf. *Mém. Inst. Français Caire*, XXXI, 118), which he was supposed to have said to his disciple (Ibn Fātik), according to 'Attār (Graham); to his sister, according to *Qawl.*, 34; to Nasr, according to Qazwīnī (cf. this edition, 1, 622).

which will threaten to engulf her at the time when his ashes are thrown into it. Which is done.[65]

The Warning. At the reading of his sentence, Hallāj stamps his foot on the ground and, addressing his judges, says "Your God is there!"[66] After the execution one of his disciples digs in the spot indicated and finds gold pieces there.[67]

The Flagellation. He is bound fast to be flagellated; and the weapon of the punishment is a stick made of thorny zizyphus.[68] After every ten or twelve blows he kisses the hand of the executioner; after each blow he says "*Ahad!*"[69]

The Mounting of the Scaffold. Hallāj is depicted walking to his death in triumph, answering all insults clearly, declaring "now comes the day of reunion with the Friend!"[70] proclaiming on the first step of the scaffold, "this is the *mi'rāj* of Sūfism!" loosening his belt and his *taylasān* to pray on high for the last time, submitting himself to the will of God, and answering a final question from his friends.[71]

The Mutilations. The legend, following the arrangement found in the genuine accounts, has Hallāj utter, after each mutilation and after the crucifixion, some sublime saying such as "*Balaghtu maqsūdī!*" ("I have attained my wish!")[72]

The different versions are in agreement in stressing a heroic gesture: with his bloody stumps Hallāj smears his face so as not to reveal his pallor, his fear of another than God,[73] and he sprinkles his arms to perform his ritual ablutions in blood.[74]

---

[65] Graham, Qazwīnī.   [66] "*Ma'būdukum hunā.*"
[67] Rousseau [bib. no. 1565-a]; Ibn Ziyān Derqawi of Oran (1923); Khashshāb 'Umar, in Cairo.
[68] *Hik.*, f. 330b.   [69] *Hik.*, 89. Baqlī, *Shathīyāt*, f. 15.
[70] 'Attār. Ibn Fadl Allāh, *Masālik* [?], "*Anā liqā al-habā'ib.*"
[71] A transposition of the account of "Shiblī's dream" (cf. this edition, 1, 633). This whole "mounting the scaffold" episode was dramatized by 'Attār (cf. this volume, pp. 361–387), who already prepared his Hallājian epic.
[72] Maqdisī, *loc. cit.* [?], 'Attār. Compare the famous utterance of Hallāj: "Though indeed You crush me with suffering, bit by bit, *ariban, ariban*, I will only love You more and more!" (Kalābādhī, *Ta'arruf* [bib. no. 143-a], 40: London ms. 888, f. 341a; and the Druze *Risāla fī'l-ridā wa'l-taslīm*, dated *Rabī'* II year II [sic] by Hamzah ibn 'Alī, perhaps 411/1020, f. 16b of my manuscript: cf. Niyāzī, *Dīwān* [bib. no. 1353-b], 14, verse 1; Hurayfish, *Rawd* [bib. no. 579-a], 143; Sarrāj, *Masāri'* [bib. no. 278-a], 115). One says to Hallāj [Qūsī [bib. no. 460-a], f. 20a): they will cut off your hand and foot and you will laugh.
[73] Cf. Bābak Khurramī, according to Nizām al-Mulk, *Siyāsatnāma* [bib. no. 1057-a], tr. p. 296. Baqlī, f. 15. 'Attār; Ibn 'Arabī, *Fut.* IV, 157, and *Mantiq al-tayr*, verses 2261–2271. *Hik.*, 40–42, 91. 'Amilī, *loc. cit.* [?], 90. Cf. "*Babad Tjerben*" (Javanese chronicle of Cheribon, Song XXXVIII, verses 2–3), which transposes this detail over to the martyrdom of Siti Jenar.
[74] 'Attār, this volume, Figure 32; cf. Nabulūsī (*Ta'tīr* [bib. no. 842-e], I, 217).

'Attār adds to the mutilations that Hallāj must have actually suffered the amputation of his nose and ears, the putting out of his eyes, and the cutting off of his tongue, while an old woman was pleading with the executioner to show no mercy to the victim.[75] This alteration forced him to move the *exposure on the cross* and the utterances that Hallāj delivered on it[76] back *before* the mutilations.[77]

The Exposure on the Cross. Legend has kept the general framework of the historical accounts, with the addition of many sayings put in the mouth of the victim, as we have remarked above,[78] and of some scenes that will be examined here:

The Flower Thrown Following Insults. After the well-known questions[79] and the insults,[80] several people throw stones at Hallāj, who remains composed; up comes Shiblī,[81] who throws a rose[82] at him; Hallāj weeps, and when people are amazed at this sign of weakness, says "it is because he knows, he especially, that nothing should be thrown at me!" In another version, it is his shaykh, Junayd, who throws the rose at him, then seeing him weep, comes to him, and kisses him between his eyes while he dies.[83]

Legend also inserts at this point an unusual scene intended to explain in an orthodox way an even stranger saying about Hallāj on the cross: "he is only half man!" a saying that makes him out to be half god.[84] Legend puts this into the mouth of his sister, Hannūna, who appears in bare feet, her face unveiled,[85] before the deceased, to reproach him for having been unable to "keep the secret of the King."[86]

The Posthumous Testimony: the Voice of the Blood. For two hours the severed head of the martyr placed between his amputated feet repeats the invocation "*Ahad! Ahad!*" (The Only One! the Only One!).[87]

His spilled blood writes on the ground in 31[88] or 35[89] places the name

---

[75] 'Attār. Cf. the "old woman with the bundle" at the execution of Jan Hus.
[76] Before his tongue was cut out.
[77] We find this inversion only in 'Attār.   [78] Cf. this edition, 1, 607 ff.
[79] 'Attār. Fātima the ambassadress (Jildakī).
[80] Qazwīnī (according to Sibt ibn al-Jawzī).   [81] 'Attār.
[82] Read: *gül* (and not *gil*, like Pavet de Courteille).   [83] *Qawl.*, 41, 42.
[84] Harīrī Marwazī, ap. Ibn Taymīya (cf. this edition, 1, 589 ff.).
[85] Since she is not in the presence of a complete man.
[86] Mustawfī (*Guzīda*), photocopy edition Browne, 776.
[87] *Hik.*, 12-61. It bounces, according to Khafājī. 'Attār. The source is probably the testimonial, referred to above, by Abū'l-'Abbās ibn 'Abd al-'Azīz (tr. this edition, 1, 602).
[88] *Hik.*, 12. Munawī.
[89] *Hik.*, 61. Maqdisī and Qāri': the earth trembled (*Sharh hāl al-awliyā'*) on account of the false hadīth "the earth trembles when an innocent is killed"; invented by Maslama, according to Ibn al-Jawzī (*Mawdū'āt, s.v. ahkām*).

"*Allāh! Allāh!*" (God! God!)[90] a legend whose source is found in Qushayrī.[91]

His hacked-up limbs repeat "*Anā'l-Haqq!*"[92]

The Testimony in Water. His ashes, when thrown into the river, write the words "*Anā'l-Haqq*" (I am the Truth) on the surface of the water;[93] and, after the waves became calm (when Hallāj's cowl was thrown into them),[94] the name "*Allāh!*"

They transmitted a particular virtue to the waters of the Tigris. In the time of al-Rifā'ī (sixth/twelfth century), a popular Baghdadian aphorism about Hallāj was often quoted:[95] "all members of the Batā'ih became shaykhs by drinking water from the Tigris where his ashes were thrown!"

Yazīdī tradition, which is even more expressive, tells us that after Hallāj's sister drew water from the Tigris where the spirit of her brother was hovering since his execution, this spirit entered her jar,[96] and when she drank, she became pregnant. And she brought her own brother into the world.

On the other hand, Yazīdī custom prescribes that neither jars, cups,

---

[90] This legendary theme has enjoyed an exceptional popularity, especially since Ibn 'Arabī (*Futūhāt* [bib. no. 421-b] II, 375, 403; *Tāj al-rasā'il* [bib. no. 421-i], 578) compared it to the blood of Zulaykhā writing "Yūsuf" (cf. Ibn Yazdānyār, Cairo ms., II, 87, f. 15b), Ibn al-Sā'ī, Dāwūd Qaysarī, Ibn Abī Sharīf and 'Alī Qāri'; so much so that Abū Yūsuf al-Qazwīnī, Ibn al-Jawzī, Ibn Taymīya, and Dhahabī believed it necessary to make detailed refutations of it based on the following reasons: (1) blood being *impure* cannot write the Pure Name (cf. this volume, p. 356; (2) the blood of the prophets and of the saints martyred before him must have written as much. To this argument of Ibn Taymīya, Munawī retorted that "the blood of Husayn, the grandson of the Prophet, had no need to defend his memory" (*Kawākib*). M-b-Mahmūd Sihāb al-Dīn Tūsī defended him: (Dhahabī, BN 1582, f. 95).
The origin of this theme perhaps should be sought in a somewhat enigmatic protest made by Hallāj upon hearing his sentence: "*Allah! Allāh fī damī!*" (Cf. *supra*, p. 268.) And the literal interpretation of the tercet on his mutilation: "*Ma qudda li 'adwun . . . illā wa fīhi lakum dhikr.*"

[91] *Risāla* [bib. no. 231-a], 1318 ed., p. 122. Cf. this edition, 1, 602; 2, 103.

[92] 'Attār (Arabic tr.).

[93] Mustawfī, *loc. cit.* [?]. His trunk says it, according to 'Attār. According to Baqlī (*loc. cit.* [?], f. 15b), his ashes say "*Allāh!*"

[94] Cf. this edition, 1, 621 ff.

[95] Kāzarūnī (d. around 790/1388) concerning Ibn Jalāl (this volume, p. 175 ff.).

[96] This could be an argument for the Sabaean source of the Yazīdis' "come from the southwest," for the Mandaeans believe that "Mary, upon drinking a particular water, became pregnant with Jesus" (Siouffi, *Subbas* [bib. no. 2217-a], p. 137). Myriam Harry (*Les Adorateurs de Satan* [bib. no. 1739-a], 1937, pp. 80-81) was told in Mosul that the banning of water jugs stems from the fact that the Yazīdīs do not want their daughters to become like the descendant of the Sabaeans (Mandaeans), Salome, who became pregnant through St. John the Baptist, whose head had been thrown into the river.

nor jugs should be used, which have either a narrow mortised neck,[97] or a material sieve used as a filter. The reason for this is the "glug glug" noise they make, for the water's gurgling is the *voice of Hallāj*, which has made the waves speak ever since his head was thrown into the Tigris by his enemies,[98] or because it echoes the noise his head made when it fell in the water.[99]

b. The Trial in the Legend

Legend, which sprang up on the evening of March 26, 922, out of popular feeling, has tended over the centuries to concentrate all of the moving elements of this tragic life story around Hallāj's execution. It has preserved the touching utterances and the extraordinary miracles, while taking pains to remove anything which might contradict strict orthodoxy and to reduce the boldness and the bearing of this religious apostolate to the sudden outbursts of a madman in love with God; finally classifying him among the "*'uqalā' al-majānin*," the "unbalanced souls," the "acrobatic mystics," the classic examples of which are still Buhlūl al-Majnūn, Sumnūn al-Muhibb, and al-Shiblī.[100]

Around Hallāj the prisoner, and afterwards when he is dying, it assembles teachings scattered throughout his life, verse from his "*dīwān*," and parables from his fables: his gibbet becomes a pulpit[101] from which the true Sūfism is expounded at great length in an orthodox and reassuring way, with a madness that is irresponsible and divine.

Grouped around the executed criminal as questioners are the leading Sūfīs of the classical period,[102] also many of his friends such as Shiblī and

---

[97] Cf. Ismā'īl Bey, Chūl, *The Yazīdī* [bib. no. 2047], p. 89.

[98] *Risāla fi'l-Yazīdīya* by Shammās 'Abdallāh of the Jabal Tur (Mosul): 'Azīz copy sent to me by R. P. Anastase. Cf. Parry and *RHR*, 1911, pp. 205-206, and n. 4. Compare the Qarmathian fable: "frogs croak (their croaking = *tasbīh*: *I'tidāl* III, 172) in every river except the Tigris" (*Farq*, 293). Frazer, *The Golden Bough*, 3rd ed., II, 70 (taboo).

[99] Lieutenant Lobéac, p. 20. We might also mention here the Persian legend of *shāb awīz*, a bird which remains all night attached by one foot only to a branch crying out *haqq, haqq*, until a drop of blood rises in its throat (Desmaisons, *Dict.* [bib. no. 2056-a], s.v.); cf. the *haqqī* pigeons in Baghdad, who make the cry *suduq, suduq* (this volume, p. 28, n. 114).

[100] The work known as "*Kitāb 'uqalā' al-majānīn*" by Hasan ibn Muhammad ibn Habīb al-Naysābūrī, d. 406/1015 [bib. no. 180A-a] (Kutubī, Gotha ms. 1567, f. 8b on Sumnūn); cf. Macdonald's article on *Buhlūl* in *E. I.*; *Tusy's List*, p. 45; P. Loosen, *ZAW* [?] XXVII, 184; Sam'ānī, f. 40b.

[101] *Crux Christi non solum lectulus morientis, sed cathedra docentis* (St. Augustine, *Oratio 119 in Joannem*).

[102] The attribution to Hallāj of the saying "*A taqtulūna man yaqūl Rabbī Allāh?*" (cf. Qur'ān 40:29) of Hāris (2nd century. Cf. Khafājī, IV, 584 ff. [bib. 811-a]) is by Baqlī (*Tafsīr* Qur'ān 7:99 and *Shathīyāt*, f. 26a).

Ibn Khafīf,[103] whose presence in that grouping history attests to or allows us to prove, as in the case of his masters al-Junayd[104] and Nūrī,[105] who had died many years before. Dhū'l-Nūn Misrī becomes his disciple,[106] and Caliph Muqtadir is confused with Mu'tadid,[107] Mutawakkil, or Mu'tasim.[108]

So it is in the legend that the trial of Hallāj becomes wholly the "trial of Sūfism." Elements characteristic of the *"mihan"* or "inquisitions" directed against Sūfīs previously, particularly in the persecution aroused by Ghulām Khalīl,[109] are incorporated into it.

Such a work is bound to alter profoundly the historical personality of Hallāj. It loses his full intellectual power, his whole dialectical subtlety, and preserves only half the passion of his religious feeling. Sūfī tradition, channeled with prudence and discipline by the great religious orders, uses Hallāj to canonize the model of the perfect religious, a man not all there, a gyrovague lost in God who, through his continual raptures, still finds the means to obey his shaykh, his spiritual director, unto death.

This new character of Hallāj is set in relief by the increasingly important role attributed in legend to two unique figures, both almost entirely legendary: his *shaykh* and his *sister.*

1. The Model of Junayd.

His shaykh is Junayd, who was in actual fact his spiritual director during his novitiate and his period of retreat (*khalwa*), but with whom he broke openly prior to beginning his public apostolate, and who died, in any case, eleven years before he did. Here Junayd emerges as the shaykh par excellence, as the model of "directors of conscience." He follows his disciple closely through his spiritual stages, the renouncing of callings for which he is not suited; and in tune with orthodoxy, he exhorts him not

---

[103] The theme of the "visits."

[104] A chronological mistake already pointed out by Pārsā, Khwandamīr.

[105] The "questions of al-Nūrī."

[106] Yesewī, *Hikam.* Qūsī, *Tawhīd.*

[107] 'Attār, Munawī.

[108] Baqlī, this edition, 1, 288, n. 86; Sārī 'Abdallāh, *Thamarāt* [?], 177.

[109] The denunciation of Ghulām Khalīl is confused with that of al-Awārijī against Hallāj. Hallāj assumes the role of al-Nūrī. (Cf. his statements in 309/922 on the "proof" [this edition, 1, 521]; to be compared with those of Nūrī as we find them in the Mālikite tradition collected by Leon the African [Giovan Lioni Africano, *Descrittione dell' Africa*, Italian text, ap. Ramusio, *Navigationi e viaggi* (Venice, 1550), I, f. 43b; Temporal French tr., reedited by Schefer (Paris, 1896), II, 146–153; Latin tr. of Florianus (Leyden, 1632), pp. 342–345], and Amīn al-Umarī; and it is because of the condemnation of Hallāj that we find Junayd casting off the Sūfī garb [this edition, 1, 75].)

to reveal the secrets of divine ecstasy, for fear of stirring up the crowd, and to remain outwardly obedient to the Law—he is the one who calls upon [Hallāj] to give himself up to become a prisoner after his condemnation, and who himself condemns him.[110]

But he did this not because he had ceased to love him, since he then put on the blue mourning clothes of mothers who have lost their children. Further, his paternal affection revealed itself when he kissed him on the eyes on two occasions: in the beginning, when he foresaw his inevitable fate, and at the end, when he expired on the gibbet.

2. Hannūna, Sister of Hallāj

The figure of the sister of Hallāj, Hannūna, is perhaps even more beautiful.[111] She plays a secondary role, without appearing in the drama in which only men act. She stays in her place, impeccable and almost unperturbed, but not insensitive. It is she, the sister of the heavenly houris, who drinks easily from the cup, a single drop from which had been enough to drive her brother crazy. She watches over him with a clairvoyant and heedful compassion, and she receives his last testament.

She acts only after his execution: with bare feet and unveiled face, she comes to reprimand the dead for his excesses of speech; then, she carries out with pious fidelity his last wishes by throwing his ashes into the angry river.

Alone at nightfall, her will falters in silence. And she weeps over him with such tears that her brother appears to her to say to her, "How long will you weep?" —"How could I help weeping after what has happened?" —"O sister, when they cut off my hands and feet, my heart was seized with love, and I knew only one thing, that that is good! When they crucified me, I contemplated my Lord and I was unaware of what they did to me. When they burned my body, the angels brought me down from heaven their wings to shield me and to carry me up beneath the Throne; then, a cry was raised from the supreme heights: 'O Husayn, God has pity on the one who recognizes His power; keeps His secret hidden, and keeps His commandments!' And I said: 'I had wanted to come to behold You more quickly!' And the voice said: 'Fill your eyes . . . I shall be hidden to you no more!' "[112]

---

[110] The legend of the *fatwā*, which grew out of the role of al-Makkī. Cf. this edition, 1, 72 ff.; p. 113 ff.
[111] *Qawl.*; cf. Khafājī; Husaynī, *Karāmāt* [bib. no. 1187-a], f. 142b.
[112] *Qawl.*, *in fine*.

III. The Model of Hallāj in Muslim
Dramatic Literature

Although the opposite was once believed, we know now that Muslim countries in which the models of Arabic literature were dominant were by no means impoverished in terms of those literary genres known as epic, drama, and narrative romance. These latter persist there in rather special forms that grew out of the grammatical demands bearing upon the presentation of ideas in Arabic. The epic form is the *qasīda*, the novella is the *maqāma*, the drama is the *qissa*, the lyric fable in which the verse recitatives of the protagonists are commented on throughout the main narrative in prose.

Overstepping gradually the specialized and narrow circle of the theological controversialist, the model of Hallāj found its way into the whole of the Muslim literary world. As it is, the legends in verse that popularize his martyrdom are not simple lectionaries for religious orders, but *qissa* outlining a dramatic perspective. Apart from his great Hallājian epics, in which any dramatic setting of the execution is thwarted by his didactic concern, 'Attār, in the 208 verses of his *Waslatnāma*, has given as intentionally dramatic a presentation of the execution in verse as he gave in presenting the same theme in prose at the end of the first recension of his *Tadhkirat al-awliyā'*. And his *Waslatnāma* is the main source of Hallājian *qissa* in Turkish and in Urdu. 'Attār, however, even when he gives in to his inclinations as a littérateur, is still a mystical author, more specialized in that respect than Rūmī, who owes much to him, but whose literary audience is much wider.

a. *Ibn al-Qārih and Ma'arrī: the* Risālat al-Ghufrān[1]

The first secular literary work in which Hallāj appears as a literary model is the "Epistle of Pardon," a subtle and skeptical response, full of veiled sarcasm, by the great blind poet of Syria to an old Aleppine littérateur, Ibn al-Qārih. The poet had received from this man a learned and disillusioned "Epistle," written rather in the manner of Jāhiz and of Lucian, on the incorrigible and absurd folly of certain human actors who make their appearance on the historical stage, beginning, as he does, with an old scholar, Zahrajī, whom he denounces rather ungratefully after hav-

---

[1] Ibn al-Qārih, ap. Kurdaly, *Rasā'il al-bulaghā* [?], 1913 ed., p. 200; Ma'arrī (Hind, 1903) [bib. no. 212-a], 150; Nicholson tr., ap. *JRAS*, 1902, p. 346; Kratchkovski, ap. *Islamica* I (1925), pp. 344-356 (critique of the theory of Asin Palacios).

ing enjoyed his "blasphemous" library in Amid, and ending, after venting his rancor against his deceased patron, Vizir Maghribī, with an unexpected anecdote about Shiblī showing the fear of Hell that he, Ibn al-Qārih, has. Meanwhile, his last line emphasizes that he still corresponds with Zahrajī.

The parade of walk-ons envisioned by Ibn al-Qārih is composed solely of famous zanādiqa, of the poet Mutanabbī, with the 'Alid ghulāt, and passing on to Bashshār, Sālih, Muqanna', Jannābī, Hallāj, Shalmaghānī,[2] Ibn al-Rāwandī, Ibn al-Rūmī, Hasan-b-Rajā, Mazyār, Bābak, each of whom is silhouetted with simple picturesque and biting anecdotes.

Ma'arrī's response, the Epistle of Pardon, completes the diptych, the dialogue between two auguries, who hardly love each other but understand each other, in guarded words. Ma'arrī begins with an elaboration of a great setting, "an excursion through Paradise." To calm the fear that Ibn al-Qārih admitted, more or less sincerely, to have of Hell, he described for him in a comic style how he was to be forgiven, how he saw him beforehand welcomed into Paradise, meeting there, along with the great figures of Islam, a host of men of letters forever quibbling over lexical matters. Then, without explicitly leaving his initial setting, Ma'arrī takes up and retouches, one by one, all of the silhouettes of the zanādiqa dealt with in the Epistle of Ibn al-Qārih, following these with his confidences about his personal relations and his travels, particularly his pilgrimages to Mecca, with the final anecdote about Shiblī, whom he gibes at in passing.

The figure of Hallāj is worked out thoroughly by Ibn al-Qārih much in the way the learned Mu'tazilites depicted it in the Shī'ite court of Baghdad in the period of its study there between 370 and 380. A daringly impulsive adventurer who wanted to overthrow empires, playing to the Shī'ism of the rich and the Sūfism of the common people, pretending to be knowledgeable in all of the sciences, yet proven guilty of ignorance by the vizir, and on top of that presenting himself as an incarnation of God, he ended up duly condemned and executed after challenging the vizir to a trial by fire.

Ma'arrī's finishing touches to this portrait bring out its aspect as caricature. He stresses the belief of some in the substitution of the Mādharā'yī's mule for Hallāj before the execution; he regards him as a model of the teaching of reincarnations who tries to divinize man, demonstrating that

---

[2] The same order, ap. Istakhrī.

he can be transformed into a mouse or a donkey—a notion which is attractive now to Nusayrīs, Shī'ites and Ismā'īlīs, but which was always accepted in India, where people are cremated to hasten reincarnation.

Hallāj's quatrain "Yā sirra sirrī . . . " shines forth in the midst of both ironic portraits with its "poetic power," which Ma'arrī recognizes apart from two quibbles that he glossed.

b. The Qādīrīyan Parables of the Flight of Hallāj

Muhyī' 'l-Dīn 'Abd al-Qādir Kīlānī (d. 561/1166), a Hanbalite in law, spoke out[3] on several occasions[4] in support of the notion of Hallāj's sainthood:

(1) The reason of one of the sages took flight one day out of the nest of the tree of his body,[5] and flew up to heaven, where it joined the legions of Angels. But it was only a falcon among the falcons of this world, whose eyes are hooded by the hood, "man was created weak." Now, this bird had found nothing in heaven that he could hunt as prey, when suddenly he saw the quarry shine forth, "I have seen my Lord!" and his resplendence grew in hearing his Objective tell him, "Wherever you turn, you will have God before you." The falcon then soared back down again, hiding on the ground what he had taken,[6] a treasure rarer in this world than the fire at the bottom of the seas,[7] but whichever way he turned, the eye of his house [= his eye] saw only the reflections (of divine resplendence). He then went back and could find in both worlds no other goal than his Beloved! He was moved to joy and he cried out, expressing the rapture of his heart, "Anā'l-Haqq! I am the Truth!" He made his song resound in a way forbidden to creatures; he chirped with joy in the Orchard of Existence, and this chirping ill becomes the sons of Adam. His voice modulated a song that exposed him to death. And deep within his conscience, these words reverberated: "O Hallāj, did you believe that your power and your will depend only on you? Proclaim now, as a representative of the sages, 'the goal of the ecstatic is the Only One! alone with Himself.' Say 'O Muhammad! it is you who are the proof of reality! you who are the image painted on the pupil[8] of existence! It is on the

---

[3] Like him [Hallāj], he contrasts *fard* with *nafal*, *'ard* with *tūl* (*Bahja*, 34).

[4] For the text of the first four quotations, see Shattanawfī (*Bahja*), 52, 73, 102, 121-122. See also this edition, 3, 217-218.

[5] Of his *nisba* (Abū'l-Hudā, Qilāda).

[6] He therefore has the divine *Rūh* in his guts (cf. this edition, 3, 164).

[7] Imitated by 'Abd al-Karīm Jīlī (Cairo ms., VII, no. 31, f. 820).

[8] Maqdīsī, *Bad'* [bib. no. 150-a], Huart tr. II, 81, line 14 ff., and *Tawāsīn*, 130, line 14. *Bahja*, 36: *insān 'ayn al-ā'lam*. Cf. the Ismā'īlī theory of Kayyāl, which has man's *condition*

doorstep of your wisdom that the napes of the sages' necks bow down! It is under the protection of your Majesty that the foreheads of creatures are humbled, altogether.' "[9]

(2) He also says of Hallāj:[10] "One of the sages flew (one day) to the horizon of the apostolate borne on the wings of "I am the Truth!" He saw the gardens of posteternity devoid of any sound and any society. He chirped for joy in a foreign language,[11] which exposed him to death. For the sea hawk came to attack him, coming out of his ambush "God has nothing to do with created worlds,"[12] and it dug its claw into his skin "Every human soul shall taste death."[13] And Solomon's law of the hour[14] declared to him, "Why have you spoken in a tongue that is not your own? Why have you made your song resound in a melody forbidden to your kind? Return now to the cage of your existence, leave the glorious way of Eternity for the narrow pass of humble temporal things, declare, uttering your confession for those pretending to the apostolate to hear, 'the goal of the ecstatic is to isolate completely his Only One!' The point on which perseverance in the straight mystical path rests is the keeping of the prescriptions of service to the Law!"

(3) *Riwāya* of 'Umar al-Bazzāz (d. 608/1211):[15] he says several times, "When my brother Husayn Hallāj stumbled there was no one in his time who took his hand.[16] But if I had lived in his time, I would have taken him by the hand. And (I declare) to all of our disciples, novices, and friends that their mount will stumble until the day of Judgment, and that I shall take them by the hand!"

(4) He was asked: "On what ground can one excuse the statement by Hallāj ('I am the Truth')."[17] He said: "Hallāj took up his position as a brigand, a highwayman on the route of love, and there he seized the pearl of the mystery of love; then he hid it in the deepest treasure-chest of his heart, pondering the risk involved. But when the sight of his inmost intuition beheld the luster of this pearl's beauty, he was blinded by it; he no longer perceived creatures; he believed he was in a place devoid of any

---

corresponding to his *sense* of sight (cf. the Buddhist correspondences between the six *senses* and the six *types* of creatures).

[9] Haytamī remarks as follows: "that is a testimony which is a glory sufficient enough for Hallāj!" Text refers to *Tawāsīn*, pp. 180-181.

[10] Reproduced by 'Alī al-Qāri', *Nuzhat al-khātir* [bib. no. 790-c].

[11] The language of the Absolute.

[12] Qur'ān 29:3.

[13] Qur'ān 3:185.   [14] Muhammad.

[15] Via Abū Abharī and Abū Khabbās.

[16] The same said by Salal (cf. this edition, 3, 215, n. 293).

[17] And to the statement by Bistāmī *Subhānī* (cf. *Tawāsīn*, index, s.v.).

being; and he confessed his larceny in a loud voice.[18] So much so that he deserved to have his hands cut off and to be executed. I swear it on your life, whosoever possesses this pearl shall be satisfied with none but the highest degree of love, which is self-annihilation!"

When Hallāj reached the Gate and knocked, someone called out to him, "O Hallāj! No one enters here without being stripped of his attributes as a creature and freed of the stigmas of humanity." Then he died of love and his body melted away with tenderness; he offered up his spirit before the gate, surrendered his soul before the curtain. Then he stopped at the stage of wonder at the feet of amazement. Self-annihilation had made him be silent, intoxication had made him speak. He cried out: "I am the Truth!" Then the chamberlain of fright answered him: "Today your fate is mutilation and death. Tomorrow it will be reconciliation and union." And Hallāj chanted, "One of your glances alone is worth more than my spilled blood."[19]

When the anxieties caused by his desires grew worse and the flames of his burning seized him, Hallāj craved union. He sat down on the rug of affliction. And it was told to him: "O Ibn Mansūr! if you are a true lover, a confessed lover, sacrifice your precious soul,[20] your noble spirit, in self-annihilation, to come to Us!" He accepted the command submissively and said, "I am the Truth!" (= the price to pay for this contract we have made)[21] in order to receive the prize at once: "Do not imagine that those who have been killed for God are dead" (Qur'ān 3:169).

Iblīs himself had said "I" in rebellion and in opposition to decrees: when the voice called out (to the Angels) "Adore (Adam!)," he responded "I am worth more than he!"[22] (Qur'ān 7:12) and thus deserved exile. "Does he not know who has created" (Qur'ān 67:14).

The gratitude of love ruled the inmost heart of Hallāj, and the power of tenderness did violence to the secret of his consciousness, and in the giddiness of his search, he cried out "I (am the Truth)!" As for Iblīs, his great pride reached to the summit of his thought; the interior of his consciousness was shaken by the proddings of his soul, and he said: "I am worth more than he!" Now, he (Hallāj) that commands the love of his Lord is worthy of being admitted into Union with Him, of being near Him, whereas he (Iblīs) who contemplates himself with a self-satisfied eye deserves to have his head cut off by the sword of damnation.

[18] He confessed "Anā'l-Haqq!" and suffered the punishment of thieves.

[19] Here, the dialogue with Bistāmī, which issues from "behind the gate," and speaks two languages of light, to him, that of tamjīd and that of tawhīd. Hallāj answers him in two languages of light, that of wijdān and that of wasl.

[20] Badhl al-rūh, the opposite reference, this edition, 3, 291, n. 89.

[21] A play on the word "qabala" (to recognize, to accept) and "haqq" (truth, debt).

[22] This has been summarized by Khafājī.

One said to him: "What is the meaning of this saying 'I am the Truth!' "[23] He answered, "I do not see any equal to whom I could disclose these high thoughts, or any confidant to whom I could reveal these secrets."

One said to him: "Iblīs said 'I' and he was removed (from God). Hallāj said 'I' and he was brought close to (God). Why?" He answered, "Hallāj was seeking annihilation through his 'I', so that the 'He' of God would be left without his 'he'; thus, he was brought to the hall of Union and, there, dressed in the everlasting robe of honor. Iblīs was seeking the everlasting through his 'I'; thus his sanctity was annihilated, his good fortune carried off, his rank lowered, his malediction proclaimed."[24]

(5) *Riwāya* of Ibrāhīm ibn Sahl al-Taghlabī Rūmī. Questioned on Hallāj, he responded: "He was a wing that soared for so long in the sky of the apostolate that the birds of the law seized him and put an end to him."[25]

Among the Qādirīya[26] who had studied the case of Hallāj, we should mention 'Abd al-Karīm Jīlī, the author of the *Insān kāmil*.[27] He has set forth in detail why Hallāj was put to death for saying "*Anā'l-Haqq*." According to him, it was because he was in too much of a hurry to speak, before he had attained the state of confirmation (*tamkīn*) in his union with God. If he had attained it (like Abū Yazīd, Kilānī, Ibn Jamīl), no one could have harmed him, for the truth of the divine attributes (dwelling within him) would have protected him[28] as it did them. When he spoke, he had within him the manifestation (*bayyina*) of God, but he did not yet have the attestation (*shāhid*) authorizing him to proclaim it. This is why God said, "The most unwelcome voice is that of the donkey (that of the novice who thinks he has arrived)" (Qur'ān 31:19). Hallāj was in too much of a hurry to speak, contrary to what the Qur'ān (75:16; 21:27) advises.[29]

23 And of that of Bistāmī, "*Subhānī*." He explains this elsewhere by "*fa haddith*" (Qur'ān 93:11).
24 A theme taken up by 'Attār, *Tadhkira* II, 145: a dialogue between Hallāj and Iblīs. Rūmī, in his *mathnawī* (II, s. 8, verse 64 and II, s. 45, verse 70), contrasts similarly the "I" of Pharaoh with the "I" of Hallāj, a comparison repeated by 'Alā' al-Dawla Samnānī and al-Qāri' (this volume, p. 39).
25 Halabī, *Ta'rīkh Qutb al-Dīn*. Vizir Jabāl al-Dīn 'UA. 'Azajī had his body exhumed and threw it in the Tigris (verses 583-584): 'Akarī IV, 313.
26 Ibn 'Arabī received this *khirqa* (Jāmī, 634).
27 He constructed his whole treatise *al-Kahf wa'l-raqīm* on a statement by Hallāj (Sul. I). Cf. this volume, p. 232.
28 God cannot cause His elect to suffer for their ecstatic words.
29 He resumed his study of the Hallāj case later in more sympathetic terms, in his *Manāzir Ilāhīya*: Hallāj arrived at the stage "*man anta*"; a laudatory parable apropos of the "*tal-*

Undoubtedly the "legend of Hallāj," as it was constituted in the seventh/thirteenth century, together with the insertion of the text of his poems within the framework of his martyrdom, was recited usually in the Qādirī order during its sessions of samā' (declamations chanted to inspire ecstasy). Proof of this is given us by an examination of the poems quoted without the authors' names as being preferred for samā' by the Qādirīya shaykhs who were contemporaries of Kilānī. At least seven poems must be attributed[30] to Hallāj.[31]

(6) A Critical Note on the Degree of These Qādirīyan Texts' Authenticity. The early form of Kilānī's maxims is given us in its simplicity in the Futūh al-ghayb, a compilation of elementary counsels[32] in mysticism attributed to his son 'Īsā (d. 573), who was the author, in addition, of a short treatise on mysticism; and in sixty-two sermons, reflecting a strict asceticism, delivered in 545–546 and published by his khalīfa 'Afīf al-Dīn ibn al-M Mubārak[33] around 590 with the title "al-Fath al-Rabbānī": the wasīya of "the one who was put on the gibbet" is cited twice in it (186): Hallāj, it is specified (199: adding a comparison between the nafs and the dog of the Seven Sleepers, which will be stylized ap. Bahja, 78); there is also an implied reference there (Khatwatāni [?], 124).

The ten Hallājian texts given in the Bahja of Shattanawfī (d. 713) are of a more complex style, as W. Braune has shown. The only one preserved exactly is the Riwāya of Bazzāz (102).

Three others, those included among the forty-four Fusūl written in florid prose in Chapter VIII (24–88, on pages 52, 71 and 73), were presented in a finished literary way in which Qur'ānic excerpts are set like pearls in jewelry. Shattanawfī tells us formally (84, cf. p. 10) that he received them at the same time, thus in A.H. 666, as the two informants, M-b-'A Karīm ibn Jarāda (to whom Mufarrij-b-'Alī Dimishqī had sent them by letter in 648), and Hasan-b-'Ali, grandson of Dulaf ibn Qūqa (d. 575), who got them from Hibatallāh-b-M ibn al-Mansūrī (d. around 635), a famous Baghdadian, khatīb in the mosque of al-Mansūr, later an

---

wī'a" stage applies probably to him. Finally, Jīlī tells of having had an ecstatic interview with Hallāj on the subjects of tahaddī and khal' al-'idhār (Recueil).

[30] Shattanawfī, Bahja, 161, 163, 171, 181, 215, 221, 231.

[31] In Egypt, Qādirism took root thanks to Ibn Kayjānī (d. 560) and to a Kurd, 'A Malik-b-'Īsā ibn Dirbas Mārānī, qādī of qādīs under Saladin (566, d. 605) (Bahja, 108). Qādirīya: Turks ('AA Eshrefoghlu, d. Isnik, 874: an ilāhi [Tāhir Bey (bib. no. 1371-a) I, 17], Nahrawānī); Malaysians (Hamza Fānsurī, d. 1630); Turks (Shams D. 'Uthmān Eff. Uskudari, d. 1311: Tāhir Bey, II, 271).

[32] Compare on murīd-murād, Fut., 151 with Bahja, 62.

[33] Grandson (Bahja, 115) or rather grand nephew of Kilānī (Bahja, 94: 'Afīf-b-Mubārak-b-Hy-b-Mahmūd Jīlī).

'Abbāsid grand *naqīb*, and holder[34] of a general *ijāza* for the transmission of all the works of Kīlānī. It must have been he who compiled the *Fusūl*, whose finishing touches indicate a Hanbalite preacher mixing Qur'ānic verses and sumptuous images with certain unusual philosophical terms (*'aql akbar*)[35] and implicit quotations from Hallāj.[36] As for the publication of his compilation, it must have been posthumous, and entrusted to his *rāwī* M-b-'Alī Tawhīdī (killed in 656, son of the sister of Grand Qādī Abū Sālih Nasr Kīlānī [d. 633], author of works written in lofty style and of poems).[37] Tādhifī, in his *Qalā'id*, gives us, I believe, the correct title of the compilation, *Durar al-jawāhir*,[38] with the name of its publisher, Abū'l-Faraj 'A R-b-Yūsuf ibn al-Jawzī (b. 604, d. 656), "*wā'iz, lahu tasānīf*,"[39] the grandson and quasi homonym of the old adversary of Kī-lānī, the famous historian who died in 597, son of a *muhtasib* who was the last 'Abbāsid *ustadhār* (Yūsuf-b-I J, born in 580, killed in 656), initiated into mysticism by the great Shaykh Ibn Sukayna and won over to Qādirism.[40]

Finally, six texts dealing with Hallāj are given in Chapter XIV (pp. 119-125), following a text on the "I" of Satan, transmitted to the author of the *Bahja* by AM Rajab ibn Mansūr Dārī in 671[41] (as having come down from a son of Kīlānī, A Nasr Mūsā, who died in Damascus in 618), in a series of "answers" by Kīlānī to questions about Iblīs and the true *tawhīd*. We no doubt are dealing here with a small collection from a single session; its redaction, written in a less finished style than that of the *Fusūl*, with a clearer sympathy to Hallāj, and a more pedagogical tone in its definitions, may, perhaps, go back to Mūsā Kīlānī.[42]

c. The Hallājian Works of 'Attār

1. The Personality of Farīd 'Attār: his *Asrārnāma*

It was above all due to the literary works of 'Attār that the Hallājian theme became one of the most famous "leitmotivs" in Iranian Muslim

---

[34] At one year (*sic: Bahja*, 112). Cf. 11, 20, 27, 54, 55, 65, 86, 99, 108, 119, 156; Fuwatī [?], 38, the master of grand qādī and grand shaykh Shams Maqdisī (d. 765). Cf. *Bi'āt al-futuwwa* [?], 37. Cf. *Nuqta khiltat al-tawhīd* [?], 32, 71. Cf. *Khadir 'aqlihi* [?], 74.

[35] Statement by Tirmidhī (*Essai*, p. 290, q. 3a), repeated by Ibn 'Arabī, *Fut.* II, 44-154.

[36] *'Arif* (b. 56), *kun* (b. 68), *khatwatānī* (b. 91), *nafal-fard, tūl-'ard* (n. 34).

[37] *Bahja*, 117.

[38] *Qal.* [bib. no. 740-a] 17: "Kīlānī's numerous statements about Hallāj have been collected in the *Durar al-jawāhir* of the *hāfiz* Abū'l-Faraj ibn al-Jawzī, who compiled the maxims of Shaykh '"AQ" therein.

[39] *'Akarī* [?], 287.   [40] *Rāwī*, ap. *Bahja*, 7, 107.

[41] *Bahja*, 82.

[42] With assonances and lines reminiscent of the Hallājian *qissa*.

poetics, wherever Islam was propagated together with a love of Persian poetry, from Turkestan and the Balkans to India and Malaysia.

"After (two) hundred and fifty years, the light (= the soul) of Mansūr (Hallāj) came to transfigure (tajallī) the spirit (rūh) of 'Attār, and it left the imprint of its makeup (murabbī) upon him," said Jalāl Rūmī.[43] This statement would place the literary activity of 'Attār after 559 (= 309 + 250); in fact, despite the latest studies of Ghazvini[44] and Ritter,[45] Fazīd al-Dīn M-b-Ibrāhīm 'Attār did not die in 586, as Mīr 'Alī Shīr Newāyī had engraved in his epitaph, but in 617/1220, according to the testimony of Nasīr al-Dīn Tūsī, who calls him "Farīd al-Dīn Sa'īd-b-Yf-b-'Alī Naysaburī al-'Attār al-'Ārif."[46]

He must have died very old, for he was born before 530/1136, seeing that he "made his decision" (= became a mystic) under Rukn al-Dīn 'Akkāf, killed in 549, quoted three times in his Musībetnāma, a disciple of A Nasr Qushayrī, who died in 514.

Furthermore, we can establish the following: his two main masters in mysticism were Abū M 'Abbās-b-M-b A Mansūr called 'Abbāsa Tūsī, who died in 549,[47] a pupil no doubt of Yūsuf Hamadhānī (d. 535: revered by 'Attār; 'Attār was supposed to have spent 17 years in Tus in close association with 'Abbāsa, then, after lengthy travels, he settled down in Nishapur); and M-b-M-b-'Alī Humrānī Qazwīnī, a disciple of Ibn Abi'l-Khayr via Fadl Rāwandī[48] and Dhū'l-Fiqār-b-Ma'bad Husaynī (465, d. 536).

The patron to whom he dedicated one of his first poetic romances, the Khusruwnāma, Abū'l-Fadl Sa'd al-Dīn ibn Rabīb, was the son of a Saljūq vizir (who died in 513), and the (younger) brother of an 'Abbāsid vizir

[43] Jāmī, 698. Such attestation is sufficient to authenticate Jawhar dhāt and Haylājnāma, two works that Said Naficy would like to transfer to a pseudo-'Attar of the ninth/fifteenth century, along with Būlbūlnāma, Ushtūmāma, and Basarnāma (which he considers childish: cf. Said Naficy, Intijā' der ahwāl 'Attār [Tehran, 1320], pp. 108, 132, 163). Moreover, at least one ms. of Haylāj dates from before the fifteenth century, from A.H. 661 (or 761).

[44] Preferred to "Tadhkirat al-awliyā'," 1905.

[45] H. Ritter, ap. DI, XXV, 1938, 134; the long epitaph of the waqf of Husayn Bayqarā' in Nishapur (Shadhyaq) was published ap. Matla' III, 104; I saw it on May 6, 1945.

[46] Ap. Ibn al-Fuwatī, Mu'jam al-alqāb, f. 114a (favorable commentary by Abbās Eghbāl): "Our master Nasīr D Tūsī saw him in Nishapur, and said: 'This was a shaykh full of shrewdness and wisdom on the subject of the maxims of mystics; the author of the famous Mantiq al-tayr and of a large Dīwān, he was killed by the Tatars.' "

[47] Caetani, Arabic onomastics no. 2065; he knew Sultan Sanjar ('Attār, Ilāhīnāma [bib. no. 1101-k], 154). 'Attār has preserved for us some violent statements on the Last Judgment by this master, when rebels will have their faces blackened (Mantiq, verse 187b), Mary will be resurrected as a male, for love, which transforms all, has taken Jesus from her, like Eve from Adam (ibid., verse 3539); "how shall I become a Muslim?" (ibid., verse 1959).

[48] Zabīdī, 'Iqd, 86, s.v. Qāsimīya.

(dismissed in 513), Abū Shujāʿ M-b-A Mansūr Rabīb, member of a vizirial family, the Rūdhrāwarī of Hamadhan, who were patrons of Hallājians.[49]

An apothecary and physician in the beginning, ʿAttār was never a conventual religious withdrawn from the world, but an artist whose eyes were enraptured by the beauty scattered throughout the universe, and a mystic at heart enthralled by the most heroic self-annihilations of love.

Did he, at the end of his life, combine with his veneration for a Sunni saint like Hallāj, a devotion for ʿAlī that would have gotten him denounced as a Shīʿite by a canonist from Samarqand to Amīr Burāq Turkman?[50] And are Shīʿite poems like Mazhar al-ʿajāʾib and Lisān al-ghayb (written in Mecca) actually by ʿAttār? Najm D Kubrā (d. 618) is quoted in these [poems], which should be noted.

His main authentic and direct disciple was Awhad al-Dīn Hāmid Kirmānī (who came to Baghdad in 632),[51] himself the master of the poet Fakhr ʿIrāqī (d. 688, in Damascus).[52] Kirmānī and ʿIrāqī, both influenced by ʿAQ Hamadhānī, emphasized the aesthetic aspect of ʿAttār's literary work, which made its way to India in that period, while the famous Jalāl Rūmī was gaining admirers for it in Anatolia.

ʿAttār, whose truly extraordinary literary fecundity (and also his facility as a mathnawī versifier) may perhaps also be explained by the flowering a century later of a cycle of pastiches, left three very different collections of authentic writings. In prose, the "Memorial of Saints" (Tadhkirat al-awliyāʾ), a magnificent sequence of hagiographical illuminations concluding with a "life of Hallāj" written with great dramatic force. In verse, first of all, some rather short and well-constructed fictionalized accounts, like Asrārnāma, Mantiq al-Tayr, Ushtūrnāma I-II, and Waslatnāma (we mention only those in which Hallāj appears); and then some amazing collections flowing with repeated lyrical outbursts, whose dimensions are as immense as the Hindu epics or the interior monologues typical of Péguy or Joyce: Haylājnāma, Jawhar al-dhāt I-II (Ushtūrnāma III), in which ʿAttār tirelessly sings of the mystical drowning of the soul in divine total-

[49] Sibt ibn al-Jawzī, ms. P. 1506, f. 288g; Rāwandī, Rāhat [?], pp. 153, 203.
[50] ʿAlī (= Haydar) is included in the isnād of the prophets of Haylājnāma (chapter 32; cf. Ushtūrnāma [bib. no. 1101-f] III, ch. 145). But the Dīwān Shams-i Tabrīz repeated that, and this is a Sunnite book. The idea of making ʿAlī the equal of Noah is, moreover, quite Ismāʿilian; the Ismāʿilis of India revere the Asrārnāma and the Jawhar al-dhāt of ʿAttār (Ivanow).
[51] Fuwatī, s.a.; he was attacked by Suhrawardī Baghdādī, cf. Eflaki [bib. no. 1131-a] I, 345.
[52] He had a monastery in Tokat and afterwards in Cairo, and died in Damascus.

ity, using Hallāj, "the highway brigand" (dūzderāh),[53] as the model and herald of this ardent annihilation.

In that land of Khurasan, where the head of the executed Hallāj, removed from the Caliphal "museum of heads" after a period of twelve months, had been paraded about, the theme of "decapitation" as a symbol of that death through love that divinizes burst forth to inspire the imagination of 'Attār. This radiant sheaf of the Hallājian legend came into view—in his Basarnāma (Book of the Beheaded), built around a vision of Hallāj in a dream that 'Attār relates to us in his Asrārnāma[54] as follows: He said to me, "this Sultan with the beautiful Name gave me this cup in place of my severed head—and whoever grasps the meaning of this cup drinks from it, —knowing that it will make him forget his own head (= his self)—and to gamble his body for his name—as I say, whosoever gambles his life, his body disappears in his name, —just as the alif disappears in bismi (llāh),[55] —when the body disappears the soul is purified; —free yourself of your soul, and annihilate yourself in the One Who is Named (by every name)."

2. His Tadhkirat al-awliyā' ("Memorial of Saints")

In the preface to this "Memorial of Saints," whose first recension concluded with the martyrdom of Hallāj, 'Attār tells us his reasons for "lifting the veil thus," which conceals from the world the beauty of the maxims and exploits of the great mystics; and he relies particularly on the authority of Yahyā-b-'Ammār, the master of Harawī, and also on Yūsuf Hamadhānī.[56] Now, the latter two, we know, were Hallājians, and the second was even one through initiation.

His purpose is above all aesthetic: he wants to make us share the admiration he has felt for their maxims; he also hopes by memorializing the saints to call forth, in accordance with the hadīth (of Wakī'), an outpouring of divine mercy.

His epigraph for Hallāj is significant: "this combatant killed by God in the holy war, this lion of the jungle of discovery, this intrepid and sincere warrior, this swallow of the tumultuous (divine) ocean, Husayn Mansūr Hallāj, may God have mercy upon him."

His notice on Hallāj is arranged as follows: a) conflicting opinions about him (among moderns, Abū Sa'īd-b-Abī'l-Khayr, 'AQ Jurjānī, A 'Alī Fārmadhī, Yūsuf Hamadhānī have a high opinion of him); the excess

[53] 'AW 'Azzām, Tasawwuf 'Attār [bib. no. 999-17] (1945), p. 68.
[54] H. Ritter, ZDMG XCIII (1939), 177, n. 1. ms. P. afp. 256, f. 8b.
[55] The alif of "(A)llāh."   [56] Cf. M. F. Köprülü [?], pp. 73-81.

of the *hulūlīya* Hallājīya in Balkh who desired to be killed in imitation of him; b) a concise biography, boiled down from Ibn Bākūyā; c) miracles, among which we find, beside the known details (Ibn Bākūyā, *Akhbār*), some accounts attributed to one of the direct masters of 'Attār, Rashīd Khired Samarqandī, and unknown elsewhere; d) forty-two maxims, a very rich and beautiful collection, only a part (eighteen) of which come from known sources (Sulamī, *Akhbār*),[57] and whose finishing doctrinal touches (*haqq* and *haqīqa*) prove that 'Attār received them from a local tradition (Yf Hamadhānī, via 'Abbāsa Tūsī); e) an account of the trial and the martyrdom. It would appear that in this part 'Attār had merely assembled the dramatic details provided him by a later literary tradition (e.g., the prisoners he had helped to escape, his eyes being put out; cf. 'Ar Iskāf), and which he was to recast later in the *Waslatnāma* and in his great Hallājian epics. This very exciting account presents some unique details concerning the attitudes of Ibn 'Atā' and Shiblī, touches lightly here and there on themes that later popular legend would deal with, and exceeds all bounds of verisimilitude with its literary outburst in the amassing punishments.

The plan is as follows: in prison (invisible for the first two nights: for he exchanges visits with *Hadra* [= the Divine Presence]; prays a thousand *rak'a* every day there; frees three hundred prisoners, and remains there); —the flagellation (three hundred blows; a heavenly voice gives him encouragement with each one; an irony connected with this subject by 'Abd al-Jalīl Saffār [Bukhārī]); before a crowd of a hundred thousand men he repeats *Anā'l-Haqq*, followed by three *wasīya* (to a dervish, to his *khādim*, to his son); walking proudly, he recites the *Nadīmī* quatrain; arriving at Bab al-Taq and turning in the direction of the *qibla*, he puts his foot on the step: "the ascent on the gibbet is the *mi'rāj* of heroes"; he buckles on his *mi'zār* and throws his *taylasān* off his shoulders; he meditates towards the *qibla* as he offers himself up. Then a series of maxims: responses to his disciples, placing devotion to the Law of his executioners before their devotion [to him], to his *khādim*, to Shiblī (Qur'ān 15:70; Sūfism; a rose thrown[58] at him when he was being stoned); a commentary on the cutting off of his hands and feet and on the blood with which he smeared his face and in which he washed his arms ("*raka'atānī fī'l-'ishq* . . . "); the putting out of his eyes; before his tongue was cut out, he

---

[57] Two from the *Tawāsīn* (3, 4) three from the *Akhbār* (5, 7, 31 = *Akhbār* 26, 73, 41), thirteen from Sulamī (15, 16, 27, 30, 31, 33, 35-37 = Sulamī, *Tabaqāt* 4, 19, 3, 21, 14, 2, 1, 12, 10; and 20, 18, 17, 19 = Sulamī, *Tafsīr*, 161, 182, 184, 199).

[58] *Ibid.*, ap. *Ushtūrnāma* III, ch. 200.

thanks God for his punishment, and speaks of his joy in the contemplation of His glory; smiling, his ears and nose cut off; stoned; beheaded at
the hour of the evening prayer (shām = 'ishā'). At the time of his stoning,
an old woman, her jug in hand (= Rābi'a?), drew near, saying: "hit him
hard, let this carder know that it is painful to speak lovingly with God."
His last words were "Hasb al-wājid" and Qur'ān 42:18. His trunk, his
ashes repeat "Anā'l-Haqq," thrown in the river; flood threatens Baghdad,
which is saved by Hallāj's khirqa being thrown in the river as he had prescribed to his khādim. Reflections: by a master, then by 'Abbāsa Tūsī (d.
549); he will return from the dead enchained, or else he will overthrow
everything (cf. Akhbār, no. 11); next by a master (a dream).[59] Shiblī's
two dreams (divulgence; his intercession on behalf of his executioners).
Dialogue with Iblīs.

3. The Early Poetic Collections: Būlbūlnāma, Ushtūrnāma I-II,
Mantiq al-tayr, Waslatnāma, Ilāhīnāma, Basarnāma

The oldest collection in which 'Attār mentions Hallāj is the Būlbūlnāma
(The Book of the Nightingale), written for his four-year-old son. It is a
short work consisting of twenty-six verses: "the nightingale's reply to
the Prophet Solomon":[60]

The nightingale replies: O prophet, our beverage has neither cup nor chalice;
—the intoxication is spiritual which overcomes me from this wine whose cup
does not hold for drinking what is not (God).
He who is ardent with the vision stays awake from evening to morning; and as
the cup-bearer pours a copious amount for him, how could he think of eating or
sleeping?
My body is weak, O Solomon—but I can speak better than other birds; that
one feels my pain who, like me, devours his liver.
Of the wine which I have drunk this morning from the hand of the cup-bearer
of the royal Court, —only a drop need be poured down the throat for reason and
thought to abandon you.
Mansūr received a mouthful of this wine, —he said "Anā'l-Haqq," and the
world became filled with tumult; as soon as he had taken the cup of union in his
hand, the muftis judged his blood lawful by fatwā [to shed].
Two hundred[61] of them signed this fatwā, abandoning any sense of shame; in
their bazaar they displayed this ecstatic, —holding his hero's head between his
hands.
Around the gibbet he went, saying "it was my jealousy (of God), not love of
others (than God), which caught me; —at dawn I went out into the streets of
love: I saw a shadow fall on the way.

---

[59] Cf. this volume, Figure 14.
[60] Ms. P., Persian supplement 811, ff. 448-453: f. 450a.
[61] 200; 380 (Waslatnāma); 300 (Yeseri).

I did not look at a forbidden face, I have taken nothing for food from any but the hand of God; —He enraptured me with just one of His glances, thereby incurring censure upon my way.[62]

Why should the lover not be so infatuated, to the point of following his beloved all around; —to one whose sun has passed through his door, how could a shadow exist to his eye?

He was hoisted onto his gibbet to be stoned, —they pelted him from every side with stones, —but complained neither of the stones, the gibbet, nor the rope, —he did not stop saying "Anā'l-Haqq" even for the space of a single hair.

Gate, wall, stone, rope, gibbet, —ropes of the tent of his severed life, —bathed in the water and fire of his love, —all resound joyously in his voice.

His ipseity was already consumed by His (divine) essence. God was the greater ipseity! A wave from the sea washed over the deserted beach, —where it split open the shell: and the pearl returned to the sea.[63]

Thousands of people have drunk this wine (of the Covenant), —but they have not revealed the divine secret.

Next comes the *Ushtūrnāma* I, in which mystical ascent is compared to the pilgrim's arduous journey to Mecca on camel. It consists particularly of anecdotes about Jesus with only one verse on "Anā'l-Haqq," words uttered without pronunciation or tongue;[64] and the *Ushtūrnāma* II, studied by H. Ritter, which contains a lyrical dithyramb on the sanctity of Hallāj inserted into the account of a mystical shipwreck of a child.[65]

Verses 2261-2272 of *Mantiq al-tayr* describe Hallāj after his mutilations smearing his face with blood to hide his pallor: "For red rose is the color of the blood of the brave" . . . "the one who goes to bed and sleeps with the seven-headed dragon in July—is playing a dangerous game, —his smallest fragment is hung on the gibbet."[66]

Next, in verses 4233-4240: "while the body of Hallāj was being burned in the fire, —a mad lover came with staff in hand—and sat down close to the handful of ashes. —He began to speak to it with a fiery tongue, —he kindled the ashes well; —and he said to them: tell the truth! —"he who shouted "Anā'l-Haqq," where is he now? tell everything that you have said and heard, —and everything that you know and have seen, —all that is only the beginning of your legend; —therefore destroy yourself, your place is not in these ruins; —you must have an Origin that is supremely free and pure, —what difference does it make to you whether or not it has boughs? —There is a real Sun that lasts forever, —may neither our atom nor our shadow continue to exist? peace."[67]

---

[62] Cf. *Akhbār*, no. 15.
[63] On the pearl, see *Tadhk*. II, 140, line 13.
[64] Ms. P. quoted *supra*, ff. 331-358: f. 332b.
[65] H. Ritter, ap. *ZDMG* XCIII (1939), 177, n. 1. This child reappears in *Jawhar al-dhāt* I (23-32) and in *Ushtūrnāma* III (130-243).
[66] Tassy tr., pp. 123-124.
[67] *Ibid.*, p. 236.

Chapter VI of *Waslatnāma* (= *Mansūrnāma*), consisting of 208 verses,[68] is devoted almost entirely to the martyrdom of Hallāj. This account, written for a wide audience, had a large circulation in Turkestan, Anatolia, and India. It is the prototype of similar works written in Turkish and Urdu.[69]

"Mansūr was in an astonishing desolation of love, —he had attained a thousand perfections on the way to realization" (v. 1).

"He had drunk the wine of union with God, —he was constantly bubbling with desire for God" (v. 4). "He kept secrets hidden for five years, then suddenly he caused a thousand uproars" (v. 14). "He said: '*Anā'l-Haqq*,' revealed his secret, and all Baghdad was thrown into confusion" (v. 15). "Three hundred eighty '*ulamā*', among the scribblers on paper of that time" (v. 17), condemned him to death as a *kāfir*; and they dragged him off before the Caliph, who felt "one hundred thousand prickles in the heart," for he loved him, had read his books; but, being fearful of the crowd and the '*ulamā*', he had him only put in prison; "I know that he is a man of God, neither blasphemous, hypocritical, nor deluded" (v. 28). In prison, he freed four hundred prisoners, who escaped through four hundred chinks in the walls; he alone stayed behind; the prison superintendent, dumbfounded, came to kiss his feet. And the '*ulamā*' got together, the crowd gathered in a mob at the prison gate, where Junayd, alerted by Shiblī, came to exhort Mansūr: keep quiet, your imagination is running away with you, you do not know how to express love; the Prophet did not say what you are saying (v. 65). Mansūr retorted: O father, Ahmad said "*man ra'nī*," "*liya ma' Allāh*," "*nahnū aqrab*,"[70] how do you know I am going astray? In wrapping yourself in the clothes of the Law (*khirqe-i nāmūs*), you are only committing yourself to the path of fraud (*sālūs*) (v. 75). The '*ulamā*' obtained a *fatwā* in which Junayd declares that outwardly he must be killed, but inwardly he knows God. The '*ulamā*' and the ignorant, making outcries, led Mansūr off to the gibbet, "he, this victim of love, this treasure of light" (v. 87). Junayd explained to him that his divulgence led to his death. [Hallāj] answered him: "O companion, I have fallen into a deep ocean—I am no longer Mansūr, no longer look upon me as such. . . . I am God, I am God, Me, God; devoid of rancor, pride, or covetousness (v. 97);[71] I annihilate my

---

[68] Ms. P., Persian suppl. 654. This title does not refer to the *Haylājnāma* (corr. S. Naficy, pp. 115, 128).

[69] Ahmadī, Murīdī; Shīvrājpūrī.

[70] Three famous hadīths.

[71] This verse is the refrain of *Basarnāma*: "*man Khudāyim* (2 folios), *man Khudā*. . . ."

own existence, I survive with the permanence even of *Haqq* (= God); I bring my body to the top of the gibbet, —even more do I bring the declaration of this Name (= *Haqq*)—so that lovers may understand that the one whom the Supreme Name burns has uttered the supreme mystery; —I come in the name of the whole universe, thus in the form of Adam. . . . I span the route of Ahmad, and thus I sacrifice myself for the way of Ahmad (v. 107); I have drunk wine from the cup of Ahmad, and I utter the creative word of the universe[72]—I have not left his route, O Shiblī (v. 111) . . . there is, in fact, a wise man who is not the Pole of the universe—he is called Kabīr (= Ibn Khafīf) in this world, he is the protector of novices and students in mysticism, —he will explain my state, —he will be here tomorrow, my son; —at this moment he is leaving Shiraz, you will see him tomorrow with your own eyes" (v. 119). Shiblī repeated this to the crowd, urging it to be patient. Kabīr arrived in Baghdad and said to Mansūr: "O man who has reached realization, why has a gibbet been erected for you . . . why have you revealed the enigma *"Anā'l-Haqq*," which has led you to the foot of the gibbet (v. 130). . . . God was a hidden treasure, and lo! you have disclosed Him, why? . . . you had steadfastly kept his secrets hidden through five years of being close to Him, —why now have you taken leave of your senses and put both worlds in an uproar?" —Mansūr answered him: "O you who know, what can I tell you that you don't already know? —the ocean of an immense Idea (*ma'nā*) has overflowed, clear, limitless, infinite (v. 136) . . . the smallest of its waves, with *"Anā'l-Haqq*," leads to the Absolute God. . . ." Kabīr resumed: "What you say is true, —I know that your essence is God." Mansūr said: "Killing me has now become *wājib* (a canonical duty), —hurry, '*ulamā*', in conformity with the Law (*sharī'a*)." —Shaykh Kabīr then repeated the *fatwā* of Junayd. The '*ulamā*', making outcries, arranged the gibbet's rope (v. 150) and lit a fire at its base— included in the huge crowd were the shaykhs, *sāliks*, *wāsils*, '*ulamā*' and the ignorant, and a great multitude of men, on this day that was as amazing as the Day of Resurrection, —with Hallāj, in the middle of it all, standing upright on the ground, —like a lion deep in the bush country. —He was not afraid . . . he cried out *"Anā'l-Haqq*," which rent the soul of everyone, overwhelming the *sāliks*, illuminating the *wāsils*, melting the bodies of Sufīs, the souls and hearts of the '*ārifs* (v. 159), separating the ascetics from their own asceticism. Then Mansūr cried out *Anā'l-Haqq* a second time, and the entire universe echoed him. —The earth,

---

[72] It is the Prophet who invites Mansūr to say *"Anā'l-Haqq"* (cf. Murīdī).

bricks, the whole of nature, in this melee, proclaimed "Anā'l-Haqq." Someone came to Mansūr, looked at his (severed) hand, saw that his blood was flowing from it writing "Anā'l-Haqq" on the ground, and said to him: "What is this mystery, this love, this sign?" (v. 168). —Then he rubbed his face with his hand, saying: "Blood is the sweat of the brave" (murdānrā z khūnest ābrū)—then, once again, he rubbed his face with his arm—he conveyed great joy in doing this, his hand had bathed his afflic-tion. His questioner said to him: "What do I see? Why do you rub your arm with your hand? —This time I am performing the prayer (namāz); I was merely doing my ablutions again with pure blood—this is the prayer of love, and this is its ablution, which is only valid when performed in blood, O man of handsome face!" (v. 173). —Then Shiblī asked him: "Explain now what Sūfism is. —You see its least important part now, as you wait for certitude in the way of God." —He asked another question: "O seeing one, tell me the way of love?" —Love, here, is to act and to suffer, and, after, to be burned in the fire (v. 177). —Such were his words, such was his state, which people talk about everywhere. —Then, after he was beheaded because of the vileness of the 'ulamā' and the faith-less ignorants, —the wind carried his ashes to the water, —where they wrote "Allāh" (v. 180).

There follows an exhortation "O brother," addressed to the reader: to arouse him to self-sacrifice.[73]

Ilāhīnāma.

When before the gibbet they severed at one blow—his two forearms, here is the way Hallāj complained:

With the blood which dripped from his arms, —he smeared his face and his stumps

And said only: "When one knows the secret of love, —one must perform the ablutions for prayer in one's blood."[74]

Someone said to him: "O ill-fated one, —why do you smear your body with blood?

If you perform this ablution with blood, —you render the essence of prayer worthless beforehand."

No, it is in this way that heroes, drawing near their beloved, —are no longer afraid of anything, of epithet or scorn, or any creature,

For every heart rooted in divine perseity, —no longer has any scrap of blame to fear.

Go, hero, be in the Act itself of God, —regard the others as nothing, be this Act itself.

---

[73] This chapter (VI) of Waslatnāma is identical to the Mansūmāma referred to by Stewart and Ethé (Persian mss. cat. Ind. Of., I, 617: same incipit).
[74] 'Attār, Ilāhīnāma, edited by H. Ritter, Bibl. Isl. XII (1940), p. 107.

Like the celestial sphere that revolves around the world, —raise yourself as a
hero above your own desire.
For if your love became lax, —your timidity would make the bond of your
vow an affliction.
If those who have the strength of many lions—are already like ants before the
strength of love,
You who are only a little ant[75] in strength and size—what makes you think you
can stand up against love?

Basamāma (Paris ms., Persian suppl. 1485, f. 1a-7a). The *Basarnāma*, a
very short poem about fifteen pages long divided into nine paragraphs,
begins as follows:

I reveal the secret of decapitation, —I am looking through the world for lovers
who have gone astray.

This is the offering of death through love; and though this poem sums
up the example of Hallāj and, in its Persian translation, repeats his "I am
the Truth" as a refrain, Hallāj himself is nowhere mentioned in it by
name. Here is the refrain that we have seen quoted in *Waslatnāma* in connection with Hallāj:

Here I am God (*man khudāyim, man khudāyim, man khudā*), here I am God, me,
God; —without any rancor (*kīna*), pride, or covetousness.

'Attār observes (VII = f. 5b) that if Satan refused to adore Adam, it
was because he did not realize that Adam was the *Rūh*; he himself
claimed to be identical with Adam and the *Rūh*. To keep the frock of the
Law (*khirqe-i nāmūs*) is to be *kāfir*; one must not venerate what is under
dilq, but be guided by God Himself (VIII = f. 6b).

4. The Great Lyric Recitatives (Hallājian Epics)

a. Jawhar al-Dhāt I-II. Book I of the Substance of Essence (*Jawhar al-
dhāt: nisf awwal*) consists of 94 chapters and 13, 262 verses.
After a eulogy to the Prophet, two hadīths (*man 'arafa nafsahu, mā
ra'aytu shay'ā*), he deals with the divine sign imprinted on man (the
beauty of Joseph; Adam; 'Alī), the form of the divine omnipotence's
manifestation (15); "if you are beheaded, you will be consumed . . . you
will be Hallāj, you will be crowned, death is better than this life . . . losing your head you will be the martyr of Karbala, Jirjīs, and Yahyā, and
will leave this world. Say *Anā'l-Haqq* to become a *wāsil* in the consummation of love. Say *Anā'l-Haqq* and you will be Mansūr scattering pearls

---

[75] Cf. the Turkish poet Zuhūrī.

of light here. Say *Anā'l-Haqq*, be prince on the gibbet. Say *Anā'l-Haqq* to become Unity. Say *Anā'l-Haqq*, and you will be 'Attār, who will entice you (by singing) from high on the gibbet. Say *Anā'l-Haqq*, overreach your heart and your soul, and scatter them for the glory of God."

In Chapter 18 (to annihilate oneself, to find the way, to become the divine dwelling place): "Be brave, cry *Anā'l-Haqq*, feigning the *kāfir*, which will bring on your death. —Be brave, cry *Anā'l-Haqq*, "I am the (Eternal) truth," so as to put yourself as a target for the arrow of love. —He who says *Anā'l-Haqq* and has the vision of God."

Chapter 19 repeats the textual account, given in *Asrārnāma*, of the dream in which Hallāj appears beheaded with a cup in his hand, and comments lyrically on it; it is the symbol of essential union. Then a short parable, of the fox and the well, is inserted; the well represents this perishable world.

Next comes the story of the mystical vocation of a very beautiful child, the son of a merchant who sailed the route to China. Taught by a wise master (*Pīr Dāna*: 23-33), he learns from Moses' burning bush to say "*Anā Allāh*": "I say *Anā'l-Haqq* before the king of Baghdad . . . I say *Anā'l-Haqq*, I am also here bringing cure to your wound of grief . . . I cry *Anā'l-Haqq* from the bottom of the sea . . ." —"Like Mansūr, this child revealed the mystery of this reality. . . ."

Chapters 37-43, 54-56, 62, 77 deal with Satan. This creature of fire, multiform flame, source of the imaginative (*khayāl*), pure jealousy of nature (*tabī'a*; "your true Satan is your *nafs*," 77), has yielded to decree (*qadā'*) and has gained the temporary mission of tempting Adam and his kin; but this is actually a dissimulation (*talbīs*) on the part of the boldest of God's lovers, whom the collar of damnation (*tawqī' la'nat*) enchains only for a time. (56: Law and reality are not in opposition to each other; speak the saying of Mansūr. . . .)

Chapters 44-66 are concerned with the creation "*'ala sūratihi*" of Adam and Eve, their nexus with the Prophet, their temptation and exile. 'Alī declares (61): "Intoxicate yourself with this wine, be Hallāj, —so that your being may offer itself to everyone as a target (*amāj*); —inebriate yourself with this wine, be Mansūr, —so that the voice of your soul may become a trumpet" (then a parallel is drawn between Mansūr and Jesus). In chapter 68 (moneity of essence and its attributes): "Mansūr's refrain was just the divine breath (Qur'ān 69:13) (in the trumpet). . . . *Anā'l-Haqq* echoed in every being and in every place." Mansūr, in answer to an unnamed person's question, shows the prostration and prayer expected of the perfect (chapter 69). To see God forever one must be on Hallāj's gibbet as a victim of love, as a target for love's arrow (chapter 71). After some chapters on Ibn Abī'l-Khayr,[76] the *Rūh al-qudus*, and Shiblī (72, 73, 78, 79), in which Shiblī[77] tells how to liberate oneself in this world: "Be ruined in reputation (*kharābāti*), be the disgrace of the world, eat the dust and pebbles of this world, —be ruined in reputation, kindle the fire. . . . Cry *Anā'l-Haqq*, be the Eternal in this world. . . . Cry *Anā'l-Haqq*, like Pharaoh secretly, like *'man ra'nī'* (= Muhammad), like Moses, like the Bush, like Mansūr. Cry the *yaqīn* in blasphemy (*kāfir*) itself, *Anā'l-Haqq*." Next, following an orison, there is a dialogue between a much-admiring Bayezid and Mansūr on the subject of self-annihilation (81, 82). Mansūr, "who is burned like a taper, like a moth," exhorts him to go further than Shiblī in *fanā'*. After a question directed at a *pīr-i tarīqa* (84), and another (how to find totality) at Mansūr (85), we have the story of a devout man guided by a *"hātif-i ghayb"* (86-87) and some statements about the essence of the Whole, the Way, and the Arrival. Chapter 92 deals with self-renunciation: "say *Anā'l-Haqq*, and you will be absolute light—the voice of 'Attār (who calls you to it) is, without any doubt, the vision of the vision—the voice of 'Attār resounds beyond the site—the voice of 'Attār is that of Mansūr on the gibbet." Then he announces "another book" in which he will explain the secret technique of this vocation, which does not come from the intellect (*'aql, hūsh*), but from the *haylāj*, the silent wisdom beneath the atoms of the universe, the spiritual Idea (*ma'nā rūhānī*), of which this other book, which will deal with the very essence of God (*dhāt-i khudā*), will speak. I shall reveal candidly this "ecstatic mystery," which remains veiled here; there I shall lift the veil on it, bringing a cure to each wounded heart; "the reality of the *haylāj* is Mansūr Hallāj"; he is the one who says now *Anā'l-Haqq*; awaken the echo of love in creation and space, comment on and explain the word *haylāj*; if you read my book here, —it will be your self, and your self will be the mystery of my veil—be assured that 'Attār is the elect, and that all things have been created through him. . . . God speaks through the heart of 'Attār. . . ."

Book II of the Substance of Essence (*Jawhar al-dhāt: nisf thānī*) consists of 67 chapters and more than 12,042 verses (120 folios 1-2; let us remember that the total number of verses in the six books of J. Rūmī's *Mathnawī* is only 25,632).

After the exordium, someone asked Mansūr the ultimate outcome and

---

[76] "This commander-in-chief of religion (*sepehsālār-i dīn*), this king of reality" says: "I sought God in sign after sign for thirty years, then he became lost in the ocean." He also says: "I have seen God, really (*yaqīn*), as butter becomes clear in milk."

[77] He also says that he sought for a long time, then realized that it was necessary to renounce every indicative sign.

the origin of Adam. —"I know them both, for I am an Adam, the Tablet, the ocean, the Intellect, love, strength . . . all the prophets and saints, and the immortal Sun . . . and the heavens and paradise" (Chapter 2). Next a definition of the unitive *nutq* of the heart and of the desire of the heart to be set afire: "Burn, O heart, which has intoxicated you like Mansūr (Chap. 4)." The illusory human form is only the talisman that imprisons the treasure of divine beauty under the appearance of suffering and pain (6). The story of Mansūr (*qisse-i Mansūr*: I) is that in his inmost self he found the Unique One, the reality of Impiety, the secret of religion. "The body comes from dust, the soul from Essence." —"Be the slave of love (*ghulāmi 'ishq*) in order to find the way . . . to become King . . . to be Adam. . . ." "Be a stove, put fire and the shining smoke of the Friend in it. . . ." Mansūr then describes the heart. "The only one who has been able to explain it is Mansūr Hallāj, —who makes a single crown out of the treasure of essences, —and, quickly putting this crown on his head, —became a diadem for the universe, —by this crown raised above him, —that no one other than he had, divine, —anything he did, he still uttered the "*lā illā*"—in his self he exhibited the "*lawlā*," —among men he placed the crown above and below, —although, according to the Law, it may only be below, —he said *Anā'l-Haqq* wearing this imperial crown, —became the sun of the seven heavens, —finally divinized, —he burned his own crown on his head, —thus did he attain pre-eternal royalty in the end, —from this royalty he came back a contemplator of reality, —in the end he found the essence of "*lā*" and "*illā*" —laying down his head and his diadem, returning to every "*ā*," —in the end finding the vision of "*qul huwa 'Llāh*," —he remembered "*sibghat Allāh* among the essences, —and seeing again he was God, —he said "*Anā'l-Haqq*" constantly in this sense (8).

Chapter 9 describes unitive emanation (*fayd*) in relation to the beauty and seductiveness of Joseph. In Chapter 10, 'Attār says the following, speaking to God: "Like your Mansūr I shall in the end be burned, —for I display your bracelets out of love, —like your Mansūr I am mad, —for the Tavern of your essence gets me drunk, —like your Mansūr I find "*Anā'l-Haqq*" again, —and I repeat it, hearing it from You . . . *Anā'l-Haqq*, I say it in a state together with You, —in which I have true vision of the essence of union. . . ."

Chapter 12 develops the following theme ('Attār is speaking here to his disciple): "You have arrived here at the stage of union without (passing through) any (other) stage." Chapter 13 (the real essence of man whose highest expression is Hallāj), "the physical nature of man in him is like the nature of Satan: it casts him into Hell; he ends up with earth, and sheds his blood." Chapter 15 details the way to find the transfiguring sun of Unity with Mansūr, by removing the veil of forms; then the problem of the whole and the parts in reality (Chapter 17), the theme of Majnūn and Laylā: "Mansūr, in fact, was Laylā and also Majnūn . . . the reality of the essence of Mansūr was no more than his soul;[78] he says Anā'l-Haqq with You, —and he will say it with You until the Trumpet sounds." Chapters 19 and 20 deal with the fiat (kun) and the "why" of God: "Why did You come to the Throne . . . among the stars? . . . in fact, You came to the bottom of the sea, —scattering shells there with the pearl "illā," but You do not dwell in all other things forever, —You did not complete the Ka'ba to last forever, —the approach to Your own Ka'ba is Mansūr, who found it, —who is celebrated for that on all horizons. . . . Come like him, like 'Attār, to union through the Prophet. . . ."

Chapters 21-28 are devoted to Muhammad and the Prophets, to the mi'rāj, and to the light of the soul (list: Adam, Noah, Abraham, Moses, Jacob, Joseph, Isaac, Ishmael, Joseph, Jirjīs, Job, Jesus, Ahmad, Murtadā, and Mansūr on the gibbet). Chapter 29 deals with the elements of this world: "I carved out a path for myself among the living. . . . I saw myself "lā" and I became "illā". . . . I shall tell these secrets in Haylāj. . . . The haylāj makes me risk my head here . . . it is through the haylāj that I have seen the mystery of Mansūr . . . like the pre-eternal Artist, I have found my essence. . . . The talisman that encloses the treasure of the essence is your heart." Chapter 30 is concerned with the hadīth "I was a hidden treasure"; Chapter 31 (cf. 62) with the cup of love from which Mansūr drank, leading to his sacrifice and his Anā'l-Haqq. He was the king of the sāliks. . . . Mansūr's death was one of love . . . having arrived at this stage, he found his self empty; he had reached the age of essential love . . . fire, earth, water and air, in everything he saw God . . . like the Prophets (Moses on Sinai) . . . attain the Arrival by proceeding from the Law (shar') like Mansūr.

Chapter 32: Mansūr answers the question "where is the cure of love?" —It is the face of God, which is both the suffering and the cure . . . the Arrival for lovers occurs without suffering. . . . He describes the Arrival, the reality of man (34): "Your beauty tempted me on sight . . . then I saw Your beauty again in my essence . . . in the stars . . . the waft of air . . . the Ka'ba of the heart. . . ." In Chapter 36 we find a commentary of Qur'ān 24:35 (Allāh nūr) and 15:29 (nafakhtu . . .); he refers to his

---

[78] The theme of "Hallāj, half man" (Recueil, p. 66; Qissa; Najm Rāzī, Mirsād [bib. no. 1107-a]). Cf. this edition, 1, Figure 8: Majnūn and Laylā.

Musībatnāma; a list of prophets . . . 'Attār says, "I am the soul, the spirit, the heart, the essence of imagination, which is not vain. . . ." Chapter 37: the secret of Mansūr and the total mystery, "tell of the Arrival at love: *Anā'l-Haqq.*" Chapter 38: the secrets of the Friend's heart, and Mansūr's secrets. Chapter 39: earth (and its thousand impressions) and the three other elements. Chapters 40-42: earth and spirit, the four seasons, heat, cold, dryness, and humidity; and Jesus (a question put to Mansūr by a master, *buzurgī*): "You are the beloved who pursues his lovers." "Like Jesus, here I am now at the foot of the gibbet, —like your Mansūr, in this situation. . . ." Chapter 43: God's call (*nidā'*) to the spirit: "in this mirror (of your form) he who is Mine casts your glance. . . ."

Chapters 44-46: the true story (*qisse*) of the soul and the heart: their dialogue: the reality of *Nūr Muhammadī.* Chapters 47-48: Mansūr explains how the *sālik* becomes *wāsil*: prostrating himself before the idol if it represents the beloved; "I practiced idolatrous worship of lovers . . . the Christian monastery is the reality for us all . . . we must therefore bow down before this king who enraptures the heart of idolaters . . . in an idolatrous prostration which may be outside the proper place . . . make your prostration (*sajda*) by contemplating Him in this form spiritually (*sūra ve ma'nā*)."

Chapter 49: Iblīs explains why he rejected the *sajda* before Adam (an idol representing God): ('Attār, *in fine* 48: "to God, damnation in this world is a parable, —as when He put His Mansūr on the gibbet in this world . . . the reality of damnation is something very beautiful. . . .") "I refused to bow down, which would have meant showing love for Adam; since the origin of my damnation is the Friend as my Beloved. —I am bound to hope in the end that He destines for me; —His word that has damned me, the Friend, dwells in my heart . . . and in my soul . . . ; why should I suffer this damnation; —His word that has damned me is in my heart and my soul, —in every moment a hundred secrets are hidden within me . . . since I know that the word of the Friend dwells in my essence, —I care no more for the creation of my universe. . . ."

Chapter 51: Husayn Mansūr, asked about that, states the following:[79] "the truth about Iblīs, in this world, remains a mystery of the Beloved . . . this lover, this consummate knight . . . has thus become the captive and the prisoner of love, —in chains of incomparable damnation . . . all of the prophets tremble before the secret of damnation in the presence of God . . . whereas Iblīs, for the sake of a single *sajda* (refused), has chosen

---

[79] The thesis of the *Tawāsīn* is different.

to suffer a wound until the Last Judgment . . . " (it was out of desire for the coming of the Prophet, before whom he bowed down, that Iblīs had refused the *sajda* before Adam) (cf. Chapters 59-60).

Chapters 52-56: questions put to Bayezid concerning the *Hadra* (= the divine presence); exclamations by 'Attār: "Muhammad has become the soul of 'Attār's heart, in which the sureness of Mansūr's secrets is immortalized . . . in the light of Muhammad I raise the crown on my head, —by this light he speaks in me, like Hallāj . . . "; then a list of the prophets: Adam, Noah, Shīth, Ibrāhīm, Ishmael, Isaac, Jacob, Joseph, Moses, John, Khidr, Jesus, Muhammad, Haydar; a second list (chapter 55) adds Ayyūb and Jirjīs. In Chapter 56, 'Attār remarks that *Haylāj* = jam' (= the Second Intellect), while the First (= *hūsh*) is Muhammad.

The last ten chapters show signs of additions having been made; the comment "here ends the *Jawhar-i dhāt*" is repeated three times, in Chapters 57, 62, and 67.

Chapter 57: " . . . you are Mansūr, see within yourself, —in a single real glance, your body and your soul, —your body is the Arrival without your knowing it, . . . here it is the Soul of the soul (= God). . . ." Chapter 59: Iblīs vis-à-vis Muhammad. Chapter 63: the *Jawhar-i dhāt* is ended, now we shall study the *Haylāj* . . . ('Attār speaks to himself): "speak of the *haylāj* and pour out your soul,—your heart and your soul for God . . . speak of the *haylāj* . . . be the essential reality of "*illā' Llāh*," —speak of the *haylāj* in the presence of the supreme Artisan, —for you have seen the central point and the compass exist . . . , speak of the *haylāj*, to point out the Friend . . . if you speak of the *haylāj* this time, lift the veil of *kufr* over your faith . . . ; I know the essential reality of Mansūr, —I have his presence and light continually. . . ." Chapter 67: "now nothing is left but the *haylāj*, nothing else . . . no more veil, God is discovered, —when I see myself, I see the Friend . . . without metensomatosis (*tanāsukh* = without His successive historical personifications). . . . O Beloved whose face is cheerful like the moon, —lift the veil from Your beauty, —that I may see Your radiant beauty, . . . living in the fragrance of the cup of love, —a trickster who reunites lovers, —with the parrot of reason . . . and the nightingale of love. . . . O Sūfī, let us assimilate purity."

b. Ushtūmāma III. In the *Haylājnāma* (32, 37), 'Attār informs us of his having previously composed an extensive monograph entitled *Ushtūrnāma* on the mental state of Mansūr. This could not refer to *Ushtūmāma* I, mentioned above, which is rather short and in which there is only one long passage about Hallāj. Paris manuscript (Persian Supplement) 1795, however, contains a huge *Ushtūrnāma* III, whose style is directly related to *Jawhar-i dhāt* and to *Haylājnāma*. We believe this is the one referred to, for we have seen no sign of *Ushtūrnāma* II.

Mujallad suyūm ez kitāb Ushtūrnāma (ff. 275b-383a of Paris ms., Pers. Suppl., 1795) = book III of the Book of the Camel, 244 chapters, around 15, 314 verses.

The text begins *ex abrupto* with a chapter "on the annihilation of one's cadaveric body and the arrival at Nearness" (1). During the whole of the 244 chapters Hallāj is suspended on the gibbet, from whence he responds to questions put to him by famous Sūfīs: Bayezid (7, 13, 29, 41, 91, 112, 128, 186, 195), Kabīr (15, 17); expressly identified with Ibn Khafīf (77, 189, 195), Junayd (3, 18, 32, 35, 38, 61, 204, 230-232), his *khādim* (199), a mysterious predestined child, who in the end vanishes in flames (130, 142, 148, 151, 234, 242-243), a mender (*pāre dūz* = *raqqaʿ*: 220). The stages of punishment are indicated: cutting off of his hands (18, his blood, pouring out, cries "*Anāʾl-Haqq*"; 32), tongue (30, 33, he continues to speak), stoning (200: a *sālik* throws a scarlet rose at him (*gūl rengīn*), and he groans (*feryād*); fire (243).

Writing in the form of definitions of *tawhīd* (2, 22, 24, 44, 48, 59), of the vision of the whole (6, 37, 46, 56), of divine love (22, 26, 30), and of the God Who is with you (57, 58), ʿAttār sketches out his first definition of the sanctity of Mansūr: based on the prophetic mission (5, 6, ʿĪsā; 11, Muhammad) and the Law (12, 52).

Chapters 60-161, while continuing to discuss *tawhīd* (108, 128, 140, 160), emphasize the prophets (81, 88 Muhammad, 90, 103, 127, 134, 145; list: Adam, Noah, Shīth, Khalīl, Isaac, Jacob, Joseph, Ayyūb, Jirjīs [his decapitation previously cited], Moses, Solomon, Sālih, Zakariyā, Yūnus, Jesus, Mustafā, Haydar), profess the (philosophical) belief in a purely spiritual resurrection (cf. 12) through the disappearance of the *sūra* (which is bemoaned, 63-69), call to mind the theme of mystical intoxication (84, 104), and prepare an initial astrological theory of the Hallājian mystery: suggesting that the couple of *khūrshīd* and *qamar* (sun and moon) equals the couple of *jān* and *dil* (= *rūh* + *qalb* = spirit and heart) (110, 118, 125, 128, 222, 235: *qalam*). The heart was explicitly defined as the divine ray's point of impact (*nazargāh ilāhī*, 110). Hallāj would therefore be in the same relation vis-à-vis the Prophet Muhammad as the moon is vis-à-vis the Sun (= Prime Intellect).

Chapters 162-244 proceed from canonical Law (*sharʿ*, *sharīʿa*, 162-166) to establish the necessity of voluntary sacrifice of one's life through divine love (169, 170, 179, 207), comment on the *shahāda* (*illā*, 184), several

Qur'ānic verses (*qul Huwa'Llāh*, 182; *qul al-Rūh*, 212; *wajh Allāh*, 213) and technical terms (*ittihād*, 179, 215; *khayāl*, 202), and end on the theme of the consuming fire, the divine burning (224, 226, 228, 233; *Anā'l-Haqq*, 239, 243).

This monograph of Hallāj did not satisfy 'Attār. The astral imagery was too physical in it (sun-moon = intellect-heart). On the other hand, Hallāj appears in it as the equal of the prophets, portrayed as a second Jesus (an old tradition drawn from the Hallājians of Talaqan), though to justify his execution 'Attār had to put *shar*' = *nūr qāhir*, and *haqīqa* = *walāya* = *nūr maqhūr*. In the *Haylājnāma*, 'Attār, so as not to contradict the latter equation and not to teach the superiority of sainthood over prophethood, abandons the parallel outlined here (which presented some Christian ambiguities) between Hallāj and Jesus, placing Hallāj instead in the second rank of prophets.

We present the following as a translation *in extenso* of Chapter 6 (f. 278a: "to explain the Whole, Mansūr speaks"):

To explain the Whole, Mansūr speaks:
God has decreed the following: —In every instant His decree is thus.
God means to express the Whole with my tongue—Gives my nature the power to speak the Whole.
Here is the Essence in my essence—While all of You remains hidden.
He has desired this act of mine from pre-eternity—Thus I offer my neck for it.
This desire was [expressed] at the time of His judgment—Let the gibbet be smeared with my blood.
It was His judgment that these hands be severed—His Hand is over every hand.
He gave me His own hand in taking these two from me—Concealing the end, both good and bad.
His judgment also aimed at all of my atoms—In their original nature.
I accepted this rank from the beginning—And I realize its fulfillment on my head.
Two of these three *sar*[80] are united together—I have exceeded being and nothingness.
Origin and rank are simply the Essence—*Lā ilāha illā* is a verse, that is all.
The sign of these atoms is Faith in Him—Whereas their essence fades away.
My spirit rests in the supreme Spirit—Let both worlds find their life-breath in Him.

This time for love of the pre-eternal mystery—I myself have offered my soul.
I am here, now, high on my gibbet—And all of these atoms in turmoil, see them.

---

[80] *Sar*(ī) means both head and origin. And *sarī* means rank.

Like Jesus (*repeat* [?]) I have reached the height of the gibbet—Having wholly preserved myself.

Like Jesus I revealed the secret in public—Which the begs, shaykhs, and the great know nothing of.

Like Jesus I came to the gibbet of certitude—To become steadfast there.

Like Jesus, raised up in the same place—I achieved the same justice in love.

Like Jesus from the peak of the gibbet of love—I repeated my profession of Love.

Like Jesus, having arrived at the destination of those who have arrived—I look directly into the Sun.

Like Jesus, I am the fixed point of everything—Myself evident and hidden.

Like Jesus, in the midst of the uproar—Everything inspires me to sing.

Like Jesus I plunge headlong into the Psalter—I have removed the veil from the face of ideas.

Like Jesus I have revived the dead—From head to foot I am drowned in light.

Like Jesus I give my life in my earthly humiliation—In order to make every living thing a pure Spirit.

Like Jesus, by raising up Five and Four—I have paid the price of Five and Four.[81]

Like Jesus to explain the Spirit of the Whole—I have found this site from where the judgment of all is proclaimed.

Like Jesus I have stabilized the gibbet—Like him, I have determined where to hang my mission.

Like Jesus, bearer of the Gospel of Love—from the height of the gibbet I have realized all the modalities of love.

Like Jesus I have plunged headlong into purity—To raise myself up as one of the guides.

Like Jesus among the impure Jews—I am suspended, the Way between before and after.

Like Jesus among the vile Hebrews—I remain bewildered in the scrutinizing daylight.

Like Jesus I am fixed (*pāydār*) on my gibbet—Like Jesus I have undertaken works.

Like Jesus here I am a master of the Way[82]—And, like Him, I am lost on His Route.

Like Jesus in the Psalter of verses of the Whole—I have said *Anā'l-Haqq*, I am the essence of the Whole.

Like Jesus in the maternal womb, like a lover—I have opened a Way through being and nothingness.

Like Jesus in time and space—I have passed beyond place and nonplace.

Like Jesus I was strengthened there—And then I took my leave of this place.

I thus attained the essence of Jesus—The Whole is enough as a point of support.

---

[81] Our five outward senses and our four humors (or our four inward senses, instead of the five as seen by Fārābī); or even the five orifices in our skull and our four limbs (or the four elements?). In any case, the reference is to the whole of humanity (see the next verse).

[82] 'Attār adopts the hierarchical ladder: *sharī'a*, *tarīqa*, *ma'rifa*, *Haqq*, *haqīqa* (cf. Thorning [?], p. 177).

My essence has become the supreme Spirit of God—His hidden Essence came under my attributes.

Like Jesus I have beheld the unified Whole—From head to foot I have become the total essence.

The beloved made me find the essence of Jesus—I found the soul of both worlds within myself.

In fact, I have the same qualifications as He—I am a comprehension without the modes of the Whole.

Like Jesus high on the gibbet, I have become Certitude (*yaqīn*)—Here on the gibbet the fruit of what I have tilled is Certitude.

A breath arose on me and my body—I do not know how.

I do not mean that Jesus may have departed at the same time completely—I do not know if this was done by command.

It is through my breath that Jesus reached the heavens—It is therefore through me that he achieved a pure heart.

The gibbet of Jesus has become my dwelling place and my home—The gibbet of Jesus has become my entire place.

Out of the gibbet of Jesus I have made a firm foundation—Made anxious by this, I have poured forth anxiety.

The gibbet of Jesus has become my royal throne—And Jesus has been raised higher in dignity by my execution.

My spirit has become the unveiled Spirit of God—And is close to the Certitude of the divine essence.

My spirit is clearly the Spirit of God—And in time space a fixed point (*pāydār*).

My spirit has given a treasure to lovers—My lovers keep it always:

Our spirit, which has become a guide for lovers and those who have arrived, and a sign for essences.

Also to be noted is the very strange role played by an anonymous child (*kudak*) who appears suddenly before the gibbet of Hallāj (130) to exhort him to fulfill his vocation: "I have drunk," he says to him, "a mouthful of your sorrow." He knows, he says to Bayezid, that Mansūr knew his state; and to Junayd (148) that he does not feel better than Mansūr. He came from Misr to Baghdad to see his end. "Here I am God like you," he says to him. He speaks to his *mi'rāj* (151), of the heart of Mansūr (159). "This very day is the essential vision" (233), and the fire of the final apotheosis consumes them together (224) in love (225-228). After Mansūr's prayer, "O Soul Who are my universe, O You, the being of my desired end" (229), there follows a canticle to the fire, "the fire of desire, which is this love of ours" (232), "the fire of desire, which throws off the spark of 'say God is the Only One,' " and a final declaration of Anā'l-Haqq (233), the child who complimented Mansūr, saying "you have held the Qalam" (*qalam* = *hadīqat-i kull* 235), and claims to have drunk from the cup of unity (*wahdat*), throws himself in the fire, where he vanishes before the dumbfounded Bayezid and Junayd (243). "His spark sets the site (of the gibbet) aflame, transforming Mansūr into the supreme Essence ('ayn-i 'ayān), —his spark looms up on every horizon, for Paradise desired Mansūr;[83] just as when Moses was on Mt. Sinai, a flood of light set creation aglow. . . ."

c. *Haylājnāma*. This book comprises 74 chapters and approximately 8,700 verses (LM ms. [dated 877]: 66 chapters, 78 folios 1/2, with 100 verses. London Or. ms. [dated 661?]: 74 chapters, 207 folios 1/2; chapters arranged as follows: 1-10, 32-54A + 54B to 54J, 11-16, 56-65, 17-30, 66). *Haylāj*, a mediaeval astrological term (Latin *hylech*; Greek *aphetes* rather than *hylikos* or *alokhos*),[84] coupled with *kadhkhudhāh* (Latin *cocoden, cholcodeam animarum datricem Avicennae*; Greek *oikodespotes*), stands for the two main planets in the genethliac theme, one determining the longevity, the other the destiny (fortunate or unfortunate), of the life of a newborn child.

'Attār tells us it is his only esoteric book, which he must have begun in secret well before he had finished *Jawhar al-dhāt* I-II, in which he refers to it (I, 92; II, 29, 63). In this work 'Attār introduces us to the immaterial world of divine Ideas, which are identified with the luminous planets of the incorruptible heavens. The pre-eternal spiritual reality of Hallāj is *Haylāj* = *'Aql-i Thānī*, the Second Intellect (= *Nūr 'alā Nūr, Sāqī-i Azal, Sajanjal* previously found in Ibn Abī'l-Khayr); identical to Khidr, who is *Shāhid-i Mīthāq*, and probably identical to Salmān (*Shāhid-i Shadd*, according to Yf. Hamadhānī). That of Muhammad is *'Aql-i Awwal*, the First Intellect; that of Jibrīl is *'Aql-i Kull*, the Third Intellect; that of 'Alī is *Haydar*, the Legislator (first among kings; designated by Muhammad as Noah, the first of the *ūlū'l-'azm* was designated by Adam). We see that 'Attār derived these symbols from an Avicennian philosophical milieu tinged with Ismā'īlian gnosticism (cf. Suhrawardī of Aleppo); however, his unitive mystical doctrine tones down its specific differentials.

Chapters 1-31, in which Hallāj is little more than the mouthpiece for 'Attār, who claims here to be constantly at one with the *Haylāj* (which he had already introduced ap. *Jawhar al-dhāt*), include the following: a *khutba*, some details about the Prophet (*na't, mi'rāj*; 1); the first four Sunnite caliphs, Hasan and Husayn (3-6), and the basic definition of *haylāj* (2, 7-10) articulated by Mansūr in response to a questioner who happens to

---

[83] Cf. the hadīth about "those whom Paradise desires" (Salmān, etc.).
[84] Saumaise said "per hilegiam et alcocodeam" (Nallino, ap. *Giom. Crit. Filos. Ital.*, VI [1925], 90); Khwārizmī, *Mafātīh* [bib. no. 1145-d], s.v.

be Junayd. "I said to him, O soul, what is your name, which God has given you measuring the longevity of your desire in this world? —It is I, Mansūr Hallāj, and my name on the astral horizons (= *āfāq*) is *Haylāj*. —O unknown divine Idea, which comes from the divine Essence. —O 'Attār, act as spokesman, transmit these secrets for me; to myself I am *haylāj*, to another I am *kadkhudā*; then you are Mansūr, and I in you am God; now write our secrets for me, so I may preserve our conversations; it is we who are speaking in your soul; you are the spokesman of love in my name." He spoke and then came near me; he came, a light in my dark heart; I kissed his hand and his head, and put the diadem of mysteries on (his) head . . . 'Hallāj said to him, put the tiara (*kulāh*), the giver of love, on your head; be glorified, O beheaded one (*basar*), at the end . . .' "(8).

Chapter 9: Mansūr explains to Junayd that the cry of *Anā'l-Haqq* comes from the stone in the wall, from the green tree (= Burning Bush), seen by Moses at night; if this tree spoke, why is it so amazing for our blood to have a voice? and for blood like Mansūr's to have had one? History is famous for it. This blood was not the reality of your God, this blood hidden under your gibbet; with the power to say *Anā'l-Haqq* remaining in the severed hand, the reality of his blood, in spilling, wielded it . . . not my hand, which was severed voluntarily, the covetousness of the good and the bad has been severed from me, severed by the hand of the horizons . . . , by the Friend; I see here only a place, a dwelling outside of creation . . . this blissful life that I contemplate in this blood . . . so too does my blood cry *Anā'l-Haqq* with the Friend.

Chapter 10: with regard to *fanā' ve baqā'*, 'Attār recalls that form does not survive; "the final tomorrow (*fardā*), by making your form disappear, will show forth your beauty."

Chapters 11-16: Mansūr defines divine Unity; it is defined as *Nūr 'alā Nūr* (Qur'ān 24:35) (15), and is manifested to Junayd as the single Sun of the soul (12). The talisman that casts a spell on the treasure must be broken, the treasure that is the reality of Mansūr; the shaykh must burn his frock (*khirqe*)[85] (13-14); the Qur'ān is the guide in this world to reality, the divine word; without the Qur'ān, you know nothing about the divine essence; without the Qur'ān, Mansūr knows nothing, he to whom this Book has been explained (*makshūf*), "*Nūr 'alā Nūr*"; . . . the reality of the Qur'ān is the vision of God (15).

Chapters 17-22 are devoted to the non-ego (*bikhūdī*), to the intoxication of the paradisiacal wine (*sharāba tuhūra*; Qur'ān 76:21) of which

---

[85] An idea used again by Hāfiz (cf. also *Dīwān d'al-Hallāj*, pp. 131, 136).

Mansūr is the lone pre-eternal cupbearer (*Saqi-i azal*; 18: as *haylāj* no doubt) in the Tavern of love (18); (here a passage on calendars);[86] the love that makes one divine (*lāhūti*) (21).

Chapters 23-31 set forth the final character of canonical Law (*sharī'a*) and of mystical reality (*haylāj*; 23, 29). 'Attār, in his commentary on the hadīth "die before dying" (*mūtū*), explains in particular that Hallāj accomplished precisely by the voluntary sacrifice of his head the decapitation that separated him from his soul (*farqa jan*) and earned him the crown (*tāj*; 26). How to see divinity (*rubūbiyat*) in *khalwa* (28-29): draw the veil back from the imperial face.

In chapters 32-65, 'Attār, in union with the *Haylāj*, continues to reveal the mission of Mansūr; Mansūr has seen God in a dream; "I saw my whole universe in this dream, all of the atoms in a deep water. He and I formed only one. . . ." 'Attār comments on this dream . . . "in union with Mansūr, like him I withdrew my hand from both worlds; the same fire that set Hallāj aflame uttered its moan (*faryād*) in my soul and my heart . . . if you are the very close (*mahram*), allowed into the privacy of Mansūr, your robe of honor will be '*nūr 'alā nūr*'. . . . I saw Muhammad in a dream," said 'Attār, referring to his *Ushtūrnāma*; Muhammad and 'Alī, those two who form only one; Muhammad is Adam, and 'Alī is Noah (32).

Keeping Hallāj explicitly as background scenery for the reader, 'Attār next groups around his gibbet several famous mystics who pose questions: Shiblī (33-36) asks if *Anā'l-Haqq* is in conformity with the Law (response: you are in *taqlīd*, I in *tawhīd*), and what is the mystery of love ('*ishq*) (response: for me love is giving up one's head) . . . I say *Anā'l-Haqq* in *Man ra'nī* (chapter 37: "I have already said, in *Ushtūrnāma*, the secret of Mansūr in another form"). Bayezid, beneath the gibbet of Mansūr, asks "this King high on the gibbet about the reality" which is the Soul of souls (= God) (38-43) (response by Hallāj: I am both *nafkh* (breath of the Spirit) and *dhāt* (pure essence of God): I am the Most High God, Mansūr Hallāj; everything needs My mercy; I am the Most High God, I am the sun and the star; everything salutes me, saying God the Most Great; I am the Most High God, here I am the Lord. . . . We are both the end and the beginning, my end and my beginning in a single utterance (*payām*): A *lastu bi Rabbikum* (= Am I not your Master? = Qur'ān 7:172 = *mīthāq*) (Hallāj reminds Bayezid of his Subhānī, 42). ("Jesus was misjudged by the Jews; so was I") (42). Shaykh Kabīr (= Ibn

---

[86] This is the first mention of this order of eccentric mystics founded by Sāwijī (killed in 618); cf. *'Awārif.*

Khafīf) rejoins Junayd and they ask questions together (44-54B) concerning the role of the Law (shar'): "We were together in India, friends," Kabīr says to Junayd, commenting on what he said about Hallāj that night (on the gibbet). An ignoramus insults Mansūr, treats him as a kāfir ("say: Huwa'l-Haqq") (47-48). Mansūr smiles and responds: "I am the sun, and you the grains of dust (= which dance in it), O simple one, O foolish one." Mansūr says to Kabīr (50): "you, O Shaykh Kabīr, Pole of the world, you know me today, the door of my cage is going to open, my veil was my form." Learned men (a'lām) come to question Mansūr while his hand is being amputated (54B-D). Junayd and Kabīr return together to interrogate him (54E-J, 65-58, 63-64). Next it is 'Abd al-Salām (who would be the son of Kabīr; variant: 'Abdallāh) and Khidr (59-62, 65) who ask why Mansūr told the king of Baghdad that Anā'l-Haqq was a saying that would last forever (response: Moses on Sinai). 'Abd al-Salām says to Khidr: this man speaks always in a state of "'ayn al-yaqīn." Khidr answers him: "you are a sālik, I am in the Essence; I am the prophet of knowledge of the Way (hidāyet; in khalwa, "'ilm ladunnī'), courage . . . generosity. . . . I have not seen Mansūr's equal, and there will be none until the blowing of the Trumpet . . . the reality of the essence of God exists in him, the yaqīn of Mansūr (= his profound self) among creatures is God . . . the fatwā of condemnation will give him access to God." When Kabīr speaks to Mansūr of the law of retaliation (qisās), Mansūr exclaims: "Ah, deliver me (by your fatwā) from the prison of this form (= his living body)" (64).

'Attār describes one more time the mysterious reality of Mansūr (65) and then concludes (66). Invested by Mansūr with his role as Haylāj, he evokes the transfigured beauty of nature, the rose and the nightingale, the morning which, after this night, is going to raise a hundred curtains: "O morning, be smiling lip to lip, with the lover whose heart is on fire, be singing the same way, since the Friend remains with me until dawn this night . . . O morning, the sun does not yet smile, there is still a little wine in the flagon, do not smile; you will smile at me in eternity, which raises its sword; together with your soul, the sword of the sun smiles at me; this night when I remain awake like a candle, I no longer have anyone for a friend; O night, do not make the door a nailed door . . . , O morning, bring life to the wounded heart . . . O night, you envelop the route to God in darkness . . . a single smile, and the universe will shine."

This esoteric book, in which 'Attār reveals to us all of his thoughts on Hallāj, is very important. It is not only a canonization, it is a total and absolute divinization—which puts 'Attār very near those Hallājian *zanādiqa* of whom he had pretended to disapprove in his *Tadhkira*. The only difference is that he does not practice direct *istiqtāl*, and that his theory of voluntary beheading depends for its realization on an unexpected and entirely personal divine invitation. He believes as they do, however, that it is the condition *sine qua non* for deification, and he prays for its coming with all of his strength.

He tells us explicitly that he had previously written another book on the Hallājian mystery, one that was constructed differently, *Ushtūrnāma* (= *Ushtūrnāma* III, analyzed above), and which did not completely satisfy him.

5. The Quatrains

A collection arranged in fifty chapters (*in fine Haylājnāma* in L.M. ms.). Three of ʿAttār's quatrains deal with Hallāj:

(Chapter VIII, no. 28): Never will you reach this true sea, —as long as you are of the earth, you will be unable to reach the water, "*Anā'l-Haqq*" —as long as you walk in multiplicity (slipping), place your feet firmly, for you run the risk of arriving only—at absolute nothingness.

(Chapter XLVIII, no. 27): The torchlight appeared and said: I have found no repose in myself, —in the chest of my self, I gasp what Hallāj said on the gibbet; —in this my trial I am like Hallāj, —hanged, burned, killed, scorned.

(*Ibid.*, no. 28): The torchlight appeared and said: why do you burn me? and being still hard to burn, do you teach me (to burn)? —I did not say "*Anā'l-Haqq*" like Hallāj, —and yet you condemn me to be killed and burned.[87]

ʿAttār wrote in a period when the theme of Husayn Mansūr Hallāj's peerless heroism, after conquering Khurasan and Turkestan, became established as a classic theme in Iranian poetry. Prior to him, Hakīm Sanā'ī, possessed of a very lofty moralism, had placed the execution of Hallāj at the summit of the "*sulūk*" on one magnificent page of his *Hadīq-i*. After him, the poetry of these Turks whom he feared, and which owes a great deal to him, would make Hallāj over into the "red rose," the standard-bearer of the Bektāshīs and the Janissaries. ʿAttār had already alluded to this symbol. Hallāj, in the initiatory rite of "*Dār-i Mansūr*," became in Balkh the intercessor and patron of a "Salmānīyan" corporation of "outlaws" from Islam, of a *futuwwa* of ʿAyyārīn inducing God to bring about the supreme ordeal of "martyrdom in holy war." ʿAttār, who is a contemplative, and who is aware of this martial fame of Hallāj, tries to portray him in his final countenance, in the perspective of the all-conquering

---

[87] Chapter XLVIII (102 quatrains) deals entirely with the "laments" of the Torchlight; and Chapter XLIX (18 quatrains) with a dialogue between the Moth and the Flame (cf. Hallāj, *Tawāsīn*, II, 2-4) (textual reference missing).

Love, at the Judgment: before the Islamic Law, which put him to death, for which he wanted to die, and which he transcends by that act: the martyred saint and substitute for the legislating Prophet, whom he completed and passed beyond by that act: the Herald of the end of the world.

d. Rūzbehān Baqlī

Baqlī is the main Hallājian to have commented on the works of Hallāj and whose commentaries, in Arabic and Persian (which is of particular importance for grasping their meaning), are extant.

He left us an autobiography in Arabic, *Kashf al-asrār*, which allows us to enter into the depths of his thought.

Born in 530 (not in 522), died in *Muharram* 606, Baqlī, seized with ecstatic intoxication at age 15, left his shop and his parents (rather coarse, though his mother was pious) in Fasa for a life of asceticism in the desert and in the mountains. Around 560, he founded a *ribāt* in Shiraz and was appointed *wā'iz* in the Jāmī 'Atīq.[88] Accused of *tashbīh*, he withdrew in 570 to Fasa, where he wrote *Mantiq*. Having called for the coming of the Salgharid amīr Tikla-b-Zanjī (575-595), he was able to return to Shiraz, where he wrote in 585 "at age 55" *Kashf al-asrār* and, after 591 (the death of Jāgīr), *Sharh al-shathīyāt*. He appears to have been cool toward Amīr Sa'd (599), whose son, Abū Bakr (623-658), however, was to venerate him (cf. the Ortoqid 'Izz Mawdūd, d. 605).

It is unlikely that he went on hajj, and his travels appear to be those of a homonym, perhaps of Baqlī Yamanī.

The following is a list of his works: 1. *Mantiq al-asrār* (written in 23 *Rabī'* II 570 at Fasa in the *ribāt* of AM Jawzak); 2. *Kashf al-asrār* (written 4 *Sha'bān* 585); 3. *Sharh al-shathīyāt* (including *Sharh al-tawāsīn*; in Persian, after 591); 4. *Sayr al-arwāh* (= *Misbāh*); 5. *Ighāna*; 6. *Abhār al-'āshiqīn*; 7. *Risālā qudsīya*; 8. *Kitāb al-nukāt*; 9. *Tafsīr al-'arā'is*. It should be noted that numbers 1, 3, and 9 glorify Hallāj, that Hallāj's name is missing from numbers 2, 4, 5, 8, and that number 6 devotes only a distich to him.

The following are the names of his masters, as taken from *Kashf*: Jamāl D Abū'l-Wafā'-b-Khalīl Fasā'ī, A Muslim Fāris-b-Muzaffar, AB Khurāsānī, AQ Darabjirdī; in *Shathīyāt* he cites only Jājīr Kurdī (d. 591), whom he was supposed to have visited near Samarra. In actual fact, he received the *khirqa* of the Kāzerūnīya before 560 from Sirāj D Mahmūd ibn Khalīfa ibn 'A Salām ibn A ibn Salība, the head in Shiraz of the Siddīqīya branch of this order (founded around 460 by a Baydāwī [through a com-

88 *FNN* II, 157.

patriot of Hallāj], Ahmad ibn Sāliba [d. 473], the grandfather of this Mahmūd). Among the visions recorded in *Kashf*, Baqlī saw Sarī' Saqatī (*hājib*), A Hy ibn Hind, Ibn Khafīf, and Ibrāhīm-b-Shāhryār, the founder of the Kāzerūnīya.

Transmission of his works remained secret; we find mention of it only in one of the Jāmīs (d. 898), Bayqarā and Witrī (d. 970). It may have been promoted in the beginning by the initiatory transmission of the Rūzbehānīya *tarīqa*, a branch of the Kāzerūnīya Murshidīya founded by Baqlī himself, and transmitted, after his son Ahmad and his grandson A Muhammad (brother of his biographer Ibrāhīm), by Farīd D 'Abd al-Wadūd ibn Dāwūd Khulwī (also initiated into the Shurayhīya, ascending to '*iqd* 65), and AF Tawūsī (d. 871), down to the Indian Qutb Nahrawālī (d. 990: a historian of Mecca), to the Qādī of Timbuctu, Ahmad Bābā' (d. 1032), to four famous chroniclers of Fez, and finally to S Murtadā Zabīdī (d. 1205).

Ivanow, guided by information taken from Ma'sum 'Alī Shāh, visited his tomb[89] in the ruins of his *ribāt* in Shiraz, at Bab Khidash-b-Mansur (present-day Mahallat Darb-i Shaykh): it had been visited by a Suhrawardian, Najīb D 'Alī Buzghush (d. 678)[90] and by Ibn Battūta.

'Attār (d. 589), a little older than Baqlī, has had the decisive role in establishing the fame of Hallāj because of the qualities of his poetic style, his broad philosophical background, and his important social and literary connections. Baqlī seems to have remained a provincial all his life, also timid.[91] After the somewhat ingenuous audacity of his action of 570, of inserting the *Sharh al-tawāsīn* into the middle of his *Mantiq*, that is to say, of inserting the complete text with commentary of a book condemned many times over, he tempered his expression of enthusiasm for Hallāj. The *Sharh al-shathīyāt*, in translating *Mantiq* into Persian, deliberately omits several passages.

Baqlī's charm, which is very Shirazian in this respect, is his joy in coming upon the beauty of nature in flowers, stars, faces. During the very severe ascetic period of his youth he partook deeply of the beauty of the stars and of flowers. This permitted him to lose himself in admiration of young faces, without the questionable ulterior motives of the aesthete, which had been a source of impurity for so many others. He spoke of this

---

[89] See the inscription engraved on this tomb, this volume, Figure 31.

[90] Cf. *Simt*, 147.

[91] Despite this, his name is the most recent among the twenty-one names of saints listed in an inscription dated (A.H.) 830 on the mosque tomb of Tawj al-Haramayn (d. 383) in Aberquh (*Tarā'iq* II, 244), rebuilt at the time by AF Tawūsī (d. 871; cf. *supra*).

in his *Tafsīr* on *sūra* 12 ("Joseph"), and he repeated it in his *Mantiq* (f. 13b) in a long and lucid commentary on the saying of Dhū'l-Nūn Misrī: "to familiarize oneself with the joy of God is to familiarize oneself with the joy found in every beautiful thing, each radiant face, each pleasant voice, each pleasing scent. That is a secret known to mystics that can only be confided to adepts; otherwise one puts oneself in a position of being punished as an example. The mystic sees no less than the radiance of the attributes of his beloved Lord in everything beautiful; specifically in the form of Adam, who was chosen for divine radiance when the angels were invited to adore him. The Prophet loved to look at beautiful faces and he said 'the red rose comes from divine glory; he who would see divine glory, let him contemplate the red rose.' And I learned that the Prophet, when he used to see a rose bud (*bākūra - güle-ahmar*), would kiss it and put it on his eyes, saying, 'this is what renews my covenant with the Lord.' "

The dreams and visions that weave through the personal life of Baqlī show him to us as a loving child filled with endless wonder in the presence of God. God tells him that He desires him, and dances with him; he sees him one day "drunk with a cup in a sea of wine," and another day, as a shepherd with a spindle who weaves a throne; another day, as a red rose between branches; He speaks to him in his maternal dialect (*Fasawī*). He consoles him in his domestic trials, during the dysentery suffered by his son Ahmad. If tears of contrition are the favorite beverage of angels (Tirmidhī had previously said that angels come and drink the prayer on the lips of beseechers), tears of desire are the beverage of God Himself. God streaks the eternal dawn with the blood of the *abdāl*; then he streaks His mercy with it ("with my blood"), says Baqlī, suddenly filled with joy, and afterwards with terror. A bad omen? No. His blood spills for the cup, and God-intoxicated dances, like a Zanj).

On the night of *al-Qadr* (of which he is forewarned; one 18 or 21 of *Ramadān*), Baqlī sees angels with long feminine tresses, earrings, and pearl necklaces; Jibrīl, before the throne, strips off his clothes in a delirium of love.

Looking at the sky, admiring the seven stars of the Big Dipper, Baqlī understands that they are the seven windows (*rūzana*) of heaven, the seven saints who preserve the world.

We are able from his works to reconstruct the list of Baqlī's documentary sources in Sūfism. First, the *Tafsīr al-haqā'iq* of Sulamī, two-thirds of which are reproduced in his *Tafsīr*, and the *Tafsīr* of Qushayrī ("al-Ustādh"; copious excerpts). Next, *Kitāb al-luma'* of AN Sarrāj, whose technical lexicon (*Luma'*, 333-374 = *Kitāb al-nukāt* of Baqlī, inserted *in fine* of the *Mantiq* f. 70b-81b) he copies (without saying so, although he quotes it for his definition of *shath*, ap. *Mantiq*; Witrī, f. 24b). This gives him the essence of archaic Sūfism. But from where has he taken the ingredients of the symbolic commentary that precede the excerpts from the aforementioned books in his *Tafsīr*, and which are the basis of his very involved exegesis of two of Hallāj's works, *Tawāsīn* and especially *Riwāyāt*? He did not invent them, and had to have taken them either from Jājīr Kurdī or from the local Kāzerūnīya tradition (though he refers in this regard only to the *Sirāt ibn Khafīf* of Daylamī) (*Mantiq* f. 8a-b; cf. also his *Tafsīr* I, 312, 504: moderns). *Shathīyāt* 14 mentions the *Tafsīr* of Bundār Shīrāzī (he seems to be unaware of the Hallājian *dhikr* that was being formed there at the same time), inasmuch as he had been initiated into it. To this source is connected the problem of Hallāj's *Riwāyāt* (who transmitted them to him?), and the even more important question of the Mansūr referred to as the son of Hallāj (whom he did not invent, since Tanūkhī refers to him, and since Najīramī told of his execution), citing a kind of commentary by him of *Tawāsīn* III, 7 (*Mantiq*, f. 69a: cf. 7b, 46a), but removing any mention of him in his *Shathīyāt*.

'Attār, with his true instinct for drama, had focused his Hallājian work on a meditation of the execution. Baqlī speaks of the execution only episodically: in folio 8b the legendary testimony of Ibn Khafīf is different from the surviving text of the *Hikāya*; together with a text, otherwise unknown, of Ibn Fātik; —in f. 55b, another legendary text, otherwise unknown, about Muqtadir, killed in punishment on the same day as the execution, the day also of the devastating flood, all of which was foretold by Hallāj: f. 3a. Baqlī believes that it was 'Alī-b-'Īsā (instead of Vizir Hāmid) who had Ibn 'Atā' killed. He has another aim clearly explained in the prologue to the *Mantiq* (abridged ap. *Shathīyāt*): "my love for Hallāj forced me to comment on his mode of ecstatic expression and of theopathic allusion to the (divine) Personality."

While 'Attār believed he was continually inspired by the "spirituality" (*rūhānīya*) of Hallāj, Baqlī restricted himself to giving us an account of a dream in which Hallāj, wearing the *kulāh* (the tiara worn by those condemned to death), came to congratulate him for his commentary on the *Tawāsīn*: "you have understood what the tiara is, you have crossed the desert of vision" (this dream is found only in the Persian version, dated after 591: *Shathīyāt*, Shehid 'Alī ms., 168; and 132 for the commentary). In the beginning of his *Mantiq* (f. 7b), Baqlī, ending the list of forty-seven Sūfī masters of *shath* with Mansūr-b-Hallāj (the son) and with his father, calls the son "the garden of wisdom, the jasmin of prediction, the rose of sapience," and his father (Hallāj himself) "the victim of preaching, inflamed with the Idea, the western phoenix of the summit of the pre-eternal Mt. Qāf, the sun of the liftings of the veil of omnipotence, the destroyer of the mask (dīmās) of matter, the plunger into the Eritrea of the absolute" (ap. Shathīyāt,[92] the three epithets of the son, expunged, are annexed to those of his father).[93] In his Tafsīr (II, 15, 128), Baqlī calls Hallāj "the sage of Fars, the shattāh of the Kingdom, the one who grappled with himself in his pre-eternity under the sign of death, and who fought the lion of the Absolute in summer, of nothingness (an allusion to the "Nadīmī quatrain"). 'Attār, for his part, had called Hallāj "that soldier killed by God in holy war, that lion of the jungle of discovery, that dauntless and upright warrior, that gulp of the tumultuous (divine) Ocean," which is related to the litanies found in a Hallājian initiatory milieu. This is easily verified by comparing it to the prologue, written in rhymed prose, of a sensitive layman like Ibn Fadlallāh 'Umarī: "Hallāj, an ocean in which only the experienced swimmer dares swim, a lion that only a tamer can drive off, he drank the cup to the bottom, and delighted in it more than he should have, he became drunk to the point of losing consciousness, he was overcome and could not get up again . . ."; here again, Baqlī seems to have been inspired by earlier models.

His admiration for the works of Hallāj is unconditional (which distinguishes him from the prudent 'Attār). Completing his commentary on the Tawāsīn "in accordance with the statements of those who have made its realization possible, and the allusions of sages" (which refers to predecessors), Baqlī adds: I used to weep, shedding the blood of the soul, at the reading of this Zend-Avesta of privileged souls, in the presence of these words that, written on the China Sea, the Eritrea of the Absolute, in alchemical reddish gold, the secret of predestination, before this discourse in which only the work of light reddening the forehead of the errant moons, engraving "the reciter of the secret of the tiara" and "witness of the desert of vision" on "the leaves of the Tūbā tree of the soul," is justified (epithets devoted to Hallāj, immediately after the previously mentioned dream).

The purpose of Baqlī's commentary on the texts of Hallāj is to elucidate the method that Hallāj follows in bearing witness to God in a seem-

---

[92] Shathīyāt, 16.
[93] Ibid., 19. Baqli adds the following: "witness of the Covenant, courier-ravisher of hearts, new-year planter of roses" (Mantiq, f. 9a has only "of lordly spirit, of spiritualized body, of eternal character, samadi'l-sifa)."

ingly paradoxical language and by means of expressions that belong to
ecstatic intoxication only in appearance, for his words are perfectly arranged, indicating an author in control of his mental state as a mystic
(*mālik hālihi*). This is the problem of the philosophical and theological
meaning of the Hallājian *shath*.

The following is the plan of the *Tawāsīn*:

1) meditation on the monotheistic testimony of the prophets: of
Moses, summoned by the voice of Holiness infused into the Burning
Bush (and "I am this Bush," Hallāj remarks; the saint is superior to the
Prophet); of Muhammad doing his utmost to measure the distance from
divine transcendence to Qāb Qawsayn, "two bowshots" (and Hallāj,
appropriating to himself the voice of "the Eternal Witness," the Spirit,
beseeches him to go further: "*ghib 'an al-awhām*," "renounce representations" in which you are in danger of drowning, rob yourself of your
imagination, enter into Union);

2) meditation on the testimony of angelic nature, protesting, through
its leader, Iblīs, against the trial of the *sujūd*, when God seems to want to
make him renounce monotheistic faith by asking him to prostrate himself before the bodily form, Adam, of a human nature in which His
incarnation—something, however, inconceivable and condemned—
would be prefigured (Hallāj, with sarcastic sympathy, analyzes the refusal of Iblīs, who claims to damn himself through love, when he per-
sists, through pride, in objecting to an order, pretends to uphold divine
transcendence in opposition to God Himself, and excludes himself, out
of a self-centered spirit and jealous self-deception, from Union, whose
modality, *nafkh al-Rūh*, shocks him). Hallāj states that Iblīs, in desiring to
differentiate Adam from God, refuses to renounce the pride of pure
thought (*fikr*: the refusal of *raf' al-'inn*), when this latter renunciation is
necessary for Union;

3) through analysis of the concept of *tawhīd*, using an intense dialectic,
Hallāj shows that the monotheistic testimonies, that of the Prophet and
that of the Angel, are inadequate and deciduous, and that only a divine
Wisdom (*ma'rifa*) engraving itself in our hearts makes them utter the true
shahāda, the authentic confirmation of the presence in ourselves of the
One.

At this point[94] psychological considerations are interposed concerning
the internal structure of the soul, *nafs*, the seat of the imagination (*wahm*);
within is found the heart, *qalb*, the seat of the intellect (*fahm, fikr*, Hallāj

---

[94] Against 'Amr Makkī.

is loathe to use the word *'aql*); in the inner wall of the heart (*shaghāf*) there flows the breath (*nafas*) of the Spirit (*Rūh nātiqa*), which can engrave wisdom (*ma'rifa*) on the inside of the heart; finally, in the center, there is an immaterial substance, the secret, *sirr*, the inner personality,[95] the virginal part (*bikr*) which must be opened only to God through love, becoming itself, through the *Fiat* (*Kun*), "the Truth" (*al-Haqq*), the creative relationship that causes it to exist and causes it to utter the divine "I."[96] Inspired wisdom, *ma'rifa*, by engraving itself in the heart, enables the inner conscience to utter the real monotheistic testimony, *tawhīd*, in the first person.[97]

Hallāj strives to present in abstract theological definitions what he experienced mystically. "The Truth (*al-Haqq*)" is the acknowledgment of the creative relationship, of our relation to a causal being whom we do not cause (Sulamī, *Tafsīr*, nos. 168, 173; Qushayrī, 161; cf. Qur'ān 6:72).

"Impiety (*kufr*)"[98] occurs essentially when God, withdrawing really from the loving soul, causes him to confess that *He is not* (dark night of the soul, a suffering that is greater than damnation, capable of burning up hell, and is the threshold of Union: *Akhbār* nos. 41, 44, 62; Ibn Sīnā repeated this idea in part).

It was very difficult to describe this divine visitation theologically, in terms of intermittent actualization in the depth of the individual conscience, without using the word *hulūl* (infusion, incarnation). Hallāj used it (with *sūra = nāsūt*), as did Fāris. But Muslim scholasticism excluded it early as implying *zandaqa*, Manichaeanism, a mixture confusing in an absurd and sacrilegious way the transcendent purity of God with created natures. And the word *hulūl* does not appear in the *Tawāsīn*. Hallāj established in it only the transforming union, the loving exchange of the "I" between God and the soul (*Taw.* II, 4-6; III, 7, 11; V, 11).

The early commentaries (cf. excerpts from the son of Hallāj, ap. Baqlī, *Mantiq*, f. 69a) accepts fully the idea that God writes His personality with that of the saint, who says "I" in His name. But 'Attār remarks (II, 136), specifically apropos of *Tawāsīn* III, 7, that it is *zandaqa* to claim that the personality of the saint is not destroyed but transubstantiated; this is the heresy of the Hallājīya *ghulāt* (cf. Khatīb VIII, 112). And Baqlī agrees with this (*Mantiq*, f. 52a), while accepting the commentary of Hallāj's son on the Burning Bush.

---

[95] *Damīr/wahdānī*.   [96] Baqlī, no. 163; *Akhbār*, 27, 29; *Tawāsīn* X, XI.

[97] For *tawhīd*, he proceeds by investigation and self-renunciation, when it is a question of the *origin* of thought. For *ma'rifa*, he reasons by *takāfu'*, spoken language, *dalāla*.

[98] *Kufr haqīqī*; cf., for *'irfān*.

With regard to the theory about the superiority of the saint over the prophet, Baqlī is obviously ill at ease (in *Mantiq* 42a he dodges it for "*uffa lakum*"): but it does not gamble against Muhammad, identified with the Spirit of holiness (*Mantiq*, f. 47a concerning *Tawāsīn* IV, 10), in accord with the Nūr Muhammadī theory.

Baqlī's commentary is very valuable for understanding Hallāj's view of the true character of Iblīs. Baqlī is not shocked by the parallel between the two missions, that of Iblīs and that of Muhammad, the one meting out the strictness, the other the mercy of God: the law in its two aspects. At an early period the moving tone given by Hallāj to Iblīs in *Tā' Sīn al-Azal* had convinced some Hallājians that Hallāj, who had been condemned, was a disciple of Iblīs, the forsaken lover who had incurred damnation through love, that both were saints content to love God from the depths of Hell. An archaic interpolation, a dispute over the "*futuwwa*, the honor of the knights" in which Hallāj is reputed to challenge Iblīs and Fir'awn on this terrain, grows out of this interpretation, which is adopted by Qushayrī, Jurjānī, and Ahmad Ghazālī—an interpretation consistent with their Ash'arite leaning toward a belief in the determinism of human actions, whether good or bad, motivated by a single agent, God. Baqlī, in agreement with Yf Hamadhānī and Kīlānī, reacts against this anomian interpretation, which abolishes all ethics. And regardless of whether it is a question of an early text of *Tā' Sīn* or of interpolation (which Baqlī accepts as Hallājian), Baqlī, analyzing the sentences minutely, shows that in actuality Iblīs, as Hallāj depicts him, is not a saint but a false "*malāmatī*," possessed of an arrogant heroism. When [Iblīs] says to Moses that God's command was only a test to tempt him (it was therefore not given in pure love), that the disfigurement that He had inflicted upon him means nothing (since God manifests Himself through beauty), that he is now serving God for His happiness (a blasphemy, for God is guileless)—all of this is only pretense, deception, and sham. In showing obstinacy in observance, Iblīs deprived himself of union with the Omnipotent; respect for divine unity caused him to fall out of this unity; the ocean of Unity threw him up onto the shore of solitude (*tajrīd*) (*Mantiq*, f. 35b, 36a; cf. 51b ff.); and he sinned in two ways: an arrogant pretension (believing himself to be superior to Adam, without considering the *nafkh al-Rūh*; cf. Nūrī, ap. Qushayrī, 126; *Farq*, 245), and a *soi-disant* resigned prescience of his fate of being damned (Hallāj had remarked that in this there was particularly a refusal to suffer more intellectually, *Tawāsīn*, VII).

In terms of the *Riwāyāt*, of which, except for one hostile Shī'ite reference, we have only Baqlī's commentary, [the latter] is so copious that we are reluctant to follow his warning (*Mantiq*, f. 35a): "I have commented on its meaning and its *isnād* in accordance with what the moment suggested to me through the movement of my thought and with what God has amassed by inward inspiration (*ilhām*) in the bookcases of my heart." He notes at the outset (f. 27b) the originality, not of the "accepted texts of the saints," but of the *isnāds* whose witnesses are not of this world (*shawāhid al-malakūt*).

e. Ibn ʿArabī

The strong intellectual personality of Ibn ʿArabī[99] dominates the entire modern history of Muslim mysticism. He is its uncontested "renewer" (*muhyī*),[100] the "master" par excellence (*shaykh akbar*), not only in the minds of Arab and Turkish Sunnites, but even those of Persian Imāmites.

In their authoritarian, formal, and pompous style, lucid in terms of syntax but crammed full of technical expressions, the general ideas and personal visions that he relates, in the same calm and cold tone, provide most valuable clues concerning the idea he held of the personality of Hallāj.

We shall examine the following in succession here: (1) the mystical rank that he assigns to him; (2) the opinion he holds of his condemnation, based on excerpts from his *Futūhāt al-makkīya*; followed by his two visions of Hallāj; (3) one related to creative causality (excerpt from *Tajallīyāt ilāhīya*); (4) the other concerning Hallāj's offense against the Prophet Muhammad.

We have already examined his discussion of Hallāj's *Anā'l-Haqq*.[101]

---

[99] Died 638/1240; married to a *Jinnīya* (Ibn Hajar, *Lisān al-mīzān* V, 313). See his tomb, this volume, Figure 16.

[100] Khunsārī calls him *"māhī al-Dīn"* derisively.

[101] *Tawāsīn*, 184-185. Ibn ʿArabī discusses him in his *Fusūs al-hikam* (p. 126) (cf. *Futūhāt* III, 626): with "creator" and "creation" being two terms united by a necessary relation, it is not the individual person of a saint, but the whole of creation which has the right *to* claim *itself* identical with God, since the wholeness of its present existence is the necessary essence of the existence of God. This is why ʿAlī al-Harīrī, a disciple of Ibn ʿArabī, wished "to swallow the Universe" to force it to confess with his mouth *"Anā'l-Haqq."*

The same idea is found in the *Wāridāt* of Simaʾūnoghlū.

Love (in *Futūhāt* II, 356-357) is total recognition, through a panoramic vision of beauty, of the necessary nexus between the creator and creation for an aesthetic actualization of God, an existentialization of God; it means to love generally, excluding any formal object, any iconographical specialization: as criticized by Ibn Taymīya: "a fugitive from his native land, far removed from his friend, weeping over the hillocks and debris, he loves without knowing whom" (*Majm. Mas. Ras.*, 163).

The divine ipseity (*huwīya*) appears to each in a form appropriate to his circle; it is wrong to think that this particular form delimits and defines the *ulūhīya* (*Tajallīyāt*, s.v. *huwīya*).

(1) The Mystery of the Distinction in Works Between "Works of Supererogation" and "Works of Obligation": this is a result of the fact that discursive knowledge is limited a priori to *two* dimensions, "length (extension)" and "breadth (comprehension)."

Ah! the one whose malady[102] is Jesus could not be sad, for Jesus is both the Creator who vivifies and the creature who is vivified. The "breadth" of the universe is physical nature (*tabī'a*), its "length" is its Spirit and its Law (*sharī'a*). This is the revealing Light, the doctrine of "umbras" and of "cycles occurring once a century"[103] which we owe to *Husayn ibn Mansūr*. Indeed, I know of no believer in the One God who could have "stitched and unstitched" in speaking of his Lord, distinguished in the twilight, the night and what it contains, and the moon when it is hidden, and arranged all of these complementary particulars among them as well as he! He was a light in the oncoming night, —God was within him, —like Moses before the Ark of the Covenant. This is why Husayn ibn Mansūr spoke of two natures, the divine "*lāhūt*" and the human "*nāsūt*," without drawing close for a single moment to those who say "the essence is one" and thereby do away with the adventitious attribute (the universe). Certainly not! Mt. Faran is not Sinai! The "breadth" (of the world) is limited, while its "length" is the shadow that darkens it; supererogatory and obligatory works are united in the same necessary relation as (man) who witnesses and (God) who is witnessed![104]

He had previously expressed his admiration for Hallāj. He included him in his strange declaration about the twelve mystical *Poles* around whom the temporal world revolves in their lifetime,[105] making him the seventh Pole (*qutb*), "the one who remains at the feet of the Prophet Job;[106] the one whose *sūra* is that of the *Baqara* [(the second) *sūra* of the Qur'ān] and whose *hāl* [inward state] is that of immensity."[107] And when he sets forth the relationships of spiritual "paternity" and "filiation" that the "Pole of *sūra* Tawba (9)" maintains with such-and-such a person, in contrast even to physical and normal genealogical order, he supports his data with a verse from an alchemistical *qasīda* on the philosopher's stone[108] attributed to Hallāj:

My mother gave birth to her father. That indeed is one of my wonders![109]

(2) His opinion concerning the legitimacy of Hallāj's condemnation is as follows:[110]

---

[102] Jesus is used here as a model of the sanctified creature who shares in the creative power of God (cf. *Futūhat* I, 187-188).

[103] *Sayhūr wa dayhūr*: cf. *Tawāsīn*, 142; and here, Chapter XIV, II, a.

[104] *Futūhāt* IV, 367.

[105] Used in the Christian sense, a very beautiful expression: they are the Elect.

[106] One of the twenty-seven great prophets (*Fusūs*). *Futūhāt* IV, 90.

[107] 'Azamat: a reference to the miracle (cf. this edition, 1, 503-505).

[108] Cf. this edition, Chapter XIV, III, c (= volume 3, 293 ff.).

[109] *Futūhāt* IV, 171.   [110] *Ibid*. II, 413.

Just as it is the duty of a *prophet* publicly to reveal his signs and his miracles for the glory of his apostolate, it is the duty of a *saint* (coming after the prophet) to conceal his. This is the commonly held view, for the saint is not an apostle; he does not need to make propaganda, for he is not a legislator, and the standard of the law is already established; and it is upheld on earth by help of scribes and scholars of the law, who render *fatwās* on worship owed to God. The latter are the masters of weighing and balancing.

As regards the saint, when he strays (inadvertently) from the norm set by the established Law, referring to his legal obligations (*taklīf*), he is considered free on account of the presumption that exists in his favor regarding the heart of the matter, which is taken into account by the law. But if he commits an act liable to a penalty, in keeping with the text of the law and the uniform interpretation of a judge, he must perforce suffer the prescribed penalty. He cannot be excused by the presumption that is fundamentally in his favor, knowing the following: that he is one of those pious men whose sins do not do harm before God, whom God allows to do acts that he has legally forbidden others to do, and whom He exempts from any penal claim in the next life, just as He said in the case of the soldiers of Badr in a hadīth[111] regarded[112] as freeing them from any interdiction (*ibāhat al-afʿāl*), and as He said, according to tradition (to the Prophet): "Do what you like, I shall pardon you in advance." He did not say, however, "I have excused you from the sanctions of the law in this world."[113] In this world, no. Also, the judge among the jurisconsults who applies the sanctions is pardoned in advance, even if the condemned (saint) is himself not guilty, like Hallāj and those who acted like him.

Ibn ʿArabī, in this matter, shares the opinion held by the Sālimīya: Hallāj was a saint, but it was just to condemn him.

(3) In his book of "divine illuminations,"[114] in the chapter[115] entitled "Illumination about the Idea of Causality," Ibn ʿArabī tells of having had the following vision of Hallāj:

In this illumination I saw Hallāj and asked him: "O Hallāj! do you accept causality as an attribute of God?" and I stopped. He smiled and said to me: "Do you not refer to the saying 'O Absolute Who has never ceased being?' " —"That is the one." —"Such a statement is that of an ignorant man.[116] Know then that God

[111] Hazm IV, 45. God forgives sins (*maʿāsī*) except for that of *kufr* without *tawba* (Rāzī, *Tafsīr kabīr* V, 230): an obligation only in the case of *kufr*.

[112] From Ghulām Khalīl, a commentary on Qurʾān 8:69 concerning the *ghanāʾim* of Badr. Cf. the hadīth "*uhillat lī al-ghanāʾim wa lam tuhall lī nabīyin qablī*" (*Shifāʾ* II, 153).

[113] Sin is only against creatures, not against the Creator; it is therefore subject only to the temporal law.

[114] The book in which he claims to converse with the masters of early Sūfism, making them progress spiritually *post mortem* (Kader [?] III, 220), thanks to his explanations. Silence on Shiblī (III, 216).

[115] Cf. Sulamī, *Radd* I, 363.

[116] Munāwī and Ibn ʿAqīl make this out of a maxim of Hallāj. It is, in fact, the beginning of a "maxim of Plato" (Amīlī, *Kashkūl*, 284; cf. 330) attributable to an Ishrāqī (cf. this edition, 3, 129, n. 38).

created the causes but is not Himself a cause. How could He accept causality, He, with whom nothing did coexist? If He were a cause, He would be part and parcel of a causal relation; and if He is conditioned in this way, God is no longer perfect. May He be exalted above what blasphemers say of Him in their stupidity![117] This is the way I understand it."[118] He repeated: "This is the way it must be understood. Remain in that position. Stick to it." I then said to him:[119] "Why did you let your house be destroyed?" —He smiled: "creatures already had their hands on it when I left it to undergo my threefold annihilation (in God); leaving Aaron as leader of my people (cf. Qur'ān 7:142). But believing that he was weak because I was no longer there, they got together to destroy my house. They had already demolished it when I returned to it after my (ecstatic) annihilation. I approached it and saw that it had fallen prey to punishments. I was ashamed to live in a house where the hand of creatures had taken hold, and I withdrew the (divine) emanation from it (Hārūn = fayze = my spirit) that I had put there.[120] Then it was said 'Hallāj is dead!' —Not at all! He is not dead, the house has crumbled but the inhabitant had already left."[121] —"Your reasoning, I observed, includes all of the proofs against him."[122] At that time Hallāj was silent, then he declared: "Over and above every learned man is God Who Knows. Enough of objections. You are right. I have told you all that I can." After that I left him.

This text by Ibn 'Arabī, it would seem, reveals a certain duplicity of thought, especially in passages underscored by commentary. He gives the appearance of blaming Hallāj in order to take the liberty of attributing two risky ideas to him that are, in fact, his own, Ibn 'Arabī's;[123] namely, that of removing from God even the name of Cause,[124] and that of reducing the spiritual self of Hallāj to pure divinity (lāhūt).

(4) Ismā'īl Haqqī of Brusa reproduced in his tafsīr[125] the following tale by Ibn 'Arabī of a vision that the latter had in Cordova concerning Hallāj:

[117] That is to say, their hasty judgment (sutūwat), the commentary observes.

[118] Ibn 'Arabī, commenting himself on this passage in the presence of Ibn Sawdakīn, notes that "it is a good exposition of tanzīh (via remotionis)."

[119] Ibn 'Arabī observes on this subject: "When one of the questioners claims to have some experience in mysticism, it is important that the other rejoin him at the point at which he claims to have arrived, by a route already known to the other and in such a way as to be able to expose the personal pretentions of the first and to paralyze his deceptions with fatigue."

[120] When Hallāj had said to the shaykh: "Stick to it" unless his rank authorizes him to speak this way to him; —the shaykh retorted: "And why. . . ." (Ibn Sawdakīn's commentary).

[121] An ironic allusion to the qasīda of Musaffar al-Sibtī (this volume. p. 415).

[122] Commentary by Ibn Sawdakīn: (cf. Nūrī, d. 646, son of a mawla of Nūr al-Dīn: Ibn al-'Adīmī, ap. Sauvaget, REI, 1933, p. 399): "Then when he saw that Hallāj in his answer had sufficiently entangled himself in his own deceptions, Ibn 'Arabī said: "Your reasoning. . . ."

[123] The Qarmathians called their created demiurge (sabīq) "cause of causes."

[124] Ghazālī, Mishkāt. In contrast to Hallāj, cf. this edition, Chapter XII (corrected here, 3, 129, n. 38).

[125] Rūh al-bayān concerning Qur'ān 93:5.

I was in the city of Cordova (praying) in a *mashhad* when God revealed to me a gathering of his leading prophets, from Adam all the way to our Prophet, Muhammad. And one of them, Hūd, speaking to me, told me why they were assembled in this way. "We are here," he told me, "to intercede with our Prophet, Muhammad, on behalf of Hallāj. For Hallāj sinned against the proprieties (= the respect due the Prophet) when he declared in his lifetime in this world: 'The thought of the Prophet did not include all rights attached to his rank.'"[126] —"And how is that?" —"God has said to him: 'Soon your Master will grant it to you (= your request); therefore be consenting (to your mission)'" (Qur'ān 93:5); which shows that he was right to give his consent only if God accepted his intercession[127] on behalf of all men,[128] infidels and faithful. But the Prophet asked only " . . . on behalf of the great sinners belonging to my nation."[129]

When Hallāj had expressed this opinion, the Prophet immediately appeared to him and said to him: "O Husayn ibn Mansūr! Is it you who have criticized my intercession?" —"Yes, O Prophet of God, you are correct." —"Have you forgotten the tradition that I said I took from God Himself: 'When I love one of my servants, I become his hearing, his sight, his tongue'?" —"Yes, O prophet of God!" —"Don't you know that I loved God?" —"Yes, O Prophet of God!" —"Well then, being the friend of God, it was He who was my tongue when I spoke, Himself Who intercedes and with Whom one intercedes, for, next to His Being, I am only nothingness. What else is there against me, O Ibn Mansūr?" —"O Prophet of God, I am sorry for what I said. What penance must I do for my error?" —"Give yourself to God as a sacrifice." —"What do you mean? Get yourself executed by the blade of my law." —And everyone knows what befell Hallāj. Then Hūd added: "Since he died, he has kept out of sight of the Prophet. Thus the assembly we are holding at present convenes to intercede with him on [Hallāj's] behalf." Now, the period from his death to this assembly amounted to more than three hundred years.[130]

f. The Sharh Hāl al-Awliyā' of 'Izz al-Dīn Maqdīsī

'Izz al-Dīn Maqdīsī (b. 577, d. 660/1262)[131] includes in his *Sharh hāl al-awliyā'* an actual poem written in rhymed prose interrupted by a verse *fī hāl al-Hallāj*, "on the state of Hallāj." He depicts him as intoxicated with

---

[126] *Himmatuhu dūna manusabihī*, cf. H in sol., ap. Qur'ān 9:43: *ta'nīs* of M before *ta'nīb*: this edition, 3, 198 and n. 126. The anecdote is characteristic, for Ibn 'Aqīl reports it, almost in the same way, in connection with Shiblī (Ibn al-Jawzī, *Talbīs* [bib. no. 370-b], 373).

[127] *Shafā'a*.

[128] Cf. this edition, 3, 213 and Bistāmī (*Essai*, 282).

[129] *Shafa'atī li-ahl al-kabā'ir min ummatī* (Tirmidhī, *Sahīh* [?] III, 71; Ibn Mājā, *ibid.* [?] II, 302); this hadīth is absent in the other four classical *sahīh*. It is found in Abū Dāwūd (and Ibn Hanbal) according to Siddīq Khān, *Sharh*, on the margin of the *Jalā*, 287.

[130] Jalāl Rūmī, repeating this theme, remarks that Hallāj held his own against Muhammad, affirming to him that he is still "a creditor," and preferring to die the next day at the hand of the executioner (Aflākī, Huart tr. [?] I, 254).

[131] An Ash'arite, attacked by the Hanbalites in Damascus around 630, he came to Egypt in 640.

divine love, incapable of suppressing his shouts of joy, imbibing in the cup of the Personality (anānīya). He [shows him] singing: "Here is the cupbearer; pass the cup around, brother! The cup that holds the drink of joy and make me a gift of it! . . ." Someone threatens him, nothing happens; he is mutilated; when his feet are cut off, he sings: "I have achieved my goal"; when he is crucified: "by the will of my Adored One!" One of these brief couplets by Maqdīsī, put in the mouth of Hallāj,[132] is quite famous:

> He allowed my blood to be shed, since my heart was allowed to reveal His name;
> Surely it is lawful for him to do what He considers lawful!
> I was not one of those who revealed their secret,
> But the thrones on which His love sits have glistened in my consciousness, and have betrayed me. . . .
> They have made me drink and they have told me: "Do not sing!"[133] but if they were to water
> Mt. Hunayn with what they have given me, surely it would sing!

In the end, his table-companions put Hallāj to death. Maqdīsī adopts the legend and the crucifixion of a substitute.

> Far from their thoughts was any idea of killing him! No, nor did they crucify him;
> But when the ecstasy of their intoxication had passed, his friends believed they had done it.
> When they approached him (the angels) had already carried him up
> To give him a pure drink and to keep silent about the secret that they had entrusted to him;
> But he could scarcely withstand the pressure they had brought to bear on him, and, overcome with intoxication, he cried out:
> "I am the one whom they have singled out in God."
> "O you who blame me, how could I conceal the love which they disclosed to me?"
> How could he hide it, this heart that they had broken with desire?[134]
> And it was said that al-Khidr passed near where Hallāj was on the cross. And Hallāj said to him: "Is this the way that saints of God are recompensed?" —"We have kept the secret and our life has been spared; you, you have revealed it: die! O Hallāj, what is your state?" —"Ah! it is such that if one of my sparks were to fly onto Mālik[135] and his hell, I would burn them up! . . ."

---

[132] Beginning with, he says, the account translated in this edition, 1, 288 (hall al-rumūz).

[133] These last two verses were previously put in Hallāj's mouth by Zakariyā al-Qazwīnī (d. 682/1283), ap. 'Ajā'ib al-makhlūqāt [bib. no. 458-a].

[134] A correction of the translation that P. Paquignon had proposed (RMM, April 1909, pp. 430-432).

[135] A demon: a reference to the sentence translated in this edition, 1, 288.

At the end of this same work, Maqdīsī recalls the crucifixion of Hallāj and ends as follows: "And this is what someone wrote on this subject who understood the universality of the divine decree[136] and its primary meaning: 'Tell me who judged it lawful to put me to death: I absolve you of it fully!' "

g. Shaykh Muhammad Iqbāl and the Jāwidānnāma

Member of a Qashmirī family, born and raised in the Punjab, professor, later lawyer in Lahore, Hanafite jurisconsult, a deeply religious mind trained in modernism during three years' residence in England and Germany, Iqbāl (1877, d. 1938) played a prominent role in Indian Islam's participation in the national awakening. He wrote in three languages, as a poet in Urdu in his youth, as a metaphysician in English, and as a philosophical poet in Persian.

He realized that the influence of Islam, as it penetrated polytheistic India, had enabled it to release its profound originality, perceiving that the experience of the faithful in a transcendent God should remove them from both the partisan formalism of the Ahmadīya and the naive rationalism of the "naturistic" ("nechari") University of Aligarh: in order to rectify the Hellenistic philosophy of the Muslim scholastics by trying to express in contemporary critical philosophical terms the subjective states of the great Muslim mystics. This position made Iqbāl an apologist of Islam, since it is extremist Sūfism, so dear to Iranians, that has been the most efficacious means of converting Hindu souls to Islam who were formed introspectively by the Upanishads and the Yogasūtra.

Iqbāl is personalistic. The amāna of Qur'ān 33:72 is for him a "divine trust," the duty to witness God by saying "I" in His place. This is the very message of extremist Sūfism;[137] and when Iqbāl was exposed in Germany to the philosophy of Nietzsche, he saw him as a Sūfī paralyzed and suffocated by a hostile milieu, as a new Hallāj.

To Iqbāl, Nietzsche's surname was a western echo of the Hallājian Anā'l-Haqq. In his Jāwīdānnāma [bib. no. 1240-a] (1932), Iqbāl has his guide, Rūmī, speak, much in Dante's manner of having Virgil speak, of "this German sage" and of "his old song played on his flute":

> Once again this Hallāj, without gibbet and rope,
> Repeats these ancient words in another form;
> Fearless words, an idea which was great;
> The blade of his word split Westerners in two.

---

[136] Amr, in the sense adopted by Ibn Isrā'īl (this edition, 3, 276 ff.).
[137] And this is the mission of Semitic languages.

As Nietzsche was killed by physicians, Hallāj was killed by mullas.

Already in Song I (Lunar), Iqbāl had borrowed the symbolism of *Tawāsīn*. Song V (Jupiterian) of the *Jāwīdnāma* introduced to the poet and his guide three famous tortured souls: Hallāj, Ghālib (the great Persian and Urdu poet, d. 1869), and Tāhire Qurrat al-ʿAyn, the proto-martyr of Babism (d. 1844); and Iblīs himself spoke at the end.

Iqbāl sees Hallāj as the one who explained to India how the union of the two oceans ("faith" and "infidelity") should be achieved; not by a conversion, but through a catalysis of the deserving asceticism of saints, through their personal "*satī*," their voluntary destruction through asceticism, fire, anathema: an ascetical autocreation causing the two antithetical parts of the canonical *Shahāda* to be stated by the divine "I" of a mahatma.

During a visit that he paid me in Paris (November 1, 1932), he told me of the importance he assigned to Hallāj, an importance that he did not bring out as clearly[138] either in the *Asrār-i Nhūdī* (1915) or in his two English works (*Development*, 1908; *Reconstruction*, 1934), as in the verses we shall cite here.

In Song V of *Jāwīdnāma*, there are three noble souls, Hallāj, Ghālib, and Qurrat al-ʿAyn Tāhire, who do not want to be put in Paradise, but revolve around the Eternal.

Iqbāl (p. 133) tells us he has surrendered to his passionate heart, which exposes him constantly to a new disaster and which, when one reaches a stopping place in one's journey, says to one, "move on. Surely for the mature man the ocean is only a reservoir; and, since the divine wonders are limitless, O traveler, where can the route end? It is the nature of knowledge to see and then to waste away, the nature of wisdom to see and then to grow."

To describe the eternal unsatisfaction of desire, Iqbāl has three great spokesmen speak.

Song of Hallāj (p. 135):

. . . in your own land seek the hidden flame, —it is unworthy (of man) to borrow light from elsewhere.

. . . I have set my gaze so much on my self, —that I cannot perceive the light surrounding the world of the Friend.

. . . and I would not give this hemistich by Nazīrī for all of the Kingdom of Jām: "whosoever has not been killed does not belong to our tribe . . ."

---

[138] However, cf. *Reconstruction*, p. 91 on Hallāj's "culminating experience" as proof of his supreme personalism; also cf. *ibid.*, pp. 92, 97, and 104.

. . . if chimerical reason has levied an army, —you, do not lose courage in thinking that Love is alone.

(p. 136) . . . Surely you know neither the route nor the stopping place, —nor what melody is lacking in Sulayma's lyre,

. . . but (I want) you to tell me a tale of capture after a hunt for sea monsters, —without telling me that our boat does not know the sea . . .

. . . I am a disciple of that vagabond who refused to follow a route where there would be neither mountain, valley, nor sea . . .

. . . join the circle of faultless drinkers, —avoid taking on a *pīr* who is not an expert in the warring fray . . .

Song of Ghālib:

. . . come, let us change the rule of heaven . . . let us refuse the dialogue with Moses and the hospitality of Abraham . . . , the king's gift, and the tax due the army. . . .

Song of Tāhire:

. . . to meet You I look at face after face, appearance after appearance . . . to see Your face, I pass by like the morning wind. . . .

Song of Hallāj (p. 139):

. . . for the free man, who knows good and evil, his soul's place is not in paradise,

. . . this paradise of mullas with its wine, houris, and ghilmān, —while the paradise of free men (*āzādegān*) is a perpetual journey . . .

. . . this paradise of mullas is to eat, sleep, and be merry, —while the paradise of the lover is to explore and to ravish . . .

. . . this resurrection of mullas is to rise from the grave and to hear the trumpet, —whereas in the case of the lover, all that upsets him is for him the dawn of the resurrection . . .

. . . this knowledge of the '*ulamā*' is fearing and hoping, —while the perfect lover no longer knows fear or hope . . .

. . . this knowledge fears the (divine) majesty in things, —while the lover goes and drowns himself in the (divine) beauty of things . . .

. . . love is free, jealous, impatient, —bold to explore and ravish. . . .

(p. 140) Our love is a stranger to lamentation, —and if it weeps, it is from ecstasy; this heart of ours, though daunted, is not subdued, —the lance which pierces us is not the gaze of houris . . .

. . . our fire, even separation revives it, —our soul, separation quickens it; to live without wounds is not to live, —one must live with fire underneath . . .

. . . to live thus is to realize one's own destiny, —one builds the Self only with his full (accepted) destiny . . .

. . . an atom of infinite desire is envied by the sun, —for it contains in itself the nine celestial spheres . . .

(The Voice of) Zenderūd:[139]

. . . both life and death are facts of fate, —who is the one who does not know a fact of fate?

Hallāj (p. 141):

. . . the one who is able to conform himself to his destiny, —his power frightens both Iblīs and death . . .

. . . to submit [to one's fate] is the religion of the sublime man, suffering is the height of strength among men . . .

. . . the mature man is ready to suffer destiny, but suffering delivers immature men into the arms of death . . .

. . . the violence of Khālid[140] turned the world into chaos, —and my violence makes religion suffer deracination . . .

. . . the fact of true men is taslīm and ridā', —raiment which is not advisable for the weak . . .

. . . you who know what rank Rūmī holds, do you not know his verses:

. . . in the time of Bayezid there was a Parsi to whom a smug Muslim said (p. 142): why don't you become a Muslim and thereby gain a thousand greetings and rewards? —If your faith, O disciple, the Parsi answered him, is like that of Bayezid, pīr of the world, I could not endure the fervor, a fire that my soul could never stand . . .

. . . our action is nothing but fear and hope to one who does not understand the ideal of taslīm . . .

. . . you who say: that will be, —your acts will actually be the mainstay of the form . . .

. . . the meaning of destiny, for comprehension, is seeing that the nonself is the negation of God.

. . . the believer implores God, saying: we shall work with You, You work with us, [Your] determination is that which created the destiny set by God, —and on the day of the battle, his arrow is the arrow of God. . . .

Zenderūd:

. . . there is an outcry at the scandal by short-sighted people, —and the servant of God is hanged on the gibbet . . .

. . . in you the hidden Existence has appeared; repeat, what finally was your sin?

Hallāj (p. 143):

. . . the sound of the trumpet was in my heart, —I saw religion on its way to the grave . . .

. . . the faithful, on account of customs and observances unfaithful, —repeating the "lā ilāha" (no god . . .)[141] but denying Him in fact . . .

. . . saying that divine Commandment is a futile text engraved—in your (man) who is only water and mud.

---

[139] The surname, in this instance, of Rūmī (p. 66): he is Iqbāl's guide here, as Virgil was Dante's.

[140] Ibn Walīd.　　　　　　　　　　　　　[141] Cf. below and Nesimī.

As for me, in His Ipseity, I have lit the fire of life, —I have told man the mystery of life.

They withdrew the construction of the universe from the Ego (= *khūdī*), —they mingled their loves with the Almighty.

The Ego is everywhere, whether apparent or invisible, —we see Him in the watery and in the igneous . . .

. . . the fires are clothed in His light, —the glory of things comes from His sphere continually; in this ancient Monastery, each heart conveys the voice of the Ego from behind the screen (of the enclosure) . . .

. . . he who does not share in His fire in this world is ignorant of himself . . .

(p. 144) India and Iran are the intimate friends of His Light, —but few of their people know His fire.

As for myself, I have spoken of His light and of His fire, —O faithful servant, see, that is my sin . . .

. . . what I have done, you are also doing it, take care . . .

. . . you too, you bring resurrection to men, take care . . .

Tāhire, Zenderūd, and Ghālib (talk to each other).

Hallāj (p. 149):

Everything you see in the world that has color and smell, —that arouses longing for His earth . . .

. . . comes either from the lustre of Nūr-i Muhammad, —or even from its eclipse . . .

(p. 150)

. . . his face touches the forehead of the universe, —God Himself calls him 'Abduh.[142]

He is beyond your comprehension, —for he is both Adam and the essence (of creatures) . . .

. . . his essence is neither Arab[143] nor non-Arab, —it is Adam and prior to Adam, he is the prefashioner of destiny, —and the rebuilder of ruined things simultaneously recreating and conquering the soul, both the empty phial and the thick rock . . .

There is another 'Abd[144] than 'Abduh, —whom we are still awaiting; 'Abduh is duration, and duration comes from him, —we are only coloration or noncoloration . . .

'Abduh has beginning but not end, —where are our mornings and evenings for him; no one knows the secret of 'Abduh, —he has no other secret than "*illā'llāh*"; "*lā ilāha*" is a sword whose point is 'Abduh, —if you want to divulge it, say "it is he, 'Abduh."

'Abduh is the how much and the how of things, —'Abduh is the inner secret of things . . .

. . . here is this distich, —for you to see from the standpoint of the "*mā ramaytu*" rank (I am not the one who produced it)[145] . . .

---

[142] Cf. *Tawāsīn*, Ch. I.   [143] *Ibid.*
[144] The Mahdī.   [145] Hadīth.

. . . ask questions and listen, O Zenderūd, drown yourself in Being, O Zenderūd . . .

Zenderūd (p. 151):

. . . what does it mean to annihilate yourself through love? —To have desire for vision, but what is vision?

Hallāj:

. . . vision means applying to oneself the Judgment that He will give on the last day . . .
. . . and living here like the Prophet of men and of genies, —to the point of being accepted by them as he was.
. . . look at him again, he is vision, —and the *Sunna* is one of his mysteries.

Zenderūd:

. . . what does it mean to see the God of the nine spheres? —He, without whose command neither the moon nor the sun turns?

Hallāj (p. 152):

. . . the sign of God is imprinted[146] first upon the soul, —and afterwards upon the universe, when the sign of the soul applies itself assiduously to the motion of the universe, —your vision of God becomes universal . . .
. . . O happy is he who, then, with his simple *huwa* does the *tawāf* in the nine heavens . . .
. . . O dervish, he who says *huwa*, —then closes his lips again and breathes back into himself the breath of the world, he will not make the command of God rule, —as long as he has not drunk from the river (?) and insisted . . .
" . . . he searched for the Monastery, he comes from Khaybar," —devoted traveler, he did not go see the Sovereign . . .
. . . the sign of God (upon yourself), rest assured, is outside the world, your inspirer; the reigns of destiny are in your hand . . .
. . . if the present century seeks a quarrel with you, —destroy the sign of God on the tablet of this ungodly one's destiny.

Zenderūd (p. 153):

. . . the sign of God (= *khūdī*) is imprinted upon the world? —I do not know how it is imprinted upon it. . . .

Hallāj:

. . . either by a lure that seduces or by the violence that forces . . .
. . . and God shows better through that which seduces, —for a lure is superior to violence.

---

[146] = *amr* = *khūdī*.

Zenderūd:

. . . speak to me again, O master, of the secrets of the East; —what is the difference between the "ascetic" and the "lover"?

Hallāj (p. 154):

. . . the ascetic is an exile from this world, the lover is an exile from the next. . . .

Zenderūd:

. . . if the end of wisdom is nothingness, —will life find its repose in annihilation?

Hallāj:

. . . if the ecstasy of lovers is allied to emptiness, —nothingness remains a stranger to wisdom . . .
. . . O you who seek an end in annihilation, —nonbeing does not end being . . .

Zenderūd (p. 155):

. . . The one who claimed he was better than Adam (= Iblīs), —has neither pickings nor dregs any more in the cellar or the granary . . .
. . . our (human) handful of earth has its place in this universe, —but where is this fire (of Iblīs), which has neither head nor body?

Hallāj:

. . . you are speaking to me of that "Lord of the People of Separation" (Iblīs), —disfigured by desire, and, from pre-eternity a "bloodstained Cup" . . .[147]
. . . we do not know if he was a Sage or not, —but his infidelity discloses this mystery to us . . .
. . . in the fall the pleasure of returning, —a regaining of life in the subsidence of grief . . .
. . . to deprive oneself of the beloved by burning in His fire, —for to burn outside His fire is not to burn . . .
. . . for (Iblīs) was foremost in love and in observance, and Adam was not let into his secret . . .
. . . break, master, the irons of taqlīd, [148] —so that Tawhīd may become (cooling) ice for him (= the burning Iblīs).

Zenderūd (p. 156):

. . . O you for whom the soul's taslīm is as easy as returning a ring around a finger, —stay a moment longer to chat with us.

---

[147] A verse by Rūmī.
[148] Servile literalism.

Hallāj:

. . . we may not stop at stages, —we fly unceasingly with desire . . .
. . . our role is to see each era's pulse beat, —to fly with neither wing nor foot is
our role.

An apparition and song of Iblīs:

. . . of whom Rūmī said: "Lord of the People of Separatior, —this everlasting
burnt one, this bloodstained cup" (pp. 156-161).

[We quote lastly] *"The Call of Hallāj"*:[149]

Seek the undiscoverable Fire in your own land,
For no other light is worthy of contemplation.
(Unfortunately) I fixed my gaze so much on myself[150] that, when the Lustre of
the Beloved
Invaded the universe, I had not the leisure to contemplate it.
I would not give (this) benediction of Nazīrī for the (price) of the kingdom of
Jamshed:
"He who does not get himself killed is not one of our tribe!"
Although falsifying Reason[151] has mobilized (its) magic army.
Be not anxious, for Love is not alone (nor without support).
It is you who are not an expert in the Way; you are ignorant of (musical)
modes,
(For) there is no melody that does not exist in the book of Solomon (?)
Tell (me) (bravely) of the capture and the hunt of sharks;
(And) do not tell (me) that our boat did not know the currents of the ocean.
I am a (devoted) disciple of one such walker (on the Way) who does not deign
to step
On a path where there are no mountains, deserts, and oceans.[152]
Join the Circle of the "Rend,"[153] (drunken)[154] drinkers of wine;
Guard against obedience to a *pīr* who is not a man of (mystic) cries.

IV. THE ATTENTION GIVEN HALLĀJ AND HIS MAXIMS
BY MUSLIM PHILOSOPHERS

a. Sijistānī and Tawhīdī

The first Muslim philosopher to have written a commentary on the Hallājian maxims was Abū Sulaymān Sijistānī (b. before 307, d. around 380

---

[149] [Poem by Iqbāl] *Ghazal*, taken from *Jāwidānnāma*.
[150] "Myself" in the antimystical sense and not the base Ego (*khud*) of Iqbālian philosophy.
[151] Literally, "Reason whose trade is (practicing) only magic and fraudulent imitation."
[152] And a thousand other dangers.
[153] This word is a favorite of Hāfiz Shirāzī.
[154] That is to say, having clouded their minds.

at the same age as Qāḍī Ibn Sayyār, d. 350). It is quite amazing for him to have perceived the essence of Hallāj's thought by this time:[1] his doctrine of the divine source and of the absolute unifying power of friendship between two souls. Sijistānī appears to have become acquainted with it in the Islamo-Christian milieu of the Qunnā'īya scribes[2] in which Mu'tazilite qāḍīs and grammarians entered into debate (as had Ibn Dāwūd in former times) with Sālimīya Sūfīs over the philosophy of spiritual love.[3]

In his *Maqāla fi'l-kamāl al-khāss bi naw' al-insān* (Kraus ms., no. 3), in which he asserts boldly that true perfection in the human species is union with God (*ittihād*), Sijistānī notes that one "sect of Sūfīs accepts the idea of union with the Essence, *'ayn al-jam''*," which is one of Hallāj's ideas referred to by the Sālimīya as dangerous.

In his conversations reported by Tawhīdī in his treatise on friendship, Sijistānī, making use of a maxim by Ibn 'Atā' and a verse by Hallāj (*Rūhuhu rūhī . . .*), comments on a maxim attributed to Aristotle concerning the unification which comes about through the union of two close friends' wills. We also know from another source that the Sālimīya circulated in learned circles one of the two magnificent "Letters to Ibn 'Atā'" from Hallāj concerning their common friendship in God.

The *Kitāb al-sadāqa* of Abū Hayyān Tawhīdī quotes a couplet by Hallāj ("*mā lī jafayta . . .* ") that was circulated as early as approximately 320 by a Mu'tazilite scholar, Qannād, and which was based on the authority of Zayd ibn Rifā'a Hāshimī (d. 372), a quasi philosopher, and probable source of the Sūfī quotations from the Ikhwān al-safā' and by Bīrūnī, a disciple of Shiblī, Hallāj's friend. With the Buwayhids strictly upholding the ban against mentioning Hallāj by name, only internal criticism enables us to discern what Tawhīdī both a philosopher and a mystic, owed to Hallāj (particularly his idea of the "*hajj 'aqlī*," already pointed out by Khūnsārī. This thesis would have caused him to be outlawed in Badhara by Vizir Muhallabī (340, d. 352); when he died in Shiraz in 414/1023, the pro-Hallāj Khafīfīya order, with AH Daylamī, author of *al-Alif wa'l-ma'lūf*, and afterwards with A Hy ibn Sālih (d. 473) as spokesman, recognized Tawhīdī publicly as a genuine mystic.

The disciples of Tawhīdī, such as Abū Shujā' Maqāridī (d. 509), were probably the source of the contact established by correspondence between the Sūfī Ibn Abī'l-Khayr and the great philosopher Ibn Sīnā, a contact that the testimony of 'AQ Hamadhānī does not allow us to put in question.

---

[1] AT, *Sadāqa* [?], 59.   [2] Ibn al-Jamāl, Nasrānī.   [3] Zayd-b-Rifā'a, a friend of Shiblī.

If the coincidences of technical terms between Avicennism and Hallāj is insufficient to prove a real connection at the time of Ibn Sīnā himself, a century and a half later the Avicennian Suhrawardī Halabī declared himself explicitly a Hallājian on a basis of "spiritual affinity" transcending time and place, as became the case among philosophers. This attempt at a "Zoroastrian" isnād, by which the latter claimed a link with Hallāj, with the "Fatā" of Bayda, is discontinuous, as is the "Hermetic" isnād by which Ibn Sab'īn and Shushtarī were later to link themselves "philosophically" to Hallāj.

b. Hallāj and Muslim Philosophical Hellenism:
Avicenna and Averroes

Ibn Sīnā (Avicenna) (d. 437/1046). We have noted the contacts that Hallāj made during the second period of his life with the Hellenistic philosophical movement, not only in order to argue better, but also to discuss ontology and political theory (*siyāsa*).

'AQ Hamadhānī is the first to call our attention to two problems, that of *kufr haqīqī* and that of *wahda*, in which Hallāj used specific philosophical definitions, which he compares to Avicennism.

Internal criticism of the Hallājian texts shows us, in fact, that Hallāj, in opposition to the *nahwīyīn* and *mutakallimīn*, had adopted the terminology of *mantiq* (Greek logic), and that he knew the ten categories, the five universals, the four causes, the logical identity (*al-huwa huwa*).[4]

Here is the definition of *wahda*, according to 'AQ Hamadhānī:[5] O *gharīb*, when one has reached this mystical stage, the subject (*shāhid*) is one, the object (*mashhūd*) no longer has a number . . . then numbers, in the One, are reduced to unity. This is the stage that was granted to Husayn ibn Mansūr when he said: "*afrād al-a'dād fī'l-wahdati wāhidun*" (= every number taken separately as having unity becomes one). Ten, in fact, is formed of ten ones, and the one included in this whole completes it.

Hamadhānī, like Ibn Sīnā, seems here to be confusing numerical unity with transcendental unity; whereas Hallāj, like Plato and like Ibn Rushd, aims, by means of this individuating (by numerical quantification) prin-

---

4 Stafr [?], n. 204.
5 'AQ Hamadhānī, *Tamhīdāt* [bib. no. 308-a], Paris ms. afp. 36, f. 63b, Persian Suppl. 1084, f. 142b. Cf. Ibn Sīnā, *Shifā'* [bib. no. 2118-a] I, 440; Ibn Rushd, *Met[aphysics]* Quiros ed., I, 38; III, 39; Fakhr Rāzī, *Mab. Mashriq* [?] I, 81; Tahānāwī, 1484. Hallāj elsewhere contrasted *fard* to *wāhid* (maxim "*hasb al-wājid . . .*," cf. T. Dantzig, *Le Nombre* [bib. no. 2050-a], p. 49, deficient number (*Akhbār*, no. 9)—*ahad* and *wāhid*—becoming one to know the one (*Sulamī, Tafsīr*).

ciple, at an individual number (the number eight, a hundred), the analogical and transcendental One, of which God is the model.[6] Similarly, in his definition of the *nuqta* point "any place where one's glance falls (on a straight line) is a point between two points,"[7] which reminds us of Dedekind.[8]

Hallāj's biography indicates specific contacts in philosophical circles, notably with the physician Rāzī, which explains the fact of his having written three treatises on political theory (*siyāsa*) (A [Akhbār], 11, 15, 38), and as many on the universals (and transcendentals: A 3, 27, 45-46). He may have known Sarakhsī (d. 286) and Mattā Qunnā'ī.[9]

Were these contacts continued by his disciples? There are some verbal coincidences between the *madīna* of Farābī[10] and Hallājism, and it was not accidental that Abū Hayyān Tawhīdī (d. 414/1023 in Shiraz) took up in a philosophical form the Hallājian idea of the "replacement of the legal pilgrimage" by a *ta'rīf 'aqlī*.

The Hallājian religious experience had a philosophical value of its own which, in spite of its archaic expression, could not fail in the end to be brought to light: for its piercing affirmation of the immateriality of the soul, outside of time and space, the notion of its transcendental substantial unity distinct from numerical unity, the mode of transnatural and direct intervention of divine action sanctifying the human creature through a love that transfigures, not only the soul, but also the body through suffering itself.

Contact was resumed[11] between the master of mysticism in Nishapur, Abū Sa'īd ibn Abī'l-Khayr (d. 440/1049), who venerated Hallāj, and the great philosopher Ibn Sīnā; their correspondence, at least in the case of the letters authenticated by 'AQ Hamadhānī, is genuine. The following is a letter from Ibn Sīnā concerning the proof (*dalīl*) needed to recognize the true religion:[12]

You are entering the reality of ungodliness, and forsake the appearance of Islam;[13] you must cast your mind's glance beyond three (created) objects (of com-

---

[6] Baqlī, *Tafsīr*, 19, *Sh.* 181; Sulamī, *Tab.*, 14; Qushūrī [?] IV, 49; *Mu'ill*, Sulamī, *Tafsīr*, 60, 168, 173.

[7] *Akhbār* 4; thus for him the point is not merely the atom of *kalām* (Tah., 1414).

[8] Proving the arithmetical continuum: a single point divides all points of a straight line into two categories (Dantzig, *Le Nombre*, p. 174).

[9] In the Qunnā'ī milieu of 280 (came to the Tustarīyīn).

[10] P. 18: *al-mahabba dhāt dhātihi* (cf. Hallāj: cf. *Essai*); *sudūr al-mawjūdāt 'anhu* (cf. Hallāj tells us, *al mawjūdāt*), an expression criticized by Ibn 'Arabī, P. ms. 6640, f. 107b.

[11] In Isfahan, in the Avicennian milieu: 'Umar-b-Sahlān, who exercised an influence over Suhrawardī Halabī; in Hamadhan, Majd, master of Fakhr Rāzī and Suhrawardī.

[12] *Recueil*, pp. 189-190. On *majāzī* Islam.   [13] Cf. 'Attār.

mon belief: paradise, hell, and a'rāf) thereby to cease being both Muslim and ungodly (= to cease saying both parts, the negation and the affirmation, of the shahāda) and to forego calling yourself "Muslim" or "ungodly" (= to enter into the pure and unique being, without specification).

One commentator, Sa'd al-Dīn Kāzarūnī (d. 758), who was affiliated with the Hallājīya tarīqa,[14] observed that this letter was Hallājian in inspiration, coming from Hallāj's letter to Jundab Wāsitī[15] concerning the uselessness of reciting the shahāda, but that its conclusion, with its perspective of existential monism, differs from it.

Apart from this, Ibn Sīnā teaches, in terms of divine love, a doctrine that is very different from that of Hallāj: there is a divine hierarchical circulation (sarayān) of love in all creatures; this 'ishq is the instinctive (gharīzī) impulse of each ipseity toward the Pure Good, which must perfect it and which draws it to Itself by an unceasing tajallī (= radiance).[16] This, we see, is a question of the ordinary expansion of divine providence, not of that transnatural love which divinizes the sanctified soul.[17] And though one can find in Ibn Sīnā the beginning of four great theses behind the Ghazālian Ihyā' concerning "the love due to God above all," one also finds in him the most categorical refusal to accept the idea of a state of mystical union. In his Ishārāt, Ibn Sīnā teaches that this union cannot really be consummated, since this supposed transformation of two into one (being neither istihāla nor tarkīb, substances) ends up in a dilemma: either the two (lovers) continue to exist (distinct from one another), or both disappear; and if only one (of the two) remains, one can no longer speak of it as union.[18]

This Avicennian argument is materialistic in its mathematical form, for it confuses ontological and structural unity with numerical unity, and it excludes the possibility of a tertium quid between being and nonbeing.[19] Nevertheless, it seemed conclusive to Ghazālī, who used it again in his Maqṣad asnā and Ma'ārij al-sālikīn to refute the hulūlī interpretation of the

---

[14] Cf. Shabistarī (ap. Sārī 'AA IV, 103).

[15] Akhbār, no. 41 (and 31), corroborated by the Kafartu verse (Dīwān, 106; of Raghib [bib. no. 276-a]). A pupil of Ibn Sīnā, Raghib Isfahānī, quoted verses of Hallāj, 196, 226, 271.

[16] Ibn Sīnā, 'Ishq, p. 87 (Cairo ed.): cf. Dante.

[17] Eckhart: "God casts His beam of contentment into creatures; but the root of all contentment He has kept entirely within Himself, for He wants us all to Himself and to no one else" (Pfeiffer ed., Sermon 43; translated by Mayrisch Saint Hubert, ap. Hermès, 1937, IV, 11). That is regarded contra ittihād, not contra hulūl.

[18] Recueil, pp. 188-189. Cf. Ibn Dāwūd, Zahra [?] XL (on the subject of Abū Tammām).

[19] = Growth in power (Aristotle, De gen. et corrupt. I, 10 [S. van den Bergh's commentary]).

Hallājian "I am the Truth": for a substance such as the soul cannot play the role of accident vis-à-vis another substance.[20] We shall see it repeated by Fakhr al-Dīn Rāzī and by Ibn 'Arabī in his *Tajallīyāt*, apropos of Junayd, and in his *Isrā'*. Only Ibn Sab'īn was to attempt to give a positive philosophical solution to the problem.

Ibn Rushd (Averroes) (d. 595/1198). A Mālikite qādī of qādīs, as well as a distinguished Aristotelian, Ibn Rushd was known to be hostile to mysticism. We have seen that one of the reasons for his spite against Ghazālī was the fact "that he had wished to pardon Hallāj." However, in his *Tahāfut al-tahāfut*, in Chapter XIII,[21] we come upon the following interesting passage dealing with divine knowledge as the cause of creatures: "creatures thus have two existences (*wujūdāni*)," one higher (= in the knowledge of God), the other lower (in this world), and the higher is the *cause* of the lower; this is why the ancient (philosophers) said 'the Creator is the whole of creation, He is its benefactor and its agent'; and this is the meaning of the saying of the Sūfī masters (= Hallāj, followed by Ghazālī):[22] '*lā huwa illā Huwa*,' 'there is no he but Him.' " And he adds that this formula is proper for those whose knowledge is sound, that it does not appear in the teaching of canon law, and must be revealed only to those who are worthy of it.

c. Suhrawardī Maqtūl and Hermeticism

With Suhrawardī Maqtūl (b. 550, d. in Aleppo in 586), a master of Persian prose, Muslim philosophy clearly defines the appropriately philosophical, metaphysical, and ontological meaning of the Hallājian case of conscience. As studied, that is, not on a basis of hearsay, but from direct quotations taken from the *Tawāsīn* (expressly named) and from *Akhbār*.

Suhrawardī had first studied Shāfi'ite law;[23] afterwards, Majd Jīlī, master of Fakhr Rāzī, in Meragha, and especially Zahīr Fārisī, in Isfahan (a pupil of the Avicennian 'Umar-b-Sahlān Sāwijī, author of the *Basā'ir*) introduced him to Hellenistic philosophy. Finally, for the last ten years of his brief life, Suhrawardī traveled about as a kind of wandering Sūfī through the Saljūq principalities of Anatolia, visiting the court of Qilij Arslan and his sons, of the amīr of Kharput Qahr Arslan, and of the amīr of Mansūr Barqiyānı. After visiting Damascus, he settled in Aleppo in close association with the son of Saladin, Malik Zāhir, who, on his

---

[20] *Ma'ārij*, f. 160a.
[21] *Recueil*, p. 191.
[22] *Mishkāt*, used previously by Ibn Sīnā.
[23] [The name of this first master has not been indicated.]

father's orders, was obliged to execute him for blasphemy (zandaqa: his refusal to say the second part of the shahāda about the mission of Muhammad;[24] this was an outgrowth of his philosophical theory of the superiority of angels to men, and of the Rūh Qudūs, the Holy Spirit, identified with the Avicennian Tenth Intellect [= Kadhkhudāh[25] "the giver of forms that are imprinted on our sublunary intellects" = Jibrīl] inspiring one directly without passing through Muhammad, particularly in order to vivify miraculously such physical effigies ['unsurī] as Jesus, Bistāmī, and Hallāj, as his disciple Shahrazūrī points out).

His worn habit of a mendicant and his theory of the Holy Spirit indeed show that Suhruwardī was acquainted with Hallāj, not through the Sūfī masters, but through the milieu of the "zanādiqa Hallājīya," which Khatīb and 'Attār tell us about, in which Hallāj was venerated as having been superhumanly transfigured in his personality.

More the impassioned metaphysician than a pure mystic, Suhrawardī intended to integrate a full explanation of Hallājian mysticism into the heart of his philosophical ishrāqī syncretism, which he constructed with Avicennian Hellenistic elements transposable into Sabaean Hermetic terms and Mazdaean terms (the Amshaspand). Suhrawardī personally revered Hallāj (whom he referred to as "my brother"), and it was in him that the Hallājian example, going beyond the limits of the Muslim setting, assumed for the first time an interreligious meaning that no Ismā'īlī thinker (not even the Ikhwān al-safā') had assigned explicitly to him.

Hallāj helped Suhrawardī prove two of his basic metaphysical ideas: that of the radical immateriality of the human soul (nonbodily resurrection), and that of transcendental unity (not the sterile atom that arithmetical analysis ends in, but the pure act that "assumpts"[26] and deifies).

Here are two prose texts:

A. T. Makkī used to say regarding his master AH-b-Sālim, "For him space has rolled in its folds, and regarding the Prophet 'as soon as a doubt beset him, space emptied of matter for him' "; and Hallāj also said regarding the Prophet, in Tawāsīn, "he blinked his eye outside the 'where,' " even though it is impossible for a physical body to do that; the limit for extended bodies is to be abstracted from extension and to "blink outside the 'where' "; similarly the following verse by Hallāj: "my essence is already defined as long as there is no more place"; and the words of a Sūfī: "I sought my essence in both worlds without finding it

---

[24] Kalimat al-tasawwuf, ms. IO, Chapter III, f. 27a. —I'tiqād al-hukamā', P. Arabic ms. 1247, f. 144b.

[25] That engender forms in our intelligences so that they may give them birth in the world (cf. Hallāj himself, and Maryam, the birth of Jesus). —'Aql Fa' 'āl of our intellects.

[26] ["Assumpts" coined by Massignon from the Assumption of Mary.]

there"; and the words of Hallāj: "all that matters to the ecstatic is to find the One singled in oneself"; and his definition of a Sūfī: unified as to essence, without any debt[27] or credit. Given the fact that every physical body is composed, its limit is to be unified, unity being indivisible; there are many statements by Abū Yazīd (Bistāmī) in this vein.[28]

The rational soul (*nafs nātiqa*)[29] is not of this world (*'ālam 'unsurī, atharī*), for an intelligent monad is not of the world of bodies, which are composed; if it were [of this world], we would not know how it could perceive the unity of the First Truth, may His Majesty be exalted; for the One is perceivable only to one who is unified (*wahdānī*);[30] as Hallāj said on the cross: "nothing which is of the world of bodies is one."

This spiritual unification can be realized totally only by shattering the body, and thus by voluntary death. This, as Suhrawardī expresses in his *Kalimāt dhawqīya*,[31] is the meaning of the Hallājian "*Anā'l-Haqq*": "the one who has looked at the sun and then looks at himself, finds he is filled with nothing else but rays of the sun and exclaims 'I am the sun.' Similarly Abū Yazīd, Hallāj, and others initiated into solitude (*tajrīd*), those moons in the sky of *Tawhīd*, when the earth of their hearts was illuminated by the light of their Lord, revealed the divine secret, which became evident to all. Then God made them speak; He who makes everything speak, expresses Himself by the tongue of His saints, as follows: 'You must break the carnal talisman (= your body), for the treasures of (divine) Holiness are enclosed in it, and he who breaks it takes possession of the (desired) Goal.' "

Suhrawardī interprets the famous verses "murder me now, my faithful friends . . ."[32] and "remove, for mercy's sake, this 'it is I' of mine from between the two of us" in the same spirit, declaring that by asking God to free him from this last physical bond, Hallāj exempted all that is not God from shedding his blood"[33] (Jīlī criticized this).

The idea of the voluntary breaking of the fleshly talisman is found with an obvious allusion to Hallāj, in the very famous *qasīda* "*Qul li'ikhwānī* . . . " that Masaffar Sibtī wrote on five verses by Suhrawardī Maqtūl.[34]

---

[27] Assumed neither by Him nor upon Him.

[28] *Kalimat al-tasawwuf*, IO ms., Chapter III, f. 26a = *Lughate mūrān*, 15 (beginning) and *Saf* [. . .], 43 (end).

[29] *I'tiqād al-hukamā'*, P. Arabic ms. 1247, f. 144b.

[30] Qushayrī, 150, Hallāj repeated these words to Ibn al-Jallā (*Hilya* X, 314).

[31] Corbin ms.

[32] *Lughate mūrān*, ap. Spies, tr. 19 (*Recueil*, p. 144). Bats, in their aversion to chameleons, expose them to the burning sun, the form of death they desire.

[33] *Recueil*, p. 148.

[34] Musaffar Sibtī, cf. *Dīwān*, JA [?], p. 131.

No less famous is the *qasīda* "*Abada tahinnū' ilaykum al-arwāh*" that must be restored to Suhrawardī Maqtūl and that also alludes to the death of Hallāj:[35]

Souls are always going with a sigh to You,
Reaching out to You are their myrtle and their wine;
These ripened hearts to love You desire You
And take pleasure only in the perfection of Your beauty.
Woe to lovers; they try to keep the secret of love, but their passion reveals it.
Now, if they give away their secret, their blood becomes lawful [to shed].
Thus is the blood of those who give it away given up. . . .

Suhrawardī Maqtūl seems to have exposed himself willfully to death.

d. Ibn Sab'īn[36]

A bitter, haughty, and tortured intelligence, an Aristotelian freed from a servile imitation of the master of whom Ibn Rushd had only wanted to be the docile commentator, Ibn Sab'īn[37] (d. 669/1270) was also a mystic. He tried, in the vein of Ghazālī, to find a criterion for classifying systems of thought[38] according to their degree of efficacy in bringing about the soul's ascension to God. He devised a more precise vocabulary, differentiating *'aql*, *nafs*, and *rūh*. Keeping the classical terms *nafs kullīya*, *'aql kullī*, and *'aql fa' 'āl*, he puts everything above a kind of divine unique and supreme emanation, reminding one of the *Rūh* of Suhrawardī Halabī. He calls it different names: *Kalima*, *qasd al-Haqq*, *annīya mutlaqa*, *himma mutlaqa*, *ihātā*. Through it, through this formative power, God individualizes, personalizes, and sanctifies beings; it is the Form (*sūra*) of the whole of created matter.

Setting forth philosophical hypotheses for modalities of the beatitude of souls,[39] Ibn Sab'īn rejects the idea that it could raise them to direct union with the First Cause; indeed, it is no longer sufficient for them to have union[40] with the universal Soul, with the universal Intellect (*'aql*

---

[35] The early recension has 23 verses (Yāqūt, *Udabā'* VII, 270; Ibn Khallikān, *Nahj* [?] III, 73; Ibn Abī Usaybi'a [?] II, 170; Shahrazūrī, pp. 103-105 of Spies [bib. no. 1801-a], has 31 verses. Abel was the first to translate a later recension having 16 verses (*Cahiers du Sud*, October 1938); cf. *Dīwān* (not identified by me).

[36] [We have let these texts on Ibn Sab'īn and Shushtarī remain here (pp. 417-420), though they were written probably at least ten years before pages 313-322.]

[37] A pupil of Shawdhī. Born in 614. Wrote *Budd* in 629. In 650 was in Bougie. In 652 in Cairo, where he saw Sadr Qūnawī. Died 669/1270.

[38] In five classes (*Budd*, f. 33a, 114a-b: cf. *Taymūr*, ms. 149, f. 440).

[39] *Recueil*, pp. 133 and 189 (in Ibn Sīnā).

[40] (*Masā'il*, f. 310b, 339b) by "substantialization" (*tajawhur*).

kullī = faṣl), or even with the active Intellect, and he shows his preference by defining beatitude as union with the absolute Ipseity (*annīya mutlaqa*), the divine Form about which we spoke previously. This leads him to deal with the Hallāj case in two long, similar, passages in the *Budd*[41] and in the *Masā'il*, which we summarize as follows:

Ascension to God is an essential undertaking, since it obtains beatitude and eternal joy. But its analytical schematization (*bi sana'at al-tarkīb*) is difficult to describe, "narrower than the edge of a sword." Aristotle had already said that the one who claims to have arrived at the First Cause to become transubstantiated in it exceeds his powers, since in this case the discursive method is no longer involved. It is useless to describe the progression of spiritual intelligences in terms of material stages when its intended goal is fixed as the central point within a closed circle, and when the powers of the soul or of the existential nexus no longer allow access to it. The one who has this end in view wants to have it shown, but has no technical preparation nor any sense of propriety, and cries out in the intoxication of believing he has arrived, "I am the Truth, praise be to Me, there is no God but Me." If he did not lose his footing, he would admit his inadequacy. For the *shattāḥ*[42] who shouts "I am the Truth" emits a cry. Is this a moment of relaxation in annihilation and a sigh of agony, or the drunkenness of a sick person becoming delirious, or the expression of sudden joy at finding oneself alive? In any case, it is not the accomplishment of what the Arrival in God will be, since the *shattāḥ* remains conscious and discursive: he has not yet died, he has not yet entered the Life of the blessed.

According to Plato, we are incapable of knowing the essence of the First Truth, since we are caught between causalized accidents and composed supposita. A statement like "I am the Truth" overlooks the fact that there are preliminary questions to be resolved, such as "does a unity exist, uniting the object, whose being is one, with the substance of things?" and "does the number add something to the nature of that which exists?" The essential preliminaries must be established in order to define the quiddity of man in general and his highest good; next, in synthesis, to determine the conditions of a real ascension to this Good which is his goal; next, after the event, through analysis, to arrive at the point of preserving this Good in oneself by verifying the difference that exists between the contingent beings to whom one returns and the Being to Whom one has been raised; and finally, to resign from oneself (*tafwīd*), to

---

[41] *Recueil*, pp. 123-128 (*Budd*, f. 69b; *Masā'il*, 316-317).
[42] The one who utters theopathic locutions.

abandon oneself in total poverty to this holy and beautiful Essence (*Dhāt muqaddasa jamīla*) which alone, then, exists. This is why Ghazālī said (in his *Mishkāt*) "there is no god except God," which is the profession of faith of the common people, and "There is no he but Him," which is the profession of faith of the intimates. And that is what is meant by the saying by Hallāj, may He be blest by God: "I am the Truth," meaning "there is no ipseity but the Unique One." When such conformity (*ittisāf*) (to God) is attained, and when it is expressed in such a way, the meaning of it appears ambiguous to the masses, and the one who uttered it is put to death, even though he is motivated in that only by the pure solitude of his naked faith.[43]

In his *Kitāb al-ihāta*,[44] Ibn Sab'īn observes that there is in man a sort of inclination to rejoin this enveloping divine Form, to transubstantiate oneself in it, due to one's "I"; and that this inclination in man conveys, on God's part, a sort of intelligible magnetic force that ends by "breaking the (corporal) talisman" in which the soul is a prisoner here below. God intervenes in the depth of the soul through this actuant Form by means of an intelligible auditory image, of a personal call "*īhi!*" "come!" calling to a *Tawhīd* more powerful than all the formulas of mystics,[45] beyond our threefold idea of the Perfect (the one who removes all illusions, brings about the true, and answers all of our prayers), "like a lover to whom one who has understood must surrender": "*īhi!*" "like the voice that awakens one who sleeps,[46] not like a sentence whose meaning one must search for in order to draw profit from it."

Repeating the Hallājian critique in a reduced form, Ibn Sab'īn taught, instead of the Muhammadian *shahāda*, this "*Laysa illā Allāh*," "Nothing but God";[47] or, more esoterically, "*Laysa illā'l-Aysa*,"[48] "Nothing except His *Fiat*." This was also the *dhikr* of his disciples who formed a congregation.

Balyānī, who was a disciple through Shushtarī of Ibn Sab'īn, gave to the *tarīqa hallājīya* that was established another form of *dhikr*, "*Lāha, Lāhi, Lāhu*."

---

[43] *Fawq al-tāmm, mufīd al-khayrāt* (*Masā'il*, f. 35a).

[44] Taymūr ms., f. 449–451; the end recalls that of the *Tawāsīn*.

[45] *Ibid.*, f. 450: particularly that of Harawī (*mā wahadda*) —His suicide.

[46] *Ibid.*, f. 454. Shushtarī repeated it in verse (Maqqārī, *Nafh* I, 417). Cf. Hallāj: *Akhbār*, p. 39; cf. *Recueil*, p. 229.

[47] Ibn Taymīya, *Majm rasā'il*.

[48] *Ihāta*, f. 474. Originally an Ismā'īlī expression: the *Nātiq* (= Adam) was *makhlūq min aysa*: the *Sābiq* was *mubda' min laysa*.

e. Shushtarī[49]

The leading disciple of Ibn Sab'īn,[50] Abū'l-Hasan Shushtarī,[51] was a great poet. Born in Andalusia, he died in Tina near Damietta[52] in 668/ 1269 leaving, in addition to his prose writings and poems written in classical Arabic, some exquisite short poems written in a very elaborate[53] (*azjāl*) Hispanic dialect whose spontaneous tone and melodies have been kept alive in the Maghrib and in Syria. Hallāj appears in a *zajal* and in three *qasīdas* by Shushtarī.[54] Furthermore, Shushtarī redacted the following important *takhmīs* on Hallāj, embellishing a canvas of Ibn 'Arabī with the ideas of Ibn Sab'īn:[55]

   I. I have established my reality, and the
      majesty of my glory that is sacred
      and elusive to the eye,
      And my tongue, speaking about me, said:
      I am the Qur'ān and the Seven Mathānī
      And the Spirit of the spirit, not the one who
      blows in the seasons.
  VI. . . . Let him who has divined the allusion
      keep the secret. Or else he will perish
      soon by the blade.
 VII. For whosoever stirs the embers of
      Truth, damns himself and sees the gate closed before him.
      While the temple of his body is demolished by the pickaxe of the Law.
      Thus did it befall Hallāj (the Carder) of Love, when the sun of reality
      Shone very close to him.
VIII. And when approaching him, the sun stood still.
      Already transfigured by the Supreme Name,
      He claimed to be one with God, without thinking
      of moving apart from Him (out of respect),
      And exclaimed: "It is I who am the Truth,
      Whose essence escapes the vicissitudes of time."

[49] [Cf. n. 36, p. 416].

[50] Other Sab'īnīya: Sāfī D. M-b-A Rahīm Hiade, shaykh of shaykhs in Damascus (d. 715).

[51] Shushtarī was born around 605. A Madyanī at the time of his conversion, afterwards a Sab'īnī (652). Goes to the East, sees Ibn Isrā'īl. Disciples: Yq-b-Mubashshir (Bāb Zuwa'īlī), Sa'īd ibn Luyūn, Zarrūq, Darqāwa. Died 668/1269.

[52] His body was embalmed in Damietta, and not transported to Cairo, where "the tomb of Shushtarī" in Musky is that of Hasan Tustarī.

[53] He attempts in this, for the adepts, who were common people, to make the divine admonition vibrate like a shock caused by brief blows. [Cf.] *Recueil*, pp. 134-137, 147-148 (Ibn 'Abbād); R. Lull, *Blanquerna*, English tr. by [E. Allison] Pears [London, 1926], pp. 375, 410.

[54] E f. 65b; L 58a; F f. 95a; M no. 13. The *qasīda* on the Christian monastery: cf. *infra*.

[55] Cf. *Dīwān*, pp. 135-137. The "demolished temple" is the "*kasr al-tilsam*."

In the *risāla qudsīya*, Shushtarī quotes Ibn Sab'īn as follows: he who says "I" mocks himself by this comparison; he who says "He" lies. Only he who keeps silent is saved. If such is the judgment of the Ruler of the E [. . .] against the one who says "I" in the manner of Husayn Ibn Mansūr, what must one's opinion be of another?

We have a *qasīda* rhymed in *nūn*[56] by Shushtarī on the mystic way (*sulūk*), in which he gives a systematic presentation of the chain of authorities (*isnād*) of the tarīqa Sab'īnīya (verses 41-67), which goes as follows: the Hermeses, Socrates, Plato, Aristotle, Dhū'l-Qarnayn, Hallāj; then, among others, not without chronological inversions that we have corrected, Ibn Masarra, Ibn Sīnā, Niffarī,[57] 'Adī Umawī, Qadib al-Bān Mawsilī, Ibn Qasyī, and Abū 'Abdallāh Shawdhī Hallawī, qādī of Seville[58] and master of Ibn Dahhāq, who taught Ibn Sab'īn.

The *isnāds* given by Ibn Sab'īn himself are less explicit; and because of the *isnād* published by Shushtarī, in which Hallāj appears, two opponents, Qutb al-Dīn ibn al-Qastallānī (d. 686/1287)[59] and Ibn Taymīya, attacked Ibn Sab'īn.[60]

f. 'Alā"l-Dawla Simnānī[61]

Born in 659, of a wealthy aristocratic family of Simnan, kinsman of Sharaf D M-b-A Simnānī, *sāhib dīwān* in Baghdad from 687 to 688, Ahmad-b-M Beyābangī (from the name of an oasis in the Lut desert), surnamed Abū'l-Makārim Rukn al-Dīn, was attracted at age thirteen to the court of the pagan ruler Arghūn. Favored in 688, he left his service, came to Baghdad to go under the guidance of the Kubrawī mystic Nūr D. 'AR Kasirqī Isfarā'ini (639, d. 719)[62] with whom he lived in Baghdad for thirty-two years. Together they composed a very beautiful symbolical commentary on the Qur'ān, *Ta'wīlāt najmīya*,[63] which Ismā'īl Haqqī

[56] *Recueil*, pp. 139-140; commentary by A. Zarrūq.

[57] Arberry published his *mawāqif*; this important text seems to me to date from earlier than the sixth century of the Hijra.

[58] Founder of the *tarīqa Shawdhīya* to which M ibn Ahlā (d. 465) of Lorca also belonged. (Marrākushī, *Dhayl al-sila*, P. ms. f. 215b, f. 174b, pointed out by G. S. Colin.)

[59] Ibn Taghrībirdī, *Manhal Sāfī*, V, 94 (commentary by M. Jawād).

[60] An Andalusian, A-b-H-b-'Alī ibn Qunfudh (*Qusamptinī*) (d. 810) transmitted this dual tarīqa along with others (Zabīdī, *'Iqd*, s.v. Sab'īnīya, Shushtarīya, Shu'aybīya, Abigharrīya, Ghamāthīya) (Kattāva [?] II, 323).

[61] Jāmī, 504, 564; *Tarā'iq* II, 292; *Durar kāmina* I, 261; Zabīdī, s.v. Ruknīya. Ivanow (ap. *JASB* XIX (1923), 299-303).

[62] Kasirqī, born in 639. A Jūrfānī (d. 669). 'Alī Ghaznawī (b. 642), known as Lālā Majd Baghdādī (d. 616). Najm Kubrā.

[63] Cairo ms. I, 134 (5 vols.).

made the basis of his *Rūh al-bayān*. Simnānī went on hajj in 689. He gave his income (90,000 dīnārs) to charity. From 720 to 736, he returned to Simnan, where his *waqf* of 500,000 dīnārs supported the Sakkākīya *khān-qāh* of "Sūfīyābād," the name he gave to his town of birth, where he was buried. He intervened several times at the Mongol court to save the great who had fallen from favor, including among others Amīr Choban, a benefactor of the holy places. He died on Friday, 22 *Rajab* [A.H.] 736.

For disciples he had Amīr Iqbāl Sīstānī,[64] who built a *ribāt* there and who published his *chihl majālis*; Mahmūd Mazdaqānī, who taught 'Alī Hamadhānī; Sharaf-b-'AA Ghawrī, who taught 'Alī Hamadhānī and Yahyā Sijistānī;[65] and two rather well-known poets, Khwājū Kirmānī (679, d. 742) and Salmān Sāwajī (700, d. 778).

His work in mysticism was important in two ways: in metaphysics, he fought openly against the existential monism of Ibn 'Arabī, both in his letters to Jamāl 'A Razzāq Kashī and in his *'Urwa li ahl al-khalwa*, in which he defends the "testimonial monism" of the Shuhūdīya against the Wujūdīya,[66] delineating the position that the Wafā'īya ('A. Karim Jīlī) and especially the Naqishbandīya of India (Sirhindī) were to defend against the anomian infiltrations of the teaching of Ibn 'Arabī. In devotion, he developed the forty-day retreats[67] to be made under a good spiritual director: they accomplish what the single soul can attain only through the Seven Sleepers' 309 symbolic years of ecstatic sleep, a model of the consummation of love, which he says in the *ta'wīlāt* (concerning Qur'ān 18:25);[68] he modified the mode of *dhikr* instituted by his master Kasirqī,[69] and also the corresponding bodily posture, a reform which we have discussed apropos of the Hallājian *dhikr*, and which plays a role even today in the recollections. He attempted to continue Tirmidhī's idea about the superiority of *walāya* (sanctity) in a manner different from that of Ibn 'Arabī.[70]

He worshipped the memory of Hallāj. Upon his arrival in Baghdad, he went at night to pray at his tomb,[71] and saw a column of light rise up from it, Hallāj being in 'Illiyīn (the highest level of Paradise); he asked God "how does it happen that the soul of Fir'awn was cast into the depths of Hell for having said 'I am your Lord Most High,' while Hu-

---

[64] Bodl. ms. 1446; Calc. ms.

[65] *Simt*, 156.

[66] Jāmī, 564; a critique (aimed against Ibn 'Arabī) of the Hallājian *anā man ahwā*.

[67] He made 140 such retreats during his last sixteen years.

[68] Bankipore ms. XIII, no. 905; Berlin 2856.

[69] Qushāshī, *Simt*, 157; *Salsabīl*, 110.

[70] Jāmī, 568.   [71] *Recueil*, pp. 144-145.

sayn Mansūr Hallāj has been carried to the peak of Paradise for saying 'I am the Truth'? Why?" (*mā'l-hikma fī dhalika?*) A voice (*nidā'*) answered him: "Fir'awn did not stop thinking about himself and forgetting Me, while Hallāj did not stop thinking of Me and forgetting himself."[72]

His master, Nūr Kasirqī, had justified Hallāj's "*Anā'l-Haqq*" on a basis of Qur'ān 28:48 as follows: the Prophet, having reached the stage of cohabitation (*'indīya*), received from God the divine name of *al-Haqq*, an allusion to his self-annihilation in the permanence of the divine ipseity, enabling him to say "I am the Truth." When such a statement is uttered by one of those who have followed him (= Hallāj), it obviously testifies to the perfect clearness of the mirror of his heart for receiving the reflection of the rays of the prophetic Sanctity (*walāyat al-nubuwwa*)[73] by placing itself before the other mirror, the heart of the Prophet. The spring of this reality is the heart of the Prophet, and the place where this water rises is the tongue of the one who speaks in imitation of him: "you have a beautiful subject for imitation (*uswa*) in the Prophet (Qur'ān 33:21)." Concluding these *ta'wīlāt*, Simnānī repeats this idea in his own way apropos of Qur'ān 112: the penultimate (*anānīya*) colored covering of the soul, when the soul is allowed to become a mirror, says "glory be to God, the Unique"; but if a trace (*baqīya*)[74] still remains of the outer covering (the grey of the mould), the voice says "Subhānī, Anā'l-Haqq," then as soon as it leaves this ecstasy "murder me now, my faithful friends."[75] "This is a very dangerous stage, one in which the *salik* must be guided closely by his shaykh, and must imitate his Prophet, so that [his shaykh may] save him from the precipice that is located in the dark sphere (*khafīya*) of the soul, by leading him to the radiance of the green covering (*haqqīya*), illuminating the preceding covering (*anānīya*). This is the danger into which Christians have fallen."

This last passage is very unusual; and it should be noted that it appears, abridged, in the *kawāhir khamsa shattārīya* apropos of the formula of the Hallājian *dhikr*, which would suggest that Simnānī knew it and that it already existed.

---

[72] 'Alī Qāri' (d. 1014) repeated this idea in his *radd* against Ibn 'Arabī.

[73] According to him, sanctity is the essence of prophesy. Cf. Haqqī VI, 411.

[74] This *baqīya* about which Suhrawardī Maqtūl had spoken, which, in reality, is the *innī* (in Latin *ecce*) whose ultimate modality 'Abd al-Karīm Jīlī specified (*Manāzir Ilāhīya*, ap. *Recueil*, p. 149).

[75] Famous verses by Hallāj that Shams D M-b-A Kīshī (d. 694, buried in the Bākitīya cemetery in Shiraz [*Shadd*, 56], a disciple in Baghdad of Jibrīl Kurdī) had specifically just included in a monograph; considered in this instance as the desire for expiatory martyrdom, which is actually the spirit behind Hallāj's last prayer.

Among his forty *majālis*, the nineteenth is devoted to anecdotes about Hallāj. Apart from the personal account of his visit to his tomb, Simnānī tells them without any concern for accuracy as to dates or even names (Muhāsibī becomes a contemporary of Hallāj, Turunghand is called Abū Nasr Sarrāj) in portraying Hallāj as a kind of madman of God, a gyrovague, towards whom God is not unbending with respect to any of his inconsistencies, when he leaves his masters one after another without warning them, when he asks God before the execution to forgive his executioners (here the text of the *du ʿā'* given in the *Akhbār* is followed by verses of *Uqtulūnī ya thiqātī* about his wish to be killed). Questioned by his disciples about this repentant confession of guilt, Simnānī tells how, after six years of trying on the hajj, he obtained a confession of this kind from another madman of God, whom he hospitalized in his monastery and who had undertaken an everlasting fast in order to be similar to God. To Simnānī, Hallāj apparently had intended to assume an outward posture of guilt, out of respect for the Law, and to suffer its judgments, although he was a saint.

One point has still to be resolved: Simnānī's attitude toward the Hallājian *dhikr*, which we have described elsewhere. Since Simnānī was the first Sūfī whose *dhikr* formula (of the Ruknīya) can be verified historically,[76] we are going to describe it. It derives from the ancient formula known as the Hammā'ilīya[77] which is performed as follows: seated with arms crossed (*tarabbuʿ*), eyes blinking, both palms on the knees, breathing from below the left breast (emptying the heart of everything other than God) while saying *lā*, declaring *ilāha* over the right shoulder (denying all idolatry), affirming *illā* over the right shoulder, and uttering *Allāh* forcefully upon returning to an empty heart. Jurjānī[78] had specified that for *lā* one must lean one's head down toward the navel, for *ilāha* raise it again, for *illā* incline it briefly toward the navel (cf. Tāj Murshidī), and turn it to the left for *Allāh*. Kasirqī (d. 719), for his part, had added that the right foot must be resting on the left leg, hands under the knees, and *illā* combined with *Allāh*.[79] Simnānī, after having copied him, modified this *jalsa*. Without changing the position of the legs, he specified that the right hand must be placed on the left hand, which holds the right leg; breath must be emitted for the *lā* from the navel (to drive the demon

[76] The Kubrawī *dhikr* (*Salsabīl*, 102) is, in fact, by ʿAli Hamadhānī (*ibid.*, 108). Qushāshī, *Simt*, 156, 157; *Salsabīl*, 105, 110 (Ruknīya).

[77] "Girdles" (for the *shadd*?). Qushāshī, *Simt*, 147, 149, has it going back via Nūr Natanzī, Barghash, and Suhrawardī to Ahmad Ghazālī.

[78] *Simt*, 155.

[79] *Salsabīl*, 106, 112; *Simt*, 155, 157.

away from the sexual organs), for *ilāha* from the nose cartilage (by "vomiting," *lāfiz*, against the demon of dreams), for *illā* from lower on the left side, and for *Allāh* from the heart: while keeping the backbone and the neck constantly straight. Tāwūsī remarks that this laborious and painful (*'usra mu'lima*) method is valuable for the inner purification and illumination of the heart.[80]

g. Hallājian Elements in the Mongol Court: the Role of Shams Kīshī in the Service of Nasīr Tūsī; the Two Leading Vizirs, Shams Juwaynī and Rashīd al-Dīn

Among the advisors to the Mongol conquerors in the court of the pagan Abaqa, alongside Shī'ite, Jewish, and Christian minorities, eager for reprisals against their former Sunnite masters, one encounters in a rather unexpected way a spirit of pacificatory gentleness toward a devastated Baghdad, combined with a special fondness for Hallāj: in the immediate entourage of two vizirs, Shams Juwaynī (d. 683) and Rashīd Hamadhānī (d. 718).

Appointed *mudarris* at the Nizāmīya of Baghdad in 666, Shams M-b-M (= A-b-'A Latīf Qurushī) Hakīm Kīshī (d. 694, Shiraz)[81] was an expert in all branches of knowledge and a persuasive moralist (he was the master of Sa'dī), as his pupil Rashīd al-Dīn informs us. He was filled with admiration for the "prayer (*du'ā'*) that Hallāj uttered at the moment of execution," a prayer that Najm Rāzī had already brought to light forty years earlier;[82] and "he wrote a *risāla* of great beauty in Persian about it (*der ghāyet khūbī*)," according to Ibn Hindūshāh,[83] also his disciple, in which he referred to the "*Uqtulūnī*" couplet of Hallāj. This *risāla* is lost, but it was following its appearance that four contemporary writers, the historian Nīkpay, Rashīd al-Dīn, and two mystics, Sa'd Farghānī[84] and 'Alā' Simnānī, focused their attention both on the prayer and on the couplet to emphasize the heroism of a martyr who interceded with God on behalf of his executioners.

Now, Kīshī was appointed to the Nizāmīya by the governor of Iraq,

---

[80] Ap. Shāh Mīr, *Musalsalāt* [bib. no. 2163-a] XLI; concerning *Simt*, 156. Other works of Simnānī [ms.] Shahīd 'Ali Pasha 1119 (*Istilāhāt al-sūfīya*).

[81] Ibn Hindūshāh, *Tajārib* [bib. no. 2100] (Eghbal preface), 6; Rashīd, P. ms. 2324, ff. 20a, 120a, 260a; Fuwatī [?], 358, 489; 'Azzāwī [see bib. no. 999-01], *Ihtil*. I, 263.—Kish = Ile Qays (west of Ormuz).

[82] *Mirsād*, ap. *Recueil*, p. 121.

[83] Twenty-five words omitted ap. Ibn Hindūshāh, 200; restored ap. Nikpay, *Ta'rīkh*, Paris ms., afp. 61, f. 424b.

[84] *Muntahā* [bib. no. 508-a], II, 30 (cf. I, 356).

'Atā' Malik Juwayni (657, d. 683), the spouse of the second marriage of the Ayyubid princess Shāhilatī (d. 679), widow of the 'Abbāsid princely heir, Ahmad-b-Musta'sim, and mother of Rābi'a-bt-Ahmad,[85] who married his nephew Hārūn-b-Shams Juwaynī (d. 685). Kīshī was a friend of the brother of Hārūn, Bahā' Juwaynī, whom he was going to join in Isfahan, and corresponded with their father, the vizir Shams Juwaynī (657, d. 683), whose son-in-law, Sadr Juwaynī (married in 671, d. 722), converted Ghāzān.

He may have been involved in the restoration of Hallāj's tomb, said to have been standing[86] near that of Ma'rūf Karkhī. For it could not have been spared by the flood of 653,[87] which ruined the *madfan* of Ma'rūf that the Juwaynīs ordered rebuilt in 678 by the inspector of *waqfs*, Asīl Ahmad Tūsī,[88] son of one of their close friends, the famous philosopher and astronomer Nasīr Tūsī, whose Shī'ite polities counseled Hūlagu in his destruction of the 'Abbāsids' Sunnite caliphate. Nasīr had been entrusted by the Mongols with the supervision of all the confessional *waqfs* of their empire, a position that stripped the grand qādīs of their duties with regard to Islam. It was in this capacity that he came to inspect those of Baghdad in 662 and in 672[89] (he died there on 8 *Hijja* 673, and was buried in Kaziman). He had developed on Avicennian principles a theory of the mystical way (*sulūk*) in which he had taken Hallāj as the ideal. And he dedicated to Vizir Shams Juwaynī a treatise in Persian, *Awsāf al-ashrāf*, in which he ended the thirty-fifth and next to last stage with three explicit quotations from Hallāj: the *"Baynī wa baynaka"* verse, the *"Anā man ahwā"* couplet, and the *"Anā'l-Haqq"* statement. Could it have been Nasīr who influenced Kīshī, his friend, to redact his Hallājian *risāla*?

The case of Rashīd al-Dīn Hamadhānī, the (Persian) vizir of the Mongols for twenty years (698-718), is even more significant. This great statesman and encyclopaedic thinker who led his sovereign, by the very enormity of the Mongol empire, to expand his horizons from China and Buddhist Tibet to Poland and Rome, envisaged in the life and especially in the death of Hallāj a religious dimension transcending the divisions between confessions, classes, races, and idioms. With him, perhaps more clearly than with Nasīr Tūsī, the Hallāj case begins to be presented al-

---

[85] These women played a role (dismissal of the prior of the Marsubānīya *ribāt*) in the restoration of the Baghdad *waqf* in 672 (Fuwatī, 410, 449; 'Azzāwī I, 269).

[86] Ibn Tiqtaqā, *Fakhrī* [bib. no. 501-a].

[87] Fuwatī, 408; 'Azzāwī I, 296. Cf. the restoration of 479 (Ibn al-Athīr [bib. no. 420-a], X, 55; Ibn Jawzī, P. ms. 1506, f. 187a-b).

[88] Fuwatī, 443. A friend of Rashīd (2324, f. 18a).

[89] Fuwatī, 350, 375.

ways as a sign of contradiction to transcend, but no longer within a closed Islam caught between Shī'ites and Sunnites or between Ash'arite theology and Hanbalite piety, rather on a general plane of intercultural humanism, of Islam open as a sign of the social mission of the true mystic, as a crucial example of sainthood.[90]

In his *Tawhīdāt* and his *Latā'if*, which presents the circumstances of his private conversations with two Mongol rulers, Ghāzān (694, d. 703), who was converted to Islam in 694 by Sadr Juwaynī (d. 722),[91] son-in-law of 'Atā' Malik Juwaynī, and Oljāyītū (703, d. 716), Rashīd al-Dīn, who did not succeed in retaining the influence over the latter that he had exercised over the former, comments[92] on a hadīth that he had used with Ghāzān: the hadīth *"al-arwāh junūd mujannada . . ."* "souls make cohorts; they form in groups according to their chosen affinities, and oppose each other according to their antipathies." This hadīth was for him an argument for establishing the doctrine of personal immortality, at the time of the body's resurrection, in his struggle against Mongol shamanism and Buddhism, which were unexpected allies of Greek philosophy. Apropos of this hadīth, he not only repeated in one of his verses a couplet of Hallāj:

> my soul is mixed and joined together with your
> soul and every accident that injures you
> injures me,[93]

and used together with Qur'ān 26:83-89 other verses of Hallāj such as *"Anā man ahwā"* and *"Uqtulūnī,"*[94] but he also affirmed that, on a basis of Qur'ān 3:169 and 2:154, Hallāj was a martyr, had his name follow the *tarahhum*, as did Kīshī, and called him *"qutb al-awliyā', al-shaykh al-rabbānī,"* "the pole of the saints, the divinely inspired master."[95]

Rashīd al-Dīn used this hadīth to exalt intellectual friendship in terms in which Hellenistic philosophy held its own with an Islamic mysticism that was unalterably purged of monism. He comments that self-sacrifice,

---

[90] The groups of qādīs approving of the vizir include, along with the great vizir (of Tabriz?) denounced by Nizām D 'Abd al-Malik Meraghī ibn Taymīya (*Fat.* IV), one great name, Baydāwī (d. 716, rather than 691), a Hallājian from Fars like Kīshī, Ibn Buzghush (Farghānī), and Baqlī.

[91] Another family from Juwayn, that of the Syro-Egyptian *shaykh al-shuyūkh*. For that of 'Atā' Malik, cf. M. Ghazvini, the preface to his *Jihān gusha* [bib. no. 2072-a], 19 (against Khwandamīr, *Dastūr al-wuzarā'* [bib. no. 1161-c], 267-295; and Khwansarī, *Rawdat* [bib. no. 2143-a], 606).

[92] *Tawdīhāt*, P. ms. 2324, ff. 72b, 132b; *Latā'if,* f. 312a (*Risāla* V).

[93] *Latā'if,* f. 72b, 158b, 139, 145b, 261a.

[94] *Ibid.,* f. 360b (*Ris.* XI).   [95] *Ibid.,* f. 325a (*Ris.* VI).

which is the very oath of love, could not be a suicide removing the existence (*wujūd*) of the lover; "on this point, the great master Hallāj said:
'*baynī wabaynaka*. . . .' "[96] This passage sums up and completes that of
Nasīr Tūsī in his *Awsāf*.

When he wrote, with a team of collaborators, his great universal history in Persian, *Jāmi' al-tawārikh*, documented first-hand on all of Asia,
he gives to the notice on Hallāj[97] nearly half of the space set aside for the
reign of Muqtadir. After reviewing the trial and execution, he observes
that "Sayyid Ahmad, who came one day to perform his ablutions on the
bank of the Tigris," drank there, in the water, the ashes of Hallāj, and
"that God raised him to sainthood because of the blessing attached to this
water." When Banākatī redacted an abridgement of *Jāmi' al-tawārikh* for
Abū Sa'īd, who had Rashīd al-Dīn killed, he cut out the notice on Hallāj.[98]

To Rashīd, a convinced Muslim and philosopher, Islam was the
fulfillment of Judaism and Christianity. His *Risāla fi'l-nāsikh* shows this
in terms of its use of honest and direct documentation, especially in the
case of Judaism. Hamadan, the city of Esther, had an ancient ghetto, and
Rashīd had a close forebear who had remained a Jew. He was reproached
on account of him, although it was his intent to integrate Jews and Christians in Islam. He may have been involved in an analogous syncretist effort by one Ibn Kammūna (d. around 684);[99] and, similarly, in the work
of transcribing into Hebrew characters for learned Jews[100] works on
Arab mysticism, such as the *Munqidh* of Ghazālī, the *Sayhūr*, and the
Dīwān of Hallāj.

v. CONTEMPORARY CRITICISM IN ISLAM

a. The "Rebellion in Hell" of Jamīl Sidqī Zahāwī

This learned Baghdadian of Kurdish origin (1863, d. 1937) represents in
contemporary Arabic literature a secularist and rationalist tendency very
similar to the Turkish *aufklärung* of the time of Union and Progress. Very
conversant in the directions of the modern spirit, he was one of the first

---

[96] *Ibid.*, f. 320a.
[97] Ms. P., Persian Suppl. 2004, f. 94b, 95a; on his collaborator AS 'AA-b-'Alī Kāshānī,
cf. Blochet ms. I, 283.
[98] Ms. P. Pers. Suppl. 210, f. 87b. It was due to Rashīd al-Dīn that Zākānī and Mustawfī
spoke about Hallāj.
[99] Fuwatī, 441; Fischel, p. 135.
[100] *Genizah ms. of Cairo* (Cambridge); Firkowitsch ms.

to call for the suppression of the veil for women, to popularize Newton's theory of gravity, and to foresee the accession of dialectal Arabic to the high position of a literary language. Denounced as a blasphemer, he ended up as poet laureate and a senator of the kingdom of Iraq.

He spoke to me about Hallāj, with some degree of hostility to mysticism, on December 25, 1907. And in 1931 he expressed the depth of his thought about Hallāj in a poem intensely hostile to the Islamic *sharī'a*, "The Rebellion in Hell *(al-thawra fī'l-jahīm)*."[1] God is depicted in it as existing only in the form of ether (thus accepted as a suitable hypothesis by physicians) (verse 131), and all of those whom the religious thought they could incarcerate in Hell in His name are going to prove his powerlessness and dethrone Him. After Laylā, 'Umar Khayyām (whom Zahāwī had translated into Arabic), and Socrates, Hallāj appears as one of the wildest of the rebels (verses 345-352):

From the depths of Hell, Mansūr al-Hallāj challenges God and scolds Him.
And I saw Hallāj then, with his eyes raised to Heaven lamenting
And saying: You alone, God, are permanent; creatures pass away
In Your presence; you are single, though multiple in Your flames.
You are the One from whom I spring, a fluttering spark in my life.
I loomed up, then disappeared in Him; He is going to appear, after having been concealed, in me.
Why did You assign damnation to me without freeing me from it, You, the liberator?
In this world my fate was to be killed, now it is cruel damnation.
You have said Your decree must be carried out, but must it if Your decree is misguided?
And so, the rebels join forces and seize paradise in a single attack.

b. In the Turkish Republic: the Hallājian
Personalism of Nurettin Ahmet Topçu (1934)

There exists in Turkish Anatolia an old tradition of mystics who are by no means quietistic, but rather men of social action, like Bedrettin Ibn Simawnā and the Melāmīler, in which the memory of Hallāce Mansūr is still venerated. Nurettin A. Topçu, a young philosopher and Turkish professor, the managing editor of the journal *Hareket* in Brusa, the organ of a reformist and social group, renewed this tradition in a doctoral thesis presented[2] at the Sorbonne on conformity and rebellion in which he openly declared himself to be a Hallājian: for reasons of personalistic philosophy similar, despite their differences in temperament, to those of the

---

[1] It appeared ap. the review *al-Duhūr* (of Ismā'īl Mazhar), Cairo, Wafā', no. [. . .], March 1931, p. 664.

[2] Thèse de Doctorat, Paris, 1934 [bib. no. 1791-a], p. 54, n. 1; p. 126.

Indian philosopher S. Muhammad Iqbāl, without their having known one another.

N. A. Topçu begins with analysis of the positive aspect of moral responsibility (of which remorse is only the negative aspect), a vital inspiring anxiety commanding action. Thought aspiring after the universal feels duty-bound to act over and beyond the instinct, self-interest, sympathy and welfare of society. "One feels one is more than the universe. . . . It is a kind of conversion to the unity of self. The self that arrives in this way at perfection is opposed to every obstacle on the path to unity. Fundamental moral action springs from this conflict, the action of rebellion, which consists in saying "I am the Truth."[3]

After an examination of the idea of freedom in Spinoza (an illusion based on pride and ignorance), in Bergson (an invention of pure spontaneity), and in Blondel (a convergence of man with God to change things and to change oneself), N. A. Topçu adds: "Action is a rebellion (against human slavery). It is the rebellion of God in us against ourselves. The one who has never rebelled, has never acted. Every free act is a rebellion."[4]

By rebellion against human slavery he means the pursuit of pleasure, the social constraint (Durkheim's criticism) of party solidarity (the division of labor), and exploitation by the police state. In the name of true responsibility, which is not at all the vain juridical survival of an ancient association of ideas of sufferance and punishment (Lévy-Brühl), but a personal imperative for action, there is a concern that deepens the conscience of the individual to act upon an object that is known, assimilated, made his own by an active working of his mind: knowledge through responsibility, true, real knowledge that we shall call belief.[5] At this point he examines belief according to Pascal, Kant, and Hamilton, of its propagation through imitation, then of aesthetic and religious faith, of mysticism. Next, N. A. Topçu adopts our thesis about the authentic Islamic origin and social force of early Sūfism: "this holy war in the heart of man and in the country is for us the only remedy for freeing the conscience and the history of the child of Anatolia from the abyss in which they are swallowed up. Only his religion begun again and infused with life by the tradition of the first three centuries of mysticism from Muhammad to Hallāj could achieve this spiritual renaissance. It will give birth in individuals to self-knowledge and to responsibility for their history."[6]

Then comes the definition of true rebellion. The duality of faith, of our

---

[3] *Ibid*., p. 12.   [4] *Ibid*., p. 40.

[5] *Ibid*., p. 70.   [6] *Ibid*., pp. 124-127.

inadequacy, and of divine attraction, is God Who denounces us for our insincerity. "He rebels against us . . . rebellion is the action of God in us,"[7] not the anarchism of Stirner, the individualism of Rousseau, or the pessimism of Schopenhauer. From an individualism without God we are raised to a personalism that tends to realize the action of God in the natural order. To do this we cling to the rebellion of a Muslim mystic like Hallāj, which is the rebellion of a God-man or the rebellion of God in man, and we affirm with him "I am the Truth" or even "I am God."[8] The last chapter, Chapter IV, "the Rebellion of God in Man" (pp. 147-155), dealing with the meaning of "I am the Truth," defines rebellion as a call from our human inadequacy to a liberating Power. By positing a liberating Power over our destiny, we are moving from the pessimism of Schopenhauer to the optimism of the Muslim mystics of whom we regard Hallāj as a model. Rebellion ends "by introducing us into the supernatural order," it is a participation of man in God . . . the mystical source from which morality springs is the will of God, the absolute will; in other words, it is the will to be God." Through suffering and sacrifice, "this pull toward salvation which no one escapes is a rebellion par excellence"; "a rebellion of the individual is needed for the salvation of history and of humanity."

"Rebellion is the conversion which, by posing to the individual the problem of his salvation being one with the salvation of the universe, demands that he participate in the historical and present immensity of the world to bear the heavy weight of universal responsibility and to prepare in himself the social revolution which proceeds necessarily from it.[9]

"Rebellion is the stance of the mystic who, attaining knowledge of his own divinity through his participation in God, and faced with a choice between the humanity that burdens him and that burdens all, and the divinity that saves him and that can save all, becomes inflamed with the passion to die accursed for the salvation of himself and for the salvation of all.

"Our God is the God of rebellion."[10]

The following is the end of his conclusion: "For a thousand years of its history Anatolia has not been lacking in heroes and martyrs who, 'waging holy war . . . not only on the frontiers, but also in the capital . . . and

---

[7] *Ibid.*, p. 129.   [8] *Ibid.*, p. 130.

[9] *Ibid.*, p. 150: "neither the individual nor society creates the person; let us reject anarchism and conformism . . . let us go beyond individualism and sociologism. . . . We choose for our point of view a personalism in which individuality is a passageway, an intermediate stage, between man and God; it is the ascension or the aspiration of man to divinity."

[10] *Ibid.*, p. 155.

in the depth of their own hearts,' have sacrificed themselves for the salvation of the community. Its children, carrying on the tradition of its mysticism, shall forever wage holy war against the tyranny of their own instincts and against the cruelty of tyrants; they shall be able to utter before their gibbets, with courage and pride, in full awareness of the meaning of these words, 'I am the Truth!' "[11]

c. In Egypt: Zakī Mubārak and Muhammad Lutfī Gum'a

The Hallāj case, recalled from time to time in brief allusions (Ahmad Deif, Ades Josipovici), has been taken up in full of late and in an original way by two Muslim critics in works aimed at the large public of the journals and Arab conferences of Cairo, a public that extends beyond Tunis and Damascus, not only to Saudi Arabia and Iraq, but also to India and Java.

Zakī 'Abd al-Salām Mubārak, known for his interesting studies of the structure of Arabic prose and of love poetry, a writer with a distinct style of his own, approached the problem of Hallāj head on in his Kitāb al-tasawwuf al-Islāmī (211-220) in 1938.[12]

He evoked at the outset the strong resemblance between Jesus and Hallāj. Both were martyrs of "existential monism." Jesus, in calling himself the "son of God," meant, according to Renan, to express a unique bond of affection between God and a beloved servant, thereby becoming entrusted with the role of mediator between the Creator and His creatures—which the Sūfīs say with regard to Muhammad (haqīqa Muhammadīya) and the Shī'ites, one of whom Hallāj seems first to have been, with regard to 'Alī.

Legend identifies Hallāj with Jesus; the actual fact of the crucifixion has been denied in both cases.

Hallāj called himself the mediator, the mediating word, between God and His disciples. In fact, he loved God to the point of annihilating himself. He wandered, poor man, from country to country changing costume and way of speech, pursuing the phantom of his forbidden Lover Whom he perceived in every creature and who brought him only desire and hypnotic trance. He loved, poor man, an elusive and inaccessible Lover, the light which blinds eyes and hearts; God, Who is too high to be love, Who is beyond images and concepts. His trial lasted a long time, he endured calumnies from critics, and ended targeted for death. He went into hiding, praying secretly to his Beloved, for years.

[11] Ibid., p. 160.
[12] Born around 1895 (cf. Brockelmann, GAL, Suppl. III, 302-305).

Hallāj's adventure with his Lord consists of unusual symbols; it causes hearts to feel pain and eyes to weep, and it teaches those who do not know that love is not a game nor a laughing matter.

And this adventure is not a legend, as has been said in the case of Jesus; it is brought too close to us by the testimonies that authenticate it. I have visited his tomb, which still stands in Baghdad. A tomb neglected, as tombs of lovers are, "so unlucky in life and in death."

Z. Mubārak then analyzes Hallāj's psychological state on the day of his execution: first, an admission of sad disappointment (*Talabtu* distich); then an evocation of the Lover, Who is an executioner to him (*Nadīmi* quatrain), and a final cry of hope in Him (*yā muʿīn al-danā*). The Lover heard this cry; He saved His lover from nothingness; the memory of Hallāj survives, of the crucified Hallāj, like the memory of Jesus crucified; the true life is the life beyond the grave (as a footnote: the account of his life exists in all languages; his name is the subject of hundreds of legends; and his portrait varies according to those who have studied him).

Like Jesus, Hallāj was punished for having divulged the secret of love. Why did he go around saying that he had become his beloved? If he had reflected on it, he would have realized that the beloved causes suffering to the one who recounts his love.[13]

Muhammad Lutfī Gumʿa, who studied law in France and, beginning in 1911, wrote a series of historical and philosophical studies, notably *Hayāt al-sharq* and *Batal al-anbiyāʾ* (on Muhammad), published in 1939 the first part of his *Muhākamat al-Hallāj* in the Cairo weekly *al-Rābita al-ʿArabīya*.[14] Seeking the way to promote an Arab renaissance of Sunnite Islam, he studied this "religious and political trial, one of the most amazing trials of history, whose *dramatis personae* consist of caliphs, viziers, politicians, jurists, Sūfīs, poets, and famous women. . . ." The following is an analysis of the first part, the only part of this study that appeared:

"The trial of Hallāj is no less famous than the trial of Joan of Arc; and since historians have endeavored to describe the social life and political and psychological conditions that surrounded Joan of Arc's vocation, heroism, and appearance before the court, to complete our understanding by showing the adverse reactions that gave rise to this unusual event,

---

[13] I, 211-220, with a photograph of the tomb (*masraʿ al-Hallāj*). Here Z. Mubārak refers to our publications.

[14] Cf. Brockelmann, *GAL*, Suppl. III, 275-276. *Rābita ʿarabīya*, numbers 132-137, 139-144 (4, 11, 18, 29 January, 1939; 8, 15 February; 1, 8, 15, 22 March; 5 April, 1939). His analysis of the *Dīwān* of Hallāj ap. *Minbār al-sharq*, 14 May, 1940.

we must in turn examine the life of Baghdad, its customs, and its culture. . . ."[15]

M. Lutfi Gum'a scores the 'Abbāsids for having been unable to follow the example set by the Umayyads in controlling the infiltration of the clever, seductive, and perverse Iranian civilization by means of the original virtues of Islam and the Arab race that they had allowed to decay. He scores the Court and their great men for enjoying all the refinements of vices[16] praised by their poets while their people went hungry; the dealers in slaves, expert stage directors, for parading the naked beauty of young women and young men (Ibn Rāmīn dared to take his "models" on hajj,[17] the caliphs being blasé Neronian fanciers, greedy, capricious, and weary). For every ardent individual protest by an ascetic poet like Abū'l-'Atāhīya, how many resigned and skeptical "confessions" like that of Abū Hayyān Tawhīdī[18] were there, or upright but empty and sterile sermons like those of Ibn Nubāta (who was twenty-five when Hallāj was put to death),[19] or literary hypocrisies by men of letters running with the fashion, singing of such and such a "lady of violets" (Mutayyam),[20] of concessions of bogus "commanders of the faithful" inclined to philosophical heresy and presiding in their harem over festivities in which their Christian concubines, all decked out, palms in hand, exhibited gold crosses on Palm Sunday.[21] Attempts at intellectual reform resulted either in the discipline of dissimulation of secret societies or in a hygienic anti-ascetical philosophy like that of Miskawayh.[22]

The asceticism recommended by the mystical code of Sūfīs, however, represented an effective remedy. Thus did Hallāj appear on the scene in 309, following a rebellion resulting from a famine, before a capricious and pleasure-seeking[23] ruler: "not in the spirit of personal propaganda nor desire to promote himself; he came with the message of the One God, of chastity, of purification of the carnal soul, and of asceticism; not against life, but against the pleasures of the world. He wanted to dam up the flood of accumulated corruption that threatened to carry off every-

---

[15] No. 132, p. 35, col. 1.
[16] The author uses the *Kitāb al-aghānī*, whose author was twenty-five at the time of Hallāj's death, and stigmatizes him for having propounded an ideal, a life like that of Ibrāhīm-b-al-Mahdī (no. 139, p. 22, col. 3).
[17] No. 135, p. 27, col. 1 (= *K. al-aghānī* X, 128).
[18] No. 142, p. 25, col. 3.
[19] No. 143, p. 30, col. 1.   [20] No. 144, p. 23, col. 1.
[21] No. 142, p. 27, col. 1.   [22] No. 143, p. 29, col. 3.
[23] No. 140, p. 26, col. 3: here the dismissal of Khaqānī is compared (mistakenly) to that of Fouquet by Louis XIV.

thing in its way. Over against him, the erotic poets were singing of impurity, denying judgment and resurrection. Reaching from the social to
the political life, the evil had overtaken the religious thought: 'godless-
ness wantonly strewed doubts in all the centers of Muslim civilization,
particularly Baghdad; will the blood of Hallãj never stop flowing, and his
memory never stop haunting consciences.' "[24, 25]

VI. HALLÃJ AND EUROPEAN THOUGHT AND ITS DISCIPLINES

The problem posed by the Hallãjian case of conscience extended, as we
have seen, beyond the Muslim setting only at the time of the Mongol
conquest, when minds like Rashīd al-Dīn, evaluating the philosophical
meaning and inter-religious importance of certain mystical experiences,
became interested in Hallãj. No doubt, certain Ismāʿīlī authors had already raised the same question; and the Ikhwān al-safā', just like the
Druze writers, being sympathetic toward Sūfism, had been able already
to study Hallãj. From another quarter, Andalusian Jewish translators,
translating into Latin texts like the Ghazālian *"Lamps luminum"* (*Mishkāt
al-anwār*) or "Destruction" of Ibn Rushd, in which Hallãj is quoted (but
not named), had begun to make some Westerners take interest in Hallãj,
of which some Arabic manuscripts in Hebrew characters discovered in
the Genizoths bears witness. But it is only after the second Renaissance,
in the seventeenth century, that the name of Hallãj appears in Europe.

Merely as a short notice to be put in its true place in the general, especially retrospective, inventory of the Muslim world prepared by cos-
mographers and encyclopaedists based on translations of the Muslim
chroniclers.

From the *Dictionary* of Bayle (continuation by Chaufepié, 1750) and
the *Universal History* of Amsterdam-Leipzig (French translation 1761
and 1782) down to Brockhaus (to the *Encyclopaedia Italiana*, Vol. XVIII),
to *Larousse*, to the *Grand Encyclopédie*, to Hastings (and before, to Chan-
tepie de la Saussaye).

Their main source was at first the Bibliothèque Orientale of Bar-
thélemy d'Herbelot (1697), whose notice "Hallage" is noteworthy for its
documentation, with errors of detail noted by Reiske.

---

[24] No. 141, p. 24, col. 3 and p. 25, col. 3.

[25] [The author left a complementary list of European polemics after 1922 that he had
planned to examine: by Schaeder, Horten, Maréchal, Dermenghem, Mazaharī, Mustafa
Jawād, including one on the influence of Zahāwī on Iqbāl, by Abdūh, Farkawī, Degrand,
and A. Schimmel.]

In completing our documentation on Hallāj with editions and translations of Eastern texts, orientalists rarely ventured on a personal interpretation of them. Influenced by Persian poetry and the cult of Hallāj in Indian Islam from Malcolm to Tholuck, some[1] have regarded him as a
complete pantheist, an advocate of "existential monism," and Kremer,
in his "leading ideas of Islam" presented him forcefully as a precursor of
Ibn 'Arabī. Whereas Barbier de Meynard, with greater subtlety, ap-
prehended an old Eastern tradition in the Hallājian doctrine of "the
incarnation of God in the adept following absolute self-renunciation and
rigorous mortifications."

In another connection, the Jacobite Christian historian al-Makīn (d.
672/1273), uncle of the secretary of state for war of the Mongol ruler
Hūlāgū (who) had possibly had his attention drawn to Hallāj by his colleague Nasīr Tūsī, left us an interesting passage in which the following
reflection is given apropos of three poems by Hallāj (*Muzijat, Subhāna,
Jubilat*): "the obvious thrust of these poems is *hulūl, ittihād*, an affirmation
of a carnal creature's divinization, thus a blasphemous profession; but
God knows more on this point about this man, whose intention may
have been other than is evident from these expressions: and it is said that
he recited the following verses going to his execution: "*Nadīmī . . .* " (the
famous love quatrain appears here). As early as 1625 Erpenius had made
a translation of it into Latin; about which A. Müllerus, in 1665, had observed "*quae quo dicta sint, facilius est conjicere, quam Elmacino, Christiano
nimium trepido, fuit alio torquere.*" A hypothesis of implicit support by Hallāj of the Christian idea of the martyr that d'Herbelot repeats in speaking
of the "sentiments of a true martyr of Jesus Christ." Which Reiske refuted with some acuteness by showing that the fourth verse of the Quatrain (which moreover is not by Hallāj) should be translated "*Ita mecum
egit deus, ut draco, cui flagrans sol venenum acuit et turgere facit*"; and he concluded "*Blasphemum est.*"

It is rather telling that the first polemic in the West about Hallāj had
thus dealt obliquely with what is, in effect, the central problem of the
mysticism of sacrifice, apropos of a quatrain that is not by him. Furthermore, though Reiske is correct in insisting on the literal meaning of
the word *tinnīn*, "venomous dragon," he was wrong to exclude its symbolism from consideration: a symbolism used by the secular author of
the quatrain, for it seems to allude to a zodiacal mansion of summer; and
a symbolism used by a Hallājian (perhaps Hallāj himself or Shiblī) who

[1] Sacy, with caution.

adapted this quatrain to mystical love, for 'Attār preserved for us a statement by Hallāj identifying *tinnīn* with *yaqīn* (= the divine substance of faith) and commented in the Persian verses (ap. *Mantiq al-tayr*) on the fourth verse of the quatrain in question in terms, not at all blasphemous, of total abandonment to the beloved.

Two centuries later, after 1913-1922 (the dates when my own research [on Hallāj] was published), the debate resumed, not so much about the borrowings of vocabulary made by Muslim mysticism from Christian sources (more or less shaded with Hellenism), which is a rather minor question, as about the social efficacy and final importance of Hallāj's death; in short, about the real meaning of his convergence with the crucial experience of Christian sanctity. What struck me, as Mukhtur Pasha Katirjoglou said in incisive Muslim terms, which do not shock me: "what struck Massignon about Hallāce Mansūr is that he achieved the myth of the crucifixion."[2] And what struck several Christian theologians, L. de Grandmaison, J. Maréchal, P. Drujon, Louis Gardet, and P. Bruno among Catholics, O. H. Thompson, H. Corbin, and C. Padwick among Protestants, is the fact, appearing outside the visible church, of a growing conformation in Christ internally with external conformities very peculiar to the circumstances of His Passion. The statement "I am the Truth." Hallāj's final vigil prayer is acceptable from a Christian standpoint only in a state of full incorporation in Christ. And there are other problems, all deriving, moreover, from a concrete sense of sanctity bursting forth outside its usual milieu of a social body sanctified sacramentally. We are not faced here with the problem of working out the definition, which incidentally would be impossible, and statics of an interreligious mysticism in the manner of Ibn 'Arabī, but, in the case of Hallāj, of establishing how union with the divine *Fiat* (*Kun*) transfigures a human life, before and after death, in its whole developing constitution, in order to configure it according to the resurrected one.[3]

---

[2] Said to Mlle. Mary Kahil. While Islam, in general, refuses to accept the fact that Jesus was really crucified (cf. *REI*, 19[?]), every Christian feels that he strips this crucifixion of meaning as long as he is unwilling to take part in it personally.

[3] One could readily draw up a significant list for Hallāj in imitation of the "liber conformitatum" that Bartholommeo Albizzi (d. 1401) made in 1399 for Saint Francis of Assisi.

APPENDIX: CRITICAL ANALYSIS OF
THE HALLĀJIAN SOURCES

Apart from the works of Hallāj himself, which will be examined further in Chapter XIV, the Hallājian sources, that is to say, the biographical
monographs concerning him, are divided into two categories:
1. collections of documents, for the most part anecdotal in nature, intended to perpetuate his memory;
2. commentaries on his biography; redacted on the occasion of a
   polemic by one or another well-known writer, either favorable or
   hostile.

I. COLLECTIONS OF DOCUMENTS

Three of these collections are extant, all three lacking an author's name
and a fixed title, which we shall designate as *Akhbār*, *Hikāya*, and *Qissa*.

a. Akhbār al-Hallāj

There have been three editions of it made, in 1914, 1936, and 1957.[1] The
1936 edition of the text was based on six manuscripts (Q, T, S, L, J, B)
described by P. Kraus on pages 7-43 and dating back earlier than the
ninth/fifteenth century. Their genealogy, the study of which I had undertaken in 1931,[2] was included in this edition by P. Kraus on page 29. I give
new references in a footnote here to be added to those found on pages
38-39 for the indirect tradition.[3] This collection contains seventy-four
prose pieces, twenty-one of which include verse, assembled more or less
artfully around a central core of twenty-four pieces concerning the ecstatic sermons in which Hallāj announced publicly in 296/908 in Baghdad
his desire for martyrdom. Number 1, ponderously constructed, appears

---

[1] *Akhbār al-Hallāj, recueil d'oraisons et d'exhortations du martyr mystique d'Islam, Husayn ibn
Mansūr Hallāj*, edited by L. Massignon: 1st. edition, 1914 (Geuthner ap. QT); 2nd. edition,
1936 (with P. Kraus, d. 1944, Larose); 3rd. edition, 1957 (Vrin, Paris). [This third edition is
subsequent to the redaction of this paragraph by the author.]

[2] Stemma ap. *Dīwān*, 2-4, by Louis Massignon.

[3] 'Attār, *Tadhkira*, Lahore (ap. Nicholson ed., II, 84, 138 = no. 6 [end]) = numbers 26,
41, 15; Nizām 'UA Zākānī (in 772; Eghbal commentary *Akhlāq* = no. 15); Siddīqī Uskudārī (in 1139), *Kashf* = no. 13 (Qush.). Ibn 'Arabī, *Tuhfa*, P. ms. 6614, f. 13b = no. 6
(end).

as the preface pleading in favor of a rehabilitation. The rest combined biographical accounts (15) with excerpts from his works (thirteen short maxims, ten doctrinal pieces, and four copies of autographs), and five short anecdotes in dialogue form belonging possibly to an early collection, one whose stylistic structure would tend to classify it in the literary genre of the "assemblies" (*maqāmāt*), in which the more or less assonanced prose sentences prepare the reader to appreciate the spiritual intention infused into the piece in the concluding verse.[4]

This collection is the basic text for anyone who wishes to understand the psychological condition of Hallāj, and, in fact, this is the way it has been used;[5] but with caution, for we are dealing with a condemned man whose works were officially outlawed. Furthermore, this text, intended, in spite of everything, to preserve his specific character, was disguised from the beginning, without title, without acknowledged author, and was tampered with in the following ways: attenuations of the bold doctrinal positions of the texts, and deliberate negligence in their chains of transmission (*isnād*).

Neither in our edition of 1914 nor in that of 1936 have we succeeded in identifying with certainty the author of this collection. [See completions in 1957 edition.] After reexamining the matter one more time, we have arrived at the following conclusions:

(1) A certain number of pieces in this collection (probably twenty-four) were assembled in the same period as Hallāj's execution and were gotten from several eyewitnesses (particularly Ibn Fātik) by a direct and fervent disciple, probably Shākir.[6] Their uniform presentation, in which a series of finely written prose maxims concludes with a verse commenting on them, attests to their literary unity. This method is found in other

---

[4] Corrigenda to the 1936 edition: p. 47, n. 4, line 13: read Abū'l-Husayn (and not Abū Yūsuf) Qazwīnī;—p. 73 (corr. n. 4 of no. 18 following Tahanāwī, 911);—no. 28, line 4 (p. 77): corr. *Mu* to read *Hu;* —p. 80 (no. 36, line 1: read: *Fāris*); —p. 108, paragraph 8: read: 'Abd al-Wāhid Shīrāzī (and not: Nīsābūrī).

[5] Kalābādhī (d. 380) quotes the verses from no. 62 (*Ta'arruf*), Baghdādī (d. 429) the first verse from no. 39. The verse pieces "*Anā man ahwā*" and "*Yā sirra sirr*" (quoted respectively ap. Kalābādhī, *Akhbār*, and Maqdīsī, *Bad'*) may have originated in numbers presently lost from the collection. It is very unusual for the collection to present the "*Juhūdī*" piece in a way that is different from that of *Tawāsīn* VI, 10; and to present a recension of the "*Wahhidnī wāhidī*" piece, already known from Ibn Khafīf (d. 371), that is different from those published by Harawī (*Dīwān*, no. 39) containing the words "*Anā'l-Haqq*," given following another presentation in the account of Ibn 'Abdallāh (= Mansūr Harawī, d. 402; or of Abū 'Abdallāh = Hy-b-A-Rāzī, d. around 350) communicated as early as 355 to Maqdīsī (*Bad'*) and to the grammarian Abū 'Alī Fārisī (d. 377). Were these corrections intentional?

[6] Under the title "*Dīwān ash'ār wa munājayāt*" (known from Qushayrī and Hujwīrī) *akhraja kalāmahu li'l-nās* (1936 ed., p. 47).

early Hallājian collections, including that of Qannād (to which I would link three separate pieces: one by Ibn Kajj on the fire altar of Tustar,[7] one by 'Abdān-b-Ahmad,[8] and the *raqs* in Ibn al-Sā'ī),[9] without implying a common source for it. The method appears to go back to Hallāj himself[10] (cf. *Tawāsīn*, except for I and XI); it is the method of the *chantefables* and of the *maqāmāt*.

(2) These early pieces underwent alterations in their uniform orientation; we have proof of this in the case of number 2 (the vigil, according to Ibn al-Haddād), whose archetype was preserved for us independently by Shāshī and Sulamī, and underwent some alteration of a much more discreet sort in the *Bidāya* of Ibn Bākūyā. In this instance, inspiration for the changes was drawn from a Hanbalite teaching evolving toward Ash'arism, which is strange.[11]

(3) Surrounding these early pieces we find pieces that are also specifically Hallājian in terms of vocabulary, but that are obviously put together as an argument for the defense. First, number 1, a labored and dense apologia shows Hallāj, not only interceding on behalf of his executioners,[12] but also thanking them for an execution that will gain him access to the true life "*Uqtulūnī yā thiqātī . . .* "[13] in what, moreover, is an improbable scenario aimed at rehabilitating his friend Shiblī, who had forsaken him (Qannād is also depicted as remaining loyal to him). Next, the corrective pieces, numbers 18-19, 60, 61, 67, 68, 71, 72, which presuppose knowledge of the notices of Daylamī and Ibn Bākūyā, in which Hallāj is criticized, and which alter them to justify his conduct. Finally, number 17, a synthetic account of the execution, also favoring Shiblī (to whom it is attributed); compared to the older account of Razzāz (preserved by Sulamī; based on AB Rāzī?), as well as to the account for which Ibn Bākūyā makes Hamd the mouthpiece, it may also date after this latter one (provided the details given by Hamd, and which he disregards, were previously included *ab antiquo* in the collection as independent pieces, in numbers 16, 20, and 65, and for that reason did not

---

[7] Ap. Z. Qazwīnī, *Athār* (ap. '*Ajā'īb* II).

[8] Naysābūrī (d. 406), '*Uqalā"l-maj.* [bib. no. 180A-a], 152.

[9] Published in *Akhbār*, 1936 ed., no. 6.

[10] Cf. the two letters to Ibn 'Atā' (*Akhbār*, nos. 2 and 3).

[11] The same prayer ("*Mutajallī*": cf. *Akhbār*, no. 8 and *Qūt*) is Hallājian, but is it in this instance in its place?

[12] Cf. already *Akhbār*, numbers 8, 44; and 'Attār II, 143, line 8 = *Akhbār*, no. 3.

[13] The "*Uqtulūnī*" verses should be included in the text of no. 1 (*Akhbār*, 1936 ed., p. 8, line 19: in accordance with the concordant depositions of Pertsch ms. 14/38, by Kīshī [d. 694: ap. Nikpāy, ms. P. afp. 61, f. 424b, and Ibn Hindūshāh, *Tajārib*, 200], by Farghānī [around 700: *Mutnahā* II, 30; cf. I, 356] and by Semnānī, Oxford ms. 1446, f. 60a).

have to be repeated). We have here a cluster of proofs conducive to identifying the collection with the *Kitāb al-intisār* of Ibn 'Aqīl (written around
451).

(4) Some chains of transmission appear in the collection, which are incidentally in a very poor state, none of which come down to Ibn 'Aqīl;
there are no more than two ends (there should be five); in numbers 2 and
5 (Abū'l-Husayn Basrī[14] before Ibn al-Haddād, Masrūq-b-Khadir after
him), 37 (Wasītī after Ibn Fātik); then in numbers 12, 41, 47-48, all of
them are said to have been dictated to an anonymous third party, which
is odd.[15] Out of the majority of unknown transmitters (thirty-four, half
of which are mere duplications; out of forty-six; which is unusual, rather
than suspect), twelve names are well known; five of them we rule out as
too well known (three hostile Sūfīs, Ibrāhīm-b-Shaybān, Nahrajūrī,
Jurayrī; one favorable, Shiblī; and an amīr, Husayn-b-Hamdān); seven
important names remain: first, Ibrāhīm-b-Fātik and his brother Ahmad,
put here as a *rāwī* on the same level; even though, thanks to Sulamī, we
know that only Ibrāhīm was a *rāwī*,[16] whereas his brother Ahmad (=
Abū'l-'Abbās Razzāz) was only an occasional transmitter of his elder.
The name itself of Ahmad appears only in Ibn Bākūyā, where he is substituted for Ibrāhīm, who was rather well known, however, at that time,
as a source of Wajihī and of A Hy Fārisī, if not of Fāris, who did not dare
refer to him by name.[17] The five remaining names are cross-checked
elsewhere as having *rāwīs*, among whom therefore one would find some
grounds for looking for the anonymous author of the collection:
Abū'l-Husayn Basrī (no. 5) appears in Khatīb (V, 29) apropos of Ibn
'Atā', and his *rāwī* is an unknown, Abū Nasr Isfahānī; "Abū'l Hy Basrī"
is, in fact, the name (cf. *Luma'*, 316) of Ibn Sālim, founder of the Sālimīya
mutakallimūn of Basra (cited ap. *Farq*, a little before the verse taken from
no. 39 of the collection). Could the collection be by Ibn Sālim? This mystic, though a Mālikite, may very well have visited the tomb of Ibn Hanbal. Next, Abū Ishāq Ibrāhīm Hilwānī (numbers 6, 7, 8), who appears in
Abū Nu'aym (ap. Sahlajī, 336, d. 430, *Nūr*, 133) with the *nisba* of
Turaythīthī, where he is given the same maxim of Bistāmī on "the saints,
the betrothed of God" that Sulamī had received (ap. Qushayrī, 139) from
Mansūr Harawī (d. 402), and who must have died, given his place in the

---

[14] Or Abū'l Hasan [Ibn Sālim al-Basrī? Cf. 1956 ed., p. 108, n. 1].

[15] A prudent precaution?

[16] This edition, 3, 245, 249, 261.

[17] This is one of the reasons why I abandoned my idea of Fāris Dīnawarī's being the
anonymous author of the collection. His date is too early (d. around 345), the style of his
Hallājian quotations (ap. Kalabadhī and Sulamī, *Tafsīr*) is much more technical.

isnād, around 375. Next, Ahmad-b-Fāris (no. 36), who appears in the *Tabaqāt* of Sulamī (twice = numbers [. . .]) as the Hallājian *rāwī* of Abū'l-Faraj 'Abd al-Wāhid-b-Bakr Warthānī Shīrāzī (d. 372), a noted Sūfī historian; as the informant of Ibn Jahdam (d. 414) for his *Bahja* (VI, f. 3a, 25a); confirmed by Khatīb III, 76); whom one is inclined to identify with AB A-b-Fāris-b-M (and not "Hasrī"?) Jajājīlī, a Sūfī from Fars (*Mantiq*, f. 16b), actually the master of Warthānī. Next, Abū Nasr A-b-Sa'd Isfījābī (no. 13 = Qushayrī, 4; cf. another Isfījābī, Qushayrī, 66), informant of Sulamī via Ibn Ghālib (not to be confused with Abū Nasr A-b-'Imrān Isfījābī, himself a *rāwī* of another Ibn Ghālib ap. Mālinī, 21). Finally, Qādī Ibn al-Haddād Misrī (d. 344; numbers 2, 5), a well-known Shāfi'ite, whose title of grand qādī of Cairo is emphasized only in two manuscripts,[18] and whose cross-reference in Sulamī shows that he could not have compiled the collection. In terms of the *isnād*, the following remain as possible authors of it: Ibn Sālim, Warthānī, Ibn Ghālib, and Abū'l-Husayn Fārisī, the principal editor of the accounts of Ibn Fātik; all four died between 355 and 380. Nothing else recommends them; and if there had been a reedition of the collection in that period, one would attribute it more likely to Nasrabādhī (d. 369), whom Khatīb[19] attests "collected" (*dawwana*), despite the official ban on Hallājian texts. Or to Ibn Ghālib, whom his other Hallājian quotations (in Sulamī) and his Ash'arite tendencies as a pupil of Ibn Khafīf bring to the fore.[20]

(5) If we concede that the collection is identical with the work done by Ibn 'Aqīl in his youth (431, d. 513), which was condemned in 465, and written as early as 451, probably under the title of *Kitāb al-intisār*, what part of it did he compose? Did he reset the texts and the *isnāds*, or did he receive them (already altered?) from one of his anti-Sālimīyan (and therefore pro-Ash'arite) masters like Ibn al-'Allāf (360, d. 442) and, via him, from Ibn Ghālib? And did he add only the deliberate corrections (no. 18, etc.; as in the case of no. 4?) when he rectified the awkward passages in Daylamī and Ibn Bākūyā? That cannot yet be determined.[21]

---

[18] This volume, p. 295.   [19] 'Aynī Welieddīn, 2386, 286.

[20] Sulamī, *Ta'rīkh*, no. [. . .]; and *Tabaqāt*, numbers 10-21; the verses that he quotes in no. 17 are those that Ahmad-b-Fāris produces in no. 36 of the collection; it therefore forms part of the early core, which Ibn Ghālib would have drawn from.

[21] In the description that Silafī gives us of the *Akhbār al-Hallāj* of Shirwānī (ap. Dhahabī, *I'tidāl* [bib. no. 530-d] II, 218; criticized by Lammens; to be completed by Ibn Hajar, *Lisān al-mīzān* IV, 205), I note that "most of the *isnāds* come from an unacknowledged book (*lā asla lahu*); and the *rāwīs* of it are unknown (*majāhil*)." "Unacknowledged" reminds one of the book of Ibn 'Aqīl, disavowed and retracted in 465; and "unknown" can easily be applied to the *rāwīs* of our collection. Dhahabī, by describing Shirwānī in this regard as an "insolent liar," is referring either to the improper use, or more likely to the apocryphal character of the framework added to this borrowing, meaning of the *Hikāya*.

(6) Is not our collection the source for the quotations found in Kalābādhī (in number 36? 42: verses) and in Baghdādī (*Farq* [. . .] in no. 39: verses), and for the references found in Mufīd (*Sharḥ 'aqā'id li'l-sadūq: āyāt wa bayyināt*)?

b. Hikāya

This collection is still, for the most part, unedited, our manuscript sources being still too lacunary. Three fragments appeared in *Recueil*, pp. 61-64.

It appears in its most complete form in ms. L of the *Akhbār* entitled *Hikāya 'an . . . Ibn Khafīf Shīrāzī* (f. 322b) and authenticated by an *isnād* that the signatory of ms. L (f. 341b: Yūsuf-b-'Alī-b-Mūsā ibn al-Zahra) gives in three terms: Shaykh Abū 'AA Husayn ibn Razīn; taken from Shaykh Abū'l Husayn-b-Yūsuf Qaraḍī;[22] taken from Abū 'AA Ahmad-b-'Abd al-Raḥmān Kirmānī,[23] who took it from *"ba'd al-fuqarā'."* Ibn Razīn was a member of the Syro-Egyptian Banū Razīn family of jurisconsults. Rather than construe him as the father, Husayn (unknown as an author, and deceased around 650), of the Shāfi'ite qāḍī of qāḍīs of Cairo, Taqī al-Dīn ibn Razīn (675, d. 680), I believe we are dealing here with this figure himself, Muhammad ibn Husayn, who, in fact, bore the *kunya* "Abū 'AA"[24] after which ms. L must have left out "M-b-"; a pupil of the famous 'Izz al-Dīn Maqdīsī (d. 660), also the qāḍī of qāḍīs of Cairo (636-640).

The *Hikāya* is basically a "story-setting," designed for pious reading, in which the Hallājian *reliquia*, poems, maxims, and anecdotes, are brought together without much order as in a gangue. This is the way the *Akhbār* were inserted into ms. L (ff. 334-341); and, inversely, the way that their mss. Q (pp. 73-81), T (pp. 5-6 and 14-16) and B (f. 41b-42a) yield us passages of the *Hikāya*.

The story setting, attributed to Ibn Khafīf, relates his six visits to Hallāj in prison, his return to Shiraz, his dream of the execution after forty days (at which, after fifteen days of anticipation, he was unable to be present), and gives in conclusion the date of Hallāj's death. It should be noted that this account preserves only a single detail (the *mandīl*) about

---

[22] It should undoubtedly be read as "Faraḍī." Who is this? The period of A 'AA Hy-b-Yf Dujaylī Faraḍī (664, d. 732: *Durar*, s.v.) is too late.

[23] This is probably the son of A Faḍl 'AR-b-M-b-Amīrūya-b-M Kirmānī (d. 544: Sam'ānī); it would be tempting to identify him as the Shaykh of the Zawzānī *ribāt* of Baghdad, A-b-'AR, a Sūfī (d. 575: Athīr XI, 305), but the latter is surnamed "Fārisī."

[24] 'Akarī, 368; Subkī V, 19. His descendants: Qāḍī 'Abd al-Laṭīf, d. 710; 'Izz M-b-'Abd al-Muḥsin, d. 748 (Subkī VI, *Dhayl Tadhk.* Huffāz, p. 121).

the historic visit that the early biographers of Ibn Khafīf, Daylamī, and Abū Ahmad Saghīr (d. 385)[25] tell us he paid to Hallāj in prison. The main purpose of this rather ingenuous account is to transmit five poems. As a supplement, a similar account of visits made by Shiblī to Hallāj in prison[26] also transmit to us several poems and maxims. These two series of visits are cross-checked, in accordance with variant omissions in the manuscripts, by three different accounts of the execution of Hallāj.[27]

Account no. 1 (ms. L, f. 324a, lines 5-19 to f. 324b, lines 9-28 = ms. H, f. 41a, line 4 from the bottom to f. 41b, line 14) is extremely important. It establishes (by a Mu'tazilite, AH Balkhī) (and by Ibn Khafīf) that Hallāj was not really crucified (like Jesus) by Vizir Hāmid while reading him the condemnation *fatwā* (signed by eighty-five jurists) stating that his execution is necessary for the peace of Islam; and it bears witness to his innocence through his spilled blood (which wrote *"Allāh"* on the ground).[28] The first reference is cited by Ghazālī (d. 505);[29] the second, known from Kīlānī (d. 561; a theory rejected by Ibn Taymīya, d. 728);[30] the third,[31] in fact, gave rise to numerous polemics beginning with Ibn al-Jawzī (d. 597) and Shihāb Tūsī (d. 596).[32] Lastly, and giving us a *terminus ad quem*, account no. 1 is reproduced in its entirety, with the story setting of the visits of Ibn Khafīf, by the Maghribin historian Tūzarī (d. around 560: *rāwī* of Silafī) in his *Iktifā'*.

Account no. 2 (ms. Q, pp. 89-91 = ms. L, f. 327a, line 12 to f. 327b, line 3)[33] depicts *ex abrupto* a mutilated Hallāj performing his ablutions with his blood, calling upon God for help (*Yā mu'īn*),[34] declaring himself *"gharīb,"* and saying in response to a Sūfī who, in this instance, is not Shiblī (*rajulun*; or Bundār, in a similar passage in ms. L, f. 323b, line 4 from the bottom) that "Sūfism is sacrificing one's spirit." This account, which was studied by 'Attār (d. 586) in Khurasan, as his *Tadhkira* proves (II, 143, lines 22 ff.), is echoed in the *Qissa*.

Account no. 3 (ms. L, f. 330b, line 1-f. 333a, line 9 = ms. T, p. 14)

---

[25] This volume, p. 182.

[26] Perhaps earlier (Shaydhala).

[27] Cf. *Akhbār*, 1957 ed., p. 28.

[28] A short independent account (ms. L, f. 328 = ms. Borgianum 3 = *Recueil*, p. 64) uses this testimony of blood as a Qur'ānic amulet.

[29] Ghazālī, *Radd 'alā'l-bātinīya*, 30, and Z. Qazwīnī.

[30] Ap. *Majm. Ras. Kub.* [bib. no. 512-j], II, 98.

[31] The formula of the *ism a'zam* given in the London ms. 888, f. 343a is the same as that published ap. [Rudolph] Strothmann, *Gnosis-texte des Ismā'īliten*, [Göttingen] 1943, p. 171, line 11.

[32] This volume, p. 171.

[33] Aya Sūfiya ms. 2144, ff. 151-154 combines it, as does ms. L, with account no. 1.

[34] This treatment of the story is found in account no. 3.

begins with a declaration by Hallāj before the caliph and proceeds, after his imprisonment, with the deliberation by the judges, his flagellation, his acts of surrender, and a brief recall of his ablution in his own blood, with a commented-upon paraphrase of a scene involving three individuals: Hallāj on the cross; Shiblī, who is dragged before him; and Fātima,[35] a mystic who agrees in the beginning to question Hallāj on behalf of Shiblī. This scene, which is older, is given separately in the sources (ms. Q, pp. 87-89 = ms. L, f. 324a, line 20 to f. 324b, line 9 = ms. T, pp. 5-6).[36] The historian Hamadhānī (d. 521) knew of it—perhaps it had been enclosed already within the story-account of the "visits" of Shiblī—for he quotes it at the same time as the "first visit" of Shiblī and the *"Nazarī badw 'illatī"*[37] distich (cf. ms. L, p. 19).

Alongside the *Hikāya 'an Ibn Khafīf* that we have just analyzed and that is partly also *"'an Shiblī,"*[38] the geographer Zakarīyā Qazwīnī (d. 682) preserved a fragment of an "account of Ibn Khafīf" which contains, following some known ingredients of the "first visit," a very strange *"ziyāra ila'l-Qadīm,"*[39] commented on by two poems (*'anīn al-murīd, al-sabb irthī muhibb*) and a summary of the Mu'tazilite Balkhī's arrival at the gibbet.

The *Hikāya* uses the same patchwork method[40] in transmitting the Hallājian poetry and maxims that the *Lawāmi'* of Qādī Shaydhala (d. 494) uses. It is quoted by historians beginning with Hamadhānī (d. 522). I believe therefore that its "invention" must be attributed to Shirwānī, and that it must be identified with the *History of al-Hallāj* that he transmitted to the great Shāfi'ite *muhaddith* Silafī prior to his departure, that is to say before the year 511.[41]

It must have been read in the Qādirīya monasteries, for all of the quotations from Hallāj's poetry contained in the biographies of Kīlānī's disciples appearing in the *Bahja* are found in it.[42]

[35] Nīsāpūrīya (T. Q. Baqlī), 'Umānīya (L.).   [36] Baqlī, *Sh.*, pp. 125-126.

[37] Hamadhānī, *'Unwān al-siyar*, excerpt ap. 'Arīb, de Goeje ed., pp. 98-101.

[38] Cf. ms. L, f. 324a, ms. Q 73; words of Baqlī, *Sh.*, p. 124.

[39] Cf. 'Attār.

[40] Which links it to a Baghdadian tradition and to the Zawzanī *ribāt*. It is certainly not Shirazian, nor Kazerunian.

[41] It gives Hallāj quotations, taken from Sulamī (*Tabaqāt*) and others, three of which concern *wajd*, taken from the *Ta'arruf* (82). (Nūrī). (L. f. 327a, beginning). Baqlī studied in the same order the following: ms. L, f. 324b (end of Nīsāpūrīya = M., f. 36b), f. 325a (Shiblī, 2 questions = M., *ibid.*), f. 325b (*ya mawdi'* = M., *ibid.*), f. 326b (*'ajibta; bayān bayāni'l-Haqq*). Baqlī gave the first Nīsāpūrīya question, as does Hamadhānī and Tūzarī (M., f. 37a). L, f. 324b, gives "Hāmid-b-Shurayh" and Baqlī regards Ibn Surayj as [an accessory to?] the maxim.

[42] The visits of Ibn Khafīf conclude by being condensed into three questions (*sabr, faqr, futuwwa*: Qūsī, f. 87b —'Umān).

c. Qissa

Because this text is still unedited (except for two excerpts included in *Recueil*, p. 66, numbers 10-11), I must give a description here of the five mss. of it that I have studied: B 2, N 2, J 2, L 2.

Ms. B 2: inserted without title in an anonymous *majmū'a*, Paris BN Arabic 1618, ff. 192a-198a (discovered by M. M. Jawād). Incipit: *"hukiya anna Husayn al-Hallāj lamma hamilat bihi wālidatuhā. . . ."* Explicit: *"Qālat lā; qāla fakadhālika anā; thumma tarakanī wa'nsarafa, rahimahu'Llāhu ta'ālā wanaffa' anā bi barakātihi; amīn."* Contains the following pericopes: 1-14, 16-25, 15, 26-27, 30-31 (abridged), 36, 29, 32, 34-35 (abr.), 37, 40-45.

Ms. N 2: a treatise of the tenth/sixteenth century, discovered in Beirut in March 1939 by Nouhad-b-Noureddine Beyhum, and given generously to L. Massignon: 8 folios recto-verso, 15 x 21 cm., 23 lines to the page. Title: *Qissat Husayn al-Hallāj/rahimahu 'Llāhu ta'ālālamīn/M/*. Incipit: *"hukiya, wa'Llāh a'lam, annahu kāna fī zamān al-Junayd imra'atun sāliha. . . ."* Explicit: (last hemistich of the dirge of Ukht Husayn: *"fayā layta yawwa'l-baynī kānat maniyatī"*). Contains the following pericopes: 1-4, 10-12, 14, 16, 20-26, 28-40, 41 (abr.), 42-44.

Ms. J 2: copy completed 28 Qa'da 1327 from a ms. of the Ahmad Eff. Jumaylī collection, owing to the generosity of M. Réouf Tchadirdji, Baghdad: 15 pages, 14x21 cm., 17 lines to the page. Title: *al-qawl al-sadīd/fī tarjamat al-'ārif al-shahīd*. Incipit: *"rawat al-thiqāt al-akhyār nāqili'l-akhbār anna Husayn-b-Mansūr, lamma hamilat bihi ummuhu, nadharat. . . ."* Explicit: *"qālat lā; qāla kadhālika anā"* (followed by *tahmīd* and *tasliya*). —Contains the following pericopes: 1-6, 7, 7b (*thaklan*), 12 (abr.), 13-16, 9-11, 12 (abr.), 26-27 (abr.), 20-24, 25 (watered down), 26-28, 32, 34 (abr. + *thaklan*), 34a (= dialogue with Shiblī), 39-44.

Ms. L 2: *risāla* no. VIII (on XXIV) of a Durzīya *majmū'a* of Chouf, copy owed to the generosity of Amīr Louis Chehab, Hammana (Lebanon). 30 pages, 13-20 cm., 10 lines to the page. Title: *Qissat Husayn al-Hallāj wamawlidihi wamaqtalihi radiya'Llāhu 'anhu*. Incipit: *"qīla annahu, lamma hamilat bihi ummuhu, nadharat. . . ."* Explicit: *"fa'mtalā qalbī farahan wa surūran"* (followed by the *Qasīda al-khamr dinnī . . .*). Contains the following pericopes: 1-3, 4 (abr.), 6 (abr.), 10-11, 12 (abr.), 14-16, 20-24, 25 (watered down), 26-27, 29-32, 34, 36-40, 42-44.

Ms. PK: *risāla* no. IV of a *majmū'a* (Cairo, Tal'at 4833, ff. 20b-28a; copy of Paul Kraus, 12 pages). Title:

[lacuna in the manuscript]

We are dealing here with a text of literature that is truly popular, with a "legend of a saint," the text of which, except for some details singled out later, must have been established rather early,[43] even before the death of the compiler of the *majmū'a* of ms. B 2 (around the year A.H. 960, since his grandfather, 'Alī ibn al-Baqarī Sa'īdī, was associated with an Ahmadī religious of Tanta, Ibrāhīm Matbūlī, 880, f. 188b). To identify its author or at least its original milieu we must follow two trails: the prose quotations and also those in verse, for in the indirect literary tradition names of founders of religious orders are mentioned in poems (sometimes important in themselves) whose pericopes are crammed full.

Initial investigation turned up formal quotations from the *Qissa* only in the *Nasīm al-riyād* of Khafājī (d. 1069) [bib. no. 811-a], Volume IV, 564-567, in which, in another recension, pericope numbers 16, 20, and 24 appear. The freeing of the prisoners theme (= no. 16) appears in 'Attār (*Tadhkira*), but without the boat. The case of no. 40 (*"werd"* thrown at the face of the executed, here by Junayd, and in 'Attār, *Takhk.* II, 143, lines 14-15, by Shiblī) is stranger. Here, in the *Qissa*, *werd* must be vocalized *wird*[44] in the sense of "rosary"; 'Attār, using a written not an oral source, read it as *"ward"* in the sense of "rose" and translated it *"gul"* (which his Uyghur translator read as *"gil"* in the sense of "mud").

Further investigation turns up about twenty poems. The following are those found in the four mss. (B, J, L, N): *"anā Husayn al-Hallāj . . . hālī"* (no. 11 = *Dīwān*, p. 141n); *"yā 'awdī min 'awdī"* (numbers N 4, L 6, J 12, B 12 = *Dīwān*, p. 152); *"Lāhat 'alā dikkati'l-khammāri asrār"* (numbers 34b and N 40 = *Dīwān*, p. 129). Two famous pieces appear in three mss. (J, L, B): *"Qul likhwānin . . . hazanan"* (no. 12 = *Dīwān*, p. 131; in its place N gives the unicum *"'Adir al-kāsāt . . . siqāma"*), —and *"Uqtulūnī, yā thiqāti"* (no. 28 = *Dīwān*, p. 33; in its place N gives an expansion to nine verses of the famous distich (given in J 12), *"Saqawnī . . . laghannati"* = *Dīwān*, p. 128). Two mss. (J, B) include borrowings from the *Hikāya*: *"Mā ziltu ajrī . . . inhattu"* (no. 16 = *Dīwān*, p. 70), *"Idhā hajarta . . . wa aqallī"* (no. 21 = *Dīwān*, p. 125). Likewise two other mss. (B, N): *"Lam uslimi'l-nafsa . . . yuhyīhā"* (no. 26 = *Dīwān*, p. 127). Also, *"Lya habibun . . . fi'l-khalawāti"* (no. 24 = *Dīwān*, p. 47); ap. ms. B. Ms. J includes in

---

[43] The *Qissa* confused the name of Vizir Hāmid with that of a Sahābi buried in Homs: Khālid ibn Walīd (mss. J,N; ms. B corrects the beginning; ms. L puts *sāhib al-shurta*) who played a role in the *futuwwa* (Thorning [?] I, 109; *"pīr al-nuqabā' "*).

Words used for Baghdadian topography show that the *Qissa* was not written in Iraq: the river in Baghdad is called *Furāt* (no. 34, mss. J,L,N: only ms. B, like Khafājī, corrects *Dijla* in no. 34 but keeps, through an oversight, *Furāt* in no. 16); *Harīm* (J 24) is in actuality the name of a palace; *Burj* (nos. 34, 43), equipped with battlements (*sharārīf*: J,L, no. 43), is possibly the Burj 'Ajamī. From the lexical standpoint, it should be noted that the Iraqi word *sindān* for prison exists only in *al-Khamr dinnī*; for footwear, the Iraqi word *qibqāb* (no. 17: re ms. B); for copper cooking pan, *hāwūn* (mss. B,L,N; and *hafīra*, ms. J; no. 24).

[44] Warda (*PK, J*).

an awkward manner a piece in which Hallāj is quoted ("*tajalla lī . . . fahayānī*," in no. 34b); it is also the only one to give a certain interesting piece, "*Sakirta min al-maʿnā . . . aʿjabu*" (no. 38 = *Dīwān*, p. 128) and the only borrowing from poems of the *Akhbār* (§ 38): "*Hawaytu bikullī . . . yā Qudsī*" (in no. 12 = *Dīwān*, p. 66).

Ms. N inserts no. 33, and ms. L adds to the final no. 44, a famous *qasīda* "*al-khamr dinnī . . . rayhānī* (*Dīwān*, p. 141); independent of the *Qissa*, related to the poem "'*Adir al-kāsāt . . . siqāma*," it will be examined here in the appendix.

The indirect tradition for the verse notices, in Jildakī (d. 743), the poem "*Anā Husayn al-Hallāj . . . hālī*" along with "*Uqtulūnī*" and, in Ibn Taymīya (d. 728), the fourth verse of "*Lāhat. . . .*"

Lastly, numbers 32-34 and 43-45 of the *Qissa*, devoted to his sister, belong to another *Qissa* which has not yet been rediscovered; a very heterodox *Qissa*, in which it is not his shaykh, but his sister, a divine *hūrī*, who initiates Hallāj (here "Mansūr") into the divine intoxication (§I), receives his last will and testament (§II), presides as an initiate at his execution ("stop transforming yourself," ap. ms. T of *Akhbār*, p. 8); "he has become a demigod" (literally: half-man, half-god) ap. Harīrī (d. 645) and Mustawfī (d. 740) (§III) and becomes pregnant by him after drinking water which he had made fertile with his ashes (§IV).[45] That this legend of Kurdish origin, spread to Iranophonic India and from there to Turkestan and as far as Java, was written down, we have a strange proof: the mistake made by the Qirghiz of Otch, who, reading in his text the same formula "*Anā'l-Haqq, Manhaqqem*," first in Arabic and repeated in Persian, believed that Hallāj, applying the Persian form to himself, said the Arabic form about his sister, that she was called "*Anā'l*," and that he claimed she had become "*Haqq*," God.

In conclusion, the four mss. (B, J, L, N) of the *Qissa* allow us only to hypothesize about its date and its original milieu. Its date: certainly earlier, not only than 1069 and 960, but also than A.H. 728, and later than A.H. 600: since three of the four mss. include the poem "*Qul li'ikhwānin*" that Ibn ʿArabī attributes expressly to Musaffar Sibtī, who died in A.H. 636 in Hama.[46] His original milieu: Damascus, among pro-mystical Hanbalite Sunnites of the Jammāʾilīyīn group (transmitters of two Hallāj-

---

[45] Fragments of §I ap. Nizām Husaynī (in 1068: cf. *Recueil*, p. 66) and two lost Indo-Persian mss. quoted by Malcolm and Graham (*Makhzan al-sārikīn, Maqsūd al-ʿārifīn*). —Fragment of §II: here, *Qissa*, nos. 32-34, 43-45. —Cf. the "soul-sister" of the Yazīdīs. She plays the role of *hājib* for the *wasīya* (ap. Z. Qazwīnī = the *khādim* ap. ʿAttār). —Fragment of §IV: Yazīdī text ap. Ismaīl beg Tchōl, *Yazīdī* [bib. no. 999-02], 1937, p. 89; cf. p. 456, and Parry.

[46] Ibn ʿArabī, *Muhādarāt* [bib. no. 421-a]; Ibn Taghrībirdī, Paris ms. 1780, f. 138b.

ian texts: *Intisār* and *Bidāya*),[47] the hosts of Mūsā Kīlānī (d. 608), *rāwī* of a
rhymed prose work on Hallāj, in rhyme *-ānī* (*Bahja*, 121-122). It was
there that ʿIzz-b-Ghānim Maqdīsī (d. 660) was to become a Hallājian; and
five pericopes of the *Qissa* (nos. 7 and 18) in ms. B, nos. 28, 37; and 46 in
ms. J) come from the *Hall* and the *Sharh* of ʿIzz Maqdīsī.[48]

The *Qissa* in ms. N is found to contain three poems that cite heads of
·congregations: Sayyidī Abū'l-Wafā' (= the Kurd Tāj al-ʿĀrifīn Kākīs
Barjasī, d. around 520: *Bahja*, 142), ʿAbd al-Qādir (Kīlānī) and Ibn al-
Rifāʿī Ahmad, ap. *ʿAdir al-kāsāt*; —ʿAbd al-Qādir, Samādī (*sic* = Rifāʿī)
Harīrī (his tomb: thus written after 645), ʿAdī-b-Musāfir (d. 558: founder
of the Yazīdī ʿAdawīya in Kurdish lands: he is said here to be of Shāmī
origin; this fact, accurate (*Bahja*, 213), proves the Syrian origin of the
poem), ap. *Saqānī min ahwāhu* (in no. 34); —Ibn al-Rifāʿī and Ibn Barakāt
(= Abū'l-Barakāt Sakhr, d. around 585, second head of the Yazīdī
ʿAdawīya, founder of their monastery in Cairo, where the Kurd
Mihranī, friend of Baybars, d. 671, lived), ap. *al-Khamr dinnī*; the connection ms. N has with the latter is underscored by mention in no. 33 of the
martyrdom of ʿUthmān, cited ap. al-Khamr, and of the *sayha* of the "*fatā
Badawī*," whom ms. L 2 calls "Ahmad Badawī."

All of that, with pro-Umayyad tone, the mention of three shaykhs
venerated by the Yazīdīs, and the mention of Ahmad Badawī of Tanta
(d. 695 and not 675),[49] who we know came to Iraq to "visit the tombs of
Hallāj and ʿAdi ibn Musāfir," therefore that he had a connection with
ʿAdawīya Kurdish monasteries in Damascus and Cairo, makes us seek
the origin of the *qasīda al-Khamr dinnī* and of ms. N of the *Qissa* in Syria
among the affiliated members of the ʿAdawīya of Damascus and of the
Rifāʿīya Harīrīya of Harran, associated with the Egyptian Badawīya (cf.
Ibn al-Baqarī).

1. Table of Contents of the Forty-five Pericopes of the
Qissat Husayn al-Hallāj
(with the 1954 edition's pagination)[50]

(1) the maternal vow (familiar theme: verified by Ibn al-Sā'igh
Dīnawarī, d. A.H. 331; cf. Siddīq Khān, *Husn al-uswa*, 378)   103

---

[47] This volume, p. 461.

[48] A parallelism in the prose pieces: with regard to the mutilations. [He] laughed at the
sayf (BN 1641, f. 252b), joy and not pain when mutilated (*ilā lamaʿān barīq al-sayf fa dahika*).

[49] Baybars (658, d. 676) came to greet him as he returned from his journey, which therefore could have taken place in 633; his direct disciple ʿAbd al-ʿĀl died in 733.

[50] *Qissāt Husayn al-Hallāj*, in *Mélanges Nyberg* [bib. no. 1695-bx].

(2) his admission to Junayd as *khādim*

(3) he inadvertently swallows the formula of the "supreme Name";
     Junayd curses the thief[51]   104

(4) sent to the market, he enters it in ecstasy

(5) he shouts his secret, then flees to the mountains

(6) returned, he inspires, without his knowing, a sermon by Junayd

(7) his ecstatic definition of love (*rid'a min thidī, jur'a*)

(8) Junayd, opening his *dalq*, discovers the wound of his heart; he
     weeps;   105

(9) he shouts the *tahlīl* in the *sūqs*; and "I am the Truth"

(10) he cards a shop full of cotton; hence, his surname; verses; threats

(11) the incident with the handkerchief (*mandīl*)   106

(12) he disappears for a year, then returns

(13) he enlarges and shrinks his body; Junayd sympathizes

(14) he disrupts traffic; Junayd makes him agree to go to prison   107

(15) there, in the presence of a visitor, he makes a pomegranate tree
     grow

(16) he exhorts his fellow prisoners, draws on the wall a "ship of salva-
     tion" which they, filled with faith, get into and escape in[52] 108

(17) he walks on the river, in *qibqāb*, pulling the ship; verses

(18) he returns to Baghdad, expressing his love of God

(19) the public, its patience overtaxed, and 70 *'ulamā'*, denounce Hallāj
     to Junayd

(20) at the time of *azān*, Hallāj shouts at the muezzin: you have lied
     about it

(21) the Caliph, prejudiced against him, orders him brought [to him]109

(22)-(24) arrested, he appears, challenges the *'ulamā'* to a test, and sits in
     a large boiling cauldron

(25) triumphant, he flees

(26) he returns to the home of Junayd: the police commissioner brings to
     the Caliph the 84 *fatwā* of the *'ulamā'* of Baghdad, Damascus, and
     Cairo "*fī qatlihi salāh al-muslimīn*"   110

(27) Junayd approves of the *fatwā* of condemnation

(28) Hallāj confirms it on a piece of paper that he throws in the air

(29) Shiblī (with 60), Junayd (with 80), and the Forty arrive

---

[51] A previously cited incident ('Attār, II, 37, 63; this volume, p. 344; cf. Mansūr-b-
Ammār, bestowed with wisdom for having respectfully swallowed the *basmala* (Ibn 'Arabī,
Jadhwa, f. 2b).

[52] (Fulk Nūh): cf. Qur'ān 11:41; cf. Noah.

(30) the crowd gathers; Hallāj has both hands cut off; his blood writes *"Allāh"* 84 times (the number of the *shuhūd*)

(31) he ablutes his forehead with his blood: "I am the Betrothed (of the Divine Presence)"; Junayd orders him to be silent   111

(32) he calls for his sister

(33) he accepts his execution, renounces making the cry of rage that would destroy everything

(34) final testament: to stop the flooding of the Tigris, throw my ashes into it

(35)-(36) he reminds Junayd of his vow to dress in black

(37)-(38) mutilation of the hand (right; left, missing)   112

(39) nailed, stoned, burned

(40) Junayd stones him with a rose; he groans

(41)-(42) Junayd kisses him between his eyes: he yields up his soul

(43) his sister threatens the Tigris, which stops flooding

(44) he appears to his sister in sleep; he expresses his joy to her

(45) if you let a bird out of its cage, to let it go free in the garden, will it be unhappy?   113

2. Filiation of Manuscripts

The stemma of the four mss. of the *Qissa*, BQ, NB, J, DR, may be arranged either by the presence of characteristic expressions in the prose parts; there are too few of them: 84 *'ulamā'* (BQ, J, NB [twice], Tūzarī), or 85 (DR), or 70 (variant BQ; cf. *"al-Khamr dinnī"*); and the name of the father of Vizir Hāmid-b-Walīd (BQ; NB, DR even give "Khālid-b-Walīd,[53] Mustawfī: Khālid-b-'Abbās; PK: Hāmid-b-'Abbās Shurayj") (Lescot, p. 231 [bib. nos. 1798, 2149]); or by the verse pieces.

BQ contains 15 pieces of verse: 7 in DR (arranged in order), 4 in NB (in order) 14 in J (in 2 orders); 13 in PK (in order).

NB contains 17: 11 in DR (9 in order), 3 in BQ (in order), 3 in J (without order); 2 in PK (in order).

J contains 17: 4 in DR (without order), 3 in NB (without order), 14 in BQ (without order); 8 in PK (out of place).

DR contains 19: 11 in NB (and in order), 7 in BQ (in order), 4 in J (without order); 2 in PK (in order).

PK contains 16: 2 in DR (in order), 2 in NB (in order), 8 in J (1 out of place), 13 in BQ (in order).

[53] Yazīdī in origin (*Lisān*, 21).

Hence, the following stemma:

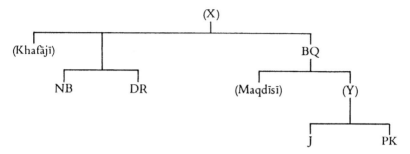

The dating of the *Qissa*, which emanates from a popular Damascene milieu venerating 'Uthmān, depends on a comparison with other Hallāj-ian collections (from which it makes no literal borrowings in prose):

a) It uses again two pieces of verse found in *Akhbār* (*Uqtulūnī*, *Hawaytu*), 5 of 80 in *Hikāya* (*Rūhuhu*, *mā ziltu*, *lam uslim*, *Idhā hajart*, *liya Habīb*), and 4 apocryphal poems (*qul limam*, by Sabtī, d. 636: J, BQ, DR; —*saqawnī*, as early as Qazwīnī, ap. NB; —*"ahruf arba‘* "), Shādhilīyan, ap. J, BQ; —*"al-khamr dinnī*," NB, DR; this *qasīda* has certain things in common with the *Qissa*: the allusion to carding, verse 5, to the cauldron, verse 4, to the muezzin, verse 10, to the 70 judges: cf. *rawd fā’iq*;

b) it uses again eleven legendary themes: theft of a book (as early as Qushayrī); the alliteration *"sudūr-qubūr"* (of Dhū’l-Nūn and Yf-b-Hy Rāzī, *Hilya* X, 243; *Luma‘*, 232; from the historian Hamadhānī); the shout *"Anā’l-Haqq"* (moderate use); the miracle of the carding (from Sulamī); the inflating episode (from Zanjī and Bāqillānī); the shrinking episode in prison on the second day (legend from Qastamūnī); the role of the Forty (with Shiblī; cf. Yesewī, Qastamūnī, Gharīb Bukhārī; *"al-khamr dinnī"*); the drops of blood (*Hikāya*); the shout *"sayha"* (*"al-khamr dinnī"*); the sister still in archaic role; expanded ap. Yazīdī, Bukharian, and Bengali legends;

c) it develops its own themes: the maternal vow; the *fatwā* "to die for the salvation of the Muslims" (cf. *Hikāya*) is divided into two parts, and God himself renders a *fatwā* confirmative (*waraqa*); the insult to the dis-tracted muezzin (as far back as Mūrīdī: the theme comes from Nūrī); the judiciary test (*mubāhala*) by the cauldron (as early as Khafājī); the escape from prison (*ibid.*, cf. 'Attār); death by stoning (cf. 'Attār: and the rose); the sister unveiled (cf. Mustawfī, *Guzīda*: ms. P., Pers. Suppl. 173, f. 266b).

We have found only one literary text, the *Sharh ḥāl al-awliyā'* of 'Izz 'A Salām-b-Ghānim Maqdīsī (Hanbalite, d. 678 in Damascus), which has a definite connection with two mss. of the *Qissa*, J and especially BQ. The piece with ten verses, *Nasama*, common to J and BQ, is to be found after 'Izz (*ḥāl*, Ibr-b-Adham) where the sequence of verses is as follows: 1-2, 9-10, a-b, 3-8 (of which two are additions). The piece with ten verses, *Ammā walladhī* (J, BQ f. 194a), is found ap. 'Izz (*ḥāl* Husayn) with five added verses (concerning Karbala: between verse 4 and verse 5). "*Uqtu-lūnī*" is watered down (J, BQ: 3 verses; *Sh*. 8). One must conclude from this that *Sharh* copied the *Qissa* (BQ f. 193a, with its snare for birds, f. 198a, which became a bird of paradise = *Sh*., f. 251a), is appended to fragments of rhymed prose, rather clumsily borrowed from *Sharh* (was it a copyist's interpolation?).

3. Excerpts from the *Qissa*

§3: One day it came to the mind of Junayd to drink the Supreme Name of God. He wrote it with musk and saffron and slipped it under his *sajjāda* to drink it with his saliva at the time of the ablution. But then, as was his custom, Husayn went in to sweep the *zāwiya*; he shook the mat, a piece of paper fell out of it; Husayn took it and swallowed it, so that God might bless it, without knowing what was written on it. Junayd, going in again found the paper no longer there, and exclaimed: "O people, who took the paper which was there?" No one responded to his repeated question. Then, by way of a threat, he said "Let him who does not return it have his hands cut off, and his feet, [let him] be crucified and burned; and let his ashes be scattered in the air." And during all of that, Husayn, standing, was crying, with his heart inflamed by the light of divine Truth.

§6: Then Husayn returned on the day of the shaykh's reception; be-cause the room was filled with many people, he remained in the hallway (*dahlīz*). Now the shaykh was eloquent, his words had touched the learned as well as the slow, therefore people liked to come there. But on this particular day what he said became so subtle that no one understood him any more. "This is no longer your way with the *fuqarā'*, someone said to him; we have understood nothing. —Nor I, said Junayd; I do not understand what I am saying; it must be a warning directed at someone who himself must understand. Look therefore in the hallway and see if there is not someone there whom this language makes weep." They looked there, they found Hallāj standing there weeping: "have you un-derstood what the shaykh has said? —Yes. —Come in, he asks for you";

and they cleared a way for him to the *minbar*: "Now then, Husayn," the shaykh said to him, "you have reached the point of grasping the divine message in the depth of consciences."

§12: He entered Junayd's lane. "What do you want?"—"I wanted to see you, to hear your words; you are the one who brought me closer to the Friend, and my separation from you saddened and caused me pain." —"Who among us has not received his share from the Beloved, who among us does not weep with desire to see the face of the Beloved? But the hearts of free men are tombs for secrets. If one spark of the Beloved's desire catches fire in the heart of the lover, it causes living flames to shine under constraint of the guarded secret." And then the shaykh opened his *dilq* (patched robe), and the blood poured out of his heart; and he wept; and his tears flowed, mingling with his blood. Before that Husayn said to him, "O shaykh, what are these tears and this blood?" —"The tears, they have flowed from desire, and the blood, it is from fear of being separated (from God). Husayn! God is merciful to one who knows His place, keeps His secret, and follows His precept." And the shaykh kissed Husayn between his eyes. Husayn answered him: "That is a constancy beyond my powers," and he left and walked the streets of Baghdad shouting, "*Allāh!*"

§16: Imprisoned, he prayed and made the prisoners pray, and said to them: "O band of Muslims! Your prison is nothing else but your sins and your heedlessness of your Beloved." Then he prayed with them at the *'ishā'* and spoke to them of God until dawn, when he performed the prayer with them. Then he got up and drew on the prison wall a picture of a ship, sat in it, and exclaimed: "let him who wants to save himself get up and enter it with me." They got up and came to him. "Cast off your ship," he said, "declare simply with me the *dhikr Allāh*, the *tahlīl!*" When they raised their voices the picture became a ship in the middle of a great river. He said to them, "O people! This is the ship of salvation (*markab al-najāt*)." They continued to utter the Name of God; when they were halfway across, Husayn took up his *qibqāb*, put them on his feet, and walked on the surface of the water, and the ship followed him until they reached the shore. He then said to them "O people, go forth wherever you wish, safe and sound."

§28: When Junayd, accepting the *fatwā* of the eighty-four judges, delivered Husayn up to the secular arm, Husayn appeared again before the Caliph and said, after looking left and right: "bring me an ink-pot and paper"; which they did; and he wrote on it: "my body is Yours, my blood is Yours, make it lawful to shed." The paper flew into the air, then returned with this written on it: "if you are full of love, submit yourself wholly to the command; if you are one of Ours and desire the intimacy of Our union, Our way, Our nature, is to put men to death, and Our Law renders their death licit (*shar'ī yuhilluhu*)."

§32: He asked that his sister be brought to him for a final admonition (*wasīya*). They went out and found her; she came with bare feet, head unveiled. "O sister, he said to her, have you no shame? Before these men veil your face." —"Where are there men, my brother? If they were men, they would not have failed to recognize (in you) the mystical states of men." —"That, my sister, is the fact of a divine preordination, the result of the curse of my shaykh Junayd. I shall be anxious to release whoever has abused, struck, stoned, nailed, and burned me. But when they have burned me, keep my ashes with you; for after three days, the Euphrates will boil over in anger against the inhabitants of Baghdad because of the evil they have done to me. Then they will come to implore you. And when the water has risen to the battlements of the Burj (*sharārif*[54] *al-Burj*), throw my ashes into it, saying to it "Husayn greets you and tells you: do not drown the inhabitants of Baghdad, because his shaykh, Junayd, is among them; do not exceed the Burj" (variant: "return to where you have come from; my brother forgives him who has done evil to him; he accepts the fate that God prepared for him for the sake of his shaykh: one alone is enough to have a thousand be spared from it").

§36 (ms. B 2 = Paris 1618, f. 196b): When they had cut off (first) his left hand, his blood wrote "*Allāh, Allāh*" in eight places on the ground, and with his blood he began to draw letters on his forehead, saying "(since) I am the betrothed of the divine Abode" (*anā 'arūs al-Hadra*) (for the marriage, the hairdresser [*harqūsa*] marks the forehead of the betrothed with scarlet, cf. J. Jouin, ap. *REI*, 1931, p. 315).

§40: And the first to stone him was his shaykh, Junayd. He stoned him with his *wird* (= rosary). And Husayn groaned "You have killed me." Junayd said to him "others have stoned you with stones, and you said nothing, but when I stone you with a rosary, you groan?" —"Lord, don't you know how much it hurts a lover to be scorned by a friend?" Then the shaykh embraced him and, kissing him between the eyes, bid him farewell.

II. BIOGRAPHIES OF HALLĀJ WITH COMMENTARIES

We are dealing here with commentaries on his biography that place it in relation to a whole, imposing on him a general form, generic, however

---

[54] *Shurafāt* (Ibn 'Arabī, *Tarjumān*).

comparative and even polemical in character, thereby delineating the favorable or hostile opinion of the authors who signed them. They can be divided into two categories:

a) works by religious writers, mystical or anti-mystical;

b) works by historians, chronological annals, biographies of individuals, dictionary-directories of notable persons (by categories).

a. Works by Religious Writers

1. Polemical Tracts Written during Hallāj's Lifetime

"*Makhārīq al-Hallāj wa'l-hīla fīhā*" = "the False Miracles of Hallāj and His Methods of Trickery" (Khatīb VIII, 124); a work composed prior to 309 by Hārūn-b-'Abd al-'Azīz Awāriji (278, d. 344), a Mu'tazilite author, a functionary in the department of finances, whose intent it was to reopen the trial. Tanūkhī (*Nishwār*) and Baqī Dānī (*Bayān wa farq*) must have made use of this work. The word "*makhārīq*" in its title evokes the famous contemporary pamphlet by the physician Rāzī.[1]

In the opposite direction, certain pro-Hallājian accounts continued at that time to be circulated in writing; at least this is what is suggested by the unusual number of separate recensions, prior to Sulamī, which have come down to us dealing with two features of Hallāj's life: his debate with Ibrāhīm Khawwās in Kufa (*Tawakkul*)[2] and his public prayer at 'Arafat during his final pilgrimage (*ta'lam 'ajzī*).[3]

2. Sulamī's Documentation and His Written Sources

Sulamī (d. 412) is the source of our knowledge of the earliest Hallājian Sūfism, with the 250 authentic (and not retouched)[4] doctrinal fragments of it that he has transmitted to us (250 out of a total of 395). He also collected biographical data on Hallāj. In spite of the traditionist fiction of *isnād*, we must try to determine the sources of all of this material.

a) *Ta'rīkh al-sūfīya*. This great historical collection of 1,000 Sūfi shaykhs was composed by Sulamī before 371, as various indications prove;[5] he was attacked for having written biographies of three

---

[1] Bīrūnī, *Répertoire . . . ouvrages Rāzī*, edited by P. Kraus, 1936, p. 20, no. 174.

[2] Kalābādhī, no. 31 (*batnak = karsh*, ap. 'Attār); Qushayrī III, 51, according to 'AA-b-M Rāzī, d. 353; Hujwīrī, tr. 205, 285, text pp. 258, 367; AH Ghazālī, *Ihyā'* [bib. no. 280-a], IV, 174, 310; Ahmad Ghazālī, *Sawānih* [bib. no. 281-c], f. 43a, '*Ishqīya*, f. 129a; Kubrā, *Tarīqat-nāma* [bib. no. 391-a]; commentary of Ibn Sīnā, *Ishārāt* II, 120.

[3] Kalābādhī, no. 29, and *Akhbār*, ms. P. 5855, f. 87a; Baqlī, *Tafsīr*, nos. 11, 17, and *Shath.*, no. 187; Sulamī, *Tabaqāt*, no. 11; 'Attār, no. 1; Shaydhala [bib. no. 259-a], no. 1.

[4] Cf. *Akhbār al-Hallāj*, 16, 40-43.

[5] He alludes in it to Ibn Khafīf (d. 371) as being alive; the work is cited by 'AA-b-Mūsā Salāmī (d. 374: ap. *Ta'rīkh*; cf. Khatīb III, 9), by A-b-M Nasawī (d. 396, ap. *Tabaqāt*), and

blacklisted men: Hallāj, Abū Hulmān and Qannād.[6] It appears lost, but Khatīb has preserved for us twenty-one fragments from it dealing with Hallāj that we published in 1914.[7] Harawī informs us that this work was a reedition of the *Ta'rīkh* of Abū Bakr M-b-'AA Bajalī Rāzī[8] (d. 376), a famous Sūfī historian, "forsaken" (*mahjūr*) following an undeserved morals charge against him;[9] and that Baqlī had had for a master Abū Bakr Paykandī, author of *tawārīkh*[10] from which he may have borrowed.[11]

It is therefore probable that, except for seven pieces derived explicitly from more recent Sūfī authors, the whole of this biography of Hallāj given in Sulamī came from Abū Bakr Bajalī, referred to elsewhere expressly as the source of numbers 12 and 24, to which must be added numbers 6 and 22, of the same *isnād*, but in which his name is omitted. It was also Bajalī who must have copied numbers 2, 5, 10, and 18 derived from the following authors respectively: Qannād, A Z Tabarī (cf. Bāk., 5), Khuldī (*Hukya*), and Fāris (via Sayyārī); for numbers 4, 17, 19-20 the borrowing is uncertain. One finds that Bajalī does not put us in direct contact with the milieu that was eyewitness to Hallāj's life.[12] It was also from him that Sulamī must have borrowed his short notice on the Hallājian Shākir (d. 311), found in the same work.

There remain seven fragments:

No. 3, taken from M-b-'AA ibn Shādhān Bajalī (d. 376), author of a *Kitāb Muzakkī* (or *Mudhakkir*), a pupil of Ibn Sālim and of Ibn Yazdānyār (Qushayrī 10, 22, 25, 31, 32; *Hilya* X, 208, 363; Khatīb V, 464); *I'tidāl* III, 85.

No. 8, taken from Mansūr-b-'AA Sadūsī Harawī (d. around 380), a disciple of Shiblī, an author attacked by Mālinī, accepted by Sahlajī and Harawī (Khatīb XIII, 85; Jāmī, 399; Sahlajī, *Nūr*, 25, 36, 131, 132, 134, 136).

---

by AS M-b-'Alī Naqqāsh (d. 412, ap. *Ta'rīkh*); cf. our *Bibliographie hallagienne*, nos. 137, 183, 180.

[6] Baghdādī, *Usūl al-dīn* [bib. no. 201-d], 316.

[7] Ap. *Quatre Textes* II.

[8] This is Ibn Shādhān.

[9] Ivanow, *JASB* XVIII, 394; Jāmī, 257; *Tarā'iq* II, 223.

[10] Kalābādhī, *Akhbār*, 5855, f. 371a.

[11] *JASB* XVIII, 394; Qushayrī, 67.

[12] Bajalī gives biographies in his *Ta'rīkh* of Kharrāz (Qushayrī, 105), Junayd (Khatīb VII, 247), Jurayrī (Khatīb VII, 248; Qushayrī, 124, 130), Kattānī (Khatīb III, 76; Qushayrī, 61, 121, 125), Ibn 'Atā' (Qushayrī, 101, 119), Ibn Shaybān (Qushayrī, 72), Abū'l-'Abbās al-Qāss (Qushayrī, 21), Khuldī (Sulamī, *tafsīr* on Qur'ān 51:1; 112:4), Yūsuf Rāzī (*Talbīs* [?], 295); cf. *Masāri'* [?], 69.

Nos. 9 and 11, taken from AQ Ja'far-b-A Rāzī (d. 378), an author quoted by Ibrāhīm Nasrābādhī (d. 364), and a *rāwī* of Ibn Abī Sa'dān (Khatīb IV, 361); no. 13, taken from Abū Bakr ibn Ghālib, whom Khatīb treats as an unknown, from whom we have three other Hallājian texts (Sulamī, *Tabaqāt*, no. 10; Qushayrī I, 45 and III, 53), who spoke of Ibn Khafīf to Kalābādhī (*Ta'arruf*, 119); this M-b-M ibn Ghālib is possibly Dāmaghānī, head of the Sūfīs of Kirman (343, d. 432: Sam'ānī, f. 358b; cf. also *Hilya* X, 253), rather than the famous *muhaddith* Burqānī (336, d. 425; Kh. IV, 373) of whom Khatīb could not have been ignorant.

No. 14, the basic account by Qādī Ibn al-Haddād of Hallāj's last vigil that Sulamī claims to have taken from the canonist Abū Bakr Qaffāl Shāshī (d. 375), an easy way of authenticating his borrowing from the *Ta'rīkh* of Bajalī, it would seem.

No. 23, taken from the *Luma'* of Sarrāj (d. 377).

Let us add that A'AA Rāzī, the *rāwī* of no. 19, is the same as Hy-b-A-b-J Rāzī (Kh. VII, 230, 248), perhaps also an author of no. 20 (*Luma'*, 316 = 808), *rāwī* of AB M-b-'Alī 'Atūfī (alive in 343, according to Sam'ānī, f. 394a), (Qushayrī, 28, 63, 112, 130, 148, 181, 192) and of nos. 9 and 11; and that Ibn Bākūyā (d. 428), successor of Sulamī as head of the "monastery" of Nishapur, recopied nine (out of twenty-one) of the Hallājian fragments from the *Ta'rīkh* of Sulamī while giving them new *isnāds*.

Lastly, Qushayrī gives others (ap. *Risāla*) in which we find two other *rāwīs* concerned with Hallāj: (III, 51) AM-'AA-b-M-b-'AR Rāzī (d. 353), the leading pupil of A U Hīrī (*Sh.* I, 119) and (IV, 19) AA-M-b-A-b-Ibrāhīm Isfahānī, qādī, d. 349, master of Mālinī (Kh. I, 270; *Hilya* X, 123, 125).

b) *Tabaqāt al-sūfīya*. At the end of his life, Sulamī abridged the *Ta'rīkh* that we have just considered in a brief collection in which the concise notices, grouped chronologically, on each shaykh are followed, without anecdotal accounts, by a selection of maxims. This still classic work, transmitted with regular *samā'* among Hanbalites,[13] was used again by Ibn Khāmīs Ka'bī (d. 553) in his *Manāqib*, by Mubārak ibn al-Athīr (d. 606) in his *Mukhtār*, by Sha'rāwī (*Tabaqāt*), by Munāwī (*Kaw.*), and by Bandanījī. J. Pedersen has begun an edition of it.[14]

Under the rubric of Hy-b-Mansūr Hallāj, the abridged biographical

---

[13] From AB A-b-'Alī Shīrāzī to 'Āyīsha Maqdīsīya (d. 816; Rūdānī, *Sila* [bib. no. 834-a], f. 91b).

[14] Fascicule I (pp. 1-10) appeared in 1938 [bib. no. 170-a]. [Published in full, Brill, Leiden, 1960. —H.M.]

notice is followed by twenty-one maxims, of which numbers 1, 6, 8 and 10 have *isnāds*:

No. 1 was taken from the *Akhbār, ahādīth wa hikāyāt* of Abū'l-Faraj 'Abd al-Wāhid-b-Bakr Warthānī (d. 372), whose biography was written by Sam'ānī (f. 580b); who took it from Ahmad-b-Fāris-b-Hasrī (= Khusraw?), *rāwī* of no. 36 of *Akhbār al-Hallāj, rāwī* of Kattānī (Khatīb III, 76), informant of Ibn Jahdam (*Bahja*, VI, ff. 2a, 25a). Warthānī was an author known for his accounts of early shaykhs (Qushayrī, 116, 145), Rudhabārī (Qushayrī, 6, 147; cf. *Masāri'*, 375) and Ibn Khafīf (Qushayrī, 24).

No. 6 came from a work by Fāris (via 'Abd al-Wāhid Shīrāzī, author of the *Tā'rīkh al-sūfīya* (= Warthānī).[15]

No. 8 came from Abū'l-Husayn Fārisī, a well-known author, died around 350, since his disciple AB M-b-A-b-Hamdūn Farrā' died in 370 (*Luma'*, 40), *rāwī* of Ibn Fātik (Qushayrī 6) concerning Junayd; and concerning other shaykhs, Ibn 'Atā' (Qushayrī, 62, 108, 171), Jurayrī (Qushayrī, 104, 107), Sarī' (Qushayrī, 113). He must be identified with Abū'l-Husayn M-b-A-b-Ibrāhīm Fārisī, a disciple of Fāris (J. Pedersen ed., 31, 45). Cf. *Talbīs*, 320 (*rāwī* of A-b-'Alī Wajīhī).

No. 10 came from M-b-M-b-Ghālib, studied above; Ibn al-Dā'ī quotes him for an answer to a "question" by Shiblī. Could Ibn Ghālib be the author of the "visits of Shiblī"?

Harawī and 'Attār gave several of these maxims.

Munāwī and Ibn 'Aqīl also. Kalābādhī give no. 11, Qushayrī nos. [. . .], Hujwīrī no. 15, and Ibn al-Sabbāgh nos. 16 and 18.

It should be noted that nos. 12 and 14 are found in Sulamī's *Tafsīr*, nos. 85 and 58 (with variants).

Sulamī, as he himself tells us, intended to give other *isnāds* here for the accounts previously published in his *Ta'rīkh*, this being the method of confirmative corroboration (*istikhrāj usūl*) by which these accounts are transformed, if their witnesses are trustworthy in other respects, into authoritative "fundamental" (*usūl*) texts (Nawawī, Marçais tr. [bib. no. 1731], f. 59a).

c) *Haqā'iq al-tafsīr*. This valuable work, in which Qur'ānic verses are commented upon by maxims of leading Sūfīs, contains 208 maxims of "al-Husayn," a prudent abbreviation for Hallāj. In his preface, Sulamī acknowledges having made use of previous attempts, those of Ja'far-b-M (= the imām) and of Ibn 'Atā' bequeathed to Abū 'Amr 'Alī Anmātī, a

---

[15] And not "Nīsābūrī" (an error in the 2nd edition of *Akhbār*, p. 108).

disciple of Nūrī. Anmāṭī, who was one of the masters of Fāris (Kalābādhī, *Ta'arruf*, 112),[16] communicated this *tafsīr* to Abū Bakr Bajalī (Ibn al-Jawzī, *Talbīs*, 354; Qushayrī, 57, 119), who transmitted it to Sulamī, who refers at least four times to Bajalī in his own *tafsīr*. Harawī describes the *Kitāb fī fahm al-Qur'ān* of Ibn 'Atā' for us as an allegorical commentary of the Qur'ānic text from beginning to end.[17] Now, we have two quotations proving that Ibn 'Atā' quoted Hallāj during his lifetime, and the second of these is found in no. 19 of Sulamī. It is possible therefore that many of the quotations from "al-Husayn" in Sulamī go back to Ibn 'Atā'. On the other hand, although Sulamī says nothing about them, his *tafsīr* had other, more recent written sources; his nos. 27 and 147 dealing with Hallāj's execution (cf. his *Ta'rīkh*, no. 22) must be restored to the *Ta'rīkh* of Abū Bakr Bajalī. Among other recent authors whom he mentions, two of them must be retained here as sources of Hallājian maxims: first, Fāris, the well-known Hallājian (d. around 345), who refers expressly to "al-Husayn" (= Hallāj) in no. 130 (cf. no. 75); then, one of his precursors, whom Fāris seems to contradict in places in terms of the meaning to be given to certain sayings of "al-Husayn" (no. 193; cf. p. 813, n. 6), Abū Bakr M-b-Mūsā Wāsiṭī (d. 331, Marw), the author of *Hāmīm al-qidam*. Sulamī appears to quote Wāsiṭī, even more than Fāris, from a continuous *tafsīr*, perhaps due to one of their disciples, Qāsim Sayyārī. Sulamī even quotes a much more recent Hallājian, Nas-rābādhī (no. 37, 'Attār II, 316).

The *tafsīr* of Sulamī, attacked violently by Wāhidī, Ibn al-Jawzī, and Dhahabī, and defended by Ghazālī (*Ladunnīya*), is cited here and there particularly for its Hallājian texts. Bīrūnī (*Hind*, 43) quotes from no. 11. Qushayrī (*Risāla* III, 53; IV, 49, 94) nos. 182, 60,[18] 14; 'Attār (*Tadhk.* II, 139 and app. 86) nos. 160, 182, 184, 199; Suhrawardī Baghdādī ('*Awārif* I, 74; II, 235) nos. 169, 184; Ibn 'Arabī (*Fut.* II, 139) no. 118; Jildakī, no. 119; "*Geniza*," no. 61; Sārī 'Abdallāh Çelebī (*Sherhé Mesnevī* II, 220, 296, 308; III, 8-9, 423) nos. 155, 43, 175, 130, 197.

Since most of the thirty-two Hallājian maxims that the *tafsīr* of Baqlī adds to those from the *tafsīr* of Sulamī must have come from a more complete ms. of this *tafsīr*, there are, in sum, 282 doctrinal pieces (out of 375) that this single source has preserved for us.

One feature will demonstrate the complexity of sources used by Sulamī; namely, the number of Hallājian pieces (at least six) of which he

---

[16] On Anmāṭī, cf. Khatīb XII, 73; Qushayrī, 57, 60.

[17] Ivanow, *JASB* XVIII, 393.

[18] Qushayrī gives an *isnād* for this no. 60 via M-b-A Isfahānī (d. 349? Khatīb I, 270).

gives us *two* (sometimes three) parallel recensions: nos. 47-93, 17-49 (cf. 204), 41-57, 110-117-150, 146-151, 51-163, 52-207, 175-193 (and *Tab.* 21), 168-173, 41-42 (and 57-152), Baqlī 31-32.

We have published these 208 numbers in the appendix of our *Essai*, pp. 359-412.

d) *Other Works*. In the *Jawāmi' adab al-sūfīya* (published ap. *Essai*, app. pp. 427-429), Sulamī gives eight maxims of Hallāj, three of which (nos. 2, 6, 7) are introduced by the clausal "*hukiya*," which may refer in terms of source to the *Hikāyāt* of Ja'far Khuldī. No. 7 = *tafsīr* no. 122.

The *Usūl al-malāmatīya* provide us with another Hallājian piece (*Essai*, p. 430).

3. Abū'l-Hasan 'Alī-b-M Daylamī

Mystic, author of the oldest manual on pure love in Arabic, *Kitāb 'atf al-alif al-ma'lūf 'alā'l-lām al-ma'tūf*, which has been studied by Ritter,[19] and whose title was taken over from Hallāj,[20] Daylamī (b. 352, d. around 415) also wrote *Tarjamat Ibn Khafīf*, a biography of a master whom he had known when young, the data for which must have been given him by Abū Ahmad Saghīr Hasan-b-'Alī Shīrāzī (315, d. 385), who was close to Ibn Khafīf from 336 to 371. This *Tarjama*, written in the *mashyakha* form, examines one by one, according to country, the many masters of Ibn Khafīf.[21] And in Section VI ('Irāq), Hallāj is fourth ahead of Shiblī (fifth) and Ibn Zīzī (sixth). Daylamī first gives the long account of Ibn Khafīf's visit to [Hallāj's] prison; next, those of his fast in the *sahn* of Mecca, of his altercation in Isfahan with 'Alī-b-Sahl, and of his departure for India; he recalls that Ibn Khafīf regarded him as a *muwahhid*, but he condemned his tercet "*Subhāna*." The seventh and final account reports the dream of Abū'l-Yamān in Wasit. Along with these seven pieces, only three of which are unfavorable, Daylamī gives two others: one in the biography of Nahrajūrī (Section IV, 6th shaykh), concerning the miracle of the cookie; the other in the biography of 'Umar-b-Shallūya (Section VI, 7th) concerning the daughter of Hallāj. He must have also given a short account of the "*Nadīmī*" quatrain and the visit to Jerusalem.

A new version in more modern Persian of this life of Ibn Khafīf was

---

[19] Ritter, *DI*, 1933, 91; Walzer, *JRAS*, 1939, p. 407; this is the Tüb. Weisw. ms. 81. Cf. excerpts of *K. 'Atf* in *Mélanges Maréchal*, Vol. II.

[20] No. [. . .] of the catalogue of his works.

[21] Classification of Section IV (Shiraz): 4th, Shaykh Abū 'Alī Wāriji (= Awāriji); 5th, A Hy Darrāj; 6th, Nahrajūrī; 7th, Abū 'Amr Zajjājī; 8th, Abū Bakr Fuwatī; 9th, 'Alī-b-'Īsā; Section V, Section VI ('Irāq): 1st, Ruwaym; 2nd, Ibn 'Atā'; 3rd, Jurayrī; 4th, Hallāj; 5th, Shiblī; 6th, Ibn Zīzī; 7th, Ibn Shallūya; 8th, Muzayīn (?). Cf. *Tarā'iq* II, 212-223.

given by Yahyā ibn Junayd (d. 840).[22] Baqlī, in his *Mantiq* (in Arabic) and in his *Shathīyāt* (in Persian), reproduced (in abridged form) 9 (of 11) of the Hallājian texts of Daylamī.[23]

4. Abū ʿAA M-b-ʿAA-b-ʿUA ibn Bākūyā Shīrāzī

Editor of the notebooks of "stories of saints" and the poet ("Bābā Kūhī"), d. 428, rather than 442. In his *Kitāb bidāyat ḥāl al-Hallāj wa nihāyatuhu*, "How Hallāj began and how he ended," he gave the first life of Hallāj with commentary. This treatise, consisting of 21 pericopes, exists in a Zāhirīya (Damascus) ms., catalogue p. 30, *Majmū*ʿ 81, *Risāla* VII, in which it was discovered for L. Massignon by Shaykh Amīn Sādiq al-Mālih, the *nassākh* and published ap. *Quatre Textes*, 1914, text (III = pp. 29-47) and introduction (pp. 13-17). Completed in (A.H.) 426, this text is authenticated in this ms. by an important *samāʿ*, analyzed later [in this book]. The treatise was used by Khatīb almost immediately (nos. 1a, 9b, 15, 14, 4, 5, 11, 21, 16, 18, 7) and by Dhahabī much later (*Ta'rīkh*, s. a. 309: nos. 1a, 1b-c, 2, 7, 9a, 10, 16, 17-19). In the seventeenth century, in the Hanbalite circles of Damascus, canonical transmission of this text was still authorized. Its *isnād* went back via Zaynab Kamālīya (646, d. 740), ʿAjība Bāqadārīya (554, d. 647), Ibn Muqarrab (d. 563), Turūrī (d. 500), and Ibn Nāsir (d. 477) to the learned Moroccan author from Sus (Rūdhānī, d. 1093, *Silat al-khalaf*, Paris ms. 4470, f. 43b), who seems to be linked to it via ʿĀyīsha Umm ʿAA-bt-M ibn ʿAbd al-Hādī (b. 723, d. 816), a famous shaykha and a relative of our copyist.

a. Sources of the Bidāya. The following are the sources used by Ibn Bākūyā for the twenty-one paragraphs of the *Bidāya*, which is the first monographic treatise on Hallāj, though it is only the fourth biographical notice on him, following those of Bajalī (8 paragraphs), Sulamī (21), and Daylamī (9 or 11).

—Nine paragraphs are taken from the *Ta'rīkh* of Sulamī, three verbatim (B8 = S2, B9a = S5, B17 = S9, B2 = S24), three established thanks to new *isnāds* (B3 = S1 = Wasit; B14 = S4 = India; B4 = S10 = anathema from Makkī), the last (B4) even being completed by three other hostile testimonies recopied from AZ Tabarī (B5, 6, 7).

—Seven are taken from Daylamī's *Tarjamat Ibn Khafīf* (B9b, 10-14, 18).

—This leaves five numbers, three of which are not found elsewhere

---

[22] Berlin Or. ms. 303, cf. our *Recueil*, pp. 81-83.
[23] *Mantiq*, ff. 7b-9a.

(B16, 20, 21); one may come from Daylamī (B15 = *Akhbār* 69) and one appears in an altered recension, ap. *Akhbār* 18 (Taymūr ms.).

—Lastly, paragraph no. 1 of the treatise, which is the most carefully fashioned of its main pieces, is presented under awkward critical conditions as direct testimony provided Ibn Bākūyā by a son of Hallāj, Hamd, who confesses having "only half understood his father"; he mentions neither his brothers Sulaymān and Mansūr nor his sister, is silent about the years 297-307 of his father's life (hence, about the trial of 301), and compresses inordinately the chronology of his life. If this Hamd really existed and lived long enough to enable Ibn Bākūyā to have him authenticate the whole of paragraph no. 1 in Tustar, the fact is that this no. 1 deals with three matters: [Hallāj's] life up to the denunciation "to Mu'tadid"; the protection [of him] by the *hājib* N Qushūrī since the time of his polemics and during his imprisonment; his vigil and the day of his execution. If, in the case of the first two, we do not know how their data was juxtaposed, in the case of the third, we have external proof that Ibn Bākūyā, without any scruple, put the following seven separate earlier testimonies in the mouth of Hamd as a direct and continuous account: the prayer of the vigil (*rāwī*: Ibn al-Haddād = Sulamī, *Ta'rīkh*, no. 14), *wasīya* (with his anonymous "son," given in a completely different form, ap. Harawī, based on Ibn Bākūyā, who had received it from Ahmad Chishtī: with his *Khādim* = Sulamī, *Ta'rīkh*, no. 22), the *Nadīmī* quatrain (Sulamī, *ibid*.; *Akhbār*, nos. 16 and 5), five hundred lashes of the whip, the invocation "*Ilāhīya . . . fika*" (Sulamī, *Ta'rīkh*, no. 17), the insult from Shiblī (quoting Qur'ān 15:70 = Sulamī, *Ta'rīkh*, no. 8, the end), and, lastly, a description of the end of the execution (attributed to Shiblī, ap. *Akhbār*, no. 17), a description known previously from Khargūshī (d. 405: he quotes "*ahwanuhu mā tarā*"). It should be noted that [this description] shifts the saying "*Hasb al-wājid*," which is put before "*nadīmī*" in the one published before 355 by Bajalī (based on Abū'l-'Abbās Razzāz, brother of Ibn Fātik). This no. 1 uses Hamd to endorse an attempt at a concordance, which would become the "vulgate."

The text of the *Bidāya*, as I published it in 1914, is, as its *isnād* proves, the (A.H.) 553 ms., and ends with its colophon, enlarged from the *samā'* of a ms. inscribed in 554 on this 553 ms. The original ms., moreover, gives two long annotations concerning its transmission: one at the beginning, the other at the end.

The first begins with the date of our ms. and the name of its copyist, proceeds with a note by Ibn Muflih, the date of Ibn Bākūyā's death, the genealogy of the 553 ms., a *samā'* (Misrī), an *ijāza* (Ibn al-Muhibb), the *waqf* emblem (Diyā'īya) of our ms., the attestation of its reading by Z Kamālīya and Ibn al-Muhibb, and of its reading by the disciples of the latter to our copyist.

The second has the *samā'* of two later copies, those of 617 and 636, follow the *samā'* of the 554 ms.

The history of consultations of our ms. can be summarized as follows: it was read on 21 *Jumāda* II 897 (= 1495) by Yūsuf ibn 'Abd al-Hādī, a well-known Hanbalite from Damascus, assisted by his wife, Būlbūl-bt-'AA and their two sons, Badr al-Dīn H and 'Abd al-Hādī.[24] Copied by him on a ms. "waqfed" in the Diyā'īya *madrasa* of Damascus, founded in Salihiya on the slope of the Qasiyun to the east of Jami' Muzaffarī by the learned Hanbalite Diyā' al-Dīn M-b-'AW Sa'dī Maqdisī (567, d. 643) for traditionists and foreign *fuqarā'*.[25] This fundamental ms., dated 638,[26] was authenticated by the reading that Zaynab-bt-Kamāl A-b-'Abd al-Rahīm Maqdīsīya (646, d. 740) gave it, as trustee of the canonical oral tradition of the text of the *Bidāya*,[27] to the *mutawallī* of the *waqf*, M-b-'AA ibn al-Muhibb Sa'dī (d. 788) on 5 *Sha'bān* 732 (May 2, 1332). The latter, a well-known Hanbalite, relative of the founder of the Diyā'īya, and disciple of Ibn Taymīya, had had it read to another Hanbalite, AB ibn Muflih (d. 763), who was pro-Hallāj, for he characterized this text as *"mubārak."*

The 638 copy was established by the Hanbalite shaykh, AH 'Alī-b-A'AA ibn al-Muqayīr, editor of Ibn 'Aqīl (563, d. in Cairo 643), and provided with an *ijāza* (indirect) from Ibn Muqarrab (d. 563) for Vizir Bahā"l-Dīn A Bayzānī, son of the famous Qādī al-Fādil, his grandsons 'AR and H-b-Qīrā'an (?), on a 617 copy.

The 617 copy was established by Shaykh AH 'Alī-b-'A Wahhāb-'Alī ibn al-Khadir Qurashī Zubayrī (provided with an *ijāza* from Ibn Muqarrab) for AB M-b-Ismā'īl-b-'AA-b-'A Muhsin-b-A ibn al-Humām Ansārī Misrī (and for his father) with the assistance of AM 'AR-b-'Umar-

---

[24] *Nā'ib* of the qādī, like his father (d. 880), born in 840, alive in 896 (Sakhāwī, *Daw'* [bib. no. 670-b], X, 308; *UV* [?], 92), master of the historian Shams M-b-Tūlūn, whom he initiated into the *tarīqa* Muhāsibīya (Zabīdī, *'Iqd* [bib. no. 862-b], 76), a descendant through his grandfather, Shihāb A-b-H-b-A-b-'Abd al-Hādī ibn Qudāma Maqdisī (born 767, died 856), of the famous Maqdisīya Jamma'illya family, a Hanbalite family from around Nablus which had come to Damascus in the sixth century.

[25] 'Ulaymī, *Anīs*, Paris ms. 5912, f. 226b; 'Akarī [bib. no. 830-a], V, 224.

[26] See Paris ms. Turkish Supplement 983; Blochet catalogue, Marceau, p. 305.

[27] I suspect that this Zaynab was trained, not only in the convent for women in Damascus called the Ribāt Safīya, which existed as early as 633 (cf. 'Ulaymī, ms. p. 5912, ff. 258a, 296a [there were four other such convents]), but also in the famous convent for women in Baghdad, the Dār al-Falak, which still existed in 725 (Fuw[atī], . . .] 934).

b-Shibāb ibn Sinjāba (?) Harrānī, A ʿAmr ʿUthmān-b-M ibn al-Hājib Mansūr Amīnī and of the son of his sister, M-b-Lū'lū-b-ʿAA Muʿaytī, 21 Qaʿda 617 in the grand mosque of Damascus; based on the 554 copy. The 554 copy had been entrusted by the uncle of the above-mentioned Ibn al-Khadir, ʿUmar-b-ʿAlī,[28] in Qaʿda 554, to Shaykh A Hy ʿAlī-b-A-B-b-ʿAlī Baghdādī: as deriving from the basic copy that he had established himself on 13 Hijja 553 (January 5, 1159) in the Haram of Mecca, from the dictation of Ahmad ibn Muqarrab Sayrafī Karkhī (480, d. 563):[29] in five copies for five hearers of note: M-b-ʿAR-b-M Masʿūdī Fanjdīhī (d. 584, commentary on Harīrī), Mahmūd-b-M Abīwardī, ʿAlī-b-M-b-A Tāhir Tarqī, AQ ʿAA-b-M-b-A Mansūr Tūsī and A Maʿālī-b-ʿAA Bādhī.

The 553 copy reproduced the text received by Ibn Muqarrab on 29 Qaʿda 493 (at age 13) from Mubārak-b-ʿAbd al-Jabbār Tuyūrī (b. 411, d. 500), as having been transmitted orally to him by A Saʿīd Masʿūd-b-Nāsir-b-A Zayd-b-A-b-M-b-Ism Sijistānī (d. 477), a direct rāwī of the original communicated to him by the author, Ibn Bākūyā, in 426.[30]

One of the two lost works by Hujwīrī (d. 475) on Hallāj, Kitāb minhāj der ibtidā' ve intihā'-i Hallāj, may have been a Persian translation of the Bidāya (Kashf, ed. p. 192; tr., p. 153).

b. Transmission of the Bidāya. It was in 426, in Nishapur, that Ibn Bākūyā gave the ijāza of the Bidāya to Masʿūd Sijzī (he seems to have been the only one to have had it explicitly). The Hanafites, persecuted from 413 to 421, now had their revenge (with the Karrāmī raʾīs of the municipality being AB ibn Mamshādh, 398-410, 421), not only against the Shāfiʿites, but also against Sūfīs (Ibn Abī'l-Khayr)—thanks to the Hanafite grand qādī, Abū'l-ʿAlā' Sāʿid-b-M Ustuwāʾī (393-98, 421, d. 431), founder of an actual dynasty of Hanafite qādīs in Nishapur that lasted until 554.

It was probably at the request of Masʿūd Sijzī, an intelligent mind and

---

[28] ʿUmar ibn al-Khadir died in 575, as qādī of the Harīm, in Baghdad. In fact, he had come there on 13 Jumāda I 553, and had settled there in close association with the leading Hanbalites, Farrā' (d. 558), Kilānī, Ibn al-Muqarrab, Ibn al-Battī, and A Najīb Suhrawardī. He lived there on intimate terms with the Banū al-Muslima, "collecting with them and for them readings of Hanbalite isnāds" (Ibn al-Dubaythī [bib. no. 422-a], ms. 5922, f. 196a, Ibn al-Najjār [bib. no. 430-a], 2131, f. 193a).

[29] Ibn Muqarrab, a Hanbalite and a mystic, trained by Hy Naʿʿālī (d. 493), preacher in Karkh, was the master of one of the B. Muslima, the Sūfī Hy-b-ʿAlī (551, d. 635), and of A Fath M-b-ʿA Bāqī ibn al-Battī (d. 564), rāwī of the Bahja of Ibn Jahdam.

[30] Since no date is given, it seems, in fact, that this is the asl (original ms. of 426) that Masʿūd bequeathed to Tuyūrī with ijāza (without dictating a new copy to him).

a critical historian of hadīth, that Ibn Bākūyā extracted from his large collection of *Hikāyāt al-sālihīn*[31] this small critical and objective dossier, giving the pros and cons of a difficult case, omitting the name of Sulamī (his main source, regarded as insufficiently sure), and going back directly to Ibn Khafīf, a surer Ash'arite *isnād*, for Mas'ūd.

—*A Sa'd Mas'ūd-b-Nāsir-b-A Zayd-b-A-b-M-b-Ism Sijzī*, born around 400, d. in 477, studied hadīth in Sijistan ('Alī-b-Sarī'), in Herat (M-b-'AR Dabbās), in Baghdad (Sarī' Fāsī, M-b-Ghaylān), in Nishapur (Ibn Hassān Rab'ī M-b-A Muzakkī, A Hafs-b-Masrūr), in Isfahan (Ibn Rabadha, d. 440), and in Wasit (A-b-Muzaffar).[32] His main masters appear to have been the following: in Nishapur, 'Abdawī (d. 417) and Ism-b-A Hīrī (d. 430), two *rāwīs* of Sulamī; in Baghdad, Abū Tālib M-b-Ghaylān Hamadhānī (346, d. 440), *rāwī* of AB Shāfi'ī (260, d. 354): the eleven *juz'* of the *Ghaylānīyāt*, and AM H-b-AT Khallāl (352, d. 439).[33]

Mas'ūd gained attention when very young, and had masters older than he as his *rāwīs*, such as M-b-'Alī Sāhilī Sūrī (382, d. 441 in Baghdad, where he had been since 418) and his friend Khatīb (391, d. 463);[34] next, M-b-'Abd al-Wāhid Daqqāq, 'Abd al-Muhassin Shīhī (401, d. 489; *Talbīs*, 214), AF M-b-T Maqdisī (Sam'ānī 2054), and especially Mubārak Tuyūrī (411, d. 500), who received from him, as had Khatīb, the *ijāza* for the *Bidāya*.

Vizir Nizām al-Mulk built a *ribāt* for him (in Bayhaq, then Tus: where Ghazālī must have met him), to study hadīth with him until his death. Zāhir Shahāmī (d. 538) accused him of leaning toward Qadarism (cf. Ibn 'Aqīl).

—*Abū'l Hy Mubārak-b-'A Jabbār Sayrafī Tuyūrī*, born in 411, died in 500,[35] was an esteemed Hanbalite traditionist (attacked by Mu'tamin Sijzī, without success). Trained by A 'Alī H-b-Shādhān (d. 435),[36] H-

---

[31] Quoted by name by 'AA-M-Q-A-Baqlī Yamanī (ms. Q 'A. M. Çelebi, 33). Source of *Talbīs*, 124, 200, 262, 209, 223, 263, 321, 333, 335, 344, 348, 360, 365, 367 (transmitted by Abū Sa'd 'Alī-b-'AA Sādiq Hīrī), 368, 370-372, 380-383, 412.

[32] *Lisān al-mīzān* VI, 27; 'Akarī, s.a. 477; Ibn Qudāma, *Tawwābīn*, ms. P. 1384, f. 132b; Dhahabī, *Huffāz* III, 27 (Hyderabad edition IV, 15; cf. III, 297); Suyūtī, *Huffāz* [bib. no. 530-h], ms. P. [. . .], f. 247b, *Masāri'* [?], 100.

[33] AM Khallāl is used by the *Tabaqāt* of Ibn al-Farrā', 114, 136, 138, 139. AB Shāfi'ī had three disciples: Dāraqutnī, 'Umar-b-Shāhīn, and Ibn Ghaylān.

[34] Khatīb (VIII, 227) quotes him.

[35] *Lisān al-mīzān* V, 9; *Tawwābīn*, ff. 102b, 130a, 132b; *Talbīs*, 39, 64, 205, 229, 239, 244, 246, 247, 302, 303, 310, 317, 322, 356. *Samā'* of the Zah. ms. of the *Bahja*. 'Akarī, s.n. quoted; Ibn al-Farrā', Tab., 138.

[36] Pupil of his father, d. 384, of his *'amm* Ibn Hayyawayh, master of Qādī M-b-'Umar Dāwūd.

b-'Alī Tanājīrī (350, d. 439), A M Khallāl (d. 439), Azajī (d. 444), Ibr. b-
'Umar Barmākī (d. 445), Sūrī, AT M-b-'Alī 'Ushshārī (366, d. 451: a
Sālimīyan and Hallājian Hanbalite), a friend of Yahyā-b-Manda (d. 511),
Mubārak Tuyūrī was not only a Sālimīyan (he transmitted the *Bahja* of
Ibn Jahdam via Azajī-Baladī in 492), but also a Hallājian. He was, in fact,
the master of AB ibn 'Arabī Ishbīlī and of two disciples of Ibn 'Aqīl, 'AA
Wāsitī (d. 544), and especially Sālih-b-Shāfi'ī Jīlī: a friend, son, and father
of friends who helped 'Ukbarī to save, along with his manuscripts, his
apologia of Hallāj. He transmitted the *ijāza* of the *Bidāya* to Ibn Muqarrab in 493.

Tuyūrī's main *rāwīs* were the following: the *muqri'* AB Makī-b-A Jīlī
(d. 514), 'A Wahhāb-b-Mubārak Anmātī, Qādī A Hy M-b-M ibn al-
Farrā' (d. 526), Mawhūd Jawāliqī (d. 540), also a Hanbalite, *imām* and
spiritual advisor to Caliph Muqtafī (d. 555); 'Alī-b-A Yazdī (d. 551: a
Shāfi'ite), Qays Suwayqī (d. 562), Sa'īd Dāraquzzī (d. 554), his brother
A-b-'A Jabbār Tuyūrī (434, d. 517: a pupil of the Sālimī Abū 'Alī
Ahwāzī). He also trained 'Abd al-Rahīm Hulwānī, an old friend of the
Sam'ānī, AN ibn Mākūlā, AB M-b-A ibn Khādiba (d. 489), and espe-
cially Abū Tāhir Silafī (475, d. 576), *rāwī* of his "Hundred *Tuyūrīyāt*" and
AR-b-M Qazzāz (455, d. 535, direct *rāwī* of Khatīb).

—*AB Ahmad-b-Muqarrab-b-Hy Karkhī*, born in 480, died in 563, a
Hanbalite, *qāri'* and *muhaddith*.[37] In the *qirā'a* of Hamza, he was the pupil
of A-b-'Alī Sawwār (d. 496) and the master (*sic*) of A Katīf-b-M Qubaytī
(563, d. 634) and of Anjab Hammāmī (554, d. 635) to whom M-b-'A
Bāqī Baltī (d. 564) transmitted the *Bahja* of Ibn Jahdam (Rūdānī [bib. no.
834-a], f. 44a); master of Hajjār (623, d. 730). Master also of the last Ibn
al-Muslima (d. 639) and of AB Mu'izz (d. 638) with Ibn al-Baltī (master
of the son of Ibn Sukayna, d. 635). In hadīth, he was the pupil of the
naqīb-qādī-vizir Tarrād Zaynabī (d. 491) and of Hy-b-A Na'ālī (d. 493).

It was Ibn Muqarrab who in 553, in the very enclosure of the Ka'ba,
gave six dictations of the *Bidāyat al-Hallāj*, thereby giving six *ijāzas* for it
to the following: 'Umar-b-'Alī-b-Khadir Zubayrī Dimishqī, M-b-'AR
Mas'ūdī Penjdīhī, Mahmūd-b-M Abiwardī, 'Alī-b-M-b-Abī Tāhir
Tarqī, AQ 'AA-b-M-b-Abī Mansūr Tūsī, and Abū'l-Ma'ālī-b-'AA
Bādhī. He must have transmitted it in a spirit of reverence for the mem-
ory of Hallāj, since, under his dictation in the *samā'*, 'Umar-b-'Alī-b-
Khadir followed the name of Hallāj with the "*tarahhum*" formula. An

---

[37] Ibn al-Jazarī [bib. no. 2104-a], II, 25, 96; 'Akarī, s.a. 563; Ibn Qudāma, *Tawwābīn*, f.
108a.

ijāza also to 'Ajība Bāqadārīya (554, d. 647) through his father, M-b-A Ghālib (d. 575).

—*'Umar-b-'Alī-b-Khadir Zubayrī Dimishqī*, born in 525, died in 575, had come precisely[38] in 533 from Damascus to Baghdad, where he resided thereafter as a guest of the B. al-Muslima vizirial family (that of the Hallājian vizir), studying hadīth there. Qādī of the Harīm in 566, diplomatic representative in 567 to Aleppo (to Amīr Zengi), he was interred at Shuniz (Ruwaym bridge). A pupil of Yāqūt Tūmī in Damascus, and of Kīlānī, Qādī Farrā' (d. 560), Ibn al-Battī, and Abū'l-Waqt Sijzī in Baghdad, he was a member of the Suhrawardian order (his *mashyakha* included eight hundred names). Through his brother, 'Abd al-Wahhāb, and his niece, Karīma (d. 641; *rāwiya* of *Luma'* with Abū'l-Waqt and 'Alī, son of Ibn al-Jawzī), both residents of Damascus, and with his nephew, 'Alī-b-'A Wahhāb, guardian of an authenticated copy, the *Bidāya* was transmitted thereafter in the Hanbalite circles of Damascus. 'Umar also gave the *ijāza* in 557 to a Baghdadian shaykh, A Hy 'Alī-b-AB-b-'Alī (ms. P. 2131). In 638, the 553 copy, preserved today in the Zāhirīya in its authenticated form established by Yūsuf-b-'Abd al-Hādī-b-Qudāma Maqdisī in 897, was "waqfed" in the Diyā' of Damascus by its founder, the famous Hanbalite *muhaddith* M-b-'AW Sa'dī Maqdisī (567, d. 643: author of a monograph on the Maqādisa of Nablus who emigrated to Damascus), with its authenticating *samā'* by Shaykha 'Ajība Bāqadārīya (554, d. 647), from Baghdad.

—*Zaynab-bt-Kamāl Maqdīsīya* (646, d. 740) *rāwiya* (at age ten) of 'Ajība, was, in another connection, at the source of the *samā'* of the *Bidāya* obtained by Rūdānī (d. 1093/1682) (cf. *Sila*, ms. P. 4470, f. 43b) when he went to Damascus. The *Bidāya*, whose role in preserving the memory of Hallāj had come to an end[39] with the appearance of the *Akhbār* among the people of hadīth (Ibn 'Aqīl, Ibn al-Qassās, popularized by Silafī), endured in this way among the Muqādisa Hanbalite *muhaddiths* of Baghdad. We have other indications: among the Maqādisa B.Qudāma, the canonist Muwaffaq D M ibn Qudāma (541, d. 620), *rāwī* of Ibn Muqarrab, a *qādirī*, wrote a *radd* against Ibn 'Aqīl, possibly concerning Hallāj (M. Jawād's theory; to be verified by Asaf ms. II, 1720, 13, 7 = Br. S. I, 689); next, his great-grand-nephew, Yf-b-'Abd al-Hādī, copying the *Bidāya* in 897, and his grand-niece, 'Āyisha-bt-M-b-'Abd al-Hādī (723, d. 816), transmitting the Hallājian treatise of Ibn 'Aqīl (via Hajjār, d. 730); the

---

[38] Ibn al-Dubaythī, ms. 5922, f. 196a; Ibn al-Najjār, ms. 2131, f. 113; 'Akarī, s.a. 575.
[39] Around 715, Dhahabī found the *Bidāya* with difficulty (in Damascus).

fact that a Maqdisī Sa'dī incorporated the *Bidāya* into his *waqf* in 638, and that another Maqdisī of the emigration, the pious shaykh Ghānim-b-'Alī (d. 631: interred in Qāsiyūn, in the *zāwiya* of his friend 'AA Urmawī, d. 631) had as his grandson, 'Izz 'A Salām-b-A-b-Ghānim Maqdisī (d. 678), the author of interesting texts glorifying the martyrdom of Hallāj (that must not be attributed to his illustrious Shāfi'ite homonym who died in 662). We do not know if the Hallājīya *zāwiya*, on which we have a text with an epigraph dated 828, should be linked to this Hallājian milieu of Damascus.[40]

After Zaynab (d. 740), the catalogue of titles of his *samā'* (with neither their full contents nor the texts!) passed by *ijāza* from 'Izz-b-Jamā'a (694, d. 767) to Ibn al-Jazarī (751, d. 833). Quraysh Basīr, Nūr 'Alī Qarāfī, Zak Ansārī (d. 926), Shamr M-b-A Ramlī (d. 1004), A-b-M Khafajī (980, d. 1069) and 'Alī Ujhūrī (975, d. 1066), who dictated it to Rūdānī (ms. P. 4470, the beginning).

5. Abū Bakr A-b-'Alī-b-Thābit Khatīb Baghdādī

Traditionist and historian, at first Hanbalite, later Shāfi'ite (391, d. 463), wrote in his *Ta'rīkh Baghdād*, or Dictionary of Traditionists of Baghdad, s.v. Husayn-b-Mansūr, the best condensed biography of Hallāj (VIII, 112-141). His 54 pericopes (no. 54, very long = account by Ibn Zanjī, published ap. *Quatre Textes*, 1914, pp. 1-8, no. 1-14) can be broken down as follows: 20 excerpts from the *Ta'rīkh al-Sūfīya* of Sulamī (= nos. 1, 3, 15, 20-26, 38-39, 42, 45-48, 50-52; published ap. *Quatre Textes*, 1914, II, 9-12, no. 17-25); 11 excerpts from the *Bidāya* of Ibn Bakūyā (= nos. 2, 16-17, 19, 27-28, 33-35, 40-41); [. . .] from the *Nishwār* of Tanūkhī (= nos. 18, 29-32, 54); 4 from the *Riwāyāt* of Qannād (= nos. 12-14; and 10, cf. ms. P. 3346, margin of f. 77b); 2 from the *Hikāyāt* of Khuldī (= nos. 9 [not omitted] and 11); one excerpt from Ibn Farrukhān Dūrī, from Ibn Jahdam (*Bahja*), from Nasawī (*Ta'rīkh*) and from Khutabī (*Ta'rīkh*), nos. 5, 6, 36, and 37. There remain six—nos. 4 (Fāris), 7-8 (A Hātim Tabarī, Sūfī), 43 (Sūrī), 44 (Abū'l-'Alā' Wāsitī) and 49 (Ibn Hayyawayh), especially the last three—which may, in fact, be depicting personal information about the author. Then two reflections (in no. 1, on the *Ghulāt*, no. [. . .] on Ibn Ghālib). And, finally, the prologue (no. 53) to the account by Ibn Zanjī, which raises several questions (which we shall deal with later).

His Monograph. Khatīb's documentation on Hallāj[41] seems to have

---

[40] *Recueil*, pp. 69-70.
[41] *Ta'rīkh Baghdād* VIII, 112-141. The authorized transmission of Khatīb's *Ta'rīkh*

taken form gradually: literary and anecdotal texts taken, from before 420, from hostile sources, such as 'Alī-b-Muhassin Tanūkhī[42] and the other disciples of M ibn Hayyawayh Khazzāz[43] (d. 382): 'UA Sayrafī,[44] AM H Jawharī,[45] Abū'l-'Alā' Wāsitī;[46] next, ingenuous poetic quotations from favorable *rāwīs*, such as A B Ardastānī[47] (d. 427), Ridwān Dīnawārī[48] (d. 426), M-b-H Ahwāzī[49] (d. 428), M-b-'Īsā Bazzāz[50] (d. 430), 'Abd al-Ghaffār Urmawī[51] (d. 433), going back particularly to the work of Qannād, followed by two excerpts from chroniclers, one from Khutabī via Ibrāhīm-b-Makhlad[52] (325, d. 410), the other from Nasawī, via his master M-b-'Alī Sūrī[53] (with one hostile anecdote), taken notice of very early (from before 410 and as early as 418 respectively). In 423, or as far back as 415, Khatīb had some important texts of Sulamī on Hallāj dictated to him by Ism Hīrī[54] (361, d. 430), a learned *qāri'* from whom Ibn Manda and Harawī received hadīths without transmitting them; and between 428 and 432 or thereabouts, Mas'ūd-b-Nāsir Sijistānī (d. 427), who also had known Hīrī, gave Khatīb the *ijāza* for the Hallāj monograph of Ibn Bākūyā, the *Bidāya*,[55] which quite interested Khatīb in terms of its collection of references to Sulamī owed to seven important texts whose *ijāza* his Hanbalite master, Abū Tālib 'Ushshārī, obtained for him.[56] He drafted this essential notice, one which was painstakingly balanced and objective, containing the pros and cons, ending with Zanjī's account of the trial of 309, and inserted it into his *Ta'rīkh Baghdād* (VIII, 112-141).

It rests mainly on the *Bidāya* of Ibn Bākūyā (whom he called "Ibn Bakwā"), in the recension of Mas'ūd, of which he gives eight excerpts, corrected and completed by twenty excerpts from Sulamī, eleven deriving from Ism Hīrī, seven from AT 'Ushshārī, and two from AB Ardas-

---

Baghdād has the following ordinary *isnād*: A Mansūr 'AR-b-M Qazzāz (456, d. 535, master of Ibn al-Jawzī); A Yumn Zayd-b-H Kindī (520, d. 614); Yf-b-Yq ibn al-Mujāwir (d. 690: author of interesting historical notes on Arabia); A Hajjāj Mizzī (654, d. 742, author of *Tahdhīb al-kamāl*) (Rūdānī, 49, cf. 'Izz-b-Jamā'a, f. 77b).

[42] *Ta'rīkh Baghdād* VIII, 119, 122, 124, 133-141.
[43] Cf. *ibid.*, 116 and 131.   [44] *Ibid.*, 131.
[45] *Ibid.*, 116 (*dalāl*).   [46] *Ibid.*, 130, 131.
[47] *Ibid.*, 117, 131 (Qannād and Walīya: via Sulamī).
[48] *Ibid.*, 115, 116 (*Tahaqqaqtuka*: verse of Ibn 'Atā').
[49] *Ibid.*, 115 (verse of AH Tabarī).
[50] *Ibid.*, 114, 116 (Dūrī, Qannād).
[51] *Ibid.*, 117 (Qannād).
[52] *Ibid.*, 126.   [53] *Ibid.*, 130.
[54] *Ibid.*, 120, 121, 128, 132, 140.
[55] *Ibid.*, 112, 118, 120, 121, 125, 126, 129.
[56] *Ibid.*, 118, 120, 121, 128, 129, 131, 132.

tānī. And after ten short literary texts attributed to Azajī[57] (d. 444), Ibn Fadāla,[58] M. Ahwāzī,[59] Ridwān Dīnawārī, H. Jawharī, M-b-ʿĪsā Bazzāz, A Ghaffār Urmawī, ʿUA Sayrafī, and Abūʾl-ʿAlāʾ Wāsitī), the excerpts from the *Nishwār* of Tanūkhī (accusations of charlatanism and the trial of 309) authenticated by his son ʿAlī, there may be sixteen masters accountable for it (with Sūrī and Ibrāhīm-b-Makhlad).

Khatīb, still a Hanbalite[60] when he began his work, became a Shāfiʿite before he had finished it (he said nothing about the opinion of Ibn Surayj), probably following the tragic death of his friend, the Hallājian vizir Ibn al-Muslima (d. 450), in whose memory he was determined to insert it into his great work on the Baghdadian *muhaddithīn*, that is to say, the generations of Baghdadian witnesses to the Muslim faith.[61] Khatīb was therefore, in reality, an advocate of the orthodoxy of Hallāj.

—*Abūʾl-Wafāʾ* ʿAlī-b-ʿAqīl-b-M-b-ʿAqīl Zafarī, b. 432, d. 513, an eminent Hanbalite canonist and learned encyclopaedist, had written in his youth—and therefore under his patron Abū Mansūr ʿAbd al-Malik-b-M ibn Yūsuf (d. 460), a personal friend of Caliph Qāʾim—a treatise (*juzʾ*) *fī nusrat al-Hallāj*, "to defend Hallāj" (Dhahabī, s.a. 591 "Azajī"; and Ibn Rajab, *Tab. Hanb.*, s.v. Ibn ʿAqīl). Threatened with death in 461, he was forced to retract it publicly, though he did not disown it privately (cf. *infra*, §10). And his Hanbalite disciples authorized its canonical transmission down to the seventeenth century, assuming it is correct, that is, as M. Jawād, who believed he had refuted it, suggested, to regard this *nusra* as the *Risālat al-intisār* of Ibn ʿAqīl that Rūdānī received at that time in Damascus with an *isnād* going back via ʿĀyīsha Maqdisīya (723, d. 816), Abū Nasr M ibn al-Shīrāzī (d. 682), ʿAlī ibn al-Jawzī (d. 630) to Ibn

---

[57] *Ibid.*, 11 (letter to Ibn ʿAtāʾ).
[58] *Ibid.*, 114 (*wasīya* according to Fāris).
[59] Ibn ʿAtāʾ *ibid.* (V., 27, 28), by Ibn Shadhān.
[60] Ibn al-Jawzī, *Muntazam* VIII, 257.
[61] Khatīb was in Basra from 412 to 413; then in Nishapur until 415; next in Isfahan, Dinawar (415) and Hamadhan. Later he went to Kufa and Rayy, but returned to Baghdad prior to 420 and remained there until 445; then, Damascus and hajj (446); Baghdad (446-450); Damascus (450-457); Tyr and Quds (457-461); (Nasr Maqdisī III, 277) via Tripoli and Aleppo, returning to Baghdad (462-463). (Dh. *Huffāz* [bib. no. 530-h], III, 312; Subkī III, 15).
In Basra, nothing (Qādī Qāsim-b-J, d. 414); in Nishapur: Abū Hāzim (d. 417), Ism Hīrī (d. 434), AQ ʿAR Sarrāj (d. 418), pupils of Asamm. In Isfahan, Abū Nuʿaym (d. 430); in Dinawar, Ridwān (*ibid.* VIII, 432); in Hamadhan, Bazzāz (*ibid.* VIII, 114); in Rayy, Ibn Fadāl' (*ibid.* VIII, 114). In Baghdad: first Hanbalites: ʿUshshārī of Bab Harb, Ahwāzī (d. 428), Sūrī (d. 441: *ibid* III, 103); Banyānī (d. 425), Urmawī (426-431: *ibid.* IX, 117); Ardastānī (*ibid.* I, 417); then, around 435-440 (*ibid.* VI, 314) Masʿūd Sijzī, a semi-Ashʿarite who convinced him to write.

Marāhib Baradānī (499, d. 583). I do not believe that the *radd 'alā Ibn 'Aqīl* (Asaf ms.) by Muwaffaq 'AA ibn Qudāma (d. 620) was aimed at his Hallājism, for Ibn Qudāma was a *qādirī* (Rūdānī, f. 77; cf. Dhahabī ms. 1582, f. 260a). We have discussed elsewhere our evidence which led us to rediscover this *nusra* in ms. T (= Taymūr) of the *Akhbār al-Hallāj* (edited in 1914, ap. *Quatre Textes*, IV; and in 1957).

6. Ibn 'Aqīl

a. Formation of Ibn 'Aqīl. He himself said, in his *Kitāb al-funūn*, of 'Abd al-Malik-b-Yūsuf,[62] "it was he who raised and sheltered[63] me until I was able to teach (*halqa*), and who then obtained a chair for me, providing mats and stately clothes, according to the conventions practiced with students, until I was about twenty years old (= in the year 451)." Shaykh Ajall. Mansūr 'Abd al-Malik (395, d. 460) was from a leading family of old Baghdadian Hanbalite stock (sepulcher near that of Imām Ibn Hanbal). He was the trusted advisor and personal friend of Caliph Qāyim, the central figure behind charitable works in those troubled times[64] (he maintained the 'Adudī hospital after having rebuilt it; he had supported the Hanbalite 'Abd al-Samad Zāhid, and pensioned the preachers and Hāshimites). Khatīb and the historian M-b-Fadl Hamadhānī confirm the eulogies of Ibn 'Aqīl.[65]

A grandson on his mother's side of a man of wealth, A Hy A-b-'AA Sawsanjardī (325, d. 402) (grandfather also of the *muqri'* M-b-'Alī Hammāmī, d. 489),[66] 'Abd al-Malik gave his full attention to the formation of Ibn 'Aqīl, who throughout his life belonged to a small group of spiritual friends consisting of Vizir Ibn al-Muslima and his famous friend Abū Ishāq Shīrāzī, Princess Urjuwān, Amīr Ibn Mahlabān, and Hājib Mardushānī. A group whose sympathies were Hanbalite but not at all fanatic, pulled toward a moral reform of popular Sūfism and toward an orthodox use of Mu'tazilite theological inquiries. Caliph Qāyim was the real center of this group, of which Ibn 'Aqīl would continue to be a member, honored publicly with this title at court under Muqtadir and

---

[62] *Funūn* (534 ms., signed by Mubarak-b-Hy b-Mahmūd ms. P. 787, f. 267a; cf. M. Jawād, ap. *REI*, p. 193 [VIII, 285]), f. 235a.

[63] After 444, when he was forced to leave Bab al-Taq (pillaged by Ghazz) and his master Farrā' (Ibn al-Jawzī, *Muntazam* IX, 212).

[64] *Muntazam* IX, 213.

[65] Sibt ibn al-Jawzī, ms. P. 1606, ff. 114a, 191b; Khatīb X, 434.

[66] *Funūn*, f. 222b specifies "'Abd al-Malik-b-M Umawī, b. 339, d. 430," which is impossible; is this his son Muhammad, d. 448, rather than his brother, AHy 'Alī, b. 328, d. 415?

Mustazhir (whose *zahīr*, Majd al-Dīn Abū Tāhir Yf, pensioned and even sheltered Ibn 'Aqīl for the last fifteen years of his life, 498-513).

The following are the masters that he chose for Ibn 'Aqīl: in Qur'ān, 'AW-b-H ibn Shītā (370, d. 450),[67] in hadīth, Ibn Bishrān;[68] in Hanbalite law, Abū Tālib 'Ushshārī (366, d. 451),[69] and, of course, the head of the rite, Qādī Abū Ya'lā Farrā' (380, d. 458); in *wa'zat zuhd*, AB Dīnawarī, AH Qazwīnī (360, d. 442: Shāfi'ite and thaumaturgist), and Abū Tāhir 'Allāf (d. 442), these latter two disciples of the mystic Ibn Sam'ūn; in *lugha*, AM H-b-'Alī Jawharī Miqna'ī (363, d. 454) and, secretly, for readings in Mu'tazilism, Abū 'Alī M-b-A ibn al-Walīd (d. 478: a personal protégé of Abd al-Malik).

This list enables us to study the conditions under which Ibn 'Aqīl set about to write an apology rehabilitating and canonizing Hallāj: a work of youth to which he held fast, since after having been forced to retract it publicly (in 465), he managed to secure its clandestine transmission (cf. Ibn Marāhib, Azajī, and Ibn al-Ghazzāl). One might imagine that he first became interested in writing it out of the same scholarly curiosity that led him to write that huge two-hundred-volume social encyclopaedia, the *Kitāb al-funūn*. But the fact that he wrote it between 444 and 450, under the vizirate of a Hallājian, Ibn al-Muslima, and in the house of a friend of the Caliph, 'Abd al-Malik, forces us to conclude that this book must have coincided, not only with the movement to rehabilitate Hallāj indicated by the efforts of Qushayrī and AJ Saydalānī, but also with a political plan of moral restoration of the Islamic caliphate pursued by Vizir Ibn al-Muslima with such upper-level assistants as Mawardī and Abū Ishāq Shīrāzī. Hallāj had offered himself up voluntarily to death to seal by his execution the laws of the City, dying "accursed" for the common good of Muslims.[70] This is the lesson to be drawn from this tragic judicial case.

---

[67] *Masārī'*, 95.

[68] Farrā' (*Tab.*, 413) adds to him, as Ibn 'Aqīl's master in hadīth, A Hy (A-b-'Alī-b-Hy) Tawwazī, qādī and *muhtasib* (b. 364, d. 442); note that the latter was a *rāwī* of Shiblī (Kh. XIV, 394), that he lived at Darb Salīm next to Vizir Ibn al-Muslima, and that he is one of the main sources for the *Masārī' al-'Ushshāq* (pp. 18-21, 29, 30, 39, 64, 77, 80, 95, 118, 119, 125, 136, 142, 146, 158, 166, 181, 216, 217, 220, 225, 237, 239, 249, 250, 262, 316, 324, 329, 342, 347, 369, 396).

[69] *Masārī'*, 5. Importance of 'Ushshārī: of Bab Harb (Kh. II, 107). His *mashyakha* transmitted by M-b-Bāqī Ansārī (d. 535 = Qadr al-Māristān = hero of the pearl diver), 'Umar-b-Tabarzad Dūraqizzī (d. 607); H-b-M-Bakrī (d. 656) (Kittanī II, 54) and his daughter Sāmiya. A pupil of: 'Alī-b-'Umar Sakkarī Khattabī (d. 386), 'Umar-b-Shāhid, H Dāraqutnī (friend of Ibn Sālim), Y-b-'Umar Qawwās, *rāwī* of Sūfīs (venerated by Dāraqutnī, *abdāl* according to Azharī, Burqānī 14, 326, and Ummī [Abī Dhurr]), A Hy-b-Habbābī, Ibrāhīm-b-M Muzakkī via AB Burqānī (Badawī, *Rābi'a* [?], 124).

[70] Cf. Iblīs (Ash'arites).

His retraction forced Ibn 'Aqīl to omit from his treatise the names of the immediate masters who helped him, and Ibn Rajab is indignant at the audacity of Ibn al-Ghazzāl (d. 615), who had dared to restore them in a reedition of the Hallājian apology. Can one restore them? First of all, it is almost certain that Abū Tāhir 'Allāf, a personal friend of Vizir Ibn al-Muslima, was pro-Hallāj, which is very likely the case with his master Ibn Sam'ūn, and therefore of his codisciple A Hy Qazwīnī. And between 437 and 442, for the first time since the death of Hallāj, doctors of the law such as 'Allāf and Qazwīnī could dare give favorable testimonies concerning him, with *isnāds* for which they were personally accountable. What is likely in the case of these two masters of Ibn 'Aqīl is verified by a third, Abū Tālib M-b-'Alī-b-Fath 'Ushshārī (d. 451), who did not hesitate at that time to transmit to Khatīb some crucial accounts[71] for which he was accountable under his own name (taken from Sulamī, an untouchable Khurasanian): particularly those concerning the convictions of Ibn 'Atā', Shiblī, and Nasrābādhī, the asceticism, condemnation, last words, and especially the final vigil of Hallāj. 'Ushshārī must surely have been quoted.

Do we still have the work by Ibn 'Aqīl? Perhaps, but retouched. It is appropriate to note first that in a collection of quotations the personality of the author can be indicated only by the arrangement of pericopes and by some deliberate internal retouchings relevant to his leanings. The place given to number 1 (Shiblī and "*Uqtulūni*") and (visit to the tomb of Ibn Hanbal) the theological retouchings in number 2[72] of the anonymous text of the *Akhbār al-Hallāj*, which we edited in 1914, 1936, and 1957, remind us rather of Ibn 'Aqīl; more than that, of a young Ibn 'Aqīl, the retouchings of the Taymūr[73] ms., with a certain youthful clumsiness,[74] and a boldness in his attempt to reshape, perhaps justified by the variants.[75] Should Hallāj's dialogue with Muqtadir, given ap. London ms., f. 350, also be traced back to his apology?[76] Later retouchings by Ibn al-Qassās.

b. Transmission of the Apology of Ibn 'Aqīl. In spite of his public retraction of 465, Ibn 'Aqīl, according to Sibt ibn al-Jawzī's remark, was supposed to have given the *ijāza* of certain condemned works. This remark

---

[71] Khatīb VIII, 118, 120, 121, 128, 129, 131, 132. 'Ushshārī received the *Kitāb al-'izz* of Ibn Abī'l-Dunyā from 'Alī-b-Akhī Mīmī and transmitted it via Tuyūrī to Ibn al-Muqayīr (Rūdānī [bib. no. 834-a], f. 95b).

[72] *Ibid.*, 42.   [73] *Ibid.*, 9.

[74] *Ibid.*, 72.   [75] *Ibid.*, 73.

[76] *Recueil*, p. 61.

refers, not to his Mu'tazilite essays (particularly on the liceity of a metaphorical divine "filiation," a revived thesis of Nazzām),[77] no trace of which has survived, but surely to his Hallājian apology,[78] for which Rūdānī[79] received the standard *ijāza* around 1070 going back via 'Āyīsha-bt-Kamāl (726, d. 816), 'Izz-b-Jamā'a (d. 767), Shihāb A-b-AT Hajjār (623, d. 730), Abū Nasr M-b-M ibn al-Shīrāzī (629, d. 723: *rāwī* of his grandfather), Badr AQ 'Alī-b-A Faraj 'AR. ibn al-Jawzī (550, d. 630: a calligrapher of low morals, *rāwī* of *Luma'*) and Abū'l-Fath M-b-Yaḥyā ibn Marāhib-b-Isrā'īl Baradānī (499, d. 583), to Ibn 'Aqīl. What did happen? During his lifetime, prior to 480, on the advice of Shāfi' Jīlī, a personal friend of Ibn 'Aqīl, 'AA-b-Mubārak ibn 'Ināl 'Ukbarī[80] (d. 528) had purchased and endowed with *waqf* the collection of Ibn 'Aqīl's manuscripts,[81] which saved them and made it possible for the grandson of Shāfi', the historian A-b-Sāliḥ Shāfi' Jīlī (520, d. 565), and afterwards Ibn al-Jawzī (d. 597) to use them. This *waqf*, resumed by the imperial concubine Zumurrud (d. 599), was managed for her at that time in the Ma'mūrīya by a *wakīl*, Abū'l-Sa'ādāt Diyā' D ibn al-Nāqid; and it was there that Ibn Marāhib[82] must have copied the authentic apology. But that caused him to be disqualified for quoting without being provided with an authentic *samā'*.

After the death of Ibn Marāhib, 'AR-b-'Umar ibn al-Ghazzāl (d. 615), a Hanbalite and an excellent calligrapher, likewise became disqualified as a *rāwī* by some for having restored the *isnāds* of Ibn 'Aqīl in a copy of the apology.[83]

---

[77] Sibt-b-J., ms. P. 1506, f. 139a; cf. *RHR*, 1941, p. 58, n. 3.

[78] Identified by M. Jawād.

[79] Rūdānī, *Sila*, ms. P. 4470, f. 76a; 'Akarī, s.n.

[80] A disciple of Baradānī (d. 498, a pupil of Ibn Ghaylān and AH Qazwīnī) and master of Mubārak. On 'Ukbarī see Ibn al-Dubaythī ms. P. 5921, f. 106a (M. Jawād).

[81] 'Akarī says: *Kitāb al-funūn* and *Kitāb al-fuṣūl* ('Akarī [bib. no. 830-a], IV, 85); Ibn 'Aqīl must have added his works to it.

[82] On Ibn Marāhib, see Ibn al-Dubaythī, ms. P. 5921, f. 175; Dhahabī, *Mukhtaṣar*, ms. P. 1582, f. 12b (commentary by M. Jawād). He was reproached as a *rāwī* for having transmitted without authorization (*sic*).

[83] According to Rūdānī ([bib. no. 834-a], ff. 56b, 100b), the *ijāza* of *Kitāb al-funūn* (very ineffective after the pillage of Baghdad in 656) came from Ibn 'Aqīl via A Faḍl M-b-Nāsir Salāmī and AH ibn Muqayyir (d. 643: the very same one who copied the Hallājian *Bidāya*); as for the other works of Ibn 'Aqīl, Ibn Muqayyir had received the *ijāza* from 'Abd al-Khāliq-b-Yf Shīrāzī to transmit them to A Nūn Dabbūsī (640, d. 729), M-b-A Mahdāwī (d. 797), A-b-Ibrāhīm-b-Sul Qalyūbī (780, d. 860).
The catalogue of titles from the *samā'* of 'Ayisha (d. 816) passed via Kamāl ibn al-Zayn (801, d. 864) to Suyūtī (d. 911) and Zak Ansārī (d. 926), and through them to 'AR-b-'Ali Suqayn, Sa'īd-b-A-Muqrī', and to Qaddūra (d. 1050), master of Rūdānī.

7. Abū Yūsuf 'Abd al-Salām-b-M Qazwīnī

An esteemed Mu'tazilite theologian (393, d. 488): "*qad jama'a akhbārahu fī mujallad waqad wasaftu 'alayhi*." He had compiled the life story of Hallāj in a bound volume that "I have examined," Sibt ibn al-Jawzī tells us (*Mir'āt*, s.v. Hallāj). This volume must have been written after 461 in order to refute Ibn 'Aqīl by using Khatīb (Ibn Bākūyā is referred to in it in the same way), and by combining with him the accounts of the historians Sūlī and Thābit ibn Sinān, the geographer Ibn Hawqal, and excerpts from Sūfī *manāqib*. Of this essential, though hostile, volume we have only a few bits and pieces, plagiarized (without so admitting) by Ibn al-Jawzī in his *Muntazam* and especially by Sibt ibn al-Jawzī, who admits partly to his grandfather's plagiarism. Qazwīnī, in correcting Hamadhānī, attributed the "*Nadīmī*" verses to Abū Nuwās. Mu'tamin Sājī, a disciple of Harawī, attacked A Y Qazwīnī.[84] His executors were Farāwī (d. 530) and Qādī 'Abd al-Malik-b-Mu'afā'.

8. 'Alī-b-A-b-'Alī Wā'iz ibn al-Qassās Shirwānī

Shirwānī (d. around 515) read his *Akhbār al-Hallāj* in Shirwan before 511: first to Sulaymān-b-'AA Shirwānī, an informant of Silafī; then to Silafī himself, who declared "*akthar mā fīhi min al-asānīd min kitāb* (variant: *murakkabāt*) *lā asla lahu*," "most of the *isnāds* given in it come from one book (variant: being from disparate sources, the whole is) without authority." This is at least the excerpt given by Dhahabī (*Mīzān al-i'tidāl*, II, 218: completed by Ibn Hajar, *Lisān al-mīzān*, IV, 205). However, I suspect Silafī was responsible[85] for the diffusion in the Maghrib via Alexandria of these *Akhbār* that I consider identical with the *Hikāya* account form analyzed above.

a. The Akhbār *of Ibn al-Qassās.* It was between 500 and 508 when Silafī (d. 576) went to Chemakha (literally, Shamākhī), capital of Chirvan (literally, Sharwan), to obtain from Ibn al-Qassās direct *samā'* of his *Akhbār al-Hallāj*. How could a biography of Hallāj have been conceived and written on the Caucasian frontier of Islam? Around 435, a disciple of the great mystic of Nishapur, Ibn Abī'l-Khayr (d. 440), Abū Nasr Sharwānī, had built a *ribāt* in Chemakha,[86] where a Hallājian center could have been implanted. And if, as we think, the *akhbār* in question were a collection of

---

[84] Ibn Haj[ar], *Lisān* IV, 12.
[85] He liked A Ghazālī, whom he had known in Hamadhān. He had accepted some *mu'ammarīn* (Abū'l-Duryā).
[86] Zhukovski [?], p. 74.

wa'z of the genre of that of Shaydhalā Jīlī (d. 494), some Baghdadian Shaykh in contact with the monastery of Chemakha—for example, the grandson of Ibn Abī'l-Khayr, AQ Tāhir-b-Sa'īd-b-Fadl Mahnawī (d. 542), prior to the Ibn Mahlabān *ribāt*—may have transmitted a secret copy of the apology of Ibn 'Aqīl to Ibn al-Qassās.

Should the political situation of Chirvan also be taken into consideration? The last of the Muslim Sharwānshāh (183-510) of Chemakh, Feridūn-b-Feribūrz, had married Tamara, daughter of the Georgian Prince David II (483/1089 to 519/1125); and his Christian father-in-law, who had undertaken successfully the conversion of the Qypchāq (Cumans), ended up by installing a bishop of Dchqondidi, Simon, as prince in place of his son-in-law. Was the redaction of the *akhbār* of Ibn al-Qassās affected by the Christianizing atmosphere dominant at that time in Chemakha? and would that explain the insertion in the text of the astonishing passage in which Vizir Hāmid, in the role of Pilate, declared to the *shuhūd* "let his blood (Hallāj's) fall on our necks." After close consideration, I regard this passage to be older[87] and even, in its original form, primitive.[88]

b. Transmission of the Akhbār *of Ibn al-Qassās.* The great Isfahanian traditionist Abū Tāhir Silafī,[89] who transmitted a notice by Qannād on Hallāj,[90] may have had his attention drawn to Hallāj by his master, Tuyūrī (d. 500), *rāwī* of *Bidāya*. After receiving, perhaps in Baghdad, the text of the *Akhbār* by Sulaymān-b-'AA Shirwānī, he intended during his excursion to Adharbayjan (in 502) which took him to Derbend, to have it reread to him in Shirwan by the author himself (when setting off again he must have left all of the documents of this trip in Salmas in 508).[91] He stated at the time that "most of the *isnāds* cited in it came from a nonauthenticated text."[92] Ibn Hajar states precisely: "most of the *isnāds*

---

[87] The chain of *isnād* of the Sa'īdīya (Zabīdī, *'Iqd*, 59): Murtā'ish (d. 328) → AN Sarrāj (d. 377) → Sarakhsī (d. in Zāhir?) → A Sa'īd-b-A Kh. (d. 440) → AN Sharwānī (d. 470) → Pīr Mardān (d. 500) → Pīr Hy (d. 530) → Dédé Mas'ūd (d. 560) → Shaykh M Mādī (d. 590) → Shaykh Nūr al-Dīn Ahmad (d. 620) → Shaykh Mu'ammar Sa'd al-Dīn Bābā (d. 650) → Abū'l-Futūh Tāwūsī (d. 871) (cf. *Takmilat al-ikmāl*, Baghdad ms. 959. Evkof [?], 79).

[88] Cf. *Akhbār*, no. 50: *laysa li'l-muslimīna shughl ahamm min qatlī.*

[89] Abū Tāhir A-b-M Silafī is the encyclopaedic master of *isnāds* in the field of hadīth (Kattanī, *Fihrist* II, 339; Dhahabī, *Huffāz* III, 39).

[90] Transmitted after him by AM A Wahhāb ibn Rawāj Iskandarānī (554, d. 640), Sharaf D Yahyā-b-Yf Misrī (648, d. 737), to 'Izz-b-Jamā'a (694, d. 767).

[91] Silafī, *Arba'īn Buldānīya*, ms. P. 722, f. 2b.

[92] *Kitāb lā asla lahu*: Dhahabī, *I'tidāl* II, 218, no. 1706.

cited in it are fabricated without any authentic foundation; and their *rāwīs*[93] are unknown (*majāhil*)."

This certainly did not prevent Silafī from transmitting this biography of Hallāj among Maghribins (hence, Tūzarī) during the sixty years (512-575) when he lived in Alexandria. Silafī's two opinions of the work should be weighed carefully. (1) It was in two parts, the main part being a copy of a nonauthenticated text (= neither *samā'* of *rāwī*, nor name of copyist); (2) the *rāwīs* mentioned in the *isnāds* are unknown. This description fits a more or less deliberately faked amalgam, which corresponds more to our existing manuscripts of anonymous *Akhbār al-Hallāj*, whose primitive core of testimonies (whose *isnāds* refer to unknown people) is enclosed by *Hikāya* of the "visits," with the general *isnād* of Ibn Razīn→Faradī→Kirmānī, which goes back to about fifty years after the death of Ibn al-Qaṣṣāṣ. The core would correspond to the disavowed work by Ibn 'Aqīl, thus be nonauthenticated.

Silafī, who died a centenarian, recorded the names of the thousand shaykhs of whom he was the *rāwī* in three *mu'jam* (Isfahan, more than 600; Baghdad; and *al-safar*). Four successive generations provided him with *rāwīs*, from Abū 'Alī Baradhānī (d. 498) to Abū'l-Khattāb-b-Khalī (d. 666). His grandson, 'AR-b-Makkī Tarābulsī (570, d. 651), the custodian of his magnificent library in Alexandria, gave his general *ijāza* (cf. 'Abd al-'Azīm Mundhirī, d. 656), which came down in this way via Hajjār (d. 730) to 'Ayisha-bt-Kamāl and Ibn Hajar. But it is doubtful if this implied the *ijāza* of a work as suspect as the Hallājian *akhbār*. The latter were more likely linked to Silafī via the initiatory *isnād* of the *tarīqa Silafīya*, which the grand qādī of Cairo, Zakarīyā Ansārī (d. 925), claimed to derive from him via a chain of six names: A Zanbānī M-b-Mukhallas, Sharaf 'Adilī, 'AA-b-M-b-AB ibn Khalīl Makkī, 'Uthmān-b-M Mālikī, AH-b-A Fath Mahmūd Mahmūdī.[94]

9. Abū'l-Faraj 'AR-b-'Alī ibn al-Jawzī

Ibn al-Jawzī (510, d. 597) says in his *Muntazam* (s.a. 309): "*qad jami'tu akhbārahu fī kitābī sammaytuhu al-Qāti' li majāli'l-lujāj al-Qāti' bi muhāli'l-Hallāj*," "I have given the account of Hallāj in a book entitled *al-Qāti'*.

---

[93] *Lisān al-mīzān* IV, 205, no. 559: that is to say, without confirming parallel recensions (cf. Nawawī, tr. by W. Marçais, p. 59, note; and Dhahabī, *Huffāz* III, 215-216).

[94] Zabīdī, *'Iqd.*, 58-59. Dhahabī: *akthar mā fīhi mina'l-asānīd min kitāb lā asla lahu*. Ibn Hajar IV, 205: *akthar mā fīhi mina'l-asānīd min kuttāb lā asla lahā* (*sic.* faulty reading) *wa ruwātuhā majāhil*.

. . ." He states precisely in his *Talbīs* (183): "I have set forth in this book the deceptions and magical tricks of Hallāj and what the *'ulamā'* have said about them. May God help us in overcoming ignorance." Ibrāhīm Sibt ibn al-'Ajamī (d. 841), commentator of the *Shifā'*, tells us that this treatise of Ibn al-Jawzī "was two *kurrās* long or a little more; I had a copy of it with me in Cairo"; and his disciple Ibn Khalīl, author of a supergloss on the *Shifā'*, adds: "Ibn al-Jawzī wrote a treatise about two *kurrās* long (= 30 pages) to refute the notion of Hallāj's sanctity and the idea that his blood could have written the Glorious Name (*Allāh*) on the ground." Two or three sentences by Ibn al-Jawzī in the *Mir'āt* of his grandson may have come from this lost work.

10. Hibatallāh-b-Sadaqa Azajī

A Hanbalite (d. 591), he wrote *Radd 'alā Abī'l-Wafā' ibn 'Aqīl fī nusrat al-Hallāj* (Dhahabī, *Ta'rīkh*, s.a. 591). This refutation must have been aimed at the aforementioned work (§6) of Ibn 'Aqīl.

11. Abū M 'Abd al-Rahmān-b-'Umar-b-Abī Nasr ibn al-Ghazzāl

A Hanbalite (544, d. 615), preacher and calligrapher, son of a *hāfiz* disciple of Kīlānī (*Bahja*, 107, 110). Ibn Rajab says (*Tab. Hanb.* [bib. no. 570], s.v.), "I have seen one piece (*juz'*) of his writing, *Akhbār al-Hallāj*, apparently composed by him, including *isnāds* going back to his masters. He tends to praise and exalt Hallāj and uses in support of him excerpts from the old book that Ibn 'Aqīl had retracted, which is a mistake on his part." Ibn al-Ghazzāl could cite as his master in it Abū'l-Waqt 'Abd al-Awwāl Sijzī (458, d. 553), a disciple of Harawī and master of Kīlānī. M. Jawād thinks that it was because of this book that another Hanbalite, Abū'l-Futūh Nasr-b-Abī'l-Faraj Husrī (d. 619), prohibited any *samā'* of Ibn al-Ghazzāl. In fact, Ibn al-Ghazzāl had two historians as *rāwīs*, Ibn al-Najjār (d. 643) and Birzālī (d. 636) (cf. Ibn al-Dubaythī, Paris ms. 5922, f. 218b), and Diyā' al-Dīn M-b-'Abd al-Wāhid Maqdisī (d. 643), founder of the Diyā'īya *madrasa* of Damascus, where the ms. of Ibn Bākūyā studied here was "waqfed."[95]

12. Abū M Rūzbehān-b-Abī Nasr Baqlī Daylamī Basā'ī

A Sunnite mystic (b. 522 or rather 530, d. 606: cf. Ivanow ap. JRASB, 1928, 1931; Ritter, ap. *DI*, 1933), who, after having been forced to leave Shiraz briefly for Fasa, wrote there in 570, in the *ribāt* of Shaykh Abū

[95] This volume, pp. 461.

Muhammad Jawzak, a monograph of *shathīyāt*, i.e., of Sūfī technical ecstatic terms, entitled *Mantiq al-asrār (Bibayān al-anwār)* = "the Logic of Hearts (Describing Ecstasies)."

This work, supposedly concerned with the *shathīyāt* of fifty masters, is, in fact, the most important work on Hallāj, his collected works, and the development of his thought. Baqlī said in f. 7b: "*Wa muntahā maqsūdī fī tasnīf hādhā'l-kitāb tafsīr shathīyāt al-Hallāj wa bayān af*ā*lihi wa aqwālihi; fa-hubbuhu hajjanī ilā ān mufassir maqalatahu fī'l-shath wa ishāratahu fī'lanānīya limuhibbiyhi wa mu*ā*dīhi; liannahu min *ā*ja'ibi shā'nihi an yakūna'lkhalqu mutahayyirin fī maqāsidi kalāmihi wa lam ya*ā*rafū daqā'iq ishārātihi . . . ,*" "My ultimate aim in writing this book has been to comment on the ecstatic sentences of Hallāj, to describe what he did and said; my love for him drove me to comment on his ecstatic mode of expression and of allusion to the (divine) Personality (= theopathic locution) for his friends and for his enemies; for, among other things, it is an admirable fact about him that all are confounded by his language and cannot discern the subtleties of his allusions" (the passage was omitted in the Persian translation).

I MUST give a description here of a ms. of this Arabic text which was rediscovered in 1930 in Tehran:

Third *risāla* of an album-size *majmū*ʿ consisting of 163 folios, 285 mm. high by 109 mm. long, 30 lines to a page, containing: (1) *Kitāb minhāj al*ā*bidīn li muzaffar* (Sibtī, d. 636), 1 + 49 + 2 ff.; (2) *'Uyūb al-nafs li'lSulamī* (d. 412) (cut off), 5 ff.; (3) *Mantiq al-asrār li Rūzbehān Baqlī* (d. 606), 81 ff.; (4) *Zīnat al-hayāt li Yūsuf Hamadhānī* (d. 535), 1 (cut off); (5) *Risāle der 'ayn-i hayāt ve Dhū'l-Qarnayn ve Khidr*, introduced, missing; (6) *Kashf al-asrār li'l-Baqlī* (written in 585), 25 ff.; perhaps 163 folios in all. The ms. is dated, *in fine*, month of *Jumāda* II, year 665 (indication repeated *in fine* [3]).

Title of (3): *Kitāb mantiq al-asrār* (f. 1a; in ornate Kufic script; with a superscription of the same date, "*Kitāb mantiq al-asrār bi-bayān al-anwār rasamahu wa sannafahu'l-imāma'l-*ā*rif shaykh al-muhibbīn wa quduwat almurīdīn bākūrat al-tajallī wa 'abhar al-uns fī dimn al-tadallī hujjat Allāh shattāh Fārs wa khātamuhum Abū Muhammad Rūzbahān-b-Abī Nasr al-Baqlī alShīrāzī, nawwara'Llāh qabrahu*"; and a modern gloss in Persian. Incipit: (basmala) *Rabb sahhil. Al-hamdu li'Llāhi'lladhī taqaddasa bisubuhāti jamāli jabarūtihi . . .* "(f. 1b). Explicit: " . . . *wahādhā mahd al-ittisāf bi'l-sifā'. Qad intahat sharh alfāz al-mushkilāt ma*ʿ *tafsīr al- shathīyāt bi 'awni'Lhāh wa husn ta'yīdihi wa hamdu lillāh kamā yanbaghī likaram wajhihi wa salawātihi 'alā*

khayr khalqihi Muhammad wa 'Ālīhi ajma'īn. Faragha min tasnīf hadhā'l-kitāb al-shaykh Rūzbahān-b-Abī Nasr-b-Rūzbahān al-Baqlī al-Shīrāzī rahmat Allāh 'alayhi (wa min kitābat al-faqīr ghaffara lahu sana 665)" (f. 81b).[96]
This work is arranged as follows: *dībāja* and eulogy of the Nabī (ff. 1b-3a); Introduction to *shath*: it is the summit of Sūfism, the third mode of expression (*lisān*: after 1. *sahw* and 1. *tamkīn*) of the third degree (*martabat haqā'iq*; after m. *tawhīd* and m. *ma'ārif*) of the third *manhaj* (*manhaj al-asrār*; after m. *mu'āmalāt* and m. *maqāmāt*). This is the *'ilm ladunnī* that Khadir taught to Moses, the fourth branch of the *sharī'a* (*haqā'iq*; after *riwāya, fiqh, nazar*); a list of saints persecuted for that (first cited, f. 3a: Hallāj): ff. 3a-5b. *First part*: a list of 50 masters; actually 47, for Thawrī, Fudayl, and Ibn Khafīf are only mentioned; the 46th is Mansūr son of Hallāj, cited also on f. 69a; the 47th is Hallāj, ff. 7b-9a: ff. 5b-9a. An examination of *shath* in the Qur'ān (*mutashābihāt al-sifāt, awā'il al-suwar*), in the cases of the *Nabī* and the *Rāshidūn*, ff. 9a-10b. An examination of 90 *shath*, of 23 of the 50 masters presented without classification, beginning with the facts taken from Abū Nasr Sarrāj (*shathīyāt*, ap. *Luma'*, 375 ff.) about Bistāmī (here 31 *shath*) and Shiblī (here 29 *shath*): ff. 11a-27b. *Second Part*: Hallāj; (1) his 27 *riwāyāt* (ff. 27b-35a), his 43 individual *shath* (ff. 35b-42b and ff. 56b-59b), and the 104 pericopes of his *Tawāsīn* (ff. 43a-56b): ff. 27b-59b. *Third Part*: *shathīyāt* "*mutafarriqa*," scattered ecstatic utterances, 72 in number, taken from 39 of the 50 masters (Hallāj reappears here, ff. 66a, 67a, 69a-b). *Appendix*: a list of about 200 technical terms, copied (without saying so) from that of Sarrāj (*Luma'*, 333-374; with the addition of terms quoted in the chapter on *shathīyāt*, *ibid.*, 375 ff.). Hallāj fills 75 of the 162 pages, almost half.

Persian translation of *Mantiq al-asrār* = *Sharh al-shathīyāt*. When he returned to Shiraz from Fasa, Baqlī decided (cf. his account, here, f. 4) to translate his *Mantiq* into Persian; the work, as a simple repository of technical terms, had become a "corpus" of *shath*. This translation, known by Jāmī (Naf. 64, 288) and Kātib Chelebi (*Kashf*, no. 7522), was rediscovered by us in Istanbul in 1911-1912, in two manuscripts (cf. H. Ritter, ap. *DI*, 1933, p. 102): Shahīd 'Ali ms. 1342, *Majmu'*, piece XIX, copied 29 *Jumāda* II 889, 185 pp. of 31 lines [each]: this is the pagination

---

[96] In f. 8a, with regard to Hallāj, "his thousand works on all the sciences, destroyed and burned by his enemies," his poems and his maxims, Baqlī adds "the blessing of God upon his life and upon his death, the mercy of God upon his brothers (*min ahl al-qissa* = involved in his trial?) and upon those who love him, until the Day of Judgment." (This passage is missing in the Persian translation.)

that we refer to here; the order is confused in two places; and Murat Mulla ms. 1271, copied after 900, 175 pp. whose order is topsy-turvy (of 27 lines).

This translation is presented as follows: *dībāja* and eulogy of the *Nabī* (pp. 1-4). A prefatory note on the composition of the Arabic original and on his translation (pp. 4-5); An *Introduction* (subdivided into *fuṣūl* and watered down) dealing with *shath*, which expresses spiritual rapture, with persecuted saints (the list reshaped in an oratorical form with prophets added at the beginning, interrupted by personal reflections): pp. 5-12. *First Part*, a list of *shath* masters; 47, in the same order, except that the 46th, Mansūr son of Hallāj, is replaced by Husrī, and the 47th, Hallāj, is dealt with separately, pp. 16-19; pp. 12-20. An examination of *shath* in the Qur'ān, in the cases of the *Nabī*, the *Rashidūn*, and the Companions (the persecution of 'Amir-b-Qays is moved here to pp. 20-26). An examination of the *shathīyāt* of 47 masters; the author has structured and classified in order here the two groups of 90 and 72 *shathīyāt* given without classification in the Arabic original; the frequent insertions of discourses on his own state (*fī wasfī*) doubles the length of this part: pp. 27-109. *Second Part*, Hallāj; (1) his *asānīd* (= 27 *riwāyāt*) pp. 109-121; (2) his 43 individual maxims, pp. 122-146, 178-181 (*asānīd* and maxims were published in the appendix of our *Essai*, 1922, pp. 337-345, 419-426); (3) the 104 pericopes of his *Tawāsīn*, pp. 147-168, with an account of a personal dream. *Appendix*: list (unchanged) of about 200 technical terms, *nukat*, pp. 168-172, 181-185. Hallāj fills no more than 64 of 185 pages, perhaps a third; Baqlī still admires him, but he omitted his two references to his son, and he seems at the beginning to put Bistāmī and Hallāj on the same level. Here he gives the name of his Kurd master, M Jāgīr-b-Dushm (d. 591), which he suppressed in 570, which shows that this translation was finished only after this date, 591.

According to Junayd the *Sharh al-tawāsīn* (here 2nd part §3) was sometimes copied separately (the Persian translation included in this *sharh* was published by us ap. *Kitāb al-tawāsīn* in 1913.

Incipit (ms. 1342 SA): "(*basmala*) . . . *wa bihi nasta'īn. Sipās ān khudhāwer dīrā kih bī azāl we abād kunh-e-dhāt we sifātash az taghāyir . . . munazzah būdh. . . .*" 1st explicit (*ibid.*, 168): ". . . *tā dil der sefā īn meydān turk tāzī kened; ākhir īn kitāb tamām shūdh bikalimātī chend kih muslih remz sūfiyān 'āsheq ast . . . mukhtasar bī tatwīl . . . tā zerāfet-e harakāt īshān bedānī kih che shīrīn we latīf ast.*" 2nd explicit (185): "*wa 'iyyākum fahm mā ashāra ilayhi al-sufīya; wa razzaqanā'l-luhūq bihim fī'l-dunyā wa'l-ākhira (taslīya; date).*"

The Hallājian Sources of the Mantiq: the sources of Baqlī's *Mantiq* for Hallāj are divided as follows:

(A = f. 7b-9a = biography of Hallāj); first, an oral tradition either Shirazian or Kurdish (in bad Arabic, cf. f. 55b) from his master Jāgīr Kurdī (d. 591; for *shath*. no. 74, combines here under his name two separate inquiries about his 1,000 works, f. 8a and f. 69a), giving unique details about his son Mansūr (f. 7b, f. 69b), repeating his trials, the hostile attitude of the *'ulamā'* and the powerful of Baghdad, his vindication by "our master and chief Ibn Khafīf" (together with Ibn 'Atā', Shiblī, and Nasrābādhī), by Ibn Surayj (rejection of *fatwā*), his 1,000 works destroyed out of envy (*tarahhum* expanded), the names of his masters, his saying, *Ilahya ta'lam 'ajzī*," his apparition coming out of the Tigris.

Beginning here, this tradition gives thirteen accounts under Ibn Khafīf's name, five of which come from the work of Daylamī (*Tarjama* = here D), an improbable source for the others: al-Hallāj miraculously unbound in prison for each ablution; A 2 he recovers the ring of Mutawakkil (*sic*; cf. the unhistorical remarks on the death of Muqtadir the day after the execution, f. 55b); A 3 the important visit in prison (= D9); his thirteen chains (= Sulamī, *Ta'rīkh*, no. 18); miracle of the wall opened onto the prison which imitates his movements in prayer; A 7 the *sahn* of Mecca (= D 10); A 8 the dream of Abū'l-Yamān (= D 15); A 9 the "*nadīmī*" quatrain followed by Qur'ān 40:28 (= D 7); A 10 mutilated, he did *tayammum* with dust (that contradicted deliberately the 'Attārian theme of Hallāj's ablution, when mutilated, in his blood); A 11, the 3,000 blows of the whip and the hand which dries (by the executioners); A 12, the flagellation, according to Ibn Fātik, during which he repeated "*Ahad, Ahad*," had flayed him alive (= perhaps the complete recension of the fragment in Sulamī, *Ta'rīkh*, no. 20); A 13, the Holy Saturday flame in Jerusalem (= D 2). (B = f. 27b-35a, 43a-59a). Here Baqlī gives us his great Hallāj texts, *Riwāyāt*, *Tawāsīn*, *Mahabba*, with full commentaries which must be only partly by him; all of them came to him from one of his masters, Jāgīr Kurdī (considering the note on f. 69a and others). (C = f. 35b-42b, 59a, 66a, 67a). Series of 43 + 5 = 48 maxims of Hallāj. Of the last 5, 4 came from Sulamī (*Tab.*, nos. 1, 2, 6, 19). The first 43 are divided as follows: 3 taken from Sulamī (*Ta'rīkh*, nos. 13, 14, 11 = C 25, 32, 39), 4 from Daylami (*Tarjama*, nos. 11, 12, 13, 14 = C 35, 36, 40, 41), one from Nisāburī ('*Uqalā*''*l-majānīn* = C 33), one from Sūlī ("*Muhlik*" 'Ad = C 44), one from *Akhbār al-Hallāj* (the "*Baynī wa baynaka*" piece, no. 50 = C 34), 2 from *Bustān al-ma'rifa* (Tawāsīn XI, 1, 25 = C 38, 42), 9 from the *Hikāya* (visits by Shiblī, Fātima before the gibbet = C 1-6, 8, 9,

37). The other 22, some of which are noteworthy, come from an un-known source (C 7, 10, 11, 12, 13 [omitted here, restored in Persian translation, no. 175], 14-18, 20-24, 26-31, 43, 49). We are forced to believe that Baqlī sometimes borrowed his commentary from others because this commentary includes sentences by Hallāj taken from texts that Baqlī himself has not given us (e.g., *Bustān al-ma'rifa*).

13. Muhyī"l-Dīn AB M-b-'Alī ibn 'Arabī Mursī

The great mystic (560, d. 638) inscribed in no. 22 of the catalogue of his works *al-Sirāj al-wahhāj fī sharh kalām al-Hallāj* (*Fihrist*, ap. Feizie ms. 2119, f. 14). This work, lost, may have only been a commentary on the words of Hallāj (cf. Asaf. Catalogue, Hyderabad, no. 352).

14. 'Alī-b-Anjab ibn al-Sā'ī

A Baghdadian historian (d. 674), Ibn al-Sā'ī was the author of the *Akhbār al-Hallāj* referred to by Kātib Çelebi (*Kashf*, no. 192), who adds *"wa huwa mujallad"*: it is a bound volume. It was therefore an important biography, all the more so given the fact that Ibn al-Sā'ī was a pupil of the historian Ibn al-Najjār, a disciple of the Hallājian Ibn al-Ghazzāl. Only one fragment is extant, ap. *Mukhtasar*, by the same author.

15. Shams al-Dīn Abū 'AA M-b-A Dhahabī Turkumānī

The famous historian (673, d. 748) indicates in his *Ta'rīkh* (s.a. 309) that he himself dealt with the *Akhbār al-Hallāj* (variant: *Sīrat* . . .) in a treatise (*"afradtuhā fī juz'in"*) that Ibn Taghrībirdī refers to ap. *Manhal* V, 86.

He must have reproduced in it the core of anti-Hallāj ideas developed in his other works.

16. Shams al-Dīn M-b-'Alī-b-A ibn Tūlūn Sālihī

A Hanafite jurisconsult (d. 953, Damascus), he inscribed toward the end of the catalogue of his works *al-hajāj min akhbār al-Hallāj*, "a quick guide to the story of Hallāj" (ap. his *Fulk mashhūn*, Damascus, 1348, 48). Probably a favorable treatise, given the fact that the author was a disciple of Yf-b-'Abd al-Hādī, a defender of Ibn 'Arabī, Raslān, and Shādhilī (*Fulk mashhūn*, 48, 41, 46); it appears to be lost.

17. Mustafā-b-Kamāl al-Dīn ibn 'Alī Siddīqī Uskudārī

A learned Turk. In the account of his journey to Iraq (*Kashf al-sadā*, Cambridge ms. 930; reference owed to M Kāzim Dujaylī), written in

1139/1727, he says, following the account of his visit to the tomb of Hallāj, "*afradtu tarjamatahu bi'l-ta'līf wa khidtu bi'l-iqrār li'l-ta'rīf; famin
muthabbiti'l-siddīqīya wa nāfin wa'l-muthabbitu muqaddam . . .*": "I wrote a
treatise on his life going deeply into the facts to better understand [him];·
for some support, others deny, his sanctity, and it is the former who are
right." A work that is lost.

Of the sixteen "lives," only four have been rediscovered.

b. Notices of Chroniclers Concerning Hallāj

There are two kinds of historical works in which Hallāj is mentioned:
those that deal with a series of specific events, in this instance the *annals of
the caliphs*; and those that are devoted to the biographies of various official
figures, in this instance the *kutub al-wuzarā'*. Both kinds emanated from a
class of bureaucratic scribes, a class of Irano-Aramaian clients. Their redaction, which was more objective and more concise in the annals, became more personal and more literary in the biographies of the people of
the court. Excerpts from biographies find their way into the annals after
a thirty-year period of obscurity. Next come the biographical dictionaries, arranged chronologically, or by country, and by profession.
As for certified documents, chancery records, and private papers, the
aforementioned sources rarely include them.

At his three trials—in 298, 301, and particularly 309—Hallāj must have
been treated by historians as a public man and not simply set down in
biographies, without any supervision, by disciples. He therefore first had
to be mentioned in the lost *Kitāb al-wuzarā'* (*dhayl* of Ibn Yazdādh by his
son, *dhayl* of Ibn Dāwūd al-Jarrāh by Thaqafī).

1. Authors Not Using the Account of Ibn Zanjī

Indeed, the first mention of his name appears in the annals of Tabarī
(ending in 302), in connection with the trial of 301 (with a brief addition,
perhaps by another hand, regarding the trial of 309). A very circumspect
and hardly enlightening reference.

Next come three closely related texts: the *Kitāb al-awrāq* of Sūlī (d. 335;
completed around 331), the *dhayl* of Ahmad ibn Abi Tāhir (written before 320) to the annals of his father, and the *dhayl* to Tabarī of 'Arīb Qurtubī (d. around 365). A careful comparison of them is called for.

Sūlī's five pages about Hallāj appear in a chapter of the biographical
sort about Muqtadir. Kratchkovsky has published them separately.[97]

---

[97] Ap. *Inst. Arch. Russes*, 1913, pp. 137-141.

Sūlī, who claims he knew Hallāj very well, does not deal with him in depth. His 45 parts of statements of characteristic statements are arranged as follows: nos. 1-3: personal reminiscence; 4-10: Hallāj the Sūfī plays the part of Mu'tazilī, Imāmī, Sunnī; *khafīf al-haraka, shu'ūdhī*, exploits *tibb* and *kimiyā; khabīth yatanaqqal min* (corrigenda: *fī*) *'l-buldān*; 11: *wakānat lahu asbāb yatūl sharhhuhā*; 12-14: his arrest by Rāsibī and transfer; 15-22: the trial of 301, the pillory, imprisonment in the palace; 23-24: *waqad qīla*: in the beginning he had preached the coming of the 'Alids (flagellated: in Jabal); 25-29: one time Sunnī, another Shī'ī, *shu'ūdhī*; stopped in the presence of AS Nawbakhtī; the musk; the dirhams (*lam yusna*); 29-30: the proceedings under Ibn al-Furāt; flight with Karnabā'ī; 31: his writings: follies, characteristic sayings;[98] 32-38: trial of 309; 39: forsaken by former disciples; 40-41: quotations: *Anā mughriq . . . Anā (sic) anta Nūh . . .* ; 42-44: caliphal sentencing and execution; date: end of 309.

We know that the *Kitāb al-awrāq* was plagiarized in large part from an earlier writer, Marthadī (d. circa 275).[99] Here numbers 23-24, 25-26 (cf. 4-10), 27-28, 31, 40-41 were copied elsewhere, as comparison with Ibn Abī Tāhir and 'Arīb confirms; likewise in the case of 12-22. Sūlī could have written only 32-38 and 42-45, concerning the year 309.

Ibn Abī Tahīr, whose notice has been preserved for us by *Fihrist*, begins with a general opinion of Hallāj, distinct and carefully constructed (we note in it *musha'bidhā*, cf. Sūlī 6 and "*yatanaqqal . . .*") = Sūlī 10. He is unaware of Rāsibī, but his expression "*huwa huwa*" comes perhaps from the letter transmitted by Rāsibī, and throws light on the words "*rubūbiya, hulūl*" from Sūlī 14. His account of the trial of 301 is closely connected with the account of Sūlī 15-22; "*waruwiya 'anhu*" introduces Sūlī 23-24; 25-26 is missing; 27-28 derives from a *recensio plenior*; 29-31 is missing; the trial of 309 is omitted, except for one allusion to Nasr (*wa-istaghwāhu*), so thoroughly that one wonders if the final lines of *Fihrist* (p. 191, lines 24-29) constituted only a part of it (cf. Ibn al-Qārih); quotations (Sūlī 40-41) are introduced by "*wakāna fī kutubihi*"; numbers 42-45 are given in less expanded form.

Ibn Abī Tāhir, earlier than Sūlī, could not have copied him, but they have common written sources.

This impression is confirmed by analysis of the third author, 'Arīb (de Goeje edition, 86-108). Writing in Andalusia around 360, 'Arīb worked on thirty-year-old Sunnite Baghdadian sources. His notice is divided into

---

[98] The Hamīd-Sāmmarī colloquy (abridged from Zanjī) is missing in I.A.T. [Ibn Abī Tāhir].

[99] *Fihrist*, 151, 129.

two parts:[100] (1) a copy of an unknown historian (86-94), and (2) (95-108)
a copy of Sūlī, numbers 1-3, 12-15 (abridgement + *hayyā* . . .), 21-22 (+
thumma'ntalaqa, an incorrect reflection), 29-30 (the name of Karnabā'ī is
missing) + *thumma zufira bihi* . . . , an incorrect reflection), 34-38, 42-45.
In comparing these two parts, one notes that 'Arīb, in recopying Sūlī,
left out only what his source A had already given him. In fact, after a
brief summary of the execution, A gives "*khabīthan, yatanaqqal* . . ." (=
Sūlī 9-10), then "*yad'ū ilā'l-ridā* . . ." (= *ibid.*, 23, badly broken up), then
he condenses Sūlī 4-8 (+ *yasta'mil al-makhārīq*), 14, 31 (+ *kufr 'azīm*),
quotations 40-41 (introduced by *wakāna fī ba'd kutubihi*), 36 (Sāmarrī:
with "*kuntum*" = the abnormal "*yakūnū*" of Sūlī), the musk and dirhams
(attributed to Nawbakhtī), no. 28. Source A, which leaves out the three
trials, does not only copy Sūlī, for its recension of 28 is that of Ibn Abī
Tāhir (*laysa bi hādirīn*).

In conclusion, we are dealing with three Baghdadian historians: Sūlī,
Ibn Abī Tāhir, and source A derived from 'Arīb (= '*Arīb-A*). All three
give numbers 23, 40-41, 42-44; Sūlī and Ibn Abī Tāhir give 15-22; Ibn
Abī Tāhir and '*Arīb-A* give 28; Sūlī and '*Arīb-A* give 4-8, 36. Ibn Abī
Tāhir alone establishes its beginning and 14; Sūlī alone establishes 29-30
and 32-38; '*Arīb-A* brings forth nothing original, is thus only a copyist.
The latter was a Baghdadian, based in 'Arīb until 319, where 'Arīb tells
us he used Farghānī. '*Arīb-A* is therefore not Farghānī. On the other
hand, we know that a *dhayl* of the *Kitāb al-wuzarā'* of Ibn Dāwūd, the one
by Mutawwaq, ends in 319. Source A of 'Arīb would therefore be the
dhayl of Mutawwaq, a fragment of which Kindī has preserved for us.[101]

The common sources of these three historians remain to be identified.
For the trial of 301 it would be the *Dhayl kitāb al-wuzarā'* of A-b-UA
Thaqafī (d. 314). For the trial of 298 it would be Ibn Yazdādh. Finally,
the three primitive fragments, 4-8 (*I'tizāl* at the beginning), 23-28 (false
miracles) and 40-41 (quotations), I believe, came from the *Kitāb makhārīq
al-Hallāj* of Awārijī, a Mu'tazilite-Shī'ite pamphlet (from no. 27, there is
an early Shī'ite recension),[102] and also a Mu'tazilite recension.

The other notices on Hallāj from this first group of historians, some of
which are extant, must be reexamined separately:

—That of Khutabī (around 340) in his annals summarizes two trials,

[100] An analogous duality of sources led him to split the famous riot of Qa'da 308 into two
parts (84, lines 5-18, and 85, lines 3-7; cf. Miskawayh, 73).
[101] *Fihrist*, 129. Ibn al-Azraq, a pupil of Mutawwaq, claims to have used his *Ta'rīkh* and
gives us the *recensio plenior* (ap. *Nishwār* I, 81) for the "hair of A.S.N. [Nawbakhtī].
[102] Going back to Umm Kulthūm, daughter of the second Imāmite *wakīl*.

that of 301 (uses the word *zandaqa*, new, along with *shu'udha*, known previously), and that of 309 (he read some documents: *jara fi dhalika kutub tiwāl*), and dates the execution of Tuesday, 23 (*sic*) Qa'da.

—That of Istakhrī (around 322-340) in his *Masālik* (geography) begins with a very important, precise, and objective theological note on the heresy of Hallāj. Next comes an equally important list of circles, offices, and professions in which [Hallāj] had gained disciples (note two words, *istaghwā* and *istamāla*, used by Khutabī); the reason for his flight in 298 is given; the arrest in 301 and the long imprisonment are referred to, but none of the trials are. As for the execution, not dated, the sentence "*fasuliba hayyan ilā ān māta*" may be either an inappropriate transfer of the pillory episode of 301, or a deliberate affirmation of [Hallāj's] exposure on the pillory in 309 (verified by the only Sūfi sources), or caution on his part lest "*suliba*" be taken here to mean "hanging." All of this, plus the serious, calm tone of the notice, makes us look behind the author for an independent and major thinker: probably Abū Zayd Balkhī (d. 340), philosopher, geographer and friend of the physician Rāzī. Unless, of course, Istakhrī had used an earlier "geography of Fārs"; Vizir 'Alī ibn 'Īsā was supposed to have written one such work;[103] he could have written the notice on Hallāj, but how can we hold him accountable for the lacunae (trials) and for the last sentence? Istakhrī was the first to say that Hallāj was born in Bayda.

—That of Mas'ūdī (abridged ap. *Tanbīh*: written in 345) specifies that Hallāj was born in Bayda, that he died on 24 Qa'da, executed on the west bank, and that his remains were displayed on the east bank (*hadhā'l-jānib*: a typical Baghdadian expression: cf. the present-day *dhāka'l-subb* = Turkish *qārsh-i yaqā* = west bank).

Can we find traces of those that are lost?

—Among annals, those of Ibn Yazdādh (up to 300), Niftawayh (d. 323), Ahmad-b-Kāmil, the qādī (d. 351), Ahmad-b-'UA Qatrubullī, 'AA ibn Asmā', nephew of Vizir 'Alī ibn 'Īsā (distinct from Ibn 'Aram-ram),[104] and 'AA ibn Khudhyān Farghānī before 370. We know only that Niftawayh and A-b-Kāmil were very concise, and that Farghānī, who wrote in 336, confused Hallājism with the 'Azāqīrī heresy.[105]

—Among biographies, only the *Kitāb al-wuzarā'* of Thaqafī (d. 314)[106] and that of Mutawwaq, the *Manāqib Ibn al-Furāt* of Sūlī, the *Akhbār al-qudāt* of Wakī' (d. 305) have been rediscovered. And a passage from Ibn

---

[103] Ibn 'Īsā, *Fāris*.
[105] Ap. Yāqūt, *Udabā'* I, 298.
[106] Cf. *Kitāb al-juz'* of Ibn 'Abbād.

[104] *Fihrist*, 139, 147-148.

Farhūn[107] makes us think that Hallāj must have figured in the biography of Grand Qādī Abū 'Umar by Niftawayh.

2. Authors Using the Account of Ibn Zanji

Beginning around 350, the great caliphal annals, from those of Thābit-b-Sinān Sābī[108] and Miskawayh to those of Sibt ibn al-Jawzī, Kutubī, and 'Aynī all use as a textual base for the trial of 309 a much more detailed source, the "account of Ibn Zanji" (taken from his father, the main clerk of the court), a recension of which we published in 1914 (ap. *Quatre Textes* I: the recension that Qādī Abū 'Alī Tanūkhī [d. 384], author of *Nishwār*, transmitted to Khatīb [*Ta'rīkh*, 1931 ed. VIII, 132-141]).

Henceforth, the personality of Hallāj is fixed according to classical history. Earlier historians, who do not seem to have made use of it, had other, direct documentary sources: archival records; official interrogations, *shahādāt bimā sumi'a minhu* (Sūlī, regarding no. 37); confiscated letters, *kutub lahu tadullu 'alā tasdīqī mā dhukira 'anhu* (Khutabī); recorded confessions, *aqarra ba'duhum bilisānihi* (Khutabī). They also knew the various and powerful supporting forces that nearly saved Hallāj (Istakhrī, Khutabī, Azrāq). Ibn Zanjī, whose account minimizes the trial, recopies none of the documents that he had nevertheless transcribed; and he eliminates prudently the interventions [on Hallāj's behalf] by implicated leading figures. His account, drafted before 311,[109] aims merely at communicating to some friends his impressions of the often picturesque sessions of the court. This is what he based its success on and what makes him valuable to us.

It was not published immediately, and its somewhat cursive script must have kept it out of the collection of *rasā'il* that Ibn Zanjī published at the end of his life. He must have restricted himself to giving the *ijāza* for it to a few contemporaries like Ibn Sangala, *kātib* of Rādī and informant of the historian 'Abd al-Rahmān ibn 'Īsā (brother of the vizir) for his annals (years 270-329);[110] like Thābit ibn Sinān (d. 366), another historian; and like Abū 'Alī Tanūkhī (d. 384), who was covetous of this genre of accounts for his *Nishwār*; and perhaps much before him to two scribes who were compilers of accounts of the reign of Muqtadir: M-b-'Abdūs Jahshyārī (d. 331) and Abū'l-Husayn-b-Hishām-b-'AA-b-Abī

---

[107] Cf. the execution.
[108] Who would have received it from Ibn Sanjala, with whom his brother had ties (*Maris*, 87: in 325).
[109] Before the death of Shākir.
[110] *Fihrist*, 129; Sābī.

Qīrāt,[111] informant of the Sābī and of Tanūkhī. I mention all these names in order to find the one among them who was the *first publisher* of the "account of Ibn Zanjī," its "prefacer."

For in our various sources this "account" is preceded by a preface without *isnād* (nos. 1-18 of the 70 sentences of the account: cf. analysis in *Quatre Textes*, pp. 1-3). It is by neither Ibn Zanjī nor Tanūkhī, their common *isnād* interposing *"haddathanā"* only in no. 14 (= Khatīb VIII, 133, line 13). It begins with *"balaghanā"* and summarizes the trial up to (the first?) *istiftā'* of the two qādīs by Vizir Hāmid. Its author seems to be unaware of the trial of 301 (just as Ibn Zanjī shifts the betrayal by Dabbās from 298 to 309), attributes to Ibn 'Īsā the arrest of M-b-'Alī Qunnā'ī, separating it (nos. 6, 10) from the arrests that Hāmid ordered (no. 34), and overlaps Ibn Zanjī in abridged form for the rest (cf. nos. 4 and 17, 6 and 25, 9 and 27, 10 and 34, 12 is perhaps identical with 37). Already Miskawayh gives part of this preface (nos. 2, 10-12) which appears in full in Ibn Sinān (d. 366) as it does in the analysis of the whole by Sibt ibn al-Jawzī (f. 73b, where there is a mistake to be corrected)[112] and in his partial quotation (f. 74a) of numbers 1-13 (including with it the number 5 that the recension of Tanūkhī omits). Is it by Ibn Sinān? I prefer to attribute the first lacunary redaction of it to his informant, to the first publisher and prefacer of the account: undoubtedly Jahshyārī (d. 331), in his early compilation of *Akhbār al-Muqtadir*, a monumental work that its author no doubt caused to be used in the *Kitāb al-'Abbāsī* of the Imāmite A-b-Ism Samaka Qummī (master of Vizir Ibn al-'Amīd: Najāshī [bib. no. 2169-a], 71).

After Miskawayh, chroniclers like Hamadhānī and Ibn al-Athīr give only numbers 2, 10-12 of this preface. Only Kutubī gives numbers 2, 6, 22, 13, 17 in succession.

Here again is the comparative list of known recensions of the "account of Ibn Zanjī":

(1) Ibn Sinān gives all of the numbers 1-70, preceded with the note *"qissat al-Hallāj mutawwala"*;[113]

(2) Tanūkhī, following the *Ta'rīkh* of Khatīb (and perhaps also the *Ta'rīkh* of Zajjāj, d. 391), omits numbers 3 (in part), 5, 10-11 (parts of each), 13, 18, 29, 35, 38, 48;

(3) Miskawayh omits 3 (in part), 4-9, 14, 15 (in part), 22, 23, 35, 37,

---

[111] Whose real source was 'AA Hy-b-'Alī Bāqata'ī (Sābī, 265, 359; Yāqūt, *Buldān* I, 476; Udabā' V, 454).

[112] "Sūlī" for "Sābī" (Ibn Sinān).

[113] Correct *Quatre Textes*, p. 1.

40, 41 (in part), 43-46, 49, 51 (in part), 55, 58, 62, 65, 66, 67 (in part), 68, 69;

(4) Hamadhānī abridges, but with care, in giving numbers 2, 3, 10, 11, 13, 15, 19, 25, 26, 28, 30, 37, 41, 42, 35 (Hāshimī is called Abū Bakr at first), 43, 46, 50-66; 63-66, 67 (in part), 69 (in part);

(5) Ibn al-Athīr gives numbers 2, 10-12, 51-54, 60, 61, 64, 66, 67 (abridged);

(6) Ibn Khallikān (*Waf.*, de Slane edition and Wüstenfeld supplement) gives numbers 25-26, 47-48, 51-67;

(7) Kutubī (copied in this instance by 'Aynī) gives in a hostile summary numbers 22, 26, 22, 13, 17, 30, 32, 47 (end), 52-55, 60, 61, 63-65, 66, 70.

The "account of Ibn Zanjī" poses one final problem. Miskawayh attributes it on several occasions ("*qāla Abū'l-Qāsim ibn Zanjī*": no. [. . .]) to Ibn Zanjī; but the *isnād* of Tanūkhī indicates that he was only its secondary *rāwī* and that it was his father, Zanjī, who wrote it and communicated it to its first publisher. Indeed, Ibn Zanjī, who died in 378, was hardly more than ten years old at the time of the aforesaid text's redaction (309-311). But his father (born around 260, died in 334), despite his more pronounced character and the literary education he received from the writer and historian A-b-M-b-'UA Thaqafī Himār al-'Uzayr,[114] left no works and would not have already omitted in the "account" the fact that Hallāj had been imprisoned from 301 to 309 and that Dabbās had betrayed him in 298 (no. 15). Other errors in the "account," however, could have come from him: deliberate errors introduced by his silence about the steps *in extremis* taken by the Sayyida, about the postponement until the next day of the *coup de grâce* for the executed criminal, and about the preservation of his head in the palace "Museum of Heads" for a year after its public display and before its dispatch to Khurasan.

In addition to using the "account of Ibn Zanjī" for the trial of 309, historians who came after 350 imitate Ibn Sinān in mentioning separately, *sub anno* 301 (or 300),[115] Hallāj's being put on the pillory.

3. Authors Using the Account of Ibn 'Ayyāsh

Besides the very valuable account of Ibn Zanjī, Tanūkhī (d. 384) has preserved for us in his *Nishwār* (I, 80-88) nine texts dealing with Hallāj and his disciples derived from a grand-nephew of Qādī Ibn Buhlūl who

---

[114] Cf. *Fihrist*, 148, and Yāqūt, *Udabā'* I, 223.   [115] This volume, p. 487.

was related to his family, Ahmad-b-Yūsuf al-Azraq (297, d. 377). The second text, lacking *isnād* and concerning AS Nawbakhtī, gives the fullest recension of an account prior to Ibn Abī Tāhir and to Sūlī.[116] Text numbers 3 and 4 emanate from Qādī Ibn 'Ayyāsh, who received them (cf. *Nishwār* 118) from one of his own paternal uncles, Abū Muhammad-b-Hasan ibn 'Ayyāsh, a *shāhid* of the grand qādī in 321. Theirs is a much more detailed account of the trial of 309 than that of Ibn Zanjī. We find in them the false propaganda document with the hierarchy "*bāb-mahdī-huwa huwa*" used as incriminating evidence in 309 by Hāmid, and, going back to 301, the scenario for the pretext of condemnation, Nasr's pronouncement on Hallāj ("*shaykh sālih*"), and "Mādharā'yī's mule" (called here "fulān"). Text 5, about his "*makhārīq*," could have come, like text 2, from Awārijī's pamphlet, but A-b-Yūsuf al-Azraq does not tell us the source.

It is very strange that no historian had used this "account of Ibn 'Ayyāsh" after Ibn Abī Tāhir ("*huwa huwa*")[117] and, possibly, Ibn Sinān ("*shaykh sālih*," note *Fihrist* 191, line 27: which may have come from Ibn Abī Tāhir).

c. Muslim Authors Who Have Discussed the Sources

In *Arabic*: no attempt at a bibliography has come down to us.

Ibn al-Nadīm Warrāq, in his *Fihrist* (190-192), gives five texts but quotes only two authors, Ibn Abī Tāhir and Ibn Sinān, and we know from whom he took the list of 47 works by Hallāj, a crucial document.

Khatīb, in his *Ta'rīkh* (VIII, 112-141), disguises in *isnāds* his consulting of at least eight works, as we pointed out above.

Abū Yūsuf Qazwīnī was the first one who attempted to assemble the sources in a systematic way; Sibt ibn al-Jawzī, in his *Mir'āt*, lists eight of them, five or six of which came to him via the plagiarism practiced by his grandfather of Qazwīnī's work: Sūlī, Ibn Sinān, Ibn Hawqal, Sulamī, *al-Manāqib* (distinct from that of Ibn Khamīs), and Khatīb.

Rūzbehān Baqlī, in his *Mantiq al-asrār*, quotes only a very small part of the works that he consulted: Daylamī (Muhammad, f. 8a, correction of 'Alī, f. 16b; for Ibn Khafīf), Abū Nasr Sarrāj (*Shathīyāt*, ff. 11a, Muhammad Jāgīr ["*ba'd al-mashā'ikh*", f. 42b, 8a = Persian translation,

---

[116] Khutabī ("*zandaqa*").

[117] This author of a *Kitāb mu'tabar fī ma'āni al-simt* (end of fifth century) was a Qarmathian. Cf. further the *Kitāb jāmi' shāhī fī'l-mawālid* of A ibn 'Abd al-Jalīl Sijzī (around 380).

p. 74, which identifies him]; we do not know where he found certain legendary pieces [Ibn Fātik, f. 8b; role of Ibn 'Īsā, f. 3b-4a; *muthla* of Muqtadir the same evening as the execution of Hallāj, f. 55b: Arabic account incorrect]; he does not tell his source for Mansūr, Hallāj's son, "*lahu lisān wa bayān wa karāmāt wa isnād*": ff. 7b, 69a), nor for the *Riwāyāt* of his father.

Nothing remains of the bibliography that Ibn al-Sā'ī must have prepared in his monograph, used by Qazwīnī.

Ibn Taymīya (d. 728) restricted himself to quoting Khutabī and Khatīb, AY Qazwīnī, Ibn al-Jawzī, and Sulamī.

Dhahabī (d. 748), even more brief, gives only references from Khatīb and Ibn al-Jawzī and the title of the *Akhbār* of Ibn al-Qassās, apart, that is, from direct recourse to Ibn Bākūyā, AS Naqqāsh, and Sulamī (*Tabaqāt*). Ibn Hajar 'Asqalānī (d. 852), in his *Lisān al-mīzān* (II, 314-315), after giving three references to Qushayrī, Khatīb, and Ibn 'Arabī, brings to light a unique text of Yūsuf Najīramī (d. 423) on the execution of a son of Hallāj in Ahwaz around 326.

We owe the following lists of sources on Hallāj, ordinary heresiographical sources, to an old tradition peculiar to Shī'ites:

(1) Mū'min Jazā'irī (d. around 1070: *khizāna*): gives Ibn Bābawayh, AJ Tūsī, Tabarsī, Mufīd, 'Alam al-Hudā, 'Allāma Hillī, Ibn Tāwūs, Ibn Fadh;

(2) Khūnsārī (d. around 1287: *rawdāt*) gives Ibn Khallikān, Nasīr Tūsī, Bahā' Amilī, Nūr Shūshtarī, Mufīd, Ibn Bābawayh, AJ Tūsī, 'Allāma Hillī, Mu'min Jazā'irī, Ibn al-Shīhna, Khwandamīr, Amīr Dāmād, Mustawfī;

(3) Khuyyī (*Sharh minhāj al-barā'a* VI, 177-178, 263, 266-269, 274) gives Qutb Dhahabī (*Fawā'ih*), Mufīd (*radd, sharh*), Ardabīlī (*hadīqa*), Khūnsārī, Ibn Bābawayh, AJ Tūsī, 'Allāma Hillī, Bīrūnī, Hajj Mū'min Khurāsānī, Ibn al-Shīhna, Khwandamīr, Dhahabī, Ibn Khallikān, Hurr 'Amilī, M Tāhir Qummī, 'Alī Shahīdī, Ism Khājūwī.

We have the following Shī'ite bibliographies also in *Persian*:

(1) Nūr Shūshtarī (d. 1019: *majālis*) gives Sam'ānī, Harawī, Rūmī, 'Allāma Hillī, Sijzī (*mu'tabar*), Pārsā;

(2) Bihbihānī (d. 1216: *khayrātīya*) gives Jāmī, Ibn al-Dā'ī, Shabistarī, Mufīd, Dūrbastī, AJ Tūsī, Ibn al-Balyānī, Abū'l-Ma'ālī Husaynī, 'Attār;

(3) 'Abbās Qummī (*Safīnat al-bihār* I, 296; II, 58) gives AJ Tūsī; Ibn Bābawayh, Mufīd, Ibn al-Nadīm, M-b-Makkī (*majmū'at*), Ibn al-Bitrīq (d. 606), Astarābādī (*manhaj*), Majlisī (*wajīza*), Bahā' 'Amilī, Mullā Sadrā (*kasr asnām al-jāhilīya*).

In *Turkish*, neither Sārī 'Abdallāh nor Hajji Khalīfa has given a bibliography on Hallāj; even a summary appears only in a few modern dictionaries. Likewise in *Urdu*.[118]

[118] Eshrefoğlu Rūmī, *makhlas* (pen-name) of the ninth/fifteenth-century Anatolian popular Sūfī poet who calls himself elsewhere 'Abdullāh b. Eshref b. Mehmed al-Misrī, suggesting an Egyptian, if not necessarily Arab, background. The details of Eshrefoğlu's life are for the most part obscure, the earliest source being Tashköprüzade's *Al-shaqā'iq al-nu'maniye*, written a century after the poet's death. In the light of Eshrefoğlu's subsequent prominence as a writer of mystical works in prose and verse, Tashköprüzade's vague but summary dismissal of his Sūfī career is curious. The popularly accepted biography (dating from the middle eleventh/seventeenth century, at the latest) links the name of Eshrefoğlu with the semilegendary *abdāls* (itinerant mystic preachers who found particular favor among the *ghazi* soldiers), with Amīr Sultan (Shams al-Din Muhammad al-Bukhari, d. 832/1429), and with Haci Bayram (d. 833/1430) the latter being virtually "patron saints" of Bursa and Ankara, respectively. Eventually Eshrefoğlu is said to have become initiated into the Qādirī order under the guidance of Sheikh Huseyin Hamāwī. Due to the influence of his own personality, Eshrefoğlu's name became linked with the branch of the Qādirī order that he founded in Iznik (Nicaea) in the mid-fifteenth century.

References to Hallāj are scattered throughout his two best known works, the didactic prose treatise *Muzekki al-nufūs*, and the collected poetry of the *Divan*. In the latter, Eshrefoğlu frequently repeats his affirmation of the "secret" of the utterance, "*anā'l-Haqq.*" While occasionally, these references seem to be merely for poetic effect, elsewhere they ring of complete sincerity and suggest a personal humiliation and suffering that the mystic likens to that of Hallāj. It is noteworthy, although difficult to explain, that in his diary Mahmūd Hüdā'i (d. 1038/1628) in several passages links the names of Hallāj and Eshrefoğlu, and in another says that the latter was killed. Such a statement is not corroborated by the other sources. [Note by Dr. William Hickman, whose doctoral thesis, Harvard University, 1971, was on Eshrefoğlu.]

Library of Congress Cataloging in Publication Data (Revised)

Massignon, Louis, 1883-1962.
    The passion of al-Hallāj.

    (Bollingen series ; 98)
    Translation of La Passion de Husayn Ibn Mansūr
Hallāj.
    CONTENTS: v. 1.   The life of al-Hallāj.—v. 2.
The survival of al-Hallāj.—v. 3. The doctrine of
al-Hallāj.—v. 4.   Bibliography and index.
    1.   Hallāj, al-Husayn ibn Mansūr, 858 or 9-922.
2.   Sufism—Biography.   3.   Sufism.   I.   Title.
II.   Series.
BP80.H27H3713   1980   297'.6 [B]   80-11085
ISBN 0-691-09910-3 (set)